EUROPEAN WRITERS

Selected Authors

EUROPEAN WRITERS
Selected Authors

GEORGE STADE
EDITOR IN CHIEF

Volume III

ALEXANDER PUSHKIN

TO

ÉMILE ZOLA

INDEX

CHARLES SCRIBNER'S SONS
NEW YORK

MAXWELL MACMILLAN CANADA
TORONTO

MAXWELL MACMILLAN INTERNATIONAL
NEW YORK   OXFORD   SINGAPORE   SYDNEY

Library of Congress Cataloging-in-Publication Data

European writers. Selected authors / George Stade, editor in chief.
    v. cm.
    Comprises 68 unabridged essays selected by the publisher from its
fourteen-volume set of "European writers" edited by George Stade,
with W.T.H. Jackson and Jacques Barzun.
    Includes bibliographical references and index.
    Contents: v. 1. Hans Christian Andersen to Johann Wolfgang von
Goethe—v. 2. Maxim Gorky to Marcel Proust—v. 3. Alexander Pushkin to
Emile Zola.
    ISBN 0–684–19583–6 (set):
    1. European literature—History and criticism.   I. Stade, George.
II. Charles Scribner's Sons.
PN501.E9   1992
809′.894—dc20

CONTENTS

Volume I

CONTENTS

Volume II

Volume III

CONTENTS

ALEXANDER PUSHKIN
(1799–1837)

IT IS SCARCELY possible to exaggerate the importance of Alexander Sergeevich Pushkin in modern Russian literature and culture. Westerners may think first of Dostoevsky, Tolstoy, Turgenev, or Chekhov. To the Russians, however, Pushkin is not only their greatest poet but also their greatest man of letters, the founder of modern Russian literature, the founder of the modern Russian literary language, and the center of Russian culture. He wrote in all the basic poetic genres, and his work in each is unsurpassed in the Russian language: long narrative poems *(poemy, povesti v stikhakh)*, the verse novel, lyrics, dramas, and even verse fairy tales. Pushkin is also the author of the first Russian prose fiction that can still be read with pleasure: each of his completed major works of prose fiction is a masterpiece of its kind. He wrote relatively little literary criticism—and most was written to sharpen his own opinions and perceptions, and was not published by him—but the criticism he did write is so important that no student of Russian literature can afford to ignore it. His letters are the best in Russian.

Pushkin's cultural influence has not been confined to literature. It is paramount in music: far more Russian operas have been based on Pushkin's works than on those of any other author. The following list, arranged according to Pushkin's basic genres, is far from complete (where Pushkin's title differs, it is given in parentheses): long narrative poems: Mikhail Glinka's *Ruslan and Lyudmila* (1842), César Cui's *Prisoner of the Caucasus* (1858, 1882), Rachmaninov's *Aleko* (*The Gypsies*, 1892), Tchaikovsky's *Mazepa* (*Poltava*, 1883), Stravinsky's *Mavra* (*The Little House in Kolomna*, 1922); novel in verse: Tchaikovsky's *Eugene Onegin* (1878); dramas: Mussorgsky's *Boris Godunov* (1872), Rimsky-Korsakov's *Mozart and Salieri* (1898), Rachmaninov's *Avaricious Knight* (1904), Alexander Dargomyzhsky's *Stone Guest* (1872; finished by Cui and Rimsky-Korsakov) and *Water Nymph* (1855); fairy tales in verse: Rimsky-Korsakov's *Tsar Saltan* (1900) and *Golden Cockerel* (1907); and prose fiction: Edward Napravnik's *Dubrovsky* (1894), Tchaikovsky's *Queen of Spades* (1890). Many of Pushkin's lyrics have been set to music, a considerable number of them more than once. Ballets have been choreographed to his works, in his own time and since. Although his dramas have never held the stage, they are presented at anniversary festivals, often with great success. His works have been used as subjects for films and have inspired many sculptors, painters, and illustrators. Moreover, his personality has been a continuing subject for interpretation as Russians have attempted to define Russian-ness. Not only biographies but novels based on Pushkin's life continue to appear.

The great Russian novelists—Turgenev, Dostoevsky, and Tolstoy—and later writers such as Chekhov and Maxim Gorky had received worldwide acclaim before the Russians' high estimate of Pushkin met with more than a polite acknowledgment of its existence outside Russia. The chief difficulty, of course, is that he was a poet. But the nature of his genius, and particularly of his characteristic literary style, even in prose, makes his work difficult to appreciate in translation. His style, poles apart from romantic improvisation or Elizabethan exuberance or the realistic piling up of what Tolstoy called "superfluous detail," is marked by the terseness, compactness, concentration, ease, simplicity, and inevitability that spring from the writer's self-imposed strictness and discipline; by the absence of images that call attention to themselves and of any lushness or striking ornamentation; and by continuing development toward further bareness of utterance.

Pushkin is at once the most cosmopolitan and the most Russian of Russian authors. His works reflect his interest in and knowledge of Western culture. He assumed that everything Russian—including literature—should be measured by European standards and that Russia, although it had its own special qualities and character, belonged to Europe. Pushkin read other authors of his own and earlier times, and he freely built onto and adapted their qualities to his needs. He combined direct connection between his life and work, on the one hand, and artistic distance, on the other, so that the merely or mainly personal is removed. Something autobiographical is hidden in almost any work, but it is usually masked and transformed. He scorned didacticism. One of his striking qualities is the presentation of unreconciled contradictions—between a work and its introduction or epilogue, or between parts of a work. It is left to the reader to infer the unified vision behind the entire work. Pushkin is the Russian author who best exemplifies the quality Keats found in Homer and Shakespeare: "negative capability," the ability of "being in uncertainties, mysteries, doubt, without any irritable reach-ing after fact and reason." Thus, just as Shakespeare, in his ability to accept the world in its multiplicity, is a different kind of writer from all other major English writers—John Milton, William Wordsworth, and Lord Byron, among others—Pushkin is a different kind of writer from other Russian writers—Dostoevsky, Tolstoy, Nikolay Gogol, Ivan Goncharov, and even Turgenev.

Pushkin's literary output is so large and so varied that individual works can be given only brief treatment; those he considered unfinished will not be considered in this essay although some are of great interest and importance.

LIFE

Pushkin was born in Moscow on 26 May 1799. The family had been nobles for more than six hundred years, and, as he liked to remember, they had taken an important part in Russian historical events—often on the losing side—under Alexander Nevsky, Ivan the Terrible, Boris Godunov, Peter the Great, and Catherine the Great. On his mother's side Pushkin was descended from Hannibal, a minor Abyssinian prince who became a ward and favorite of Peter the Great. By Pushkin's time his family had lost its influence, but it still had a recognized, though hardly important, place in the Russian nobility. Young Pushkin was taught at home by a series of foreign tutors and governesses, but the chief source of his early education was his father's library of seventeenth- and eighteenth-century French classics.

In 1811 he was selected to be among the thirty students of the first class of the lyceum at Tsarskoe Selo, the site of the summer palace, near Petersburg, established by Alexander I to educate scions of prominent families for important state positions. At the lyceum he received the best education available in Russia at the time. In 1815 his poem "Recollections in Tsarskoe Selo" earned the approval of the venerable Gavril Derzhavin, the greatest eighteenth-century Russian poet, in a public examination at the lyceum. While still a student Pushkin became active in Arzamas, an elite literary society that included such leading poets as Vasily Zhukovsky, Konstantin Batyushkov, and Prince Pyotr Vyazemsky, and he was accepted as a full member in September 1817. Upon graduating from the lyceum that year, he was given a sinecure in the Collegium of Foreign Affairs, in Petersburg. He was warmly received in literary circles; among guards-style lovers of wine, women, and song; and in groups where political liberals debated reforms and constitutions. Between 1817 and 1820 he voiced liberal views in privately circulated "revolutionary" poems: "Liberty: An Ode," "In the Country," and a number of poems on Alexander I and his minister Aleksei Arakcheev. At the same time Pushkin was working on his first large-scale work, *Ruslan and Lyudmila.*

In April 1820 the views expressed in his political poems led to interrogation by the Petersburg governor-general and exile to southern Russia in the guise of an administrative transfer in the foreign affairs service. Pushkin's chief, General Inzov, allowed him to make an extended trip to the Caucasus and the Crimea, together with the family of General Raevsky, a hero of the Russian defeat of Napoleon in 1812. Two months spent at spas in the Caucasus and a month in the Crimea gave Pushkin his first acquaintance with mountains and with primitive peoples. At the same time, under the Raevskys' tutelage he fell under the spell of Byron's poetry. In September he arrived in Bessarabia, ceded to Russia by Turkey only eight years before. There, and at Kamenka, the estate of the Davidov family, in the province of Kiev, Pushkin became acquainted with the more radical leaders of the secret political societies. He witnessed Alexander Ypsilanti's unsuccessful attempt in 1821 to invade European Turkey from Bessarabia, in order to free Greece from Turkish rule.

During his nearly three years in Kishinev, Pushkin wrote his first romantic, or Byronic, verse tales, *The Prisoner of the Caucasus* (1820–1821) and *The Fountain of Bakhchisaray* (1821–1823). He interrupted work on these for *The Gabrieliad* (1821), in which the Annunciation is treated with the levity that Homer accords the gods of Olympus. And two months before leaving Kishinev he began his verse novel, *Eugene Onegin* (1823–1831), chapters of which appeared as separate books from 1825 to 1832.

Through the aid of influential friends, Pushkin was transferred in July 1823 to Odessa, where his literary creativity continued; there he completed *The Fountain of Bakhchisaray* and chapter 1 of *Eugene Onegin,* and began *The Gypsies,* the most polished of his romantic verse tales. But soon he was embroiled with the Russian governor general, Count Vorontsov, who ordered him to perform the duties of his governmental position, hitherto purely nominal. Pushkin angrily attempted to resign from the service. In the meantime, postal officials had intercepted a letter in which he remarked that atheism, though "not so consoling as it is usually thought," is "unfortunately [the most] plausible" belief. In czarist Russia an offense against religion was an offense against the state: he was dismissed from the service and exiled, in open disgrace, to his mother's estate, Mikhaylovskoe, in northern Russia.

The next two years, from August 1824 to August 1826, Pushkin spent at Mikhaylovskoe under the surveillance not only of the police but also of the father superior of the nearby Svyatye Gory Monastery. Pushkin's family happened to be at Mikhaylovskoe when he arrived, and violent family dissension arose when his father undertook surveillance over him for the government. After the family left in November he had the companionship of the family of the widowed Madame Osipova, on the nearby estate of Trigorskoe, and of his aged peasant nursemaid, Arina Rodionovna. However unpleasant he may have found his virtual imprisonment in the village, his literary productivity continued. During 1824 and 1825 he finished *The Gypsies* and wrote *Boris Godunov,* the humorous *Count Nulin,* and chapter 2 of *Eugene Onegin.*

When the Decembrist uprising took place in Petersburg on 14 December 1825, Pushkin was still in Mikhaylovskoe. Though he had suspected the existence of the Decembrist groups, he had never obtained direct knowledge of them and was never asked to join. But he soon learned that he was implicated, for all the Decembrists had copies of his early political poems. In the late spring of 1826 he sent the czar a petition asking to be released from exile. On 4 September Pushkin was ordered to leave immediately with a special state messenger for an audience with Nicholas I, then in Moscow for his coronation. On 8 September, still grimy from the road, he was taken before Nicholas I. Pushkin left the interview jubilant; he had been released from exile, and Nicholas had agreed to be the personal censor of his works. Pushkin thought that he would be free to travel and to participate in the publication of journals, and that, except in cases he himself might consider questionable and wish to refer to his royal censor, he would be exempt from censorship. But Count Benkendorf, chief of gendarmes, gave him to understand that without explicit permission he could not travel, participate in any journal, or publish—or even read in literary circles—any of his works. In 1827 Pushkin was questioned by the police about his poem "André Chénier," written in early 1825 but now being interpreted as referring to the Decembrist uprising. In 1828 he was subjected to unpleasantness because of *The Gabrieliad.* Later he had to defend his poem "The Upas Tree" (written 1828; published 1832) against the allegation of "hidden political allusions" and the satirical "On the Convalescence of Lucullus" (1835), an "imitation of the ancients," against the charge that it had contemporary application.

Still, he was free from exile; and he spent the years 1826 to 1831 chiefly in searching for a wife and preparing to settle down. He sought no less than the most beautiful woman in Russia for his bride. In 1829 he met Natalia Goncharov; he presented a formal proposal to her mother in April of that year, and when he received an indefinite answer, he set off without authorization for the military front of the Russo-Turkish War. He obtained the Russian commander's permission to visit the army and entered captured Erzurum, in Turkey—the only time he was ever outside the Russian Empire. On his return to Petersburg, the czar himself asked how he had dared to visit the military front and the army without his express permission: "Don't you know that the army is mine?" Pushkin renewed his suit for the hand of Natalia Goncharov, and in April 1830 his proposal was accepted. As a kind of wedding present, after four years of waiting Pushkin was given permission to publish *Boris Godunov* under his "own responsibility." He was formally betrothed on 6 May 1830.

Financial arrangements arising from his father's wedding gift to him of the right to mortgage half the serfs on Kistenevo necessitated a visit to the elder Pushkin's neighboring estate, Boldino, in east-central Russia. When Pushkin arrived there in September 1830 he expected to remain only a few days, but for three months he was held in quarantine because of an epidemic of Asiatic cholera—the first European invasion of what was to be perhaps the most deadly disease of nineteenth-century Europe and America. These three months were literarily the most productive of his life. During his last months of exile at Mikhaylovskoe he had completed chapters 5 and 6 of *Eugene Onegin,* but in the four subsequent years, of his major works he had written only *Poltava* (1828), the unfinished novel *The Blackamoor of Peter the Great* (1827), and chapter 7 of *Eugene Onegin* (1827–1828). During the autumn at Boldino, Pushkin wrote the five short stories of *The Tales of Belkin;* the verse tale *The Little House in Kolomna;* his four "Little

Tragedies"—*The Covetous Knight, Mozart and Salieri, The Stone Guest,* and *Feast in Time of the Plague;* the first of his fairy tales in verse, *The Tale of the Priest and His Workman Balda;* the last chapter of *Onegin;* and, among other lyrics, "The Devils."

Pushkin was married to Natalia Goncharov on 18 February 1831, in Moscow. In May they moved to Tsarskoe Selo and in October to Petersburg, where they lived for the remainder of Pushkin's life. Madame Pushkin's beauty caused an immediate sensation in society; her admirers included the czar himself. Pushkin petitioned for permission to do historical research in the government archives, and on 14 November, after writing and quickly publishing nationalistic poems on the Polish revolution of 1830–1831, he was officially enrolled in government service to do historical research at a modest salary. As Pushkin worked in the archives, his interest moved from Peter the Great to the revolt led by Emilian Pugachev in 1773–1775. The result was two quite different books: one, a piece of expository historical research, and the other, a work of prose fiction, a historical novel. In the fall of 1833 he traveled to the Pugachev country of the Urals. On the return trip he stopped at Boldino, where he settled down to another of his fruitful literary periods. Since 1830 he had completed only one major work, the verse fairy tale *Tsar Saltan* (1831). In a month and a half he now wrote the long narrative poem *Angelo,* a recasting of Shakespeare's *Measure for Measure,* and his verse masterpiece *The Bronze Horseman;* he also wrote his prose masterpiece *The Queen of Spades,* and finished *The History of Pugachev.*

On 30 December 1833 Nicholas I made Pushkin a kammerjunker, an intermediate court rank usually reserved for youths of high aristocratic lineage. Pushkin, now thirty-four, was deeply offended, all the more so because he was convinced that the appointment had been made not for any quality of his but only to make it proper for his beautiful wife to attend court balls. Pushkin could ill afford the cost and the time required by court duties. His worries increased when, in the autumn of 1834, his wife's two unmarried sisters came to live with them indefinitely. In addition, in the spring of 1834 he had taken over the management of his improvident father's estate and undertaken to settle the debts of his spendthrift brother. The result was cares, annoyances, and even outlays from his own pocket before he gave up trying to set things in order in mid-1835. After considerable negotiation, Pushkin obtained permission to publish the literary quarterly *Contemporary,* beginning in 1836. The journal was not a financial success, and it involved endless editorial problems and difficulties with the censors. During a short visit to the country in 1834 he wrote his final verse fairy tale, *The Golden Cockerel;* in 1835 he revised his travel notes of 1829 for *A Journey to Erzurum;* in 1836 he completed his historical novel *The Captain's Daughter,* also based on his research on Pugachev, and wrote a number of his finest lyrics.

The final part of Pushkin's tragedy was played out against the background of court society. Madame Pushkin loved the attention that her beauty attracted; she was fond of flirting and of being surrounded by admirers. In 1834 she met a young man who was not content with flirtation, a handsome French royalist émigré in Russian service who was the adopted son of the Dutch ambassador, Louis van Heeckeren. George d'Anthès-Heeckeren pursued Madame Pushkin for two years, finally so openly and unabashedly that by the autumn of 1836 his conduct had become a scandal. On 4 November Pushkin received copies of a "certificate" nominating him "coadjutor of the Order of Cuckolds and Historiographer of the Order." He immediately challenged d'Anthès-Heeckeren to a duel. Pushkin twice allowed postponements and then retracted the challenge altogether when he learned "from public rumor" that d'Anthès-Heeckeren was "really" in love with his wife's sister, Ekaterina Goncharov. On 10 January 1837, contrary to Pushkin's expectations, the marriage to his sister-in-law took place. Pushkin refused to attend the wedding or to receive the couple in his home, but in society d'Anthès-Heeckeren pursued Madame Pushkin even more openly. He arranged a meeting with her by persuading her friend Idalia Poletika to invite her for a visit; Madame Poletika left the two alone, but one of her children surprised them. Madame Pushkin managed to get away, but on hearing of the rendezvous Pushkin sent an insulting letter to the elder Heeckeren, accusing him of being the author of the "certificate" and the "pander" of his "bastard." A duel with d'Anthès-Heeckeren was now inevitable. It occurred on 27 January 1837. D'Anthès-Heeckeren fired first, and Pushkin was mortally wounded; after he fell, he summoned the strength to fire his shot and slightly wounded his adversary. Pushkin died two days later, on 29 January.

As Pushkin lay dying, and even after his death, court society, except for a few friends, sympathized with d'Anthès-Heeckeren. But thousands of people from all other social levels came to Pushkin's apartment to express sympathy and to mourn. The government feared a political demonstration. To prevent public display, the funeral was moved from Saint Isaac's Cathedral to the small Royal Stables Church, with admission by ticket permitted only to members of the court and of diplomatic society. Then the body was sent away in secret, at midnight. The coffin was carried on a simple cart accompanied only by an old family friend, by Pushkin's serf "uncle," and by a captain of gendarmes. At dawn on 6 February 1837, Pushkin was buried beside his mother at Svyatye Gory Monastery, near Mikhaylovskoe.

WORKS

Pushkin's works can be grouped by genre: long narrative poems; verse novel; lyrics; dramas; verse fairy tales; and prose fiction. In the first three groups the poetry is "lyrical" in a special way: a first-person narrator or speaker (the poetic "I") represents "Pushkin"—who is often quite stylized—or else such a figure is implied. This use of the first person in short lyrics is hardly surprising, but its use in long narrative poems or a novel in verse is one of their most striking features. In the three remaining genres, Pushkin's personality as such is absent. His characters speak for themselves. In his dramas no single character is a mouthpiece for the author; rather, Pushkin plays all the roles. In his verse fairy tales the implied poet-narrator is a peasant teller of fairy tales, miraculously granted the ability to tell them in sparkling verse rather than the customary prose. In his prose fiction there is almost always at least one fictional narrator, and much of the plot, including its climax, may be related in direct speech by one of its characters.

Long Narrative Poems

Pushkin first attained fame with the publication of *Ruslan and Lyudmila* (1817–1820), an effervescent work in a form that had not hitherto appeared in Russia: a "romance epic" (*romanicheskaia* or *romanticheskaia poema*), a poem of serious themes but largely comic tone utilizing legends of Kievan Rus (old Russia) as a Russian counterpart to the Western use of the Roland story, especially in Ludovico Ariosto's *Orlando Furioso* and Torquato Tasso's *Jerusalem Delivered.* Instead of being simply mock-heroic, *Ruslan* treats the serious themes of knightly quest, constancy in love, and heroism in combat. Like almost all Pushkin's long narrative poems, it is written in iambic tetrameter with alternating masculine and feminine rhymes, in verse paragraphs rather than stanzas; this at once became the model for long narrative poems.

Ruslan, set in the court of Prince Vladimir of Kiev, relates the exploits of *bogatyrs* (heroes), the nearest equivalent to Western knights in the Russian folk epic *(bylina)* and fairy tale *(skazka).* The poem proper mingles themes and diction common to folklore; the prologue, added in the second edition (1828), is a bravura verse setting of genuine folkloric material from prose fairy tales told to Pushkin by his peasant nursemaid, Arina Rodionovna. Some characters' names are borrowed from Russian folklore, but the story is apparently Pushkin's. Along with the fantastic and the legendary, the poem utilizes a historical event, the attack on Kiev by the Pechenegs. Dedicated to "young ladies," it is almost continuously humorous and urbanely ironic, except for the prologue and Ruslan's battle with the Pechenegs.

Unlike that of the verse fairy tales, the manner of narration prevents the suspension of disbelief: the story is told by a narrator who interrupts the action from time to time, expressing cool, modern reactions to situations and events, and even rejoicing that "in our time there are no longer so many magicians" (4.1–4). The poem tells of the quest of Ruslan and three other contenders for Lyudmila, who has been abducted by the magician Chernomor on the night of her wedding to Ruslan. In perhaps the most carefully plotted long work in Russian literature, each contender is followed separately before he is overcome. Ruslan remains heroic in combat and faithful in love; Lyudmila is a delightful mixture of faithfulness in love and feminine flightiness, as in her irresistible impulse to see a mirror reflection of herself wearing Chernomor's magic cap of invisibility. In the second edition of the poem Pushkin also added a first-person lyrical epilogue informing the reader that he had felt drained on completing the poem and that he hoped as a "seeker of new impressions," to find fresh inspiration in the Caucasus, where the epilogue was written (1820).

Ruslan and Lyudmila seemed especially original when it appeared, in part because it broke with eighteenth-century expectations of style by mixing the humorous and the serious, the mock and the heroic. *The Gabrieliad* (1821) is, by contrast, a one-canto, consistently mock-heroic epic. It is a travesty of the biblical story of the Annunciation culminating in the sensuously presented visitation to Mary of God in the form of a dove, just as Leda is visited by Zeus in the form of a swan. The biblical account is changed in significant ways, perhaps on the basis of apocryphal sources. Naive, ignorant, innocent Mary is married to aged, impotent Joseph. She has had a vision of heaven, where she sees God but prefers Gabriel. While Gabriel is on his way to inform Mary of God's "love," Satan seduces her by telling the "true" story of his visit to Eve, which resulted not in her fall but in her salvation through learning of a "limb with two marvelous apples." The biblical battle of angels in heaven is parodied by a battle between Satan and Gabriel, which Gabriel wins by taking advantage of the vulnerability of the "limb by which Satan has sinned." Mary accepts Gabriel's embraces gladly but God's reluctantly. Then she muses that she has experienced "love" three times in one day. The poem ends by stating that God accepted the child as his but Gabriel continued to visit Mary. Early in the poem the poet-narrator addresses this story to a modern-day Jewish girl whom he similarly wishes to seduce by telling it; at other times, he addresses "brethren" in parody of a sermon. First-person digressions are interspersed with the action, and the poem ends with the poet-narrator's prayer to Joseph asking that after marriage he be granted "unconcern, meekness, much patience, peace in the family, and neighborly love." On the surface the poem appears blasphemous; however, it is devoid of the polemical or tendentious cast of comparable eighteenth-century poems (especially those of Evaniste Parny and Voltaire). It is written not in the iambic tetrameter of *Ruslan* but in rhymed iambic pentameter with caesura (obligatory word-end after the fourth syllable of each line). It is a joyous and ribald acceptance of the flesh and is particularly amusing in its parody of God's "Oriental, varicolored style" and in the mock prayer to Joseph—all too prophetic of Pushkin's own situation years later.

Pushkin's southern, or romantic, verse

tales sharply contrast with *Ruslan and Lyudmila* and *The Gabrieliad* by combining elevated seriousness of tone with strong lyrical involvement of the poet-narrator in events, setting, and characterization. Each depicts a region that Pushkin had visited in 1820 and that seemed exotic to Russians because it was newly incorporated into the empire or was in the process of being incorporated: *The Prisoner of the Caucasus* (Russian conquest of the area was completed only in the 1850's); *The Fountain of Bakhchisaray* (set in the Crimea, annexed in 1783); and *The Gypsies* (set in Bessarabia, annexed in 1812). For these poems Pushkin consciously adapted the type of lyrical narrative used by Byron in his "Oriental" poems, especially *The Giaour, The Corsair,* and *The Bride of Abydos,* in which only high points of action are presented, usually in fragmentary fashion. Background, character, and motivation are shrouded in mystery; the reader is left to imagine much that happens. A highly lyrical tone conveys strong passions against an exotic background, and the narrator identifies himself with a disenchanted hero. Pushkin adopts all these devices, but unlike Byron he builds into the poem, or establishes through an epilogue or other accompanying materials, a contrasting or contradictory illumination to the main story. Moreover, he moves from a single voice and style in the first poem, *The Prisoner of the Caucasus,* to different voices for each character in the final poem, *The Gypsies.*

The Prisoner of the Caucasus (1820–1821) introduces to Russian literature a disenchanted contemporary hero in an exotic setting. The unnamed Russian, seeking freedom from the bonds of civilization as well as from an unrequited love, is captured by tribesmen in the Caucasus. While the warriors are raiding Russian border settlements, he is freed from his chains by a native girl who has fallen in love with him. When he has swum the swift boundary river, circles appear on the water's surface, suggesting to him and the reader that the girl has drowned. "Liberated," the hero rejoins the Russians. The first part of the poem centers on an ethnographic depiction of the mountaineers in their native habitat, including a description of their cruel sports; Pushkin himself called the passage an hors d'oeuvre, but it implies the bravery and self-control of a hero who shows no fear, though he is in danger of becoming a victim of their cruelty himself. The center of the second part is the "night visit" in which the hero and heroine meet while her father and other adult males are on a raid attacking a Cossack border settlement. The Russian confesses his inability to love her; she tells of her own "imprisonment" in the mores of her people, which will force her into a loveless marriage with another native mountaineer. The poem is narrated in the third person, but in a lyrical manner that identifies the implied narrator with the Russian protagonist. The poet speaks in his own person in the epilogue, which, in contrast to the poem proper, celebrates the Russian military leaders participating in the conquest of the Caucasus. Thus the poem deals with the overt contrast but underlying similarity between a man of civilization and the primitive exotic: however much the exotic is poeticized, the mountain girl is a prisoner of her "civilization," just as the Russian is of his. This marks the first presentation in Russian literature of the disenchanted or dissatisfied hero and also of his "confession," a theme that would become the center of nineteenth-century Russian novels by Pushkin himself (*Eugene Onegin*), Mikhail Lermontov, Goncharov, Turgenev, Dostoevsky, Tolstoy, and many others.

The Fountain of Bakhchisaray (1821–1823) has the exotic setting of a Turkish harem at a time when Turks still ruled the Crimea. The poem presents two contrasting heroines, both Christians, captured and put in the harem. One, Zarema, is from Caucasian Georgia; brunette, southern, sensual, passionate, and violent, she has adopted the religion and mores of Khan Girey. The second, Maria, is a Polish girl, northern, chaste, and entirely ignorant of the passions. Hoping to win Maria's love, Girey has abandoned Zarema, his former favorite. In the central scene Zarema confronts Maria, threatening to kill her with a dagger if Girey does not return to her. Through a suggestive indirect use of narration, we are told that "Maria ceased to be" the "same night" Zarema was executed; the implication is that Girey had Zarema put to death for carrying out her threat. Girey goes to war again, but even in the heat of battle he cannot forget his tormenting love for Maria. The poem ends with the poet speaking of his own visit to Bakhchisaray, where he saw a "vision"—a love of his own. He asks himself which of the two heroines she is like. In the subsequent editions of the poem, Pushkin added a letter in which he recalls his visit to the locale in a very different mood. He also added a travel account in which the story of the Polish girl's capture is termed a legend. Thus the poem and Pushkin's accompanying materials give contradictory illuminations. During Pushkin's lifetime, *The Fountain of Bakhchisaray* was his most popular poem.

Pushkin's final southern, or romantic, verse tale, *The Gypsies* (1824), is his masterpiece in the genre. It is a tale of love and infidelity, of violence and peacefulness, of aggressiveness and passivity, of civilization and law versus the state of nature and freedom. Much of the poem is in dramatic form, and there are four chief speakers, each with a different voice: Aleko, the Old Gypsy, his daughter Zemfira, and the poet-narrator. Indeed, each has two quite different ways of speaking: homely, succinct, matter-of-fact, ordinary speech, and a more figurative and elaborate manner when emotionally aroused. Aleko, fleeing civilization and pursued by the law, is taken by Zemfira as her mate and accepted by the gypsies. After two years, Zemfira tires of him and uses "Mariula's song" to let him know that she "hates him and loves another." The Old Gypsy tells Aleko that Zemfira's mother sang the same song to him, after only a year of happiness, and then ran off with another. But un-

like the Old Gypsy Aleko insists on revenge; in fact, it is suggested by Zemfira's overhearing him talk in his sleep that Aleko is fleeing the law because he has already exacted revenge for infidelity in "civilization." Aleko catches Zemfira with her gypsy lover and kills them both. The Old Gypsy ostracizes Aleko from the band, and the gypsies leave; Aleko's cart remains in the field alone, like a wounded crane when the flock has migrated. Thus the poem presents the attraction of the state of nature to the civilized, and the converse. Woman's inconstancy in love is common to both, and it earns two responses: the civilized man's aggressive revenge, resulting in ostracism from both societies; and the natural man's passive acceptance, with his memories of the single bright spot of his lifetime. In the epilogue the poet-narrator remembers warmly his own wanderings with gypsies, when he too heard Mariula's song. He concludes by noting that "even under your tattered carts there are tormenting dreams, and there is no defense against the fates."

Interpretations of *The Gypsies* have varied radically since the poem first appeared. Some assume that Aleko (whose name is a form of Alexander, Pushkin's first name) is the key to interpretation; others (especially Dostoevsky) have argued that the Old Gypsy's final speech ostracizing the "European wanderer" presents the poem's central idea. (One wonders what Dostoevsky would have thought if he had known that, in the story Pushkin is reported to have drawn on, the jealous young gypsy murdered the gypsy girl who had abandoned the European—Pushkin himself—for him.) Whatever one concludes, it should be noted how clearly and how successfully Pushkin presents irreconcilables without choosing among them.

Byron, after writing his Oriental verse tales, turned their manner upside down in *Beppo*. The tense, highly lyrical presentation of strong passions and violent action—love, jealousy, revenge, suicide, murder—against an exotic, primitive background is replaced by a relaxed, still subjective, but humorously digressive and urbane presentation of civilization, and the expectation of strong emotion or violent action is humorously and anticlimactically dispelled. Following Byron's example, Pushkin, as he himself acknowledged, turned the manner of his own southern verse tales upside down in *Count Nulin* and *The Little House in Kolomna*.

Count Nulin (1825) has a first-person narrator who in no way identifies with the characters or situations, except for a brief lyric expressing the lonely country-dweller's eagerness for visitors. The materials of *Count Nulin* are to a considerable degree those of *The Prisoner of the Caucasus*, but with a completely different, largely ironic, presentation. Count Nulin (from the Russian for "zero") is returning from "civilized" Paris, where he has spent his "future income" on the latest fashions. He becomes an overnight "prisoner" on a Russian country estate when a wheel of his carriage breaks; his hostess is glad of company in the absence of her husband, who is off on a "raid" hunting hares; thus the way is open for a "night visit" from Nulin to his hostess, Natalia. The milieu is presented ethnographically in direct, "low" detail—muddy farmyard, squabbling animals, turkey hens following a wet cock, ducks in a puddle. The heroine's way of observing this scene implies her character, as did the Russian's observing the customs and cruel games of the mountaineers in *The Prisoner of the Caucasus*. Instead of the "primitive," uncultivated person Nulin expects to find in the desolate Russian countryside, Natalia is a lady of some pretension who has been educated in an émigrée Frenchwoman's pension, and her clothing is *almost* in the latest fashion. Nulin is so taken with her that he decides she implied willingness for their conversation to continue in her bedroom. But instead of words of love or an embrace, she gives him a slap in the face (in contrast, the poem points out, to Lucrece's reaction to Tarquin—an allusion to Shakespeare's *Rape of Lucrece*, which is also being

parodied). The next morning, although the husband returns and asks him to stay longer, the count "escapes." Then the wife tells the story to all. The husband becomes angry, but young Lidin, a neighbor from the next estate, is amused. The poem ends with a tongue-in-cheek comment that "in our times, it is not surprising to find a woman faithful to her spouse." Thus the image of the "old man" requiring the "native" girl to marry the ethnic neighbor, though she falls in love with the visitor from "civilization," is turned upside down. Nulin's French culture is all style. From another point of view, the story is in direct contrast to the sentimental novel—described by the narrator as "long, long, long" and lacking the "tricks" of "romantic works." In the poem the tricks of romantic works are given a farmyard and manor-house setting, rather than an exotic one. The most ordinary has replaced the unusual.

Stanzaic narrative poems in Pushkin's day were expected to be ballads, with immediate action and terse storytelling. *The Little House in Kolomna* (1830) uses ottava rima and digresses in the Byronic *Beppo* style, beginning with a long digression on poetic technique that takes up almost a third of the poem; then the story is told in such a manner as to direct attention *away* from what is really going on. It is pointedly written in iambic pentameter, without the French caesura. The narrative begins with a diversion as the poet-narrator, in Kolomna, a suburb of Petersburg, remembers a rich, haughty, beautiful, and unhappily married countess. The story of the poem will be, in contrast, about "good, kind Parasha," a poor widow's daughter, a "fair maid" who looks with admiration on guardsmen and is so looked on by them. But: "Which did she love? We'll see." The story is told through the "imperceptiveness" of Parasha's mother, who wishes to hire a cook as cheaply as possible after her own cook dies. Parasha brings in a cook who is willing to work for whatever Parasha's mother will pay. She is tall and ungainly and, it turns out, cannot cook or sew.

On Sunday the mother and daughter go to church; the mother rushes home, thinking that the cook may be robbing them. There she discovers the cook shaving "her" face "just like my late husband." The cook flees, and the poem ends with "no serious damage done." At "a critic's " desire, the poem ends with mock-serious morals: "it's dangerous to hire help for nothing"; "one cannot conceal one's sex indefinitely; a man will have to shave"; and "you cannot squeeze more out of the story." Critics have tried. The poem is a humorous defense of the poet's right to choose subject, theme, and poetic form. There is a remarkable technical feat at the climax, where a line is omitted from stanza thirty-six—the cook jumps *over the omitted line* to escape.

Pushkin's last two verse tales to be considered here have historical settings and deal with Peter the Great. *Poltava* centers on the battle of the same name (1709), in which Peter defeated Charles XII of Sweden and preserved a multinational empire by retaining the Ukraine. *The Bronze Horseman* presents Peter as he conceives of establishing Petersburg (founded 1703), and then it shifts to November 1824 for a "Petersburg story" of the flood.

Pushkin carefully "followed history" in *Poltava* (1828). The poem tells the story of the love of the Ukrainian hetman Mazepa and his goddaughter, Maria, against the background of the famous battle. The unity of the plot (including the love story and the battle) turns on Maria's recognition of who Mazepa is and is not. Maria's parents reject "old" Mazepa's marriage proposal as incestuous in the eyes of the church. After Maria elopes with him, her father, Kochubey, knowing that Mazepa intends to lead the Cossack Ukraine in a revolt for independence, denounces him to Peter. But Peter delivers Kochubey to Mazepa, who has him executed. When Maria learns that her father has been killed by her husband she disappears. The battle of Poltava is won by Peter; Charles XII and Mazepa escape. As Mazepa flees past the Kochubey estate, Maria, now mad, appears to him. In an epilogue written in the present tense, from the viewpoint of a hundred years later, Peter's glory is extolled; Mazepa is said to be forgotten except for an annual anathema pronounced by the church; and Maria is remembered in folk songs.

In a central scene Maria learns of Mazepa's military plans; she expects him to be "czar of his native land," shares his ambition, and, it is clear, is attracted by his heroic qualities. Mazepa takes the opportunity to make her admit that she loves him more than her father; she feels confused, yet does not understand that she has unwittingly consented to her father's execution. At the battle of Poltava Peter is described in the style of the encomiastic ode; when Maria sees Mazepa after going mad, her language too closely follows the earlier description of Peter to be accidental:

Peter (poet speaking; emphasis added)

> His *eyes*
> Shine. *His face is horrible.*
> His movements are rapid. *He is handsome.*
> He is all like God's storm.

Mazepa (Maria speaking)

> I took you for another, old man.
> Leave me.
> Your *gaze* is mocking and *horrible.*
> You are ugly. *He is handsome.*
> . . .
> His moustaches are whiter than snow,
> But blood has dried on yours.

Maria's speech to Mazepa shows the prescience of madness, as will the hero's speech to the statue of Peter the Great, in *The Bronze Horseman.* Maria, in falling in love with Mazepa, had taken him for a great military leader and statesman who would unite and lead his country, a man merciful and generous to his opponents. She had taken him as being, for the Ukraine, what the narrator sees Peter the Great as being for Russia. In this passage, she recognizes the real Mazepa as being quite different from the ideal she fell in love with.

That Mazepa was old and had white moustaches, but this one is a beast of prey with her father's blood clotted on his moustaches. Maria is described throughout the poem and in the epilogue in terms symbolic of nature in the Ukraine and taken from folklore. In the symbolic structure of the poem Maria represents the "young Ukraine" "seduced" by Mazepa into joining him and opposing Peter.

Poltava is the only one of Pushkin's long narrative poems in which the poet-narrator does not speak in the first person, although his voice is implied by the lyrical descriptions of Maria and of Ukrainian nature (especially the night), by the author's direct address to his characters, and by the use of rhetorical questions. The Russian nationalistic strain of the poem is reflected in the use of the first-person plural ("we," "our") when speaking of Peter's forces at the battle. Pushkin said later that he regretted having presented Mazepa as "evil" but that he was following history. He avoided the pitfall of such one-sided characterization of important historical figures in his other completed works dealing with Russian history: *Boris Godunov, The Bronze Horseman,* and *The Captain's Daughter.*

Although *Poltava* in the poem proper gives a picture of the events of 1709, its epilogue is set in the narrative present. The introduction to *The Bronze Horseman* (1833) begins on the eve of Peter's founding of Petersburg (1703); then it shifts to the immediate narrative present, while the poem proper goes back slightly in time to 1824, the year of the Neva flood. The introduction presents a highly encomiastic picture of Peter envisioning the city. Then the poet catalogs what he " loves" about Petersburg, not only in heroic but also in everyday terms: ships from all fleets, victorious troops, winter that makes girls' cheeks red as roses, white nights. Peter is presented as creating the city because "nature commanded" it; the flood is presented as nature rebelling against him. The story is an account of the flood as experienced by a poor clerk, Eugene— perhaps a descendant of the old nobility but now a minor member of the bureaucracy established by Peter—whose "dream" is to obtain a slightly better position in the service and then to start a family with his bride, Parasha. As soon as the floodwaters recede a little he crosses over to the suburb of Kolomna to visit Parasha, but when he discovers that the house has been washed away he goes mad. The next fall, now a wandering beggar, Eugene finds himself standing before a statue of Peter the Great, the Bronze Horseman, and in the "horrible illumination" of madness he sees Peter, founder of the city and its bureaucracy, as responsible for his plight. He shakes his fist at him—"You'll get yours"—and then turns and flees, pursued, he thinks, by the thundering hoofs of the Bronze Horseman's steed. At the end of the poem Eugene's body is found on a bare island at the mouth of the river, on the threshold of a rickety house, obviously Parasha's. He is given a pauper's burial. The poem draws no conclusions: it presents the grandeur of Petersburg and the poet's love for it; it also presents the suffering of Eugene and his death as a consequence of the flood and of Peter's creation. Admiration for Peter's accomplishment is balanced by pity for a victim of it. Perhaps nowhere can one find such a stark presentation of the claims and demands of the state, through the figure personifying it, balanced by the legitimate claims and demands of the individual. Nicholas I did not permit this poem to be published during Pushkin's lifetime; Pushkin was allowed to publish only the introduction (with a few omissions)—the encomium to Peter and his city. *The Bronze Horseman* is perhaps the poem in the Russian language that best meets Matthew Arnold's criterion for the grand style: "The grand style arises in poetry, when a noble nature, poetically gifted, treats with simplicity or severity a serious subject."

Verse Novel

Pushkin's most popular and influential work is *Eugene Onegin,* not a novel, he said, but a novel in verse, "a devil of a difference." It was on *Eugene Onegin* that he worked the longest: more than eight years, from 1823 to 1831. The individual chapters appeared separately from 1825 to 1832; the entire novel was published in 1833 and again early in 1837. The writing of the novel coincides with and reflects Pushkin's maturing as man and poet; while working on it he produced masterpieces in quite different styles and in all of his genres: serious and humorous verse tales, all of his completed dramas, the first of his verse fairy tales, a multitude of lyrics of different kinds, and even his first completed works of prose fiction. *Eugene Onegin* reflects more aspects of Pushkin's poetic personality than does any other of his works, ranging in tone from the matter-of-fact, to the humorous and urbane, to the ironic (on a multitude of levels), to the parodistic, to the lyric outcry of the heart.

Pushkin's point of departure for a stanzaic-verse novel in varied styles was Byron's *Don Juan*, but *Eugene Onegin* differs sharply in type of narrator, style, characters, and plot. *Don Juan* is an adventure-type, episodic novel; *Eugene Onegin* has a single, well-developed plot. Pushkin's characters are not puppets manipulated by the author; the reader accepts them as having authentic existences. And unlike *Don Juan*, as Pushkin notes, *Eugene Onegin* does not have a "drop of satire"; its qualities are quite different from Byron's "tempest anger, tempest mirth." *Eugene Onegin* is written in Pushkin's most intimate and relaxed style (far more relaxed than even his personal letters); however, the poetic effect is by the line and stanza rather than merely by the page, and even the digressions on themes suggested by the characters and action, which constitute about one-third of the novel, are subordinate to and harmonious with its design and structure.

The plot of *Eugene Onegin* turns on twice-rejected love: early in the novel Onegin rejects Tatiana's love; at the end she rejects his. But the poignancy and tragedy of the situation is that their love was, as Tatiana sensed, fated—but ill-fated because ill-timed. "Happiness was so near, so possible," she says at the end; it was prevented (as it usually is in Pushkin's works with contemporary heroes) not by external obstacles but by the hero's character. The two main characters, Tatiana and Onegin, grow and develop during the novel, as does the author-narrator himself.

Tatiana, a rural young lady (*baryshnia*), falls in love at first sight when Onegin arrives from Petersburg to settle on a nearby estate. She sends him a letter confessing her love, but he rejects her. Her love, however, not only continues but deepens as she learns more about him, although they have parted, she thinks, forever. Having no hope of a love match, she consents to a marriage of convenience; the commitment, freely taken, is for her a permanent and binding one. In the final chapter Onegin returns to Petersburg and meets Tatiana, now a great lady and the center of the highest society. He falls in love with her and, in turn, writes a letter. In a subsequent interview Tatiana admits to Onegin that she still loves him, but she has the strength and integrity to remain faithful to her marriage vows. This candor, strength, and integrity have made her perhaps the favorite among all Russian fictional heroines. (Tatiana's character and story are in sharp contrast to those of the heroine of Tolstoy's *Anna Karenina*, written some fifty years later. Anna makes a marriage of convenience before she discovers her potential for love; when she falls in love with Vronsky, she cannot countenance even the idea of a covert affair. But after she abandons her husband and son to live with Vronsky, she is unable to endure the ensuing social ostracism, which ends with her suicide.)

Onegin, like the heroes of Pushkin's *The Prisoner of the Caucasus* and *The Gypsies*, is a disenchanted man of civilization. Instead of going to an exotic land, the city-bred Onegin goes to a remote rural region of Russia; instead of having previously entertained an unrequited love or having been deceived in love,

Onegin has been all too successful in amorous affairs, but he has not found real love and has no hope that he will. However, unlike Pushkin's earlier contemporary heroes, Onegin is able to grow and develop. When he meets Tatiana again after his years of wandering, he falls in love with her. Once he acknowledges this love to himself and to her, we sense that it will be as constant as hers. The genuineness of his feeling is shown in his dreaming of her—now unavailable to him—not as the great lady she has become but as the country girl he remembers at the window of her rural home. The novel leaves unclear whether Tatiana understands how much Onegin has changed, whether she misunderstands him now as much as he had misunderstood her earlier, and what either of them will now do. This open ending is one of the most important characteristics of *Eugene Onegin* in terms of the development of the Russian novel.

In contrast to Onegin, the rural landowner-neighbor Lensky is a young poet, educated in Germany and full of youthful enchantment and enthusiasm. He becomes engaged to Tatiana's sister, Olga. Lensky and Onegin become friends "from having nothing to do," and Lensky introduces Onegin to Tatiana and Olga. In a moment of pique at Lensky, Onegin thoughtlessly provokes his jealousy and causes his friend to challenge him to a duel; Onegin accepts the challenge and kills Lensky. Onegin then leaves on his wanderings; the commonplace Olga quickly forgets Lensky and marries another.

The characters, including the poet-narrator, live in a particular time and place, but in their essence they could live anytime, anywhere. Thus the novel is both a social novel and a work of universal import. Pushkin makes explicit at the beginning of the novel that Onegin typifies a Petersburg young man of 1819–1820, with particular qualities of dress (a dandy) and manner (the disenchanted "Byronic" youth). Tatiana is a rural Russian girl, responsive to but unspoiled by French sentimental novels and Russian chapbooks, and brought up on folk stories told by her peasant nurse. At the same time, as the novel specifically states, she becomes Pushkin's muse, and his novel in verse is to a considerable degree a love poem to her. That Lensky falls in love with Olga instead of Tatiana is noted, even by Onegin, as an implied deficiency in Lensky as a poet (and, it is implied, as a man); Onegin's failure to fall in love with Tatiana on meeting her is a failure of character, however much it may also be a matter of timing. That Tatiana is "Russian in soul," loving her peasant nurse and what pertains to the Russian folk, suggests that she is to be understood in even broader terms, as a symbol of Russia itself, permanently attracted to and in love with a representative of Europe (a Westernized Russian) but nevertheless, in the end, faithful to her Russian spouse, her real destiny. This aspect of *Eugene Onegin* was continued by Goncharov in *Oblomov*, by Tolstoy in *War and Peace*, and by Turgenev in his novels.

Tatiana's change from an ingenuous country girl to a great lady in Petersburg is presented as a social development that reflects no basic change in her character: she is still as simple, natural, and unaffected, as direct in feeling and expression, and she still has the same values and ideals. The male characters, in contrast, represent stages of maturing; the implied question is how a man can mature and yet remain, or once again become, poetic. They are imperfect, human, particularized, social representations of the ideal figures of the "young poet" and the "demon" in Pushkin's lyric "The Demon" (1823). Lensky is an enthusiastic young man, the poet of exalted love and friendship. Onegin's deliberate arousal of Lensky's jealousy results in Lensky's disenchantment with friendship (Onegin) and, temporarily, with love (Olga). The novel suggests that for Lensky to become a great poet he would have needed to survive Onegin's "demonic" temptation, and this would have required more depth of character than he possessed.

The characterization of Onegin is more

complex: on the one hand, he provides a "demonic" temptation for Lensky; on the other, he represents a man arrested at the stage of disenchantment, which for him came too soon and has lasted too long. By the final chapter he has regained the ability to feel, and he dreams of Lensky's death and Tatiana at the window: betrayed friendship and rejected love. We are not told what he may do at this new stage of maturity. Judging from the poet-narrator's direct intrusion (which includes presenting himself briefly, early in the novel, as a friend of Onegin's in Petersburg), his lyrical passages, and his multilevel irony, Onegin has also succeeded in revaluing meaning and value, in a new stage of mature re-enchantment.

Eugene Onegin is a triumph of plot and characterization, but its uniqueness—as Vladimir Nabokov has shown in his voluminous commentary on the novel—lies chiefly in its style. The novel is both symmetrical and controlled, on the one hand, and whimsical in the extreme—in a manner somewhat reminiscent of the work of Laurence Sterne—on the other. There is continuing deceptive play on literary form, predicated on the illusion of "gentlemanly carelessness," although everything is precisely planned and worked out, in measure and proportion; when form and expectation are broken, it is for poetic purposes and inevitable surprise. The novel is written in a special stanza form that Pushkin invented for it and called the *Onegin* stanza. Like a sonnet, this stanza has fourteen lines, but it has three varied quatrains and a concluding couplet in the rhyme scheme *AbAb CCdd EffE gg* (capital letters indicate feminine rhymes). Each stanza is a poetic miniature of scene, action, or comment. Typically, the initial quatrain introduces a theme, the other two quatrains develop it, and the final couplet supplies a definite, witty, epigrammatic conclusion. The play on structure includes the clearly indicated omission of stanzas or parts of stanzas here and there; the reader is left to imagine their content. The eight chapters of the novel are followed by a sort of appendix, "Onegin's Journey" (unfortunately omitted from the English verse translation of the entire novel), important in the implied characterization of Onegin. The mode of narration in the novel is in a class of its own. The first-person narrator introduces his characters and comments on their situations and actions; characterization is accomplished largely through authorial comment and attitude, especially by the use of stylistic coloring appropriate to the individual character. But in the plot's central passages the characters' words are presented directly: Tatiana's letter and Onegin's response; Onegin's letter and Tatiana's response; Onegin's thoughts prior to the duel with Lensky; Lensky's poem on the eve of the duel; Tatiana's dream.

Eugene Onegin is incomparable as a novel in verse, although neither its verse form nor its use of a lyrical narrator resulted in further important developments in the Russian novel. But as a novel based on social realities, with the hero reflecting his time and the heroine embodying the country and its ideal aspirations, it founded a tradition continued in the prose novel of Pushkin's successors. *Eugene Onegin* toys with many ideas, including the notion of the "prosaic," but the entire novel suggests the importance of the poetic. Perhaps the fundamental question of the novel is how a man may develop to maturity and remain, or once more become, poetic. The great Russian novels of the late nineteenth century are in prose, in both style and conception. *Eugene Onegin,* the first great Russian novel, is probably best viewed not as a transitional or anticipatory work but as the most controversial and influential novel, and the one nearest to perfection, in Russian literature.

Lyrics

Pushkin's lyrics are astonishing in their number, variety, and excellence; no other Russian poet's work can compare. We classify as lyrics all poems not included in the other poetic genres; they constitute almost exactly half of his entire poetic output (some 21,716 of the 42,541 lines of verse in the complete textual edition). The early lyrics build directly on those of two older poets, Zhukovsky and Batyushkov, whom Pushkin quickly outstripped and then eclipsed. He was always conscious of literary tradition, including genres and the use of poetic form on all levels, but he rejected the eighteenth century's strict expectations for style and form in each genre and moved on to new effects, including the mixture of genres and deliberate breaking with formal expectations to achieve particular effects. Apart from the technical qualities achieved in his lyrics—his mastery of verse and of stanzaic form—even as a young man he moved Russian poetry toward more purity in rhyme, flexibility in rhythm, and variety in meters.

The most appealing of his lyrics are probably those in which the poet-persona, the "I" of the poet, presents an individual experience in narrative form. However, the first-person lyrics are of many other varieties, and Pushkin was also master of lyrics in which the first person does not appear, such as the ode and the literary ballad. But the "I" of Pushkin's lyrics is of a special kind: his lyrics are not about what I think and feel but about what I *think* and *feel*. Experience is re-created and thought is felt so that the reader may share them directly. Pushkin's manuscripts show that, in revising, he consciously removed the merely personal or all-too-personal, so that there are both poetic immediacy and artistic distancing, even when (as is often the case) we know of the biographical moment reflected. Pushkin wrote some poems in the many lyric genres he inherited from the eighteenth century—odes, poetic epistles, epigrams, satires—and from the early nineteenth century—ballads, elegies, and the "anthological" poem (based on the poetics of the Greek Anthology). He put his imprint—not only a high level of poetic excellence but an individual tone, quality, and poetic construction—on any genre he used.

The main body of his lyrics, however, defies genre classification: some are personal lyrics, with the "I" of the poet directly expressed; some are meditative; some are experiential; others use third-person narrative.

One of the most characteristic qualities of Pushkin's lyrics of direct experience is their extreme brevity. Batyushkov, in some of his later poems, introduced direct sensuous poetry typical of the Greek Anthology. Pushkin further developed and refined such poetry, beginning with "Nereida" (1820), a short narrative poem in which a satyr watches a sea nymph rising from the water (with the clear implication that the sea nymph is human and the satyr is the poet-voyeur); the situation is intensely felt, yet the poet invites impersonal interpretation not based on his personal history by calling such lyrics "imitations of the ancients." Among these are "The Burned Letter"(1825), which with absolute unity of time presents the burning of a letter and the accompanying thoughts, including the visual detail of the ashes of the letter, with white writing on black; "Night" (1823), in which the poet hears "my voice for you" saying "I'm thine, I'm thine"; and, the masterpiece of this kind, "Bacchic Song" (1825), in which reason (here "wisdom") is celebrated as encompassing enjoyment of wine, women, and song—in complete contrast to eighteenth-century ideas of reason. Greek myth could be used to imply personal situation and attitude, as in "Arion" (1827), which clearly reflects Pushkin's relationship to the Decembrists. These poems are brief, almost epigrammatic. Some include a universal statement, such as "The Wagon of Life" (1823), which presents in plainest Russian the three stages of a man's life through the image of Time driving a jolting wagon.

Many of Pushkin's personal lyrics are related to love, incipient, current, or remembered; they can be intensely sensuous and physical, or idealistic. Many of them deal with actual experiences. The most famous is, no doubt, the one to Madame Kern, "I Remember a Wondrous Moment" (1825), about meeting, forgetting, and meeting again a "genius of pure beauty," and the resurrection of inspiration and love. The lyrics can be delightfully teasing, as is one on a slip of a young lady's tongue, "Thou and You" (1828). Love can be expressed in light and capricious terms, as in "I Love You, Though I Am Enraged" (1829), or in terms of self-abnegation, as in "I Have Loved You" (1829). One of the most powerful lyrics, " Under the Blue Sky" (1826), is about the absence of any feeling on hearing of the death of a former passionate love; four years later, in "Bound for the Shores of Your Distant Country" (1830), the same woman is called back from the grave to give the poet a promised kiss. Love may be potential rather than actual—now married, he must not let love arise in response to a beautiful woman: "The Beauty" (1832) and "I Thought My Heart Had Quite Forgotten" (1835). The most intensely sensual of all Pushkin's lyrics is "No, I Do Not Value" (1830), in which orgasms with two sharply contrasting types of women are experienced (Pushkin apparently considered calling this an Anthological poem; he never published it). Jealousy is presented in narrative form in "The Dismal Day Has Flickered Out" (1824), a lyric in which the "I" imagines what a far-off loved one is doing; its two climaxes are indicated by omissions and by a broken-off line and sentence.

Pushkin's poems on friendship are related to those on love. Outstanding among them are poems celebrating the anniversary of the founding of the lyceum at Tsarskoe Selo, especially the first, "October 19" (1825). But poems in the form of poetic epistles are perhaps his best memorial to friendship; they transform the discursive, ratiocinative expectations of the genre into the familiar and intimate.

The poems that caused the most difficulty during Pushkin's lifetime are those with overt or implied political themes. Under an autocracy, as in a totalitarian state, individual thinking on political themes is considered subversive or revolutionary. Pushkin's "Liberty: An Ode" (1817) is a panegyric to an idea rather than, as expected, a person: the poem celebrates "Liberty" with "Law" and opposes the breaking of the "Law" by autocrat or mob. "In the Country" (1819) presents in its second part a strongly negative picture of village life for the serfs and expresses hope for their emancipation through a "gesture" from the czar; the first part, in contrast, presents an idyllic visit to the countryside by a "lover of mankind" (it is curious that when Pushkin was refused the right to publish the whole poem, he nevertheless was willing to publish the first part). "Fairy Tales: A Noël" (1818), in the genre of French parodies of Christmas carols, dismisses as "fairy tales" the idea that Alexander I would give a constitution to Russia. "Napoleon: An Ode" (1821), which Pushkin later called "my last liberal delirium," is by no means a panegryric ode; it praises Napoleon because he "pointed to the high lot of the Russian people and bequeathed eternal liberty to the world." "The Dagger" (1821) celebrates that weapon as the "last judge of infamy and insult" and gives instances of its use: the assassination of Julius Caesar by Brutus, of Jean Paul Marat by Charlotte Corday, and of August von Kotzebue by the student Sand. That Pushkin no longer had hopes for radical reform, abroad or in Russia, is reflected in "Freedom's Sower in the Wilderness" (1823). When the Decembrist uprising failed, Pushkin again hoped for reforms "from above." In "Stanzas (In Hope of Fame and Good)" (1826) the figure of Peter the Great enters Pushkin's poetry; Peter is celebrated not so much for his reforms as for pardoning those who had opposed him. The theme recurs in "The Feast of Peter the Great" (1835), as well as in *Poltava*. In "To Siberia" (1827) Pushkin sends greetings and hope to the Decembrist exiles; and, as suggested above, in "Arion" he, the singer miraculously preserved, "still sings the former songs." In one of his final poems, entitled "From Pindemonte" (1836)—suggesting a translation from the earlier Italian poet Ippolito Pindemonte—but obviously expressing Pushkin's views, the poet sees no difference between the tyranny of one (autocracy) and the tyranny of the people (democracy). Pushkin had read Alexis de Tocqueville's writings and, like him, feared the "tyranny of the majority"; Pushkin calls instead for inner freedom. No freedom of any kind is attainable in "God Grant I Not Go Mad" (usually dated 1833).

Pushkin wrote a number of poems on poetry and poets. In early poems the poet appears in the conventional image of the mournful "singer" of unrequited love, as in "The Singer" (1816). In "A Conversation Between a Poet and a Bookseller" (1824) the poet heatedly protests that his "inspiration" is not for sale, but the bookseller manages to convince him that—with no contradiction—he can sell the completed "manuscript." "The Prophet" uses images from the book of Isaiah (1:1–6) to present a prophet being called from on high; the poem has been interpreted from Pushkin's day to ours as referring to the poet receiving the divine call. The "prophet" is called by God to "burn with the Word the hearts of men," but the poem does not reveal what the "Word" is. In "The Poet" (1827) the poet is the most ordinary of men, until the "godly word" touches his keen ear and he goes to "desert waves" and "wide-rustling groves" to listen and write. In "The Poet and the Mob" (1828) the poet-devotee sings to the "undedicated, cold, proud mob" and scorns its desire that he "teach" and be "useful"; he was born for "inspiration, sweet songs, and prayers." In "Echo" (1831) Pushkin condenses a poem by Barry Cornwall, adding the idea that the poet, like the echo itself, evokes no echo. The final poem in this group is "I Have Raised to Myself a Monument" (1836), an adaptation of Horace's *Exegi monumentum*: Pushkin will be remembered as long as a single poet lives; he will "long" be remembered by the "people" because he sang of "kind feelings" and "freedom," and "called for mercy to the fallen." "Freedom" here can be construed as either political or inner freedom; the poem suggests

that Pushkin expected to be remembered, as far as the general populace is concerned, for a tiny part of his work; by poets, or those who can appreciate poetry as poetry, he would be remembered for much more. However, those who can appreciate poetry without a message, as well as poetry with one, have come to constitute a much larger group than Pushkin suspected.

Pushkin was not a religious author, a desperate seeker reflecting his search in his work, as were Gogol, Dostoevsky, and Tolstoy. He began as an agnostic in "Unbelief" (1817). We have seen that *The Gabrieliad* travesties the story of the Annunciation and that Pushkin's exile in 1824 was caused by a letter in which he stated that atheism was the most "plausible" faith. However, in *The Fountain of Bakhchisaray* Maria is presented as an earthly embodiment of the biblical Mary, with her purity, innocence, and ignorance of the "passions." In 1825 Pushkin wrote two songs based on the Song of Songs: "In My Blood Burns the Fire of Desire" and "My Sister's Garden." As we have seen, "The Prophet" builds directly on Isaiah. In *Poltava*, Kochubey dies a specifically Christian death. The pain of remorse is powerfully presented in "Remembrance" (1828). "Once There Lived a Knight" (1829) is a ballad about a knight who has a vision of the Madonna and falls in love with her (as in stories of nuns who feel physical love for Christ), forsaking all women; Mary intercedes for her "paladin" when he dies. In the sonnet "Madonna" (1830) the poet celebrates a painting of the Madonna and identifies his own fiancée with her, suggesting that earthly love can be "pure." "The Pilgrim" (1835), based on the first part of John Bunyan's *Pilgrim's Progress*, transmits the urgency and loneliness of spiritual quest. In a cycle written in 1836, one poem, "Secular Power," bitterly criticizes the use of police force to keep the populace from "crowding the merrymaking gentry" when the common people try to see a painting of the Crucifixion of the one "whose execution redeemed all the

ALEXANDER PUSHKIN

tribe of Adam"; another poem, "Desert Fathers and Spotless Virgins" (1836), embodies the Lenten prayer of Ephraim the Syrian, which Pushkin had parodied many years earlier, at the end of *The Gabrieliad.* Pushkin's spiritual quest was implicit from the beginning.

Pushkin's poetry has rightly been characterized as primarily of this world rather than the one beyond. He calls for the participation of the reader and by no means makes everything explicit, but he does not subscribe to the romantic inexpressibility that Zhukovsky celebrates in "The Inexpressible" (1819). However, Pushkin's use of supernatural imagery should be noted. In the early poetry such imagery centered on the use of Greek myth (the Muse, Apollo, and the like). In *The Gabrieliad* supernatural creatures (anthropomorphically imagined) include Satan, Gabriel, and God himself. In "The Prophet" a seraph appears to the poet-narrator, and at the end he hears the voice of God. In "Demon" (1823) the spirit of temptation is identified as the spirit of disenchantment with all creation. Both an angel and a fallen angel appear in "The Angel" (1827). In an original "Scene from Faust" (1825) Pushkin's Mephistopheles taunts his Faust by suggesting that when he caressed Gretchen there was not the "union of two souls" as well as bodies, but merely conquest followed by boredom. In "I Remember a Wondrous Moment" (1825) a beautiful woman is celebrated as a "genius of pure beauty." "Remembrance" (1828) presents a personified Remembrance unrolling the long scroll on which the poet "reads his life." In "The Devils" (1830), a ballad, the traveler and his peasant coachman have "lost their way" in a snowstorm; they see a swarm of devils singing mournfully in the clouds and leading them astray.

Fantastic themes also appear in *Ruslan and Lyudmila,* in the verse fairy tales, and in Pushkin's prose. His biographers have much to say about his superstitiousness, which indeed is reflected in his letters. However, the lyric "Portents (I Was on the Way to You)" (1829) views "superstitious portents" as "concordant with the feelings of the soul." The poem depicts a joyous trip to, and a despondent one from, a loved one; it is built on the Russian superstition that to see the moon over the right shoulder is a good sign, over the left a bad one. (Pushkin commented to a contemporary that of course the moon was on the left when he returned, because he was going in the opposite direction.) The "magic" quality of the talisman in the poem of that name (1828) turns out to be not mastery of the forces of nature, but a sign and measure to prevent the poet from falling in love again, unworthily.

Pushkin's poems on nature, or nature and human beings, are among his best. These lyrics may deal with what is exotic to the Russians: the mountains, as in "Monastery on Kazbek" (1829), where the monastery and mountain are a symbol of spiritual aspiration; the sea, as in "To the Sea" (1824), where the sea is the "free element" as opposed to the "chains" of land; "The Storm" (1825), where the storm is the symbol of turbulent, rebellious man and is less beautiful than a "girl on a cliff." But most deal with Russia itself. The beauties of "Autumn" (1833) are, like a consumptive girl, the more beautiful for being short-lived. In these poems nature is of interest always in connection with human beings: as a place in which to live, to experience life and inspiration, to escape from cares and tribulations—not to seek impulses from vernal woods. In "Winter Morning" (1829) Nina is awakened to see the beauty of dark trees against the dazzling snow; in "Winter. What Is There to Do in the Country?" (1829), a chronicle of winter-day activities is given, culminating in a family visit that includes two sisters and a kiss that "burns in the cold." Nature is not always beautiful or enjoyed: in "Winter Evening" (1825) the exiled poet calls on his old peasant nurse to dispel boredom by singing folk songs and having a drink with him; in "Winter Road" (1826) the boring road is enlivened by the coachman's mournful folk song, before all becomes silent and boring again.

There are many poems dealing with conventional nature images. "The Flower" (1828) is typical: the subject is not the flower itself, but the question of who put it in the book, and why. A nature image is used to epitomize man's inhumanity to man in "The Upas Tree" (1828): a prince sends a slave to the upas tree for poison; upon delivering the poison, the slaves dies from it. Then the prince uses it to attack his neighbors. "Wide-rustling groves" provide not impulses for poetry, but rather a suitable environment for creativity ("The Poet," 1827). In one of his final lyrics Pushkin contrasts a city graveyard with a rural one where "instead of vain urns and little pyramids, a spreading oak stands, quivering and rustling" ("When, Lost in Thought," 1836).

Pushkin experimented with imitations of folk poetry and folk meters in his "Songs of Stenka Razin" (1826) and "Songs of the Western Slavs" (1834); these poems also imply a folk-type peasant narrator. They duplicate folk style and themes more successfully than any other poems in Russian—another sign of his versatility as a poet. In adapting the folk or folk-type ballad from the West, Zhukovsky had changed its tone and diction to that of his personal lyrics; Pushkin, in his literary ballads, reintroduced an implied narrator whose thought and speech were drawn from the common people, especially in "The Bridegroom" (1825), which is echoed in Tatiana's dream in *Eugene Onegin;* and in "The Drowned Man" (1828). Pushkin is much more brusque, direct, and suggestive even than the Scottish original in "Raven to Raven Flies" (1828), an adaptation of a poem in Sir Walter Scott's *Minstrelsy of the Scottish Border.*

Dramas

Pushkin's completed dramas include *Boris Godunov* (1824–1825) and four "Little Tragedies" completed in 1830: *The Covetous Knight, Mozart and Salieri, The Stone Guest,* and *Feast in Time of the Plague.* All follow Shakespeare in using unrhymed iambic pentameter. In *Boris Godunov* there is a caesura after the fourth syllable of each line, according to the French model. The later plays depart from earlier Russian practice by omitting the caesura entirely, according to the English model; the result is remarkable flexibility.

In *Boris Godunov* Pushkin consciously adapted Shakespearean principles of characterization and dramatic structure instead of following the neoclassical unities of time, place, action, and, as he noted, the "fourth unity" of style. Pushkin's aim was to write both a tragedy of character and one of *coûtume,* that is, a historical play accurately reflecting its times. Pushkin's play has twenty-three scenes and is not divided into acts; some scenes are in prose. It mixes the serious and the comic. Like some of Shakespeare's plays, *Boris Godunov* spans several years and has scenes set in widely separated places: Moscow, the Lithuanian border, Poland, and other locales in the Russian Empire. Pushkin consciously follows Shakespeare in having Boris speak differently in the family circle, among courtiers, and before the populace. However, there is considerable stylistic difference between *Boris Godunov* and Shakespeare's plays: Pushkin's language has no "purple patches" and avoids the saturated metaphorical style so characteristic of Shakespeare at his best. (Translations of Shakespeare into Russian have obviously been influenced by the style of *Boris Godunov;* even those by Boris Pasternak tend to sound more like Pushkin's play than like Shakespeare's originals.)

Boris Godunov is, unlike *Macbeth,* a play of dynastic, rather than personal, ambition. It extends from Boris' election as czar in 1598 to his death and the end of his dynasty in 1605. The first three scenes show how Boris contrives to be elected; the last three lead from his own death to that of his son and thus the end of the dynasty. As a tragedy rooted in Boris' character, the drama traces the path of guilt and expiation, of crime (the murder of the rightful heir, the True Dimitry) and punishment (not only Boris' death but that of his son). Pushkin follows the historian Nikolay Karamzin in assuming Boris' guilt in the murder of Czarevich Dimitry in 1591. (The Rurik dynasty had come to an end with the death of the childless Czar Feodor just before the play begins; the Romanov dynasty began in 1613, at the end of the Time of Troubles, eight years after Boris' death.) Boris' attempts to be a good ruler are thwarted by famine and pestilence, for which the ruler is blamed as reflecting evil in the state, a theme as old as Sophocles' *Oedipus the King.* And in Boris' attempts to be a good ruler he institutes changes that have both immediate and long-lasting evil consequences. One of these changes is the abolition of Saint George's Day—when peasants had the right to move from one landowner to another—thus establishing serfdom, disliked at once by both nobles and the peasantry. Another is the granting of rank and responsibility by merit rather than birth, an anticipation of the reforms of Peter the Great, a century later, which did away with the power of the old nobility. Ironically, the ambitious Basmanov, who owes his military promotion to precisely this change in policy, is false to his oath of allegiance almost immediately.

Grigory Otrepiev, the False Dimitry, is presented as an amiable, light-hearted adventurer rather than a man of serious ambition. He is a novice in a monastery when he decides to make rather than write history (unlike his mentor, the monk-chronicler Pimen), though a prophetic dream presages his fall as well as his rise. His central scene presents him risking all in order to discover whether he is loved for himself rather than as czarevich, and he agrees to masquerade as the True Dimitry only when the Polish heroine, Marina Mniszek, threatens to reveal his identity. The character of the play who most openly displays personal

ambition, she succeeds in her attempt to hasten the pretender's attack on Russia by promising to be his bride when he has conquered Moscow.

Perhaps the most unusual thing about *Boris Godunov* is that the title character never meets his rival, the False Dimitry; Boris dies of a sudden seizure rather than in a direct confrontation. The unifying factor in the play is the "spirit" of the True Dimitry, which has tormented Boris in his dreams for some thirteen years. It is a terrible irony that Boris, who would have reason to fear for his throne if the pretender is indeed the True Dimitry, feels reassured when Shuysky tells him that he himself saw the True Dimitry dead after the murder. The description of the undecayed corpse presages the revelation—just before Boris' sudden seizure and death—that the True Dimitry has become a wonder-working saint. When Marina Mniszek threatens to reveal the identity of the pretender, for the only time in the play the text identifies him not as Otrepiev or the pretender or the False Dimitry, but as "Dimitry": he assures Marina that the "shade" of Ivan the Terrible has made him his son, "Dimitry, the Czarevich."

Crowd scenes play a considerable role in the play. At the beginning the crowd is manipulated into calling for Boris' election. In the middle the crown seems convinced that the pretender is the True Dimitry; the one exception is the Holy Fool, who accuses Boris to his face of being a Herod, slaughterer of the innocent, and refuses Boris' request that he pray for him because the "Mother of God forbids." In the final scene the crowd, on learning of the death of Boris' son, responds with silence when called upon to cry, "Long live Dimitry." Thus the end of *Boris Godunov* contrasts sharply with the usual end of a tragedy: instead of being serene, it is ominous.

Each of Pushkin's "Little Tragedies" is based on a tight knot of irreconcilable contradictions in characterization or motivation, as revealed by their titles: in *The Covetous*

Knight, the contradiction between covetousness and knightliness; in *Mozart and Salieri,* the "idle" man of genius versus the hardworking man of talent; in *The Stone Guest,* the animated statue; and in *Feast in Time of the Plague,* celebration during calamity.

Pushkin's *Covetous Knight* is usually considered only in terms of the literary tradition of the miser, particularly Molière's *L'Avare.* However, Pushkin's subtitle suggests his real meaning (and reveals his knowledge of English): "Scenes from Chenstone's *The Covetous Knight*"—the title of the tragicomic "source" is given in English. In fact, no such play by a "Chenstone" or Shenstone is known. In Pushkin's *Covetous Knight* there are two main characters, a father and his son. The central conflict is between father and son over inheritance, anticipating Dostoevsky's *Brothers Karamazov* (which directly alludes to and builds on Pushkin's work): the "covetous" son who desires to inherit from his father; the "covetous" father who withholds inheritance from his son. The title adjective, *skupoi,* covers a whole range of English meanings, from "miserly" to "stingy," "avaricious," "niggardly," and "covetous." The "miserly" father is "stingy" to his son, who in consequence sees himself as "covetous" of a jousting opponent's helmet in attempting to play the knightly role to which his birth entitles him.

The middle scene of three is a long soliloquy—perhaps the most Shakespearean passage in all Russian literature (*too* Shakespearean, Turgenev thought)—in which the miserly old knight gloats over his wealth, and especially over the pain and grief it has caused others. His imagery is sexual, of whoremongering and even rape, and there is a suggestion of a black mass before his coffers. He sees in his wealth not only glitter but also potential power. His pleasure, however, is spoiled by the idea that the gold will be inherited by his "wastrel" son, who has not earned the money and hence the right to enjoy it. In the first scene the young knight indignantly rejects the

idea of hastening his inheritance through the use of poison; however, the duke, to whom he resorts for help in the third scene, does not succeed in conciliating father and son. The father accuses the son of wishing to kill him or steal from him, and the son calls the father a "liar" and "greedily" accepts his challenge to a duel. But the father suddenly dies of a seizure, and the son is banished. Thus the conflict between father and son is here irreconcilable.

Pushkin thought his own father stingy toward his sons (but that improvident man could hardly be considered avaricious or miserly or covetous). *The Covetous Knight* thematically reflects the conflict between Pushkin and his father in 1824 (see his letter of 31 October 1824 to Zhukovsky), when he was exiled to his mother's estate, Mikhaylovskoe. However, that conflict was reconciled before he wrote the play six years later, in 1830, at Boldino, his father's estate, where Pushkin went to mortgage the serfs, a gift from his father to make his marriage possible. Publication came only after another six years, in Pushkin's journal *Contemporary,* following his mother's death; but even then the author was identified only as "P," which could be read as Cyrillic *R* or Latin *P.*

Mozart and Salieri, a play of theodicy, the justice of God, uses the legend that the composer Salieri poisoned Mozart from jealousy. Salieri, in the first lines of the play, poses the question directly: "There is no justice [*pravda*] on earth or above." *Pravda* can mean either "truth" or "justice": justice and truth (and injustice and untruth) operate as verbal-thematic echoes throughout the play. God's justice is tested by the confrontation between Salieri, a hard-working man of talent who has given up normal life (represented by Izora, his beloved) to devote himself to music, and Mozart, the natural genius who can live a normal family life and effortlessly compose masterpieces. Salieri recognizes in the first scene that he has become jealous of Mozart; such jealousy is ironic because Salieri has success, position, and fame, whereas Mozart lives in such poverty that, after his death, he will be buried in a pauper's grave. Salieri tells himself that music advances as each composer learns from other gifted composers, as he himself had gladly learned from Puccini, Gluck, and Haydn; but he argues that Mozart's music is not "useful," for nobody can learn from it (this is patently false; early Mozart learned from Haydn; late Haydn learned from Mozart). When Mozart, as a joke, brings a blind fiddler who mangles some of his own music, he is amused, but Salieri is so offended that he decides that for the good of music Mozart must die.

In the second scene Salieri pours into Mozart's cup the poison Izora gave him twenty years before, when he abandoned all else to serve art. Mozart plays from his most recent composition, the *Requiem.* Seeing Salieri's emotion, Mozart identifies the two of them as "the elect, happy idlers who disdain vile usefulness, devotees of the beautiful alone." Thus Mozart is also a devotee not of art as craft but of the "beautiful alone." Salieri is left with the agonizing question of whether Mozart's dictum "genius and evildoing cannot coexist" is true—for the question then arises whether he himself is a genius. On the face of it, Pushkin's sympathy seems to be completely on Mozart's side. But one image shows how Pushkin plays all the roles in the "Little Tragedies": Salieri says that it is not funny to him when a "mountebank" dishonors Dante; the Russian word for "mountebank" is *figliar,* which to Pushkin at this time meant the despicable police spy and *littérateur* Faddey Bulgarin (attacked as "Figliarin" in one of Pushkin's epigrams), who had managed to get access to Pushkin's *Boris Godunov* before it was published, to borrow from it for a work of his own, and then to charge that Pushkin had plagiarized his work. The final scene of *Mozart and Salieri* makes use of the subconscious: Mozart is tormentingly aware, just below the level of consciousness, of the implication of his feeling that Death is sitting with the two of them,

and that he has composed and is playing for Salieri his own *Requiem.*

In *The Stone Guest* Pushkin gives his own version of the story of Don Juan (or Don Guan, as he has it), just as he had given an original turn to the miser theme in *The Covetous Knight.* Pushkin uses an epigraph from Mozart's *Don Giovanni,* suggesting that his version be compared with that one. Pushkin's Don Juan is quite different from earlier ones: he is an artist in lovemaking; instead of being a liar, a rapist, a despoiler of virgins, one who applies force and deception, he pays court until willing consent is obtained, insists on being loved as and for himself, and remembers previous loves with pleasure. Doña Anna, the only woman character taken from the traditional story, is the widow, not the daughter, of the commander. The commander has been killed "honorably in a duel" by Don Juan—we are not told the cause of the duel—instead of dying, as in Mozart, by Don Giovanni's hand over a brazen attempt to seduce his daughter, Doña Anna.

Pushkin's play opens as Don Juan returns to Madrid (not Seville) from exile without permission—his "friend" the king had exiled him to protect him from the commander's family. The play deals with three loves of Don Juan. He remembers with pleasure Doña Ineza, now dead, whom he courted for several months before winning her; he discovered "too late" that her husband was a "stern goodfor-nothing." He visits the actress Laura, who has just accepted as lover Don Carlos, brother of the commander. Laura is attracted to Don Carlos because in his anger and hatred toward Don Juan he reminds her of Don Juan himself. Don Carlos insists on a duel then and there; he falls, and Don Juan plans to take the body away the next morning. (The implication is that the presence of the corpse does not prevent him and Laura from enjoying each other.) This scene shows Don Juan as an artist (he wrote the song that Laura sings), a brave man, an accomplished duelist—"always guilty without guilt." In the first scene Don Juan sees Doña Anna; later, disguised as a monk, he manages to get her attention as she visits her husband's tomb, which is ornamented by an oversized statue of the deceased. In the presence of the statue Don Juan declares his love and obtains permission to visit Doña Anna; with bravado he invites the statue to attend. It nods assent. In the final scene Doña Anna says that the only man she hates is the one who killed her husband, although she admits that she did not marry for love. When Don Juan reveals his identity she finds that she nevertheless loves him and she agrees to another meeting. As Don Juan is about to depart, the statue of the commander enters and asks for Don Juan's hand; he fearlessly offers it, saying that he is ''glad'' the statue has come. As they fall through the floor Don Juan calls out, ''Doña Anna.''

Thus three triangles are presented in *The Stone Guest:* the retrospective one of Don Juan, Doña Ineza, and her husband, in which Ineza has died; Don Juan, Laura, and Don Carlos, in which Don Carlos dies; and Don Juan, Doña Anna, and the statue, in which Don Juan dies. There is no suggestion that Don Juan is married; Doña Anna is the only one of the women whom Don Juan might have married (Doña Ineza was already married; he would hardly have married an actress; peasant girls are spoken of, but they would be no match for a grandee). The play leaves ambiguous to what degree Don Juan's love for Doña Anna is mere momentary physical attraction, to what degree his role with her is acting, to what degree his feeling is genuine and lasting, and whether he might propose. The audience must decide.

The last of the ''Little Tragedies,'' *Feast in Time of the Plague,* is a rarity in world literature: part of a scene from John Wilson's *The City of the Plague* (1816) is translated and slightly adapted, and two songs are completely rewritten, to transform a work now almost forgotten in English into a Russian masterpiece. Thus all four of these plays are on themes from Western literature, with which Pushkin was consciously competing. In his letters Pushkin used the word ''plague'' several times to refer to the epidemic of Asiatic cholera that quarantined him at Boldino while he was writing these plays. *Feast* is Pushkin's play in the sense that he obviously took complete responsibility for everything in it. His two original songs are central. Mary's song, referring to an earlier visit of the plague to Scotland, suggests submission and self-abnegation. The girl in the song prays that, should she die of the plague, her beloved, Edmund, will stay away from her grave until the pestilence is past; she will pray for him from heaven. The Master of the Revels' ''Hymn in Honor of the Plague'' is about the exhilaration, the joy, of taking risks—of being on the edge of the abyss, being endangered by a hurricane, or kissing lips perhaps infected with plague. But when the Priest comes and urges the Master of the Revels to leave this ''feast'' in the name of his mother and wife, who have recently died, he admits that his hymn was really inspired by despair. Nevertheless, he refuses to follow the Priest but leaves the revelers and remains alone, deep in thought.

Verse Fairy Tales

Pushkin's verse fairy tales are the most popular of his works in Russia—popular in the sense of appealing to everyone, uneducated and educated, young and old. Pushkin lived at the time that folklore was beginning to be of interest to all levels of society. While he was in exile at Mikhaylovskoe he jotted down several précis of fairy tales told him by his peasant nurse, Arina Rodionovna, who was obviously an accomplished storyteller. Russian fairy tales (including Pushkin's) imply a peasant narrator (*skazitel'* or *skazochnik*) who identifies with the story and its action—in complete contrast to the separation between materials and narrator in *Ruslan and Lyudmila,* where only the prologue is popular in this sense. In these fairy tales there is suspension of disbelief and immediate acceptance of a poetic world that includes a mixture of magic and the homely everyday, where characters and their motivations are simple (good, evil, envious, greedy, and so on), and where czars, princesses, *bogatyrs*, priests, and peasants are seen as simple people see them. Conventional symbols, epithets, similes, fixed expressions and images, and formulaic repetition, often with incremental additions or changes, characterize their style. Pushkin may use Russian materials alone or present a mixture of Russian and foreign materials or adapt foreign materials, but each story is told in Russian fashion. Each contains themes of universal interest and is related dispassionately.

The Tale of the Village Priest and His Workman Balda (1830) follows closely one of the stories told to Pushkin by Arina Rodionovna. It celebrates the hard work and, especially, the wiliness of the peasant laborer Balda, and it ridicules the village priest who tries to hire him cheaply and then avoid payment by giving him an impossible task. The central part of the poem tells how Balda outwits and overcomes an Old Devil *(bes)* and a Young Devil, and collects from them the quitrent owed to the parish priest. In the end Balda collects his "pay" with a vengeance: three fillips on the priest's head. Three typical folk themes are here combined: the wily peasant worker, the stupid parish priest, and minor devils who amuse rather than frighten. The poem is written like a *raeshnik*, a typical verse form with irregular beats like doggerel or rhymed prose, with emphasized rhyme-words in couplets, and with the rhyming parts of the rhyme-words (rhyme-elements) varying from one to four syllables.

Pushkin combined Russian and international materials in *The Tale of the Fisherman and the Fish* (1833), which treats the theme of the compliant husband and his overreaching wife. The fisherman's wife is dissatisfied when she learns that her husband has caught and released a golden fish that can talk and that offered as ransom whatever he wished. She sends her husband back again and again with ever greater demands: that their broken trough be replaced by a whole one, that their hut be changed into a cottage, that she be made a noblewoman, that she be made a czaritsa, and, finally, that she be made ruler of the sea and have the golden fish at her beck and call. Then everything returns to its former condition: she is left in front of their mud hut with a broken trough. Pushkin departs from the Grimms' version (1812–1814) in omitting the wife's desire to be pope (which would mean nothing to an Orthodox Russian peasant) and in having her treat her obedient husband as a mere lackey who ultimately is not even allowed to associate with his wife, rather than having the couple share their improved status. However, he follows the Grimms in having the sea progressively darken as the fisherman returns with ever greater demands. The poem uses a Russian folk verse form: three-stress accentual verse in lines of different numbers of syllables, with penultimate final stress.

Perhaps the most charming of the verse fairy tales is the one with the long and characteristic title *The Tale of the Tsar Saltan, of His Son the Glorious and Powerful Bogatyr Prince Gvidon, and of the Beautiful Swan Princess* (1831). This is the first of three delightful verse fairy tales in trochaic tetrameter with couplet rhymes—trochaic verse was considered folkish—and is the longest and most leisurely. Saltan and Gvidon are characteristic of the heroic *bogatyr* type: gigantic, powerful, and simple-hearted. The story concerns Saltan's wronged wife, slandered by her two sisters and mother; the Swan Princess's rescue from the Sorcerer-Kite by Saltan's son, Gvidon, who matures suddenly; and the Swan Princess, who helps Gvidon through magic to attract Saltan to visit his city, full of wonders, so that father, mother, and son will be united. Marvels typical of Russian folk tales are incorporated: a city constructed magically on an uninhabited island for Gvidon to rule; a squirrel that gnaws nuts with golden hulls and emerald kernels; thirty *bogatyrs* who come up out of the sea with their leader, Chernomor; and a princess who "eclipses the day," and has a moon in her hair and a star in her forehead—the Swan Princess, who becomes Gvidon's bride. Visiting merchants see Gvidon's city and the other wonders that are created there. Gvidon sends an invitation to Saltan to visit him. He himself visits Saltan three times—in the form of a midge, a fly, and a bee—and punishes the two sisters and mother in turn, as they deprecate the marvels reported and tell what a *real* marvel would be like. There is charming incremental repetition: a *real* marvel is described; Givdon asks the Swan Princess whether it actually exists; he sees it after she has created it by magic; visiting merchants come and see it and the previously created marvels; and the merchants report to Saltan the marvels they have seen. In the conclusion Saltan sees all the marvels himself and, finally, his wife and son.

The Tale of the Dead Princess and the Seven Bogatyrs (1833) is a Russian version of the familiar story of Snow White, with the seven dwarfs replaced by seven *bogatyr*s. It includes such traditional material as the jealous stepmother, the magic speaking mirror, the abandonment of the princess in the woods to die, her sojourn with seven males, the witch with the poisoned apple, and the princess's final awakening from a deathlike sleep. But significant details of story and characterization are unique to Pushkin: The seven *bogatyr*s, true to peasant psychology, are convinced that their visitor is a princess because of the way she has cleaned and straightened up their house before they return; they all fall in love with her and ask her to marry whichever one of them she prefers, but with great tact she refuses because she is already affianced to Prince Elisey. After she "dies" of the poison she is placed in a crystal coffin high on a steep mountain. Prince Elisey seeks her, asking the Sun and the Moon fruitlessly whether they know where she is; finally the Wind informs him. He finds her in her coffin and breaks it open; the piece of poisoned apple is dislodged, and

she comes back to life. The stepmother dies of anguish when she discovers that the girl is alive; the marriage is celebrated with feasting. The theme of constancy in love is one we have seen in Pushkin as early as *Ruslan and Lyudmila.* Pushkin's adaptations indicate that, as he suggested in a letter to his wife, no matter how much he loved beauty of face, he loved beauty of soul even more.

The story of *The Tale of the Golden Cockerel* (1834) is adapted from Washington Irving's "Tale of the Arabian Astrologer," in *The Alhambra* (1832). Irving's story is a charming, ironic just-so type of story explaining why Granadans are so prone to be sleepy: it is because they hear through fissures in the rock the Gothic princess playing her lyre and singing to the Arabian astrologer deep underground. The Arabian astrologer had set up a magic horseman with a lance who would warn the king when his enemies were approaching by pointing in the direction from which they would come. After all military threats are disposed of, it points to the Gothic princess. When the king refuses to give her up to the astrologer, she and the astrologer disappear into a cleft in the mountain. Pushkin substitutes the golden cockerel as "talisman" (both "golden" and "cockerel" are suggested by other talismans mentioned in Irving's story), and it focuses on only one danger, which turns out to be the beautiful princess of Shamakha. After Czar Dadon's two sons successively lead armies to meet the threat but do not return, he follows them. When he arrives at a mountain meadow, he finds that they have killed each other. He then meets the princess of Shamakha, over whom they have obviously fought, and he too becomes enthralled by her. When Dadon returns with her, the astrologer demands her as his promised reward. The czar, in anger, kills the astrologer, whereupon the golden cockerel swoops down from its pinnacle, pecks the czar to death, and soars away. The princess laughs "hee-hee-hee" and "haw-haw-haw," and disappears. The poem ends by stating that it has a hint for "fine good fellows." The story is told tensely and tersely; it is the least "Russian" of Pushkin's fairy tales in verse. Interpretation has been the subject of much debate; many have suspected political satire. It should be noted, however, that in Irving's story nobody's death is caused by the Gothic princess; in Pushkin's tale the "magic" of a beautiful and heartless woman results in the destruction of all the male characters—the czar's two sons, the astrologer, and the czar himself—and also in the disappearance of the golden cockerel.

Prose Fiction

Pushkin wrote the first prose fiction in Russian that can still be read with pleasure. The works he completed and published himself are still perhaps the finest of their kind in Russian and compare favorably with anything similar in world literature. They include a collection of short stories, *The Tales of the Late Ivan Petrovich Belkin;* one long short story, or novella, *The Queen of Spades;* and a historical novel, *The Captain's Daughter.* Pushkin left unfinished a number of prose works that are, unfortunately, often published in both Russian editions and translation as though they represented Pushkin's standards of artistry in the genre.

The most characteristic quality of Pushkin's prose fiction is the absence of anything that might ostensibly relate thought or incident to the ideas or life of Alexander Pushkin. There is a whole series of masks in *The Tales of Belkin* (1830). The introduction, purportedly giving information on Belkin, is written by an obviously fictional "A. P.," the publisher, who certainly is no Pushkin. We are told that from "lack of imagination" Belkin used stories told to him by others (identified by initials, sex, and social position or status). Obviously, "A. P." or Pushkin himself must be thought to have made editorial changes and to have supplied the epigraphs, some of which could hardly have been supplied by Belkin. There are allusions to works that appeared

after Belkin's "death." Two of the stories are told in the first person: "The Shot" by a figure similar to Belkin as he is represented, and "The Stationmaster" by a Russian civil servant whose career is quite unlike Belkin's. The others are told in the third person, with hints of stylistic residues from those who "told" them to Belkin.

The stories are models of varied storytelling, something like extended revelatory anecdotes about unusual individuals and occurrences set against a background of the everyday and the ordinary. The prose is simple, direct, and extremely economical. Pushkin's refusal to point a moral or make explicit the stories' implications led them to be greatly undervalued in the nineteenth century. In the twentieth century they have gradually been recognized as masterpieces of their type, and their implications are now seen as being as complex and worthy of study as those of Pushkin's verse.

"The Shot" is a story about delayed revenge. An envious hussar intentionally provokes a duel, and when his opponent unconcernedly eats cherries while waiting to be shot he has the "malicious idea" of delaying his shot until his opponent's marriage, whenever that may be. All of this is told to the narrator by Silvio, the vengeful man himself, six years after the event. The second part of the story is told to the narrator by the second principal, the count, five years after the incident that he, in turn, relates. During the count's honeymoon, Silvio appeared and insisted on resuming the duel; he persuaded the count to draw lots, by which the count was awarded the first shot. The count missed, his bullet piercing a painting on the wall. Then, although the count's wife had come in, Silvio completed the duel by shooting his bullet into the hole made by the count's shot. The story ends with the bare statement that Silvio is rumored to have died in the war for Greek independence. Two-thirds or more of each section of the story is devoted to setting up the situation in which each principal will tell the narrator his part of the story. Thus there is the suggestion that a two-stage "recognition" is what the story mainly concerns: whether to a mature man or a young one, "valor is the acme of human virtues and an excuse for all possible vices."

"The Snowstorm" is striking in both its use of a natural phenomenon and its mode of narration. The story relates parallel adventures: Vladimir and Marya Gavrilovna, influenced by French sentimental novels and in love with love rather than with each other, plan to elope to a remote church. The hussar Burmin, unaccountably impelled to go out in the snowstorm, gets lost and arrives unexpectedly at the same church, where he substitutes himself for the delayed bridegroom with "incomprehensible levity." The Napoleonic invasion of 1812, another natural force outside their control that affects the characters' lives, removes Vladimir by taking his life but returns Burmin, a wounded hero. As a result of this second "snowstorm" Burmin has been given an opportunity to mature: he regrets his hussar prank and falls passionately in love with the unknown woman he had married in the church. Like "The Shot," this story combines two narratives; but they are told quite differently and at different times. The narrator follows Vladimir's consciousness, his night of mental and physical agony as he gets lost in the snowstorm and arrives at the church hours later than he had expected. Burmin tells his own story years later as he recalls and regrets the incident, as part of his declaration-confession to the heroine. The climax and resolution are combined: revelation of what happened in the church results in immediate recognition by the lovers, who are already wed.

"The Stationmaster" presents still another hussar escapade: an elopement with the stationmaster's pretty daughter. However, the emphasis is not on the hussar Minsky but on the stationmaster and his daughter, Dunya. The story is told through the observations and conversations of the narrator in a series of visits to the station. It is a model of sympathy and detachment combined, of sentiment without sentimentality. The story is built on the expectations aroused by pictures of the parable of the Prodigal Son on the station wall, on the one hand, and the stationmaster's view of himself as the Good Shepherd whose duty it is to go after the "lost sheep" (his daughter) on the other. When the "lost sheep" is unwilling to be brought back, he cannot imagine that she will return voluntarily. He goes back to the station and, over a period of time, drinks himself to death. But she does return—not in rags and tatters like the Prodigal Son but as a lady with a fine coach, rich clothing, three children, and a wetnurse. Her visit is recounted uncomprehendingly to the narrator by a small boy, to whom (along with other boys) the stationmaster had been kind after his daughter left. The story ends with the narrator rejoicing at what he has learned. In this parallel to the parable of the Prodigal Son the narrator plays a role comparable to that of the older brother—not the older brother of the parable, but the parable's suggestion of what the older brother should have been like. *The Stationmaster* is the most influential of the *Belkin* tales. It is often regarded as the source of the "natural school" in Russian literature, exemplified by Gogol's "The Overcoat" and Dostoevsky's *Poor Folk*.

"The Undertaker" is an ironic presentation of a serious-minded, unimaginative undertaker who, at a get-acquainted party after he has just moved into a new neighborhood, becomes incensed when other tradesmen drink to their clients' health and laughingly urge him to do the same. He decides to invite his "clients" to a party. They come from the grave and, one after another, accuse him of having cheated them. Only the next day does he discover (along with the reader) that the visit of the corpses was a dream. To the reader, the accusations of the corpses show that the undertaker's conscience is involved; however, the story ends with the irony—left without comment—that after his dream the undertaker immediately returns to life as usual, even in unaccustomed good humor, without having learned anything from the experience. The story has often been interpreted as a satire on the class of tradesmen or as a parody of conventional ghost stories; however, there are hints in it that on some level Pushkin himself is the "undertaker" and his works the coffins in which the corpses—his characters—have been "cheated" of a proper "burial."

"Mistress into Maid" is a charmingly indulgent story of how two country squires settle their "manorly feud," and of how their respective son and daughter put on and remove masks or disguises and, finally, make a match. As a lighthearted comedy of manners it has no parallel in Russian literature. The son returns to the country from the university posing as a disenchanted, Byronic young man in the presence of young ladies; he drops his pose to frolic with peasant girls. To make his acquaintance, the daughter assumes the disguise of a peasant girl; he "educates" her, and they gradually fall in love. When their parents become reconciled, she assumes still another disguise—that of false curls and paint—to avoid being recognized by him. The fathers decide to marry their children to each other, whereupon the young man finds himself so much in love with the "peasant" that he writes her a "mad" letter. When he goes to persuade the neighboring father or his daughter to let him marry someone else, he finds his peasant love in morning dress, reading his letter. There is an amusing interchange of manor styles and disguises between fathers and children: the father of the son with the Byronic (Western, English) mask is a Russophile; the father of the daughter who disguises herself as a (Russian) peasant is an Anglophile. The parallel situations of the disenchanted young man and the unspoiled country girl in this story and in *Eugene Onegin* have often been noted. The essential difference lies in the relationships of mask and character.

The Queen of Spades (1833) is the most enigmatic, controversial, and profound of Pushkin's works of prose fiction. Critics disagree completely about whether the fantastic element in it should be interpreted as "real" or as a figment of the hero's imagination. The work makes use of supernatural themes but is firmly grounded in social and psychological reality—although, as always in Pushkin, the psychology is implied rather than explicit. It is the story of a man's character as his fate, of calculation versus imagination, of the conscious versus the subconscious, of chance versus possible supernatural causation. Pushkin was aware that, in gambling, chance becomes fate, and that the nonprofessional gambler feels the need to test chance/fate, and, ultimately, to lose. Hermann, an army engineering officer of German extraction, has been able to restrain the "imagination" of a "born gambler" by the "German" quality of "calculation," until he hears about an old countess who knows a secret system of three cards that, played in sequence, will win each time in faro. By paying court to her young female companion Hermann obtains access to the countess, but the "old witch" dies—without revealing the secret despite his efforts at persuasion and his threats. However, the countess's ghost appears and gives him the sequence and instructions for using it. The identity of the cards (trey, seven, ace) has already been in Hermann's consciousness and is suggested by the mode of betting in faro. That the ace culminates the series shows the height of Hermann's ambition; a collateral meaning of the Russian word for ace (*tuz*) is a "fat cat" or "big shot," a prosperous, high-ranking, influential man. When he goes to play the sequence Hermann's first two cards win; to win with the third he must hold the ace, as he intends; but when he shows the queen of spades he is told, "Your lady has been killed." Hermann cries out, "The old woman!" Hermann loses not only his winnings and his patrimony but his mind. It should be noted that Hermann is the only character in the story who witnesses the fantastic: the dead countess winking at him from her coffin, her ghostly visit, and the identification of the queen of spades as the "old woman," whom Hermann had called, to her face, "old witch." Thus the countess as "witch" is even more enigmatic than the witches in *Macbeth*, who embody Macbeth's ambition and guilt and presage his rise and fall. Unlike Macbeth and other literary figures who make a conscious or unconscious pact with the forces of evil, Hermann at no time enjoys success. Through natural or supernatural influence, depending on how one chooses to interpret the story, he shows the wrong card at the climax of the story, and the moment of victory becomes the moment of defeat.

The Captain's Daughter (1833–1836) is a historical novel set at the time of the Pugachev Rebellion (1772–1775) and related as the memoirs of Pyotr Grinev forty or fifty years later, during the reign of Alexander I; the two eras are contrasted directly and by implication. There is also a brief epilogue by the "publisher," dated 19 October 1836, in which he states that he has tried to give a suitable epigraph to each chapter and has changed some of the personal names. Thus the novel is cast in a triple time perspective: the events at the time of their occurrence; as they seemed two generations later, in another reign; and as they seem in a still later reign. *The Captain's Daughter* is a historical novel that attempts to evoke a time past; it is a memoir and a family chronicle; and it is a novel of the development of Grinev from boyhood to maturity (a bildungsroman). Thus events are put into deep perspective, and there is a constant play of irony at the expense of the hero's own callow youthfulness and past imperfections, alternating with a serious presentation of such vital experiences as Grinev's prophetic dream, the execution of the Mironovs by Pugachev's men, Grinev's meetings with Pugachev, and Masha Mironov's meeting with Catherine the Great.

Like most historical romances since Sir Walter Scott initiated the popular genre with *Waverley* (1814), *The Captain's Daughter* presents fictional characters and story against the background of actual events; historical personages may appear, but they are not the primary characters in the story. The main theme and central image of the novel are expressed in its epigraph: "Watch over your honor while you are young, and your coat while it is new." Young Grinev, on the way to military duty in the Urals region, gives his *old* hareskin coat to a peasant who has guided him safely through a snowstorm. This gift results in the sparing of Grinev's life when Pugachev (the peasant) and his men take the fortress where Grinev is serving. There is a twofold test or measure of Grinev's "honor": first, fidelity to his oath of allegiance to Catherine II as an officer, and, second, his "knightly" honor, to protect the life and honor of Masha, daughter of Captain Mironov, commander of the fortress. (Neither of the claimants to the throne of Russia had any legitimate claim to it: Catherine, a German princess, had usurped it when her husband, Peter III, was deposed and assassinated in 1762; the peasant Pugachev claimed to be Peter III.) Grinev remains true to both kinds of honor, although after the struggle appearances lead to his arrest and conviction on a charge of treason. Unlike Scott's character Waverley, Grinev never fights on the opposing side and never breaks his oath of allegiance. Pugachev's rewards to Grinev for the hareskin coat are indeed great: he not only halts Grinev's execution but rescues Masha from the villain Shvabrin and gives Masha and Grinev a safe conduct through his lines. Grinev is found guilty because he is so protective of Masha's honor that he will not mention her name at the trial; to do so might free him, but it might also lead to false charges that would tarnish her honor. Grinev's honor of both kinds is in direct contrast to the lack of honor of Shvabrin, another officer at the fortress. He slanders Masha, joins Pugachev's forces, imprisons Masha and attempts to force her to marry him, and slanders Grinev after both men are arrested.

Masha realizes why Grinev has been found guilty. At the end of the novel proper, Grinev recounts her story: Masha goes to Tsarskoe Selo, where she manages to meet a "lady" with a dog in the garden and to tell her the true story; the "lady" is revealed to be Catherine II, who then pardons Grinev and provides a dowry for Masha. Thus the novel is balanced; just as Pugachev serves metaphorically as "father substitute," Catherine serves as "mother substitute" and brings Grinev and Masha together in marriage. Through direct witnesses the novel presents Pugachev and Catherine II as human beings, fallible but appealing, and, as regards Grinev and Masha, just and even merciful. In *Poltava*, as we have seen, Pushkin follows historians in presenting Mazepa as evil. Pushkin had done his own historical research for *The Captain's Daughter* (when preparing his *History of Pugachev*, 1833); the characterization of Pugachev is built on what Pushkin discovered in documents and in the memories of surviving witnesses.

Selected Bibliography

FIRST EDITIONS

Stikhotvoreniia Aleksandra Pushkina. St. Petersburg, 1826.
Stikhotvoreniia Aleksandra Pushkina. 4 vols. St. Petersburg, 1829–1834.
Povesti, izdannye Aleksandrom Pushkinym. St. Petersburg, 1834.
Poemy i povesti Aleksandra Pushkina. 2 vols. St. Petersburg, 1835.

MODERN EDITIONS

Dnevnik Pushkina, 1833–1835. Edited by B. L. Modzalevsky. Moscow, 1923.
Dnevnik Pushkina (1833–1835). Edited by V. F. Savodnik and M. M. Speransky. Moscow and Petrograd, 1923.
Pis'ma. Vols. 1 and 2, edited by B. L. Modzalevsky. Moscow and Leningrad, 1926. Vol. 3, edited by L. B. Modzalevsky. Moscow, 1935. Letters 1815–1833, with exhaustive commentary.
Pis'ma poslednikh let, 1834–1837. Edited by N. V. Izmailov. Leningrad, 1969. Exhaustive commentary.

Polnoe sobranie sochinenii. Edited by M. A. Tsiavlovsky and Iu. G. Oksman. 6 vols. Moscow, 1936–1938. Best commentary.
————. Edited by V. D. Bronch-Bruevich et al. 17 vols. Moscow, 1937–1939. "Large academy edition," including all variants and information on sources of texts.
————. Edited by B. V. Tomashevsky. 10 vols. Moscow, 1949; 2nd ed., 1956–1958; 3rd ed., 1962–1966; 4th ed., 1977–1979. Texts based on 1937–1939 edition, with succinct commentary.
Pushkin. [*Sobranie sochinenii.*] Edited by S. A. Vengerov. 6 vols. St. Petersburg, 1907–1915. Extensive accompanying articles.
Risunki Pushkina. Edited by T. G. Tsiavlovskaya. Moscow, 1980. Reproduces and studies Pushkin's drawings on manuscripts.
Rukoiu Pushkina: Nesobrannye i neopublikovannye teksty. Edited by M. A. Tsiavlovsky et al. Moscow and Leningrad, 1935.
Sochineniia Aleksandra Pushkina. Edited by V. A. Zhukovsky et al. 11 vols. St. Petersburg, 1838–1841. Vols. 1–8 reprinted from original editions; materials in vols. 9–11 collected for first time.
————. Edited by P. V. Annenkov. 7 vols. St. Petersburg, 1855–1857. Much new material from manuscripts.

TRANSLATIONS

All of Pushkin's longer works in verse have been translated (with the exception of *Angelo*), but many of the lyrics have not. Various verse translations of the poetry have long been out of print.

VERSE AND VERSE-AND-PROSE COLLECTIONS

Alexander Pushkin: Collected Narrative and Lyrical Poetry. Translated and edited by Walter Arndt. Ann Arbor, Mich., 1984. Ninety-eight lyrics and twelve narratives, plus "Onegin's Journey," each in the prosodic form of the original. Recommended.
The Bronze Horseman: Selected Poems of Alexander Pushkin. Translated and edited by D. M. Thomas. New York, 1982. Thirty-eight lyrics and ten longer verse works.
The Poems, Prose, and Plays of Pushkin. Edited by Avrahm Yarmolinsky. New York, 1936. Prose and verse translations by various hands of forty-six lyrics and ballads, plus longer works.

Pushkin. Translated and edited by John Fennell. Harmondsworth, 1964. Russian texts and prose translations of forty-eight lyrics, plus four longer works in verse.

Pushkin: A Laurel Reader. Edited by E. J. Simmons. New York, 1961. Prose and verse translations by various hands of forty-seven lyrics and ballads, plus longer works.

Pushkin Threefold. Translated by Walter Arndt. New York, 1972. Russian with two English translations, one linear and one metrical, of seventy-six lyrics and ballads, plus four longer works in verse.

PROSE COLLECTIONS

Alexander Pushkin: Complete Prose Fiction. Translated and edited by Paul Debrezceny. Stanford, Calif., 1983. All the finished and unfinished prose fiction, plus *The History of Pugachev.* Recommended.

The Captain's Daughter and Other Tales. Translated by Natalie Duddington. London and New York, 1933.

The Complete Prose Tales of Alexandr Sergeevich Pushkin. Translated by Gillon R. Aitken. London, 1966; New York, 1978.

The Prose Tales of A. Poushkin. Translated by T. Keane. London, 1915. Reprinted Freeport, N.Y., 1971.

The Queen of Spades; The Negro of Peter the Great; Dubrovsky; The Captain's Daughter. Translated by Rosemary Edmonds. London, 1958, 1962.

The Queen of Spades and Other Tales. Translated by Ivy and Tatiana Litvinov. New York, 1961.

EUGENE ONEGIN

Eugene Onegin. Translated by Walter Arndt. New York, 1963. Revised edition, New York, 1981. Includes five articles written by four critics. Recommended.

Eugene Onegin. Translated and edited by Vladimir Nabokov. 4 vols. Princeton, N.J., 1964. Revised edition, Princeton, 1964.

Eugene Onegin. Translated by Charles Johnston. London, 1977. Reprinted Harmondsworth and New York, 1979.

Evgeny Onegin. Translated by Oliver Elton. London, 1929.

OTHER WORKS

Alexander Pushkin: The History of Pugachev. Translated and edited by Earl Sampson. Ann Arbor, Mich., 1983.

Alexander Pushkin: Mozart and Salieri. The Little Tragedies. Translated by Antony Wood. London, 1982.

Boris Godunov. Translated by Alfred Hayes. London, 1918.

Boris Godunov. Translated by Philip L. Barbour. New York, 1953.

The Critical Prose of Alexander Pushkin. Translated by Carl. R. Proffer. Bloomington, Ind., 1969. Selection of Pushkin's critical articles.

A Journey to Arzrum. Translated by Birgitta Ingemanson. Ann Arbor, Mich., 1974.

The Letters of Alexander Pushkin. Translated by J. Thomas Shaw. Philadelphia, 1963. Reprinted Madison, Wis., 1967.

Pushkin on Literature. Translated by Tatiana Wolff. London, 1971. Critical articles and criticism from diary and letters; includes catalog of foreign-language books in Pushkin's library.

Pushkin: Three Comic Poems. Translated by William E. Harkins. Ann Arbor, Mich., 1977.

Pushkin's Fairy Tales. Translated by Janet Dalley. London, 1978. New York, n.d. Prose paraphrase adaptations.

The Russian Wonderland. Translated by Boris Brasol. New York, 1936. Three fairy tales.

Six Poems from the Russian. Translated by Jacob Krug. New York, 1936. Includes three long narrative poems by Pushkin.

Verse from Pushkin and Others. Translated by Oliver Elton. London, 1935. Includes all the fairy tales, *The Bronze Horseman,* and two lyrics.

BIOGRAPHICAL AND CRITICAL STUDIES

Bayley, John. *Pushkin: A Comparative Commentary.* Cambridge, 1971.

Briggs, A. D. F. *Alexander Pushkin: A Critical Study.* London, 1983.

Debreczeny, Paul. *The Other Pushkin: A Study of Alexander Pushkin's Prose Fiction.* Stanford, Calif., 1983.

Jakobson, Roman. *Pushkin and His Sculptural Myth,* translated by John Burbank. Paris, 1975. Reprinted in Jakobson's *Selected Writings,* vol. 5. The Hague, 1979. Pp. 237–298.

Lavrin, Janko. *Pushkin and Russian Literature*. London, 1947.

Lednicki, Waclaw. *Pushkin's "Bronze Horseman": The Story of a Masterpiece*. Berkeley, Calif., 1955.

Lezhnev, Abram. *Pushkin's Prose,* translated by Robert Reeder. Ann Arbor, Mich., 1983.

Magarshack, David. *Pushkin: A Biography.* New York and London, 1967.

Mirsky, D. S. *Pushkin.* London, 1926. Reprinted New York, 1963.

O'Bell, Leslie. *Pushkin's "Egyptian Nights": The Biography of a Work.* Ann Arbor, Mich., 1984.

Richards, J. J., and C. R. S. Cockrell, eds. and trs. *Russian Views of Pushkin.* Oxford, 1976. Contains twenty-six essays written between 1834 and 1968.

Setschkareff, Vsevolod. *Alexander Puschkin: Sein Leben und sein Werk.* Wiesbaden, 1963.

Simmons, E. J. *Pushkin.* Cambridge, Mass., 1937. Reprinted, without notes or bibliography, New York, 1964.

Troyat, Henri. *Pushkin: A Biography,* translated by Nancy Amphoux. New York, 1970.

Vickery, Walter N. *Alexander Pushkin.* New York, 1970.

————. *Pushkin: Death of a Poet.* Bloomington, Ind., 1968.

BIBLIOGRAPHIES

Cross, Samuel S. "Pouchkine en Angleterre." *Revue de littérature comparée* 17:163–181 (1937).

Fomichev, S. A. "Soviet Pushkin Scholarship of the Last Decade." *Canadian-American Slavic Studies* 11:141–154 (1977).

Shaw, J. Thomas. "Recent Soviet Scholarly Books on Pushkin: A Review Article." *Slavic and East European Journal* 10:66–84 (1966).

Terry, Garth M. "Pushkin, Alexander Sergeevich." In his *East European Languages and Literatures: A Subject and Name Index to Articles in English-Language Journals, 1900–1977.* Oxford, 1978.

Wreath, Patrick J., and I. April. "Alexander Pushkin: A Bibliography of Criticism in English, 1920–1975." *Canadian-American Slavic Studies* 10:279–304 (1976).

Yarmolinsky, Avrahm. *Pushkin in English: A List of Works By and About Pushkin.* New York, 1977.

J. THOMAS SHAW

FRANÇOIS RABELAIS
(ca. 1494–1553)

S ET WITHIN AN imaginary universe peopled by giants, humanists, scholars, peasants, practical jokers, and kings, François Rabelais's five books invite the reader to journey through a unique literary world that is both notorious and renowned for the problems, the laughter, and the ideas it has inspired over its four centuries of existence. Born of an especially fertile time in European cultural history and the equally rich imagination of a lawyer's son, who became a priest, doctor, scholar, author, humanist, and diplomat, the five books evolve, along with the French Renaissance itself, from heady, optimistic affirmations of human potential in the early 1530's to the more somber, guarded perspectives of the mid-century. Destined for the Lyons trade fairs, the village *veillée* (story night) at the local tavern, the humanist's study, and the king's chamber, Rabelais's books contain specific allusions and indirect references to traditional philosophy, metaphysics, and popular legend, to the Bible and biblical commentary, and to works of classical antiquity and contemporary scholarship that were probably as baffling to their original audience as they still are to us.

In the works themselves giants stomp, joke, and eat their way about the countryside in pursuit of amusement, adventure, and knowledge; splendiferous lists of banquet dishes, malodorously intellectual books, and catalogs of fools, games, and sexual organs lure us into a fantasy world that never lets itself be fully charted or explained. Extremely varied in its style and content and full of images that are rarely as straightforward as they might at first appear, Rabelais's text presents an especially difficult challenge to the reader who wishes to organize and interpret its vast outpourings of human language and experience in the hope of perceiving its creator's design. Sentences, themes, episodes, and the entire work catch us in quicksands of shifting emphasis and meaning; the text promises profound commentary on ethical and aesthetic values and yet also sabotages its own display of lofty ideas, evident meaning, and systematized wisdom. But even when we are not sure of the message, we are directed to witness and indeed participate in an ongoing act of creation that combines history and imagination, content and style, author and reader. Every excursion through Rabelais's text, every interpretation brought to bear on it, testifies to a relationship in which the author both encourages and defies his readers to enjoy and to understand the measure of new ideas communicated by him.

Our journey might best begin literally, with historical fact, when French noblemen were freed from the economic constraints and demographic, political, and personal ravages of the Hundred Years War and followed their kings Charles VIII (1483–1498), Louis XII (1498–1515), Francis I (1515–1547), and

1375

Henry II (1547–1559) over the Alps to claim sovereign rights to Milan and Naples. This series of so-called Italian wars soon brought surprises and undreamed-of adventures; the French invaders discovered a civilization far more sophisticated than their own. During the fourteenth and fifteenth centuries, Italy had welcomed refugee scholars of Greek, classical Latin, and Hebrew who helped to develop the intellectual, artistic, and philosophical legacy of antiquity, applying classical ideas in a way that respected their origin yet also added personal energy and vision to traditional form. Time and space, human capacity and needs, had come to be acknowledged as a valuable part of the cosmos and as worthy subjects of artistic concern: Brunelleschi, Donatello, Giotto, and the Venetians had experimented with perspective, anatomical and expressive design, and color in art; Petrarch had written amiable letters to Cicero and Caesar, dispensing personal advice and criticism to illustrious figures of the past in Ciceronian Latin; Boccaccio had produced a comic *Decameron* of stories (ten days of ten stories each) emphasizing his protagonists' ability to get themselves in and out of trouble by manipulating their wits and their native language; Pico della Mirandola had created syntheses of theological and mystical concepts that elevated man to such a high position on the metaphysical ladder that he became the virtual equal of God; Machiavelli had looked back to Herodotus and Pliny and then ahead in a treatise on statecraft that pitted a prince's wits and will *(virtù)* against the winds of fortune.

Back to France came soldiers, ideas, and texts, as well as scholars and artists such as Leonardo da Vinci and Primaticcio, and enthusiastic Frenchmen dreamed that their new cultural inheritance *(translatio studii)* would be matched by the transfer of political power from Greece to Italy to France *(translatio imperii)*. Francis I treated state-building as a serious enterprise as well as a theoretical art: the king constantly attempted to increase the prestige of his court and his governmental power. Armed conflict with the king of Spain and Holy Roman Emperor Charles V contributed to a rise of French nationalism, and funds borrowed from French, German, and Italian banking houses allowed Francis to expand the royal treasury, finance expeditions to the New World, improve his army through the use of artillery and gunpowder, and act as a patron to the writers and scholars known as the French humanists. Initially a group of philologists dedicated to the restoration of classical Latin, Greek, and Hebrew letters by means of careful linguistic study and responsible commentary on the original texts, some humanists, such as Guillaume Budé, Étienne Dolet, Jacques Lefevre d'Étaples, the king's own sister Margaret of Navarre, and Rabelais himself, soon ventured onto the risky terrain of interpreting sacred letters, joining forces with the German Hebraicists Johann Reuchlin and Philip Melanchthon and the cosmopolitan Dutch biblical scholar, stylist, and spokesman for religious reform Desiderius Erasmus.

Like Erasmus, the French Evangelicals favored a return to religious practice based on the imitation of Jesus' life and mission and the early Christian communities. Since this *imitatio Christi* often contradicted such traditional church practices as the cult of the saints, veneration of relics, pilgrimages, and accepting centuries of secondary glosses on the Bible as "holy word," the Evangelicals promptly incurred the wrath of the Sorbonne's reactionary and influential faculty. This conflict was to become sharper still as Martin Luther's theses (1517) and John Calvin's *Institutes of the Christian Religion* (1536) led to a radical break with the Catholic church, and the Evangelicals found themselves caught in the middle of a schism they had hoped to avoid through peaceful reform from within the church.

As Charles V gained power and territory, Francis vacillated in his tolerance of Evangelical humanists and French Huguenots according to the shifting balance of international alliances. The same ill-fed and roughly clothed public that indulged in the feasts and merriment of pre-Lenten carnival, the mumming of guild fraternities, and the momentary splendor of a royal entry into a host city soon witnessed another form of diversion: the burning of heretics. From the 1540's to the end of the century, the early humanists' faith in man's ability to grow and to perfect himself through education and moral discipline, and their hope that one might rise above mortal limitations as much through willed self-transformation as by the gift of divine grace, would be replaced by intolerance, skepticism, and religious persecution. Transformation was to be reserved as the sole prerogative of God, and confidence in secular development through ethics and education was circumscribed by the contingencies of the here and now, the incursions of invading armies, the reality of drought and plague, the recurrent massacres known as the Wars of Religion, and the uncertainty of a world in which traditional values were constantly challenged without being replaced. Even the most courageous and imaginative of voyagers were aware that temporal flux brought shipwreck as well as adventure; these fears, problems, and hopes all found a place in Rabelais's evolving literary production even as they did in the writer's own life.

In itself that life is one of the best illustrations of personal development and humanistic endeavor to be found in sixteenth-century France, even though it is often difficult to arrive at precise dates and specific events in Rabelais's biography. His eagerness to explore new ideas and to seek out a community with which to share them is as evident in his own existence as in the prologues he wrote, inviting readers to partake of healing laughter and consoling drafts from the inexhaustible barrel of good wine and good hope. The fourth child of a lawyer from Chinon in the Loire Valley, Rabelais was born around 1494 (although perhaps as early as 1483) and soon came to possess the wit and the wisdom that his books were later to preach. He received a religious education in the Franciscan minorite monas-

tery at Fontenay-le-Comte in Poitou, replete not only with cumbersome scholasticism and the sacrosanct legacy of glosses written upon glosses that he would later mock in his fiction, but also with the livelier techniques of good preaching and audience manipulation for which the Franciscans were renowned: a stock of secular anecdotes, strategic delaying devices, and picturesque turns of phrase guaranteed to catch even the most jaded of worldly ears. But Rabelais's education also included the Renaissance new learning as well. With his friend and fellow minorite Pierre Amy, he began to study classical Latin, Greek, and Hebrew. Soon thereafter he sent elegant Latin letters full of Greek phrases to Budé and to Erasmus himself, translated the Greek satires of Lucian into Latin, and attended the erudite discussion groups in Fontenay held by the lawyer André Tiraqueau and the liberal bishop Geoffroy d'Estissac. When the Sorbonne put a ban on the study of Greek in France to counteract the spread of Evangelical doctrine, and Rabelais's Greek texts were temporarily confiscated by his Franciscan superiors, he changed orders, following d'Estissac to the Benedictine monastery at Saint-Pierre-de-Maillzeais, where he remained for two years (1524–1526).

But it was neither Rabelais's nature nor his destiny to remain in one place with one calling. Already well conversant with theology and law, the forty-year-old priest spent the next decade of his life in transit, living irregularly either as a secular priest or as a layman and studying medicine first at Paris, then at Montpellier. Medical studies in the Renaissance were far more concentrated on the scholarly presentation of newly discovered texts than on clinical proficiency; Rabelais's translations of and commentaries on Hippocrates' *Aphorisms* and Galen's *Ars parva* and his preface to Manardi's *Epistolae medicinales* earned him such a reputation that he was appointed chief physician to the well-known Hôtel-Dieu de Notre-Dame de la Pitié in Lyons on 1 November 1532. There is one theory that six months earlier Rabelais had come to Lyons to try his hand in the printing trade, to work as an editor and proofreader in order to finance the remainder of his medical studies. The publication and overnight success of a rambling, roughly written, but amusing chapbook about the adventures of a family of giants created by Merlin the magician in order to protect King Arthur, entitled *The Great and Inestimable Chronicles of the Great and Enormous Giant Gargantua* (1532), brought forth in Rabelais's mind other ideas for instant income and fun to boot; in the summer of 1532 Claude Nourry put on sale the first edition of *Pantagruel*, Rabelais's spoofing "son of Gargantua" sequel, ostensibly produced by a loquacious huckster-narrator called Alcofribas Nasier (an anagram of François Rabelais), as well as a *Pantagrueline prognostication* for 1533 featuring Master Alcofribas's ludicrous astronomical predictions for the coming year. Sales were so good that a second, revised and augmented, edition of *Pantagruel* and another *Pantagrueline prognostication* for 1534 appeared in 1533. Five years of drought and ruined crops, the periodic devastation of the Black Death, and man's futile hope to know the will of the stars and the shape of his future were foiled by an always thirsty, always articulate giant, by a jaunty rogue named Panurge, and by a solemn reminder that God alone rules the planets, the stars, and the lives of men:

> *Et ne aura Saturne, ne Mars, ne Jupiter, ne autre planète, certes non les anges, ny les saincts, ny les hommes, ny les diables, vertuz, efficace, ne influence aulcunes, si Dieu de son bon plaisir ne leur donne. . . .*
>
> (*Pantagrueline prognostication . . . pour l'an perpetuel*, p. 898)*

Nor will Saturn, Mars, Jupiter, or any other planet, nor will angels, nor saints, nor men, nor devils have any potential, effective power or influence if it does not please God to give them these things. . . .

The challenge of forming the self in order to collaborate actively with God and within one's community would become a major theme both in Rabelais's second book, *Gargantua*, published by François Juste in 1534 (followed by a second edition in 1535 and a reprinting with *Pantagruel* in 1537), and in the sequence of events that widened the humanist doctor's circle of ideas, adventures, friends, enemies, and patrons. On 15 January 1534 Rabelais left Lyons on his first trip to Rome as the private physician of his second patron, the bishop and future cardinal Jean du Bellay. He would make at least four more journeys to Italy, either to Rome with the bishop (1535–1536, 1540, 1547–1549) or to Turin and the Piedmont region (1540–1542) with Jean's brother Guillaume, the diplomat, soldier, and governor of Piedmont who served as Rabelais's model statesman-warrior. During his stay in Rome, Rabelais arranged to receive papal absolution for his earlier "apostasy" from the Benedictines, so that he could first be reinstalled in Jean du Bellay's abbey at Saint-Maur-les-Fossés and then become a lay priest in good standing when that abbey was secularized in February 1536. In 1540 he also obtained a papal bull relieving his two children, François and Junie, of the stigma of illegitimacy; around this same period his third child, Théodule, was born in wedlock (the identities of the mothers are unknown).

Already renowned as one of the best anatomists in France, Rabelais was granted his doctorate in medicine on 22 May 1537, lectured in Montpellier, and later practiced briefly in Metz (1546–1547); the greatest part of his time, however, was spent on international missions with the Du Bellay family, serving them not only as physician but as go-between in their efforts to reconcile Catholics and Protestants. But the times worked against Rabelais and his patrons. Rabelais lost his infant son, Théodule, in the early 1540's, as well as his

---

* All quotations from the original works are taken from J. Boulenger and L. Scheler, eds., *Oeuvres complètes* (Paris, 1955), the Pléiade edition.

patrons Geoffroy d'Estissac (30 May 1543) and Guillaume du Bellay (9 January 1543). Both Francis I and his successor, Henry II, adopted increasingly severe attitudes toward religious dissent, and judicial suppression of heresy led to executions and massacres such as the slaughter of the French Protestant Vaudois in April 1545. When the Sorbonne was authorized by the Parlement of Paris to draw up a list of books to be censured, both *Pantagruel* and *Gargantua* figured among the titles condemned for "obscenity" by the theologians, despite Rabelais's attempts to tone down the jibes against the "Sorbonards" in his expurgated edition of 1542. But regardless of the Sorbonne's displeasure, a royal *privilège* for the printing of the *Third Book* was granted in 1545, and the work was printed by Christian Wechel in Paris in 1546.

Radically different in content, style, and structure, Rabelais's *Third Book* questions and even undercuts the enthusiastic optimism found in *Pantagruel* and *Gargantua.* Scenes of copious abstract verbal debate and arcane erudition force both protagonists and general readers to acknowledge the limits of human community, wisdom, and ability to communicate in a world full of inextricably entangled moral, philosophical, and rhetorical problems. The *Third Book* promptly appeared on the December 1546 list of condemned books, most likely because the Sorbonne did not like Rabelais's propaganda against monks and clandestine marriage. Yet Rabelais continued to write, leaving the eleven-chapter manuscript of his "partial" *Fourth Book* with the printer Pierre de Tours when passing through Lyons in 1547 on his way to join Jean du Bellay in Rome. Published in 1548, the *Fourth Book* reads like a rough draft; it contains bitter attacks against the diabolical censors who slandered the author and a storm episode that supports Jean du Bellay's stand against the doctrinaire Council of Trent and also emphasizes the importance of free will and human cooperation with God. These were beliefs held by Rabelais, the Du Bellays, moderate Lu-

therans, and the humanist Evangelicals. Consequently, the Sorbonists called Rabelais a Lutheran and the Calvinists maligned him as a renegade and an atheist; still, supported by Cardinal Odet de Châtillon, Rabelais obtained a royal *privilège* for all his works from Henry II in August 1550 and set about revising and completing the *Fourth Book,* adding twice as many new chapters and numerous stylistic improvements to the 1548 edition. Given the virulent criticism to which the now famous author was subjected by both sides of the religious opposition, one can well understand why the prologue to the new book contains a plea for moderation *(médiocrité)* and a prayer for health; Rabelais was approximately sixty years old when Michel Fezandat printed the expanded *Fourth Book* on 28 January 1552. Again the Sorbonne censured his work, and the Paris Parlement ordered it to be withdrawn from sale in March 1552, but the allegorical adventures of Pantagruel and his followers on bizarre islands en route to the temple of the Holy Bottle were so popular for their satire that the official ban once again proved ineffectual.

Much remains unknown concerning the details and precise chronology of Rabelais's journeys within France and abroad, his private life, and his writing; the circumstances of his death and the posthumous publication of the *Ringing Island* and the *Fifth Book* are equally enigmatic. We do know that Rabelais received the benefices of Meudon and of Saint-Christophe-du-Jambet from Jean du Bellay in 1551 and that he resigned these curacies on 9 January 1553. He died approximately three months later, in April 1553, and was buried in Saint Paul's Church, rue des Jardins, Paris. Did he end his life a pauper, "seeking the great Perhaps" or sardonically remarking, "Lower the curtain. The farce is over," as legend would have it? No documents provide us with definite answers, but the remarkable curiosity, variety of interests, and tolerance shown by Rabelais throughout his life suggest a less bitter ending: that he died as a Christian humanist, aware that mind, body, and soul need health and laughter as well as charity and community, that the full process of human growth and development also includes death and decline, and that infinite possibilities for transformation are promised to those with faith in God's will and the courage to act in that faith.

Following Rabelais's death, chapters 1 to 16 of the *Fifth Book* were published in 1562 under the title *The Ringing Island (L'Isle sonante)* by M. Francoys Rabelays, with no mention of a publisher. In 1564 there appeared *The Fifth and Last Book of the Heroic Deeds and Sayings of the Good Pantagruel (Le Cinquiesme et dernier livre des faicts et dicts héroïques du bon Pantagruel)*, again ascribed to Rabelais and again without the name of a publisher. Scholars have long and noisily debated the authenticity of the *Fifth Book,* marshaling subjective impressions, stylistic and thematic analyses, and even computer printouts of vocabulary and sentence structure in an attempt to show to what extent Rabelais was responsible for the voyage's final episodes and the concluding visit to the oracle of the Holy Bottle. Our own choice is to seek a golden mean and accept the hypothesis of a good number of scholars: that the Ringing Island and Grippeminault chapters and most of the Holy Bottle episode were written or at least sketched out by Rabelais. In the Holy Bottle section, descriptions of the temple door, murals, lamp, and fountain borrowed from Lucian and from Francesco Colonna's *Dream of Polyphile* could well have been marginally indicated by Rabelais but actually translated, arranged, or inserted by a later editor. At stake here are various possibilities for a conclusion to Rabelais's work: readings ending with the *Fourth Book* leave the voyagers on the high seas off the island of the Antimuses; inclusion of the *Fifth Book* and the Holy Bottle episode forces us to deal with the symbolic and perhaps satiric meaning of the word *trinch,* which is pronounced by the Holy Bottle and interpreted by

its oracle, Bacbuc, as the key to the Pantagruelist's quest for knowledge.

"*Trinch,*" said the clerk, and the peddlar showing the book around the tavern grinned toothlessly at the faces half-hidden in the corners of the public room. He couldn't read the figures called words shaped on the page like a long, lovely bottle, but he could certainly see that bottle! The folks nearest the hearth stretched and stared and tried to guess just what that fellow Rabelais was up to with his giants, grotesque islands, outrageous puns, and arcane ideas. The serving woman remembered with a sigh the Pantagruelic wedding feasts described to her some thirty years earlier; for they were unlike anything she'd ever seen or heard tell of since, even in the kings' lives or the church's golden book of saints. Then she'd heard parts of the *Third Book* and hoped that that hypocrite scoundrel of a Panurge would get his due share of cuckoldom, like the worried old men with young, pretty wives in the farces played ever since she could remember in the town square. The local lord, come for the latest reading with his pages, yawned and wondered just what manner of epic or antiepic heroes were these giants Pantagruel and Gargantua, at first as uncouth as bumpkins, now as wise and even more silent than the Christian sages described by the Evangelical preachers on their country rounds. To his mind's ear *Pantagruel* and *Gargantua* had followed the exact order of the old epics and later adventure romances recording the birth, childhood, and chivalric feats of a young hero. Moreover, those two books contained characters and turns of phrase that reminded him of Folengo's burlesque epic *Baldus;* but the valiant master's secretary had fudged on his reading, skipped every other line; and no one was any too sure if there really were any esoteric secrets about philosophy, astronomy, politics, astrology, alchemy, medicine, and music to be found in the text. The lord had also heard the *Third Book* years ago, but that had been a disappointment because all that consulting about whether to marry or not to marry and all that heaped-up wisdom got awfully boring after a while and made one feel very stupid. Now all this mumbo jumbo about an initiation into the rites of a Holy Bottle deep in the earth brought back memories of Holy Grail stories, except that Perceval had never sat with flour on his face, two codpieces and three bagpipes around his waist, and his ass twosquare on the ground.

A visiting merchant, who even in his youth had chortled a bit uneasily over Panurge's repertoire of dirty tricks and off-color jokes reserved for the dignified Paris citizenry in *Pantagruel,* asked a fellow traveling tradesman if the Holy Bottle's oracle was speaking to them as well, suggesting riches hidden in the earth and journeys meant to profit the body and, well, yes, also the soul. Had Cartier or da Gama or Magellan seen the magical islands, or had this Rabelais made up the whole story, spinning tales on his way to Metz or to Rome when dodging the censors? But still, Panurge's last trick on the sheep seller Dindenault was really taking matters a bit too far. After all, Dindenault was one merchant who knew how to hawk his wares, even if he was a bit insulting in the bargain.

Not so, answered the village clerk, notary, and scribe, who had read the Dindenault story from the *Fourth Book* ten years earlier and very much liked the idea that the underdog could turn the tables on anyone and avenge insult and arrogance by a happy combination of wit and words. In a way, he thought, Rabelais's anecdotes were quite similar to the best of the traditional French *fabliaux* that he had learned from his grandfather: verse tales of sharp wit, deception, and clever language with a brief moral added at the end, after lusty young clerks triumphed in love, war, and money over boorish burghers, and lecherous friars plied and lied to the ladies, be they virtuously naive or wise and willing. Since the clerk was the only man in town besides the curate who could read, this was his night to shine. And Rabelais's books had always been favorites of his, because they contained wonderful passages that, even when read, sounded more spoken than bookish; every Renaissance rhetorician knew that this was the secret of winning audiences. This particular clerk also fancied himself quite an actor and especially loved Rabelais's many dialogues, hymns of praise, and patches of prose written in foreign tongues (even though he himself could understand only church Latin and a bit of Italian), for then he could proclaim, declaim, exclaim, and gesticulate *ad libitum,* to the delight of his audience. When he looked at the printed page, Rabelais's prose very often reminded him of that flashy poetry in vogue earlier in the 1500's, when the *Grands Rhétoriqueurs* such as Melin de Saint-Gelais dazzled the eyes with rhymes, puns, and the way words looked in print.

At first the village curate seated near the tavern hearth was not sure whether to laugh with his flock at the sacrilegious humor of this priest-turned-buffoon or consult with his superiors about the exact meaning of the words "scandal" and "heresy." He knew well enough that his parishioners were far more likely to listen when he told a good story to prove a point in his daily sermon; he suspected that Rabelais, too, had meant to lead his audience from surface narrative to deeper moral and spiritual meaning. But no sure glosses, no authority or reliable tradition spelled out the way to understanding. There was no doubt in his mind that Rabelais had meant to mock superstition and intolerance, but as in the case of Erasmus' *Praise of Folly,* it was hard to tell where satire left off and Christian folly began. As he walked home later that night, the curate thought of many questions for his next sermon: What did it mean to be human? To pour forth words as wine and to claim the beds and the wives of the gods? To invent the printing press and gunpowder too? To dance in the Chinon meadows and to deliver a harangue at the Sorbonne? And what did it mean to seek God? To die with the knowledge that the intellective soul is immortal and that one's progeny would guarantee a kind of bodily continuity? To read the Holy Scriptures and to practice their precepts in the world? To dream of God's kingdom here on earth, the material splendor of *Gargantua*'s utopian Abbey of Thélème and the Holy Bottle's temple at the end of the last book? The curate guessed that these questions fitted together, and he sensed that the quiet around him contained as many ideas as individuals, as many traditions as innovations, as many reflections on the meaning of the Bottle's "*trinch*" as memories of carnival revels, the bitter cup of Gethsemane, and the goblet of Easter communion.

From the quiet of this and other moments of speculation emerged a reputation and a history of interpretation that now cover four centuries of effort to grasp the presence and the meaning behind Rabelais's comic masks. According to Marcel de Grève, Rabelais's skills as a satirist and inventor of striking turns of phrase brought him immediate fame. Other storytellers borrowed freely from his repertoire of themes, images, and vocabulary: Bonaventure des Périers and Noël du Fail, the moralists and religious propagandists Agrippa d'Aubigné, Étienne Tabourot, and Henri Estienne, and the poets Clément Marot and Mathurin Régnier. The sixteenth-century general reading public in France and the French-speaking Netherlands eagerly exhausted editions of all five books, while its view of Rabelais gradually evolved from that of a drunken fool to that of an early freethinker and a brilliant historical allegorist whose references to contemporary events and personalities were hidden beneath fictional names requiring explanatory "keys."

Condemned for their length and obscenity during the following two centuries by readers accustomed to standards of order, measure, and decorum, Rabelais's works were nonetheless admired, alluded to, and borrowed from by Jacques de La Fontaine, Denis Diderot, and Voltaire in France and by Ben Jonson, Jonathan Swift, and Laurence Sterne in England; they were also very freely translated and adapted by Urquhart (books I–III, 1653, 1693) and Le Motteux (books IV and V, 1694) in the second half of the seventeenth century. The French romantics of the nineteenth century reinstated Rabelais as an author of genius; Chateaubriand, Victor Hugo, Goethe, Coleridge, Swinburne, Balzac, Flaubert, Charles Kingsley, and Michelet celebrated the Rabelaisian depth of vision, freedom of thought, grotesque comedy, and richness of verbal invention.

In the twentieth century, twenty-four new editions were printed between 1901 and 1922; three journals devoted solely to Rabelais studies have appeared in succession; French writers such as Anatole France, Jean Giono, Jean Giraudoux, Marcel Proust, Louis Aragon, and Louis-Ferdinand Céline have tried their hand at parodies; and in 1967 the actor-producer Jean-Louis Barrault created *Rabelais,* a multimedia play that unites sections from all five books in an energetic, enthusiastic synthesis of laughter, language, and cultural background. Rabelais has been hailed as a hero of the people in Communist countries. He has also been called a kindred spirit with the modern master of wordplay, James Joyce.

Far easier to discuss from the critic's chair than to imitate successfully, Rabelais has never lacked interpreters and evaluators. While translations and scholarly studies are listed in the Bibliography at the end of this essay, it is useful to note here that to date there have been three major directions in the evolving history of Rabelais criticism. The first of these covers four hundred years of attempts to unearth the factual "reality" underlying Rabelais's entire work, and includes the criticism of Motteux, Voltaire, Ginguené, and Johanneau and Esmangart. This approach culminated in the pioneering but incomplete critical edition produced by Abel Lefranc and his team of collaborators (1913–1955). Their supporting commentary on the text from *Pantagruel* to chapter 17 of the *Fourth Book* combines profuse philological and lexicological notes with correspondences binding history to fiction: according to them, the Picrocholine war is "in fact" a local Chinon skirmish over fishing rights; Panurge's quandary in the *Third Book* may be explained by a contemporary debate over the status of women in society; and the journey of the last two books can be charted on Renaissance navigational maps.

A second scholarly approach progressed from the strictures of a literal reality to the broader domain of thematics and cultural history. Mikhail Bakhtin's *Rabelais and His World* pioneered the way by presenting Rabelais as a "son of the people" imbued with marketplace humor and the festive spirit of carnival; scholars such as M. A. Screech, Thomas Greene, Gérard Defaux, and Florence Weinberg have studied the importance of Christian humanism and church tradition in the five books.

Beginning in the 1960's, a third group of critics, including Michel Beaujour, Alfred Glauser, Jean Paris, and Floyd Gray, began to apply modern structuralist theories and perspectives to Rabelais's works, presenting his texts as self-contained entities and focusing attention on his use of language and style as a self-reflexive commentary on the process of writing. Most recently, an increasing number of scholars, such as François Rigolot and Terence Cave, have begun to combine cultural context, narrative theory, and a text's internal unfolding in light of Renaissance rhetorical theory and practice. There are still many gaps to bridge and many questions to answer concerning cultural background, criteria for humor and "obscenity," narrative strategies, and rhetorical play. A long way removed from Rabelais's first audiences, we are nonetheless still asked to react as they did: with heart and mind, memory and intelligence of words past and ideas yet to come.

In the prologue to the *Third Book*, Rabelais offers his readers an inexhaustible wine barrel containing what he claims is a brew of joyfulness, mirth, and good hope. The narrator's invitation to drink encourages each guest to come to the barrel in liberty and to choose a personal style of drinking, provided that the result be a happy, consoling one. The wine Rabelais describes is then directly associated with the verbal content of the *Third Book;* we are in fact being asked not just to appreciate the heady power and pleasure of good words, as of good wine, but also to contribute a personal style of reading to a bottomless text. The challenge is formidable, for the five books were written by an artist whose curiosity, humor, and eagerness to experiment are as present in his literary work as in the rest of his life; each successive text builds on the lessons of technique and content set by its predecessor. Our goal in the remaining pages is to follow the general evolution of Rabelais's works, book by book, while focusing on a very limited number of problems and episodes so that the adventurous reader may savor some of the complications that arise when human development, transformation, and the extravagant jesting found in tall tales are brought into play with and against each other, both as important themes in the books and in the act of narration itself.

The first of Rabelais's comic works about giants chronologically reverses generations and begins with the life and exploits of Gargantua's son, Pantagruel. Written during a period of abnormally dry, hot weather, recurrences of the plague, and much puzzlement about what to do with the French language as a literary vehicle, *Pantagruel* presents itself as a tongue-in-cheek transformation of drought to rich and novel draught. This book is derived in content and conception from *The Great and Inestimable Chronicles of the Great and Enormous Giant Gargantua* and several other popular chapbooks of the same ilk; its hero's name, "Panta" ("all") and "gruel" ("thirsty"), is borrowed from a little devil who tossed salt in the mouths of drunkards in Simon Gréban's mystery play *The Acts of the Apostles. Pantagruel* vaunts a handy cure for the pain of toothache, childbirth, syphilis, and acute boredom and then sets out a dazzling display of how language can both promote and subvert human communication. The story of the giant Pantagruel's birth, youth, and deeds embraces not just a famous "Hymn to Renaissance" that celebrates man's intellectual passage from Gothic darkness to humanistic illumination through the revival of neglected belles lettres (chapter 8); it also includes a parade of secondary characters who add their vocabularies to the book's composite sketch of languages in search of a heritage and a future: a pretentious Limousin student who embellishes slovenly manners and morals with a facade of fancy pig-Latin (chapter 6); an equally ostentatious "lady" who listens to the language of seduction only if it is couched in courtly niceties and promises material reward (chapters 21–22); an earnest yet naive English scholar who seeks esoteric meaning in earthy, mostly obscene gesture (chapters 18–20); and a crafty master-of-all-tricks (and all languages) aptly named Panurge ("good for everything") who quickly outdistances his good master, Pantagruel, and even his colleague, Alcofribas, with his ability to make language everything from a gratuitous instrument (his incomprehensible languages in chapter 9) to a close substitute for the sex act itself (the old lady and the lion anecdote in chapter 15).

Pantagruel's first chapter presents a mythical upside-down world of temporal and spatial chaos: August arrives in May, three Thursdays fall within a week, the sun stumbles across the sky, and Abel's blood fertilizes the earth, causing the soil to give birth to oversized medlars. Consumed by the inhabitants of the region, the fruits enlarge various parts of the human body and ultimately produce Pantagruel's ancestors. Generation has begun, and fiction has announced its own origins in the nontime and nonspace of a tall tale. This creation story, Rabelais's invention, comically reverses the biblical account of man's Fall in Genesis: whereas Adam ate the apple and so fell into sin, these first-cousin crab apples absorb Abel's blood and are offered up in turn as new fruit to be consumed in an atmosphere of optimism, good will, and celebration. Instead of reducing man to the stature of a fatigued, guilty tiller of the earth, the medlars cause those who eat them to grow in size until they become giants. The new owners of barrel-like stomachs are proclaimed the ancestors of such festive characters as Saint Paunch (Pansart) and King Carnival himself, Mardi Gras; their appetite is and remains heartily physical. That the play on words *ventrem omnipotentem* (all-powerful belly) should designate a belly as round as a hefty barrel ("ventre bossu comme une grosse tonne": p. 172) is not out of keeping with the major emphasis of chapter 1 and of *Pantagruel* in general: rather than scornfully attacking the divine Father, this parody of the Credo *(patrem omnipotentem)* in the Catholic Mass jokingly situates *Pantagruel*'s brand of humor in the nontranscendent, material world.

In fact the extraordinary vitality of Rabelais's first book comes from the author's deliberate focus on the physical aspects of human existence. In the first chapter body parts and exterior objects are linked through verbal "like" (*comme*) comparisons that encourage the reader to imagine a whole constellation of images that transform limbs and organs into ships, stills, wine barrels, flamingos, and mountains. The phallus, for example, is not only personified as "nature's laborer" (*le laboureur de nature*) but also inspires a variety of visual analogues. It is metaphorically transformed into an oversized belt paradoxically able to hold up the very breeches worn to conceal it, the comb of a rooster or game fowl, a ship sailing before the wind, and a poised jousting lance. The dynamic forward thrust of physical renewal is thus carried on as much through words as through theme, as the giants establish their existence and (re)produce a genealogy.

Seven chapters later the themes of generation, transformation, and growth of body and mind receive more formal, eloquent elaboration in Gargantua's letter of fatherly advice to the young student Pantagruel. The tone of chapter 8 modulates to a more solemn key and the style generates Latinisms rather than puns, but Gargantua's discussion of the limited immortality available to those who beget offspring, the almost unlimited possibilities for acquiring knowledge in a new age of restored letters, and the necessity of combining learning with faith and charity reflect back on the whole process and rationale of a genealogy. The very notions of restoration and progress introduce the movement of history and a basic opposition between the changes brought by life's constant flow and the relative stability of an organic, intellectual, and spiritual chain linking generations through seminal substance, shared ideas, and common faith. Subject to the vicissitudes of time, man is an image of the finite: he ages and dies, unable to escape his destiny. Yet chapter 8 constitutes a resounding *Te Deum* for the "gifts, graces, and prerogatives" awarded by God to men; emphasis shifts from the mortality of an individual to the continuity of civilization, the hope of understanding the past and perfecting the future through the study of classical languages and texts, and delight in the physical and transitory aspects of life, which here receive a deliberate place and purpose in the divine scheme of things.

It is in light of the metaphysical implications of (re)production that the letter's style, as well as its content, are best understood. Although the letter is far from original by modern standards and may very well parody overly enthusiastic and optimistic humanist programs of study, it also refers readers to a linguistic heritage shared by generations. Cicero's stylistic influence, the Latinate vocabulary, and the many literary subtexts that echo in the letter's lines convey the no-tion of ancestors, both verbal and human, appearing and disappearing with time, yet maintaining an unbroken bond from father to son, from text to text, from Latin to French: the text itself acts as progeny perpetuating the essence of its ancestors by conserving previously voiced themes and classical stylistic techniques within the full movement of historical chronology. As different texts are juxtaposed and their shared content noted, there occurs a momentary fusion of voices, an act of literary (re)production that transcends time; fiction, like men and giants, can be renewed by generating more of its kind before passing into oblivion.

But the transcendent tendencies that create giants and suspend time through the power of generation and common roots, both genealogical and literary, are achieved by the same general means: the reader must abandon the contingencies of reality, enter into the imaginative domain of art, and allow the cohesive power of analogy to overcome the divisive, dispersive flow of time. The divine gift of identity through reproduction parallels the workings of metaphor and simile: art's own eternity founded on the shared essence of compared substances and juxtaposed texts. But elsewhere in *Pantagruel* the timelessness that depends on artistic means often seems more like a sleight-of-hand trick designed to entertain than a deliberate, serious affirmation of the author's creative powers. For example, Épistémon's miraculous resurrection following a visit to the underworld (chapter 30) celebrates an absolute victory over death and heralds the intervention of a language able to send knowledge (*épistémé*) to the grave and retrieve it for the living as inspired prophecy. Yet even as Panurge reattaches Épistémon's severed head with a few strategic stitches and Épistémon recounts his vision of hell, we know that Épistémon's death is not death at all and that the language of transcendent truth in fact serves as the text's most eloquent commentary on its own artificiality. The real miracle of the episode occurs in an offhand slip of the tongue, a reversal of the grammatical function of words in the chapter title thanks to which the noun ("head") and the verb ("chopped") exchange places and rob death of its seriousness: "Comment Epistémon, qui avoit la couppe testée, feut guéry habillement par Panurge, et des nouvelles des diables et des damnéz" (How Épistémon, who had his chop headed off, was skillfully healed by Panurge, and some news from the devils and the damned). Death is no more than a play on words, a literary accident to be corrected by an artificial resurrection; Panurge's nonchalant performance mirrors the blasé aplomb of an author who can bring characters in and out of his story at will, create a week of three Thursdays, and otherwise depart into imaginative fantasy whenever a new verbal experiment comes to mind.

In the event that the reader misses the point in chapter 30, later episodes provide additional evidence of fiction's powers. The Utopians' journey to the land of the Dipsodes ("the thirsty ones") is suspended until the beginning of the *Third Book,* and *Pantagruel*'s heretofore chronological sequence of adventures suddenly trails off, leaving the reader in midair (or more exactly, in mid-route), with a double thematic repetition of descent and return: in chapter 32 Alcofribas travels into Pantagruel's mouth and in chapter 33 a team of peasants is lowered into the giant's stomach to remove a mountain of ill-digested waste. Both adventures contain familiar themes of discovery, inversion (perspectives of the old world and the new), healing, and reward; both project images of even more far-fetched descents into tall tales.

The entry into Pantagruel's body, especially the final descent into the "horrible pit" of his belly, returns us to the primeval and biological chaos whence arose the medlars, the genealogy, Pantagruel, and the book itself. And in this final mirroring of the book's beginning, knowledge brings illumination. The main narrative, so apparently horizontal in its progress, has attempted to fool the reader into believing that it has faithfully represented the natural processes of growth and renewal. By its very display of temporal and spatial impossibilities, chapter 1 heralds the text's fictional origins; the transformations of nondescript men into ancestors of giants, of worthless medlars into magical fruit, of sacred history into comic myth, and of the prankster Panurge into a healing doctor all belong to the same abyss of art's "unsettling" miracles that permits the narrator, Alcofribas, to be swallowed up as a character by his own creation. Characters, narrator, supporting cast of bystanders, and amused audience take turns at being mystified. Yet Rabelais's interpretive game is meant to be played in good cheer, even in moments of doubt and sheer confusion. For *Pantagruel*'s reward lies not only in its optimistic celebration of human progress but also—and especially—in its power to elude the pathos of time, age, and death by spinning out tall tales and tiny comparisons, myriad anecdotes and lessons of (pro)creation, new life from verbal chaos and, notwithstanding our inability to understand some of its messages, the promise of more generations to come.

Gargantua answers that promise with yet another series of riddles that delve more deeply into the issues first raised in *Pantagruel*: the possibilities of growth and renewal for an individual, a community, and language itself; the nature and range of literary symbols; and the interpretation of a text that constantly proclaims its ambiguity while it solicits our efforts to decode its secrets. In many ways Rabelais's second book reflects and even repeats the narrative structure of *Pantagruel*: the life and deeds of Gargantua are related in a linear narrative that leads from his birth within a verbose community of happy drinkers ("bien yvres") to a detailed plan for his education and wartime exploits with his anti-monk ally, a crozier-swinging master of sexual double entendre, gluttony, and uncouth insult and injury named Friar John of the Minced Meat. The book closes with a radical about-face: a new, sophisticated, and quite uncharacteristic community, the Abbey of Thélème. Yet in this, Rabelais's finest book of growth, evolution, and metamorphosis, language itself is allowed a continuity and a stable abundance of meaning that were suggested but not developed in the course of *Pantagruel*'s linguistic and stylistic experiments. *Gargantua*'s cast of characters is smaller, but Rabelaisian reductions are always to be suspected of paradoxical expansion. The illustrious drinkers ("beuveurs très illustres") and pox-ridden feasters ("véroléz très précieux") invoked in the first sentence of the prologue and the book's closing quip point the way both literally and figuratively to enigmatic depths that frame the text: *Gargantua* begins and ends with (an image of) the grave. Early in the first chapter Alcofribas explains that the giants' genealogy was discovered in a tomb containing nine flasks and a book; beneath the Abbey of Thélème lies another grave containing a cryptic message to be deciphered. Communities of drinkers and communities of readers join in intellect as they consider symbolic relationships linking wine and words, bottle and text: if we know how to read well, we will learn how to drink; if we know how to drink fully, we will discover the joys within the mirages of reading.

Neither activity is straightforward and simple to understand. In a prologue justly renowned for its difficulty, images set up as parallel analogues move from outer surface to inner substance, from gaily painted boxes to the precious drugs stored within them, from Socrates' merry yet ugly countenance to the divine wisdom, outstanding virtue, and incomparable sobriety of his inner nature, from the bone to the marrow, from the bottle to the draught, from *Gargantua*'s emphasis on merriment and bodily pleasures to its serious "Pythagorean symbols" said to contain "a different savor and more secret doctrine that will reveal very high sacraments and awesome mysteries, as much concerning our religion as about the state of our government and economic life" (p. 5). The prologue then reverses

itself: the reader is cautioned not to look for hidden allegories, for Alcofribas claims to have composed his work only during the time he took to eat and drink. His book is not meant to reek of oil from the scholar's lamp. Rather, it is to suggest "the scent of wine . . . appetizing, laughing, prayerful, more celestial and delicious than the smell of oil"; indeed, the prologue ends with the call for a drinkers' mutual toast between reader-audience and author-narrator: "do gaily and comfortably read the rest . . . and remember to drink to me . . . and I shall return the favor to you on the spot" (p. 6). Yet the drinker has already spilled his share of scholar's oil; a second glance at the avalanche of "inner-outer" images provided as refreshment reveals that the apparent division between frivolous, jesting exterior and meaningful interior is far less clear-cut than we are first led to believe:

> *Et, posé le cas qu'au sens litéral vous trouvez matières assez joyeuses et bien correspondentes au nom, toutesfois pas demourer là ne fault, comme au chant de Sirènes, ains à plus hault sens interpréter ce que par adventure cuidiez dict en gayeté de cueur.*
>
> (p. 4)

And, even in case you find joyous and appropriate reading material on the literal level [of my book], still you ought not to stop there, as if you were held spellbound by the Sirens' song, but rather interpret on a higher level those things that you believe are said only with a merry heart.

In fact neither manner of reading excludes the other; just as the wine's fragrance inspires earthy joviality ("appetizing," "laughing," "delicious") it also suggests the vertical, metaphysical dimension of communion ("prayerful," "celestial"). Fused in the fictional time and space of the narrator's refreshment, writing and drinking offer delight to the senses and, at the same time, nourishment for the spirit and the imagination.

The importance of the wine/word metaphor as a meeting place for drinking and reading, as well as for an exchange of literal and figurative meaning, is further illustrated in the first chapter's parody of what was previously celebrated with much solemnity in Gargantua's letter to Pantagruel: the very principles and ideals of erudite humanists who wish to restore the lost works of antiquity. Equipped with spectacles and Aristotle's nonexistent volume on the deciphering of "invisible" letters ("lettres non apparentes"), Alcofribas helps unearth a bronze tomb containing nine bottles and a moldy yet cute, big yet little, half-chewed book that he then "translates." The haphazardly juxtaposed book and flasks are united both in the space of the tomb and in the reader's mind, thereby expanding the metaphorical meaning of the "Etruscan" words *hic bibitur* ("here one may drink") engraved on the tomb. What is more, Alcofribas's disclosure of the tomb, the goblet, and the little book may well allude to some of the central symbols of Christian faith: the book of Scripture written by an understandably invisible author, a reflection of the "word" of God; the goblet of the Eucharist; the empty tomb following Jesus' resurrection. Although such religious references are by no means certain, they do remind us that communion, like a symbolic text, serves a twofold purpose. First of all, it invites men to transcend their mortal condition and participate in a ritual, atemporal act. But communion then sends men back into time: its function, like that of the book and the flasks, is also to renew and refresh human beings for future struggle. Likewise, to conceive of a symbol without considering its temporal and physical consequences is impossible: the whole of *Gargantua* exists as evidence that the act of reading can take place only within history; the bond between wine and words is expressed not only through the metaphysical vocabulary of the sacraments but also in terms of human needs and appetite. As an art of interpreting symbols, reading may promise glimpses of transcendence; yet at the same time, as Alcofribas's role as "translator" and our own experience

confirm, it remains a fundamentally human act, an ongoing immersion in (and reaction to) a movement of images that continually appear and merge with each other.

The desire to include both secular development and spiritual striving toward transcendence as meaningful human activities is expressed directly in the young giant's personal motto, taken from Saint Paul (1 Cor. 13:5): "Charity does not insist on its own way," and in the author's ongoing attempt to dramatize this motto through the activities of various communities in *Gargantua*: village folk united by drink and good cheer; countrymen joined in war; a young prince and his retinue united by friendship, the will to learn, and mutual service; the evil king Picrochole and his advisers united by greed for power; and finally, the select community of Thélème united by personal refinement, universal accord, and the famous motto "Fay ce que voldras" (Do as you will). Commentary about Thélème diverges widely in the assessment of exactly what ideals are celebrated in the abbey, what sort of will or desire governs its inhabitants, and, still more fundamentally, whether the episode as a whole should be read as a serious statement or as a parody of utopias, for Thélème is generally considered one of Rabelais's least typical creations. The chronology of Gargantua's education and the varied circumstances under which it took place give way to uncharted hours, elegant, well-born young people who dress and act alike, geometrically flawless architecture, and imposing towers that, for all the diversity of their elaborate names, appear the same. The dynamic process of metaphoric linkage and exchange between images characteristic of the rest of *Gargantua* is replaced by harmonious sameness, reiterated abstract adjectives ("beautiful," "magnificent"), and the timeless stasis of the verb "to be" in the imperfect tense. The text becomes immobilized by perfection and the reader, more likely than not, gets bored. Why then, he wonders, was Thélème conceived in this way?

Just as the inscription *hic bibitur* encourages both a literal and a symbolic interpretation of the tomb's contents, so does the etymologically "buried" root *thelēma* focus attention on some of Thélème's possible meanings. The linguistic cornerstone of both the abbey's name and its motto, "Fay ce que vouldras," *thelēma* is usually translated from the Greek as "will" or "desire." It may be read simply as an expression of human desire for ease, material comfort, and sensual pleasure; it may indicate a wider ethical and social context of moral conscience, corporate responsibility, and personal development brought to such perfection (*per/facere*) that renewal and growth are no longer possible; it may derive from the Lord's Prayer (*Genēthētō to thelēma sou*, or "Do Thy will on earth"), thereby suggesting an ideal vision of the divine kingdom come "on earth as in heaven," bringing to full flower the Evangelical (as well as humanistic) hope of man's peace with others, with God, and with himself. Still other interpretations associate *thelēma* with the author's struggle to "do his own will" and exteriorize personal vision, to "translate" inspiration into communicable literary form, or else to deceive his reader into believing any or all of these hypotheses; for the most apparently profound of symbols could well function as ambivalent lures that undercut their own highest designs by offering false promises of meaning. If in fact all is fiction, Thélème's very impossibility is perhaps the text's best conclusion: a clever admonition to the reader who misread *Gargantua* by taking its semblance of life far too literally, constructing reality out of castles in the air.

The book's last prophetic enigma found in a tomb beneath the abbey (chapter 58) contains no answers, but it does provide a final lesson in reading as an act of (re)creation. Borrowed in part from the poet Melin de Saint-Gelais, the rhyming riddle engages *Gargantua*'s two main characters in opposite interpretive directions: Frère Jean views the poem as a literal paraphrase of an athletic contest; Gargantua chooses to find in its images of fire, strife, and encouragement to perserve a symbolic admonition to persecuted Evangelicals. Rabelais provides no central authority to arbitrate between the text, its opposed interpreters, and the outside reader: Alcofribas has disappeared from the scene, leaving us to decide alone just how we wish to "translate" the riddle. The text multiplies its meanings: the enigma is and is not an athletic match ("jeu de paume"), is and is not an allusion to divine truth, and is and is not both or neither of these. Alcofribas's "translation" of the past—indeed, the creation of *Gargantua* as a whole—belongs (and does not belong) to the same deceptive, arbitrary domain of tall tales as do the medlar myth, Épistémon's resurrection, *Gargantua*'s books and bottles, and the Abbey of Thélème. Books enclosed in the tombs yield "histories" of process and symbol that, having run their course, spawn self-reflected images of another tomb and another inscription, rendering past and future, horizontality and verticality, transformation and stasis equivalent in an internal play of mirrors.

Yet despite the fact that Rabelais's text can at any moment give itself the lie and mean the opposite of what it claims, irony cannot truly be said to possess or even dominate *Gargantua*. Even though founded on artifice, the text still reflects valid lessons of human experience, and the tension between fiction and symbol's truth enriches it with elusive promises of revelation: promises that mark the beginning of human struggle with symbol's infinite meaning, promises that slyly remind the reader of his own finite limits, promises that thereby guarantee a difference in each new reading. Even as one attempts to grasp the seemingly inexhaustible possibilities of wine as organic substance, as symbol of communion with the divine, and as artistic inspiration; of the book as a "moldy little volume," as the revealed word, and as fiction itself; of meaning as wholly arbitrary, as an allusion to transcendent truth, or as a frivolous joke, the work imparts its most important lesson: that its own rebirth can occur only as the reader reenacts Alcofribas's first miracle by breaking into unillumined depths and becoming personally immersed in the difficult but indeed perpetual process of interpretation.

Fourteen years after the publication of *Pantagruel* Rabelais appears ready to take up where he left off at the end of that book: "You shall have the rest of the story . . . wherein you shall see how Panurge was wed and cuckolded in the first month of his marriage" (*Pantagruel*, p. 311). But Panurge never reaches the altar. Instead the *Third Book* pursues the problem with which we were left at the end of *Gargantua:* that of human struggle with interpretive choice and ultimate meaning. *Pantagruel*'s optimistic proclamation of intellectual victory over Gothic darkness seems, at least on the level of our understanding of Rabelais's *Third Book*, to have been reversed; the linearity typical of the first two books gives way to a complicated circling that passes from Panurge's praise of debts to a long, erudite series of consultations about his future, then to a new hymn of praise to the Pantagruelion plant. All of these sections are heavily laden with learned references, numerous subtexts, and contradictory meanings. Accumulated wisdom and the desire to read "as one wills" end in futility and frustration; no longer a mere literary game, the act of reading/interpreting causes in Panurge a quite modern "existential" anguish: for him the text has become a matter of life and death, while for us it raises questions about rhetoric as an expression of moral choice and as an evasion of responsible action.

These problems are introduced as early as chapter 3 of the *Third Book*, when Panurge squanders his worldly resources and delivers a masterly eulogy of debts. Like the inscription on Thélème's portal that banishes from the abbey's inner sanctuary all agents of divisiveness, illness, and unnatural vice before welcoming the elect, Panurge begins by casuistically (and paradoxically) condemning the solitary world of the debtless (who owe nothing to no one and are owed nothing in return). He then consigns chaos, devils, death, and darkness to a realm of isolation and unrelatedness from which he is—by basic definition of money owed and prayers for long life bestowed by his creditors—safely excluded. Antithetically juxtaposed with this first chilling tableau of monsters, universal disarray, and nonreciprocity, Panurge's second world is ordered by the debtors' perfect circle of reciprocity; its cosmology follows perfectly Panurge's basic definition of debts: "comme une connexion et colligence des cieulx et terre, un entretenement unicque de l'humain lignaige . . . [et] par adventure celle grande âme de l'univers, laquelle scelon les Académicques toutes choses vivifie" (like a connection and colligation of heaven and earth, the universal preservation of the human race . . . [and] perhaps that great soul of the universe which, according to the Academics, imparts life to all things: pp. 340–341).

Panurge endows cosmos, earth, and man with debts' double properties of sharing and exchange: on the one hand, the stability of a mutual bond ("a connection and colligation"); on the other, the movement and animation implicit in the process of giving life. His lists of the benefits debts confer on human society blend spiritual qualities ("peace," "love," "mutual affection") and the physical pleasure of nourishment and reproduction; we cannot help but recall the best moments of dynamic exchange and vertical impulse toward higher meaning found in earlier books. Thélème in particular readily comes to mind as Panurge's vision fuses with the myth of a paradise transcending time and space; once more, absolutes and abstractions in a "blessed world" point to a perfect concurrence of harmony in human community and obedience to divine will: "Charity alone reigns, rules, dominates, triumphs" (p. 344). But this time paired images are kept in dynamic movement through the constant sharing of the debtors' active exchange, and movement through history is presented as exclusively positive: only the debtless are subject to the negative effects of temporal change. Stylistically, one might say that Panurge, as inspired poet, has achieved the impossible: within the spheres of his debtors' cosmos, polarities of stability and exchange, process and permanence, immanence and transcendence are bound together by the power of perfect metaphor.

An impressive hymn to creation and creativity, this triumphant vision of a world that includes yet transcends human time and space nonetheless poses some fundamental problems. However meaningful its message of charity, however valid its celebration of universal reciprocity, Panurge's vision is above all else a fiction in the most basic etymological sense of the word (Latin, *fictus:* formed, invented). The eulogy constitutes a sustained exercise in pure artistic representation: his image of the world is built out of nothing more than figures of speech that admit all shades of meaning except the literal. And since in fact Panurge incurs debts but returns nothing to his creditors, Pantagruel notes that his friend's "beautiful rhetorical figures and designs" also conceal a serious moral problem: incurring debts is a vice akin to lying. Like "Satan's angel disguised as an angel of light" (p. 380), Panurge praises charity while from behind the rhetorician's mask come words that betray self-centered love:

> *"Suidez-vous que je suis aise, quand tous les matins autour de moy je voy ces créditeurs tant humbles, serviables et copieux en révérences . . . ? Il m'est advis que je joue encores le Dieu de la passion de Saulmur accompaigné de ses anges et chérubins. Ce sont mes candidatz, mes parasites, mes salueurs, mes diseurs de bons jours, mes orateurs perpétuelz."*
>
> (p. 340)

"Can you believe how happy I am when every morning I see my creditors so humble, so ready to serve me, so profuse in their bows, all crowded around me . . . ? It seems to be that I'm still playing God in the Saumur passion play, ac-companied by his angels and cherubim. Those creditors are my office seekers, my parasites, my saluters, my greeters, my constant petitioners."

Panurge manipulates language to usurp the prerogatives and power of the divine Creator and to proffer the "Word" that re-creates the universe in images that satisfy his own desires. Yet beneath the unquestionable moral turpitude of his egotism lie a wish and a fear that will reveal themselves time and again throughout the *Third Book.* Panurge's attempts to confuse representation with reality, to turn creditors into intercessors who will preserve him from death, and to take refuge from the ravages of time in an imaginative and often very entertaining collection of sexual fantasies all reflect the same human anxiety, the same ultimate blasphemy, the same impossible fiction of immortality: to reign as God in a world where death does not exist.

When a literal-minded Pantagruel overrides his subordinate's protests and relieves Panurge of his debts, the text undergoes a radical change in style, and its ideal sphere of reciprocity becomes a circle of doubt and non-communication. By a sort of poetic justice infused with profound irony, the now debtless Panurge becomes the quarry of precisely those powers of death and separation that he himself had previously consigned to his fictional world without debts: social ridicule and isolation, degeneration, devils, and impotence repeatedly appear as themes in conversations with friends and learned authorities. No longer an overwhelmingly positive force of growth and renewal in the Rabelaisian universe, the passage of time now comes to reveal its darker side, mocking the man who would forget his own mortality by taking refuge in the world of fictional illusion. The narrator's vague reference to his own "shipwreck at the lighthouse of bad fortune" in the prologue suggests that Rabelais might also have wished to ironize, if not reject outright, his own early "blessed world" of superficial *pantagruélisme;* for it is exactly the sequence of transparent images spiraling toward perfection, the naive desire to rise above human limits and embrace an ideal through fiction's transcendence, that are first incorporated into Panurge's eulogy, then put into question as his cosmos falls apart. The pleasant universe of *Pantagruel* and *Gargantua* is superseded by serious reflection on human existence and transcendence. No longer an innocent pastime designed purely for the reader's amusement, fictional diversions become, at least in part, ethically questionable evasions that allow one to substitute empty words for responsible action.

The text's most obvious demonstration of the limits imposed by human existence also begins where *Gargantua* ended: with an enigma demanding interpretation. Panurge's anxious attempt to resolve the question of his future and know the consequences of marriage introduces a lengthy series of consultations drawing upon multiple sources of wisdom and divination, from the most eminent to the least sane. Beneath its formidable display of erudition, the *Third Book*'s middle section explicitly thematizes a truth already experienced by *Gargantua*'s reader: interpretation is necessarily an incomplete act dependent on the contingencies of time and the limits of human comprehension. Just as it was impossible to choose one correct reading of Saint-Gelais's riddle at the end of *Gargantua,* so Panurge's efforts to know his fate with certainty are doomed to failure.

But it would be a mistake to limit a reading of the *Third Book* to a profession of doubt, for the work offers an explicit affirmation of a Power that transcends the conditionals of time and space that shape human destiny. According to Pantagruel, the theologian Hippothadée, and the judge Bridoye, man's limited ability to predict and control life's chance events is meant to be complemented by the faith expressed in the Lord's Prayer: "Thy will be done on earth as it is in heaven." Yet unlike Thélème's transparent "heaven on earth" in which the elect easily and naturally comply

with divine precepts of charity, the *Third Book*'s version of "Fay ce que vouldras" insists on the painful ambiguity, the tenuousness, and the shadows that separate divine from human will. Granted only a glimpse of God's revealed will through Scripture, man must choose his path and then act, even in the face of doubt. Pantagruel encourages Panurge to trust in God and accept the responsibility of choice, but Panurge stubbornly persists in his longing to remove all risk and negativity from life and to regain his lost paradise by substituting words for action; his fascination with marriage is itself an evasion, a refusal to "arm" for life's battles. Pantagruel's understanding, tolerance, and affection for his confused companion serve as testimony to genuine *caritas*, but the *Third Book* nonetheless belongs to Panurge, the self-centered dreamer who copes badly with obstacles, moving in a vicious circle of flight from circumscribing reality and an inevitable fall back into it. In an age of increased preoccupation with self, solitude, and power, we are especially sensitive to the negativity of experience and to the personal obsessions of a protagonist haunted by the grim specters of old age, impotence, and death.

His fictions repeatedly crushed by the overwhelming force of existence, the hapless yet guilty Panurge finally breaks out of his impasse through an encounter with the madman Triboullet, who hands him an empty bottle. Panurge converts the literal image of drunken debauch into a magically personified symbol: he vows to undertake a journey in order to consult with the oracle of the Holy Bottle. Doubt and frustration give way to constructive decision and a definite goal, and the *Third Book* ends in a burst of optimistic lyricism. Pantagruel agrees with Panurge's metaphorical reading and accepts the proposed journey; the narrator-author intervenes here for the first and only time in the book, lending his approbation to the proceedings through his observations as an eyewitness and confirming the text's renewed promise of symbolic resolution in his eulogy of the Pantagruelion plant (chapters 49–52). Exactly like Panurge, the narrator chooses to read metaphorically; as he expounds upon the name and qualities of the plant through the use of rhetorical figures such as synecdoche (the use of a part to represent the whole) and comparison, the pedantic narrator-persona dependent upon Pliny's taxonomy from the *Historia naturalis* is transformed into a poet who imaginatively interweaves plant life with the gods and heroes of antiquity, exotic geography, human body function, and natural phenomena through the juxtaposition of images. Improving upon Panurge's solely figurative use of metaphoric links in the eulogy of debts, Rabelais's narrator-persona constructs a network of bonds as literal as they are figurative: he ascribes to the Pantagruelion plant the organic properties of hemp, flax, and asbestos in order to work its magic as a medium able to capture the winds, link nations together, and even produce a new herb that will allow mortals to visit the beds of the gods.

But the plant's greatest virtue, we are told, is its ability not only to withstand fire but also to be purified by it. Like the bottomless barrel offered to the reader in the prologue to the *Third Book* and Gargantua's Evangelical interpretation of Saint-Gelais's riddle, the Pantagruelion embodies and extends "good hope" in the face of trial and destruction. Wholly consonant with Pantagruel's example and advice to Panurge throughout the *Third Book,* the closing episode encourages man in his passage through the flames, promising support in struggle and even in death through the "divinity of this holy Pantagruelion" (p. 510), a symbol that, like wine, moves our thoughts in a vertical path. Yet Panurge remains in limbo, unaware of the Pantagruelion's transcendent properties. Only the reader has "heard" the eulogy composed and delivered by "M. Fran. Rabelais, Docteur en Médicine." In fact Pantagruel's herb belongs neither to the text's past nor to its present: like the promised word of the Holy Bottle, the Panta-

gruelion offers only tentative fragments of meaning to Pantagruelists, who are invited to "carry away the seed of this herb" (p. 513). Its flowering is deferred, its fruition held in reserve, for the end of the journey to come.

In the temporal and spatial margins of that future revelation one discovers the most fantastic, complicated series of tableaux in all of Rabelais's works: a formidable textual detour leads from the giants' familiar territory to an open sea and islands of bizarre singularity. Just as the Israelites were promised a land of milk and honey but were allowed to enter it only after forty years of trial and struggle in the desert, so Rabelais's wandering pilgrims are periodically reminded of the oracle's promised word; yet they continue to wander for an additional two hundred pages. In the course of their visits to islands, most often grouped in antithetical pairs, Rabelais extends and deepens the meditation on human frailty and transcendent power begun in the *Third Book,* transforming fiction into a vehicle for allegory's truth. Voyagers and readers encounter temptations of diverse form but related essence, artificial idols cast in the trappings of nature, and violent metamorphoses that reverse the positive themes of earlier books, ending not with growth and renewal but rather with the death of body and spirit. We shall focus very briefly on two such episodes related by their use of food imagery: the Gaster episode in the *Fourth Book* (chapters 57–62) and the confrontation with Grippeminault in the *Fifth Book* (chapters 11–15). No longer heady drafts of light-hearted banquet banter, personal restoration, refreshment, and healing, these passages contain ambiguities and negative, threatening depths that must be fathomed before the Bottle's message can be heard and deciphered.

At first glance the presence of a character named "Sir Stomach" appears to indicate a return to the festive atmosphere found in the first two books, when country folk consumed medlars and giants welcomed Mardi Gras and

"Saint Paunch" in the context of birth, growth, and respite from warfare. But as "Saint Paunch" makes way for "Sir Stomach" the inadvertent consumption of medlars in a burlesque paradise is replaced by an Eden no sooner rediscovered than lost. The narrator soon learns that the "Island of Delights" is ruled not by love, nor by moral excellence, nor even by a jolly embodiment of feasting and sensual enjoyment. Rather it falls under the dominion of sheer physical necessity, personified in the demanding tyrant Gaster. The narrator's naive eulogy of "an isle admirable beyond all others" soon reduces all creative enterprise to a single refrain: "Et tout pour la trippe!" (And all for the gut). Human development, like the body itself, has become ambivalent, full of threat as well as promise.

There follows a difficult series of thematic and structural shifts in which Gaster is alternately praised as a source of imagination and vilified as Manduce, a voracious set of jaws designed to terrify children at carnival time. The joking reference to the first giants' *ventrem omnipotentem* (*Pantagruel*, chapter 1) becomes a concrete image as Gaster's worshipers elect him their "ventripotent god" and pay homage to his wooden effigy. With an irony that only gradually reveals its full scope, the author transforms natural body function into a grotesque idol by reintroducing the same stylistic device once used to convey creative exuberance: the famous, quasi-inexhaustible Rabelaisian list. In and of itself the menu of banquet fare in chapters 59–60 combines the best of natural imagery with the culinary imagination of a master chef. In context, however, the list not only expresses the Gastrolaters' misplaced reverence but also contributes the most to the metamorphosis of Gaster into a false god. Art's excess has distorted nature: the Gastrolaters' offerings of food end up as a grotesque celebration of unnatural gluttony.

The notion of an idol worshiped as "ventripotent" points as well to a clear-cut opposition between things human and things divine. The Gastrolaters' error and Gaster's subsequent negative role as the monster Manduce may be explained both in rhetorical terms as an ironic misuse of synecdoche—the deification of only the lowest physical part of man's total being—and, concomitantly, in metaphysical terms as a blatant act of egotism. The narrator's quotation from Saint Paul's epistle provides a direct condemnation of those enslaved by the flesh: "For many walk. . . . Whose end is destruction, whose God is their belly, and whose glory is in their shame, who mind earthly things" (Philippians 3:18–19). Ambivalent even in its closing anecdote about the excellence and purity of sound of wild elder-bush reeds that grow farthest from civilization and closest to God, the Gaster episode offers no word personal yet powerful enough to resolve conflicting tensions between the music of earthly substance and that of celestial ideas. Only the faintest of harmonies contained within the lines of the banquet list suggests a possible synthesis in the act of communion, a union more fully realized in the meal served aboard ship at the end of the *Fourth Book* (chapters 64–65). But no sooner is such a promise half glimpsed than it is obscured by moral darkness. Only Pantagruel grasps the transcendent significance of the communal meal; his companions, like the Gastrolaters, look for no nuances of meaning beyond the literal slaking of physical appetite.

The most negative moment of the voyage occurs when the Pantagruelists arrive at the lair of Grippeminault ("Grabpuss") and his Furrycats. The old beggar who greets the travelers outside the cats' lair provides a guiding motto that grows in meaning and menace as Rabelais's indictment of corruption in the courts of law is revealed: "Pour le signe de mon pronosticq, advisez que léans sont les mangeries au-dessus des rastelliers" (As proof of my warning, notice that herein the mangers are above the bench: p. 777). Out of context, the beggar's phrase evokes the literal image of cats grasping and devouring (*mangeries*, from *manger*: to eat) what appears to be some sort of trapped rodent (*râtelier*: rattrap); as such, it suggests a natural regenerative cycle not foreign to *Gargantua*'s feasts of slaughtered oxen or the baby giant's instinctive eating of cows (*Pantagruel*, chapter 4). However, the legal setting of the episode demands that the phrase be read as a figurative technical description of legal mangers (*dossiers*) collected and filed in bins (another meaning of *râtelier*) above the judge's bench. These apparently divergent interpretive possibilities fuse as Grippeminault is presented as a catlike monster equipped with bloody claws for seizing and disposing of hapless victims. Grippeminault's hunger is neither for food nor for justice, but rather for gold. Once agents of renewal and exchange, both food and the flow of money here become negative, one-way indicators of perverted appetite.

The *mangeries* within the *rastellier* grow increasingly more sinister as the episode progresses. Grippeminault's riddle about "an Egyptian son born like a viper, having eaten through his mother's body" (p. 779) and Panurge's correct interpretation of the enigma further develop the interwoven themes of hell, hunger, and death: a black weevil born by eating its way through a white bean would receive by metempsychosis the soul of a Furrycat, were these monsters human and had they souls; for already in this world Grippeminault and his minions devour all they can grasp. After the Pantagruelists helplessly throw down their gold as a bribe for freedom and return to port, they discover shiploads of treasure destined for the judges, among which are an abundance of game birds and animals. Operating the same sort of metempsychosis as mentioned in the weevil riddle, Rabelais achieves the worst inversion of all, the final illumination of the beggar's phrase:

> *Les âmes d'iceux* ["chefs de guerre"; "bons gentilshommes"], *selon l'oppinion de Grippeminault, après leur mort sont entrées ès sangliers, cerfs, chevreux, hayrons, perdrix et autres tels animaux, lesquels ils avoient, leur première vie durant, toujours aymé et cherché. Orez ces*

> *Chats fourréz, avoir leurs chasteaux, terres, dommaines, possessions, rentes et revenuz destruit et dévoré, encores leur cherchent-ils le sang et l'âme en l'autre vie. O le gueux de bien, qui nous en donna l'advertissement à l'enseigne de la mangeoire installée au-dessus du râtelier!*
>
> (pp. 783–784)

The souls of these men [noble-born hunters and warriors], according to Grippeminault's opinion, enter after their death into boars, stags, roebucks, herons, partridges, and other such creatures as they have always loved and pursued during their lives. So, after destroying and devouring their castles, estates, domains, possessions, rents, and revenue, these Furrycats still seek to have their blood and souls in the other life. What a truthful beggar that was who warned us of this by telling us of the manger up above the bench!

Their spirits transferred into the bodies of animals, the aristocrats who once graced Thélème are destroyed both physically and symbolically: the nobility's loss of wealth and honor at the hands of rapacious magistrates is rendered by a nightmarish about-face of Pantagruelic feasting in which monstrous animals turn the tables and consume human souls.

Grippeminault's voracity constitutes an active, direct force that both terrifies and overpowers his victims. Far more grim in its images of cruelty and death than most of the other adventures in Rabelais's books, this episode also marks the pilgrims' deepest plunge into moral turpitude. Impotence is no longer a theme confined to the limited context of cuckoldry. Rather, it has become the only reaction possible in the face of evil grown beyond human power to correct it; one can only hope, like the beggar, for some eventual punishment from heaven. In this Luciferian hell where language itself is inverted, vice is called virtue, and moral authority is usurped from God, there reigns a darkness that precludes all possibility of transcendence. No word but the clatter of coin ("Or sà," meaning both "Let's see now'' and ''Put the gold here!'') echoes in Grippeminault's den, and the only possible interpretation of the monster's cannibalistic feasting described in the weevil riddle is proffered by Panurge in the name of the devil: ''or de par le diable là.''

Although the Pantagruelists' itinerary presents a great variety of other ports of call, including Islands of Abstractions, Papimaniacs, Sausages and Chitterlings, Boxed and Bashed Bailiffs, and even philosophical Quintessentials, their journey maintains an underlying coherence of mode and meaning. By its subject matter, its lack of verisimilitude, and its specific use of figurative language to illustrate a moral lesson, the text duly adheres to the prescriptions of allegory. Drawing on the two themes most traditionally associated with the allegorical mode, the journey and, to a lesser extent, conflict between paired adversaries, Rabelais develops the idea of *médiocrité* (moderation) both as a dynamic ongoing search for many possible interpretations and as a struggle to avoid extremes and rigidly fixed meaning. First introduced in the prologue to the *Fourth Book*, the ''golden mean'' of *médiocrité* governs both the humble woodsman Couillatris's wise choice of his own lost hatchet over silver and gold axes offered by the Olympian gods, and the author-narrator's wish for good health rather than for riches or power. But in the course of the voyage, *médiocrité* disappears from view, and one is left to ponder the insularity of each polarized community, the absolute demands of a doctrine, belief, or style of life that isolates its adherents, and the impasse in communication between uncompromising extremists and restless Pantagruelists. The synthesis and the diversity implicit in *médiocrité* are ignored by all but the sage Pantagruel, whose role in the *Fourth Book* consists precisely in suggesting the numerous interpretive possibilities one can find in a text, on an island, or in any adventure.

That the last two books deal both with the literal risks of imminent physical peril and with the figurative dangers of intolerance, moral darkness, and spiritual blindness may well reflect not only the historical problems of the midcentury, when censors leveled diatribes against Rabelais and the hymn ''When Israel Fled from Egypt'' evoked the exile of those advocating Evangelical reform, but also an early use of allegory to project a character's inner state. The reader cannot help but recall *médiocrité*'s first nemesis: the Panurgic ego prone to excess of pride, the deadliest of all sins. Since the voyage originates in Panurge's imagination (his interpretation of Triboullet's gesture), it may well be in the projection of his fundamental selfishness that Rabelais's last two books find their unity. The wilderness is extended into and through the domain of allegory as an *itinerarium mentis*: an itinerary of the mind or soul. In essence the *Fourth* and *Fifth Book*s function as a psychological landscape laid out in prismatic reflections of its source: Panurge's obsessive self-love and his desire to possess without giving to others. Projected through secondary characters and inverted themes that consistently reveal the reversed signs of vice's excess, the fragmented ego haunted by the idea of self-apotheosis displaces worship of the divine onto physical idols, calls vice a virtue, and takes up its lonely exile in sin. Like an unclean spirit the Panurgic ego enters Rabelais's last books as Legion and casts its negativity into the islands' grotesque monsters, marking the text with the image of death transformed from a simple fiction into a spiritual reality.

As the journey's futile circling comes to an end and its graphic allegorization of irreconcilable forces gives way to hopeful anticipation of resolution, the voyagers' path shifts in direction and dimension. The Pantagruelists descend vertically into the Holy Bottle's temple, and the reader becomes involved in a parallel search for meaning that involves two contrary yet simultaneous interpretive processes. On the one hand, the narrative branches out thematically as its hidden depths are illumined, bringing to mind other related scenes of renewal and transformation; on the other hand, the Holy Bottle episode channels these themes and their attendant images into a central symbol and encourages the reader to grasp the ambiguous word that lies at its center. Having crossed a vast expanse of text in which comedy seldom appears without satire's bitter social and moral overtones, we cannot help but notice the positive nature of the laughter that resurfaces in the *Fifth Book*'s closing chapters. The parody of mystical quests and heroic descents to the underworld, the hocus-pocus of Panurge's initiation rites, and the celebrating of inspired drinkers surround and complement the metaphysical lessons presented in this final episode. For Panurge's simultaneous recovery of rhyme, reason, and vision at the end of his visit to the Bottle invites us to reconsider the notion of fictional invention neither as a gratuitous piece of virtuosity nor as moral evasion, but rather as a source of healing, a creative release from anxiety, and a bridge between imagination and the imperative to meet life's challenges.

Upon their arrival on the oracle's island, the voyagers pass by Bacchus' vineyard, an ancient archway designed as a drinkers' memorial, and a barrel-shaped trellis bearing both grapes and "five hundred various artificial forms" interlaced with ivy. The narrator launches with renewed enthusiasm into enumerations of regional wines, drinking vessels, and spicy appetizers. Interwoven with the growth and cyclical regeneration of plant life and the discriminating drinkers' gustatory and visual recollections is a negation of time: the image of eternal spring that is Bacchus' special benediction. The trellis and archway are also literally rooted in nature but have been so carefully arranged by an invisible hand that it is difficult to distinguish between natural growth and artificial display, between what is sculpted and what is real: the products of art and agriculture here coexist in the distinct yet curiously unified apposition. These descriptions seem to suggest a relationship between nature and art quite different from that found in the earlier books. For all its reminders of past banquets and exuberant lists, the Holy Bottle episode does not project the flippant yet deliberate ease with which Rabelais contrasted nature and fiction in the scene of Épistémon's resurrection. What is more, artifice also appears to have lost the negative connotations associated with it ever since Panurge first attempted to dodge real issues by spinning elaborate tall tales. One need only juxtapose the ironic eulogy of gunpowder and human greed in the Gaster episode ("Nature herself was amazed and confessed herself vanquished by art": *Fourth Book*, p. 710) with the images of children sculpted on the rim of the temple lamp, "expressed so ingeniously by art that nature could do no better" (*Fifth Book*, p. 871). Art here enhances and extends nature's beauty and design; the tension between domains has become a complementary relationship that hints at the fulfillment of a heretofore absent ideal: the harmonious equilibrium of *médiocrité*.

As grapes and vine leaves are removed from the monuments, eaten, and placed in the voyagers' shoes, there results a corresponding upward resurgence of both the human spirit and the symbolic potential of wine. Descent has become a reversed route toward transcendence, and the reader who has already struggled with *Gargantua*'s invitation to drink/read from a bottle/book retrieved from a tomb, with a barrel full of "metaphysical wine" in the *Third Book*'s prologue, and with Panurge's figurative interpretation of Triboullet's proffered bottle, now prepares to explore further those themes associated with wine: the nature of human thirst, imagination, and creative drinking. As they pass to the center of the temple, the Pantagruelists change guides: the lantern is replaced by the priestess Bacbuc ("bottle" in Hebrew), a personified image of wine's container and verbal content. Like the lantern in the vineyard, Bacbuc teaches about "the contemplation of things divine" not by denying the importance of concrete reality and sensory experience, but rather by building upon them. Invited to sample the water in the fountain, the voyagers at first drink/read with strict literality, as all but Pantagruel have done throughout their journey. But at the point at which their physical need is strongest, the priestess reveals a second dimension of thirst:

> "Jadis une cappitaine juif, docte et chevalereux, conduisant son peuple par les désertz en extrême famine, impétra des cieulx la manne, laquelle leur estoit de goût tel par imagination que par avant réallement leurs estoient les viandes. Icy de mesme: beuvens ceste liqueur mirificque, sentirez goust de vin tel que l'avez imaginé. Or, imaginez et beuvez!"
>
> (p. 878)

> "As once a learned and valiant Jewish captain leading his famished people across the desert received manna out of the skies, which to their imagination tasted exactly as their food had tasted in the past, so it is for you now: drinking this miraculous liquor, you will perceive the taste of whatever wine you may imagine. Now, imagine and drink!"

Bacbuc's analogy challenges the Pantagruelists to move beyond literal substance and (re)create a world closer to their hearts' desire through the use of images ("imag(e)-ination"). At the same time, such human effort and aspiration are associated with a transcendent source that reveals its divinity in the physical world: the gift of manna was sent from heaven; Jesus' first miracle at Cana was to transform water into wine.

Having thus suggested a meeting point of axes through the combined presence of imagination and inspiration, the text honors its long-deferred promise and reveals "the word of the Holy Bottle." This second, central part of the adventure is also its most disconcerting section, for one can never be sure what to make of the word "trinch." Is it an anticlimactic, gratuitous return to the flat horizon-

tality and simple imagery of other books, a word of infinite meaning, or the fulfillment of a promise made at the journey's beginning: that man, having been purified by trial, may eventually find himself in the presence of divine being(s)? Unlike the Pantagruelion eulogy, however, the Holy Bottle's word does not long remain out of Panurge's grasp. Bacbuc pours a "gloss" down Panurge's throat, thereby activating one of Friar John's favorite puns on bréviaire as both a (prayer)book and "a venerated, true, and natural wine flask" (p. 883). The images reappearing here are exactly those first unearthed in *Gargantua*'s first chapter: book, bottle, and *hic bibitur*. But here the book/bottle works magic within Panurge, causing doubt and a difficult question to be resolved in a new outpouring of confidence, illumination, and poetry. The hero's fears of impotence, which underlay his uneasy performance jokes and hesitation about marrying a young wife, now vanish as he once again wears his codpiece. His sexual restoration is completed and complemented by the intellectual and spiritual gifts of wine: insight, joy, and wisdom.

As Bacbuc continues to explain the meaning of the oracle's word, it becomes clear that *trinch* is no mere facetious toast to the newly rejuvenated Bacchic initiate:

> Et icy maincterons que non rire, ains boyre est le propre de l'homme: je ne dis boyre simplement et absoluement, car aussi bien beuvent les bestes; je dis boyre vin bon et frais. Notez, amys, que de vin divin on devient, et n'y a argument tant seur, ny art de divination moins falace. . . . il emplist l'âme de toute vérité, tout savoir et toute philosophie.
>
> (p. 883)

And here we maintain that not laughter but drinking is the proper lot of man: I do not mean drinking simply and literally, because beasts also drink in that way; I mean drinking good cool wine. Note, my friends, that by wine one becomes divine, and there is no surer argument, no art of divination less fallacious. . . . wine fills the soul with all truth, all knowledge, and all philosophy.

This statement encourages us to reflect further on the relationship between verticality ("becoming divine") and man's thirst *(altérité)*. For Bacbuc's purge not only turns physical need into the creative thirst of imagination; it also renews man's desire *(theléma)* for transcendence, a desire finally met through the mediating presence of wine capable of "making one divine." One of the most important aspects of this gloss on the meaning of thirst is its emphasis on transformation as a reciprocal relationship between human will and divine grace. The vertical pathway leads upward, marking man's struggle to envision the infinite ("imagine"), but it must also move downward, bringing transcendence into the domain of personal experience ("drink"):

> *Car tous philosophes et saiges anticques, [pour] bien sûrement et plaisamment parfaire le chemin de congnoissance divine et chasse de sapience, ont estimé deux choses nécessaires: guyde de Dieu et compaignye d'homme.*
>
> (p. 889)

For all ancient philosophers and sages have judged two things to be necessary to safely and agreeably complete the journey on the road to divine wisdom and knowledge: the guidance of God and the company of men.

At the center of the temple, horizontal and vertical axes cross: will and faith, human imagination and divine transformation, concern for community and trust in God combine in a final manifestation of *médiocrité*.

Predicated on man's experience as well as on divine grace and guidance, the word of the Holy Bottle returns us to the physical and temporal world. Panurge is once again asked to read/drink/choose for himself, and this time he trusts in the oracle and resolves to act, deciding to marry and creating a poem to express his newfound confidence. Having literally taken to heart the Holy Bottle's prophecy, the voyagers communicate universal vision—the precepts of charity and the miracle of inspiration, the ethics of a generous, responsible society implicit in Aesop's parable of the sack mentioned as a symbol of human need (p. 883), and the transformative power of wine— in a distinctly personal manner: "O Dieu, Père paterne,/Qui muas l'eaue en vin,/Fais de mon cul lanterne,/Pour luyre à mon voisin" (O God, holy Father,/Who turned water to wine,/Make of my ass a lantern,/To shine for my neighbor: p. 885).

Trinch invites renewal of the self in artistic as well as spiritual and reproductive terms. After passing beyond islands dominated by the "words" of others, the voyagers at long last discover and affirm words of their own. Thus the *Fifth Book* does not close with a repudiation of human limitations; no perfect symbol provides the pilgrims with the key to the "domain of celestial signs" mentioned in the Pantagruelion eulogy. Rather, the upward movement of symbol is balanced by the revelation of the divine in the most common of material substances: water and wine. Indeed, the beauty of the book's conclusion is largely the result of the author's return to images evoking concrete objects and down-to-earth rejoicing.

By the conclusion of his work, Rabelais has come to reveal the full (re)creative potential of his literary draft. Read in their entirety, the five books satisfy *altérité* in all its dimensions: literal and figurative thirst; the power to change and the faith to act; concern for others, humble acceptance of mortal limitations, and moral charity discovered and affirmed after a struggle with egotism and spiritual darkness. No gloss poured from a *bréviaire* could convey any more profound vision, any more complete message about the kingdom of God to be sought by men on earth, any more immanent meeting of divine purpose and human *theléma* within the temple of the heart:

> *Vos philosophes nyent estre par vertuz de figures mouvement faict: oyés icy et voyez le contraire.*

Par la seulle figure lymacialle que voyés bipartiente, ensemble une quintuple infoliature mobile à chacune rencontre intérieure (telle qu'est en la vène cave en lieu qu'elle entre le dextre ventricule du cueur), est ceste sacrée fontaine escoulée, par icelle en harmonye telle que oyés, monte jusques à la mer de vostre monde.

(p. 877)

Your philosophers deny that movement can arise from the power of figures: but listen now and you will see that they are wrong. Merely by that two-part corkscrew figure that you see there, combined with a fivefold pattern of leaf-work that moves at every inner joint (as the hollow vein does at the point where it enters the right ventricle of the heart), this sacred fountain flows in the harmony that you can now hear, and rises up to the sea of your world.

As the voyagers sign their names and take leave to return to Touraine, the reader understands that the last words about death and renewal, nature and art, time and transcendence are to be his. For the first witness at *Pantagruel*'s birth out of chaos is also the final creator of the text's total gloss: the reader retains the privilege and the responsibility of interpretive choice. If one has been careful to note the figure revealed at the center of the fountain's converging fluid pathways ("infoliature mobile"), as well as the lesson of *Gargantua*'s enigmas and Panurge's long struggle, it should come as no surprise that the greatest treasure within the Bottle's sanctuary is the image of the human heart. Among the "gifts, graces, and prerogatives" transmitted from Creator to author to reader is the personal freedom and, indeed, the admonition to drink, imagine, and create interpretive "words": words that may, to be sure, ironize the text's symbols and embrace ambiguity; words that celebrate the drinker's joyful return home and, in relating human growth to that which is eternal, would make of each end a new beginning.

Selected Bibliography

EDITIONS

Gargantua. Edited by Ruth Calder. Geneva and Paris, 1970. With a preface by V. L. Saulnier and an introduction and commentaries by M. A. Screech. Textes Littéraires Français. The best available critical edition.

L'Isle sonante. Edited by Abel Lefranc and Jacques Boulanger. Paris, 1905.

Oeuvres. Edited by Abel Lefranc et al. 6 vols. Paris and Geneva, 1913–1955. A critical edition with copious footnotes, but incomplete; includes books 1–4, chapter 17.

Oeuvres complètes. Edited by Jacques Boulanger and Lucien Scheler. Paris, 1955. The Pléiade edition.

————. Edited by Pierre Jourda. 2 vols. Paris, 1962.

————. Edited by Guy Demerson. Paris, 1973. Editions du Seuil. Bilingual modern and Middle French on facing pages; very good for students.

Pantagruel. Edited by V. L. Saulnier. Paris, 1946. Textes Littéraires Français. The best available critical edition.

Pantagruel, Gargantua, Tiers Livre, Quart Livre, Cinquiesme Livre. Edited by Pierre Michel. 5 vols. Paris, 1965. Folio, undated. Livre de Poche.

Pantagrueline Prognostication. Edited by M. A. Screech. Geneva, 1974. Textes Littéraires Français. The best available critical edition.

Quart Livre. Edited by Robert Marichal. Geneva, 1947. Textes Littéraires Français. The best available critical edition.

Tiers Livre. Edited by M. A. Screech. Geneva, 1964. Textes Littéraires Français. The best available critical edition.

TRANSLATIONS

All the Extant Works of François Rabelais. Translated by Samuel Putnam. 3 vols. New York, 1929. Parts available in *The Portable Rabelais.* New York, 1946. A lively, colloquial translation.

Gargantua and Pantagruel. Translated by J. M. Cohen. Harmondsworth, 1955. Penquin Classics edition. One of the most accessible for students.

Gargantua and Pantagruel (Books 1–4). Translated by Thomas Urquhart and Pierre Le Motteux. New York and London, 1929. Everyman's Library edition. Books 1–2 (1653) and book 3 (1693) edited by Urquhart; books 4–5 (1694) edited by Le Motteux. Urquhart's contribution adds humorous material ''in the style of the original''; Le Motteux also departs from the letter of Rabelais's text, but with less wit.

Gargantua and Pantagruel: The Five Books by François Rabelais. Translated by Jacques Leclercq. 5 vols. New York, 1936. Limited Editions Club. New York, 1944. Modern Library edition.

The Five Books and Minor Writings. Translated by W. F. Smith. 2 vols. London, 1893. 2nd ed. of vol. 1: *Gargantua*. Cambridge, 1934.

CRITICAL STUDIES

BOOKS

Bakhtin, Mikhail. *Rabelais and His World*. Translated by Helene Iswolsky. Cambridge, Mass., and London, 1968. A Marxist approach to Rabelais; very good on popular humor and festive imagery.

Beaujour, Michel. *Le Jeu de Rabelais*. Paris, 1969.

Bowen, Barbara C. *The Age of Bluff: Paradox and Ambiguity in Rabelais and Montaigne*. Urbana, Ill.; Chicago; and London, 1972.

Cave, Terence. *The Cornucopian Text: Problems of Writing in the French Renaissance*. Oxford, 1979.

Coleman, Dorothy Gabe. *Rabelais: A Critical Study in Prose Fiction*. Cambridge, 1971.

Defaux, Gérard. *Pantagruel et Les sophistes*. The Hague, 1973.

Dieguez, Manuel de. *Rabelais par lui-même*. Paris, 1960.

Febvre, Lucien. *Le Problème de l'incroyance au XVIe siècle: La Religion de Rabelais*. Paris, 1942. A systematic refutation of Lefranc's allegations that Rabelais was an atheist.

Frame, Donald H. *François Rabelais: A Study*. New York and London, 1977. A fine general introduction to the main themes and episodes in the five books.

Gilson, Étienne. *Les Idées et les lettres*. Paris, 1932. A ''rehabilitation'' of Rabelais as a Catholic writer.

Glauser, Alfred. *Le Faux Rabelais*. Paris, 1975. A negative approach to the question of the authenticity of the *Fifth Book*.

—————. *Rabelais créateur*. Paris, 1966.

Gray, Floyd. *Rabelais et l'écriture*. Paris, 1974.

Greene, Thomas M. *Rabelais: A Study in Comic Courage*. Englewood Cliffs, N.J., 1970. An excellent introduction to the humanistic and Christian themes developed in the five books.

Grève, Marcel de. ''L'Interprétation de Rabelais au XVIe siècle.'' *Études rabelaisiennes* 3 (1961).

Kaiser, Walter. *Praisers of Folly: Erasmus, Rabelais, Shakespeare*. Cambridge, Mass., 1963. Part 2, pp. 101–192.

Krailsheimer, A. J. *Rabelais and the Franciscans*. Oxford, 1963. Very good on educational influences and sermon techniques.

Lefranc, Abel. *Rabelais: Études sur Gargantua, Pantagruel, le Tiers Livre*. Paris, 1953. The source of the theory that Rabelais was an atheist.

Masters, George Mallary. *Rabelaisian Dialectic and the Platonic-Hermetic Tradition*. Albany, N.Y., 1969.

Paris, Jean. *Rabelais au futur*. Paris, 1970.

Plattard, Jean. *Vie de François Rabelais*. Paris and Brussels, 1928.

Putnam, Samuel. *François Rabelais, Man of the Renaissance: A Spiritual Biography*. New York, 1929.

Rigolot, François. ''Les Langages de Rabelais.'' *Études rabelaisiennes* 10 (1972). Contains an excellent discussion of the linguistic styles of the characters in the five books, especially the hymns of praise.

Sainéan, Lazare. *L'Influence et la réputation de Rabelais*. Paris, 1930.

Saulnier, V. L. *Le Dessein de Rabelais*. Paris, 1957.

Screech, M. A. *Rabelais*. Ithaca, N.Y., 1979. A series of close readings of numerous selected passages from Rabelais's works.

—————. *The Rabelaisian Marriage*. London, 1958. Provides excellent insights into the moral and marriage questions raised in the *Third Book*.

Villey, Pierre. *Marot et Rabelais*. Paris, 1923.

Weinberg, Florence. *The Wine and the Will: Rabelais's Bacchic Christianity*. Detroit, 1972. An interesting study of Christian symbolism in Rabelais's books.

ARTICLES

Auerbach, Erich. ''The World in Pantagruel's Mouth.'' In *Mimesis*. Translated by Willard Trask. Garden City, N.Y., 1957. Pp. 229–249.

Brault, Gerard J. "'Une Abysme de Science': On the Interpretation of Gargantua's Letter to Pantagruel." *Bibliothèque d'humanisme et renaissance* 28:615–632 (1966).

Defaux, Gérard. "De *Pantagruel* au *Tiers Livre:* Panurge et le Pouvoir." *Études rabelaisiennes* 13:163–180 (1976).

————. "Rabelais et son masque comique: Sophista loquitur." *Études rabelaisiennes* 11:89–136 (1974).

Gray, Floyd. "Ambiguity and Point of View in the Prologue to *Gargantua*." *Romanic Review* 56:12–21 (1965).

————. "Structure and Meaning in the Prologue to the *Tiers Livre*." *L'Esprit créateur* 3:57–62 (1963).

Jeanneret, Michel. "Les Paroles dégélées (*Quart Livre*: 48–65)." *Littérature* 17:14–30 (February 1975).

Kittay, Jeffrey S. "From Telling to Talking: A Study of Style and Sequence in Rabelais." *Études rabelaisiennes* 14:111–218 (1977).

La Charité, Raymond C. "The Unity of Rabelais's *Pantagruel*." *French Studies* 26:257–265 (1972).

Marichal, Robert. "Commentaires du *Quart Livre*." *Études rabelaisiennes* 1:151–202 (1956).

————. "Notes pour le commentaire des oeuvres de Rabelais." *Études rabelaisiennes* 6:89–112 (1965).

————. "*Quart Livre:* Commentaires." *Études rabelaisiennes* 5:65–162 (1964).

————. "Le Quart Livre de 1548." *Études rabelaisiennes* 9:131–174 (1971).

Nykrog, Per. "Thélème, Panurge et la Dive Bouteille." *Revue d'histoire littéraire de la France* 3:385–397 (July–September 1965).

Petrossian, George A. "The Problem of the Authenticity of the *Cinquiesme Livre de Pantagruel:* A Quantitative Study." *Études rabelaisiennes* 13:1–64 (1976).

Rebhorn, Wayne A. "The Burdens and Joys of Freedom: An Interpretation of the Five Books of Rabelais." *Études rabelaisiennes* 9:70–90 (1971).

Regosin, Richard. "The Artist and the *Abbaye*." *Studies in Philology* 68:121–129 (1971).

Rigolot, François. "Cratylisme et Pantagruélisme." *Études rabelaisiennes* 13:115–132 (1976).

Saulnier, V. L. "L'Enigme du Pantagruélion ou: Du *Tiers* au *Quart Livre*." *Études rabelaisiennes* 1:48–72 (1956).

Screech, M. A. "Some Reflexions on the Abbey of Thelema." *Études rabelaisiennes* 8:109–114 (1968).

Spanos, Margaret. "The Function of the Prologues in the Works of Rabelais." *Études rabelaisiennes* 9:29–47 (1971).

Spitzer, Leo. "Le prétendu réalisme de Rabelais." *Modern Philology* 37:139–150 (November 1939).

————. "Rabelais et les 'Rabelaisants.'" *Studi francesi* 4:401–423 (1960).

————. "The Works of Rabelais." In *Literary Masterpieces of the Western World*. Edited by Francis H. Horn. Baltimore, 1953. Pp. 134–146.

SHARLENE POLINER

RENAISSANCE PASTORAL POETRY

INTRODUCTION AND BACKGROUND

THE PASTORAL LITERATURE of the Renaissance is both an episode in the larger history of a literary mode and a unique moment with its own formal and thematic character. As a culmination of classical and medieval pastoral, it was retrospective; but insofar as it adapted, modulated, renovated, and transformed the inheritance, it represented a new stage of and a fresh approach to the tradition, looking to an even brighter future development of genre and type. As matters turned out, however, the reaction against pastoral in the post-Renaissance eras of Enlightenment and romanticism (or, as some would argue, the submersion and reappearance of the pastoral impulse or ethos in unconventional modern dress) meant that the pastoral activity of the Renaissance was in fact a climax.

Renaissance pastoral (from the Latin word for shepherd) was written in incredible abundance. The production of pastoral poetry, drama, and fiction in neo-Latin and in the European vernaculars is staggering, especially if one counts not only the recognizable pastoral types but the other genres that the pastoral ideal infiltrated or subverted or in which it appeared as an episode. The Renaissance used pastoral, traditionally a lowly and simple literary form, to express most of its key ideas, typical sentiments, and loftiest aspirations. It is therefore a crucial index to Renaissance culture.

To understand the enormous appeal of pastoral to the Renaissance one must take into account the universal attractions of the pastoral mode, the fact of its classical pedigree, and the potential it contained for exploitation as a vehicle of Christian and humanist ideas.

The Renaissance response to pastoral was due to the psychological, social, and philosophical appeal of its lovely natural setting, simple shepherd protagonists, easy rural life, and omnipresent song. Paradoxically, this simple environment could contain and dramatize not only such essentials as love, death, and art but also such concepts, attitudes, and myths as "soft" primitivism, noble savagery, the golden age, Eden before the Fall, and the division between nature and art, town and country, courtier and rustic. Arcadia proved infinitely attractive and useful as an imaginary pastoral country to which one could travel, if he were not a native, and in which one might stay temporarily, if he could escape the obligations of civilization. Its very simplicity and harmony provided a contemplative respite from urban tensions and clarification by contrast to complex personal and political issues, not to mention a persuasive literary softening of harsh social and religious satire. The Renaissance pastoralists were also aware of the frailty of a form that lent itself so easily to obsequious panegyric or praise, mere pretty artifice, or blatant self-advertisement. They knew too that Arcadia largely reflects the character of those who inhabit it or invade it. As John Donne (1572–1631) and Andrew Mar-

vell (1621–1678) both asserted in the opening stanzas of their poems "Twickenham Garden" and "The Garden," the *locus amoenus*
(pleasance or lovely grove) is easily contaminated by those who come to it with their fallen
natures and trailing worldly burdens. Refreshment and insight are available in the pleasance, but one must always return to the real
world.

As for classical pedigree, Renaissance pastoral is incomprehensible without an awareness of its debt to ancient pastoralists, especially Theocritus, Vergil, and Longus; in
addition, these and other Greco-Roman poets
provided their successors with terminology
and a rich assortment of motifs, themes, formal devices, and types. Renaissance neoclas-
sicists insisted that the classical authors had
discovered eternally valid literary forms,
which must be imitated or adapted according
to their internal laws, or decorum. The model
career of Vergil, the tenets of classical literary
criticism, and the obviously lofty subject matter and tone of tragedy and epic argued that
pastoral poetry was a beginner's kind of literary activity, a chance to test one's wings before trying the more difficult flights of tragedy
and epic, but especially the latter. At the same
time such celebrated specimens as the allegedly prophetic fourth eclogue of Vergil could
remind its practitioners of pastoral's potential
for large and somber meanings. The Christianization of pastoral, exemplified by the interpretation of it as treating the coming of
Christ, along with other medieval modulations of classical pastoral and exploitations of
biblical analogues, gained entry for it into the
Renaissance classroom, where it soon became
a pedagogical aid for humanist schoolmasters.

Pastoral was born sophisticated and literary. Though its origin in Greek poetic imitations of country life or in other literary genres
and types such as comedy and mime is murky,
its earliest known manifestation in the Sicilian Theocritus (*ca.* 308–*ca.* 240 B.C.) is self-
consciously artful despite its seemingly fresh

approach to a naive rural milieu and simple
rustic characters. Written in the urban literary
atmosphere of the Hellenistic culture that
flourished most notably at Alexandria, the
Idylls of Theocritus present us at once with
what would become the crucial Renaissance
tension between town and country, nature and
culture. The thirty *Idylls* (from the Greek for
"little pictures") by or attributed to Theocritus are all written in the dactylic hexameter
used for epic, but offer a bewildering variety of
different types of short poem, from recognizably pastoral songs with refrains to mimes
and *epyllia* ("little epics" or brief mythological narratives). The pastoral poems have a
pleasant natural setting, with shepherds and
goatherds, even fishermen, conversing and
singing or piping. The important themes include the lament or dirge for a dead shepherd,
amatory complaint, and song contest. The latter may involve mere juxtaposition of songs,
or *amoebean* dialogues (from the Greek for
"responsive verses": the technical term for
contests in which the shepherds vie with each
other by exchanging and trying to cap each
other's short verses), before a judge who may
award a prize, declare a winner, or courteously
announce a tie. By using archaic Doric dialect,
simultaneously "rustic" yet literary because
of its use by previous lyric poets, Theocritus
raised a question that would plague the Renaissance: How should shepherds talk? Or,
what are the requirements and limits of realism in pastoral?

Renaissance poets also knew the extant
idylls of two other poets, Moschus and Bion,
the former a Syracusan writing in the mid-sec-
ond century B.C., and the latter, from Smyrna,
at work possibly some fifty years later. Among
the mainly mythological rather than pastoral
poems attributed to these followers of Theocritus are two of special interest and influence: the *Lament for Bion* and the *Lament for
Adonis*. These, along with Theocritus' *Lament
for Daphnis*, helped establish a pedigree for
the Renaissance pastoral elegy, which reached
a climax in what many believe to be the last

and best pastoral poem of the Renaissance, John Milton's *Lycidas* (1637).

Some Renaissance poets could read Theocritus in the Greek original and others in Latin translation; but for the essentially Latinate culture of the time the key pastoral work was the set of ten eclogues (from the Latin for "select pieces") published in 39 B.C. by Vergil (70–19 B.C.). Here the Renaissance found the stylish elegance of writing and tone it cherished. Along with elaborations in smooth hexameters of the now conventional Theocritean themes of love complaint, elegy, singing contest, and panegyric or praise, Vergil arranges the eclogues in a symmetrical structure of alternating monologues and dialogues. There are also occasional allusions to contemporary events and real people, thus encouraging future assumptions that symbolism and allegory were inherent in the form. The praise of fellow poets and powerful patrons also comes to the fore as a major theme that Renaissance authors would seize on for both profit and pleasure. The fourth eclogue mentioned above, probably a celebration of the coming birth of the emperor Octavian's child, flatters the parents by suggesting that the event heralds the return of the golden age—but it was interpreted in a messianic Christian key later as foretelling the birth of Christ, thus giving Vergil a special status as a pagan graced with prophecy.

Although alluded to briefly in Theocritus, Arcadia, the foremost pastoral country, was first given currency in Vergil's eclogues, for which it is the setting. The actual Arcadia in Greece is rugged mountain terrain, but since Polybius and Pausanius had said that its shepherds were singers, there was a basis for choosing this remote place and its ancient inhabitants as the realistic underpinnings for what was, in fact, an entirely imaginary green world, a landscape of the mind.

After completing the *Eclogues* and before finishing his great epic the *Aeneid*, Vergil produced in 29 B.C. a didactic poem, the *Georgics* (from the Latin *georgica*, or agricultural themes), which is in the tradition of the Greek poet Hesiod's *Works and Days* but is related to pastoral in ways that led to a fusion of its topics and tone with more strictly pastoral literature. In four books of hexameters, the *Georgics* combine a manual for farmers and shepherds (dealing with the care of animals and crops) with a philosophical meditation on the nature of things and on the advantages of living and working in the peaceful natural milieu. At the same time Vergil brings in a good deal of mythology and imbues his rural landscape with a sense of the supernatural through the invoked presence of the gods (as he had done earlier, in contrast to Theocritus, with the Arcadian landscape of the *Eclogues*). Both the emphasis upon the advantages of rural retreat and the saturation of Arcadia with mythology were to become standard associations or fusions with pastoral. Although kept separate at times, the pastoral poem and the mythological poem often merged, with the result that Arcadia could be peopled by allegedly real shepherds in a landscape swarming with those deities and semideities especially associated with the woods and forests, headed by Pan, the chief god of Arcadia, patron of shepherds and inventor of their pipe, who was merged with their own god Faunus by the Romans.

Among Vergil's contemporaries and successors these modulations of pastoral received further impetus. Thus Horace's insistence on the advantages of *otium* (rural retreat or leisure), far from urban tensions, over *negotium* (worldly affairs) reinforced the idea of pastoral as blessed refuge. At the same time, the satiric approach that he and, more harshly, Juvenal could take toward the ills of urban existence helped admit moral and political satire into pastoral, where otherwise the amused irony of Theocritus and the understated, implied critique of Vergil might have prevailed. The fusion of pastoral and mythological landscapes and protagonists mentioned above also received impetus from the collecting and memorable retelling of the many woodland myths by Ovid in his famous *Metamorphoses.* Thus Renaissance pastoral, so called and accepted as such, often blends somewhat incongruously Arcadian landscape and characters with Ovidian deities and myths, and often combines details of or allusions to husbandry and the agricultural cycle of the seasons with the ideals of the city dweller longing to put aside commerce for the leisure of the country villa and its rustic charms.

In addition to the terms already mentioned (pastoral, idyll, eclogue), the Vergilian milieu used at least two others that came down to Renaissance poets and critics in the vocabulary of literary pastoral: bucolic and rustic. Bucolic, from the Greek *boukolos* (herdsman) or *boukolika* (herdsman songs) and the Latin *bucolica* (pastoral poems), was preferred by the Renaissance to idyll, which was rarely used apart from reference to Theocritus' works, and only quite late as a designation for mythological poems. Rustic, from the Latin *rusticus* (of the countryside), might refer in Renaissance parlance to rustic songs (*rustica carmina*) about actual country scenes, dwellers, and activities; but as often as not it was used synonymously with pastoral and bucolic.

As was the case with Theocritus, the Renaissance poets knew of the pastoral works of two followers of Vergil, Calpurnius and Nemesianus. The former, a poet during Nero's reign in the first century A.D., wrote seven eclogues that in their courtly, panegyric, rustic, and didactic contents reinforced the Renaissance tendency to vary widely the content and style of the eclogue. His praise of Nero as harbinger of a new golden age also set far too attractive a precedent to be ignored by those Renaissance poets who lapsed into verse of lavish proportions. Calpurnius has also been credited with an important contribution to the debate between town and country as a key pastoral motif. His follower, Nemesianus of Carthage, flourished at the end of the third century A.D., but his four extant eclogues, known to and of some influence in the Renaissance, were long thought to be part of the canon of Calpurnius. His merger of the motifs of lament and praise into the celebration of a friend or patron in his first eclogue has been noted as a precedent for the development of the pastoral elegy.

The dominance of the eclogue in hexameters in the works of the classical pastoral poets should not blind us to the existence of a large body of other lyric poetry, Greek and Latin, in a variety of meters and forms, from epigram to elegy, that survived into the Renaissance. Some were part of ancient collections of pastoral verse; others were known through the *Greek Anthology*, a late-classical gathering of several thousand brief poems, mostly epigrams and epigraphs. But whether mainly amatory and mythological, or only marginally pastoral (a pastoral setting or protagonist, a bucolic allusion or image), these sources too came into the wide net cast by Renaissance pastoralists, who tended both to expand blithely if not overload the eclogue and generously pour pastoral contents into other lyric containers of a classical or nonclassical pedigree. Among the neo-Latin poets of the Renaissance as well as those writing in the various European vernaculars, there was a special appeal to be found in light and witty verse of the kind that survived in the *Anthology* and other collections, with or without pastoral trappings. They called their collections of Latin imitations of such poems *lusus pastorales* (pastoral vignettes or games). In the vernacular this light pastoral vein appeared in such forms as the quatrain, octave stanza, and sonnet, with more weighty matter reserved for the formal eclogue in Latin hexameters and elegiac distichs or in equivalent vernacular meters. In sum, the Renaissance had ample precedent in antiquity for writing pastoral verse or near-pastoral verse in a whole range of lyric styles.

Apart from some analogues in the situations or settings of classical comedy and satyr play, the pastoral dramatists of the Renaissance could not look to an ancient source and had virtually to invent the genre. But for the pastoral prose romance, there was not only the precedent of the late Greek or Byzantine novel with pastoral interludes but also the *Daphnis and Chloe* of Longus, which was more important than the other romances in its use of a pastoral setting and characters for the bulk of the plot. Written sometime between the second and third centuries A.D. by its otherwise unknown author, the romance has the familiar motifs of oracles and prophecies, foundlings who turn out to be of high birth, pirate raids, attempted rapes, hairbreadth escapes, postponement of erotic satisfaction until much trial and tribulation have been undergone, and the crowning of long suffering with marriage and general reconciliation. Renaissance writers were not much interested in its central feature, the anatomy of budding love between innocents, since they were not interested in adolescence as such. What did attract Renaissance readers was the issue of nature versus art (Longus claims in the prologue that he is describing a painting), the contrast of nature and nurture, town and country; the alternation of narrated action and idyllic description; the plot motifs and machinery of romance. Longus also purveys an ironic yet sympathetic tone, an Ovidian tongue-in-cheek kind of humor, and a skill at psychological analysis of love that were also duly noted. But although one hears echoes of these qualities in other Renaissance amatory works, they do not occur often enough in the pastoral romance, which sometimes tends to a wearisome solemnity of theme and tone.

There was a good deal of pastoral and quasi-pastoral literature written during the Middle Ages, and some of it was classical in inspiration. The Renaissance poets and scholars knew very little of it, however, and by humanist prejudice were not prepared to give it serious attention when it was discovered. From a purely literary point of view, the best pastoral literature of the medieval period was its vernacular lyrics, shepherds' plays, and romances rather than the Latin eclogues of churchmen or schoolmasters imitating the classics. Nevertheless, up to the time of and including Boccaccio and Petrarch, it was the scholars and poets who Christianized and otherwise shaped the pastoral eclogue in ways that made it a different thing from its ancient source. Even a romance form like the medieval *pastourelle* (a lyric centering on an amatory encounter between knight and shepherdess), differing as it does from classical pastoral in its social contrast and erotic content, was an influence on Renaissance pastoral.

The Christianization of pastoral was in several ways as natural and inevitable as it was consciously forged by individual poets. The word "pastoral" itself had the dual meaning of shepherd and priest. The metaphor of shepherd and flock had biblical associations with Jesus, the lamb of God. The Nativity narrative gave a central role to shepherds and their animals. In the Old Testament there were shepherds from Abel to David, and the pastoral life provided a familiar context for events, settings, parables, and figures of speech. The *Song of Solomon*, both an epithalamium and dream-pastoral, could be and was allegorized to spiritual abstraction, hence suggesting a way to moralize pastoral scenery and sentiment. No wonder that by the time of the Renaissance, pastoral could be seen as both a pure classical genre and an especially appropriate vehicle for Christian ideas and feelings veiled in allegory.

DANTE, PETRARCH, AND BOCCACCIO

A curious revival of classical pastoral occurs in the correspondence between Dante (1265–1321), poet of the *Divine Comedy*, and a Bolognese professor of rhetoric, Giovanni del Virgilio (*ca.* 1270–*ca.* 1330), dating from 1319 to 1321. The issue was Dante's use of Tuscan instead of Latin in writing his great poem, and, in spite of that alleged mistake, an invitation to be crowned with the laurel at Bologna extended by del Virgilio. In his reply, a short poem in Latin hexameters, Dante pens in effect an epistolary eclogue, responding to "Mopsus" as "Tityrus," and promising to send the gift of ten pails of milk (cantos of *Paradiso*). In a second epistolary eclogue, also in Latin hexameters but of doubtful authenticity, Dante replies to a return letter from del Virgilio and uses pastoral cypher to refer to his exile from Florence and contemporary politics.

Between 1346 and 1357 Petrarch (1304–1374) wrote most of his dozen eclogues in Latin hexameters. In line with the medieval theory of poetry that he and Boccaccio shared, which emphasized allegorical cover for literal meaning, and his desire to obscure allusion to contemporary events and persons, Petrarch wrote virtual pastoral cryptograms. In fact, despite his providing keys to their meanings, many of the details still baffle scholars. The general subjects, however, are fairly clear: classical versus Christian poetry; worldly pursuits versus monastic life (1, 9); corruption at the papal court (6, 7); laments and praise for dead patrons and his beloved Laura (2, 3, 10, 11); the art of literature (4); and contemporary politics (5, 8, 12). It is obvious that Petrarch had expanded the range and altered the character of the classical eclogue, not to mention its length, as in the 413 hexameters of eclogue 10. Their fusion of medieval ideals and Vergilian form, their weighty classical learning, and their obscure allegory assured the eclogues' attraction for later Renaissance poets.

In his celebrated lyrics in the vernacular, as in his many autobiographical letters, Petrarch also includes many descriptions of and allusions to the real landscape of his beloved Vaucluse and the imaginary landscapes of medieval poetry. In these, and in a Latin treatise on the solitary life, he may be said to have introduced the theme of solitude, which was to have strong links with pastoral and was to be quite influential on Renaissance lyric poets. Unlike the Horatian *otium*, however, Petrarch's solitude is neither convivial nor hedonistic or epicurean, but instead a secular alternative to monastic contemplative isolation, a meditative aloneness surrounded by natural scenery that the mind may find sympathetic (the pathetic fallacy) or symbolically suggestive, a stimulus to renewed creativity or to sorrowful memory of past and passing joys.

Boccaccio (1313–1375) also wrote eclogues in Latin, some sixteen of them in the usual hexameters, entitled *Bucolicum carmen* (Bucolic Song). Neither as polished nor as interesting as those of Petrarch, they nevertheless had impact because of some attractive features and the fact that they were the work of an acknowledged disciple of Petrarch and coworker with him in the field of revived classical learning. Apart from the obligatory amatory praises and laments (1, 2), politics (3–9), art (10, 12, 13), and autobiographical treatment of literary and spiritual crises (1, 15, 16), there are two startlingly unusual themes treated in eclogues 11 and 14. In the eleventh, entitled "Pantheon," Boccaccio presents the conversation of two shepherds, Myrtillis (the Church) and Glaucus (Saint Peter), including a bucolic version of the life of Christ, from the Nativity to the Second Coming, which was to have numerous pastoral progeny. In the more famous fourteenth eclogue, Olympia, the poet, as Sylvius, has a vision of his dead daughter Violante and her heavenly dwelling place that he describes in no fewer than 285 hexameters. It has been noted that there is both genuine personal feeling and sincere religious sentiment in this poem, rarely found in the pastoral eclogue, which generally eschews domestic themes.

Boccaccio's contribution to Renaissance pastoral also rests on two vernacular works, the poem *Ninfale fiesolano* (*The Nymph of Fiesole*, or, literally, The Fiesolean Nymphal), and the prose romance *Ninfale d'Ameto* (*The Nymph of Admetus*, or Admetus' Nymphal). Boccaccio used the curious term "nymphal" for these two works on the analogy with pastoral and bucolic, since the heroines of both are allegedly nymphs. The *Fiesolano* (1348?) blends the popular minstrel form of the narrative in octaves with the characteristics of an erotic novella, and Ovidian explanatory myth with the rustic elements of the pastoral tradition, as it narrates the tragic love of the rustic Affrico for the nymph Mensola. The poem has been called the first Italian idyll. It was quite popular in the Renaissance, with many Italian editions and translations into French and English. Not the least of its influential features was the suggestion of modern myth-making, for the names of Boccaccio's hero and heroine come from and are therefore made to explain the origin of two actual streams, the Affrico and the Mensola, that run down from the hills of Fiesole into the Arno near Florence. And their descendants are said to have played a role in Florence's early history and to have survived among the population of that city in Boccaccio's own time. Thus a history of the Renaissance idyll understood narrowly as a mythological or Ovidian narrative, and running from Lorenzo de' Medici to Marlowe and Shakespeare, might well begin with Boccaccio's *Ninfale.*

The *Ameto* (ca. 1342), also known as the *Commedia delle ninfe fiorentine* (Comedy of the Florentine Nymphs), is a prose romance interspersed with verse. Its pastoral touches have led to its designation as the first Italian pastoral romance and therefore as the pioneer in the tradition that runs from Jacopo Sannazaro to Jorge de Montemayor. The regenerative love of the crude hunter Ameto for the nymph Lia acts as a frame for the amatory autobiographies she and six other nymphs tell for Ameto's edification. That they represent the seven virtues as well as seven actual Florentine ladies, combining obvious moral allegory with real-life identities it is up to the reader to decipher, is all too predictive of what would follow in Renaissance bucolic literature. Boccaccio was perhaps not the actual father of the bucolic masquerade (playing at pastoral may go back to Theocritus, book 7), but the *Ameto* is undoubtedly a link in the infamous tradition of pastoral play-acting that eventually doomed the genre. Finally, we may note the occurrence in chapter 14 of the *Ameto* an early specimen of vernacular eclogue, a singing match apparently of the classical type, between two shepherds, Alcesto and Acaten. Though not allegorical, this eclogue raises some interesting questions about its classical quality if one looks at it more carefully. For one thing, its alternating terza rima does not have the effect of antiphonal hexameters; also, the theme of the song contest is the very medieval one of the ascetic versus the worldly life. Then, too, the tone and other features of the exchange remind us of the Provençal *tenson* (a lyric in which a topic is proposed and discussed) and the European-wide medieval genre of the moral debate. In sum, as we turn to survey the pastoral literature of the Renaissance, under the convenient generic headings of lyric, drama, and romance, we should be alert to the complex interweaving of classical and medieval forms and motifs, but especially to the contemporary impulse to make the tradition responsive to the needs of Christian humanism and to the needs of the creative imagination in the many poets, dramatists, and novelists who attempted pastoral song.

PASTORAL LYRIC

For the purposes of our survey, we shall include in the category of pastoral lyric not only formal eclogues in Latin and in the vernacular, but also Latin and vernacular poems of other formal lyric types that have a pastoral or rustic setting and characters and, more crucial, embody the pastoral ethos. We omit poetry that merely alludes to the green world and springtime and shepherds, or that is primarily mythological or amatory or both. On this premise we can begin with the influence of the three major Italian poets already discussed, on one another and on their successors writing in Latin and Italian during the fifteenth century.

That influence established nothing less than an enviable standard of Latin and vernacular composition. The followers of Petrarch and Boccaccio especially include eminent men of affairs as well as lesser figures. Thus we know of eclogues written by the Florentine chancellor Salutati (1331–1406) and the papal secretary to Pope Urban VI, Giovanni Quatrario (1336–1402), as well as vernacular lyrics by Franco Sacchetti (ca. 1330–1400), better known perhaps as the author of *novellas*. Most readers would now willingly exchange the ponderous Latin eclogues for the freshness of Sacchetti's pastoral *ballata* beginning "O vaghe montanine pasturelle,/Donde venite sì leggiadre e belle?" (O lovely mountain shepherdesses,/ Where do you come from, so graceful and so beautiful?). Indeed the question of Latin or vernacular composition was to vex the latter part of the fifteenth century, when a powerful burst of vernacular literature, including pastoral, assured that Latin would not dominate the literary scene.

A particularly vital center of this activity was the Florence of Lorenzo de' Medici (1449–1492), whose literary output included several pastoral efforts. Lorenzo followed the Boccaccian lead in composing two vernacular idylls, the *Ambra* and the *Corinto*. The former recounts in Tuscan octaves the love of Ombrone (a river) for Ambra (a nymph eventually turned to stone), against a rural setting that evidences Lorenzo's known affection for and knowledge of the countryside outside of Florence, where there were two family villas. The *Corinto*, which some would call the first Italian pastoral (as opposed to mythological) idyll, concerns the amorous plea, in terza rima, of the shepherd Corinto to his beloved Galatea, culminating in the motif of *coglia la rosa* (gather ye rosebuds) from the carpe diem theme of Latin love poetry. Lorenzo also composed an *Altercazione*, or debate, in terza rima, divided into six *capitoli*, or sections, which features himself and a veteran shepherd, Alfeo, arguing about the pastoral life. Alfeo, a "hard" primitivist, counters Lorenzo's praise of rural existence with a descrip-

tion of its hardships. The intervention of the philosopher Marsilio Ficino raises the discussion to the philosophical consideration of the supreme good for man but weakens the bucolic frame. A final, less strained contribution of Lorenzo to pastoral occurs in his *Selve d'amore* (Amatory Improvisations), two poems in octaves, the second of which has a pioneering vernacular treatment of the pastoral theme of the golden age.

Within the Lorentian milieu was the precocious scholar and poet Angelo Poliziano (1454–1494), whose brilliant poetry in Latin and the vernacular has some pastoral elements; but for our purposes, more notable are his hexameter *Sylvae* (1489), actually public lectures, in two of which he deals with Vergil, the *Georgics*, and contemporary rustic life. By contrast, within that same cultural environment, there was a rage for sophisticated parody of rustic love. A flurry of poems about the peasant Vallera's crude courting of his shepherdess Nencia from the village of Barberino (the best known of these once attributed to Lorenzo himself) was a harbinger of one kind of favorite Renaissance pastoral humor, culminating in Don Quixote's love for Aldonza Lorenzo transformed into Dulcinea del Toboso, in Cervantes' *Don Quixote*. The whole point of such parody is a response to the question: If one could overhear real rustics in love, what would they sound like?

At the end of the century, in other cultural centers outside of Florence (Naples, Ferrara, Rome, Venice, Mantua, Milan), innovative pastoral composition was a prominent part of a general and flourishing literary activity in Latin and the vernacular. At Ferrara there was Matteo Maria Boiardo (1441–1494), best known as author of the *Orlando innamorato*, the chivalric romance continued by Ariosto in his celebrated *Orlando furioso* but also the composer of ten Latin eclogues (1463–1465), many of a courtly kind that anticipate the taste of the next century. At Naples, Giovanni Pontano (1424–1503), luminary of the local academy and friend of the equally famous poet Sannazaro, was an innovator of the pastoral epicedium, or dirge, in his widely imitated eclogue *Melisseus,* on the death of his wife. His *Lepidina,* another Latin eclogue, also deals with a conjugal theme, in this case the happy union of Macron and Lepidina and the impending wedding of the nymph Partenope (Naples) and the river Sebeto, followed by a spectacle that the scholar W. Leonard Grant has treated in terms of pastoral masque and a very early example of play-within-play (see Bibliography).

At Mantua, also in the closing decades of the fifteenth century, we find the curious figure Giovanni Battista Spagnolo or Mantovano (1448–1516), also known as Baptista Mantuanus and in English as Mantuan, but not to be confused with the infinitely greater Mantuan, Vergil. In fact this prolific writer of neo-Latin verse and prose (it has been estimated that he wrote some 60,000 lines of Latin verse, and quickly) was held in such high esteem by his contemporaries that some, including Erasmus, did not hesitate to place him on a par with the other Mantuan as a writer of Latin eclogues. He was also a Carmelite monk, several times elected to the headship of his order, and may be the only pastoralist ever beatified by the church (1885). Born at Mantua of a Spanish father (hence Spagnolo or sometimes Spagnoli), he began work on his eclogues while a student at Padua, where he was acquiring his immense learning, but did not publish them until revised and expanded, in 1498. Though barely known today, and mainly to specialists, this author and his ten longish hexameter eclogues were better known than any other modern pastoralist and pastoral poetry in the Renaissance, largely because the poems were used as a Latin primer in the schools of Europe, especially in Germany. Widely read, translated, quoted, and adapted, the eclogues were so familiar to readers of the time that Shakespeare could have Holofernes in *Love's Labor's Lost* (4.2) ac-

tually quote the opening lines in Latin of the first eclogue, and then exclaim: "Old Mantuan, old Mantuan! Who understandeth thee not, loves thee not."

The themes of these eclogues that Holofernes expects us to know and love offer a clue to their popularity. The first four eclogues deal with contrastingly joyous and miserable love: the courtship and happy marriage of Faustus and Galla (1); the wretched plight of Amyntas, plunged into illicit love (2); the miserable end of Amyntas, whose sinful story is here concluded (3); a culminating rhetorical exercise, a satire on the evil nature of women (4). The fifth eclogue, in a welcome shift of emphasis, takes up the favorite Renaissance literary topic of the niggardliness of patrons in rewarding poets; and the sixth, the by now venerable stock pastoral theme of town versus country. The last four eclogues are religious or devotional in subject: young Rollux, warned by a vision of the Virgin Mary, flees the world to Mount Carmel, that is, the Carmelite order (7); then, in continuation of the Marian motif, eclogue 8 offers praise of the "nymph" Mary and an exhortation to observe the sacred days in her honor; next, the Roman curia is denounced for its corruption, much to the delight of later Protestant readers (9); and finally, in the tenth eclogue, there is the strangely nonpastoral subject of a debate between two rival factions of the Carmelites, the Discalced and Conventuals, about the proper rule for the order. There is clearly in these eclogues a wide range of material to choose from, a mix of humanist and religious topics, plentiful recognition in allusions to Vergil, Petrarch, and other predecessors, and, without allegorical obscurity, a sufficiently credible maintaining of the usual pastoral characters, setting, and activities. The Latin style, though not always "correct," has a flavor, due to its gnomic utterances, surprising realism, and occasional humorous exaggeration, that apparently greatly satisfied Renaissance taste, not excluding that of Spenser and Milton.

RENAISSANCE PASTORAL POETRY

The sixteenth century witnessed the flowering and culmination of Italian Renaissance culture and its transmission to the other countries of Europe. The same may be said for pastoral, which became all pervasive in that culture and its transalpine imitators. The triumph of the vernacular did not diminish the flow of pastoral lyric, since many poets simply wrote in both Latin *and* Italian or French or English, thereby doubling the pastoral output. As we shall see, pastoral drama and romance took their place in the generic expansion of the bucolic mode, as the mixing and interpenetration of genres so typical of Renaissance literary activity proceeded apace. The mature Italian and European pastoral lyric both swelled and contracted as new demands were put upon it, and as it interacted with them it became increasingly difficult to isolate pastoral from other flourishing lyric modes and types, especially mythological and Petrarchan poetry. The eclogue, an average of eighty lines in length in Vergil, now grew to hundreds of lines to accommodate almost every Renaissance need, private and public, occasional and commemorative. It deals with births, weddings, deaths, courtly panegyric and moral satire, public and domestic events, not to mention Christian subjects and themes. Eclogues in Latin and the vernacular were virtually composed and sent as greeting cards are today, and they even began to be treated as scripts for dramatization or libretti for musical setting. At the same time, as though in reaction to the confining limits of the original and simple pastoral setting and protagonists of the eclogue, it now became fashionable to admit any other outdoor activity and its protagonists, from fishermen to vinegrowers, with appropriate substitutions of scene and characteristic labor. Simultaneously, as the eclogue swelled to encompass these new interests, the short bucolic lyric in Latin and the vernacular, the *lusus,* or epigram, and the madrigal condensed the pastoral scenario into a few lines, distilling its essence in a brief dramatic scene or monologue or description. Finally, it became a requirement in longer, nonpastoral works like the chivalric romance to include pastoral interludes, both for their own aesthetic sake and for their usefulness in conveying larger meanings.

A glance at some examples of these major trends might begin with Baldesar Castiglione (1478–1529), author of the celebrated guide to ideal courtly conduct *Il cortegiano* (*The Courtier*), which has been called an urban pastoral. More conventionally pastoral, however, is his Latin elegy *Alcon,* in 155 hexameters, written to honor the memory of a young friend by sounding the conventional notes of regret at the early demise of so much promise. As the shepherd Iolas, the author calls on the other shepherds and the woodland nymphs to join him in memorializing the dead youth Alcon: "Since the cruel fates have stole him away, the very hills weep and the day has turned to night: all light is dark, all sweet is bitter" (153–155). As may be imagined, this poem impressed Milton enough to influence both his vernacular *Lycidas* and Latin *Epitaphium Damonis* (Lament for Damon), both composed also in memory of the poet's dead friends.

We have had occasion to mention the quasi-dramatic eclogue of Pontano, *Lepidina;* and in the same category of budding dramatic or theatrical adaptation of pastoral we should include the eclogue *Tirsi,* written by Castiglione in collaboration with a cousin and performed at Urbino during the carnival of 1506. In dialogue form, and totaling fifty-five octave stanzas, the eclogue flatters the Urbino rulers and court by praising them under pastoral guise with appropriate words, song, and dance from shepherds and chorus.

Jacopo Sannazaro (1456–1530), a pioneer of pastoral romance, may be considered also as another representative of the new uses—and, often, abuses—of pastoral lyric in the High Renaissance. His very popular five piscatorial eclogues, and a fragment of a sixth, are written in Latin hexameters of decent Vergilian length. The mainly amatory contents and formal structures of these fishermen's eclogues remain Vergilian and Petrarchan (the idea of the marine eclogue, however, goes back to Theocritus, book 21). What makes them piscatorial is an ingenious transposition from land to sea, from Arcadia to an idealized Bay of Naples. From this shift of scene follows others: fishermen instead of shepherds, fishing instead of pasturing, marine deities (tritons, nereids, naiads, Neptune, Glaucus, Proteus) instead of woodland spirits. Despite the fish and nets and boats, however, it would seem that fishermen sing and play the pipes and engage in doleful complaints about cruel or dead beloveds, or in lively amoebean contests, very much as their land brethren do in Arcadia. But the wide appeal of this transposition was such that soon piscatorials were being written in the vernacular, for example, by Bernardino Rota (1509–1575) in Italian (1533), and by Phineas Fletcher (1582–1650) in English as well as in Latin (1633). The great popularity and European-wide influence of Sannazaro's experiment assured not only the development of piscatorial poetry but also the exploration of other, analogous areas of rural life, such as hunting, farming, gardening, and sailing. At the same time Sannazaro's works gave impetus to an equally literary expansion of bucolic domain by his transfusion of eclogue with domesticated Ovidian myth, as in his Latin hexameter poem *Salices* (Willows). Here, the transformation into a willow of the nymph Salix, fleeing Pan, occurs in a very familiar Neapolitan landscape, reminding us of a Vergilian precedent, but the tale of metamorphosis is pure Ovid within an eclogue frame.

Among the practitioners of the Latin "little eclogue" called *lusus pastoralis* (and variously translated as epigram, vignette, sport, playful piece, toy), three Venetians were outstanding: Pietro Bembo (1470–1547), Andrea Navagero (1483–1529), and Marcantonio Flaminio (1498–1550). Flaminio's modern biographer has defined the *lusus* as "a fairly short poem in elegiac couplets on pastoral themes or on love in a pastoral setting" (C. Maddison, *Marcantonio Flaminio. Poet, Humanist, Reformer*, p. 55). The best known of these was Navagero's *lusus* beginning "Florentes dum forte vagans mea Hyella per hortos" (While my Hyella was by chance wandering in her flowering garden), which was everywhere imitated, adapted, and translated. Here is the original:

Florentes dum forte vagans mea Hyella per hortos
  Texit odoratis lilia cana rosis:
Ecce rosas inter latitantem invenit amorem:
  Et simul annexis floribus implicuit.
Luctatur primo: et contra nitentibus alis
  Indomitus tentat solvere vincla puer.
Mox ubi lacteolas, et dignas matre papillas
  Vidit, et ora ipsos nata movere deos:
Impositosque comae ambrosios ut sensit odores:
  Quosque legit diti messe beatus arabs:
I, dixit, mea, quaere novum tibi, mater, amorem,
  Imperio sedes haec erit apta meo.

(*Lusus* 21.40–42)

While my Hyella was by chance wandering in her flowering garden, weaving white lilies and fragrant roses, suddenly she came upon Cupid himself, and entangled him in her garland of flowers. At first he struggled and, fighting back with his wings, the unyielding little boy tried to loosen his chains. But then, seeing her milky breasts, worthy of his mother, Venus, and her lips, created to dazzle the very Gods, and sensing from her hair the ambrosial fragrance which the wealthy Arab gathers in plentiful harvest, he said: "My mother, go seek a new Love for yourself. *This* will henceforth be the fitting place from which to exercise my power."

The vernacular madrigal, akin to the Latin epigram and *lusus*, is another miniature arena within which Renaissance poets displayed highly condensed versions of the protagonists, descriptions, and sentiments often expanded in the more generous space of the eclogue. The following example by Torquato Tasso (1544–1595) manages to weave the pastoral, amatory, and mythological threads we have been discussing into a fabric of just eight lines:

> *Sovra un lucido rio*
> *si dolea per amore*
> *un pastorel mirando il suo bel viso:*
> *"Perché" diceva "anch'io*
> *non mi converto in fiore,*
> *benché non ami come fé Narciso,*
> *che 'n quella forma almeno*
> *mi raccorrebbe la mia donna in seno?"*
> (*Opere*, vol. 1, Maier ed.: *Rime*, no.
> 318)

By a lucent stream a shepherd lad was gazing at his image and complaining of love: "Why," he said, "do not I also transform myself into a flower, though I do not love as Narcissus did, for at least in that form my lady would gather me to her breast?"

Tasso is also of course the author of the celebrated epic-romance *Gerusalemme liberata (Jerusalem Delivered)*. That poem, like its rival, the earlier *Orlando furioso* (Orlando Mad) of Ludovico Ariosto (1474–1533), contains an obligatory pastoral interlude. The idyll occurs beginning with canto 11, when the princess Angelica, dressed in lowly pastoral attire, comes upon the wounded Medoro and falls in love with him; they marry under the roof of a simple herdsman's hut and spend the following rapturous weeks exploring every stream, meadow, and cave, carving their names on every tree and rock. And it is these signs of pastoral amatory bliss that trigger the jealous madness of the hero, Orlando. Tasso's pastoral interlude occurs in the seventh book of his epic, when the princess Erminia, in love with but unable to join Tancredi, finds herself taking refuge in a shepherd's cottage on the banks of the Jordan River. Here she stays awhile, refreshed by the soothing praise of the simple life spoken to her by a wise old shepherd and delighting in unaccustomed pastoral chores, which relieve her grief. In the same

vein, there is Spenser's book 6 of *The Faerie Queene* (1590–1596), influenced by both Italian poems, and using the pastoral interlude for the expression of some of his epic's key moral ideas.

Before turning to other countries, we should note that Renaissance Italy also gave birth to the first modern histories and theories of pastoral, as J. E. Congleton has pointed out. Though hardly as thorough scholars as W. W. Greg and W. L. Grant, or as interesting critics as William Empson and Renato Poggioli (see Bibliography), Poliziano and, later, Marco Girolamo Vida (*ca.* 1485–1566) and J. C. Scaliger (1484–1558) did lay the foundations, however tentative, of subsequent inquiry into the origins and literary conventions of pastoral from antiquity to their own time.

As Renaissance culture spread outside of Italy in the sixteenth century, the pastoral lyric was widely and abundantly cultivated as one of the key literary indices of the arrival and absorption of the new humanistic and aesthetic ideals. Several factors conditioned the European reception and assured that there would be something more than mere copying of the classical and Italian models. First, in several countries, especially France and England, there were strong native traditions of pastoral that had already inspired many medieval plays and poems, and these retained a powerful hold on the literary imagination. Second, the Italians had developed the lyric to a high degree of artfulness by expansion, condensation, fusion with other forms and modes, and utilization of musical and dramatic setting. The European poets knew these works but also the sources (Theocritus, Vergil, Catullus, Horace, Ovid, the *Greek Anthology*, Petrarch, Neoplatonism) that the Italians had used to brew novel recipes for the eclogue and epigram. Still another new ingredient, the poetry of Anacreon, was available from 1554, when the first edition was published at Lyons, late for the Italians but just in time for the further enrichment by cross-fertilization of pastoral lyric. Hence the Europeans attempted to display the required skills but also to achieve novelty by the same means employed earlier in Italy: imitation, according to which one manipulates the familiar so that it remains always recognizable yet novel, a fresh and creative adaptation but not utterly or shockingly new. Third, the sheer, self-conscious artfulness of pastoral, present from the beginning with Theocritus and now intensified by excessive production, meant an increase of satire, allegory, generic self-scrutiny (pastoral questioning the meaning of pastoral), and symbolization (pastoral as metaphor).

In France the pastoral lyric is prominent among the literary works inspired by the new interest in classical and Italian forms. Clément Marot (1495–1544), a transitional figure between the medieval traditions of lyric poetry and the contemporary ideals of the Pléiade poets, penned several court eclogues, notably one on the death of Louise of Savoy and another on the birth of a son to the dauphin, both among the very first written in France. At the same time, he could write a *ballade* for Christmas Day in which he addresses the native shepherds Colin and Margot and invites them to rejoice. The classical landscapes of literary pastoral and images of the French countryside thus are evoked alternately or blended by Marot in his poetry, exemplifying a key feature of the best French Renaissance pastoral lyric.

The sister of Francis I, Marguerite of Navarre (1492–1549), whom Marot had served, is best known for her *Heptameron*, a collection of Boccaccian tales; but she also wrote an eclogue on the death of her brother and an imitation of Sannazaro's *Salices*. Another major figure of the time, the poet Maurice Scève (1500–1560), author of a celebrated collection of love lyrics, *Délie*, also composed in 1547 a pastoral work entitled *La Saulsaye: Eglogue de la vie solitaire* (The Willow Grove: An Eclogue of the Solitary Life), which combines the bucolic and Petrarchan motifs, along with Sannazaro's modern myth, in a meditation on the nature and virtues of solitude,

"loin des cités vie tumultueuse" (far from the tumultuous life of the cities). And in 1536 a collection of memorial poems for the dead dauphin included probably the first French specimen of an *eglogue marine*, by Hughes Salel (1504–1553). By 1544 Sannazaro's *Arcadia* had been translated, followed in 1559 by a rendering of Longus' *Daphnis and Chloe*. Thus, earlier than and apart from the appearance of the Pléiade poets, there was a good deal of pioneering pastoral being written and circulated to court and salon, or through printing to a wider literary audience, from Lyons to Paris.

The *Défense et illustration de la langue française* (The Defense and Making Illustrious of the French Language) appeared in 1549 from the pen of Joachim du Bellay (1523–1560). This treatise, announcing a literary program for a small and loose band of young poets known subsequently as the Pléiade, included pastoral among the classical and Italian forms recommended as a challenge to the modern French poet who wished to glorify his vernacular tongue and achieve personal fame. Du Bellay himself has many pastoral touches in his lyrics, whether Petrarchan sonnets or imitations of *lusus pastorales,* and at least one Latin eclogue, *Iolas,* in hexameters. His *Divers jeux rustiques* (Diverse Rustic Diversions), published in 1558, includes poems like the well-known *chanson* "D'un vanneur de blé aux vents" ("From a Winnower of Corn to the Winds"), in which the speaker, the winnower of the title, offers gifts of flowers to the passing winds that they might fan him with their cool breezes while he labors in the heat of the day. Redolent of the countryside yet hardly realistic, this poem is a typical example of the way in which Renaissance "rustic" poetry often becomes the ground of a clash between pastoral tradition and observed contemporary rural life, with few clear victories for the latter.

The leading Pléiade poet, Pierre de Ronsard (1524–1585), has numerous pastoral elements scattered throughout his vast lyric production, many of these found in eclogues of the kind that commemorate through allegory the various occasions marking the life of the French court. There are also other bucolic poems, or *bergeries,* written for such special festivities as the carnival season celebrated at Fontainebleau. But it is perhaps in his love poems that Ronsard, who really knew and loved the countryside as well as he knew and loved the pastoral poets, achieved a stable balance between nature and art. For instance, the poems written to Marie in his avowedly "beautiful low style," while occasionally laboring under the initial fiction of a love relationship between the poet and a peasant girl, do manage to evoke a simpler world and something of that erotic innocence which allegedly prevailed in the golden age, one of Ronsard's favorite myths.

As though given the chief assignment in the area of pastoral production, Remy Belleau (1528–1577), another Pléiade poet, wrote the most considered bucolic work of the group, his *Bergeries* (1565, 1572). Divided into two *journées,* or days, it has a prose matrix consisting of descriptions of the château of Joinville and its environs. Embedded into this setting are the varied pastoral poems themselves, some, such as the much anthologized "Avril," a brief ode to the gifts of spring, containing a few delightfully realistic touches that recall the Elizabethan lyricists. It is interesting to note too that this translator of Anacreon also published in 1576 a group of *eclogues sacrées.* There are pastoral poems and ingredients in the works of other poets associated with Ronsard and du Bellay, especially Jean Dorat (*ca.* 1502–1588) and Jean-Antoine de Baïf (1532–1589), but none of outstanding merit. The popularity of the court poet Phillipe Desportes (1546–1606) was a phenomenon of the later decades of the sixteenth century, but like his predecessors of the Pléiade he continued the cultivation of pastoral in his *Bergeries* (1594). A full history of the pastoral lyric in France would have to include also the eclogues and idylls of Henri Estienne (1511–1598) and the

Foresteries (1555) of Vauquelin de la Fresnaye (*ca.* 1535–1606), as well as Scévole de Sainte-Marthe's paraphrases of Flaminio's *lusus.* Fresnaye and Sainte-Marthe (1533–1623) take us into the seventeenth century and such Baroque extensions of biblical pastoral as the *Moyse sauvé (Moses Saved)* of Girard Saint-Amant (1594–1661), subtitled *Idylle héroique* (Heroic Idyll) and published in 1653. The significant poems on solitude of Saint-Amant and Théophile de Viau (1590–1626) are further proof that the pastoral lyric tradition was not yet engulfed by the inanities that would provoke satire and scorn, and that its conventions could still inspire gifted French poets to utilize it in interpreting themselves and their world.

The proliferation of Renaissance pastoral lyric in Spain may be conveniently dated from the publication in 1543 of the works of Juan Boscán (*ca.* 1490–1542) and Garcilaso de la Vega (1503–1536). Earlier, the dramatist Juan del Encina (1468?–1529) had used the term *égloga,* probably for the first time in Spanish, for his secular and religious pastoral plays; and in 1492 he had penned an eclogue, imitating Vergil's fourth, heralding the birth of a child to the monarchs Ferdinand and Isabella. These tentative efforts may stand for the kinds of limited experiments in pastoral lyricism made prior to the 1543 volume of Boscán and Garcilaso.

That volume, initially inspired by a conversation between Boscán and Andrea Navagero, who had urged upon the Spanish author the imitation of Italian Renaissance forms and themes, marked the introduction of the latter on a large scale. A good many of its pages are taken up by three Vergilian eclogues of Garcilaso. The varied meters and the Castilian language are in the service of some familiar themes: amorous complaint (*el dulce lamentar*), exchanges of song, interpolated Ovidian myths, sonorous descriptions of idealized landscape, minimal allusion to rural activities, and obligatory courtly panegyric. There is also a strong moral emphasis—the second eclogue extols marriage and service to the faith exemplified by the career of the duke of Alba, as against the pains of obsessive and frustrating erotic passion (see Rivers ed., *Renaissance and Baroque Poetry of Spain*, p. 16), if not as yet the religious concern that appears in much Spanish lyricism of the time. This latter impulse is evident in the poetry of Fray Luis de León (1527–1591) and San Juan de la Cruz (1542–1591).

The friar Luis de León translated into Spanish verse the eclogues and part of the *Georgics* of Vergil, and also accommodated the Horatian ode and its sentiments (the "retired life") to quasi-mystical Christian ideals, a "conversion" of secular to religious form and content quite widely practiced at the time, especially in the more obvious way of transposing actual texts, word and image, in a sacred key (*a lo divino*). In Luis de Léon and Juan de la Cruz there is less self-conscious transposition than complete absorption of sources and models by spiritual force. Thus Juan de la Cruz's *Cántico espiritual (Spiritual Canticle)* recalls the *Song of Solomon* and has touches of secular pastoral, but these are successfully fused by mystic fervor. The fourth song, "El Pastorcico" (The Little Shepherd), is announced as composed *a lo divino* but proceeds to describe in typical pastoral fashion the plight of a shepherd saddened because his love is unreciprocated. By the end of the fifth and last quatrain of the poem, however, this shepherd has climbed a tree to die there, fastened by his widespread arms, and we suddenly see that it is Christ and his love for man that was meant from the start.

In these middle- and late-sixteenth-century poets and their contemporaries and followers in the next century—including Fernando de Herrera (*ca.* 1534–1597), Lope de Vega (1562–1635), Luis de Góngora (1561–1627), and Francisco de Quevedo (1580–1645)— pastoral images and motifs make their presence known not only in the formal eclogue but also in other, usually brief lyric forms, whether of classical inspiration (ode, epi-

gram), Italian Renaissance (*canzone*, sonnet, octave, terza rima), or native (*romance, letrilla, copla*). As in other European pastoral literatures, there is a constant tension among the claims of pastoral art, of recognizable imitation, and the powerful lure of contemporary reality, especially for Spanish artists. The premium put on wit in the poetry of the seventeenth century, at the peak of Spain's *siglo de oro*, or golden age, adds still another dimension to the problem of pastoral style. A famous painting by Velázquez (1599–1660) entitled *Los borrachos* (literally *The Drunkards*, but usually called in English *Homage to Bacchus* or *Bacchus and His Companions, ca.* 1630) features a classical nude Bacchus surrounded by very realistic, earthy peasant types. Though based on Dutch precedents, this mingling of the worlds of mythology and contemporary reality typifies a very Spanish trend. Though the tension may be reconciled at the level of symbolic meaning, there remains an inevitable irony in such juxtapositions and sometimes a release into satire and parody, if not burlesque.

Lope de Vega, known primarily as a prolific author of hundreds of plays, including *comedias pastoriles*, also wrote a pastoral novel, *Arcadia* (1598), and many pastoral eclogues and short lyrics. In these poems the figures of Filis, Belisa, and Amarillis have been interpreted as referring to his various loves, though they are conventional enough. A poet of *rimas sacras* as well as *rimas humanas*, Lope also wrote a religious novel, *Los pastores de Belén* (*The Shepherds of Bethlehem*, 1612), perhaps in counterpoint to his earlier, and secular, *Arcadia*.

With Góngora and Quevedo we are in the full tide of late Spanish Renaissance or Baroque lyric style, with its obscurities, conceits, recondite allusions, syntactical distortions, and occasional, searing realism. Góngora's short lyrics have the expected pastoral touches, but more significant are his longer poems, such as the 1602 romance *Angélica y Medoro*, a thirty-four-quatrain version of the

Medoro, a thirty-four-quatrain version of the famous pastoral interlude from Ariosto's poem, retold with no little amount of amused irony. Both of Góngora's acknowledged masterpieces, the *Fábula de Polifemo y Galatea* (*The Fable of Polyphemus and Galatea*, 1613), in octaves, and the unfinished *Soledades* (*Solitudes*, 1613), in the irregular *silva* stanza, have strong pastoral credentials. The former represents a kind of culmination of the fusion of pastoral and mythological poem, with a pastoral frame serving to introduce and embellish the familiar Ovidian tale. The *Soledades,* another poem in the European tradition of praise of the solitary, retired life, surpasses all others of its kind in richness and complexity, mainly due to Góngora's habit of enameling landscape, transforming nature by metaphor and periphrasis into a glittering quasi-surreal aesthetic world. By contrast, his rival Quevedo, burdened with a darker vision of things, did not find the bucolic convention congenial except for the opportunities it presented to satirize human lack of awareness of time, decay, and death. As befits the author of a grimly realistic picaresque masterpiece, *El buscón* (*The Sharper*, 1626), Quevedo was uncomfortable with the ideals and sentiments of the pastoral mode:

> *Salime al campo, vi que el sol bebía*
> *los arroyos del hielo desatados;*
> *y del monte quejosos los ganados*
> *que con sombras hurtó su luz al día.*
>
> . . .
>
> *y no hallé cosa en que poner los ojos*
> *que no fuese recuerdo de la muerte.*
> (*Penguin Book of Spanish Verse,*
> 1956 ed., p. 269)

I went to the fields, and saw that the sun was drinking up the streams from the melted frost, and the cattle complaining to the trees that they stole the light of day with their shadows. . . . And I found nothing on which to cast my sight that did not remind me of death.

The pastoral lyric also flourished in northern Europe. Formal eclogues and briefer forms were written in Latin and the vernaculars by many German, Dutch, Scots, and English authors of the sixteenth and seventeenth centuries, although only the English poets of the Elizabethan period and their Baroque and neoclassical successors tend to be well known to us today. At the time, however, there were poets, scholars, schoolmasters, critics, and celebrated intellectuals writing in Latin whose reputations were such that their pastoral efforts attracted attention and exerted influence. Among these one might cite Joachim Camerarius (1500–1574), author of twenty eclogues; Daniel Heinsius of Ghent (1580–1655) and his epicedium on the death of Scaliger (1640); Hugo Grotius (1583–1645), the distinguished Dutch law specialist and also author of a marine eclogue; John Leech of Montrose and Aberdeen (*ca.* 1590–1630) and George Buchanan (1506–1582), both Scots who penned Latin eclogues along with other well-known works read throughout Europe. Through renewed study by such scholars as W. L. Grant, and reprinting of texts in recent anthologies (see Bibliography), the international production of neo-Latin pastoral and its relationship to the vernaculars has now emerged as a crucial feature of the northern literary scene.

In England the appearance of Edmund Spenser's *Shephearde's Calendar* (1579) was so significant that it overshadowed for his contemporaries (and still does for us) earlier and subsequent efforts at establishing a tradition of English eclogue. As early as 1514 Alexander Barclay (1475?–1552) had completed the first eclogues in English, based largely upon Mantuan. In 1563 Barnabe Googe (1540–1594) published another batch, followed by the 1567 translation into English of Mantuan by George Turberville (1540?–*ca.* 1610). Within a decade of Spenser's work, both Theocritus and Vergil had been translated, thus completing the formation of a body of vernacular eclogue for stimulation and emulation.

Spenser also composed a pastoral elegy, *Astrophel* (1595), on the death of Sir Philip Sidney, and an extended eclogue, *Colin Clouts Come Home Againe* (1595), dealing with the English court and the literary scene under the guise of a shepherd's report on a journey he has made. Eclogues of note were also written by several other major Elizabethan poets and their seventeenth-century heirs in the wake of Spenser's experiment; for example, *Idea, the Shepherd's Garland* (1593) by Michael Drayton (1563–1631), "fashioned in nine eclogues," and the works of John Milton and Phineas Fletcher. Needless to say, however, the bulk and the best of English Renaissance pastoral lyricism lies outside the formal eclogue. The "informal" pastoral lyric, usually though not always brief, either isolated or loosely packaged with others of its kind, both songlike in its smooth clarity and also at times incredibly subtle and complex, is the real glory of English pastoral poetry. The impetus to such poetry from the native tradition, from Spenser and continental poetry in Latin and the vernaculars, reached a climax in the anthology *England's Helicon* (1600), but pastoral lyrics had already infiltrated other kinds of literary works in prose and verse and were serving as texts for musical setting.

It is *England's Helicon* that offered perhaps the best known of all English pastoral poems, Marlowe's "The Passionate Shepherd to His Love" and Sir Walter Raleigh's "The Nymph's Reply to the Shepherd," in which the pastoral ideal of erotic freedom and happiness is charmingly proposed and devastatingly demolished. A third contribution to the debate, by John Donne (1572–1635), is a poem entitled "The Bait" (appearing in his *Songs and Sonets*, 1633, but probably written several decades earlier). Donne scoffs at Marlowe's plea and Raleigh's questioning of the validity of the pastoral argument by offering instead a dazzling piscatorial piece of flattery designed to prove that the nymph can be won by superior wit rather than by bucolic clichés that invite skepticism, however smoothly expressed. Among the heirs of Donne and Ben Jonson (1572–1637), customarily referred to as Metaphysical or Cavalier poets, the pastoral lyric often has the kind of irony, wit, and generic self-consciousness evidenced by Donne's poem. In many of these poets, nevertheless, the Elizabethan fondness for a clear, unruffled, songlike expression at the surface and relatively straightforward, conventional notions just below often alternates or competes with the warped density typical of Donne's kind of wit or the tightly packed terseness of Jonsonian wit. It is perhaps the chief attraction *and* frustration of the pastoral poetry of Andrew Marvell (1621–1678) that he manages in such poems as "The Garden" and his so-called Mower lyrics to fuse the two styles and at the same time suggest that pastoral itself is a key metaphor in the cluster of his meanings. With this kind of involuted complexity, not to mention the thick referentiality of Milton's *Lycidas*, it is not surprising that neoclassical critics later argued that the pastoral lyric is overburdened, that like the love lyric it has become subtilized beyond its own decorum and the norms of art.

English poets also shared in the European fashion of including a pastoral interlude or oasis in longer poems of a different generic stamp. Here the best example would be Spenser's creation of a pastoral oasis in the sixth book of his epic *The Faerie Queene*. Unlike Ariosto, Tasso, and the Portuguese poet Luíz Vaz de Camoëns, whose heroes and heroines enjoy idyllic moments that fulfill long cherished fantasies of escape and recreation, Spenser has his knight of courtesy, Calidore, enter the pastoral world only to learn of its frailty. Linking visions of love, civility, *otium*, and artistic creativity on the one hand, and opposing these with the violence of brigands and savages and the poisonous slander represented by the Blatant Beast, Spenser argues that the pastoral ideal, like any literary creation, cannot by itself withstand the onslaught of evil in the world after the Fall. As in Milton, whose scenes of Eden in *Paradise Lost* constitute another pastoral oasis, it is the *locus amoenus,* or paradise within, earned by experience that is the only possible and enduring Arcadia. Art, and therefore pastoral poetry, can acknowledge the powerful appeal of the ancient dream of a golden age returning or to be found even now in some remote primitive place. But it must do so in order to alert us to the passing beast, still unchained and trampling the flowers as he roars by.

PASTORAL DRAMA

In *The Oaten Flute* Renato Poggioli has argued that "the poetic of the pastoral fully reveals that all of its subgenres must be reduced to the common denominator of the lyrical mode. The *epyllion* is not epic; the pastoral romance is not narrative; pastoral drama is not dramatic; tragicomedy is neither comic nor tragic" (p. 39). This suggests, correctly, that the popularity of pastoral lyric caused it to invade alien generic territory, with mixed aesthetic consequences. We have already noticed the way in which mythological poem *(epyllion)* and pastoral lyric were juxtaposed, or interpenetrated each other, from the beginning. With drama and romance, however, there were only the classical precedents of the Greek satyr play, known from the *Cyclops* of Euripides, and the *Daphnis and Chloe* of Longus. Other ancient romances known to the sixteenth century might have pastoral interludes but were not essentially pastoral.

Despite the lack of a generic tradition, and given the opportunities this might present for innovation, both pastoral drama and romance instead begged and borrowed from other established genres to pad their lyrical plots, and quickly established new hybrid norms. A few especially popular examples of the new subgenres—Sannazaro's *Arcadia,* Montemayor's *Diana,* Tasso's *Aminta,* Giambattista Guarini's *Pastor fido*—were endlessly imitated as "classic" models of the arguably legitimate new subgenres. But there is nothing like the bewildering variety and creative vitality evident in the development of pastoral lyric. As Poggioli implies, it is clear that even if the Renaissance produced some successful works in the new subgenres, the price paid was a kind of lyric stasis that cried out for music, dance, spectacle, and other types of theatrical support, eventually to be provided by interlude, masque, and opera.

There was no doubt in the minds of late Renaissance critics that the *Aminta* of Tasso, first performed in 1573, put the new subgenre on the literary map, nor have their modern successors disputed the claim. Early manuscripts and printed editions (the first of hundreds to follow) variously describe the *Aminta* as a *favola boschereccia* (sylvan fable), *commedia pastorale* (pastoral comedy), or simply *pastorale* or *ecloga,* and this terminological confusion reflects uncertainty about the origins, precedents, and generic nature of the work. A hundred years earlier, Angelo Poliziano's *Orfeo* (1471), a curious mixture of Ovidian myth and medieval mystery play, had established a precedent for the performance of mythological plays. With renewed interest in classical comedy and tragedy, and with the vogue for the eclogue (including, as we have seen, recital or performance), there soon developed a kind of play in which classical rather than medieval form and structure were used for a plot based on myth with pastoral properties, or one that featured pastoral protagonists and sentiments with some mythological background and intrusions.

Thus as early as 1487 Correggio's *Cefalo* dramatized the Ovidian story of Cephalus and Procris (a *favola*) in five acts in a production at Ferrara, destined to be the home of many such experiments. Casalio's *Amaranta* of 1538 bore the subtitle *comedia nuova pasto-*

rale (new pastoral comedy), but it is more likely that Argenti's *Sfortunato (The Unfortunate One)* of 1568, called a *favola pastorale,* was better known to Tasso. Guarini himself and others credited Beccari's *Il Sacrificio (The Sacrifice),* performed at Ferrara in 1554, with pioneering what he considered to be the new pastoral subgenre, rejecting the several precedents of mythological plays. Further, he argued that *Aminta* and his own *Pastor fido,* though essentially comedies, had tragic features and other refinements that entitled them to be called tragicomedies. Eventually the kinship of pastoral drama and tragicomedy would be taken for granted and indeed the tragicomic mold assumed to be its official form. But the plays of Tasso and Guarini, and the theorizing of the latter, were themselves shaped by earlier experiments and debates that need to be understood.

Briefly, the issue was whether tragedy and comedy were "pure" generically. One could cite Aristotle's *Poetics,* Cicero, Horace, and some classical dramas to defend purity; one could also point to "mixed" plays and to other statements by the same ancient critics that seemed to allow for them. At the same time the nature of the satyr play, "mixed" in its protagonists and tone but thought to be fundamentally tragic by Renaissance critics, brought the related pastoral into the discussion. And so, for example, Giambattista Giraldi (1504–1573), also known as Cinzio or Cynthius, wrote a satyr play, *Egle* (named after its heroine, a nymph), in 1545, along with a critical treatise on this type of play in which he argued that it partakes of comedy and tragedy and is thus a third, "mixed" kind, but also that it is historically a forerunner of tragedy and remains essentially so, thus requiring an unhappy cathartic ending to purge the passions after its lighter moments. Giraldi also wrote several tragedies "with a happy ending," which he defended in influential discourses (1543, 1549). Guarini would argue later that tragicomedy was not Giraldi's trag-

edy "of double issue" (morally satisfying because unlike some ancient plays, the wicked are punished *and* the good rewarded), but essentially an elevated comedy in which dignified personages and themes, plots with Aristotelian recognitions and reversals of fortune, and the narrowly averted catastrophes of romance would blend and terminate in a single happy resolution to make a new kind of "modern" comic structure. It would also meet Giraldi's argument that audiences loved happy endings. Also, left unspoken but most important, a fundamental comic plot would also be more appropriate to traditional pastoral subject matter: love lost and won.

Thus, shaky literary history, Christian moral concern, neo-Aristotelian generic "laws" misinterpreted out of the *Poetics,* and the practicing dramatist's desire to please his audience all combined in an attempt to cope with the popularity and define the legitimacy of a new subgenre, with results that are not as reliable and illuminating as we would like but that do provide us with some valuable insights into the nature and intentions of the works themselves.

The formal and thematic properties of Tasso's *Aminta* reveal its eclectic lineage in the monologues and dialogues of the eclogue tradition, the plot of amorous intrigue and the five-act structure of neoclassical comedy, and the sentiments of contemporary Petrarchism and Neoplatonism. Tragedy, pastoral romance, and mythology also contribute to what is nevertheless a play celebrated for its overall simplicity and clarity of design and action. It has a prologue spoken by Amor in pastoral garb; in its five acts there are choruses, confidants, messengers and reported offstage action, dialogues and choral passages in rhymed and (mostly) unrhymed lyric measures.

Amor, signifying by his arrival a stimulus to love, explains that he has come in flight from his mother and has endowed the inhabitants of the play's world—actually and in the plot the island in the Po outside Ferrara where the play was performed—with unexpected poetic speech, thus settling an old pastoral issue right off. From mythology comes the background opposition of the Diana and Venus principles and the character of the satyr, representing a third force, violent lust. Silvia, devoted to Diana and chastity, rejects love and procreation out of hand, despite the pleas of the experienced Dafne. Aminta, the timid shepherd of the title, has loved Silvia in vain for three years but does not heed the advice of his confidant, the experienced poet Tirsi (suggesting Tasso himself), to seek someone else to love. Dafne and Tirsi, the confidants, will now plot together to help their charges, but they themselves seem not to have achieved with their wisdom the happiness they recommend to others, and this reinforces the sense of a world out of joint. Certainly the famous chorus at the end of act 1 has reason to lament the passing of the golden age, a time when love was free of such impediments as the tyrant Honor, and when the rule was "s 'ei piace, ei lice" (if it pleases, it is licit). In any event, despite the efforts of Dafne and Tirsi, and Aminta's rescue of Silvia from the lascivious satyr, she is won over only when she hears that Aminta has (presumably) killed himself in the erroneous belief that she has been devoured by wolves. The recognitions and reversals provided by these two averted catastrophes bring together at last (we are told) the two lovers, who do not in fact meet once on stage during the entire course of the play. Creaky as some of this may now seem, especially when abstracted from the saving grace of the splendid poetry, there is no doubt that the *Aminta* struck its contemporaries as a miniature miracle, evidenced by hundreds of printed editions, a host of translations and adaptations (the whole play or excerpts like the "golden age" chorus), and countless allusions and references in every European literature.

Equally if not more influential was the *Pastor fido* (Faithful Shepherd) of Giambattista Guarini (1538–1612), the successor to Tasso as court poet at Ferrara. Written between 1580 and 1584, published first in 1589 and definitively in 1602, it is more than three times as long as *Aminta* and infinitely more complicated in background and action.

The scene is set in Arcadia and, as the Arcadian river god Alfeo tells us in the prologue, back in the golden age. But the inhabitants, pastoral aristocrats, labor under a curse of Diana, who has decreed an annual sacrifice of a maiden to propitiate an earlier offense by a faithless nymph, until such time as an Arcadian couple of divine stock marry and a faithful shepherd makes amends for the ancient lapse. In the meantime, also, any maiden or woman proved faithless must die unless someone takes her place. The hunter Silvio and the nymph Amarilli being descended from Hercules and Pan, their fathers, Montano and Titiro, have arranged a match between them, but Silvio is not interested. Mirtillo, the hero of the play and a stranger in Arcadia, loves Amarilli in vain, as does Dorinda the indifferent Silvio. A third love-action is added with the wicked Corisca's passion for Mirtillo, which causes her to betray her friend Amarilli while she herself is being pursued by an amorous old satyr and fruitlessly wooed by the shepherd Coridone. All of this we learn in solid Terentian fashion from the expository monologues and dialogues of the first two acts.

In the third and fourth acts, the complications introduced earlier intensify toward climax and denouement. Persuaded to meet Amarilli in the memorable game of blindman's buff (with a ballet and choral lyrics set to music), Mirtillo is caught by her and reveals his love, only to be rebuked (3.2, 3). Corisca now conspires to bring Mirtillo and Amarilli together in a cave and fatally compromise her friend. When the jealous satyr blocks the entrance to the cave and the two young people are discovered inside, both are arrested, and Amarilli is condemned to death according to Diana's law. Silvio, meanwhile, having killed a ferocious boar, exults in his feat by praising Diana over Venus and is mocked by Echo

(4.8), another famous scene often imitated. Then Silvio accidentally wounds Dorinda, and the resulting remorse reveals to him his love for her. At the end of act 4, the chorus sings its praise of the golden age, opposing Tasso's version with Guarini's idea that the wonderful time was characterized by an identity of desire and instinctive virtue: "piaccia, se leice" (it is pleasing, if it is licit). In the last act Mirtillo's identity as the long-lost eldest child of the priest Montano is revealed just as the latter is about to sacrifice him in place of Amarilli, as Mirtillo has wished. A blind seer, Tirenio, now appears to justify the ways of providence by pointing out that Mirtillo and Amarilli as a couple fulfill the oracle, and that Mirtillo's faithfulness properly atones for the old offense. Now Amarilli and Mirtillo, like Silvio and Dorinda, are united in marriage, and a penitent Corisca is forgiven. The closing chorus reminds the audience that true joy is possible only when it springs from virtue after suffering.

Guarini called his play a *tragicommedia pastorale* and defended the genre in two separate critical treatises and the dense annotations he prepared for subsequent editions. Its refined verse and lofty sentiments, endlessly poured out, its clever plotting and richness of allusion to other works, classical and contemporary, appealed strongly to late Renaissance taste. Modern taste may well find, paradoxically, that the *Pastor fido*, compared to the eclogue, is not pastoral enough. Like the *Aminta* it removes all bucolic props from the scene— no animals, crooks, pipes, shepherds' labors—and aims at tragic dignity through noble characters and a style that echoes the classical poets. Without being aware of the contribution he was making to the eventual demise of pastoral by making its underpinnings increasingly preposterous, Guarini argued that golden-age society was hierarchical, topped by a noble class of shepherds and shepherdesses, not to mention nymphs and other sylvan deities, along with semidivine products of frequent unions between gods and mortals (note the lineage of Mirtillo and Amarilli). There is also the problem of excessive length, hoary plot devices and complications drawn from Greek romance, and the several allusions to other dramatic works. For example, the pillaging of *Oedipus Rex* for the last act seems awkward to us, but Guarini eagerly pointed it out, not only because he wished to show classical precedent but also because he knew his audience would enjoy the experience of recognizing and savoring the parallel.

That Guarini knew what he was about is evidenced too by the work's incredible popularity. In Italy, by itself and in conjunction with the *Aminta* (they were often published together), there were many imitations, though only the 1607 *Filli di Sciro* (Phyllis of Scyros) of Guidobaldo Bonarelli (1563–1608) came close to matching the two masterpieces. In France, where Guarini's influence was felt rather quickly, there were three translations between 1593 and 1666 and numerous elaborate editions of the *Pastor fido* thereafter. The combination in Guarini's play of pastoral and tragicomedy appealed especially to such dramatists as Alexandre Hardy (*ca.* 1569–1632), author of no fewer than five pastoral plays, who professed his indebtedness to Tasso and Guarini in the preface to his *Corine* (1626); Honorat de Racan (1589–1670), disciple of François de Malherbe and author of the *Bergeries* (published in 1625); Jean Mairet (1604–1686), whose *Sylvie* (1626) and *La Sylvanire* (1630) also reveal the influence of Guarini's masterpiece and theories, which continued to be felt until the time of Molière and the modulation of pastoral play into opera libretto. (This was of course ultimately the common fate of both mythological play and pastoral play; witness the beginnings of opera in Italy at the end of the sixteenth century, when such plays were the first libretti.)

Elsewhere there was equal enthusiasm: translations into Spanish (1602), German (1636), and, much later, Dutch and Portuguese. An Italian edition of the *Pastor fido* was published in London in 1591, and there were two translations into English prior to the splendid version by Sir Richard Fanshawe (1647). By the time he wrote *Volpone* (1607), Ben Jonson could chide English poets for stealing from the play (3.2). English imitations or adaptations include such works as Samuel Daniel's *The Queen's Arcadia* (1605) and *Hymen's Triumph* (1614), both produced at court; Phineas Fletcher's *Sicelides, a Piscatory* (1615), set on the Sicilian shore and featuring fishermen; John Fletcher's *The Faithful Shepherdess* (1609); and Thomas Randolph's *Amyntas* (1638). Masques such as Milton's *Arcades* (1632) and *Comus* (1634) would also figure in a broadened survey of less direct influences.

The play by John Fletcher has attracted attention because of its imitative title and feisty preface in which he chided his first audience for not understanding literary pastoral and then proceeded to lecture them on the generic nature of tragicomedy. English audiences apparently liked their pastoral native and rustic with generous good humor, not loftily tragic. There is certainly no humor in Fletcher's version of Guarini; and despite the effective verse, one feels the weight of heavy moralizing, virtually allegorical, thanks mainly to the unfortunate impact of Spenser's *Shephearde's Calendar* and *Faerie Queene*. Jonson's unfinished *The Sad Shepherd* (1640), set in Sherwood Forest and including Robin Hood and his crew among its protagonists, contrasts vividly with Fletcher's very literary concoction, though Jonson greatly admired *The Faithful Shepherdess*. In England as elsewhere there were mythological plays or pastoral plays and masques, or plays with pastoral interludes, that did not necessarily follow the pattern of the *Pastor fido* or of tragicomic form. The obvious examples in English, Shakespeare's *As You Like It* (*ca.* 1600) and *The Winter's Tale* (1610), are both based on pastoral romances, reminding us that still another subgenre was flourishing and could have its impact on pastoral drama.

PASTORAL ROMANCE

Like the drama, Renaissance pastoral romance was mainly the creation of two authors, the Italian Sannazaro and the Spaniard Montemayor; the chief disciples, Sir Philip Sidney and Honoré d'Urfé, were English and French: hence the four authors neatly illustrate its international vogue.

The Neapolitan patrician and courtier Jacopo Sannazaro began his *Arcadia* by composing youthful eclogues, to which he added prose matrices and additional poetry until, by 1489, he had a version in ten chapters and ten eclogues. By 1502 an unauthorized edition had appeared, followed by an approved one in 1504, expanded to twelve chapters and eclogues. The mixture of prose and verse had many ancient and medieval precedents, most recently the *Vita nuova* of Dante and the *Ameto* of Boccaccio. But the eclecticism of the *Arcadia*'s sources is such that not only the whole previous pastoral tradition but also the major Greco-Roman and modern lyric and epic poets are everywhere evoked and imitated. Nevertheless, the essentially lyric plot is fairly simple. Sincero (the poet himself) has come to Arcadia from Naples because of unhappiness in love. Along with the shepherds and other inhabitants he participates in or observes hunting and herding, song contests, religious rites, and memorial games. His own melancholy finds its echo in the mostly sad amatory songs and experiences of his fellow shepherds. Finally, after an ominous dream, a nymph leads him via a subterranean passage back to Naples, where he learns the bitter news of the death of his beloved. In an epilogue he addresses his pipe and urges upon it, now that Arcadia is no more, the modest satisfactions of the retired life.

The complexities of this apparently straightforward story lie in the tension between its ambiguous autobiographical signals and its ultrasophisticated literary artifice, creating several unresolved issues. Sannazaro obviously sees Arcadia as a projection of mental life, and a sojourn there as a means of exploring the psychology of love and the related passion for poetry: both bring joy and sorrow, both are ideals that must contend with change and death, both raise questions about the risks and penalties of personal engagement. By putting himself into two separate characters, the narrator Sincero and the shepherd Ergasto—aloof spectator and stranger in, even disdainer of, rustic Arcadia as well as typical inhabitant—Sannazaro is able to test the two worlds of reality and imagination, action and contemplation, *otium* and *negotium*, for himself and other Renaissance minds preoccupied with the same crucial oppositions. He proudly claims third place in the succession of pastoral poets from Theocritus to Vergil to himself, and aims like the Roman poet at loftier song, but he does not feel at home in Arcadia; then, on the death of his beloved, he wishes he had never left. And finally, as we have seen, he insists Arcadia is dead and urges his pipe to curb its aspirations. It should be noted, too, that there are also singing shepherds encountered upon the return to Naples, which thus cannot easily symbolize reality or suggest the end of a journey in quest of a vocation or personal identity.

Autobiography contends with artifice also in the form of an allusive style that often makes Sannazaro speak his mind in the words of previous poets. In addition, there are numerous descriptions, catalogs, and set pieces; some of these are pastoral, like the famous bird-trapping scene (7) later imitated by Garcilaso and the English poet Barnabe Googe; others, less exclusively pastoral, include detailed descriptions of temple paintings (3) and storied vessels (4, 11), one of the latter said to be by Mantegna. Lists of trees, birds, rivers, shepherds' laws and labors, and a compilation of magical lore from Pliny's *Natural History*, not to mention the textbook variety of lyric measures and forms used in the eclogues (from terza rima to double sestina), all suggest a young author addicted to and engrossed by literature, yet attempting to express or dramatize an inner struggle, a contest between art and life already won by art.

Sannazaro, typically, professed to be disturbed by the great popularity of the *Arcadia*, believing it to be too easily won. But as we have had occasion to note several times, its influence was far in excess of his wishes. Yet none of its progeny maintained its lyric plot and modest length. Like pastoral drama, the romance moved toward narrative density and richness or aspired to the generic status of tragedy and epic. Hence the immediate effect of the *Arcadia* was the flood tide of eclogues, and the idea of a cycle of such poems, as in Spenser. The formal mixture of prose and verse actually had more of an impact on subsequent romance. That the work was seen as essentially poetry might also account for the paucity of outstanding translations beyond the two French versions known (1544, 1547), and a Castilian rendering from the same time. Finally, there is the undoubted importance of Sannazaro's work as part of his model career—that of a servant of the Aragonese dynasty who managed to be a nonprofessional man of letters at the same time (one thinks of Castiglione, Montemayor, D'Urfé, and Sidney). Then too, there is his participation with Pontano and others in the Neapolitan literary academy; Pontano directly, the others more obscurely, are referred to briefly in the *Arcadia*, thus making it an innocent forerunner of the later, much maligned *pastorale à clef*, or pastoral conceived as a cipher of actual living identities.

With the Italians engrossed in the development of the pastoral drama, it was in Spain that the fragile lyric romance of Sannazaro was lengthened and thickened in the direction of pastoral novel. The key figure is Jorge de Montemayor (1520?–1561), a Portuguese poet and courtier in the service of the Spanish royal family who wrote, mostly in Castilian, *Los siete libros de la Diana* (The Seven Books of the Diana), published in 1559 and left unfinished on his death in Italy as a result of a duel. The book is often referred to simply as the

Diana, and includes two sequels, both from 1564, the *Segunda parte de la Diana* (The Second Part of the Diana) by the Salamancan physician Alonso Pérez, and the *Diana enamorada* (Diana in Love) by the Valencian poet Gaspar Gil Polo; the latter's addition is still highly esteemed. These two sequels are complemented by more than a dozen imitations in Spain alone. Thus, coming at a time when the Spanish sentimental and chivalric novels (the famous *Amadis of Gaul* and its numerous progeny, for example), had enjoyed and were perhaps beginning to lose favor in the Iberian peninsula, Montemayor's novel clearly initiated a new vogue there and, soon after, throughout Europe.

Like most Renaissance attempts at lengthy prose fiction, the *Diana* has a narrative structure that is meandering and episodic. There is an initial plot thread provided by the frustrated love of the shepherd Sireno for the shepherdess Diana, following the pattern of separation, journey, and reconciliation found in Sannazaro and a host of other romance sources. There is also the thematic thread of the search for felicity through love purified or made virtuous by trial and travail. From Sannazaro also came the eruption of prose narrative into pastoral eclogue and song, and its regular interruption by tales, mostly unhappy love experiences, told by actual or masquerading shepherds and shepherdesses who encounter or join a swelling group of characters (including nymphs and "wild men") as they journey about. Their immediate goal, reached in book 4 near the midpoint of the larger story, is the Temple of Diana, a magical place presided over by the sorceress and priestess of Diana, Felicia, who dispenses wisdom and magic potions that will enable the travelers eventually to find resolutions of their woes. Thereafter Montemayor follows individual characters in the style of Ariosto, weaving Sireno's and their separate adventures into the complex narrative fabric that is the last three books. As has been noted by critics, the *Diana,* for all the movement suggested by a plot summary, remains essentially static, with sentiment replacing chivalric action. A good deal of its narrative time is spent in song, amatory gestures like carving names on trees, listening to stories, and above all endlessly discussing love in the courtly and Neoplatonic terms made fashionable by Italian treatises on love and works like Castiglione's *Book of the Courtier* and Marguerite of Navarre's *Heptameron.* Needless to say, Montemayor's shepherds never do any real pastoral work.

The *Diana* and its sequels were immediately and immensely influential. Between 1570 and 1620 alone there were many translations and adaptations of the individual poems and stories, or the whole, in French, Italian, German, and English. Among the Spanish imitations were Luis Gálvez de Montalvo's *El pastor de Filida* (1582), Gonzalo de Saavedra's *Los pastores del Betis* (1633), Lope de Vega's *Arcadia* (1598), and the first part of Cervantes' *La Galatea* (1585), his earliest work, never completed as promised. In fact the reader may have first encountered the *Diana* in the sixth chapter of part 1 of *Don Quixote,* where it is mentioned along with *La Galatea* in the Inquisition on the books of the Don's library as worthy of being saved provided Felicia and her magic liquid are purged. (There was a "sacred" version of *Diana, a lo divino,* completed in 1582 to mitigate its allegedly dangerous appeal.) It will be remembered also that in that same sixth chapter there is a fearful forecast of the Don's flirtation with the pastoral life after the failures of the chivalric. Indeed, the pastoral ideal is so prominent in *Don Quixote* that it almost competes with the chivalric ideal for parodic exploitation. The popularity of Montemayor surely influenced as well Cervantes' ironic contrast of real and pretended bucolic characters in the Don's discourse on the golden age to the goatherds, the affair of Marcela and Chrysostom (1.11–14), and the encounter with would-be shepherds (2.58) who are studying the eclogues of Garcilaso and Camoëns. We know too from one of his *Exemplary Novels*, "El Coloquio de los perros" ("The Dialogue of the Dogs"), where the dog Berganza comments sharply on the discrepancy between real and literary bucolic life, that Cervantes was both scornful of the pastoral vogue and hopelessly obsessed with it, from the time of *La Galatea* until the last pages of *Don Quixote*.

As we saw above, the *Diana* left Spain for other European countries with two sequels. Different as these inevitably were, in attitudes to the central theme of love, in narrative development, and in style, and despite the fact that only Gil Polo's *Diana enamorada* is worthy of its predecessor, there was enough of continuation in characters and situations to satisfy those who sampled the Montemayor books and wanted more. Another item that appeared in subsequent editions was an anonymous story added to book 4 of the *Diana*, a now famous "Moorish" tale, the first and perhaps the best known of its type: *Abindarraez y Jarifa*, of still uncertain authorship.

In England Googe had included adaptations of Montemayor's among his own pioneering pastoral poems, and there were several partial and full translations, including Bartholomew Yong's rendering of the whole published in 1598. In the anthology *England's Helicon* some two dozen poems from the *Diana* in Yong's translations constituted the largest block of poems from any single source. The story of Felix and Felismena, told in the second book of *Diana* by the shepherdess Felismena and probably derived from Matteo Bandello, apparently became the plot of an anonymous play (1585) whence it attracted the eye of Shakespeare for the plot of his *Two Gentlemen of Verona* (1590). The Pérez sequel seems especially to have influenced some of Spenser's characters and incidents in book 6 of *The Faerie Queene*, just as the Gil Polo sequel and the lyrics of Montemayor affected the plotting and lyrical insets of Sidney's *Arcadia*.

Sir Philip Sidney (1554–1586) began writing his celebrated *Arcadia* in 1577, completed the five books of this "Old Arcadia" in 1580 (not published until 1912), then began redrafting books 1, 2, and part of 3, with many additions and reshufflings of materials and with a new emphasis on heroic love and valor, fulsome rhetoric, and intricate plotting. The incomplete revised version was published in 1590; and in 1593 Sidney's sister, the countess of Pembroke, published the incomplete revision fleshed out by the "old" version, somewhat emended and with a gap between the two, later papered over (1621). It is clear that Sidney wished to write a pastoral romance, but his revisions also indicate a desire to go beyond Sannazaro and Montemayor, the latter his chief pastoral source, in the direction of chivalric romance and heroic epic. In other words, *Amadis of Gaul* and the late Greek or Byzantine romances (Heliodoros' *Aethiopica* and Achilles Tatius' *Clitophon and Leucippe*) have intervened.

In France, where the *Diana* of Montemayor and its sequels, as well as Sidney's *Arcadia*, were well known, it remained for Honoré d'Urfé (1567–1625) to compose effectively the last pastoral novel of European-wide appeal and influence. Plays like Alexandre Hardy's *Félismene* (1626?) and Jean de Rotrou's *Celimène et Filandre* (1633), and other evidence gathered by scholars indicate that the *Diana* had its impact on every genre, but it was D'Urfé's novel *L'Astrée (Astrea)* that best showed how Montemayor could be transformed to the needs of French aristocratic and literary fashion. For like the other pastoralists discussed above, D'Urfé was well connected. Scion of an important patrician family of Forez (the setting of *L'Astrée*), related through his wife to the house of Savoy, a soldier and amateur man of letters, D'Urfé moved easily in the aristocratic and courtly worlds of Turin and Paris, both reflected in the thinly layered pastoral disguises of his lengthy novel. With him pastoral completes its earlier and tentative gestures in the direction of social fashion and becomes a manual for salon conversation and manners.

Early in his career D'Urfé composed a narrative poem, *Sireine,* whose title and content announce the infatuation with Montemayor's *Diana* that was to inspire the subsequent composition of the *Astrée,* published from 1607 to 1619, and its fourth and last part posthumously by his secretary, Baro, in 1628. Dedicated to the "sovereign shepherd" Henry IV and presumed to reflect D'Urfé's love for his sister-in-law Diane de Chateaumorand, *Astrée* has a central theme in the love, separation, and reconciliation of the shepherd Céladon and the shepherdess Astrée, set back in fifth-century Gaul, with Druidism the prevailing philosophy and faith. But since the *Astrée* is not only the longest pastoral novel but also one of the longest narratives ever written (a modern edition required five volumes), its thousands of pages are stuffed with the type of digressions, episodes, and incidents familiar from the works of Montemayor and Sidney. The many other shepherds present pass their time in singing, exchanging letters, listening to or narrating amatory histories, and, especially in the *Astrée,* debating endlessly the finer points of the experience of love, always struggling with an ideal of its refining power. Though warfare and other violent incidents occur, it is this casuistry of love that finally overwhelms with its sheer bulk the other ingredients of the novel. Certainly, however much its first audience delighted in the huge surplus of amatory sentiment and debate, the subsequent loss of interest in the *Astrée* (Jean de La Fontaine and Nicholas Boileau-Despréaux were the last to say anything nice about it, until Jean Jacques Rousseau) is stark proof that the pastoral genre had also reached its bursting point; the simple assumptions of the early eclogue were no longer able to sustain the massive burden pastoral tradition had placed upon it. If, as some argue, post-Renaissance pastoral still thrives in other, more recent dreams or nightmares of simplicity, innocence, and harmony, it is a tribute to the tenacity of the ancient ideal and its grip on the literary imagination.

Selected Bibliography

EDITIONS AND TRANSLATIONS OF INDIVIDUAL AUTHORS

Boccaccio, Giovanni. *Eglogue.* In *Poesie latine minori.* Edited by Aldo Francesco Massèra. Bari, 1928.

―――――. *Tutte le opere.* Vol. 2. Edited by Antonio Enzo Quaglio. Milan, 1964. Vol. 3. Edited by Armando Balduino. Milan, 1974.

Dante Alighieri. *Eclogues.* In *The Latin Works.* Translated by Philip H. Wicksted. London, 1904. Reprinted 1940.

D'Urfé, Honoré. *L'Astrée.* Edited by Hugues Vaganay. 5 vols. Lyons, 1925–1928.

England's Helicon. Edited by Hugh Macdonald, London, 1949.

Guarini, Battista. *Pastor fido.* Translated by Richard Fanshawe with an introduction by John Humphreys Whitfield. Edinburgh, 1976.

Longus. *Daphnis and Chloe.* Translated by Moses Hadas. New York, 1953.

―――――. *Daphnis and Chloe.* Edited by Paul Turner. Harmondsworth, 1968.

Mantuan. *Eclogues.* Edited by Wilfred P. Mustard. Baltimore, 1911.

―――――. *Eclogues.* Translated by George Turberville (1567) and edited by Douglas Bush. New York, 1937.

Montemayor, Jorge de. *Los siete libros de la Diana.* Edited by Francisco López Estrada. Madrid, 1962.

―――――. *Los siete libros de la Diana.* Translated by Bartholomew Yong (1598) and edited by Judith M. Kennedy. Fair Lawn, N. J., 1968.

Navagero, Andrea. *Lusus.* Edited and translated by Alice E. Wilson. Nieuwkoup, 1973.

Petrarch, Francis. *Bucolicum carmen.* Edited and translated by Thomas G. Bergin. New Haven, Conn., and London, 1974.

Polo, Gil. *Diana enamorada.* Translated by Bartholomew Yong (1598) and edited by Raymond L.

Grismer and Mildred B. Grismer. Minneapolis, 1959. The sequel to Montemayor's *Los siete libros de la Diana.*

Sannazaro, Jacopo. *Arcadia.* Edited by Enrico Carrara. Milan, 1926. Reprinted Turin, 1967. Translated with piscatory eclogues by Ralph Nash. Detroit, 1966.

Sidney, Sir Philip. *Arcadia.* Edited by Maurice Evans. Harmondsworth, 1977.

Spenser, Edmund. *The Complete Poetical Works.* Edited by R. E. N. Dodge. Cambridge, Mass., 1936.

Tasso, Torquato. *Aminta.* In *Opere.* Vol. 1. Edited by B. Maier. Milan, 1963.

————. *A Translation of the Orpheus of Angelo Politian and the Aminta of Torquato Tasso.* Translated by Louis Eleazer Lord. London, 1931.

Vergil. *The Pastoral Poems.* Translated by Emile Victor Rieu. Harmondsworth, 1949.

————. *The Pastoral Poems.* Translated by C. Day Lewis. New York, 1952.

ANTHOLOGIES OF TRANSLATIONS

An Anthology of Neo-Latin Poetry. Edited by Fred J. Nichols. New Haven, Conn., and London, 1978.

French Poetry of the Renaissance. Edited by Bernard Weinberg. Carbondale, Ill., 1954.

Greek Pastoral Poetry. Translated by Anthony Holden. Harmondsworth, 1974. Contains Theocritus, Bion, Moschus.

The Latin Poetry of the English Poets. Boston and London, 1962.

Maddison, Carol. *Marcantonio Flaminio. Poet, Humanist, Reformer.* London, 1965.

The Pastoral Elegy. Edited by Thomas Perrin Harrison. Austin, Tex., 1939. Reprinted New York, 1968.

The Penguin Book of French Verse. Vol. 2. Edited and translated by Geoffrey Brereton. Harmondsworth, 1958.

The Penguin Book of Italian Verse. Edited and translated by George Kay. Harmondsworth, 1968.

The Penguin Book of Latin Verse. Edited and translated by Frederick Brittain. Harmondsworth, 1962.

The Penguin Book of Spanish Verse. Edited and translated by John Michael Cohen. Harmondsworth, 1956.

The Poetry of France. Edited by Alan Boase. 2 vols. London, 1964, 1973.

Renaissance and Baroque Poetry of Spain. Edited and translated by Elias L. Rivers. New York, 1966.

Renaissance Latin Verse: An Anthology. Edited by Alessandro Perosa and John Sparrow. Chapel Hill, N.C., 1979.

CRITICAL STUDIES

Avalla-Arce, Juan Battista. *La novela pastoril española.* Madrid, 1959.

Carrara, Enrico. *La poesia pastorale.* Milan, 1907.

Cody, Richard. *The Landscape of the Mind.* Oxford, 1969.

Congleton, James Edmund. *Theories of Pastoral Poetry in England.* Gainesville, Fla., 1952.

Cooper, Helen. *Pastoral: Medieval into Renaissance.* Totowa, N.J., and Suffolk, 1977.

Empson, William. *Some Versions of Pastoral.* London, 1935.

Frye, Northrup. *Anatomy of Criticism.* Princeton, N.J., 1957.

Genouy, Hector. *"L'Arcadia" de Sidney dans ses rapports avec "L'Arcadia" de Sannàzaro et la "Diana" de Montemayor.* Paris, 1928.

Grant, W. Leonard. *Neo-Latin Literature and the Pastoral.* Chapel Hill, N.C., 1965.

Greg, Walter W. *Pastoral Poetry and Pastoral Drama.* London, 1905. Reprinted New York, 1959.

Hardin, Richard F., ed. *Survivals of Pastoral.* Lawrence, Kans., 1979.

Herrick, Marvin T. *Tragicomedy.* Urbana, Ill., 1962.

Lambert, Ellen Zetzel. *Placing Sorrow: A Study of the Pastoral Elegy Convention from Theocritus to Milton.* Chapel Hill, N.C., 1978.

Lincoln, E. T., ed. *Pastoral and Romance.* Englewood Cliffs, N.J., 1969.

Levin, Harry. *The Myth of the Golden Age.* New York, 1969.

Marinelli, Peter V. *Pastoral.* London, 1971.

Patrides, C. A., ed. *Milton's "Lycidas": Tradition and Poem.* New York, 1961.

Perella, Nicholas J. *The Critical Fortune of Battista Guarini's "Il Pastor fido."* Florence, 1973.

Poggioli, Renato. *The Oaten Flute.* Cambridge, Mass., 1975.

RENAISSANCE PASTORAL POETRY

Rosenmeyer, Thomas G. *The Green Cabinet*. Berkeley, Calif., 1969.

Sole-Leris, Amadeu. *The Spanish Pastoral Novel*. Boston, 1980.

Tayler, Edward W. *Nature and Art in Renaissance Literature*. New York and London, 1964.

Toliver, Harold. *Pastoral Forms and Attitudes*. Berkeley, Calif., 1971.

Williams, Raymond. *The Country and the City*. Oxford, 1973.

Young, David. *The Heart's Forest*. New Haven, Conn., 1972.

JAMES V. MIROLLO

RENAISSANCE SHORT FICTION

INTRODUCTION: DEFINING THE NOVELLA

IT IS TEMPTING to identify the short fiction of the Renaissance, ranging from witty anecdote to picaresque tale, wholly with the *Decameron* tradition; that is, with the Boccaccian novella (Italian, *novella*; French, *nouvelle*; Spanish, *novela*; German, *Schwänk*). And we will succumb to this temptation, at least to the extent of giving it focal attention in this essay, for two reasons. First, for sheer quantity and, what is more important, quality of production, the vernacular novella is the outstanding type of short fiction in the period roughly encompassing the fifteenth and sixteenth centuries. Second, for extent of creative influence on contemporary and subsequent literature, the novella, or brief fictional narrative in prose, has no peer. Nevertheless, the use then and now of the label "novella," with its suggestion of generic clarity, is in fact deceptive. The word itself (from the Italian for "news" or "story" or even "fresh bit of gossip") was not widely used outside the romance languages (for instance, English and German) until later, and then with reference to longer kinds of modern fiction such as the novel or short novel. Giovanni Boccaccio himself, in labeling his stories in the *Decameron* proem, speaks of a hundred "novelle, o favole o parabole o istorie che dire le vogliamo" (novellas, or fables or parables or histories or whatever we want to call them).

Apart from the slipperiness of the term "no-vella," there is also the awkward fact that, beginning with the *Decameron*, many European Renaissance collections of short fiction contain several different types of brief narrative and a thematic range not comfortably assembled under any single generic rubric. And it should be noted that as the secular literature of the Renaissance developed across Europe, the type of brief fictional narrative we usually call a "novella" was, in actuality, sometimes composed in verse, at great length, and in Latin. Nor was it entirely fictional, in the sense that varying amounts of historical data could be included and frequent claims of historicity voiced. Thematically, even if one has recourse to a simpleminded division of narrative content into realism and romance, it would be difficult thus to classify, neatly, fictional materials that came to include mere jokes, witty anecdotes, folktales, scabrous accounts of successful erotic intrigue, tear-stained melodramas of erotic suffering, and sordid picaresque adventures. As this list indicates, too, both the comic and tragic modes can be found in the novella collection, and it does not hesitate to draw its inspiration from popular or subliterary as well as sophisticated literary sources.

The most recent study of the novella, *Anatomy of the Novella* by Clements and Gibaldi (see Bibliography), emphasizes its oral tradition and oral character along with a theory of the novella to be found in the rhetorical tradition and a few Renaissance critics, but mostly in the novella collections themselves.

The oral ingredient is important for the frame, since it invariably reproduces storytelling situations that mirror, however idealized, contemporary custom. Both in the *Decameron* and later, however, the oral character of the tales themselves—the references to recent events circulating as stories; the consciousness of a listening audience; the brevity and conciseness in handling character and action; the reliance on familiar and simple narrative formulas for beginning, complicating, and resolving the plot—yields to the exigencies of artistically conscious composition and an increasingly literate reading public, its size further increased by the availability of the printed book. It is nevertheless true that storytelling continued to be a prominent feature of Renaissance social life, virtually a requirement for those who wished to display good manners or needed to employ oratorical skills, but also necessary for the cohesiveness provided to the social group by oral communication. There was thus an interchange between recited and written novella, and both were officially required to provide useful or honest delight. But it is unlikely that even one of Count Baldesar Castiglione's talented courtiers at Urbino could recite stories as complex in plotting and style as Matteo Bandello's, although the latter pretends he heard his novellas on various social occasions and then transcribed them. Here the alleged oral situation has become largely an obligatory formal gesture.

Because the novella had no generic standing, Renaissance critics—the few who deign to discuss it at all—either force it into awkward juxtaposition with official types such as comedy and tragedy or take it up when dealing with rhetorical technique and style. Unlike these critics, who tend to make the novella either a minidrama or the stuff of the orator's repertoire, the novella authors themselves frequently have their storytellers comment on what makes a good story in and of itself. But these scattered remarks, in the *Decameron* and elsewhere, do not so much define the no-

vella as delineate the ideal of novella performance. Their emphasis on brevity, clarity, verisimilitude, and stylishness does not so much tell us what a novella is as sets forth the essential requirements for any tale of any kind to seize and hold the attention of an audience engaged in listening as a pastime.

Even a definition of the novella based on external form, such as the use of a frame story—so that we could cheerfully designate all stories within a fictional frame as novellas—would not hold up in view of the fact that in the later Renaissance it became desirable and acceptable to abandon frame stories and compose unframed groups of longer, more complex tales or even single, isolated tales in prose or verse. To the former category belongs the *Novelas ejemplares* (1613) of Miguel de Cervantes, for example; to the latter, the celebrated story of *Romeo and Juliet* by Luigi Da Porto (*ca.* 1530), as we shall see.

Our best course, then, is to use "short fiction" as an umbrella term for the various types known and practiced in the Renaissance, but we should also use the term to make some helpful distinctions. One of these would involve the *Decameron* and its tradition; another might be to isolate for analysis within that tradition one of its mainstays, say, the comic tale of erotic intrigue. Or one could chart the interpenetration of Renaissance tale collections by older types of short fiction, literary and subliterary, such as the classical anecdote, the oriental folktale, the medieval fabliau. All of these approaches would be necessary for a lengthy, wide-ranging, and comprehensive survey of the totality of Renaissance short fiction, not to mention the specific phenomenon of the novella.

For our more limited purposes, however, and since the novella is our focus, we need only a working definition that will enable us to select and describe the most important specimens. And so we shall say that a Renaissance novella is a type of secular fiction, usually (though not always) brief and in prose, that mirrors or is alleged to mirror an oral culture generally, but specifically a storytelling situation in which there is need to pass the time in honest recreation. The often elaborate frame story, where it exists, sets forth the occasion and topics of the stories. Where there is no frame, this same information is offered by a dramatized narrator who is in varying degrees of thin disguise the actual author. The general subject matter of the stories may be divided into two broad categories: (1) plots in which there occurs the frustration of human desire for life, love, wealth, and fame by fortune, social and religious norms, or the intransigent wickedness of other human beings; (2) plots in which there occurs the eventual fulfillment of such desires thanks to the power of human ingenuity and perseverence. Their action and tone may be fundamentally satiric, tragic, or comic. But narration of an intensely focused plot usually takes precedence over individualization of the small cast of characters or detailed description of setting. The milieu and characters may be drawn from any class level. The scene may be set in a peasant hut, the bourgeois interior of an urban dwelling, or the exotic landscapes and stormy seascapes of romance. Sometimes the events of the story are close to the actual historical present; at other times, a more remote past is evoked with nostalgia. Brutal realism and lofty idealization may occur in either the bourgeois or the aristocratic milieu, and many stories have themes and settings that involve a confrontation or interpenetration of these two worlds. The style of narration of the briefer kind of novella is characterized by an objective narrator's voice, swift pace, and concise dialogue, though these norms are often violated in late Renaissance examples by intrusive and digressive comment and description or, worse, lengthy rhetorical set pieces. The authors and their creations, the tale-spinners, frequently assert the genuine historical truth and moral utility of their stories, while also defending them as recreational. Finally, we could not complete our working definition without noting that however far it may stray from the Boccaccian

model, the Renaissance novella rarely eludes the shadow, or light, of the *Decameron*.

CLASSICAL AND MEDIEVAL ANTECEDENTS

To understand not only the generic fluidity but also the cultural and aesthetic significance of the novella, one must begin with a survey of the tradition of short fiction bequeathed to the Renaissance by classical and medieval authors. There, too, will be found an explanation of the insistence on verisimilitude and the discomfort about offering pure fictional entertainment voiced by novella authors from Boccaccio to Cervantes. And if the essential ingredients of a tale collection may be said to be its frame story, salient themes, and narrative style, all of these will be seen to have their influential antecedents, if not actual sources, in both the classical past the Renaissance proudly claimed to have revived and the medieval heritage it professed to scorn but continued to exploit, albeit often unknowingly.

Antiquity knew and practiced many types of brief narrative, oral and written, in verse and prose. These included literary as well as subliterary types: myths and legends, apothegms (anecdotes), *facetiae* (jokes or jests), brief romances or lays, apologues (beast fables), folktales, parables, licentious tales of erotic intrigue, and fantastic yarns dealing in magic, witchcraft, and other kinds of traffic with the supernatural world. Extant or referred to in biblical, oriental, and Greco-Roman texts, these types of narrative persisted through the Middle Ages and into the Renaissance as accepted kinds of short fiction or as novellas. Distinctions could be made between oral and written, popular and sophisticated literature, but the subliterary types (jests, folktales, licentious stories) that did survive were preserved in written texts of greater artfulness and respectability. That short fiction should be perishable and disreputable is not surprising. It had no generic status, hence no critical standing; it was usually written or told in prose rather than verse, and its brevity, medium, artlessness, and subversive content relegated it to the status of the transient and popular. This stigma attached itself with special vigor to the licentious tale of erotic intrigue aimed at the sheer entertainment of its listener, as we shall see.

Having little social or aesthetic standing, short fiction could survive to influence Renaissance literature in three ways: first, by incorporation into the repertoire and art of rhetoric; second, by insertion into a longer fictional or nonfictional work; third, by collection and framing with a frame story. The last way was more typical of, and successful with, the oriental than the Western tales, but all three continued into the Renaissance as a means of presenting short fiction. It should be added that in the case of the explicitly didactic Aesopian fables in verse, survival depended on the medium and the content rather than on incorporation or framing; but they had little impact on the novella proper, except insofar as fable collections sometimes attracted other types of short fiction and thus passed them down to later readers or were themselves absorbed into later miscellanies of brief narrative.

The transmission of such short fictional types as the joke or jest and the more serious moral anecdote or apothegm in the rhetorical tradition is exemplified by the works of Cicero, Quintilian, and Valerius Maximus, among many others. Cicero, for instance, discusses witticisms and witty anecdotes, or *facetiae*, in the second book of his *De oratore* (On Oratory), dating from 55 B.C.; and Quintilian devotes a chapter of book 6 of his *Institutio oratoria* (The Education of an Orator), *ca.* A.D. 95, to the pungent anecdote culminating in a witty deed or words. This influential division into deed and word was also used by the first-century-A.D. compiler Valerius Maximus, whose *Facta et dicta memorabilia* (Memorable Deeds and Words), an anthology for orators, was to provide medieval and Renaissance successors with a storehouse of moralizing and witty anecdotes about the actions and utterances of the illustrious figures of antiquity. Other editors or enthusiasts of this same kind of material included Caesar, Plutarch, Aulus Gellius, and Ambrosius Theodosius Macrobius, so that the Greco-Roman treasury of anecdotes was varied and full. As we shall see, both the materials themselves and their use in discussions of wit and humor and other modes of persuasive communication would have their impact in the modern period.

Closer to the fully developed Renaissance novella than the anecdote is the erotic tale. Significantly, the best-known collection has not survived, so that we have to look in longer works to find out from incorporated material what the so-called Milesian tale and Milesian mode of storytelling were about. Associated with a certain Aristides of Miletus, these second-century-B.C. Greek tales seem to have been notorious for their licentious content and trick endings. Indeed, Plutarch tells how the Parthian Surena expressed some surprise at finding a Latin copy of them in a Roman officer's baggage after the battle of Carrhae in 53 B.C. We also hear of a lengthy romance, the *Milesiaca*, set in Miletus and translated into Latin, and it too was very popular with the Romans, which probably led to the term "Milesian" being applied to a marvelous or fantastic fictional mode. That such works were considered unworthy of preservation tells us something about the disreputable status of this kind of short fiction, and also why "Milesian" could still be used in the Renaissance thus to characterize fiction. For example, in *Don Quixote*, part 1, chapter 47, the canon of Toledo associates the cursed books of chivalry with "Milesian fables" because, he says, they are fantastic tales whose purpose is to amaze but not to instruct. The dismissal of short fiction that does not follow the Horatian formula of pleasing *and* instructing (as understood by the Renaissance) was thus given the sanction of antiquity.

Both the Milesian tale and the Milesian

manner have survived, in all probability, in such longer works as the *Golden Ass* of Lucius Apuleius (second century A.D.) and the *Satyricon* of Gaius Petronius (first century A.D.). Apuleius says he is writing in the Milesian manner, and among the many types of inserted short fictions he includes—ranging from the brief romance of Charite and Tlepolemus and the Cupid and Psyche myth it encloses to the bawdy tales of book 9—it is likely that the latter most closely resemble the celebrated Milesian tales. They were also well known to and used by Boccaccio, not only for their comic plots and the motifs of successful or discovered adultery but also for their framing. Lucius' stay at the mill serves as a frame story for the boxed tales that follow, in themselves serving as a centripetal frame for the innermost story. For the most part the technique of boxed stories, also found in Ovid's *Metamorphoses* and in such oriental collections as the *Thousand and One Nights,* was not used by Boccaccio and his disciples, most of whom preferred the single encompassing frame story and discrete tales, though it did have its impact on a few later works. Undoubtedly more influential, especially for Boccaccio, was the brisk and spare style of narration Apuleius employs for the tales of erotic intrigue in book 9 and elsewhere, since this accounts in large measure for the shape and pace of the Boccaccian novella.

In the "Eumolpus" section of the *Satyricon* there occur two important antecedents of the novella tradition. Like the *Golden Ass,* the *Satyricon* as a whole serves as a story frame for inserted materials; in the "Eumolpus" shipboard scene, we have something closer to the Boccaccian type of frame story, for the assembled travelers listen to and comment on the famous tale of the Widow of Ephesus in order to pass the time. (One might call this a symposium type of frame story as opposed to the dialogue type found frequently in Apuleius, when two individuals encounter each other and listen to or exchange stories.) The tale itself, a veritable ur-novella, assures the careless listener that women are far too lustful and clever to be trusted, since it involves a widow's betrayal of her husband's memory in response to the advances of a virile centurion. But the more careful listener would note that the widow's decision to accept first food, then sex, represents the triumph of life-force over sterile rituals of mourning, of gratification over denial. Her clever stratagem, next, to save her lover's life by misusing her dead husband's body represents the triumph of ingenuity unleashed by passionate desire. Here may be found the underlying plot and ethos of the novella of erotic intrigue that ends in the immediate and continuing satisfaction of sexual desire.

For the kind of novella in which erotic suffering endures until trial and tribulation either lead to the relief of legal union or terminate in frustration and death, one must look elsewhere, especially to the influence of Greek romance, New Comedy, and classical tragedy and epic, all of which were well known to the Renaissance and had long before crossed the ill-defined and therefore vulnerable borders of short fiction. We should not be surprised, then, if at times in the action and characters of a Renaissance novella we recognize descent from the *Odyssey,* the *Aethiopica, Daphnis and Chloe,* Terentian comedy, the Jason and Medea of Euripides and Seneca, or the Dido and Aeneas of Vergil.

Much of this material was known also to the Middle Ages, which transmitted it to the Renaissance as is, or accompanied by Christian schemes of interpretation. Two other medieval developments were crucial: the absorption of oriental fiction into European tale collections, and the creation of new types of short narrative such as the fabliau and saint's legend, both contributors to the *Decameron* tradition. One should add, too, that the treatment of short fiction as exemplary, which to some may seem a distortion for the sake of moralizing, nevertheless helped to preserve and transmit a good deal of sheer fictional stuff that might otherwise have perished. And if it is argued that much of this deserved oblivion, it can be replied that given the art of adapting and revivifying plots, so well known and so essential to Renaissance authors of novellas, an abundance of existing specimens, no matter how familiar and unpromising, can serve as crucial grist for the creative mill.

From the early *Panchatantra* to the late and better-known *Thousand and One Nights,* the oriental tale collections that reached the West through translation and adaptation share a tradition of modest but very influential frame stories. Usually of the dialogue type, these frame stories include the motif of learning through exemplary tales and also the motif of postponing or averting an undesirable fate through diverting storytelling. The outcome of the frame-story situation may depend on what is learned from the stories themselves or on the skill of the storyteller at recollecting and spinning out a succession of tales. There was thus inserted into the concept of a narrative frame the idea that telling stories could be educational as well as recreational, that tales might both enhance and save life, or at least delay or mitigate disaster—all potent suggestions for the novella frame of the Renaissance.

Two examples of medieval collections influenced by Eastern materials are the twelfth-century *Disciplina clericalis* (Instruction for Living) of Petrus Alfonsi, adapted from Arabic sources, and Don Juan Manuel's fourteenth-century *El conde Lucanor* (The Book of Count Lucanor and Patronio), also arising out of the peculiarly Spanish mix of Arabic, Jewish, and Latin scholarship. In the Latin *Disciplina*, each of the thirty-four anecdotes, fables, and tales is introduced as a cautionary example, a so-called sweetener to inculcate piety and virtue. Similarly, the fifty-one tales in Spanish of *El conde Lucanor* are set within an instructional dialogue frame and their moral utility stressed. The combination of didacticism and entertainment afforded by these exemplary tales will reappear in less obvious ways in the Renaissance novella collection just as the tales themselves will echo in the individual plots of authors such as Boccaccio, Hans Sachs, and Cervantes, to name but a few who benefited from their preservation.

The same may be said for that *summa* of medieval short fiction known as the *Gesta Romanorum* (Deeds of the Romans), first published in 1473 but probably compiled much earlier. Depending on the manuscript or edition at hand, it contained anywhere from a hundred to two hundred anecdotes and tales in Latin prose. The title refers not to the historical Romans but to the fact that many of the stories are set arbitrarily and anachronistically in the reign of a Roman emperor. Each of the essentially secular tales is followed by an application, or allegorical reading, of its plot, which stresses its value as pious example *(exemplum)*. The frame here is an implied one, since the application is addressed to an audience listening to, or assumed to be listening to, a sermon by a priest Also significant is the variety of short fictional types this collection offered to readers and clergy. There are the usual serious and moral anecdotes about the words and deeds *(gesta)* of the illustrious, from biblical and pagan heroes, emperors, kings, philosophers, and saints to ordinary, nameless folk identified merely by profession. Some of these anecdotes narrate a serious or humorous situation leading to a pungent comment or extraordinary gesture; others merely give the setting for a witticism (what X said when he met Y on a certain occasion). But in addition to the anecdotes, fables, folktales, and witticisms there are also a few novella-type tales of comic trickery and deception, practical jokes as well as carefully plotted and adulterous stratagems (for example, numbers 6, 28, 56, 118, and 122).

Conspicuously lacking in the *Gesta* are tragic tales of erotic suffering and the amatory romance generally, probably because these lack either the necessary brevity or plot simplicity, though certainly not an "applicable" content; in any event such stories were not regularly part of medieval collections of *exempla,* though they would come to dominate the Renaissance counterpart. A famous and influential exception found in the *Gesta*, the lengthy romance of Apollonius of Tyre (153), has its erotic motifs and episodes, but its exemplary feature was perceived to be its plot line—the long series of earthly trials and tribulations leading at last to reward here and in heaven. The conviction voiced by Apollonius' saintly daughter, that God will not permit the tears of his virtuous servants to be shed in vain, and the plot that typically illustrates the conviction are found, of course, in the saint's legend. Gathered in and known from such collections as the *Legenda aurea*, the lives of the saints seem at first glance to have little to do with Boccaccian novellas. The link between the two can easily be seen, however, by comparing the story of Saint Julian in the *Gesta* (18), for example, with *Decameron* 2.2, the tale of Rinaldo d'Asti's tribulations. Like the patron saint of hospitality he invokes with confidence on his travels, Rinaldo encounters misery and despair that subsequently turn to joy, albeit the material one of bodily comfort and erotic satisfaction. This tale, then, like others in the *Decameron* tradition, is a secular parody of the saint's legend, made more explicit in this case by the ironic invocation of the saint himself in his traditional role as protector of travelers.

It is arguable that the French fabliaux (as well as their German analogues, the *Märem*, and Latin counterparts, the *comoediae*) constitute the most significant type of medieval short fiction, original or transmitted, that contributed to the development of the Renaissance novella. This may seem surprising in view of the fact that the fabliau is in verse, often anonymous, usually a single unframed story that may or may not be collected with others and, most important of all, rather raucous in plot and language. Nevertheless, the more stylistically elegant novella owes to the fabliau a good deal of its basic narrative stuff. In addition to a host of plots and plot motifs, the novella could find also in its predecessor several formal ingredients to emulate, especially swift narrative pace and generous use of dialogue. Thus, revealing comparison and contrast can be made between a typical fabliau, "The Miller and the Two Clerics" (Hellman and O'Gorman, pp. 51–58), and the versions of Geoffrey Chaucer and Boccaccio in "The Reeve's Tale" and *Decameron* 9.6. The Chaucer version, rich in late Gothic realistic detail and with deft touches of social and individual characterization, is subtle and sophisticated in its comic artistry, though it retains some of the original's physical brutality. The compact and precise Boccaccio version eschews social and individual characterization as well as Chaucer's more complex plotting in order to emphasize the favorite theme of erotic gratification achieved and potential discord reconciled by human ingenuity—quickly, effectively, and with lasting results. It was Boccaccio's stylistically and formally elegant version of the plot that then inspired a host of imitations, from an Italian novella to a *Schwänk* by Hans Sachs to an eighteenth-century Danish broadside (see Benson and Andersson, pp. 79–201). But in the beginning was the fabliau.

THE DECAMERON *TRADITION AND OTHER SHORT FICTION IN ITALY*

The tradition begins long before the *Decameron* with a work Boccaccio knew well, the *Cento novelle antiche* (Hundred Ancient Tales), the first Italian collection of proto-novella materials. Written or compiled by an anonymous Florentine in early Tuscan prose in the closing decades of the thirteenth century, and also known as *Il novellino* (Little Book of Novellas) from a title given it in the nineteenth century, this gathering of mostly brief anecdotes and tales was published for the first time in the sixteenth century. A subtitle appended later in that century has come down to our own day also, so that modern editions will add to *Cento novelle antiche* the phrase *Libro di novelle e di bel parlar gentile*

(Book of Novellas and Beautiful Noble Speech). For once, an unauthorized title is welcome, since it reflects both the emphasis within the collection on witty and wise sayings and quick responses *(motti arguti)*, Boccaccio's *belle e pronte risposte,* and the perceived role of the collection as a storehouse of useful anecdotes, stories, legends, and myths for private edification or public performance, courtly or rhetorical.

From the viewpoint of the Renaissance, the anticipation of the anecdotal kind of novella in the *Decameron,* along with the overall secular tone, gives the *Novellino* a place at the head of the novella line; but despite its undoubted transitional role, the collection is quintessentially medieval in its materials and values. The sources include the Bible, Greco-Roman history and myth (wonderfully garbled, as when Socrates is made a Roman philosopher in number 61), Arthurian romance, fabliaux, Provençal biographies of and commentaries on poets, and local oral gossip about individuals of varying professions and status. The point of view is often, as in one of Boccaccio's moods too, chivalric and aristocratic, even nostalgic for a time when noble spirits like Alexander, Trajan, Charlemagne, Frederick II, and Saladin did and said marvelously generous and wise things (for example, 4, 69, 18, 24, and 30). At the same time, the *Decameron*'s other interests are anticipated in anecdotes about local and recent personalities drawn from the worlds of Italian civic, social, and professional life and peninsular politics—from nameless merchants (97, 98) to the famous tyrant Azzolino da Romano, whose lazy *novellatore* (court storyteller) recites and breaks off a novella, a well-known version of the "let the sheep pass over" motif (31), whereby the teller refuses to continue his tale until all the many animals who must cross a river or stream in the plot, one by one, actually do so.

Though in the minority, anecdotes of an anticlerical and erotic (57) stamp are included, one of the latter (59), in fact, a moralized ver-

sion of the "Widow of Ephesus" tale, and another (14), a primitive telling of Boccaccio's story about Fillippo Balducci and his son offered in the introduction to the fourth day as proof that sexual attraction is natural. Comparison of the two stories (the earlier one a brief paragraph in length) reveals how far Boccaccio has advanced in narrative art beyond his source, but also reminds us that an anecdote, though not a fully developed novella, nor intended to be, is often the matrix of a novella. The anecdotes and other generally brief stories of the *Cento novelle antiche* therefore presage both the vernacular novella collections and the separate anthologies of "pure" anecdotes in Latin and the vernacular that emerged when the novella came to be understood as Boccaccian, emphasizing plot as well as recorded event, story as well as history.

Some fifty years after the *Novellino,* following the plague that struck Florence in 1348, Boccaccio completed the *Decameron.* Its immediate and widespread success undoubtedly encouraged the imitations that began to appear before the end of the century. These and others to follow in the Italian Renaissance have their virtues, and in some instances exerted important influence, but none equals the virtually sacred text as a literary masterpiece. In the wake of its popularity, the *Decameron*'s successful blend of frame story, theme, and narrative style was never repeated; indeed it was often ignored or resisted, or at best fragmented, as though the Boccaccian blend or formula amounted to no more than the idea of collecting and publishing a group of stories for their instructive and recreational value.

Typical of the first wave are the late-fourteenth-century novellas of Franco Sacchetti (*ca.* 1335–*ca.* 1400), Giovanni Sercambi of Lucca (*ca.* 1348–1424), and the obscure author known as Ser Giovanni Fiorentino, active in the century's last decades.

The *Libro delle trecentonovelle* (Book of Three Hundred Novellas), written in the 1390's by Sacchetti, a Florentine poet of some learning and much prominence in the city's affairs, uses no frame and is unpretentious in tone and style. Despite the number promised by the title, and although the last extant tale is number 258 (in the surviving manuscripts and in all modern printed editions and translations), there are lacunae and fragments, so that only two hundred and twenty-three whole tales actually survive, closer in length and complexity of plot to the tales of the *Decameron* than to those of the *Novellino*. But unlike Boccaccio, Sacchetti consciously insists on his personal involvement in his materials. Even when a story has obviously been manipulated artistically, he stresses the anecdotal, saying that he himself saw, knew, or at least heard about the event. Acting as his own frame, Sacchetti, especially in the chatty preambles and moralizing conclusions of his novellas, draws the reader's attention to others, thus knitting the collection together by personal cross-referencing and running moral commentary. The informal style, lively dialogue, and contemporary Florentine setting of many of the tales have given him a modern reputation for realism and freshness, though there is significant evidence of his artfulness and narrative conventionality.

Sacchetti includes anecdotes about celebrities, whether Bernabò Visconti (4), Giotto (63), or Pope Boniface (35, 203), but his best stories are dominated by those dealing with the "characters" of his day: Lappaccio di Geri, who slept with a corpse (48); Bonamico the painter, whose work was defaced by a monkey (161); and seventy-year-old Agnolo di ser Gherardo, who, Quixote-like, tried to go jousting, with disastrous results (64). From their misadventures the pious Sacchetti invariably draws moral conclusions, occasionally fusing his sources in the *Decameron* and the medieval exemplary tale, as when he notes at the end of novella 254 that the effective witticism of an ordinary person shows how powerful words are, then asks us to consider how much more powerful must be prayer.

Sercambi's 155 novellas, also written in the last decades of the century but untitled, and unpublished until 1816, are better known than Sacchetti's because of their elaborate symposium frame story and its curious resemblance to Chaucer's contrivance. A lost manuscript of one hundred tales possibly dating from the 1370's would allow for Chaucer's knowledge of Sercambi; but in its absence and with the evidence only of a later manuscript (*ca.* 1400), it is difficult to prove that Chaucer had access to Sercambi for his frame. The resemblances, however, remain intriguing. Sercambi posits a *brigata* (company) of men and women (including clergy) fleeing a plague in Lucca and traveling about from Naples to Venice to Genoa and back to Lucca. Stories are told on the way or in some of the hundred or so towns they stay at during the journey. But they are told by one individual, a narrator who is appointed by the leader, Alvisi, to recite his tales, according to a scheme proposed by him upon his election to leadership. An acrostic sonnet reveals that this narrator is Sercambi himself. Also, there is non-narrative activity, such as singing, dancing, and playing musical instruments, enjoyed by the group in towns they stay at on their journey.

The tales themselves are not as uniformly interesting as the frame, though several attract attention because they originate or transmit famous plots or merit study as sources and analogues of greater writers. Thus, Sercambi's 31 follows *Decameron* 8.1 and is an analogue of Chaucer's "The Shipman's Tale"; novella 111, from oriental sources and on the apparent misfortunes of Landra, recalls Sacchetti's 196 and reappears in later European works; novella 7, telling how Rinaldo Buondalmonti attempts to keep his wife chaste with a suit of armor, also echoes in French and Spanish treatments of the favorite novella theme of the useless precaution. Similarly, novella 126 treats the famous "snow baby" theme that had originated in a Latin poem that became a French fabliau: an adulterous wife tries to persuade her merchant husband that the bastard child she bore while he was away was conceived by her eating snow. When the husband takes the child away and disposes of it in a southern climate, he reports to his wife on his return that the child melted in the heat. Sercambi's version then shows up in details of later interpretations by Italian, French, and German writers. Novella 128 passed on from its Spanish source to Italian and European writers the celebrated tale of the painter who brushes an image of a lamb on his wife's stomach to ensure her chastity. As these examples indicate, the novellas of Sercambi are a quarry for scholars; still being debated are the scholarly problems of his relationship to Chaucer and how his versions of these traditional plots, or his apparently original ones, were circulated and could be imitated before their very late printing.

Equally problematic is the identity of Ser Giovanni Fiorentino and the precise meaning of his title, *Il pecorone*. An epilogue sonnet to his novella collection gives both bits of information, and the proem refers to the year 1378 as the beginning date of the composition, but this is all we know about Ser Giovanni the Florentine. The work itself, whose title (The Numskull?) may refer to the foolishness of the author, the story characters, or the interlocutors themselves, was not published until 1558 in a revised and altered state, but in time for later Renaissance exploitation. Under the influence of Boccaccio, the author contrives a dialogue frame story involving a nun, Saturnina, and a chaplain, Auretto, who meet for twenty-five days in the parlor of a convent at Forlì to console each other for their prohibited love by exchanging one story each, for a total of fifty. Each storytelling session is concluded by the recital of *ballate* that invariably deal with love themes, sometimes ironically. Like Boccaccio, too, the author explains in his proem that he, a political exile and understanding sufferer from love, hopes to console with his tales. And indeed as matters turn out, Auretto and Saturnina sublimate their passion very nicely, allowing themselves no more than touching of hands, although there are suggestions of strain—when Auretto suggests

(5.1) they abandon love themes for moral ones and when, before telling the final scurrilous story about a love finally consummated between a gentleman and a nun, he remarks that Saturnina will get the message.

Remarkable too is the tension between tale and anecdote. Of the fifty stories told, fully thirty-two are simply recastings of historical episodes from the *Chronicle* of Giovanni Villani (*ca.* 1275–1348). Of the remaining eighteen, barely a dozen belong to the central novella tradition: both 3.2 and *Decameron 7.7* treat the fabliau motif of "beaten and cuckolded"; 4.1, "Giannetto and the Lady of Belmont" must have been read by William Shakespeare in the original for his *Merchant of Venice* plot, since the English translations from Ser Giovanni in William Painter's *Palace of Pleasure* (1566) were of Ser Giovanni's 1.1 and 9.1. A comparison of 9.1 with Sercambi's similar tale (58) or with the general style of Boccaccio and Sachetti, both sources for Ser Giovanni, reveals that he is not fond of complicated and subtle narrative; he tells a story straightforwardly and with a simplicity of tone and moral attitude that may be more artful than naive, like the parlor game of Auretto and Saturnina.

The fifteenth century begins with this legacy of novellas and the problematic figure of the Sienese Gentile Sermini (*ca.* 1390–*ca.* 1450), whose forty unframed novellas have not been highly regarded, though Bishop chose to translate two of them (2 and 13) at the head of his *Renaissance Storybook* (pp. 3–16). Not published completely until 1874, the collection is characterized by a vivid colloquial style, the use of Sienese dialect, a relentless anticlericalism, and a predominance of meandering plots of erotic intrigue, some of these having been the special targets of obscenity charges from past critics. Sermini also tries to ignore Boccaccio's plots and style, though it is obvious he is exploiting one *Decameron* vein to exhaustion. Nevertheless, despite the Boccaccian length and appearance of his novellas, Sermini has few direct confrontations with the *Decameron* (a rare one, number 13, "Giannetto, Pellegrino, and Gallaziella," challenges *Decameron* 10.8). Certainly he did not learn from Boccaccio how to tell a story well.

There is a lull in fifteenth-century vernacular novella activity between the works of Sermini and the impressive *Novellino* of Massuccio (completed by 1475). But these were also the decades of flourishing Italian Renaissance humanism, with much literary energy channeled into composition in Latin under classical influence. One famous example is the *Historia de duobus amantibus* (The History of Two Lovers, 1444) by the Sienese humanist Enea Silvio (Aeneas Sylvius) Piccolomini (1405–1464), who became Pope Pius II in 1458. This famous man of letters wrote his lengthy story of two lovers while serving as imperial secretary in Vienna. It is told in the form of a letter to a friend relating an incident that actually occurred in his native Siena when the emperor was staying there during the period 1432–1433. Eurialo, a member of the imperial entourage, contrives a passionate affair with Lucrezia, wife of a local magnate appropriately enough named Menelaus. Equally smitten, the lovers are able with much effort to consummate their passion, but soon their forced parting causes her death and his apparently inconsolable—though, as it turns out, temporary—grief. Piccolomini frequently expresses moral concern, but the essence of the work is its fulsome style, rich in classical allusion, psychological realism, amatory rhetoric, and sensual detail. These undoubtedly accounted for its immense European success, with many editions and translations into Italian, French, German, and English.

This was not the first Latin novella, of course; the medieval fabliaux, or *comoediae*, had created a tradition, and there had been fruitful interpenetration of Latin and vernacular tales—a famous example being the twelfth-century *Comoedia Lidiae* used by Boccaccio in *Decameron* 7.9 and by Chaucer in "The Merchant's Tale." Piccolomini's achievement was to combine Boccaccio and Ovid and, by virtue of his great personal prestige and admired style, raise the novella to literary respectability. By focusing, too, on the single tragic tale of erotic suffering, as opposed to the plot of comic erotic intrigue, he assured that almost every subsequent European novella to tell at length the tribulations of two passionate but ultimately defeated lovers would owe a debt to his pioneering effort.

This was also a period in which the classically inspired, serious anecdote and the *facetia* (joke), in both Latin and the vernacular, found renewed popularity; along with witticisms *(motti)* of all kinds, these blood relatives of the novella, sometimes indeed, as we have seen, barely indistinguishable from it, flourished anew to a degree that suggests a collectors' and readers' mania.

If any single book may be said to have sparked the revival of the *facetia* all by itself, it would surely be the *Liber facetiarum* (Book of Jokes) of the celebrated Florentine humanist Poggio Bracciolini (1380–1459). This famous scholar, translator, man of letters, and papal secretary enjoyed an international reputation based as much upon his book of jokes as his discovery of lost classical texts. Written between 1438 and 1452, though not published until 1470, his 272 Latin anecdotes became widely known even before printing assured their European diffusion. Poggio claims the *facetiae* were exchanged by papal secretaries during their "breaks" in a place he calls the *Bugiale* (Lying Room); and indeed there is a contemporary flavor to most of them—not what Alexander or Diogenes said and did but what Dante said (27, 56, 57, 220) or how the cardinal of Avignon replied to the king of France (226). Like his classical and medieval predecessors, too, Poggio favored the kind of anecdote in which an ordinary or lesser personage gets away with a sharp retort to a king or duke or pope, the sheer wit or wisdom involved causing laughter or shame and thus diffusing danger, or even earning approval (as in *facetiae* 13, 20, 50, 107, 130, and 210, for example). There are also quite a few anecdotes recounting wondrous events, such as a cow giving birth to a dragon (30) and other monster stories (31–33); also, miracles (97, 98, and 218) and omens (166–167). The majority of the *facetiae*, however, deal with peasants and townspeople, wives and husbands, friars, priests, doctors, merchants, apprentices, students, and an assortment of local "characters" and regional types as well as traditional comic foils, young and old. These enact humorous, sometimes bawdy and vulgar pranks *(burle)*, or serve as satirical targets, or are made to mouth witticisms and repartee that occasionally have real satiric bite. The relationship to the comic novella is clear in such *facetiae* as the one about a widow and a lustful friar (5); or about why the Perugian woman would never break in her new shoes (65); or Francesco Filelfo's vision, the famous story of Hans Carvel's ring (132); or how a friar seduced a woman by pretending to cure his hurt finger (194); or the clever scheme of a Florentine woman who was caught *in flagrante* (265). To add to this narrative plenty, Poggio even includes specimens of folktale (for example, 58) and beast fable (78). No wonder the *facetiae*, told in a pleasingly colloquial Latin, enjoyed a staggering popularity, as evidenced by editions, translations, and adaptations. Their impact is evident, for instance, on the pioneering French *Cent nouvelles nouvelles* (One Hundred New Tales, 1456–1462), the English *Hundred Merry Tales* (1526) and *Tales and Quick Answers* (1535), and the Latin anecdote collections of Heinrich Bebel (1495) and Desiderius Erasmus (1531), to name just a few. Typical is the publication by William Caxton in 1484 of an edition of Aesop to which he added translations of thirteen *facetiae* from Poggio, derived from a French translation that had in turn been translated from the Latin and German versions of a German editor (*ca.* 1477).

The mania for collecting and writing anecdotes in Latin or the vernacular persisted throughout the fifteenth and into the sixteenth centuries. Thus, among the more celebrated Italian practitioners were Angelo Poliziano (1454–1494), who wrote over four hundred anecdotes in the vernacular; Giovanni Pontano (1426–1503), another celebrated humanist, whose influential *De sermone* (On Discourse) of *ca.* 1499, a Ciceronian treatise on the art of polite conversation, included anecdotal materials of contemporary and classical provenance; Leonardo da Vinci himself (1452–1519), who recorded a few dozen, mostly bawdy anecdotes in his varied writings; and, of course, Castiglione, who inserted many examples of witticisms and practical jokes into the discussion of social humor in book 2 of *The Courtier* (1525). Among lesser-known anthologists of importance are Ludovico Domenichi (1515–1564), whose final edition of his *Facetie, motti et burle* (Jokes, Witticisms, and Pranks, 1564) contained close to a thousand items, padded out with anecdotes by Poliziano and translations of the Latin and German of Pontano, Bebel, Erasmus, and Johannes Gast. Also influential was the *L'hore di ricreatione* (1568) of Ludovico Guicciardini (1521–1589), nephew of the historian, who included many of the famous Italian and northern sources in his "Hours of Recreation"; translated and printed in bilingual editions, it served as an effective language manual. In his *Wit and Wisdom of the Italian Renaissance* (1964), the American authority on this material, Charles Speroni, has also highlighted anecdotes centering on individuals, wits, or pranksters, such as the Florentine Priest Arlotto (1396–1484) or the Ferrarese court buffoon Gonnella (mid-fourteenth century). Unlike Boccaccio's Calandrino, who is the butt of *burle* and *beffe* (pranks and taunts), these two characters are famous for their legendary repartee and jests directed at others, including those above them in station. Unlike their northern jestbook cousin, Tyl Eulenspiegel, however, the Italians, especially Priest Arlotto, rely on verbal rather than physical jests, on the pungent witticism as opposed to the scabrous exploit, often contained within a genuine story. The *motti* and *facezie* of Arlotto were published from the early sixteenth century on, sometimes accompanied by the buffooneries of Gonnella, though a few of the latter had already appeared among the novellas and anecdotes of Sacchetti, Poggio, and Pontano. Multiple editions and translations into other languages assured the European diffusion of these masters of the quip and jest.

In the last quarter of the fifteenth century, the lull in production of vernacular novellas ended with the appearance of the most important collection since Boccaccio, the *Novellino* of Masuccio Salernitano (completed 1475). Tommaso de'Guardati (better known by the diminutive of his first name and his home town) was born between 1410 and 1415, and died in 1475, shortly after assembling fifty novellas for publication. In the service of the Neapolitan nobility most of his life, he claims in the prologue to his work that he had sent single novellas to distinguished individuals over a long period of time and had now decided to gather them together. Undoubtedly, the novellas were written over such a period, but it is pure convention to address noble patrons and offer them individual works; hence it is likely the dedications prefacing each of the fifty tales were part of the final editing, as was also the decision to dedicate the whole to the princess of Calabria. Masuccio, in addition, divided his fifty novellas into five parts of ten each, according to theme and tone, but not rigidly maintained, especially in the alternation of serious and comic stories. Thus, the first part treats the misconduct of clergy; the second, the varied effects of jealousy. In the preface to the third part, Masuccio describes a dream vision out of Dante and Boccaccio in which Mercury instructs him to follow in the footsteps of Juvenal and Boccaccio in dealing with wicked women and their wiles, the theme of the stern and jocose stories to follow. The fourth part mixes "tearful and wretched" matter with "pleasing and light-hearted" stuff, whereas the final section narrates instances of princely magnanimity. This nod in the direction of Boccaccian thematic structure is obvious, though Masuccio avoids the *Decameron* frame story and thus allows himself complete control over his stories and the right to moralize and comment before, during, and after each of them. In the epilogues he wrote for each of his stories, he also refers to the next story; hence they serve as links. At the end of his collection, Masuccio adds a *parlamento* "conversation" with his book in which he refers to the death of his patron, the prince of Salerno, as the reason why it does not contain more stories—indicating that the *Decameron* total was a challenging norm.

There are not enough memorable tales in the *Novellino* to make the collection as a whole successful. The story of how a friar's breeches became relics (3) is amusingly anticlerical; as is the tale of how Friar Ieronimo persuaded a congregation that he had the arm of Saint Luke in his possession (4), a plot destined to reappear as an episode in the picaresque *Lazarillo de Tormes*, among other places. The story of Viola and her three lovers (29) is a well-known analogue of Chaucer's "The Miller's Tale," and reminds us that despite his aristocratic bias and strong moral bent, Masuccio did not rule out, and indeed has more than, the usual quota of licentious or obscene novellas. Perhaps the best novella of the collection, however, is a tragic one (31) telling how two lovers, Martina and Loisi, meet horrible deaths when they take desperate refuge in a grim community of lepers. But even here, Masuccio strains after the pathetic, insisting on telling us before, during, and after his tale how terrible the events were. In fact, despite his frequent pleas of artlessness, Masuccio is too artful at times and at others not artful enough for the sake of his stories. He lacks the inventiveness and stylistic vivacity that can rescue familiar materials from tedium; despite an interesting infusion of dialect, his writing is monotonous.

Masuccio's place in literary history is secure, nevertheless, if only because his story of Mariotto and Ganozza (33) is a crucial link in the evolution of the Romeo and Juliet story. Before Masuccio there were many individual stories of two hapless lovers by Boccaccio and his followers, including Piccolomini; then, closer to Masuccio's invention, there was an anonymous novella of Ippolito and Leonora. But it was Masuccio's version that led the Vicentine soldier Luigi Da Porto (1486–1529) to write the classic story of Romeo and Giulietta about 1520, with some help from Ovid's tale of Pyramus and Thisbe. Subsequently, the versions and translations in prose and verse of Bandello, Pierre Boaistuau, Arthur Brooke, and Painter reached a culmination in Shakespeare's masterpiece.

Masuccio's *Novellino* was also popular enough in Italy during the following century to go through many editions, influence a host of novella writers, and earn itself a place on the church's Index of Prohibited Books. Outside of Italy, it proved especially useful to Spanish and Elizabethan authors, traces of its plots having been located in such diverse works as, for example, Mateo Alemán's *Guzmán de Alfarache* (Masuccio 32, 41) and Shakespeare's *Merchant of Venice* (14), to name only two that are well known. The long list of other Italian and European authors of novellas and plays indebted to Masuccio would include Bandello, Girolamo Parabosco, Painter, Francis Beaumont and John Fletcher, María de Zayas y Sotomayor, and Paul Scarron, among many others.

Before the fifteenth century came to an end, at least one other collection of novellas appeared, more significant for its interesting continuation of the *Decameron* frame story tradition than for the originality or sparkle of its Boccaccian tales. The sixty-one novellas (1478) of the Bolognese Giovanni Sabadino degli Arienti (*d.* 1510) are entitled *Le Porretane* (Tales from the Baths at Porretta), from the resort where his noble *brigata* meet during a four-day holiday and pass part of their time in storytelling. Dedicated to Duke Ercole of Ferrara, the *Porretane* are noted for their occasional realistic glimpses of the contemporary world, whether in the novel frame story, featuring the historical personage Count Andrea Bentivoglio and his entourage, or in the novellas themselves, where not only historical figures but actual places, customs, and "characters" are sometimes evoked with skill (for example, 13, 22, 45, and 60).

The sixteenth century in Italy witnessed an enormous output of novellas, surpassed only by the flood of Petrarchan sonnets. The eighty-odd Latin *Novellae* (1520) of Girolamo Morlini marked a culmination rather than a continuation; henceforth the vernacular novella held the field largely to itself. The Boccaccian collection of tales proliferated, though the single novella, like Machiavelli's *Belfagor*, continued to be written and attract notice. Several authors, defeated by time, circumstance, or lack of inspiration, left behind unfinished though imaginatively conceived schemes for framing and incorporating tales. Novellas began to infiltrate other literary types, especially the plots of drama, and in turn to be invaded by them. The novella interpolated into a longer work of poetry or prose now became standard, as in the several utilized by Ariosto in the *Orlando furioso* (1532) and by Antonfrancesco Doni (1513–1574) in *I marmi* (The Marbles), published in 1552 and purporting to reproduce dialogue and conversation overheard on the marble steps of the Florentine cathedral. Doni, an unfrocked priest, scholar, and literary journalist, dispersed other novellas throughout his many works, but they were less significant than his role in still another sixteenth-century trend: curiosity about the Eastern and other early sources of modern short fiction. Thus, he made an Italian translation of the *Panchatantra* from its Latin and Spanish versions, following upon an adaptation (1541) of the same work by the Florentine monk Angelo Firenzuola.

Firenzuola (1493–1545) is also one of the earliest of the sixteenth-century writers of novellas to merit attention. He was famed for his prose style, as evidenced by an adaptation of Apuleius (another ancient novella source), and his Neoplatonic treatises in dialogue and epistolary form on women and their beauty. His unfinished *Ragionamenti* (Discussions), however, was to be his grand novella collection. The frame story posits a gathering of a small *brigata* in 1523 at the villa of Possolatico outside of Florence; made up of six persons, the group is hostessed by Costanza Amaretta, Firenzuola's beloved, and includes among the three men himself as Celso. The first of six planned *giornate* (days) features discussion of Platonic love, among other equally literary topics, and the recitation of six dull novellas mostly on amatory subjects. This first *giornata* and a fragment of the second, consisting of two tales, were published posthumously in 1548, all that remained of the original scheme.

More successful in completing his plan was Gianfrancesco Straparola, about whom we know little beyond his birthplace, Carravaggio, and that he lived in the last few decades of the fifteenth and into the mid-sixteenth centuries, dying sometime after 1557. In 1550 the first volume of his novellas, the *Piacevoli notti* (Pleasant Nights) was published in Venice; the second volume came out in 1553. The time period of the delightful frame story is the last thirteen nights of the Venetian carnival season of 1536, and the place is the island of Murano, where the daughter of Ottaviano Maria Sforza, Lucrezia Gonzaga, entertains a noble company. The double impulse of carnival and Ottaviano's taking refuge from political turmoil in Milan creates an atmosphere wherein music, dancing, games, conversation, and storytelling are especially welcome. Lucrezia commands five ladies to draw lots and tell stories each of the thirteen "nights"; furthermore, each story must conclude with a riddle or enigma in ottava rima to be solved by the company. The five stories told on each of the thirteen nights and a few additional ones told on the last night by male guests make for a grand total of seventy-five.

The importance of Straparola's tales can hardly be overestimated. Like all sixteenth-century novella authors, he faced the problem of a genre in full bloom and requiring creative innovation in structure, theme, or style to make an impact. He chose to make his bid for attention by expanding the conventional novella domain through the inclusion of folk and fairy tale. Thus one can find in Straparola either the first European appearance or significant versions of some famous folktales: "Puss-in-Boots" (11.1); "Beauty and the Beast" (2.1); "The Magic Fish" (3.1); "The Singing Apple, Speaking Bird, and Dancing Water" (4.3). This puts him in the important line that runs from Basile to Charles Perrault and later folktale spinners and collectors. He also includes two tales told in dialect, an Aesopic fable (10.2), and stories dominated by magic and fantasy (8.5; 5.2; 7.1). But his story about how three nuns demonstrated their fitness in vying for the position of abbess (6.4) is as indecent as a traditionally salacious novella can be. Among the best of his stories, however, are the unsalacious 9.3, telling of a harrowing adventure of Francesco Sforza; 10.4, an amusing tale about how a wicked usurer made his will; 8.2, using the "taming of a shrew" motif; 7.2, about poor Margherita and her hermit-lover, Teodoro. By the end of the century, these and other tales in his collection had made Straparola's Italian and European reputation, as evidenced by widespread imitation and translations into French, Spanish, and English.

The carnival motif of Straparola's frame story was to prove especially attractive; it reappears, for example, in the otherwise negligible *Giuoco piacevole* (Pleasant Play) of Ascanio de' Mori (1585) and Scipione Bargagli's *Trattenimenti* (Entertainments) of 1587. But its best adaptation is to be found in the colorful frame story of *Le cene* (The Suppers), an unfinished collection of novellas by Antonfrancesco Grazzini (1503–1583). This Florentine playwright and editor of traditional Tuscan poetry was also known by the academic name "Il lasca" (The Mullet). The frame of *Le cene* has a *brigata* of ten meet at the house of a Florentine widow for supper and storytelling on each of three successive carnival Thursdays. The planned total of thirty stories was not reached, however, and only twenty-two are extant. The frame story has a "first" in its description of a snowball fight among the *brigata* on the first Thursday, a blustery, cold January day. Begun in the 1540's, the tales themselves reveal Grazzini's Florentine experience, since the city dominates his settings, and the Florentine love of *beffe* (mean tricks) his plots. His ability to tell a tale with verve is illustrated by the grim story of Fazio the goldsmith and his family, brought to a horrible end by greed and jealousy (1.5); and, in an amusing vein, by the story of the *beffa* played on Doctor Manente (1.1), translated in our time by D. H. Lawrence. Since the novellas of Grazzini were not published until the eighteenth century, their influence until then was limited to their circulation in manuscript.

The leading novelist of the century was undoubtedly the Lombard Matteo Bandello (1485–1561). He entered the Dominican order early and eventually became bishop of Agen, in France, but he also managed a life of court and diplomatic service that immersed him in Italian politics and culture, especially at Rome, Milan, and Mantua. His literary scholarship and creativity produced some secular poetry, among other works, though his fame rests on the bulkiest and most influential collection of novellas of the time, appearing in 1554 (parts 1–3) and 1573 (part 4). The total of his novella production, 214, is impressive enough when one considers how some other writers had difficulty writing a mere dozen or two; but equally impressive is the overall quality of his novellas and the record of their widespread influence, especially outside of Italy, away from the Italian fussing about his Lombardisms.

Bandello's success is due to the skill with which he chose and told stories that constitute a vivid record of the hectic world he inhabited. Bandello knew just about everybody who mattered then, and he was involved in many of the crucial events of the time. Out of his living experience and his reading in the *Decameron* tradition he concocted a blend in theme and style of the literary and the real that responded effectively to the old problem of justifying the creation of novellas in the face of their low generic standing and dubious moral content. It was essential for him in this regard to eschew the by then all-too-literary frame story and insist instead that he had written down stories actually told by others and heard by him on various occasions. And to each of the 214 novellas Bandello prefaces an epistolary dedication to one of the illustrious of his day and of his acquaintance recalling the occasion. What is more, he stresses that the events of the novellas really happened (supported by the historical personages, settings, and actions of many of them) and that he owed to his patroness, Ippolita Sforza, the impetus to write them down in the first place (in his poor style) and later to collect them for publication. As both history and story, they will *giovare* and *dilettare* (be useful and delight), Bandello says in the proem, manipulating the Horatian formula simultaneously to disclaim purely literary intentions and responsibility for activity inappropriate to a cleric, and to claim authority as a mere chronicler and obedient servant of the courtly world. He does *not* mention Masuccio Salernitano's *Novellino*, which arose from a similar courtly milieu and utilized a similar "realistic" frame, for to do so would be to invoke literary tradition and upset the delicate balance of fiction and reality he has sought to achieve. Even the occasional moral digression or laudatory description that appears in the dedications or the tales retards matters sufficiently to suggest the leisurely nonfictionality of the whole enterprise.

As might be expected from their numbers alone, Bandello's novellas themselves vary considerably in type and tone, if not in style. The familiar staples of the novella tradition are abundantly present: historical anecdotes, tragic romance, incidents of magnanimity, exotic or fantastic adventure, misbehavior of the clergy, comic erotic intrigue, witty sayings and clever tricks, even the pranks of Gonnella. The range in time and place is also great, though the majority of plots are European and contemporary in reference. Of outstanding interest in the midst of all this plenty are several of the "historical" novellas: on Niccolò III d'Este (1.44); Henry VIII (3.60 and 62); the duchess of Amalfi (1.26), well known as the source of John Webster's play; Edward III (2.37); Alfonso X of Spain (4.9); Mohammed (1.10; 2.13); William of Aquitaine (4.15); the origins of the house of Savoy (4.19), dedicated to fellow novelist Marguerite of Navarre; the painter Lippo Lippi (1.58); and the poet Alain Chartier (1.46). In the preface to 1.40, Bandello tells a famous anecdote about Niccolò Machiavelli's failure to put into practice his vaunted military theories, and elsewhere he mentions other famous literary contemporaries such as Ariosto, Pietro Aretino, and Castiglione. In sum, a whole panorama of Italian and European history, politics, and culture is evoked in the dedications and ensuing novellas.

In these historical tales and in the tragic romances, Bandello exploited a vein of melodrama—anger and frustration, deception and treachery, or mere cruel chance leading to suicides and brutal murder—that assured his popularity with dramatists and thrill-seeking readers. With his eye for realistic detail and keen sense of the terrible extremes to which passion can drive its victims, he gave new, violent force to familiar amatory plots, many of which provided playwrights with good theatrical pieces: for example, Shakespeare's *Romeo and Juliet* (Bandello 2.9), Webster's

The Duchess of Malfi (1.26), Beaumont and Fletcher's *The Triumph of Death* (1.42). To compare the latter with Grazzini's grim tale of Fazio the goldsmith is to see how far beyond the norms of horror Bandello could go, for in his story the betrayed Violante avenges her honor by dismembering the bigamous Didaco alive, then going happily to her own death by decapitation.

As Shakespeare's *Much Ado About Nothing* and *Twelfth Night* also indicate, however, Bandello could provide less gruesome plots (for these plays, see 1.22; 2.36), and indeed his influence was enormous, not only on the Elizabethan and Jacobean dramatists but on playwrights and novelists throughout Europe. His impact came quickly and was aided by translation. As early as 1559, Boaistuau had freely translated a half dozen of the novellas into French, followed by François de Belleforest's four volumes (1559–1570) of adaptations of some seventy of them; there were other translations in French and Spanish by the end of the century, and the French versions especially often served as intermediaries for the English versions of Painter (1566–1567) and Geoffrey Fenton (1567).

Perhaps it was inevitable that Bandello not have any real rivals, considering the scope and skill of his collection; but to Giovanni Battista Giraldi (1504–1573), known also as Cinthio or Cinzio from his Latin pseudonym, Cynthius, must go some credit for attempting to renovate the Boccaccian model of a novella collection. This Ferrarese professor, playwright, and literary critic achieved a reputation for his Senecan tragedies and his treatises on drama and romance-epic, though he is best known today for providing Shakespeare with the plot of *Othello* through his novella "The Moor of Venice" (3.7). That celebrated plot comes from Giraldi's *Gli ecatommiti* or *hecatomithi* (published 1565), a collection of over a hundred novellas written between 1528 and 1565. The title is a Greek coinage of the author's for "The Hundred Stories," though by including a prefatory group he in fact achieved a total of 113. The engaging frame story has a group of Romans flee the sack of 1527 by ship to Marseilles and pass time aboard and at mooring points by engaging in song, dance, and storytelling. The *brigata* has twice the requisite number, with ten men and ten women, but only ten stories are told on each of the ten days required to make the journey.

Giraldi's relentless pursuit of the *Decameron* model and, at the same time, peace with the censor provides us with some interesting features. His preliminary description of the sack of Rome, though perhaps suspect in its moral outrage, has vivid detail. The prefatory justification and Latin inscription prefixed to the tales are almost a parody of Boccaccio's various defenses, but they are, in fact, quite seriously intended to ward off criticism from Counter-Reformation zealots. Giraldi argues, not without some insincerity, that there is no offense to morality or religion included or intended in his stories. In this regard, too, we might note that Giraldi has all of his *brigata* either married or widowed, to avoid even a hint of scandal (one recalls that Boccaccio's unmarried group took pride in having avoided unseemly behavior of its own moral accord). In fact, the stories of Giraldi are not as licentious as those of his predecessors, especially Bandello, but that churchman published his tales before the impact of the Council of Trent began to be felt, whereas Giraldi had to justify his decision to publish them in a more tense period.

The hundred tales making up the main body of the work are divided by subject into ten *deche* (decades): the first *deca* allows any pleasing subject; the second proposes the subject of love, secret or against the wishes of parents, leading to joyous or sorrowful ends; the fidelity and infidelity of wives and husbands (*deche* 3 and 5) frame the theme of 4, how treacherous acts are revealed and punished; acts of courtesy (6), witty replies (7), ingratitude (8), fortune (9), and chivalrous deeds (10) provide the themes of the remaining *deche.*

Among the influential stories—and one refers to plots since Giraldi is a dull storyteller—are the aforementioned "Moor of Venice" (3.7) and the novella of Juriste and Epitia (10.5), which he later made into a play and George Whetstone turned into the English play and story of Promos and Cassandra (1582), whence Shakespeare adapted it for *Measure for Measure.* Apparently Shakespeare did not know the Italian original or the French translation of Giraldi made by Gabriel Chapuis de Tours (1584) entitled *Les facétieuses journées.* Another link with the English and French playwrights was Giraldi's tragedy *Orbecche,* based on his own novella (2.2) and first performed in 1541 in the vanguard of European experiments with revived Senecan tragedy.

Were it not for the imposing figure of Basile looming on the horizon, one might say the quality of novella production in the second half of the sixteenth century confirms the end of the *Decameron* tradition in Italy. Henceforth, nevertheless, there will be little to note except an occasionally felicitous frame story idea or an appealing individual novella. Thus, Girolamo Parabosco's *I diporti* (The Diversions), left unfinished at his death in 1557, with seventeen of the hundred planned novellas completed, has the novel frame of a hunting and fishing expedition that turns to indoor storytelling when the weather intervenes. Pietro Fortini's *Novelle* (*ca.* 1560) surprisingly includes some classical myths among the eighty stories of the collection. And Sebastiano Erizzo's thirty-six novellas (1567) utilize an innovative frame featuring noble young students at the University of Padua who take six summer days off from study to pass the time in storytelling.

The last outstanding Italian Renaissance author of novellas is also among the first of its Baroque artists, since his work takes us into the next century and embodies a new aesthetic ideal. Giambattista Basile (*ca.* 1575–1632), a Neapolitan soldier, courtier, and feudal governor, completed in 1634 a collection of fifty tales in Neapolitan dialect he called *Lo cunto de li cunti* (The Tale of Tales), later called also *Il pentamerone* in reference to its five days of storytelling. The dialect and subtitle, "The Entertainment of Children," point to the domination of the collection by folklore material but hardly prepare us for its delightfully sophisticated form and style. To begin, Basile signed his work with an anagram of his name: Gian Alessio Abbatutis. Then, in a humorous parody of the Eastern and the Boccaccian frame story, he created a *brigata* of ten ugly old women who entertain the pregnant wife of Prince Taddeo with stories after dinner. The wife, a Moorish slave, has deceived the prince into marrying her, thereby usurping the place of Princess Zoza, who has employed magic to set up the storytelling situation. Finally, on the last day, Zoza substitutes for the tenth tale her own story, thereby revealing the deception of the slave and bringing about the latter's death and her own marriage to the prince. In sum, we have a frame story that is itself a folktale enveloping the first true collection of such short fiction.

Outstanding features of Basile's collection are the pioneering tales themselves and the style of their narration. The tales include some of the great favorites, either told here for the first time or given in an early version: "Cinderella" (1.6), "Puss-in-Boots" (2.4), "The Golden Goose" (5.1), "Rapunzel" (2.1), "Sleeping Beauty" (5.5), "Hansel and Gretel" (5.8), and many others. The style is full of witty conceits, rhetorical flourishes, and extravagant imagery in the manner of the Italian Baroque poet Giambattista Marino, especially in the zany descriptions of dawn and evening: "the sun, tired of playing the canary all day in the fields of heaven, having chased out the stars to the torch ball, had retired to change his shirt" (*The Pentameron of Basile*, Burton trans., p. 257). Needless to say, Basile holds an important place in the succession of folktale authors and collectors that runs from Straparola through himself to Perrault, the brothers Grimm, and Hans Christian Andersen. A translation into modern Italian made by Benedetto Croce (1925) and several translations into English (including Sir Richard Burton's of 1893) and into other languages have made Basile as accessible as his sprightly work deserves to be.

THE DECAMERON *TRADITION AND OTHER SHORT FICTION IN EUROPE*

The French Renaissance novella (*nouvelle*) may be said to have begun when a confluence occurred of a still vital native tradition, a humanist interest in revived classical types such as the *facetia* and the rhetorical anecdote, and finally but most importantly the impact of the *Decameron*. The native medieval tradition of long and short narrative, in prose and verse, was particularly rich in France; and what with the *lais*, fables, fabliaux, *exempla* (in Latin and the vernacular), and the oriental *contes* available in translation, there was no lack of short fictional models and materials. In the case of the fabliau, as we have seen, the novella was in a sense coming home. Already in the early decades of the fifteenth century the humanist scholarly activities and the vernacular as well as Latin works of Petrarch and Boccaccio were being absorbed, and, of special note for our purpose, the *Decameron* was translated into French by Laurent Premierfait (1414). The first collection of *nouvelles* to reveal indebtedness to Boccaccio's collection was completed by 1462, nearly a hundred years before the publication of the *Heptaméron* of Marguerite de Navarre (1558), regarded by many as the highlight of the Boccaccian influence in France. In between there were constant if tentative experimentation, translation, and adaption of what was regarded as the Italian or modern mode of storytelling.

The collection completed in 1462 is the *Cent nouvelles nouvelles*, begun in 1456 by an anonymous author some would identify with Antoine de La Sale or one of the other of the thirty-six actual historical personages the au-

1449

thor has recite the bulk of his tales. He says he is modeling his work on Boccaccio, though like so many other French novelists he finds it very difficult to manage a coherent frame story, or perhaps he prefers not to have one. In any event, apart from the names of the reciters and their association with the court of the Burgundian duke Phillipe le Bon, there is little indication of a larger setting and occasion. The stories themselves, however, told as part of each reciter's memories and experiences, are in fact drawn from such mixed sources as Boccaccio, Poggio, the *Disciplina clericalis*, and the fabliaux. Favorite themes of the international novella supply are present: "The Self-Made Cuckold" (9), "The One-Eyed Husband" (16), "The Snow-Child" (19), and "Great Expectations" (80), this last based on Poggio's joke about the new bride who is disappointed in her husband's sexual apparatus (43). There are the usual Chaucerian analogues (18, of "The Shipman's Tale"), many anticlerical tales (for example, 21, 32, and 46), and a version of the "Hans Carvel's Ring" story (11) to go along with other, mostly indecent *nouvelles* of erotic intrigue. There are also the usual jibes at the expense of the black-coated professions, with a combination in one case (2) of a friar and a physician in the same wicked person (see also 20, 79, and 96). Generally, unlike its medieval predecessors, the *Cent nouvelles* aims consciously at pleasure rather than either wisdom or morality; its liveliness comes from closeness to an oral tradition that still echoes in its dialogues. Though his skill at storytelling is not of the highest, the anonymous author tells one memorably chilling tale, long and tragic (and in both these ways unique in the collection), about two noble lovers who wander into a lower-class milieu and find violent death (98). It recalls the fate of Masuccio's two lovers among the lepers (31), mentioned above.

From the publishing and manuscript evidence of the last decades of the fifteenth century to the first half of the sixteenth, it is obvious that there was a new rage for short fiction. In 1493 appeared a French translation of Piccolomini's *Historia de duobus amantibus.* Shortly afterward, a series of anthologies of old and new tales began to be published in Paris or Lyons bearing such titles as *Parangon des nouvelles honnestes et délectables* (Model of Honest and Delectable Tales, 1531), *Les joyeuses adventures* (Joyous Adventures, 1555), *Les joyeuses narrations advenues de nostre temps* (Joyous Stories That Have Happened in Our Time, 1557), *Recueil des plaisantes et facétieuses nouvelles* (Collection of Pleasant and Witty Tales, 1555), and *Les comptes du monde adventureux* (Tales from the Adventurous World, 1555). The last of these even has a Boccaccian frame of sorts involving tales told on a journey. Like the others, it also uses the plots of the *Decameron*, along with those of Masuccio and the other Italian and French sources (including the *Cent nouvelles nouvelles*) that were then common pillaging ground. In view of the continuing dubious status of short fiction, however, it is not surprising that authorial anonymity was preferred.

When authors are known, they are likely to be bourgeois. Among the minor figures of interest though not of real artistry in this period are Phillipe de Vigneulles (1471–1527?); Madame Jeanne Flore, known only from her *Comptes amoureux* (ca. 1532); and Nicholas de Troyes, also known only from his "great model" or *Grand parangon des nouvelles nouvelles* (1537). Vigneulles, a hosier from Metz, knew the *Decameron* well (see, for example, his 71 and *Decameron* 8.2), and was also determined to recall the *Cent nouvelles nouvelles* by calling his work *Les cent nouvelles nouvelles de Phillipe de Vigneulles* (written 1505–1515). This so-called second *Cent nouvelles*, not published until our time, has a vague frame story about a group of garrisoned gentlemen soldiers who tell stories during a truce. Madame Flore, noteworthy as a female author of novellas before Marguerite de Navarre, has in her *Comptes amoureux* the first real French example of a frame story, since her seven otherwise undistinguished stories are recited and discussed by a *brigata* of ladies. Nicolas de Troyes, a saddler established at Tours, began his collection of 180 surviving tales in 1535. Though not published until the nineteenth century, they are interesting in their extensive use of fabliaux, Boccaccio, and the first *Cent nouvelles nouvelles;* a rare incorporation of popular speech and folklore motifs; and a probable influence on Marguerite and Des Péiers.

The one writer of this early period who now draws critical attention as an outstanding figure along with the last two named is Noël du Fail (1520?–1591), a country squire and jurist who had a special attraction to and keen ear for the nostalgic chatter of rustic types. He recorded their alleged conversations and stories in his rather brief *Propos rustiques* (Rustic Talk, 1547) and *Baliverneries d'Eutrapel* (Cock-and-Bull Stories of Eutrapel, 1548). "Eutrapel," from the Greek and meaning "witty," is his name for himself as participant. A later work, his *Contes d'Eutrapel* (1585), focuses rather on memories of student days. The stories floating in these seas of reminiscences are, paradoxically, more often than not to be found in literary sources, along with the powerful influence of François Rabelais as storyteller and master of the "overheard" oral style. The tendency among French novelists to blur frame and story and to aim at representing conversation, the flow of "real" talk, owes much to Rabelais. In du Fail, however, accurately recording village talk often produces an obscurity that offsets his attractive rendition of the flavor of Breton village life.

In 1545 Antoine Le Macon published a new translation of the *Decameron* at the behest of Marguerite, sister of King Francis I and queen of Navarre (1492–1549). Her interest in Boccaccio had earlier manifested itself in a desire to write a French *Decameron*, its stories more true to life than those of the original and certainly more of a vehicle for expressing her reformist and evangelical religious ideals, not to mention her personal intellectual and spiritual conflicts. Begun probably after 1540, her *Heptaméron* was left unfinished at her death, with seventy-two of the planned one hundred novellas completed.

The frame story is easily the best of its kind outside of the *Decameron* itself. A *brigata* of aristocrats has been stranded by floods in a Pyrenean abbey after visiting the baths at Cauterets. Before reaching the safety of Notre Dame de Serrance, each of the ten ladies and gentlemen has suffered personal danger and loss, so the ten days of storytelling, planned to pass the time while the floods subside and a bridge can be built over the swollen river Gave, offer a respite in an oasis, an opportunity to prepare—morally, spiritually, and psychologically—to face life again. The aristocratic *brigata* has five male members (Geburon, Hircan, Simontault, Saffredent, and Dagousin) and five females (Parlament, Oisille, Normerfide, Ennasuite, Longarine); Parlamente and Hircan easily stand for Marguerite herself and her husband, just as the older Oisille is Louise of Savoy, her mother, and the others are similarly identifiable with known historical figures. It is Parlamente who proposes the storytelling to pass the time in a pleasant and virtuous way. There are, however, prayers and Bible reading instead of the gay entertainment that precedes or follows storytelling in other novella frames.

Marguerite's narrators are characterized by the mostly amatory stories they choose to tell and their stands during the discussion that follows each recital, which is often more intriguing than the stories (become *exampla*) themselves. Thus, we learn that the attitudes of the men range from the male chauvinism of Hircan to the pure idealism of Dagousin; among the women, there is the pious widom of Oisille to offset the youthful restlessness of Nomerfide. Parlamente herself tries to steer a course between or to fuse flesh and spirit, to uphold love and marriage in a context of individual fulfillment and conformity to Christian ideals. These unique debates, recalling at times not the *Decameron* links but the medieval questions of love and the more recent Italian treatises of a Neoplatonic stamp dealing with love in a quasi-philosophic way, do not reach any clear conclusions. The often exhilarating exchange of opinions remains its own end, possibly reflecting Marguerite's own inconclusive struggles.

The novellas themselves, varied in type and quality, reveal a sinful world much in need of redemptive grace. The topics are familiar: the tricks men and women practice on each other (1); *ad libitum,* or a tale on any topic one chooses (2); chaste love and its opposite (3); patient and virtuous women and prudent men who accomplish marriage or preserve honor (4); virtuous maids and wives and their opposites who prefer pleasure to honor (5); the deceits men and women practice on each other (6); those who have done the opposite of what they desired (7); and instances of the most flagrant follies imaginable (8). As can be seen, the topics allow for the usual anticlerical tales, here evoking both intense loathing and scathing denunciation because of Marguerite's reformist beliefs (5, 11, 22, 31, 33, 56, and 72). Erotic intrigue abounds, but women are given far more credit than in other collections for chastity and a sense of honor (2, 4, 9, 15, 35–37, 42, and 67). In the stories and debates, women are seen as victims who justly take revenge but are not licensed to revolt against convention (3, 10, 13, 40, and 42).

In view of Marguerite's professed desire to tell only stories based on real events, it is inevitable that readers have sought to identify historical persons in the tales. It is fairly sure that she tells several about herself (4, 22) and her family (7, 17, and 66), and some others refer to actual happenings with varying degrees of concealment (25, 42). But in fact sources and analogues have been found for many of Marguerite's stories in Poggio, Morlini, Masuccio, Fortini, Sabadino, Sercambi, Castiglione, and Bandello; hence, the collection can hardly qualify as a history of the times. This abundant literary tradition proba-

bly accounts in part for her lack of verve as a storyteller, especially since she seems to have been more stimulated by the issues raised than by the narration of the plots themselves. Among her outstanding stories, nevertheless, are some of the best of the French Renaissance: the tragic story of Rolandine (21), a tale of incest (30), how the virtuous widow, Marguerite herself, fends off a rape (4), the lord of Avannes' frustrated love (26), the chaste boatwoman (5), the cruelty of Bernage to his unchaste wife (32), the English lord who wears a lady's glove on his doublet (57), and how the lust and hatred of a duchess leads to the death of her lovers (70).

Marguerite's novellas were published posthumously by Boaistuau in 1558, then again, more faithfully and with their current title, the following year. By 1566, Painter had included sixteen of them in his *Palace of Pleasure;* Bandello had borrowed from several of them (for example, compare her 17 and 25 with his 4.13 and 1.39); and other French and European authors had begun to absorb her influence. As a patron of authors, such as Clément Marot and Rabelais, and, in particular, her valet-de-chambre Bonaventure des Périers, Marguerite also encouraged literary production by others. In the case of Des Périers (1510?–1544?), one result was a significant collection entitled *Nouvelles récréations et joyeux devis* (Novel Pastimes and Merry Tales, 1558).

Des Périers was a humanist scholar of reformist beliefs who helped translate the Bible into French and edit classical texts. He entered Marguerite's service in 1536 and worked on his tales between 1537 and 1540; an allegorical work attributable to him and expressing hostility to both sides of the religious conflict was published anonymously in 1537 but was quickly recognized and castigated as his. By 1544 he was dead, apparently by suicide, at the age of thirty-two. The tales, published posthumously in 1558 (containing ninety in all) and again in 1568 (with the addition of thirty-nine more, many from Henri Estienne's

Apologie pour Hérodote, 1566), hardly suggest the serious and troubled spirit whose life we have sketched. Closer to *facetiae* than novellas, they are told in a cheerful, relaxed way, with a real sense of sharing with the reader delight at the humorous spectacle of mankind bumbling along. Though not quite as exuberant and fecund as Rabelais, Des Périers has the same fascination with language, and he adapts the latter's oral style, nudging the reader into his confidence. Indeed, his high-spirited narrator's voice *is* his frame, barely distinguishable from the tales and anecdotes it tells in a terse manner, but in the most casual and even chaotic of sequences. The comic variety is plentiful: animal stories (24, 31, 81, and 91); anticlerical satire (33–36, 40, 60, 62, and 79); plots based on semantic behavior: verbal wit, plain flubs, and various kinds of verbal misunderstandings (3, 7, 14, 43, 58, 69, 75, and 83); erotic trickery (5, 8, 16, 54, 64, and 84); urban bourgeois and provincial or peasant stupidity (9, 19, 20–21, 27, 30, and 46); and even anti-Italian sentiment (24, 78, and 88). Add merciless exposure of the foibles of the academic and professional worlds, and one has a panorama richer and far less sober than Marguerite's.

Des Périers often botches his stories by eliminating exposition, trailing off instead of finishing crisply with a climax, and piling up old and new anecdotes, even within other stories or anecdotes, according to a common theme. What saves and pleases, nevertheless, are the sheer vitality and spirit of the telling and of the spoken dialogues within the tales. We share his joy in human folly revealed. Yet much of his material came from by now familiar sources: Poggio, Erasmus, Bebel, and Castiglione, among others. He in turn was popular enough to have many French editions in the sixteenth century and at least one translation abroad, an English version of thirty-nine of the tales (1583) by a "T.D." who may have been Thomas Deloney.

In the last half of the sixteenth century, novella activity continued apace, with the afore-mentioned translations of individual Italian novelists (Bandello, Straparola, Giraldi, and others), more anthologies, and several individual collections. Two among the latter deserve note: those by Jacques Yver (*ca.* 1520–*ca.* 1571) and Bénigne Poissenot (*b.* 1558?). Yver's *Le printemps* (Spring, 1572) has a frame story featuring six principals who take refuge from the civil wars to tell and discuss stories during five days spent at a château in Poitou. Published posthumously and with seventeen editions to 1618, it offers proof of the enduring appeal of the Boccaccian frame story and the new attraction of Marguerite's linking debates. Similarly, Poissenot's *L'Esté* has three law students from Toulouse who vacation and tell stories in various country places in or near Narbonne during summertime. But as in so many other failed collections of novellas, it is the incidental natural descriptions provoked by the frame story and not the tales themselves or their relation to the frame that attract our attention here and remind us of the pastoral fiction to come.

Like their French counterparts, Spanish authors of the sixteenth century could look back to a rich medieval tradition of fiction in prose and verse. And as we have seen, Spain was particularly influential in the transmission of oriental story materials in the form of exemplary tales. We have also noted that some of the Italian novella writers were being translated well before the end of the sixteenth century, a sure sign that the *Decameron* tradition as well as knowledge of Boccaccio's masterpiece itself would soon stir novella production in the Renaissance mode of short fiction in prose. Nevertheless, the full tide of the novella in Spain (*novela*) came late, essentially in the seventeenth century, when Spanish literature was in its so-called golden age and had passed from Renaissance to Baroque. And novella production was so completely dominated by Cervantes' twelve *Novelas ejemplares* (*Exemplary Novels,* 1613) that we forget there were other authors and other reasons for their failure to create memorable individual stories or collections. Surely one reason was the very lateness of the surge, making innovation and creative adaptation of the many existing European predecessors difficult. Then, too, pressure from state or church authority, or the author's own pious conscience, limited the deployment of licentious material, though less rigidly than one might suspect given the reputation of Spain for stern Counter-Reformation morality. There was also competition from other popular types of literature, especially the drama; and many authors who practiced both types, like Lope de Vega and Tirso de Molina, wrote far better plays than novellas.

In the preface to his *Novelas ejemplares,* Cervantes averred that he was the first to write them in Castilian, arguing that those in print and in circulation were all translated from foreign languages. This was largely true, but, more important, it suggested that a new vein of fiction was opened for exploitation; and in the flood of imitations that followed, Cervantes himself joined the Italians as a frequent source. Though by this time the French novella production of the sixteenth century was over and its fruits available, there does not seem to have been on the Spanish side anything like the consistent and systematic exploitation by the French of Spanish plots, in short fiction as well as drama.

In the sixteenth century prior to Cervantes' collection, there were several important developments that concern short fiction. Two longer types of prose narrative, the chivalric romance and the pastoral romance, were enormously popular. The rediscovery of Heliodorus also helped promote a taste for the intricacies of the Byzantine novel. The habit of intercalating or merely inserting short stories into these longer plots, especially those of pastoral romance, is a sure sign of new interest in the novella. A famous example is the Moorish tale of the *Abencerraje,* known also as the love story of Abindarráez and the beautiful Jarifa, which appeared in a miscellany of 1565 and in Montemayor's celebrated pastoral romance *Diana* (1561 edition). Against the background of the Andalusian border wars between Christian and Moor, the story tells how the love of the Moorish couple and the chivalry of the Christian captain Rodrigo de Narváez resulted in a rare moment of courtesy and friendship between erstwhile enemies. Equally famous are the stories Cervantes himself incorporated into *Don Quixote,* such as the memorable "Tale of Foolish Curiosity" in part 1 of his masterpiece. Like the *Novelas ejemplares,* Cervantes' tales in *Don Quixote* tend to be long and intricate, in this respect unlike the Boccaccian model but quite typical of late Renaissance preferences, especially in England and Spain. The habit of inserting novellas into miscellanies of prose and verse, themselves not collections of novellas and without traditional frame stories, is also typical of one kind of Spanish production.

The sixteenth century also witnessed the birth of the picaresque novel in *Lazarillo de Tormes* (1554). This fresh kind of realistic fiction, featuring a rogue who tells his story of a life led among the dispossessed of his society and of how he learns to survive in a cruel world, enjoyed great and immediate success with Spanish and European writers and readers. Before the century ended, Mateo Alemán's *Guzmán de Alfarache* (1599) had already initiated the long series of novels about the assorted adventures of a host of rogues or vagrants (*pícaros* and *pícaras*) that would make up the roster of the new fictional mode. Though none of its progeny was as short and simple in structure as *Lazarillo,* many retained its autobiographical narration and episodic structure. That novellas could serve as such episodes is evidenced by at least one of the adventures, told rather than experienced by the hero, in the fifth episode of *Lazarillo,* an anticlerical novella closely resembling one of Masuccio's (4). We have also referred to Alemán's intercalated novellas from the same Italian author. It should be noticed, however, that the use of a first-person narrator in a picaresque romance precludes acting out a novella plot inimical to the character and setting; hence the resort to *hearing* a novella told, or having the hero experience it as an encountered and unfolding event, as in *Lazarillo* and *Guzmán.*

By 1567, the Valencian bibliophile Juan de Timoneda (1490?–1583) had already succeeded in adapting the Boccaccian novella in three different collections of anecdotal stories, mostly from others, as Cervantes argued. The best of these three, entitled *El patrañuelo* (Trifling Tales, 1567), is nevertheless, as the title implies, insignificant stuff. Of the many collections that followed upon the masterly novellas of Cervantes (1613) a few deserve notice. The *Casa del placer honesto* (1620) of Alonso Jerónimo de Salas Barbadillo (1581–1635) is sometimes called the first genuine Spanish imitation of Boccaccio, though the author of this "House of Virtuous Pleasure" is better known as the creator of several picaresque novels of wide influence. Alonso de Castillo Solórzano (1584–1648), the most prolific writer of novelas and picaresque fiction of his day, left no fewer than eight collections of novellas written between 1625 and 1650, all with a frame and other features of the Boccaccian tradition. The titles alone suggest the escapist nature of the materials despite the familiar and necessary claim that the *placer* they offer is *honesto: Tardes entretenidas* (Entertaining Evenings, 1625), *Jornadas alegres* (Joyous Days, 1626), *Noches de placer* (Nights of Pleasure, 1631), *Fiestas del jardín* (Festivities in the Garden, 1634), and so on. Castillo Solórzano could be this prolific in part because of his reliance on the formulaic tale of serious amatory intrigue called by Spaniards the *novela cortesana;* like the contemporary cape-and-sword drama, this kind of lengthy novella uses interchangeable characters and endlessly repeated plots involving love, honor, revenge, and ultimate *desengaño* (disillusionment with sensual love). He also makes use of and adapts with some ingenuity the many frame-story types already noted: spring or summer pastimes, journeys, winter nights, holiday seasons, or festive occasions. Typical also is the focus on five or six days of storytelling, fewer and longer stories than the Italian norm, and the juxtaposition of the tales with other, quite diverse and challenging entertainments, including not only the usual singing and dancing but also the recital and acting of both sacred and secular plays.

Some straining after original frame-story settings is indicated by the *Historias peregrinas y ejemplares* (Strange and Exemplary Histories, 1623) of Gonzalo Céspedes y Meneses (1585?–1638), each of whose "strange and exemplary" novellas is told in a different city of Spain, each duly described. Strain of another kind is evident in Francisco Lugo y Dávilla's *Teatro popular* (1622), which has a proem dedicated to proving that the novella is defensible in Aristotelian terms as a legitimate literary form. Still another kind of tension is evidenced by Juan Pérez de Montalbán's *Sucesos y prodigios de amor en ocho novelas ejemplares* (Amatory Happenings and Wonders in Eight Exemplary Novellas, 1624), since one of his stories (4), "La mejor confusión," caused its author to be brought before the Inquisition because the plot seemed to suggest the church condoned the "confusión" of incestuous marriage. Though rare, such incidents did serve to remind authors of limits.

The two most interesting Spanish authors of novellas after Cervantes are undoubtedly Gabriel Téllez, or Tirso de Molina (1584?–1648), and María de Zayas y Sotomayor (d. 1661?). Tirso, of course, is best known for the Don Juan play *El burlador de Sevilla* and other masterpieces of drama; but here we refer to his *Cigarrales de Toledo* (Country-Houses of Toledo, 1624), an intricate miscellany with intercalated novellas, and *Deleitar aprovechando* (To Enjoy Profitably, 1635), whose Horatian title refers to pastimes of the last three days of carnival. The *Cigarrales* attract attention because of their inclusion of Tirso's anticlassical opinions about drama and of at least one tale, "Los tres maridos burlados" (The Three Tricked Husbands), that continues the novella motif of the *burla* in worthy Spanish fashion. María de Zayas y Sotomayor also inserted her opinions in the preface to her *Novelas amorosas y exemplares* (Amatory and Exemplary Tales, parts 1 and 2, 1637–1649), in which she defends women against the oppression of men and, in particular, argues that women would otherwise be perfectly capable of being scholars and writers. Like Marguerite, she also insists that her stories in part 2 especially are true and illustrate *desengaño* (moral awakening). Utilizing familiar frame settings (part 1 has five days of storytelling; part 2 has ten carnival days), Doña María attempts the unconventional feat of blending progressive feminism and the rigid Christian moralism of her day. Many of the stories in part 2 make clear her sympathy for exploited women; but typical of the necessary ambiguities her approach entails is the intricate novella entitled "El prevenido engañado" (The Mistaken Precaution, 4), in which we have, much complicated, the typical novella situation of an old husband who tries to keep his young wife sexually innocent only to end up wiser but cuckolded. In her comment on the tale, the author argues both that women can and should be educated, and be free to make proper moral choices, and that, as Green has pointed out, an intelligent woman can at least be counted on to be discreet. Inevitably, as we are reminded by the title of her other work, *Desengaños amorosos* (Amatory Disillusions, 1647), Doña María's social and moral milieu guaranteed in any case considerable disillusionment for those who failed to adjust fictional amatory ideals to Spanish reality.

The contribution of Dutch and German authors to Renaissance short fiction, already alluded to several times above, effectively begins with the humanist figures of Erasmus of Rotterdam (*ca.* 1466–1536) and Heinrich Bebel (1472–1518). Earlier the *Decameron* had been translated into German in 1472 by Heinrich Schlüssfelder of Nürnberg; and Heinrich Steinhöwel, the town doctor of Ulm, had translated parts of Poggio and the Griselda story from the *Decameron* in 1473. Poggio's *Facetiae* had also been translated by the chancellor of Wurtemberg, Niclas von Wyle, by 1478.

It would be difficult to exaggerate the widespread influence of Erasmus, since it was felt deeply and everywhere throughout Europe, in classrooms as well as libraries. For short fiction, his role was to disseminate Latin anecdotes in the form of his *Apophthegmata* (1531) and incidentally in his *Adagia* (1500 and 1508). At the same time, and closer to the Poggio model, the Tübingen professor Bebel published his popular and elegantly styled *Libri facetiarum* (1508–1512). Also in Latin, we have the German humanist spoof of 1515 known as the *Epistolae obscurorum virorum* (Epistles of Obscure Men), to which was appended in later editions a version of the plot of Chaucer's "The Reeve's Tale." But as was the case elsewhere, Latin anecdotes and *comoediae* were destined to retreat before the surge in vernacular production of anecdotes and novellas (*Schwänke*), many of these, as we have noted, indebted to Italian, French, and Spanish sources but also at times exerting their own influence elsewhere.

A transitional work between the still powerful medieval didactic tradition and the Renaissance novella is Johannes Pauli's *Schimpf und Ernst* (Wit and Solemnity, 1522), a collection of anecdotes and exemplary tales by a Franciscan monk. A more obviously Boccaccian or Italianate tradition then begins to establish itself with a succession of more worldly, often licentious works published in rapid order during the middle years of the century. Typical of these are Jörg Wickram's *Rollwagenbüchlein* (Coach-Traveler's Companion, 1555), by an Alsatian town secretary who even has a frame story featuring travelers who exchange stories; Valentin Schumann's *Nachtbüchlein* (Bedtime Reader, 1559); Jacob

Frey's *Gartengesellschaft* (Garden Party, 1556). Most of these authors of *Schwäncke* also wrote *Meisterleider* and other kinds of poetry as well as Shrovetide plays and longer prose works. Chief among the multitalented creators of *Schwänke* was, of course, the Nuremberg cobbler Hans Sachs (1494–1576), whom we have referred to earlier as the beneficiary of fabliau and Italian novella plots. Like his middle-class predecessors, Hans Rosenplüt and especially Hans Folz, a Worms barber and surgeon, Sachs used tales not only for his *Schwänke* in verse but also for the lyrics and plots of his *Lieder* and Shrovetide plays. Though without framing or other signs of conscious collection, Sachs's tales are outstanding in their time if not often memorable in themselves.

Insofar as the long prose work centering on the escapades of a single individual may involve adapted novella material for its various episodes, we should at least mention such a work as *Tyl Eulenspiegel* (1515), a jest-cycle dealing with the pranks of a wise fool who mocks and deflates pompous middle-class types. Not surprisingly, scholars have listed among the sources and analogues of these pranks the jests of Gonnella, the *facetiae* of Poggio and Bebel, and other novella collections. The considerable thematic and artistic difference between this work and the later, more realistic *Simplicissimus* (1669) of Hans von Grimmelshausen (1625–1676) is due in part to the intervention of the Spanish picaresque, which was enormously popular in Germany. At the same time, older novella sources such as Boccaccio and Bandello still had their impact (see 4.4–5). Indeed, reminding us as it does of the picaresque novel and the novel generally, about to prevail with European authors and readers, *Simplicissimus* may as much attest to the continuing vitality of Renaissance short fiction as remind us of its absorption into other literary kinds and the end of its independent vitality.

Selected Bibliography

ANTHOLOGIES OF EDITIONS AND TRANSLATIONS

GENERAL TRANSLATIONS

Elizabethan Love Stories. Edited by T. J. B. Spencer. Harmondsworth, 1968.

The Literary Context of Chaucer's Fabliaux. Edited by Larry D. Benson and Theodore M. Andersson. Indianapolis and New York, 1971.

Medieval Comic Tales. Translated by Peter Rickard, Alan Deyermond et al. Totowa, N.J., 1973.

William Painter. *The Palace of Pleasure*. Edited by Joseph Jacobs (1890). 3 vols. Reprinted New York, 1966.

————. *The Palace of Pleasure*. Edited by Harry Levtow and Maurice Valency. New York, 1960.

A Renaissance Storybook. Edited by Morris Bishop. Ithaca, N.Y., and London, 1971.

ITALY

Great Italian Short Stories. Edited by P. M. Pasinetti. New York, 1959.

The Italian Novelists. Translated by Thomas Roscoe. 4 vols. London, 1825.

Novelle del cinquecento. Edited by Giovanni Battista Salinari. Torino, 1976.

Novelle del quattrocento. Edited by Giuseppe Guido Ferrero and Maria Luisa Doglio. Torino, 1976.

The Penguin Book of Italian Short Stories. Edited by Guido Waldman. Harmondsworth, 1969.

The Wit and Wisdom of the Italian Renaissance. Edited by Charles Speroni. Berkeley and Los Angeles, 1964.

FRANCE

Conteurs du XVIème siecle. Edited by Pierre Jourda. Paris, 1966.

Early French Novella. Edited and translated by Patricia F. Cholakian and Rouben C. Cholakian. Albany, N.Y., 1972.

Fabliaux. Edited by Robert Hellman and Richard O'Gorman. New York, 1965. Contains illustrations by Ashley Bryan.

Three Sixteenth-Century Conteurs. Edited by A. J. Krailsheimer. New York and London, 1966.

SPAIN

Coleción selecta de antiguas novelas españoles. Edited by Emilio Cotarelo y Mori. 12 vols. Madrid, 1906–1909.

GERMANY

Die deutsche Märendichtung des 15. Jahrhunderts. Edited by Hans Fischer. Munich, 1966.

Volks-und Schwänkbücher. Edited by Heinz Kindermann. 3 vols. Leipzig, 1928–1936.

Schwänke des 16. Jahrhunderts. Deutsche National-Litteratur (Stuttgart), 1898–

PRINCIPAL AUTHORS: EDITIONS AND TRANSLATIONS

ITALY

Bandello, Matteo. *Le novelle.* Vols. 1–2 of *Tutte le opere.* Edited by Francesco Flora. Milan, 1952.

—————. *Certain Tragical Discourses.* Translated by Geoffrey Fenton. London, 1567. Modernized by Hugh Harris. London, 1924.

—————. *Novels.* Translated by John Payne. London, 1890.

[Bandello, Matteo]. *The French Bandello.* Edited by Frank S. Hook. Columbia, Mo., 1948.

Basile, Giovanni Battista. *Il pentamerone.* Translated by Richard Burton. London, 1893.

—————. *Il pentamerone.* Translated and edited by Benedetto Croce (1925). Reprinted Bari, 1974.

—————. *Il pentamerone.* Translated by Norman Mosley Penzer. London, 1932.

Boaistuau, Pierre. *Histoires tragiques.* Edited by Richard A. Carr. Chapel Hill, N.C., 1977.

Da Porto, Luigi. *Romeo and Juliet.* Translated and edited by Maurice Jonas. London, 1921.

Ser Giovanni Fiorentino. *Il pecorone.* Edited by Enzo Esposito. Ravenna, 1974.

—————. *Il pecorone.* Translated by William George Waters. London, 1901.

Giraldi, Giovanni Battista. *Gli ecatommiti.* Turin, 1879.

Grazzini, Anton Francesco. *Le cene.* Edited by Riccardo Bruscagli. Rome, 1976.

The Hundred Old Tales. Translated by Edward Storer. London, 1925.

Masuccio Salernitano. *Novellino.* Translated by William George Waters. London, 1895.

—————. *Novellino.* Edited by Giorgio Petrocchi. Florence, 1947.

Il novellino. Edited by Guido Favati. Genoa, 1970.

Pius II (Aeneas Silvius Piccolomini). *Historia de duobus amantibus.* Anonymous translation. London, 1596.

—————. *Historia de duobus amantibus.* Translated by Charles Allen. London, 1639.

—————. *Historia de duobus amantibus.* Edited by Rudolf Wolkan. Vienna, 1918.

Poggio Bracciolini. *Liber facetiarum.* In *Opera omnia.* Edited by Luigi Firpo. 4 vols. Turin, 1964–1968.

—————. *Liber facetiarum.* Translated by Bernhardt J. Hurwood. New York, 1968.

Sacchetti, Francesco. *Trecentonovelle.* Translated by Mary G. Steegman. London, 1908.

—————. *Trecentonovelle.* Edited by Vincenzo Pernicone. Bari, 1946.

Sercambi, Giovanni. *Il novelliere.* Edited by Luciano Rossi. Rome, 1974.

Straparola, Giovanfrancesco. *Piacevoli notte.* Translated by William George Waters. London, 1894.

—————. *Piacevoli notte.* Edited by Bartolomeo Rossetti. Rome, 1966.

FRANCE

Conteurs du XVIème siècle. Edited by Pierre Jourda. Paris, 1966. Contains Marguerite de Navarre, *Heptaméron*; Bonaventure Des Périers, *Nouvelles récréations et joyeux devis; Les Cent nouvelles nouvelles*; Nöel Du Fail, *Propos rustiques, Baliverneries*; excerpts from Yver, *Poissenot.*

De Vigneulles, Phillippe. *Les Cents nouvelles nouvelles.* Edited by Charles H. Livingston with Francoise R. Livingston and Robert H. Ivy, Jr. Geneva, 1972.

The Heptaméron Tales and Novels of Marguerite Queen of Navarre (1886). Translated by Arthur Machen. London, 1959.

The Hundred Merry Tales. Translated by Russell Hope Robbins. New York, 1960.

Novel Bonaventure Des Périers's Novel Pastimes and Merry Tales. Translated by Raymond C. La Charité and Virginia La Charité. Lexington, Ky., 1972.

Le Parangon de nouvelles. Edited by Centre Lyonnais d'Étude de l'Humanisme. Geneva, 1979.

RENAISSANCE SHORT FICTION

SPAIN

El abencerraje. Edited and translated by Francisco López Estrada and John E. Keller. Chapel Hill, N.C., 1964.

Alemán, Mateo. *Guzmán de Alfarache.* In *La novela picaresca española.* Edited by Francisco Rico. Barcelona, 1967.

Castillo Solorzano, Alonso de. *La garduña de Sevilla.* Edited by Ferdinando Ruiz Morcuende. Madrid, 1922.

————. *Noches de placer.* Edited by Emilio Cotarelo y Mori. Madrid, 1906.

————. *Tardes entretenidas.* Edited by Emilio Cotarelo y Mori. Madrid, 1908.

————. *Journadas alegres.* Edited by Emilio Cotarelo y Mori. Madrid, 1909.

Cervantes, Miguel de. *Novelas ejemplares.* Edited by Francisco Rodriguez Marín. 2 vols. Madrid, 1917.

————. *Novelas ejemplares.* Translated by Harriet De Onis. Woodbury, N.Y., 1961.

————. *Novelas ejemplares.* Edited by Walter Starkie. New York, 1963.

————. *Novelas ejemplares.* Edited by C. A. Jones. Harmondsworth, 1972.

Céspedes y Meneses, Gonzalo de. *Historias peregrinas y ejemplares.* Edited by Yves-René Fonquerne. Madrid, 1970.

Lugo y Dávila, Francisco de. *Teatro pupular.* Edited by Emilio Cotarelo y Mori. Madrid, 1906.

Pérez de Montalbán, Juan. *Sucesos y prodigios de amor en ochos novelas ejemplares.* Madrid, 1949. Reprint of 1624 ed.

Salas Barbadillo, Alonso Jerónimo de. *Casa del placer honesto.* Edited by Edmund B. Place. Boulder, Colo., 1927.

Timoneda, Juan de. *El patrañuelo.* Edited by Ferdinando Ruiz Morcuende. Madrid, 1930.

Tirso de Molina. *Cigarrales de Toledo.* Edited by Victor Said Armesto. Madrid, 1913.

Vega y Carpio, Lope de. *Novelas a la señora Marcia Leonarda.* Edited by Francisco Rico. Madrid, 1968.

La vida de Lazarillo de Tormes. Edited by José Caso González. Madrid, 1967.

Zayas y Sotomayor, María de. *Novelas amorosas y ejemplares.* Edited by Agustín G. de Amezúa. Madrid, 1948–1950.

————. *Desengaños amorosos.* Edited by Agustín G. de Amezúa. Madrid, 1950.

GERMANY AND THE NETHERLANDS

Bebel, Heinrich. *Libri facetiarum.* Tübingen, 1542.

————. *Faceiten.* Edited by Gustav Bebermayer. Leipzig, 1931.

Erasmus. *Apophthegmatum libri* (1531). Translated by Richard Taverner. London, 1540.

————. *Apophthegmatum libri.* Translated by Nicholas Udall. London, 1542.

————. *Apophthegmatum libri.* In *Opera omnia.* Edited by Peter Vander. Rotterdam, 1703.

Frey, Jacob. *Gartengesellschaft.* Edited by Johannes Bolte. Berlin, 1896.

Pauli, Johannes. *Schimpf und Ernst.* Edited by Johannes Bolte. 2 vols. Berlin, 1924.

Sachs, Hans. *Sämtliche Fabeln und Schwänke.* Edited by Edmund Goetze and Karl Drescher. Stuttgart, 1900.

————. *Merry Tales and Three Shrovetide Plays.* Translated by William Leighton (1910). Reprinted Westport, Conn., 1978.

Schumann, Valentin. *Nachtbüchlein.* Edited by Johannes Bolte. Berlin, 1893.

Wickram, Jörg. *Das Rollwagenbüchlein.* In *Samtliche Werke.* Edited by Hans-Gert Roloff. Vol. 7. Berlin, 1967.

CRITICAL AND HISTORICAL STUDIES

Auerbach, Erich. *Mimesis.* Princeton, N.J., 1974.

Bourland, Caroline B. *The Short Story in Spain in the Seventeenth Century.* New York, 1973.

Clements, Robert, and Joseph Gibaldi. *Anatomy of the Novella.* New York, 1977.

Crane, Thomas F. *Italian Social Customs of the Sixteenth Century.* New Haven, Conn., 1920.

Ferrier, Janet M. *Forerunners of the French Novel.* Manchester, 1954.

Gerlernt, Jules. *World of Many Loves: The "Heptaméron."* Chapel Hill, N.C., 1966.

Green, Otis H. *Spain and the Western Tradition.* 4 vols. Madison and Milwaukee, Wis., 1963–1966.

Griffith, T. Gwynfor. *Bandello's Fiction.* Oxford, 1955.

Hartley, Kelver Hayward. *Bandello and the "Heptaméron."* Melbourne, 1960.

Kuttner, Gerhard. *Wesen und Formen der deutsche Schwankeliteratur.* Berlin, 1934.

Leibowitz, Judith. *Narrative Purpose in the Novella.* The Hague, 1975.

Pabst, Walter. *Novellentheorie und Novellendichtung.* Berlin, 1953.

Paine, J. H. E. *Theory and Criticism of the Novella.* Bonn, 1979.

Polheim, Karl Konrad. *Novellentheorie und Novellenforschung.* Stuttgart, 1965.

Pruvost, René. *Bandello and Elizabethan Fiction.* Paris, 1937.

Rotunda, Dominic Peter. *Motif-Index of the Italian Novella in Prose.* Bloomington, Ind., 1942. Reprinted New York, 1973.

Rodax, Yvonne. *The Ideal and the Real in the Novella of Italy, France and England.* Chapel Hill, N.C., 1968.

Sieber, Harry. *Picaresque.* New York, 1977.

Stone, Donald. *From Tales to Truths: Essays on French Fiction in the Sixteenth Century.* Frankfurt am Main, 1973.

Tetel, Marcell. *Marguerite of Navarre's "Heptaméron."* Durham, N.C., 1973.

Whitbourn, Christine J., ed. *Knaves and Swindlers.* New York, London, and Toronto, 1974. Essays on picaresque.

JAMES V. MIROLLO

RAINER MARIA RILKE
(1875–1926)

IN 1927 THE Austrian novelist Robert Musil said of Rainer Maria Rilke, who had died at the age of fifty-one on 29 December 1926: "This great lyric poet did nothing other than to make the German poem perfect." For all the debate Rilke's work has generated since then, Musil's judgment retains its suggestiveness. Rilke's "perfection" can, in fact, be understood in at least three ways. First, there is the extraordinary logic of his biography: Rilke saw his vocation as that of a poet and simply refused to compromise for any reason, not for human relationships and certainly not for an ordinary job to support his writing. As a result he can sometimes seem rather precious and aloof in his huge correspondence: he makes emotionally committed statements only to withdraw subsequently, through stylization and careful modification of his own words, into a self-absorbed and self-justifying artistic isolation. Some of his letters to wealthy (usually female) admirers are actually thinly disguised requests for money; but when one thinks of today's research scientists and their open dependence on public grants, one has to concede that Rilke was simply assuming a comparable public significance for poetry, and indeed his decorous letters can be read as quite businesslike grant proposals. There is in fact something daring about Rilke's determination to live exclusively as a poet, for at the moments in his life when he felt most tempted to make a full commitment to a woman, he made it very clear that he was not an ascetic, that his renunciations were genuine and painful. Rilke had no preconceived model of a poetic vocation. What he did know was that poetry, in order to be great, must speak of the entire historical experience of an age— and that the poetry of his time, with its inherited hostility to middle-class civilization, was gradually ceasing to be effectively rebellious and becoming merely decorative, a voluntary exile from history. Poetic language either registered every nuance of feeling and perception, or fell silent, paralyzed by the fear that poetic subjectivity had become detached not only from the norm of experience in industrial society, but from the very objects words sought to designate. This so-called language crisis (*Sprachkrise*) was articulated by many turn-of-the-century writers, notably Hugo von Hofmannsthal in his "Chandos Letter" of 1902.

In order to "perfect" his poetic vocation, then, Rilke had to forge a language that would embody precisely the historical experience of language's failure. His success in doing so is what Musil most clearly refers to when he says that Rilke made "the German poem perfect." For Rilke achieved an astounding linguistic virtuosity, an ability to make the German language burst through the limits of what had been expressible in the nineteenth century. This achievement is comparable only to that of Johann Wolfgang von Goethe and Friedrich

Hölderlin at the end of the eighteenth century. These poets had emancipated the language from a provincialism of stylized feeling and tasteful word-painting. A century later German poetry seemed mired in a new provincialism, a self-conscious intimacy dissolving all clarity into gestures of dream; and to a large extent it was Rilke who, by opening words simultaneously to the "hardness" of external objects and to the perceptual fragmentation threatening human subjectivity, propelled German poetry into a full-fledged international modernism. Only the very greatest modernist poets—Stéphane Mallarmé, Paul Valéry, T. S. Eliot, Ezra Pound, Wallace Stevens, Boris Pasternak, Federico García Lorca—can be considered Rilke's equals. And the remarkable fact is that Rilke's early writings are marked by the worst provincialism of the 1890's. Although with hindsight one can see the origins of the poet's mature preoccupations and motifs, Rilke's early collections (in his ambitiousness he published too much too soon, as he himself rapidly realized) are emotionally decadent and linguistically diffuse. But this very weakness is intimately linked to the miracle of Rilke's "perfected" style. For very early on he realized that he could take nothing for granted, that it was not just a matter of learning how to express himself: his expressive goals were completely inseparable from his technical needs, his poet's vocation. His personal history thus coincided with the history of the poetically possible in his time; clearly perceiving the weakness of his earliest publications, Rilke took the crucial second step of treating language as raw material, words as entities to be isolated, molded, polished. Rilke's linguistic virtuosity is thus rarely an end in itself. It is born of historical necessity, the necessity that linked poetry decisively to the visual arts (the works of Auguste Rodin, Paul Cézanne, Pablo Picasso), the necessity we have come to know as modernism. For the way out of the language crisis of the 1890's did indeed prove to be the epochal shift from an aural and suggestive to a visual and sculptural model of language, or, in other words, from impressionism to expressionism.

If Musil is right, then Rilke's bringing the German poem to perfection has a third kind of significance, as an ongoing provocation of the question: what is poetry and what is its function in the twentieth century? This question involves more than just the traditional assertion of premier rank for that which is perfect. Raphael is often called a perfect painter and is in no danger of losing his high rank; but there are epochs and schools of painting for which Raphael is without interest. With Rilke indifference seems impossible. In 1910 the violent expressionist Georg Heym termed Rilke's poetry effeminate; and the years immediately after Rilke's death are dominated by assertions, like that of Bertolt Brecht in 1927, that "all great poems have documentary value." In other words, Rilke's uncompromising insistence on the autonomous function of art is confronted in our century by equally uncompromising points of view that subordinate art to social claims, whether humanistic or frankly political, and regard the idea of artistic autonomy as meaningless. The very notion of artistic perfection is viewed as a mask for conservative politics. This conflict is in a sense perennial. What is new is the emancipation of both sides from overtly religious programs. Rilke's aesthetic absolutism uses religious motifs but refuses all gestures of belief; conversely, when his detractors attack Rilke's emphasis on individual isolation and social stability as inherently conservative and elitist, a gesture of belief is implicit in the attack, namely the belief in the need for social change.

Interestingly, although Rilke would hardly reject the labels of conservatism and elitism, his poetic achievement is such that young, "political" writers, like W. H. Auden in the 1930's, repeatedly drew nourishment from its integrity and linguistic radicalism—in short, from its perfection. In a time when the prestige of literature is becoming a dim memory, we only have to open Rilke's texts to be challenged again to think and feel on a large scale.

For although the theory of aesthetic autonomy was central to Rilke's own productivity, it is in no sense a prerequisite to reading him. And the essential reason is that Rilke repeatedly staged, in his poems, the very crisis of value and language for which the texts themselves are to embody momentary solutions. Rilke has been linked to every kind of politics and philosophy, not because he was an original political or philosophical thinker, but because his writing is so intimately attuned to the new century's intellectual currents that the agendas of all the various disciplines enter his work by historical osmosis. For Rilke the poem makes its claim to irrefutable value only through emotional, perceptual, and linguistic struggle; without such struggle there is no viable poem. A poem neither records nor expresses; rather, it uses a moment of intense awareness to invoke the entire set of questions as to what feeling and observing, expressing and recording, involve exactly and how they are intertwined.

René Maria Rilke (he began calling himself Rainer in 1897) was born in Prague on 4 December 1875. His childhood was characterized by strong contradictions that haunted his later life and led to a deeply ambivalent attitude toward childhood (as inaccessible innocence and well-remembered horror) in his poetry. On the one hand his overprotective mother dressed him in girls' clothes for even longer than was the custom at the time; and on the other hand his father insisted that he be sent to a military academy, from 1886–1891, where mindless discipline and spiritual desolation permanently affected the poet. Moreover his parents separated in 1885. One can see that he internalized these clashing experiences as poetic sources: he idealized women, particularly their capacity for love, while transforming his wholly negative experience at the military school into a quest for supposedly noble ancestors—and into an allegorical celebration of the hero figure. The latter interest resulted in Rilke's biggest "best-seller," a prose poem entitled *De Weise von Liebe und Tod des Cornets Christoph Rilke* (*The Lay of the Love and Death of the Cornet Christoph Rilke*, written in 1899, first published in 1906).

Rilke's biographer Wolfgang Leppmann terms his education "fragmentary": he spent a year at business school in Linz (1891–1892), then studied privately—and successfully—back in Prague from 1892–1895 to achieve his diploma. The most important event of these years, however, was the growing realization that his vocation was literature (his first published book, *Leben und Lieder* [Life and Songs], came in 1894). In 1896 he moved to a genuine metropolis, Munich, where in May 1897 there occurred the decisive encounter of Rilke's life, the meeting with Lou Andreas-Salomé, a married woman of Russian descent who, already a prominent intellectual, had been in Friedrich Nietzsche's circle and was to become a leading student of Sigmund Freud. Rilke and Lou were lovers for three years and remained close friends and correspondents throughout the poet's life. They made two trips to Russia together (in 1899 and 1900), visiting eminences such as Leo Tolstoy as well as the sites of Lou's girlhood. Most important about these trips was the impact of Russian religious services on Rilke: while not inducing belief in him, these ardent ceremonies can be linked to an enduring theme in his poetry, the sense that there exists an ancient, vital, communal way of life no longer imaginable in Western European cities. The Russian experience is fundamental to Rilke's first important poems, contained in *Das Stundenbuch* (*The Book of Hours*), written in three parts in 1899, 1901, and 1903, and published in 1905. Essential to these lyrics is the notion of "building God": the imagery for such building is drawn from the literal building of cathedrals as well as from figurative structuring of an ascetic life (the first part of the work is entitled *Das Buch vom mönchischen Leben* [*The Book of Monastic Life*]). But the central impulse of these poems, in the context of Rilke's mature achievement, is the metaphysical claim they implicitly make for language as such. The texts' religiosity can quickly be decoded as aesthetic ambition: poetic language is to fuse silence and ceremony, individual and community, daily living and ritualized dying.

In 1900 Rilke joined an artists' colony in Worpswede, near Bremen. There he met two young women, Clara Westhoff (whom he married in 1901) and Paula Becker, who married another member of the colony, Otto Modersohn, and whose death in 1907 (from childbirth complications) resulted in one of Rilke's most moving long poems, "Requiem für eine Freundin" ("Requiem for a Friend," 1908). Although they never divorced, Rilke and Clara did not live together long: their daughter, Ruth, was born in December 1901, but in August 1902 Rilke moved to Paris alone. He and Clara maintained friendly relations and were together from time to time throughout his life; some see Rilke's marriage as "liberated" while others view it as typifying his emotional limitations. In any case the move to Paris crystallized two enduring themes of his life and work: on the one hand the horror and anonymity of mass existence in a metropolis (in vivid contrast to the communal vision of Russian religion); and on the other hand the ideal of the artist's existence as a ceaseless and solitary working relationship with the human and natural environment. This ideal was embodied for Rilke in the sculpture of Rodin, whom he met in 1902 and whose secretary he became for a time in 1905–1906. These two themes dominate in counterpoint the great achievements of Rilke's Paris years: the dark, obsessive prose work, often called a decisive influence on the modern novel, entitled *Die Aufzeichnungen des Malte Laurids Brigge* (*The Notebooks of Malte Laurids Brigge*), completed and published in 1910; and the sculpturally conceived, linguistically taut *Neue Gedichte* (*New Poems*), published in two parts in 1907 and 1908.

The contrast between the fluid softness of *The Book of Hours* and the rigorous flexibility of *New Poems* is striking; an intermediate collection, however, *Das Buch der Bilder* (*The Book of Pictures,* first edition 1902, second edition 1906), illuminates the continuity of Rilke's maturing process. It is tempting yet slightly misleading to adopt the poet's own excited perspective on his goals, emphasizing the production of poems as linguistic objects, as self-contained, as hard and existent as ordinary "things." As we shall see, the problem of how and whether language expresses the external world, as well as Rilke's increasing insistence on a text's social-didactic function, were ceaselessly being worked through, as much in the "thinglike" poems as in their rhapsodic predecessors.

Already in the Paris years Rilke became a restless wanderer, setting a pattern for his poet's existence, which assigned a representative quality to the sites he visited and the countries he lived in. Rilke came to discern in this geographical network a Europe that had once existed and must urgently be reimagined. An entire book by Eudo Mason has been devoted to the intricate nature of Rilke's Europe. As his fame grew, the poet himself became conscious that his evident rootlessness opened the possibility of a symbolic rescue of European values, that the countries most important to him (Russia, Spain, the Scandinavian countries) were, despite or perhaps because of their location on Europe's periphery, spiritually central to the European idea, as Rilke saw it. Rilke's attachment to Italy was not as strong as that of many writers; and his attitude toward both Germany and his native Austria ranged from ambivalence to hostility. He disliked both militaristic nationalism and the bureaucratized soullessness he saw in the final decrepitude of the Habsburg Empire. He seems to have sought a valuation of national roots (such as he perceived in Russian religion) fused with a cosmopolitan culture. Indeed he thought he discerned such a fusion, near the end of his life, in the program of Benito Mussolini, whom he praised in a controversial 1925 letter. For Rilke himself, however, "roots" were out of the question; the poet's vocation necessitated both travel and tranquil isolation. The most important of the aristocratic ladies willing to help him achieve these goals was Princess Marie von Thurn und Taxis, whose invitation in 1912 to her castle at Duino, near Trieste, proved decisive. There he wrote the first poems in the *Duineser Elegien* (*Duino Elegies*, 1923), which he could not complete as a set until 1922; immediately, however, he realized that they were to be his life's crowning task.

In retrospect Rilke's wanderings through Europe during the decade 1910–1920 can be seen as the basis of his final "perfect" achievement. The experience itself was a prolonged crisis for the poet, a tormented awareness that he and the civilization he cherished had lost their way, perhaps definitively. Rilke himself felt that he had identified the poetic enterprise too closely with the visual arts; both in his essays on Rodin (1903 and 1907) and in his rhapsodic reception of a Cézanne exhibition (documented in letters to Clara, October 1907), he had developed an intensely spatial vision of art as a kind of colonization of the physical environment, an absorption into itself of wind, gravity, atmosphere. He began to think, in the crisis years, that his concentration on the visual had somehow atrophied his capacity to tap the traditional sources of poetry, particularly his capacity to love. Thus he wrote in a famous admonition to himself in the poem "Wendung" ("Turning-Point," 1914):

> *Werk des Gesichts ist getan,*
> *tue nun Herz-werk.*

> The work of the eyes is done,
> do now the work of the heart.
> (2. 83)[1]

In literary terms we can identify a powerful new influence: Friedrich Hölderlin, whose po-

etry was being rediscovered and reissued in a modern edition by Norbert von Hellingrath in these years before 1914. The impact of Hölderlin's hymnic, syntactically complex, and open-ended style can be seen everywhere in Rilke's work at this time, notably in the first two Duino Elegies. But the demands of a hymnic, cosmological poetry were particularly difficult for Rilke to fulfill after his close identification with Rodin's craftsman ideal. Moreover he was becoming aware of emotional limitations in himself, habits of withdrawal that seemed to condemn him to a sterile rather than productive isolation. Did the artist's vocation *have* to mean a deliberate stunting of life feelings, as Rilke's near contemporaries Thomas Mann and Franz Kafka thought? In the early months of 1914 Rilke made his greatest attempt at "breaking out" of his self-imposed emotional solitude, in an intense involvement with the pianist Magda von Hattingberg ("Benvenuta"). But his rigorous poetic vocation was by then too clearly established: the more Rilke imagined spending his life with her, the more Benvenuta became frightened at the demands such a role would place on her, and so she gently disengaged herself.

And then there was World War I. Rilke joined in the general enthusiasm for the war in August 1914, writing the "Fünf Gesänge" ("Five Songs") in the hymnic mode of Hölderlin, for whom the national idea had been important at the time of the Napoleonic Wars. But his disillusionment was immediate, and Rilke became an explicit pacifist. Drafted into the Austrian army in late 1915, he was spared active service at the front thanks to the efforts of friends such as his publisher, Anton Kippenberg, and his wife, Katharina, and influential writers such as Hofmannsthal and Karl Kraus. Instead he was assigned duties deemed appropriate to a writer at the Imperial Archives, where he was to engage in "hero-trimming"— rewriting news dispatches so that the Austrian cause would appear just and flourishing. But there was clearly no basis for accommodation

[1]All references in the text are made to the authoritative six-volume critical edition edited by Ernst Zinn (1955–1966).

between Rilke and the Austrian army. Released from service in June 1916, Rilke returned to Munich, his base during most of the war years.

Since leaving Paris in 1910, he had been traveling more and more; his growing fame (and the generosity of Kippenberg) made such travel financially possible. But his increasing mobility and his creative difficulties were intertwined. As the war dragged on, Rilke became ever less able to write, ever more aware that this horrific transformation of the world, far from being a release from stagnation (as it continued to appear to the younger, expressionist generation), threatened everything he valued. The inner link between his poetic language and the historical moment, which had so nourished his achievement, now became a heavy destiny: Rilke simply could not work amid the destruction; indeed, Leppmann says he spent the year 1916–1917 "in a state of suspended animation." Like others at this time, Rilke became interested in occult matters as a temporary escape from the relentless rhythm of impersonal, technological death. There was a brief creative spell in November 1915, when Rilke completed the Fourth Duino Elegy; and the posthumous publication of the poems and sketches he worked on in these years reveals continuous experimentation, a quest for the new language he had glimpsed in 1912 (I shall be analyzing this process in some detail). But Rilke came to see the war years as a necessary vocational torment, a time of negation and sterility both in himself and in the world; if he could fully internalize this negativity, then, he felt, he might find his way forward to a historically adequate language. Always he resisted suggestions from his friends that he undergo psychoanalysis (although he met Freud on several occasions, for the last time in December 1915). As Rilke put it, if they drove out his devils, they would drive out his angels also. This might be acceptable if he were to give up writing. But writing was his very essence; he had no other existence.

After the end of the war Rilke remained for nine months in Munich, still unproductive, and ambivalent about the workers' revolution erupting around him. On the one hand he was impressed by the new ability of ordinary people to view social structures with clarity and by their willingness to cooperate and utilize talent purposefully, all of which suggested to him the return of the communal idea, of a large social vision. But on the other hand he was appalled by the violence, the ruthlessness, the dominance of an opportunistic minority; without gentleness, without spiritual change, there could be no "revolution" as Rilke understood the term. And how could these qualities be expected after the years of senseless killing? In 1919 Rilke and his friends became preoccupied with the need to find him an appropriate place to live, a place where the "double rescue" could be achieved: the personal rescue of everything Rilke felt unfinished and open about his past, particularly the past embodied in the unfinished Duino Elegies; and the reclaiming in language of certain stabilities of prewar Europe, particularly the high valuation of art and nature as key sources of human inspiration. The country of destiny turned out to be Switzerland, where Rilke was invited to give a series of lectures in the fall of 1919. After extensive travels and a return visit to Paris it seemed Rilke had found, in November 1920, the right place to live—Castle Berg am Irchel, near Zurich. The continuity with the past and the quietness of the present seemed ideal, yet Rilke still could not settle down fully. He began translating Valéry's poems into German, an important exercise that culminated not only in a friendship with Valéry but also in his own series of poems in French, written in his last years. He left Castle Berg in May 1921 and, with his last significant lover, Baladine Klossowska ("Merline"), began to look for a replacement home. Near Sierre in the Valais region they stumbled upon what turned out to be the ideal place, a small thirteenth-century castle named Muzot, lacking water or electricity. Rilke's friends did everything possible in terms of money and creature comforts to make this new "relationship" work, and gradually, as 1921 wore on, Rilke and Muzot developed a complete symbiosis.

Then, in the single month of February 1922, fulfillment came: Rilke completed the ten Duino Elegies in a sustained burst of inspiration. To the public at the time the miracle must have seemed even greater than it does now, since Rilke had published virtually nothing since the *New Poems* in 1907–1908 and the novel *Malte* in 1910. Although he had written important individual poems, he was dominated by the idea of the completed cycle. (Musil's notion of perfectibility certainly applies to Rilke's view of himself.)

Of the Elegies themselves, the first two had been written at Duino in 1912, the Third in Paris in 1913, the Fourth in Munich in 1915; preliminary versions of the Sixth and Tenth also existed. But some of the most astonishing were both conceived and completed in these weeks: the Fifth, with its harrowing evocation of the inauthentic lives of circus people (Rilke had been profoundly moved by the famous Picasso painting *Les saltimbanques*); and the Seventh and Ninth, with their grandiose development of the themes of "rescuing" past values and experience and of fulfilling the world's secret, innermost longings by reproducing things as "invisible" poetic language. And what Rilke had not anticipated was the simultaneous production, in the three weeks between 2 and 23 February, of fifty-five *Sonette an Orpheus* (*Sonnets to Orpheus*, 1923). Many regard these poems as even greater than the Elegies because they are pure "achievement" (*Leistung*, a favorite Rilkean term), containing the high aspirations of the Elegies and the immediacy of a localized event within the disciplined parameters of the sonnet form. To be sure, these sonnets are not rhetorically symmetrical in the manner of Shakespeare's sonnets. Often the outpouring of images is so overwhelming that the reader, as it were, "forgets" the sonnet form. But looking back

from the fourteenth line, one sees the balancing procedures, the structure that sustains the flow.

Rilke saw the sonnets as a "gift," while the Elegies were the completion of his life's central task. In his last years he engaged several times in explication of the Elegies, particularly of the controversial figure of the Angel, who is to be understood as an image of perfection always already achieved, in no sense as a mediating figure in the Christian tradition; the essential text in this respect is the long letter from Rilke to his Polish translator, Witold Hulewicz (13 November 1925). Opinions will always differ about a work making such uncompromisingly cosmic claims as the Elegies; but there can be no doubt that Rilke's life and work culminate in them and that a viable Rilke interpretation cannot sidestep their less accessible passages. In his last years Rilke concentrated on short poems, not often sonnets but clearly developing the concise style of the *Sonnets to Orpheus*. Intellectually the late poems are even more compressed, while the experience celebrated (*Rühmen* [to celebrate; to praise] is another key word for Rilke) often has a new, delightful simplicity, an absorption in the seasonal processes around Muzot. Rilke also wrote a large number of poems in French (over two hundred pages in the critical edition, edited by Ernst Zinn); these can be readily linked to his growing "Europeanness," his awareness of his own representative role as bearer of civilized values in a world threatened by political turbulence and ill-understood technology. ("All past achievements are threatened by the machine" is the opening line of one of the *Sonnets to Orpheus*.)

Rilke's biographer, Leppmann, argues that the exhaustion felt by the poet at the completion of the Elegies lasted in a sense the rest of his life. He continued to sleep unusually long hours after February 1922, and his health became increasingly problematic. At the end of 1923 he experienced a real collapse, probably the first impact of the leukemia that killed him three years later. Thereafter, periods of energy and productivity alternated with spells of depression and visits to the sanatorium at Val-Mont, where Rilke died in December 1926. For a poet whose texts continuously invoke the need to integrate the processes of living and dying within consciousness, the preparation for his death was typically complex. Thus he wrote a famous epitaph for himself, a masterly drawing of dying into the infinite life-symbol of the rose as

> *reiner Widerspruch, Lust,*
> *Niemandes Schlaf zu sein. . . .*
>
> pure contradiction, delight
> in being no one's sleep. . . .
> (2.185)

But a text also survives from the month of his death, his very last poem, which concludes thus:

> *Bin ich es noch, der da unkenntlich brennt?*
> *Erinnerungen*
> *reiss ich nicht herein.*
> *O Leben, Leben: Draussensein.*
> *Und ich in Lohe. Niemand der mich kennt.*
>
> Am I still the one burning there unrecognizably?
> I cannot grasp memories into myself.
> O life, life: to be outside.
> And I being consumed by fire. No one there who
> knows me.
> (2.511)

Rilke experienced an intense fear of death, and he felt the urge to avoid facing it that is common to us all. But he was not untrue to the life goals projected by his poetic production, and at the same time his despair neither cancels nor is cancelled by the aesthetic perfection of the rose epitaph. The only way Rilke could reach such perfection was through enduring the long seasons of sterility as well as drawing out the sweetness of the creative moment.

The fact that Rilke withheld from publication so many complete and fragmentary poems written between 1906 and 1926 gives the reader a special opening into his world and his cosmology. For the more Rilke came to define his goals in terms of the completed cycle of the Elegies, the more clearly we can discern, in the poems that in his judgment did *not* achieve those goals, the perceptual, ethical, and linguistic problems with which he continually struggled. Two versions of Rilke's career are thus available to us: the documented achievement of the poetry authorized for publication (in which the stylistic differences between early, middle, and late periods become somewhat exaggerated through the omission of "in-between" texts); and the probing, often completely unprotected articulations of the problems confronted by a poet as soon as he attempts to circumscribe an experience and situate it in language. We will begin with the latter series, the "workshop" poems, juxtaposing poems that illuminate the developing relationship between specific motifs and the problem of writing itself. Even though years may separate these texts, they can readily be understood as stages in a single, exceptionally complex creative struggle.

A section of a poem entitled "Improvisationen aus dem Capreser Winter" ("Improvisations from Winter on Capri"), written in December 1906, reads as follows:

> *Gesicht, mein Gesicht:*
> *wessen bist du? für was für Dinge*
> *bist du Gesicht?*
> *Wie kannst du Gesicht sein für so ein Innen, drin*
> *sich*
> *immerfort das Beginnen*
> *mit dem Zerfliessen zu etwas ballt.*
> *Hat der Wald ein Gesicht?*
> *Steht der Berge Basalt*
> *gesichtlos nicht da?*
> *Hebt sich das Meer*
> *nicht ohne Gesicht*
> *aus dem Meergrund her?*
> *Spiegelt sich nicht der Himmel drin,*
> *ohne Stirn, ohne Mund, ohne Kinn?*
>
> Face, my face:
> whose face are you? for what kind of things

RAINER MARIA RILKE

are you the face?
How can you be the face for such an interior,
  where
beginnings perpetually join
with dissolvings to produce a transient fixity.
Does the forest have a face?
Does not the mountains' basalt
stand faceless?
Does not the sea
crest without face
as it rises from its depths?
And is not the sky mirrored therein,
without forehead, without mouth, without chin?

(2.12)

The human face is an essential symbol for
human destiny: it insists on unity, form, symmetry. And the paradox is that, on the one
hand, nothing in nature seems to insist on a
complete unity—phenomena are comfortably
ensconced in fluidity and multiplicity—and,
on the other hand, if we look within ourselves
we find a virtual chaos, a perpetual motion of
thoughts and instinctive reactions that seems
to contradict utterly the persistent, symmetrical, and logical unity of our face, as others see
it and as we may contemplate it in a mirror.
What unity then is our face expressing?
Clearly it is the unity that our perceptions and
our language impose on the world. The great
human achievement is to describe that unity,
to integrate natural phenomena, first at the
minimal level of language and then, dynami-
cally as civilization unfolds in time, in the
intuitive and majestic gestures of art. But is
the unity expressed in our face then a unity
that exists only *outside* our individual being?
Is that not an impossible paradox? It is certainly one that fuels Rilke's entire metaphysics
of art; and virtually all his poems are metaphysical in that sense, posing the question of
their own status in the very process of their
unfolding. Two months after this first text,
while still on Capri, Rilke wrote, on 15 February 1907, "Ein Frühlingswind" ("A Springtime
Wind"):

*Mit diesem Wind kommt Schicksal; lass, o lass
es kommen, all das Drängende und Blinde,*

*von dem wir glühen werden—: alles das.
(Sei still und rühr dich nicht, dass es uns finde.)
O unser Schicksal kommt mit diesem Wind.*

*Von irgendwo bringt dieser neue Wind,
schwankend vom Tragen namenloser Dinge, über
  das
Meer her was wir sind.*

*. . . Wären wirs doch. So wären wir zuhaus.
(Die Himmel stiegen in uns auf und nieder.)
Aber mit diesem Wind geht immer wieder
das Schicksal riesig über uns hinaus.*

With this wind comes fate; let, o let
it come, all the thrusting, blind urges,
which will cause us to glow: all that.
(Be still, don't move, that it may discover us.)
O our fate comes with this wind.

From somewhere far this new wind brings,
  unsteady
from bearing so many nameless things,
across the sea to us—our very being.

. . . If only that's what we were. We'd be at home.
(The heavens would rise and fall within us.)
But with this wind fate rushes perpetually
through and beyond us, immense, remote.

(2.16)

The shift from imagery of face to imagery of
wind is the crucial shift from space to time. The
paradox of the face can, in one sense, be resolved by this shift: the unity of a person's face
is the unity of experienced time, the order imposed by an individual on that experience. But
in another sense the paradox is merely displaced. For what *is* experience? Once again,
what seems to be inside us is essentially outside, a series of disorderly events that exercise
an impact on our sensorium: our minds impose
an order on these events and declare them to be
our own, indeed our personal fate.

In this poem we encounter Rilke's curious
use of the word "fate," which receives its best-
known explication at the start of the Ninth
Elegy. Essentially he inverts Aristotle. Fate is
precisely not something deep within us working itself out through a series of predestined,
dramatically sequenced events. On the con-

1469

trary, fate is the pure externality of events, the things that happen to us without any necessity whatever, simply because we conduct (and mentally unify) our lives in time. We wish this apparently meaningful sequence were really meaningful; as Rilke puts it in the Ninth Elegy, echoing the word's traditional usage, we "long for fate."

But Rilke is not simply demystifying our self-importance; the double movement of the poems shows very clearly that he is determined to master the situation, to reformulate the question of our being, of our ontology. We should welcome fate as it pours in on us, the random gusts of a windy spring; but we must also, somehow, internalize its otherness, center our experience in the irreducible fact that events do not belong to us or to anyone. For even as nature imperiously ignores us, something non-random is happening; human history and civilization are realities as actual and enduring as nature's indifference. Again and again, over the centuries, human beings have had the courage to confront that indifference and to assert the value of their being nevertheless. Very often such assertions have had a religious basis, but this has not diminished their validity. For Rilke religious answers are not available in themselves, but their cultural expression is very much available; it constitutes the history of human achievement that lives in the world, not only in books and museums but also in the natural world as it has been subtly modified by civilization. The forces that impel nature, which we would so like to transfer by analogy to our own lives, are utterly alien from us; but the traces of human resistance to those forces are everywhere to be seen, forever yielding in defeat yet never eliminated. Their perpetually precarious survival constitutes what we call civilization. Thus Rilke is able to sustain his original paradox, the paradox of the face: it *does* make sense to say that our face is the face of the world outside us, for in the spots and moments of that world the essence of our inner being is after all to be found.

Rilke sees himself as very much the inheritor of the fragmented story of civilization. Those whose courage and energy produced that civilization were generally nourished by religious or comparable illusions. Rilke is resolved to jettison all illusions; for him the only way forward is through grasping and actualizing the civilizing drive itself. He is not a detached anthropologist, working without commitment. On the contrary, the productions of art and civilization that Rilke invokes in his poetry are all creations of the past that have entered his experience. (His many travels, particularly to Russia, Spain, and Egypt, were indispensable to his artistic program.) Rilke was especially interested in letters of women long dead, letters that express, through the gradual purification and transcendance of a hopeless love, the essence of an entire human existence; in such letters he saw the potency of civilization, which is not confined to the production of artworks but rather extends, through the power of the transforming impulse, into every detail of an ordinary life—when it is consciously lived as such. We have reached the word "transformation" (*Verwandlung*), a notion indispensable to Rilke's metaphysics, indeed to the metaphysics of anyone whose project is to justify the world without God. For it is only through transformation that the double movement of the poem we are studying makes sense: we are to absorb fate as it rushes in upon us and release it again as it transcends us. If there is to be meaning in this sequence it can only be through the idea of the transforming consciousness: *something* of what hurtles through us is retained and *something* of the wind's destination is glimpsed through a flash of recognition, a momentary glimpse of a fragment of civilization as it is battered once again by nature's indifferent power.

If we broaden the perspective on this metaphysical enterprise beyond Rilke himself, we immediately think of Nietzsche; Erich Heller early pointed out the parallels between Rilke's and Nietzsche's thought. But the differences are almost as significant as the parallels, and the fundamental one is that whereas Nietzsche wills the end of the metaphysical tradition (his "transvaluation of all values"), Rilke embraces it, wills its rescue: "transformation" is but a means to that end. Thus for Nietzsche art is an instrument of radical change, a way of galvanizing the redirected will; humanity is deemed a transitional stage, a bridge leading to intensified Being; and our very understanding of time is to be revolutionized by the thinking of the Eternal Return. It is not necessary to explore Nietzsche's thinking any further to discern Rilke's wholly different points of emphasis. For Rilke the goal of art is not to change the world but to enter it, to participate in the processes of transformation always already going on—and to fulfill the function preordained for art in the invisible order of things. Rilke saw it as his life's work to articulate that function, and in doing so to actualize it, to make it exist. Human beings, in Rilke's eyes, are in a remote exile from the spirituality of their essential existence, which is both communal and solitary, sensuous and ascetic. One thinks of the imaginary monastic ideal of the *Book of Hours,* or of the Russian religion, which was seminal for Rilke; or indeed of the idea of continuous, dedicated work embodied in the sculptor Rodin, whose slogan, adopted by Rilke, was "Toujours travailler!" (Always work!). Certainly this is a conservative ideal. In contrast to Nietzsche, Rilke dreamed of reactivating human possibilities that have *always been there*; his goal is not transvaluation of value but gradual, patient, ascetic recovery of values that have already been fully imagined.

Andras Sandor has pointed to a kinship between his thought and that of Walter Benjamin, rooted in the concept of "rescue"; certainly their ideas of time, crucial to the structure of poetry, are closely linked. Like Benjamin, Rilke focuses intently on the past in quest of that moment of intersection, of electric flow from present to past and back; in such moments the past ceases to be past and the present is emancipated from its continuous defeat both by natural forces and (more ominously) by the indifference of technological time. Whereas Nietzsche imagines a transformation of time as such, Rilke (and Benjamin in his very different way) seek only to reactivate and guarantee the immense images of human time that civilization has generated in profusion but that have become enigmatic, inaccessible to the "progressive" uniformity of commodified, complacent modern time.

Transforming the raw material of experience, rescuing the achieved moments of civilization, these are key ingredients in Rilke's conception of the poem as the "face" of what is outside as well as what is inside the self. Another idea crystallizing during the fruitful winter on Capri is that of accepting, indeed celebrating, limits; the poem "Sonnen-Untergang" ("Sunset") was written in Paris in August 1907:

Wie Blicke blendend, wie eine warme Arene,
vom Tage bevölkert, umgab dich das Land;
bis endlich strahlend, als goldene Pallas-Athene
auf dem Vorgebirg der Untergang stand,
*   verstreut von dem gross ihn vergeudenden Meer.*
Da wurde Raum in den langsam sich leerenden
*   Räumen;*
über den Bergen wurde es leer.

Und dein Leben, von dem man die lichten
*   Gewichte gehoben,*
stieg, soweit Raum war, über das Alles nach
*   oben,*
füllend die rasch sich verkühlende Leere der Welt.
Bis es, im Steigen, in kaum zu erfühlender Ferne
sanft an die Nacht stiess. Da wurden ihm einige
*   Sterne,*
als nächste Wirklichkeit, wehrend
*   entgegengestellt.*

As if gazing with blinding force, like a warm
    arena,
inhabited by the day, the land surrounded you;
until, radiant at last, a golden Pallas Athena,
the sunset stood poised on the outer rock,
    dispersed, squandered by the extravagant sea.
Then the surrounding spaces began to be emptied
    out;

above you, above the houses and trees,
above the mountains the void grew.

And your life, all its light attachments loosened,
rose above everything, as far as the space opened,
filling the world's rapidly cooling emptiness.
Until, rising, at a scarcely imaginable distance,
it encountered the night. Then certain stars,
now its closest reality, were placed in resistance
   to it.

                       (2.28–29)

The image of the soul soaring off into the sky on its own is highly traditional (see, for example, Joseph von Eichendorff's famous "Mondnacht" [Moonlit Night]), and tradition is indeed crucial to Rilke's purpose here. For the rescue of the tradition is to be accomplished by a double reactivation of imagery. On the one hand powerful symbols of motion and strength are frankly invoked and given new life as abstractions: thus the springtime wind of the previous poem becomes impersonal fate, while the dissolution of visual forms at sunset becomes, in the present text, explicitly a void, a vast opening for imaginative flight. Meanings that are merely implicit in the traditional images are spelled out by Rilke. How then does he avoid the dryness of purely abstract language? The answer lies in his counterstrategy, what I have called his celebration of limits. This complementary use of traditional motifs involves the use of those cosmic realms that are nominally outside experience—and presenting them in highly concrete, even intimate language. In our previous text we read, in a confidential parenthesis: "(The heavens would rise and fall within us)." Rilke is speaking, of course, of what in actual experience does *not* happen; but in linguistic terms it *does* happen, the conscious naïveté of the fantasy draws us close to the self as it is swept aside by its tempestuous, impersonal fate.

    This imagining of limits, of otherness, of what lies outside human potential enables Rilke to give new life to the entirety of the tradition, not just to its last phase, that moment of his youth when striving was becoming a mem-

ory, dissolving into dreamlike passivity. What he does is to re-stage the rising, striving motion as an open fiction: the opening word of this poem, *Wie* (as if), launches a typical Rilkean sequence. But the suddenly intimate tone at the very limit of the rising sequence converts the fiction into a new kind of reality, situating it in an almost primitively concrete universe. In "Sunset" we encounter "certain stars" at the limit of the self's ascent; indeed they are explicitly "placed in resistance to it." The stars are absolutely other, as they have always been to the primitive imagination; and Rilke here converts the fictive rise to "a scarcely imaginable distance" into an awed closeness to the alien cosmos. The effect is actually not playful, since the whole momentum of the poem is thrust against this limit. "Stars" and "angels" are of course well-known Rilkean symbols of otherness. My concern here is to show how they actually work for him, how such ancient symbolism lives again inside a technological universe. Primitive imaginations fear stars; they loom without distance. For Rilke, a constellation is a "known figure" (*gewusste Figur*); the imagery of tradition is never employed with false innocence. But the knowing does not alter the fact of otherness. In accelerating the metaphysical rush to the limits and then pausing there, hovering with only the support of language, Rilke makes us share his longing not to transcend limits, but to populate the emptiness with words from the everyday. The historical and physical distances that always surround human experience are simultaneously opened up, through drastic abstraction, and drawn back down again, through the intimate imagining of limiting zones.

    It should be clear that for Rilke there is no distinction between metaphysics and poetic craft: the poem *is* the realization of his speculative moves. While that could perhaps be said of most philosophical poets, what is specific to Rilke is the third element, which is in equally complete interdependence with the other two: namely the project of rescuing, reactivating the entire Western tradition of myths and forms. The self who addresses us in Rilke's texts is no stranger to us; he knows our everyday anxieties. But at the same time he has a mission both to enlarge the possibilities of experience and to persuade the reader, often quite didactically, to join him on that mission. We have only to recall the erratic and provincial quality of Rilke's own education to see why his autodidactic enthusiasm is so infectious.

His quest for a language adequate to his project of rescue is paradoxically a rather humble enterprise. Rilke continuously discovered and absorbed, as the key to his ever more self-conscious poet's life, the excitements of the tradition for himself. At the same time, as the vast scope of his poetic goals became clearer to him, he developed a language more in harmony with those goals, indeed one of astounding flexibility. The developing dynamics of his language—the new virtuosity with which his poetry valorizes that zone between the soaring aspirations of human experience and the silence, the otherness that limits it—is evident in "An die Musik" ("To Music"), the only poem Rilke completed in 1918:

Musik: Atem der Statuen. Vielleicht:
Stille der Bilder. Du Sprache wo Sprachen
enden. Du Zeit,
die senkrecht steht auf der Richtung vergehender
Herzen.

Gefühle zu wem? O du der Gefühle
Wandlung in was?—: in hörbare Landschaft.
Du Fremde: Musik. Du uns entwachsener
Herzraum. Innigstes unser,
das, uns übersteigend, hinausdrängt,—
heiliger Abschied:
da uns das Innre umsteht
als geübteste Ferne, als andre
Seite der Luft:
rein,
riesig,
nicht mehr bewohnbar.

Music: breath of statues. Perhaps:
stillness of pictures. O language where languages
end. O time,

standing vertically against the flow of mortal
  emotions.

Feelings for whom? O transformation
of feelings into what? Into audible landscape.
O strangeness: music. Zone of the heart
grown away from us. Our most intimate being
thrusting beyond us, transcending us,
sacred farewell:
when our inner world surrounds us
as distance shaped through practice, as other
face of the air:
pure,
immense,
no longer habitable.

                              (2.111)

A paradox of Rilke's poetry is that it resists as far as possible the atmosphere of paradox, of contradictory realities. Rilke's goal is to expand his reader's mental landscape to the point where contradictions dissolve, where the irreconcilable is reconciled, either at the spatial limits of the cosmos or in the overlapping time zones of history or memory. As Beda Allemann has pointed out, this reconciling movement in Rilke distinguishes him sharply from Mallarmé, with the latter's invocation of "the flower absent from all bouquets." One can call Mallarmé's insistence on absence either uncompromising aestheticism or rigorous neo-Platonism; it is certainly very different from the absence that pervades our present text. Rilke's absence remains a longing for and intimation of possible presence; it is never at rest like Mallarmé's white purity. As critics noted early on, Rilke's perpetual motion is akin to the imagery of another great modernist, Eliot. In section two of "Burnt Norton" (1935), the first of the *Four Quartets*, Eliot imagines the simultaneity of ordinary, repetitive reality with a rhythmic affirmation of that same reality:

Below, the boarhound and the boar
Pursue their pattern as before
But reconciled among the stars
. . . And do not call it fixity,
Where past and future are gathered. Neither
    movement from nor towards,

Neither ascent nor decline. Except for the point,
   the still point.
There would be no dance, and there is only the
   dance.

Even more than Eliot, Rilke refuses to transcend the everyday. The more seemingly remote his images, the more they throw tendrils back toward the familiar earth. The phrase "Zone of the heart / grown away from us" illustrates this process in "To Music." Music is expressive in ways of which ordinary feeling hearts no longer seem capable. But this means that music is *not* "other" than ourselves; through a historical process our powers have atrophied, but musical achievements recall those powers and challenge us to embark on a mission of recovery. "Grown away" (*entwachsen*): this typically Rilkean participle loosens the web of paradox that the poem itself has constructed ("O language where languages / end"), redefining the text as inside rather than outside history, a narrative both of loss and of movement toward recovery. Music is a central version of the "face" outside ourselves: not only does it activate our most elemental rhythmic responses, it requires equally our most highly developed formal understanding in order to impose itself on human time. Thus even as it transcends us, it must carry us with it, impelling us to contemplate what has become of the inwardness with which we have lost contact in ordinary existence. As Rilke celebrates this particular limit, the limit of sublimely organized music, he opens the poem back toward the possibilities of memory and the actualities of momentary exhilaration. It is the very formality of music that forces the buried connectedness of our experience into consciousness. And thus the final phrase, "no longer habitable," has an impact diametrically opposed to Mallarmé's remoteness; what is no longer habitable is in fact a dwelling rising again into "invisible" existence, built out of new word structures for music's movement, for the "language where languages / end."

    Rilke consummated this "ultimate" language in the miraculous month of February 1922. It seems appropriate, then, that our last look into his "workshop" should focus on an untitled poem written on the first day of that month:

. . . Wann wird, wann wird, wann wird es genügen
das Klagen und Sagen? Waren nicht Meister im
   Fügen
menschlicher Worte gekommen? Warum die
   neuen Versuche?

Sind nicht, sind nicht, sind nicht vom Buche
die Menschen geschlagen wie von fortwährender
   Glocke?
Wenn dir, zwischen zwei Buchern, schweigender
   Himmel erscheint: frohlocke . . . ,
oder ein Ausschnitt einfacher Erde im Abend.

Mehr als die Stürme, mehr als die Meere haben
die Menschen geschrieen . . . Welche
   Übergewichte von Stille
müssen im Weltraum wohnen, da uns die Grille
hörbar blieb, uns schreienden Menschen. Da uns
   die Sterne
schweigende scheinen, im angeschrieenen Äther!

Redeten uns die fernsten, die alten und ältesten
   Vater!
Und wir: Hörende endlich! Die ersten hörenden
   Menschen.

When will, when will, when will it suffice
The lamenting and telling? Have there not
   already been
masters in the weaving of the human words?
   Why the
new attempts?

Are not, are not, are not human lives
battered by the book as by a ceaselessly ringing
   bell?
When between two books the silent sky looms up:
   rejoice . . . ,
or a sector of simple earth at evening.

Above the storms, above the seas have human
   cries
resounded . . . What extra dimensions of quiet
must dwell in the universe, that the cricket
   remained audible
to us, us clamoring humans. That the stars
seem silent, in the ether bombarded with our
   cries!

O that the most distant, most ancient ancestors
    could speak to us!
And that we would finally hear! Would be the
    first hearing humans.

(2.134–135)

The immensities of time and space traversed by this poem are matched by its visionary summation of the history of language. The exhaustion of language arises from the repetitive ordinariness of fear and grief. Yet this ordinariness has already been distilled by the great poets of the past. We can see what might be termed Rilke's sliding use of paradox at work: the poem asserts simultaneously the pointless repetition of the language of pain and the pointlessness of trying to match the masters of that language. Clearly the two kinds of pointlessness do *not* reinforce each other; the image of an already fulfilled poetry actually subverts the notion of repetitious complaining. Certain unique "complaints" endure. And so the paradoxical style "slides" to a new negative vista, the idea (already promulgated by Feodor Dostoevsky in *Notes from Underground* [1864]) that human feeling is inauthentic, the mere product of books.

This sliding from authentic-but-repetitive to feeling as mere reproduction is highly instructive in terms of the metaphysical movement we have noted throughout the "workshop" poems. As before, the language is abstract but passionate, and it thrusts toward a limit, this time a downward limit, a minimizing of human potential. And at this limit the language changes from abstract to concrete: the bell rings, glimpses of evening silence are vouchsafed. And the possibility of utter silence, freedom from words, is imagined. But how could such imagining be articulated? Of course in language, the language of "rejoicing." In our previous text music is praised as the "language where languages end"; Rilke's poetry can only aspire to that status. The evocation of wordlessness at the center of this poem can only be verbal.

But to stop there, to take refuge in "moments," would be to betray the opening rheto-ric. This poem asks questions about the entirety of human speaking, the ongoing history of noise as well as the silence that defines it by contrast. And so the abstract language resumes, with another slide in the paradox. Human history is now inscribed in a spatial image, the image of the universe filled with human outcries. The paradox, as it now appears, is that the concept of silence has survived at all, given the senseless accumulation of pain that crowds out all the more gentle modes of feelings. Rilke has thrust against another limit. And as is typical with him, the intense bleakness of the vision instantly softens at the edges, the sliding of the paradox continues. For everything about this "hopeless" vision suggests grandeur: the accusing human cry (which opens the First Elegy, written ten years earlier and answered here); the glimpses of simplicity (the cricket) and serenity (the stars) that persist through the racket; indeed the very act of imagining the entirety of history as a single spatialized event.

For even though Rilke has insisted on the unmeaning, the repetitious darkness, of this history, the actual movement of his poem continually points in other directions, opening the dimension of the possible. Thus far in the poem, that dimension has been confined to the extrahuman, the little silences outside history. But we have noted how the very processes of linguistic evocation undermine such limiting, and thus, as the inferno of human history is gathered up into a single moment, the poem seems to drive beyond that moment, to insist on release. And Rilke's conclusion is adequate to the challenge; suddenly this compression of history is not a confused babble but a lucid conversation between the beginning and the end of the time humanity has so far traversed. The man of today is released from speaking; he becomes the pure receiver of meaning. The mood is subjunctive, to be sure—the world of the last lines cannot yet be. But Rilke has achieved a marvelous image of how his mission as a poet might be fulfilled. His "hearing" is of course poetic "speaking"; anti-language remains language. But such speaking would be a genuine rescue of history as a whole, neither adding more laments to the babble nor escaping into the magic moments of twilight: the translation of the most ancient human experiences into a language that distills both the darkness and the light from their history— this is the goal Rilke finally articulated for poetry, and that he achieved in the remaining days of February 1922. In that month he completed both the *Duino Elegies* and the *Sonnets to Orpheus.*

The purpose of this traversal of Rilke's "workshop" (my usage of this term does not imply ranking: some of his greatest poems belong here, including "Es winkt zu Fühlung" [A Summons to Feeling], in which the famous term *Weltinnenraum* ["world-inner-space"] is coined) has been to establish continuities. We have seen how an extremely fragile and vulnerable poetic self is both challenged and fulfilled by the vision of the Western tradition as a whole. On the one hand the myriad voices of the past crowd in on the individual sensibility, threatening to drown out all personal language. But on the other hand the poet becomes ever more adept at shaping poetic structures out of the very process of being "drowned"; the initial paradox of the face "outside" the self becomes less and less paradoxical and more the simple reality of poetic existence. And matching this metaphysical continuity is a continuity of method: traditional images (stars, sunsets) are invoked in an abstract mode, one that includes their traditional roles and probes their structure; conversely the extreme enigmas, the limiting zones of human existence, are explored as if it were in fact possible to explore them, through the spare, minimal imagery of irreducible, "meaningless" concreteness. A much-discussed 1914 poem, "Ausgesetzt auf den Bergen des Herzens" ("Exposed on the Mountains of the Heart"), provides a virtual map of this poetic landscape. As the poet ascends the mountain of feeling, passing above the zone of

language into ever more forbidding regions, he notices that the "void" is in fact populated:

Hier blüht wohl
einiges auf; aus stummen Absturz
blüht ein unwissendes Kraut singend hervor.

Here something
blooms; from out of a silent crevice
an unknowing weed emerges singing into
    existence.

(2.94)

Understanding these continuities of style and metaphysical project helps us read all of Rilke's published poems, particularly the early ones. But it is important not to limit ourselves to the study of how poetic texts unfold through reflection on their own reason for being. Such a procedure might be justified in the case of Mallarmé (to pursue once again Allemann's comparison of Rilke with another master modernist), for Mallarmé's language wills its own otherness from all everyday concerns. But Rilke is quite different: both his intention and his historical impact are emotionally intimate as well as urgently didactic. He wants his poems to have an effect on the world; and this they have certainly achieved. He would welcome the questions: Well, so you've summed up, "rescued" the Western tradition—but why? What good is it to us? And what do you yourself have to tell us? It is important to shift our focus from structural to thematic concerns, and one good reason is that Rilke's two great themes are ultimately inseparable from his metaphysics of poetry. That is, his themes are "life-ideas," to be used by ordinary people in everyday existence, but their impact is guaranteed by their poetic shaping (*Gestalt*) precisely because Rilke's own response to his life challenges was to live the poet's life as an endless task and inescapable responsibility. The special quality of his writing is to force us to modify our traditional usage of the word "aesthetic." To Rilke the very existence of aesthetic objects, of art as such, represents an inescapable imperative: human beings *must* live their daily lives in some sort of harmony with the great achievements of the past. It is the responsibility of the poet to match those achievements directly; it is the responsibility of the rest of us not to live trivial lives, not to be mocked by art.

Rilke's perennial themes can be summarized as willing change and making objects or, more abstractly, as intervening in time and intervening in space. Clearly they fit the poet's own activity very well: the poem, a compression of experienced time, is to be inserted into the spatial flux as an independent object laying claim to permanence. But in Rilke's eyes the twin themes fuse the two poles of human action in the world, a polarity well understood by the Greeks and other ancient civilizations yet forgotten by a technological age in which human and natural time are sundered while the distinction between object and image disappears in the commodity, in the texture of illusion and consumption. Time is the element in which human beings must live, but it is inert and sterile, unless they concentrate their energies on it, drawing the time of the organic world, the time of the human past, and the fragile time of the individual present into some kind of productive unity. And to think such a unity is already in some sense to think spatially. As the romantic thinker Novalis put it: "Space is the precipitate of time." In the world around him Rilke saw a space almost infinitely contaminated by the inauthentic: cities of identical houses forcing the organic qualities of humanity into an industrial world designed to kill them and replace them with a "life" of prepackaged commodities, and images dominated by advertising and politics, pictures aiming always to substitute an imaginary life for reality, utterly alien to the traditional function of physical images as fulfilling and celebrating the real. Rilke's countermove, his insistence on "intervention," on marshaling all the powers that are dormant within us, is thus essentially anti-political, at least as politics is normally understood. But it is not opposed to the "politics of community" that, at a deep level of idealism, nourishes socialist and conservative thought alike. To engage the organic realm, as in the following early text, "Eingang" ("Entering," 1900), is to be involved by definition in an urgent human dialogue:

Wer du auch seist: am Abend tritt hinaus
aus deiner Stube, drin du alles weisst;
als letzes vor der Ferne liegt dein Haus:
wer du auch seist.
Mit deinen Augen, welche müde kaum
von der verbrauchten Schwelle sich befrein,
hebst du ganz langsam einen schwarzen Baum
und stellst ihn vor den Himmel: schlank, allein.
Und hast die Welt gemacht. Und sie ist gross
Und wie dein Wille ihren Sinn begreift,
lassen sie deine Augen zärtlich los . . .

Whoever you are: step out in the evening
from your room where all is known to you;
your house is just this side of great distances:
whoever you are.
With your eyes which, exhausted,
barely free themselves from the worn threshold,
you raise up, slowly, a black tree
and place it against the sky: slender, alone.
And you've made the world. And it is vast
and like a word which ripens still in silence.
And as your will begins to grasp its meaning,
your eyes release it gently . . .

(1.371)

Written in February 1900 in Berlin-Schmargendorf, this is the first poem, the "entrance," to the *Book of Pictures*. And immediately a subtle Rilkean tension is established with the opening gesture. For the "entering" is actually a leaving, a moving out of the known into the forever "unknown" fullness of the natural world. The contrast between internal and external, human and natural, might seem oversimple except that Rilke immediately causes all opposites to slide, almost to rotate around the creative principle as it is gently activated, both in life and in the book of poems. For the self or reader being addressed does not "find" anything outside his home. He simply intervenes in life, draws together the powers dissipated by the familiarity of things; and this creative move is open to anyone—*all* houses are "just this side of great distances." In comparison with later texts already discussed, this poem is soft-edged: the negative image of the familiar ceases to be necessary for the later Rilke, and the notion of "releasing" the world that eyes have constituted in the tree seems rather precious, excessively ritualistic in the manner of much early Rilke. But if the contrast is made with even earlier (as opposed to later) poems, the significance of this "entering" is more clearly perceptible. Just a few months before, in October 1899, Rilke had completed the first part of *The Book of Hours—The Book of Monastic Life.* There the ritual apparatus is much more elaborate: in its monk's persona, the self insists on ascetic regularity ("I live my life in growing rings"), and the outcome of the various intensities is nothing less than the "rebuilding" of God. In other words Rilke's poetic beginnings are encumbered both with an excess of subjective pomposity and with elaborate "objective" goals, images of purified new/old divinities.

The present text, then, endeavors to focus the act of intervention, which is synonymous with creation, in a way that Käte Hamburger has termed "phenomenological." To concentrate one's powers on a tree is to "create" that tree, to isolate and realize its being, which cannot meaningfully exist without human intervention. The only requirement of the self is that it delve inward and release its powers; and the tree refers to nothing but its own existence. Neither purified subjectivity nor a larger project are necessary. But what certifies Rilke's text as poetry rather than phenomenological thought is the way in which the tensions involved in the concentration on the tree ripple into the open toward the end of the text. The tree's isolation is stressed, but "you've made the world." The very informality of the phrase points in opposite directions: Rilke is being playful about his own imagery but is simultaneously "embracing the limit," acknowledging the human impetus toward ulti-

mates. In the very creation of the tree, questions about both the meaning of the natural order and the status of the questioning consciousness continue to reverberate. They point to the aspiration of the poem itself, the paradoxical urge of language, the quintessential man-made system, to "ripen" like an organism with a guaranteed place in the world. (Jacob Steiner has shown the frequency and thematic importance of Rilke's references to "the word"; here, even in the prevailing soft image-making, the simile has a slightly disruptive effect, as if the poem's organic ambitions were being prevented by a consciously strained analogy.) And the questions readmit the human agent: "tired" at the outset of the poem, his "will" is now engaging the "meaning" of what is essentially his own performance. The term "will" reminds us also of the continuing quest of the self, its need to interpret and criticize its own productive moment. None of these tensions are stressed: what Rilke does is to imagine the perfection of an aesthetic act, an obvious analogue to his own poem, *and* to open the moment of achievement into the continuity and dissatisfaction of living. The title thus gains an extra dimension: this text really is an "entrance" into both the integrity and the perpetual struggle of Rilke's poetic maturity. The creative gaze at its center becomes, in the poem "Archaïscher Torso Apollos" ("Archaic Torso of Apollo," 1908), almost infinitely dynamic and nuanced:

Wir kannten nicht sein unerhörtes Haupt,
darin die Augenäpfel reiften. Aber
sein Torso glüht noch wie ein Kandelaber
in dem sein Schauen, nur zurückgeschraubt,

sich hält und glänzt. Sonst könnte nicht der Bug
der Brust dich blenden, und im leisen Drehen
der Lenden könnte nicht ein Lächeln gehen
zu jener Mitte, die die Zeugung trug.

Sonst stünde dieser Stein enstellt und kurz
unter der Schultern durchsichtigem Sturz
und flimmerte nicht so wie Raubtierfelle;

und bräche nicht aus allen seinen Rändern
aus wie ein Stern: denn da ist keine Stelle,
die dich nicht sieht. Du musst dein Leben ändern.

We never knew his unimaginable head,
wherein the eyeballs ripened. But
his torso glows still like a chandelier
in which his gaze, but forced back inwards,

maintains itself and shines. The thrusting rib
    cage
could otherwise not blind you, and in the gentle
    turning
of the hips a smile could not go
to the body's procreative center.

This stone were otherwise disfigured, cut short
under the shoulder's transparent plunge
and would not shimmer like a predator's mane;

and would not burst from all its confines, like
a shooting star: for there is no spot there
which does not see you. You must change your
    life.

(1.557)

Another "opening" poem, this one was written
in the early summer of 1908 and placed at the
head of the second part of the *New Poems,*
where it faces the volume's dedicatory note: "A
mon grand ami Auguste Rodin." It is one of
Rilke's great achievements, showing how easily the idea of the "thing-poem" (*Dinggedicht*)
can be misunderstood. Certainly the texture
and monumental presence of Rodin's sculpture were revelations to the poet; certainly,
too, one of Rilke's great themes is the need
to intervene in space. But this need is never
separable from the explicitly poetic intervention in time; Rilke's experiences of painting
and sculpture in his Paris years enable him
to transform the metaphysical, self-conscious
space of the poem written in 1900 into a
concreteness that blends the multiple textures
of earth, air, light, and stone. But he is also
emancipated from the need to "include" the
theme of poetry in his meditation; this poem
knows that it is language, that language is the
vehicle of time, and that its relationship to
sculpture can never be one of mere transcription or evocation.

The text weaves four distinct temporal dimensions together, not in smoothly artificial
harmony but in a series of linguistic tension

points, "interventions" through which the
sculpture is reborn into a complexity of time
zones. There is first the time of the absent
head, the lost past of the original statue, the
art-historical dimension that might logically
open backward into the conditions of the archaic past. However, Rilke instantly reverses
direction: in its absence the statue's gaze is all
the more "present"; the god Apollo himself
lives with increasing, not diminishing intensity as time passes and, as it were, adheres to
the torso, compressing ever more history into the same space. The third dimension is the
movement of the observer's eye down and
around the torso: in contradiction to the traditional aesthetic tenet (Gotthold Lessing's) that
a visual work of art is perceived as a whole in
a single instant, what we witness is a dramatic,
conflict-ridden passage over the torso's surface, a movement in time equivalent to the time
of the poem itself. Finally there is the time of the
observer's own life: this life is "absent" in an
exactly complementary sense to the absence of
the statue's head. As that absent gaze insists on
its presence in every detail of the surface, so the
private life of the spectator, hiding initially in
the anonymous "we" of the first line, is drawn
into an ever more intense involvement with the
gaze—until the "we" of the opening becomes
the "you" of the conclusion.

In the poem "Entering" the notion of "ripening" is strategically assigned to the (poetic)
world, but here the ripening is withdrawn
entirely from the known world; it names the
entrance of the god himself into the absent,
indeed unimaginable eyes of the statue. But
the very flexibility with which Rilke uses this
organic term underlines its importance to
him. It connotes the poem's ambition to become a "thing," to intervene and take root in
space. And whereas in 1900 Rilke still favored
a soft-edged, gradual movement in his lines—
that is, an "imitation" of ripening—here the
text moves immediately to a rhythm of growth
that imitates nothing and belongs entirely to
the movement of language itself. The poem is a
sonnet and exploits all the conventions of the

sonnet to convey both the charged weaving of time dimensions and the torso's powerful presence in space. Enjambment, the spilling-over from one line to the next, is central to its rhythm. Thus the "growing" of the god's gaze in the first quatrain is embodied in the way lines turn in on themselves, expanding yet not released. Release comes in the transition from the first to the second quatrain: one has to "see" the sonnet structure in order to feel the powerful self-assertion of the verbs that open line five. This instant establishment of the god's gaze is in turn essential to the strong image of "to blind." Given the detached, narrative tone of the poem's opening, there is an almost shocking impact in the arrival of this verb in line six: it is a spurt of "growth" in which the observer is suddenly enmeshed. Skillfully Rilke immediately mitigates the shock, shifting the verbs to the more controlled subjunctive mood and, as the poem nears its center, stressing the statue's gentleness. The god's gaze becomes a smile; and a balance between god and observer is struck as the lines use a smooth enjambment to achieve a "turning" motion, a graceful arabesque both in the torso's texture and in the observer's move around it.

The opening of the tercets seems to maintain the balance, as the observer meditates on the aesthetic necessity of god's gaze: without it the torso would be incomplete, shapeless. But as the observer enters into the realm of the gaze, the momentum of growth resumes, the relation of enjambment between the lines begins to express acceleration. The image of the predator suggests the observer's loss of freedom. And at the opening of the final tercet the enjambment literally evokes the "bursting" of the statue's power out into the observer's life: the god's gaze has always been expressed as light; now it is a shooting star, invoking absolute otherness and strangeness (Rilke's constant attributes for stars), that nevertheless overwhelms the observer with its immediacy. The balance at the poem's center has shifted drastically: the spectator may have "produced" the gaze initially, by unlocking

the history compressed within the torso, but by the end of the poem he is wholly within its power. The time zones of both archaic history and aesthetic contemplation have culminated in radical "un-freedom," which is what makes the final phrase so remarkable. The poem's "growth" has proceeded through drastic shifts and decelerations to this most extreme of all shifts. From "un-freedom" the command issues forth: regain control, act in freedom. These words are spoken in all four time zones at once: the archaic world of authentic gods addresses the modernity of alienated lives; the god's gaze, compressed within the torso, is finally interpreted by the observer—the oracle speaks, and the visual culminates in the verbal; the act of contemplating the torso and simultaneously producing the poem has resulted not in harmony but in the intervention of the statue/poem in life itself; and finally, the words can be heard as accusatory, a charge from god to observer that instantly translates to the reader. As the god's gaze has overwhelmed the observer, so the simultaneously emerging poem overwhelms the reader. But this overwhelming sets all merely aesthetic force relations radically into reverse: the transparency of the stone (line ten) is a historical and social transparency, a linkage of eras rendering museums and even statues irrelevant to the ethical imperatives that produced oracular language—and hence poetry. These last words express the single "truth" that oracles of all times and places have spoken. The aesthetic is the only "godlike" authority we have left: without the ethical charge, which is both premise and purpose of all creation, we will have nothing. And in Rilke's later poems, he repeatedly explores this moment of fusion between the interrogative and the imperative, the aesthetic and the ethical, the temporal and the spatial. This exploration is particularly characteristic of the *Sonnets to Orpheus*, for example of sonnet 18 of part two:

Tänzerin: O du Verlegung
alles Vergehens in Gang: wie brachtest du's dar.

*Und der Wirbel am Schluss, dieser Baum aus
   Bewegung,*
*nahm er nicht ganz in Besitz das erschwungene
   Jahr?*

*Blühte nicht, dass ihn dein Schwingen von vorhin
   umschwärme,*
plötzlich sein Wipfel von Stille? Und über ihr,
*war sie nicht Sonne, war sie nicht Sommer, die
   Wärme,*
diese unzählige Wärme aus dir?

Aber er trug auch, er trug, dein Baum der Ekstase.
Sind sie nicht seine ruhigen Früchte: der Krug,
reifend gestreift, und die gereiftere Vase?

*Und in den Bildern: ist nicht die Zeichnung
   geblieben,*
die deiner Braue dunkler Zug
*rasch an die Wandung der eigenen Wendung
   geschrieben?*

Dancer: you transmutation
of all fading into motion: how you shaped that
   role.
And the whirl at the end, this tree of movement,
did it not wholly contain the year's vibrating
   essence?

Did not its tip blossom, responding to the
   embrace of your emotion,
suddenly into stillness? And above that,
was it not sun, was it not summer, the warmth,
this infinite warmth from in you?

But it sustained also, it sustained, your tree of
   ecstasy.
Are they not its peaceful fruits: the jug,
ripened by a passing touch, and the more fully
   ripened vase?

And in the pictures: has not the drawing
   remained,
which the dark movement of your brow
quickly sketched on the screen of your own
   turning?

(1.763)

Written between 17 and 19 February 1922, this sonnet distills, in the figure of the dancer, the essence of Rilke's great interlocking themes of "intervention" in time and in space. In certain respects Rilke draws closer to Mallarmé's pro-cedures in his final period (perhaps his contact with Mallarmé's disciple Valéry had an effect); the elaboration of internal verbal relationships, particularly assonances, makes the movement of certain lines almost impossible to translate; and there is an increasing exploration of what is superficially absent from empirical reality, such as the dancer's "tree of movement." Yet to notice the proximity to Mallarmé is again to notice the gulf that divides the two poets. There is never a significant shift, in Rilke, toward a hermetic poetics, a sealing of language into its own realm of pure play. Rilke never breaks faith with the ethical imperative of Apollo's torso. The evocations in this sonnet of the dance's traces, the residues of time in space, are designed not to draw us into an esoteric realm but, on the contrary, to expand our understanding of all those realities that we limit by abstract description: movement, time, action, feeling. The Apollo poem transforms our very definition of the word "statue" by embedding the torso in the dynamic "absence" of the god's eyes; an object in space becomes shot through with multiple tracks of time. In the Orpheus sonnet the poetic movement is in a sense the reverse: the poem is willed to "become" its theme, the dance. Far from being structured as a magisterial continuity from archaic past to the opening into a possible future, the present text whirls in self-limiting circles, stopping, restarting, adding new images instead of drawing out the old, compressing time into space. A comparison of the uses of enjambment is instructive: in the Apollo sonnet almost every one is structurally important, accelerating or decelerating the virtuosic forward movement; here, by contrast, no enjambment is stressed—each line seems to be relished in its self-containment as emblem of the dancer's quicksilver turns.

With Apollo a statue becomes movement; with Orpheus movement becomes a statue. The equation is oversimple, but it points to the unity of Rilke's concerns. The imperative to "change your life" resounds in the Orpheus sonnets also; but instead of a response to history's infinitely deep surface, the injunction here is to insist on the movement, to imagine the myriad changes in the world activated by the dance's fulfilled movement. Here it is pertinent to quote again Eliot's lines: "Except for the point, the still point, / There would be no dance, and there is only the dance." We cited this previously in relation to music; here, of course, the relevance is explicit: Rilke's sonnet revolves around a "still point," an invisible rhythmic center that represents a "limit" embraced as intensely as the transcending structures of music. The center is the generative power of the dance itself, a fruitfulness inaccessible to the dancer's personality. But Rilke did have a specific dancer in mind, the dedicatee of the sonnets, Wera Ouckama Knoop, who had died three years before at the age of nineteen. Thus even as he moves toward the limit at her center, that ancient rhythm that she cannot "know," his goal is to re-invent very specific, simple things in the room around her, to give back to her in homage what her movement has brought into existence. Here Rilke diverges from Eliot (as, in a different sense, we have seen him diverge from Mallarmé): unlike Eliot, Rilke never ultimately celebrates abstraction; his embrace of limits is always part of a rhythm of return—return to concreteness, to individuality that, however focused and refined, can and must live in multiple relationships.

The poem begins by naming the center, qualifying it only with the abstractions that give dance its possibility of meaning. In a sense we are immediately at the Rilkean "limit"; in his late poetry Rilke is impatient to launch the return. The word "fading" is an inadequate rendering of *Vergehen,* which links aimless motion to the process of mortality itself: the dancer does not resist mortality, but she intervenes in the process, accelerating it into a single dance. As we have noted in relation to motifs like stars and angels, Rilke's imagining of the dance is deeply and affirmatively traditional. Into these brief abstractions he compresses all the meanings elaborated in

past dance images—and begins his quest for a language of specificity. It is no accident that he begins at the end of the girl's performance. He seeks to locate the secret of the dance after it has ended, to add another time dimension (that of memory), and to strive for precision in defining exactly how the dancer alters space. Thus the imagery at the end of the first quatrain, the "tree" of movement that distills the essence of the year just past, is still much too general for Rilke. His poem merely describes the pattern of the dance it wishes to consummate.

The second quatrain is made of two very differently phrased questions. The first is elaborate, circling around the dancer's final pirouette, focusing on the "tip" of the tree, presumably her upstretched hands. Perhaps it is there, at the point of symbolic aspiration and conclusion, that the medium of language can find legitimacy, can respond to some need expressed within the perfection of the dance. The second question is probing, still general but less closed than the question in line four, as if sensing the possibility of precision in the energy given off by the dancer's hands. The repetition of "was it not" is tentative; the repetition of "sustained" is suddenly confident. At the center of the poem occurs the shift from question to answer. Rilke finds his answer within the traditional imagery of the dancer as living tree. The dancer's arms are "branches"; they give off energy flows during the dance as well as at the conclusion, imparting to the jug and vase the "organic" legitimacy that a casual eye can see in them but cannot explain. We are here at the center of Rilke's mature concerns: at stake in this dance is the poetic argument of the Ninth Elegy, the notion that the essence of human language is to speak the meaning already compressed into the simplicity of domestic objects, as well as the accumulated cultural meaning ready to be unlocked in Apollo's torso. This sonnet is thus acting out, or rather dancing, the metaphysic of the Elegies: the wholeness and the rightness of simple objects derives from the graceful movements that have occurred and, in their repetition, accumulated in the space around such objects.

Rilke's "answers" continue, of course, to be phrased as questions. One is reminded of the use of the subjunctive mood in the Apollo sonnet: the more intensely concrete the imagery, the more important it is to the poet to retain links to the reader's world, to co-opt the reader's doubts. Here the shift to the present perfect tense at the start of the last tercet has a double effect: the question, with the key thematic term "remained," becomes more assertive, but simultaneously the dance itself, which until now seems to have just finished, moves a little further into the past. This is explicitly a remembered moment, and it is through memory that Rilke reaches most boldly into the specificity of the dancer's intervention in space. To express his meaning he has to impel the language toward a new kind of abstraction, one whose assonances ("Wandung . . . Wendung") cannot be translated. This is non-generalizable abstraction, however, language of a given moment coined to re-imagine that moment only—and its residue in space. The dancer's movements generate energy and simultaneously harness that energy into enduring "drawings," sketches bound to a particular place (like frescoes in that respect) but living in the observer's mind (where art must always live). The poem remains a sequence of questions.

Unlike Eliot, Rilke never stabilized his aesthetic "theory." Theorizing is a continuous element of his poetry, but it is always only a moment, an embrace of limits from which a return must follow. Rilke's truth is always that of the Apollo sonnet: "You must change your life"—in the direction of fuller life. In the sonnet to Orpheus that fuller life is in the dance—which is thus far too important to be passively admired. Awareness of fullness means new responsibility, responsibility to remember it and to draw it back into daily usefulness. For Rilke, the man of words, the responsibility is to enlarge continuously the scope of what poetry can do along these lines. And as his words reach their readers, they become equipment for the task of focused life-change that is everyone's.

This double journey through Rilke's development (through the "workshop" and then through the landmark collections) has, I hope, demonstrated the extraordinary unity between his work on perfecting poetic language and the work of living itself. His "ideas" leap from the text to the reader's mind precisely because they are not exactly ideas at all, but intuitions of meaning produced by a particular moment and guaranteed by the integrity with which that moment has been transformed. Their flexible, even chameleonlike quality derives from their rootedness in the language of experience. They may sound abstract, but often the abstraction (like the famous "world-inner-space") is simultaneous with the event of thinking and hence itself a kind of temporal object. And far from confining Rilke's impact, this essentially experimental quality renders it inescapable. For he so expanded the expressivity of the German language that his verbal nuances, even his personal agenda, reverberate through it whenever ordinary people try to say what they feel. His influence on poets is clear: it is obviously at work in the linguistic inventiveness of, say, Paul Celan and Karl Krolow, two major German poets of the years immediately following World War II; and one can equally say that the sober, militant style of such conscious opponents of Rilke as Brecht, Hans Magnus Enzensberger, and Erich Fried is dialectically involved with what it opposes. (Dominant figures of the 1960's, Enzensberger and Fried frequently defined political poetry through polemics against Rilkean "aestheticism.") But the "perfection" of Rilke's achievement implies even more than that. His is a language forged in a crisis of historical change, both reflecting and resisting that change. And the continued convulsions of German history since his death seem to have reinforced the staying power of his language.

Some of his formulations may seem over-aesthetic, even precious (an analogy with Virginia Woolf suggests itself); but when people struggle to express their sense of crisis, of alienation, or of secret continuities, Rilke's words are simply *there,* a repertoire to be shaken out, adapted, perhaps angrily rejected, but never discarded.

The objection is sometimes heard that Rilke hasn't really earned this status, that his linguistic virtuosity masks an excessive self-absorption, even an insincerity. If the goal of Rilke's quest is always ultimately poetic language, so the argument runs, then he has trapped his readers in a vicious circle: they cannot challenge the quality of his expressed "meaning" since that meaning is ultimately inseparable from its linguistic vehicle, the poem. In my survey of Rilke's development I hope to have shown how profoundly the poet was aware of this problem, how his mature achievement is conditioned by ruthless self-criticism, indeed for much of the decade 1912–1922 by a sense of almost certain failure. In fact I think the "vicious" circle can be restated as a "hermeneutic" circle: Rilke's achievement is certified by the fact that his texts continually demand interpretation, provoking readers spontaneously to make his language their own. The works' authenticity is demonstrated by the public's continued involvement with them: there are many poetic virtuosi (one thinks of Rilke's near contemporary Stefan George) whose texts do not reverberate in this manner.

But there is one further argument to be made. During Rilke's Paris years, when his poetic project found its fulfillment in the *New Poems* (which include the magisterial "Archaic Torso of Apollo"), he produced simultaneously an extraordinary prose text, *The Notebooks of Malte Laurids Brigge,* completed in January 1910. This book is the dark shadow against which the sunlit *New Poems* are to be read. Rilke always saw it as autobiographical, therapeutic, to be read "against the grain" (it includes portions of his letters virtually unchanged). Although it is not "formless"—

much recent criticism has been devoted to its eccentric structural symmetries—it is an extremely loose text, seemingly always threatened by disintegration and silence. Since the *New Poems'* chief characteristics are integration and eloquence, a comprehensive "rescue" of images both immediate and inherited, it is easy to see why *Malte* needed to be written. Its language is very like that of the poems, but it speaks of impossibilities, the impossibility of holding the intensity of experience in language, the impossibility of asserting any value against the indifferent weight of time. Above all it speaks of horror: the disease and decay lurking just beneath the surfaces so lovingly celebrated in the *New Poems.*

Although *Malte* is usually called a novel, it challenges the very notion of the traditional novel: a central theme is that it is no longer possible to "tell stories." And in challenging formal conventions the book has played a significant role in this century's fictional developments, linking Rilke to the contemporary innovations of Hofmannsthal, Musil, and James Joyce. The prose of *Malte* is stylistically homogeneous, but the forms inhabited by its voice include the extremes of intimate reflection, documentary impression, theological speculation, and a romanticized yet esoteric historical fable.

Malte is a young Dane living in Paris. Obsessed by a childhood he feels he has not digested, he is equally vulnerable to the repressed horror of ordinary lives in the metropolis, the ways in which death, now the modern world's only obscenity, erupts onto the surface of a life becoming ever more deathly as it strives to refuse death's truth. Malte's "notes" oscillate between exploration of the negativities, which seem to consume his own existence, and memories, ostensibly from childhood, where definable values existed. A key figure here is his grandfather, who died a "great death," a ritual performance from which no one in the community could escape. In his grandfather's time, too, stories could be told, sequences of authentic experience. And in a memory from his childhood, his Aunt Abelone crystallizes some of these stories—stories of women, of medieval nuns, and also of Goethe's friend Bettina von Arnim, whose love transcended its object and hence could fill the world with its intensity instead of being consumed. But these fullnesses of death, love, and storytelling are not simply played off nostalgically against present decay. The shifting, skeptical quality of Malte's writing is such that the closer he comes to a stabilized truth, the more it seems to dissolve into doubt and into a new quest into the penumbra of the past.

Judith Ryan has called the narrative mode "hypothetical," based on the refusal of even the smallest certainty. And it is in this dissolving of its own true-false antithesis that the text gains its authenticity. Malte's quest for his own life must remain unfulfilled: the novel ends with a version of the story of the prodigal son that refuses an ending, refuses the pretence of love and community. But precisely in Malte's lack of "own-ness" lies the strength of his perceptions: Malte's experience is vicarious; he tells stories that he *cannot* know to be true, stories of his fellow-sufferers within the inauthentic. His project turns out to be a rescue operation complementary to that of the *New Poems.* Where the poems rescue the achieved moments of civilization as well as the quiet simplicities that are being lost to technology, Malte rescues all that has failed in the past and the present, the "living" that hardly deserves the name.

To give a sense of the text I quote excerpts from a fairly long early section set in Paris:

It is good to say it out loud: "Nothing has happened." Again: "Nothing has happened." Does it help? . . .

I have always been on the move. God knows in how many cities, sections of cities, cemeteries, bridges, and alleyways. Somewhere I saw a man pushing a vegetable cart. He cried, "Chou-fleur, Chou-fleur," the "fleur" with a strangely opaque "eu" sound. Beside him walked an angular, ugly woman, who jabbed him from time to time. And whenever she jabbed him, he cried out. Sometimes he cried out of his own accord, but then it turned out to have been pointless, and right away he had to cry out again, because a house that might buy had been reached. Have I already said that he was blind? No? Well, he was blind. He was blind and cried out. I'm falsifying when I say that, I'm leaving out the cart he was pushing, I'm acting as if I hadn't noticed that his cry was about vegetables. But is that essential? And even if it were essential, isn't it a question of what the whole thing meant to me? I saw an old man who was blind and cried out. I saw that. Saw it.

. . . You could see the inside [of demolished houses]. On the various stories you could see internal walls to which the hangings still clung, here and there a fragment of wall or ceiling. Next to these walls there persisted, along the whole outside wall, a dirty-white space, and through this there crawled, in revolting, serpentlike, softly absorbing patterns, the open, rusted duct of the toilet pipe. . . . The resistant life of these rooms refused to be stamped out. It was still there, hanging on to the remaining nails, standing on the remains of the floors, barely a hand's width, creeping into the attachments of the corners, where one could still speak of an interior. You could see that it inhabited the color which it had slowly, year in, year out, transformed: blue into moldy green, green into grey, and yellow into an old, worn out, decaying white. . . .

For a while yet I can note all that down and tell of it. But there will come a day when my hand will be far from me, and when I order it to write, it will write words which I don't mean. The day of a different interpretation will dawn, and no word will stay attached to the next, and all meaning will dissolve like clouds and pour down like water.

(4.748, 749–750, 756)

Just as Rilke's project of rescue is discernible in *Malte,* so too we can speak of the structure of limits. But instead of the limits that control the human imagination, toward which the poetry thrusts and which it strives to inhabit, Malte explores the limit at the very beginning of consciousness, the ability to connect one thing with another, on which poetry depends. Beneath that limit lies the threat to all language, hence to consciousness itself—a world where all old connections are corroded, to be replaced by a kind of prehistorical, inhuman causality. This is Malte's world. In all the quoted descriptive passages we see his drive to record and connect the sequences of this quasi-life ignored by everyone. But the very process of translating the inarticulate into language forces him to look at what he's doing, to ask why and to realize that he has no answer. Anticipating Beckett he can only reiterate: "Saw it." Significantly, the most elegant, coherent imagery—that of clouds and rain—is generated by the moment when all connections are to be lost forever.

For Malte one absence leads to another: from the vestigial life of the blind man he can only move to the disgusting, meaningless traces of past human living in the demolished, gaping interiors. In this world the very thought of presence and fullness is suspect, with its apparent ignoring of time's absolute corrosive power. And this desolate world is the ultimate ground of Rilke's poetic achievement. His celebration of moments of joy, of the wonders of imagining long past, of the incredible toughness of the human spirit (the same spirit that won't let go of rusty nails)—all this celebration is conditioned by the fear, indeed the certainty of loss. And in the world of Malte, our world, such loss knows no possibility of rescue: the movement from half-life into death is without ritual, barely noticeable. To have produced a language of celebration that never denies the radical darkness of this knowledge: this is Rilke's lifework and usable legacy.

Selected Bibliography

EDITIONS

INDIVIDUAL WORKS

Leben und Lieder: Bilder und Tagebuchblätter. Strassburg and Leipzig, 1894.

Larenopfer. Prague, 1896.

Wegwarten: Lieder, dem Volke geschenkt. Prague, 1896.

Traumgekrönt. Leipzig, 1897.

Advent. Leipzig, 1898.

Am Leben hin: Novellen und Skizzen. Stuttgart, 1898.

Ohne Gegenwart: Drama in zwei Akten. Berlin, 1898.

Mir zur Feier: Gedichte. Berlin, 1899.

Zwei Prager Geschichten. Stuttgart, 1899.

Vom lieben Gott und Anderes: An Grosse für Kinder erzählt. Berlin and Leipzig, 1900. Second (1904) and subsequent editions are entitled *Geschichten vom lieben Gott.*

Das tägliche Leben: Drama in zwei Akten. Munich, 1902.

Die Letzten. Geschichten. Berlin, 1902.

Das Buch der Bilder. Berlin, 1902; 2d, much-expanded edition, 1906.

Worpswede: Fritz Mackensen, Otto Modersohn, Fritz Overbeck, Hans am Ende, Heinrich Vogeler. Bielfeld and Leipzig, 1903.

Auguste Rodin. Berlin, 1903.

Das Stundenbuch, enthaltend die drei Bücher: Vom mönchischen Leben, Von der Pilgerschaft, Von der Armuth und vom Tode. Leipzig, 1905.

Die Weise von Liebe und Tod des Cornets Christoph Rilke. Berlin, 1906.

Neue Gedichte. Leipzig, 1907–1908. Published in two parts.

Requiem. Leipzig, 1909.

Die Aufzeichnungen des Malte Laurids Brigge. Leipzig, 1910.

Das Marien-Leben. Leipzig, 1913.

Erste Gedichte. Leipzig, 1913.

Die weisse Fürstin: Eine Szene am Meer. Berlin and Steglitz, 1920.

Puppen: Mit Zeichnungen von Lotte Pritzel. Munich, 1921.

Duineser Elegien. Leipzig, 1923.

Die Sonette an Orpheus: Geschrieben als ein Grabmal für Wera Ouckama Knoop. Leipzig, 1923.

Vergers suivi des Quatrains Valaisans. Paris, 1926.

Ewald Tragy: Erzählung. Munich, 1929.

Späte Gedichte. Leipzig, 1934.

Aus dem Nachlass des Grafen C. W.: Ein Gedichtkreis. Wiesbaden, 1950.

COLLECTED WORKS

Gesammelte Werke. 6 vols. Leipzig, 1927. Volume 6 contains Rilke's translations ("Übertragungen"), of which the following are the most important: *Elizabeth Barrett-Brownings Sonette aus dem Portugiesischen* (1908), *Maurice de Guérin: Der Kentauer* (1911), *Portugiesische Briefe: Die Briefe der Marianna Alcoforado* (1913), *André Gide: Die Rückkehr des verlorenen Sohnes* (1914), *Die vierundzwanzig Sonette der Louise Labé, Lyoneserin, 1555* (1918), *Michelangelo-Übertragungen* (1913–1921), *Paul Valéry: Gedichte* (1925).

Sämtliche Werke. 6 vols. Edited by Ernst Zinn. Wiesbaden, 1955–1966. The standard critical edition, fully annotated.

Übertragungen. Edited by Ernst Zinn and Karin Weis. Frankfurt, 1975.

CORRESPONDENCE AND DIARIES

Briefe. Edited by Karl Altheim in cooperation with Ruth Sieber-Rilke. 2 vols. Leipzig, 1950. This selection has remained standard, being reissued in a single volume in 1980. However, many complete correspondences have appeared subsequently.

Briefe an Auguste Rodin. Leipzig, 1928.

Briefe an eine Freundin [Claire Goll-Studer], *1918–1924.* Edited by Richard von Mises. Aurora, N.Y., 1944.

Briefe an eine junge Frau [Lisa Heise]. Leipzig, 1930.

Briefe an einen jungen Dichter [Franz Xaver Kappus]. Leipzig, 1929.

Briefe an Nanny Wunderly-Volkart. 2 vols. Edited by Niklaus Bigler and Rätus Luck. Frankfurt, 1977.

Briefe an seinen Verleger [Anton Kippenberg], *1906–1926.* 2 vols. Wiesbaden, 1949.

Briefe und Tagebücher aus der Frühzeit, 1899–1902. Leipzig, 1933.

Briefwechsel [Hugo von Hofmannsthal]. Edited by Rudolf Hirsch and Ingeborg Schnack. Frankfurt, 1978.

Briefwechsel in Gedichten mit Erika Mitterer. Wiesbaden, 1950.

Briefwechsel mit Helene von Nostitz. Edited by Oswalt von Nostitz. Frankfurt, 1976.

Briefwechsel mit Inga Junghanns. Edited by Wolfgang Herwig. Wiesbaden, 1959.

Briefwechsel mit Katharina Kippenberg. Edited by Bettina von Bouchard. Wiesbaden, 1954.

Briefwechsel mit Lou Andreas-Salomé. Edited by Ernst Pfeiffer. Zurich, 1952.

Briefwechsel mit Marie von Thurn und Taxis. Edited by Ernst Zinn. Zurich, 1951.

Die Briefe an Gräfin Margot Sizzo, 1921–1926. Wiesbaden, 1950.

Gesammelte Briefe. 6 vols. Edited by Ruth Sieber-Rilke and Carl Sieber. Leipzig, 1936–1939.

Lettres à Merline [Baladine Klossowska], *1919–1922.* Paris, 1950.

Lettres à une amie vénétienne [Mimi Romanelli]. Verona, 1941.

R. M. Rilke—André Gide Correspondance, 1909–1926. Edited by Renée Lang. Paris, 1952.

So lass ich mich zu träumen geben: Briefe an Magda von Hattingberg. Gmunden, Bad Ischl, 1949.

Über Gott: Zwei Briefe. Leipzig, 1933.

TRANSLATIONS

Since the question of Rilke's reception in the English-speaking world is inherently interesting, the listing of early and current translations is extensive, and is given in chronological order. Many early translations, particularly those by Leishman, MacIntyre, and Norton, are still widely available in paperback editions.

Poems. Translated by Jessie Lemont. New York, 1918.

Auguste Rodin, Part I. Translated by Jessie Lemont and Hans Trausil. New York, 1919.

The Life of the Virgin Mary. Translated by R. G. L. Barrett. Würzburg, 1921.

Ten Poems. Translated by B. J. Morse. Trieste, 1926.

Two Duino Elegies. Translated by B. J. Morse. Trieste, 1926.

The Story of the Love and Death of Cornet Christopher Rilke. Translated by B. J. Morse. Osnabrück, 1927.

The Notebook of Malte Laurids Brigge. Translated by John Linton. London, 1930.

The Journal of My Other Self. New York, 1930.

Elegies from the Castle of Duino. Translated by Victoria and Edward Sackville-West. London, 1931.

Stories of God. Translated by Nora Purtscher-Wydenbruck and M. D. Herter Norton. London and New York, 1932.

Letters to a Young Poet. Translated by M. D. Herter Norton. New York, 1934.

Poems. Translated by J. B. Leishman. London, 1935.

Sonnets to Orpheus. Translated by J. B. Leishman. London, 1936.

Later Poems. Translated by J. B. Leishman. London, 1938.

Translations from the Poetry of Rainer Maria Rilke. Translated by M. D. Herter Norton. New York, 1938.

Duino Elegies. Translated by J. B. Leishman and Stephen Spender. London, 1939.

Fifty Selected Poems. Translated by C. F. MacIntyre. Berkeley, Calif., 1940.

Poems from the Book of Hours: Das Stundenbuch. Translated by Babette Deutsch. Norfolk, Conn., 1941.

Primal Sound and Other Prose Pieces. Translated by C. A. Niemeyer. Cummington, Mass., 1943.

Sonnets to Orpheus and Duino Elegies. Translated by Jessie Lemont. New York, 1945.

Letters of Rainer Maria Rilke 1892–1910. Translated by Jane Bannard Greene and M. D. Herter Norton. New York, 1945.

Letters of Rainer Maria Rilke 1911–1926. Translated by Jane Greene and M. D. Herter Norton. New York, 1948.

The Notebooks of Malte Laurids Brigge. Translated by M. D. Herter Norton. New York, 1949.

From the Remains of Count C. W. Translated by J. B. Leishman. London, 1952.

Letters of Rainer Maria Rilke and Princess Marie von Thurn und Taxis. Translated by Nora Wydenbruck. Norfolk, Conn., 1958.

New Poems. Translated by J. B. Leishman. New York, 1964.

Duinesian Elegies. Translated by Elaine E. Boney. Chapel Hill, N.C., 1975.

Rilke on Love and Other Difficulties. Translated by John Mood. New York, 1975.

Duino Elegies and Sonnets to Orpheus. Translated by A. Poulin. Boston, 1977.

The Roses and the Windows. French poems, translated by A. Poulin. Port Townsend, Wash., 1978.

Nine Plays. Translated by Klaus Phillips and John Locke. New York, 1979.

Selected Poems. Translated by Robert Bly. New York, 1981.

Poems 1912–1926. Translated by Michael Hamburger. Redding Ridge, Conn., 1981.

Selected Poetry of Rainer Maria Rilke. Translated by Stephen Mitchell. New York, 1982.

The Lay of the Love and Death of Cornet Christoph Rilke. Translated by Stephen Mitchell. San Francisco, 1983.

Sonnets to Orpheus. Translated by Kenneth Pitchford. Harrison, N.Y., 1983.

The Notebooks of Malte Laurids Brigge. Translated by Stephen Mitchell. New York, 1983.

Prose and Poetry. Edited by Egon Schwartz. New York, 1984.

The Book of Pictures. Translated by Stephen Mitchell. New York, 1984.

Rilke: Between Roots. Translated by Rika Lesser. Princeton, N.J., 1986.

New Poems. 2 vols. Translated by Edward Snow. Berkeley, Calif., 1984, 1987.

Sonnets to Orpheus. Translated by David Young. Middletown, Conn., 1987.

BIOGRAPHICAL AND CRITICAL STUDIES

Allemann, Beda. *Zeit und Figur beim späten Rilke.* Pfullingen, West Germany, 1961.

————. "Rilke und Mallarmé: Entwicklung einer Grundfrage der symbolistischen Poetik." In *Rilke in neuer Sicht,* edited by Käte Hamburger. Stuttgart, 1971.

Andreas-Salomé, Lou. *Rainer Maria Rilke.* Translated by A. Von der Lippe. Redding Ridge, Conn., 1984. (German original published 1929.)

Baron, Frank, Ernst S. Dick, and Warren R. Maurer, eds. *Rilke: The Alchemy of Alienation.* Lawrence, Kans., 1980. An important recent collection of articles in English. Contributors include Hans Egon Holthusen, Stephen Spender, Lev Kopelev, Walter H. Sokel, Andras Sandor, and Erich Simenauer.

Butler, Eliza M. *Rilke.* Cambridge, England, 1941.

Demetz, Peter. *René Rilkes Prager Jahre.* Düsseldorf, 1953.

Guardini, Romano. *Rilke's "Duino Elegies": An Interpretation.* Chicago, 1961.

Hamburger, Käte, ed. *Rilke in neuer Sicht.* Stuttgart, 1971. This important collection includes articles by Eudo C. Mason, Beda Allemann, and Jacob Steiner, and Käte Hamburger's own seminal study, "Die phänomenologische Struktur der Dichtung Rilkes."

Heller, Erich. "Rilke and Nietzsche." In *The Disinherited Mind.* Cambridge, England, 1952.

Hendry, J. F. *The Sacred Threshold: A Life of Rainer Maria Rilke.* Manchester, England, 1983.

Holthusen, Hans Egon. *Rainer Marie Rilke: A Study of His Later Poetry*. New Haven, Conn., 1952.

Jayne, Richard. *The Symbolism of Space and Motion in the Works of Rainer Maria Rilke*. Frankfurt, 1972.

Leppmann, Wolfgang. *Rilke: A Life*. New York, 1984.

Liebnitz, Jennifer, and John E. Holmes. *Rilke and the Visual Arts*. Lawrence, Kans., 1982.

Mason, Eudo C. *Rilke, Europe, and the English-Speaking World*. Cambridge, England, 1961.

Musil, Robert. *Rede zur Rilke-Feier in Berlin am 16. Januar 1927*. Berlin, 1927.

Ritzer, Walter. *Rainer Maria Rilke Bibliographie*. Vienna, 1951.

Rolleston, James. *Rilke in Transition: An Exploration of His Earliest Poetry*. New Haven, Conn., 1970.

Ryan, Judith. *Umschlag und Verwandlung: Poetische Struktur und Dichtungstheorie in Rainer Maria Rilkes Lyrik der mittleren Periode (1907–1914)*. Munich, 1972.

Salis, J. R. von. *Rilke: The Years in Switzerland*. Berkeley, Calif., 1964.

Sandor, Andras. "Rilke's and Walter Benjamin's Conceptions of Rescue and Liberation." In Baron et al. (see above).

Schnack, Ingeborg. *Rilke Leben und Werk im Bild*. Frankfurt, 1966.

Steiner, Jacob. *Rilkes Duineser Elegien*. 2d ed. Berne, 1969.

Webb, Karl E. *Rilke and Jugendstil*. Chapel Hill, N.C., 1978.

Wood, Frank. *Rilke: The Ring of Forms*. Minneapolis, 1958.

JAMES ROLLESTON

THE *ROMANCE OF THE ROSE*
AND
MEDIEVAL ALLEGORY

MEDIEVAL POETRY, PARTICULARLY that produced by learned poets for a sophisticated audience, is highly conventional. The poet customarily works in an established genre and with a traditional theme and incorporates the work of his predecessors to a degree that may well seem hard to understand today, when originality is generally accepted as one of the criteria of artistic achievement. Medieval poets, like medieval painters and architects, took the traditional nature of their work for granted. They were equipped with a vast repertory of conventional signs, motifs, and formal patterns, and in learning to control this material they learned as well that genuine and profound originality can take the form of a series of minute adjustments to a traditional model, adjustments that may be invisible to one who does not know the language, the symbolic code that artist and model possess in common. Where innovation occurs on a larger scale, it typically takes the form of a new ordering of traditional elements, the juxtaposition of themes and motifs from different works or traditions in such a way as to suggest interrelations and complexities that had been inexpressible previously.

The *Romance of the Rose* provides a classic example of this re-creative originality. Guillaume de Lorris, who began the poem, is by medieval standards a boldly innovative poet; he assures us that his subject matter is new, yet he achieves his originality through a synthesis of conventional material that had been brought to a high level of refinement by earlier poets working in a variety of separate forms. The extraordinary influence of his work, though due in great measure to its appropriation by Jean de Meun, is also due largely to Guillaume's success in providing a new conventional model to serve as a foil to the innovations of others.

The *Romance of the Rose* was by far the most popular and influential work of medieval French literature. Over two hundred manuscripts of the complete poem survive, an extraordinary number for any work of medieval vernacular literature. (*The Canterbury Tales* survives in eighty-three manuscripts, many of them fragmentary, and the *Decameron* in eighty-two.) It appeared in one printed edition after another well into the sixteenth century. Its effect on the formal and thematic character of the French poetry of succeeding centuries was profound, and it had an immense influence on other literatures. The two greatest poets of the later Middle Ages, Dante Alighieri and Geoffrey Chaucer, knew the poem intimately and used it extensively, and the names of both have been persistently associated with versions of the *Romance* in their own languages.

THE *ROMANCE OF THE ROSE* AND MEDIEVAL ALLEGORY

The *Romance,* set in the form of a dream and narrating the Dreamer-Lover's quest for possession of the beloved represented by the Rose of the poem's title, is the work of two very different poets. Concerning Guillaume de Lorris, whose name is assumed to refer to the village of Lorris near Orléans, we know only that he produced, evidently between 1225 and 1245, a poem of some 4,000 octosyllabic lines describing the Dreamer's initiation into the joys and pains of love and tracing his early unsuccessful attempts to gain access to his Rose. When Guillaume's poem breaks off, the Rose has been immured in the castle of Jealousy, and the Lover is seemingly on the point of succumbing to despair. The poem is assumed to be incomplete, but we cannot tell how much longer it would have become, nor even, despite a number of optimistic hints from the narrator, whether it would have ended with the union of Lover and Rose.

Even in its fragmentary state, Guillaume's poem seems to have enjoyed a considerable success, but it became world famous when taken up and "completed" by Jean de Meun. Also from the region of Orléans, Jean evidently spent much of his adult life, presumably as a teacher, in Paris, where he died in 1305. He produced a number of French translations of Latin writings, including surviving versions of Vegetius' treatise on warfare, Anicius Manlius Severinus Boethius' *Consolation of Philosophy*, and the famous letters of Pierre Abélard and Héloïse. Contemporary allusions, notably a reference to Charles of Anjou as "now king of Sicily," enable us to date his continuation tentatively between 1268 and 1285. To Guillaume's original 4,000 lines, Jean added nearly 18,000, expanding the Lover's private quest into an elaborate campaign conducted by the God of Love and involving a cast of characters whose natures and associations provide occasion for extended digressions on the mores of lay and ecclesiastical society, church politics, and the state of learning in Jean's day. Jean's narrative ends decisively with the Lover's awakening from his dream after a graphic account of his final sexual conquest of the Rose.

Though Jean's grafting of his own work onto that of Guillaume was a stroke of genius, and the meaning of the *Romance* is greatly enriched when the two authors are read in combination, Guillaume and Jean are of importance for later medieval poetry in two quite distinct ways. Guillaume's achievement was the creation of a new and extremely influential paradigm, a virtual archetype for the presentation of psychological experience. Jean's largely satirical extension, in which Guillaume's delicate, polysemous construct is exposed to a merciless onslaught of social and sexual realism, may be seen as a critique of Guillaume's model and a serious challenge to its implicit claim to have revealed a potentially spiritual significance in human love. Guillaume is the father of a tradition of "love visions," allegorical dramatizations of imaginative experience that attain their finest form in the early works of Chaucer; his rendering of the Lover's initiation informs Chaucer's masterpiece on the theme of love, the *Troilus and Criseyde,* and deeply affected Dante's treatment of certain major stages in his love of Beatrice. The work of Jean did a great deal to enlarge the satirical and didactic range of vernacular poetry, and it made possible such major experiments in comic realism as Geoffrey Chaucer's *Canterbury Tales* and ultimately the work of François Rabelais.

This essay, which is concerned with the *Romance* as allegory, concentrates mainly on the work of Guillaume. To consider his poem against the background of earlier medieval poetry is to observe a sudden and remarkable realization of ideas and poetic techniques that had previously been only tentatively explored. Not only does his work represent a striking new departure in the use of allegory as a vehicle for the dramatization of psychological themes, but it is the first major narrative poem in the vernacular tradition to take love as its central and sole theme. After Guillaume, and perhaps as much because of his work as that of any other poet, love becomes once and for all, in the words of Erich Auerbach, "a theme worthy of sublime style, indeed its principal theme," capable of inspiring a Dante.

The Narrator of Guillaume's poem opens by affirming the prophetic power of dreams, for his poem will recount a sweet dream of his own that corresponded in every detail with events in his subsequent life. Love bids him write: his romance will describe love's art and, he hopes, will find favor with one who is herself worthy to be called "Rose."

The dream is set in May, the "amorous season." The Dreamer-Narrator, a young man of fashion, wanders outside the city and comes upon a walled garden, decorated on the outside with portraits of personified qualities, female figures whose common trait seems to be their antipathy to youthful pleasure-seeking. Some of these—Hatred, Felony, Villainy (that is, boorish or lowborn conduct), Covetousness, and Avarice—have a broad social orientation. Others are related more pointedly to the courtly love world the Dreamer is about to enter. Envy lives for news of the shaming of noble persons and cannot bear to hear grace or beauty praised. Sorrow, disheveled and unconsolable by dance or song, suggests the sufferings of love: her pain and anger are a "martyrdom" that love will visit on the Dreamer himself.

The fullest portrait is that of Old Age. Her ugly and useless state is not spared, but there is pathos in details such as her hair, "white as if it were floured" *(florie)*, a wordplay that hints at a time past when the whiteness might have been that of a garland. The Narrator interrupts his description with a digression on time and death, and then returns in a more humane spirit to note the signs of wisdom and capability that still appear in her feeble state, and the heavy wraps that protect her from the cold.

Two final portraits, *Papelardie* ("Pope-Holy," or religious hypocrisy) and Poverty, make a pair. Both are lean and humble in appearance, but the contrast between Poverty, who can never hope for preferment in this world, and *Papelardie*, whose feigned austerity will never gain her admission to Paradise, is the contrast between secular and spiritual indigence. The pairing, like the series of portraits as a whole, suggests dimensions of human experience that the courtly world ignores, hints at its preoccupation with material splendor and mock-religious idealism, yet tactfully refrains from discrediting the courtly ideal by offering a positive alternative.

The beautiful lady Idleness admits the Dreamer to the garden, and her dazzling portrait is his introduction to the life within. She speaks the final word about the portraits on the wall: "they are neither charming nor graceful," she says, and this aesthetic judgment sets the tone for the Dreamer's initiation into courtly society. The garden was created and enclosed by Sir Delight, and nothing in its life is merely natural. No peasants tend it, and in it the songs of birds become "dances of love" that gradually evolve, as the Dreamer is drawn forward, into the harmony of actual musicians. The inhabitants of the garden first appear engaged in a dance. Sexuality itself is first prefigured aesthetically by maidens who seek to draw Sir Delight into the dance by the grace of their dancing with one another.

Drawn into the dance himself by Courtesy, the Dreamer becomes aware of other dancers and offers a new sequence of portraits of the attributes of the courtly life, to balance those inscribed on the outer wall. The God of Love is described wholly in terms of his clothing, a robe of flowers, "made by delicate loves," and a garland of roses with nightingales perpetually flying about it. His portrait is followed by a digressive account of the weapons borne by his attendant, Sweet Looks: two bows, one gnarled and black, the other slim, pliant, and gaily painted; five golden arrows, whose wounds represent the process of attraction by which one falls in love; and five iron arrows, which convey the effects of various forces hostile to the survival of love. No mention is made of clothing in the portrait of Beauty, who accompanies the God of Love in the dance, but the memory of her grace can still bring sweetness to the Dreamer's heart. Wealth exercises a different attraction. Her yellow hair is the only detail of her appearance we are given, but her robes and jewelry are described at length, with special emphasis on the protective and curative powers of certain precious stones. Where Beauty has a radiance of her own, Wealth is adorned by a carbuncle whose radiance illumines her face and everything around her. Largesse, whose generosity is at once a function of wealth and a gift of God, has given away the jewel that had closed her robe at the throat, but the loose collar only serves to set off the intrinsic brightness and purity of her body's beauty. The beauty of Franchise, the frankness, openness, and softheartedness that make a lady receptive to love, is less a matter of form than of attitude: in her eyes there is laughter, and her manner is amiable in every way. Her appeal is complemented by her robe, the style of which sets off her grace and charm, its whiteness "signifying" her sweet and open nature. Courtesy and Idleness are briefly dismissed, and the dance ends with another tentative reminder of the erotic orientation of the Dreamer's experience in the behavior of Youth, a child of twelve who exchanges kisses with her partner in mutual and guileless innocence.

The Dreamer now goes off alone through the garden. Curiously half aware that the God of Love is "stalking" him, he strays among endlessly varied trees and flowers and discovers, beneath a pine tree, a fountain with the inscription "Here died the fair Narcissus." In what follows it becomes difficult to tell the actual experience of the Dreamer from the Narrator's retrospective account of this experience. The Narrator tells the story of Narcissus and his fatal infatuation with his image in the pool and then describes the Dreamer's reaction to the inscription: an initial timidity followed by a sudden unexplained renewal of confidence that makes him approach the foun-

tain. After a moment of suspense as the fountain and its setting are described, we learn the properties of two crystals that the Dreamer sees at the bottom of the pool: in sunlight they become a mirror, and from any angle they reveal one half of the garden in all its rich detail. This account is followed by a sudden outburst against the "perilous mirror," which instills madness in its victims, and this in turn by a rueful reflection on the Narrator's own fate. Delightful though it was to gaze into this mirror, it was an unlucky day when he did so:

> Alas! how much have I sighed since then because of it! The mirror deceived me: had I known beforehand what its force and power were, I would never have drawn near. But now I am fallen into the trap that has caught and betrayed so many men.
>
> (1606–1612)

Seeing in the mirror a group of rosebushes set off by a hedge, the Dreamer at first feels "rage," an indiscriminate desire to approach and pluck a rose. Fearful of offending the lord of the garden, he reflects on the delicate and transitory beauty of roses and finally focuses his desire on a single perfect bud, which then and there becomes the beloved object of the quest that the remainder of the *Romance* describes. But thorns, briars, and nettles prevent his reaching out for it, and as he pauses, the God of Love draws his bow and launches the golden arrow of Beauty, which pierces his eye and lodges in his heart. The wound only quickens his desire for the Rose, and he drags himself forward as he is struck successively by the arrows of Simplicity, Courtesy, and Companionship, the growing effects of proximity to the object of his love, which urge him forward at the same time that they render him helpless. A final arrow, Fair Appearance, defines his condition more clearly, for it has the power of healing even as it wounds, quickening desire but at the same time rewarding it with the promise of continued contemplation of the beloved. In this suspended state he is seized and claimed as vassal by the God of Love, who approves his humble and courteous speech of formal submission and confirms it by locking up his heart with a golden key. The god then teaches the Lover (as we must now call him) his "commandments," the rules of behavior proper to lovers, emphasizing courtesy, humility, grooming, cheerfulness, and generosity. After imposing the "penance" of unceasing devotion to thoughts of love without repentance, he discourses on the pains to which love gives rise: an inability to endure the pain of separation from the beloved, balanced by an equally painful inability to speak and act in a forthright way when she is present; and sleepless nights and anxious days. Then he describes the remedies for these pains, beginning with a sort of homily on Hope, who endures indescribable pains in expectation of a reward a hundred times greater. Sweet Thought, Sweet Speech, and Sweet Sight—the Lover's memory of the beloved, occasions for speaking of her or hearing her praised, and opportunities to meet her—are Hope's companions.

The God of Love vanishes at this point and the Lover experiences a moment of uneasiness at his abandonment. He is baffled as to how to proceed until Fair Welcome, son of Courtesy, appears, to guide him through the hedge and bring him almost to the point of being able to touch the Rose. Fair Welcome might be defined as a lady's receptiveness to polite attentions, and his encouragement draws the Lover into revealing that he desires ultimately to possess the Rose. At this, Fair Welcome recoils in horror and Danger leaps out of hiding to drive the Lover away, shamed and intimidated.

The quality called Danger is, as I will suggest further on, more complex than is usually allowed, but he is most obviously a lady's active resistance to sexual advances, a *vilain* who meets any hint of "villainy" in the Lover's conduct on its own terms. He is motivated by three qualities that define the atmosphere of mistrust created by any threat to the lady's chastity: Evil Tongue, Fear, and above all Shame, born of Reason and conceived by the mere glance of Misdeed. Shame has Fear, Evil Tongue, and Jealousy at her command, for though she herself is "simple and honest," virtuous instincts, her power is reinforced by an aura of undefined guilt and a fear of malicious gossip that menaces all courtly dalliance. It is this complex of forces that accounts for the sudden indignation of Fair Welcome and the vivid appearance of Danger, whose fiery eyes, coarse appearance, and stout club come close to wholly demoralizing the Lover:

> Then Fair Welcome took flight, and I was left, utterly abashed, ashamed, and defeated; and I repented that I had ever spoken my mind. I recalled my folly, and saw that my body had been given up to misery, pain, and martyrdom.
>
> (2935–2941)

Words like "repented" and "folly" suggest a dawning moral perspective, and they help to account for the sudden appearance at this point of "the lady of the High Vantage," Reason, who descends from a tower and comes straightforward to meet the Lover. We have heard nothing of Reason until now, and the vivid description of her angelic beauty and paradisal origin is as surprising as the earlier apparition of Idleness. She seeks to draw the Lover away from love, explaining how the menace of Danger is reinforced by Shame and her attendants, and dwelling repeatedly on the folly that is the real condition of all lovers. But the Lover replies, briefly and with a certain dignity, that he is powerless to withdraw his feelings from love's dominion, and in any case he would rather die than be so disloyal. Reason withdraws.

In urging the value of Sweet Speech, the God of Love had advised the Lover to find a trustworthy Friend. This the Lover now does, and on the Friend's advice he seeks Danger's pardon for his earlier presumption. Pity and Franchise persuade Danger to allow a renewal of contact with Fair Welcome, and the Lover now seeks leave to kiss the Rose (who has matured and grown more beautiful in his absence). When his appeal is reinforced by the appearance of Venus, brightly arrayed and bearing her torch, Fair Welcome relents and grants him his first and only reward.

Evil Tongue has been spying on the Lover and immediately awakens Jealousy, who rushes to accuse Fair Welcome of treachery. Shame apologizes for Fair Welcome and defends his good intentions, but Shame is then persuaded by Fear to reawaken Danger, who once again banishes the Lover. Jealousy now constructs around the rose garden a moated castle that is described at length. Danger becomes chief warden; Evil Tongue walks the battlements singing defamatory songs about the lecherous propensities of women; and Fair Welcome is imprisoned in the tower. The Lover reflects on the high cost in suffering of the joys of love and on the workings of Fortune in general; he concludes Guillaume's portion of the *Romance* with an appeal to the absent Fair Welcome to remain true to him, breaking off on a note of near despair.

Though the *Romance* must have struck its audience as new in a number of often startling ways, the most obvious and the most striking of Guillaume's innovations is his having made erotic love, of a kind traditionally the province of lyric poets, into the central theme of a narrative poem that exhibits many of the characteristics of chivalric romance. Johan Huizinga (in *The Waning of the Middle Ages*) calls attention to the social significance of this adjustment: the enshrinement of love as a central and all-embracing concern constitutes the highest expression of an "aspiration to the life beautiful" that expresses itself also in ceremonial and in the code of chivalry. But the significance of such poetry is not merely social: the Lover who serves as first-person narrator of Guillaume's poem offers a number of hints that his story contains a deeper significance, a "buried truth," that underlies and transcends the erotic and social concerns of

the surface narrative, more or less as the Grail theme enlarges the meaning of Arthurian romance. In making this suggestion, Guillaume is not only thinking of the precedent provided by such romances but also invoking a tradition of learned Latin poetry concerned with the place of human love in the order of things, natural and divine, and an emerging vernacular tradition of religious poetry in which the settings and imagery of romance were used to express a religious truth that could be "discovered" by the systematic application of the sort of interpretative technique ordinarily associated with the doctrinal meaning of biblical texts. Though Guillaume's poetry can never be reduced systematically to the expression of a doctrinal message, and its underlying meaning remains tantalizing and elusive, the suggestion is strong that this new poetry centered around the experience of love is to be understood as possessing an autonomy and a potential symbolic value that comparison with religious symbolic systems may help to illumine, though its meaning will always remain peculiarly its own.

It is in the light of these implicit claims that we should read the couplet that announces both the name of Guillaume's poem and its central theme:

> ce est li *Romanz de la Rose,*
> ou l'art d'Amors est tote enclose.
> (37–38)

The "art of love" is a notion that had an almost boundless suggestiveness for medieval courtly poets. Love as an art, art in the service of love, love as a stimulus to art, and art as a stimulus to love—the variety and ambiguity of the couplings of these ideas do not begin to suggest themselves if we make only the too obvious association with a too obvious reading of Ovid's *Art of Love* and gloss art as "technique" and love as "seduction." For the poets of the medieval courtly tradition and the conventional lover who is the subject of their songs, art and love are in collaboration from the first stirrings of erotic or aesthetic feeling. Art at this primary level is a means of articulation, a vocabulary and a set of images in terms of which we first realize imaginatively the condition of loving. Love and the impulse to trace its movements exercise a constant pressure on the poet-lover, and it is extremely difficult to distinguish the aspect in which this condition can be viewed as a spontaneous response to an external phenomenon from the aspect in which it is one's own imaginative response to the promptings of convention. Hence the concern of so many medieval poets with the relationship of love and poetry; the virtual identification, in many courtly lyrics, of the impulse to love with the impulse to sing; the preoccupation of lovers in romances with the foreshadowings of their joys and sorrows in the stories of other lovers.

In the great flowering of lyric love poetry in the twelfth century, the central achievement is what critics have agreed to call the "grand chant courtois" (very roughly, "high courtly song"), the Provençal *canso* perfected by Bernart de Ventadour and its French counterpart and offspring, the *chanson* of the trouvères. In its characteristic form, the "grand chant" is the delineation of a paradox, in that it enshrines an ideal, a love of the highest refinement, a *fin amor,* within a charmed circle from which the poet-lover is himself excluded. His emotion defines and in a sense comprehends this circle, but the articulation of emotion is at the same time explicitly a suspension of the movement toward possession or union, the ostensible object of his yearning. His state is one of vacillation between the poles of joy and pain, emotions that engage him in paradoxical ways. So good is the beloved that the pains she causes are pleasurable; so great is she that to consider a response to her salutation arouses doubt and fear. The poet's antithetical emotions tend to define themselves as complementary, delineating a state of balance within which he can preserve a continuity of feeling, now aspiring to the ecstasy of contemplation, now therapeutically ministering to pain by a

revivifying consideration of its source in the love he feels. Thus, the troubadour Bernart de Ventadour:

> Tan n'aten bon' esperansa
> ves que pauc m'aonda,
> qu'atressi sui en balansa
> cum la naus en l'onda;
> ("Tant ai mo cor plede
> joya," 37–40)

I have placed such good hope in her who grants me so little relief that I am equipoised like a boat on the sea.

The synthesizing tendency of his emotions becomes a complement to the act of poetic creation, defining a lyric world from which everything but the poet's love is excluded. Again Bernart:

> Although I lose, due to men's flattery, the assurance of the joys of *fin amor,* yet if one were to offer me the universe in exchange I would still prefer this joy by which I am beguiled.
> ("Ja mos chantars no m'er onors," 45–48)

The "grand chant courtois" has its source, as Paul Zumthor has suggested, in "the archetypal heart," and to its role as pure expression any referable action or emotion bears only an accidental relation. The series *chanter-chant-chanson,* the impulse, process, and completion of the act of song, defines the "procession" or emanation of a pure emotion whose only meaning is itself. But in an age fascinated by its rediscovery of the possibilities of literary form, the very ingenuity and ambiguity of the "grand chant," its profession of erotic desire and its emulation of spiritual unity, inevitably provoked analysis and led to new uses of its paradigms. The ways in which the conventions of courtly lyric were appropriated vary widely, but it is important to see that the "grand chant courtois," in providing the imaginative nucleus for the delineation of larger patterns of experience, has a fundamental role in the development of serious poetry in the vernacular.

It is Guillaume's achievement to have given a new narrative form to the experience of love "enclosed" in the courtly lyric, a form that enabled him to analyze in terms of a sequential psychological process the stages through which the emotional complex of *fin amor* manifests itself and the alternatives it presents to a lover or reader imaginatively attuned to its nuances. Guillaume does full justice to the private, privileged aspect of the love world portrayed in his poem, the sense in which it is the highly artificial creation of a social elite. He makes us aware at the same time of the archetypal character of the experience to which his Lover is introduced, the aspect in which his experience brings him into contact not only with nature and the forces that sustain and renew the order of nature but with an intuition of something divine. The Lover is in a state of constant suspension, always in danger of lapsing into a mere narcissistic infatuation with his own condition as lover, but at the same time dimly aware of a powerful symbolism that seems to invite both Lover and reader to recognize a deeper significance in his experience.

There is also, of course, a sense in which the *Romance* is about the art of love on the practical level, the indoctrination of a lover whose pursuit of his lady in accordance with a prescribed strategy constitutes the plot of the poem. We see the Lover instructed in the rules of love, warned about the pains to which love can lead, and advised as to the remedies for these pains. We think inevitably of Ovid, whose "manuals" on these subjects were widely read and even used as school texts in the medieval period. The courtly poets of the twelfth and thirteenth centuries were fascinated by Ovid's doctrinal approach to love, but because they rarely exhibit anything like Ovid's posture of deliberately outrageous cynicism about the women and institutions of Rome, it has been assumed all too readily that they were unappreciative of it. It has become the rule to cite C. S. Lewis' astute but misleading suggestion (in *The Allegory of Love*) that

the sort of courtly formulation of the rules of love that Guillaume presents can be explained as "Ovid misunderstood," a taking seriously of what Ovid himself had intended as wholly ironic. But it is always dangerous to see medieval poetry as naive in this way. There is plenty of evidence that courtly poets were capable of taking a skeptical view of the lover's code. Certainly the famous *Art of Courtly Love* (*ca.* 1185) of Andreas Capellanus, which contains such rules as "the lover regularly turns pale in the presence of his beloved" and which apologizes for the lecherous tendency of clerics on the grounds of their abundance of food and free time, is cheerfully responsive to Ovid's irony. And certainly Guillaume, whose Lover is far too easily awed and unnerved to be capable of the slightest degree of detachment or cynicism, seems to have seen as clearly as Ovid himself that the notion of an art of love is finally a contradiction in terms.

Indeed it is possible to see the frequent haplessness of Guillaume's Lover and the insistent bravado of Ovid's as complementary, two responses to the same hard facts about love. For there is a sense in which Ovid's elaborate irony is neither cynical nor satirical, but simply a preferred substitute for mere pathos—a deliberate, even a principled and humane response to the difficult realities of human passion, a taunt aimed not at the respectable matrons of imperial Rome but at the destructive forces that make emotional balance and happiness in love so difficult to attain. Sophistication and self-assertion are in this view a willed alternative to the recognition that restless frustration and mistrust are all too often the results of the pursuit of love, as well as to the darker realities implied by the myths of Pasiphae and Ariadne. Guillaume, too, as we will see, raises serious questions about his Lover's psychological adequacy to the challenges of the "new rage" without measure or restraint that seizes him before the fountain of Narcissus. His treatment of passion is much more subdued and tentative than Ovid's, and he has obviously refined away some of the coarser aspects of Ovid's pragmatism to give an outwardly more moral emphasis to his "teachings on love." But we may safely assume that in defining his own theme as "the whole art of love," he fully appreciated the paradoxical nature of Ovid's claim to have reduced love to a body of doctrine.

But of course Guillaume's Lover is by no means simply the product of an Ovidian indoctrination and its consequences. Although he values the practical advice of his Friend and the God of Love and does his best to apply their strategies, he preserves an essential innocence that has no equivalent in the carefully restricted world of Ovid's *Art of Love* (though there is much of it in the *Metamorphoses,* which Guillaume also knew). His pursuit of his Rose is inspired at the primary level by an imaginative vision of love that, though only dimly glimpsed, is highly idealistic, one that his more pragmatic goal of sexual conquest never destroys. Indeed, the visionary and sexual impulses seem at certain moments to be in conflict and to imply distinct, alternative ways of resolving his quest.

A curious passage, one of several in which Guillaume invites us to consider the conclusion toward which his uncompleted poem is tending, serves to set these two aspects of the Lover's view of love in relation. Preparing to narrate the final major episode of his poem as we have it, in which Jealousy, at the instigation of Shame and Fear, and in retaliation for the Lover's having succeeded in kissing the Rose, builds a castle and imprisons the Rose within it, Guillaume's Lover-Narrator offers the following reflections:

> At this point it is proper that I tell you how I became embroiled with Shame, who then caused me great grief; and how a wall was erected, and that rich and strong castle which Love later took by force. I wish to tell the whole story through, and it wearies me not at all to write it, and so I think it may bring pleasure to that beautiful one—may God keep her!—who will be better

able than any other to reward me, when it shall please her to do so.

> (3481–3492)

It is hard to see the God of Love's taking of the castle of Jealousy as anything but a prophecy of the successful conclusion of the Lover's sexual campaign, and this, we may reasonably assume, would have been as likely a resolution as any for Guillaume's narrative. But the reward that the Lover hopes to receive at the hands of the "beautiful one" whom he invokes in the final lines of this passage is referred to a less definite future, apparently outside the confines of the poem's narrative time, as though the consummation of the Lover's quest (for the "truth" of which the Narrator vouches at several points) were only the foreshadowing of something more real and more significant. A similar disjunction between the poem's quest and the Narrator's relation to a "she" outside the text is suggested by the dedication of the poem that follows the declaration of its title and theme:

> Now may God grant that she for whom I have undertaken it receive it in good spirit. For she is of such value, and so worthy to be loved, that she herself should be called "Rose."

> (40–44)

In relation to this vaguely adumbrated female figure ("she" in the lines just quoted; "that beautiful one" in the passage quoted above), the Rose is seemingly relegated to a symbolic status, reduced here to an honorific title for the lady, as in the later passage its attainment within the poem seems only to prefigure her *guerredon,* or reward.

Deferring for the moment any further speculation about the seeming gap in the Lover's experience, we may note that the juxtaposition of the quest, which is the poem's literal theme, with hints of the ongoing pursuit of a more ideal object is in conformity with the tendency of the poem to develop hints latent in the most serious of earlier courtly poetry.

The extreme conventionality of the terms in which the Lover's emotional condition is realized lends his experience the character of ritual, a passage through preordained stages that can be viewed half cynically in terms of Ovidian indoctrination or, alternatively, as a rite of initiation with intimations of a symbolic rebirth. To the extent that the Lover's imaginative participation in this ritual is dominated by the sophistication of the God of Love, who provokes his will to possess the Rose, he is led forward more or less obsessively; his vision does no more than isolate the desirable aspect of the object of his love and draw his other conscious faculties into the service of his desire to possess it. But on another, more primary level, the Lover's imagination responds to an aesthetic impulse and tends, in its storing up of the images of sensory experience, to enhance that aspect of their attractiveness which approximates the ideal. To the extent that he remains free of the contaminating influence of physical desire, his imagination dwells on this aspect of what it loves in an increasingly reflective way. The ritual of his experience tends to become the cultivation of an ideal that is sensed as present in or symbolized by the Rose.

When this tendency toward idealization in a courtly lover's experience reaches full development, as in Dante's *Vita nuova* (*New Life*) or Chaucer's *Troilus,* love becomes almost a mystical experience. The lover moves toward a level of apprehension so intense as to suspend the activity of the will. At this level he seems to intuit in what he loves something that makes him yearn beyond possession, perhaps toward an ideal of which the beloved appears as a foreshadowing, or perhaps, nostalgically, toward a purity or a state of emotional integration that humanity has lost, and for which the ideal of union with the beloved serves him, consciously or not, as a substitute. The experience of Guillaume's Lover is never developed on this ideal plane, but from the moment of his entry into the garden there are strong suggestions that his initiation into the world of courtly love is a version, spiritually attenuated and disguised by an overlay of sophisticated eroticism, of the dream of Paradise, the desire to return to a sacred source. His experience at the fountain of Narcissus, which translates his vague imaginative yearnings into sexual terms, is potentially the means of contact with the origins of life at a deeper level of uncontaminated vitality and beauty. The Lover's failure to realize these implications of his experience is the imaginative equivalent to the abortive result of his sexual quest as Guillaume's fragmentary poem presents it, and the two failures together point up something fundamentally contradictory, a self-betraying tendency in the cult of highly refined love, or *fin amor,* that shapes the Lover's awareness of the experience of love. Though Guillaume never underscores these implications of his narrative, the Lover's quest reveals a psychological inadequacy to the challenge of love that has deep moral and spiritual implications.

To consider these larger implications of Guillaume's love theme is to raise the question of the possible bases for his claim that his poem contains a deeper significance. Here it becomes necessary to take up in some detail the question of "allegory," a word that was current in several senses in Guillaume's day but that, so far as we can tell, would not have occurred to him to apply to his own poem. In using this term, as in speaking of the "courtly" view of love, we are using a modern critical notion to locate an element common to works and genres that medieval readers and writers may well have seen as quite different from one another. But just as the *Romance* can fairly claim to contain "all the art of love" as French courtly society understood it, so its synthesis of romance, lyric, and Latin and vernacular vision poetry incorporates a broad range of those devices that we call allegorical. Thus the poem offers an unusually representative illustration of the term.

It is common to locate the origins of allegory in the attempt of Greek philosophers from the early classical period forward to systematize the mass of traditional myths concerning the gods and to make them yield a coherent body of doctrine. It is evident, however, that a certain amount of such systematic thinking had already influenced the roles played by the gods in Homer and Hesiod. Thus from the earliest times, it is probably impossible to establish a clear and consistent distinction between allegory as a method of interpretation and allegory as a mode of fiction. Certainly they are inseparable in the work of Plato, who, while strongly critical of the use of allegory to explain away barbaric or absurd behavior in the traditional gods, employs myths of his own to express his intuitive sense of the nature of reality.

Study of the work of Jean de Meun shows that interpretative allegorization of classical myth remained an important determinant of the uses to which myth was put in postclassical poetry; but by the beginning of the Christian era certain distinctions could already be made. Interpretative allegory assumed an increasingly separate role, as in the work of Philo of Alexandria and other Jewish scholars, who found the essence of Greek philosophical and religious thought expressed in the Bible, and later when the work of Christian allegorists was concerned with showing that the truths of Christianity were adumbrated in the events and imagery of the Old Testament. "Creative" allegory, usually in the form of personified abstractions, is a recurrent element in the imagery of Augustan and later Roman literature and emerges full-blown in such a work as the tale of Cupid and Psyche inserted into the *Metamorphoses* of Lucius Apuleius. In the medieval period, though certain types of historical and hagiographical writing were designed to be read typologically as part of the continuum of sacred history, the allegorical interpretation that centered on the Bible and the imaginative literature that incorporated traditional resources of allegorical fiction can be regarded as separate traditions.

A brief look at literary allegory in general may be useful before examining the background and major elements of Guillaume's allegory. In broadest terms, allegory is that literary mode in which the terms and structures that at one level give a work its formal coherence serve at the same time to represent another dimension of meaning (*allos* means "other"), an idea or process (moral, religious, historical, psychological) that it analyzes into terms which are then represented by images and "characters" in the structure or plot of a work of literature. In Northrop Frye's words, "a writer is being allegorical whenever it is clear that he is saying 'by this I also (*allos*) mean that.'" But of course some allegories are clearer than others. At the simplest level there is a mechanical correspondence between the characters in a simple fiction and the situation they are intended to illustrate: Desire discovers itself suspended between Hope and Fear; Pluck and Enterprise defeat Slackness and Diffidence in the course of a journey toward Accomplishment. From such simple structures we move through works such as the *Romance*, Spenser's *Faerie Queene*, and Bunyan's *Pilgrim's Progress*—more elaborate and harder to read systematically since the truths they dramatize are more complex—to a *Samson Agonistes* or *Divine Comedy*, where the personae and literal action are so engaging in realistic terms as to distract most modern readers from the recognition of their intricate relation to a preexistent body of doctrine that is the poem's underlying significance. A work may make occasional use of allegory, as when, in Henry James's *The Portrait of a Lady*, Isabel Archer imagines her marriage as a walled enclosure, without light or air, overlooked from a small high window by the "beautiful mind" of Gilbert Osmond, rather as Reason and the God of Love seem always to have the Lover of the *Romance* in view. Or, as in Dante's *Divine Comedy*, with its three worlds where figures from among Dante's own acquaintances and from recent Italian history coexist with famous saints and sinners and exemplary figures from ancient history and legend, a single fiction may bear a coherent relation to several kinds or levels of allegorical meaning.

Finally, as the allegories I have mentioned suggest, certain narrative patterns lend themselves particularly well to allegorical use. The two that seem most basic and that are most clearly suggested by the plot of the *Romance* are the battle and the journey, "symbolic actions" that, even in works with no preconceived allegorical purpose, tend to invite allegorical interpretation.

To introduce a term like "symbolic action" (I have borrowed it from Angus Fletcher's excellent theoretical study *Allegory: The Theory of a Symbolic Mode*) and to allow allegorical fiction a life as organic and outwardly convincing as that of any other fictional mode is to make assumptions that criticism has not always taken for granted. It has been common even in recent times to deprecate allegory as the most artificial form of imaginative writing. Its fictions are seen as necessarily contrived in such a way as to conform to a preconceived system of ideas that severely limits their thematic range, the interrelations of their characters, and the plausibility of their settings and imagery. To a great extent this is due to a historical accident: notions about allegory tend to reflect the enduring influence of two great critics, Goethe and Coleridge, both of whom viewed allegory as an inferior kind of imaginative exercise and contrasted it with a truer and more poetic kind that they called "symbolic." A symbol is something real in which we sense, consciously or unconsciously, the presence of something more—a larger, more complex, or more significant reality. Symbolic perception is spontaneous and intuitive, a natural process by contrast with the "mechanical" activity of allegorizing, which involves a deliberate and more or less systematic correlation of imagery with the concept or process to be represented. For Goethe it is the difference between choosing particular images to represent general truths

in a merely exemplary way and seeing these truths actually expressed in particular things. For Coleridge the distinction between allegory and symbol is closely bound up with the distinction between "mechanic" form, predetermined and externally imposed, and "organic" form, which develops itself from within as the unique response to a genuine intuition. For both critics the best poetry is symbolic in character; its images have a direct, living connection with the reality they express, whereas there is inevitably something at once contrived and arbitrary about the imagery of allegory.

It is easy enough to see in such views the romantic tendency to exaggerate the role of imagination in artistic creation, to value ingenuous and "unmediated" vision while remaining highly suspicious of the contaminating effects associated with convention and deliberate artifice. But there has been a tendency to define the allegory of medieval poets in terms that have something of the same insidious effect, even in the work of critics who deeply appreciate the aims and capacities of allegory. C. S. Lewis, who has written the nearest thing we have to a history of medieval allegory, has offered his own version of the allegory-symbol formula. Symbolism, for Lewis, is "sacramental," an expression of the belief that the world we know by sense and reason is only the shadow or copy of an invisible, transcendent reality. Symbolism is "a mode of thought," whereas allegory is only "a mode of expression," restricted to talking about reality at one remove, in terms of "that which is confessedly less real, which is a fiction." (See Lewis' discussion in *The Allegory of Love* 2.1.)

As an illustration of the limits of allegory, Lewis cites a passage in Dante's highly allegorical history of his love for Beatrice during her life on earth, the *Vita nuova*. In this passage the poet discusses his personification of Love as a character in his allegory. He has spoken of Love throughout as "a thing in itself," a person capable of thought and motion, when in fact Love has no substantive reality but is only an "accident" to which human nature is susceptible. This, says Lewis, clearly indicates that medieval allegory is not mysterious, and also corrects the naive belief that Dante is groping romantically toward "some transcendental reality which forms of discursive thought cannot contain."

But the passage to which Lewis points occurs at a crucial moment in the *Vita nuova* and must be read in context. It follows close upon Dante's account in chapter 24 of a day on which he had seen Beatrice pass by, preceded by a beautiful lady named Giovanna, who was known because of her beauty as Primavera. As Dante watched the two ladies, Love seemed to speak in his heart, explaining to him that Giovanna-Primavera (*prima verra*, "she will come first") preceded Beatrice as her namesake, John, had been the precursor of Christ. The scene ends with Love's declaration that a subtle thinker would assign to Beatrice herself the name of Love.

This scene and the sonnet that summarizes it constitute the final appearance of Love personified in the *Vita nuova*. It is this figure whom Dante dismisses in chapter 25 as the mere personification of a passion, an accident occurring in a substance. But it is clear that the *Vita nuova* dismisses Love in this inferior sense only to make way for the more significant embodiment of Love in the figure of Beatrice herself. It seems equally clear that in the total scheme of the *Vita nuova* this shift marks an ascent from one level of meaning to another—what we might describe in Lewis' terms as an ascent from allegory to sacramentalism or symbolism—and that both levels are integrally part of a single allegorical construct.

The new aspect in which Beatrice now appears recalls Guillaume's foreshadowing of the conclusion of the *Romance*, in which the love mediated by the God of Love, even as its fulfillment is promised, seems to become a mere prelude to the reward that "the beautiful one" may bestow. In both cases a shift of perspective points to the possibility of an evolution, and potentially a total transformation, of the Lover's awareness of the meaning of what he sees. Evolution in this psychological sense is one of the most fundamental of allegorical themes, a natural complement to the basic narrative patterns of quest and conflict, and it provides us with a way of resolving the seeming dichotomy between mere allegorical device and genuine symbol, in the recognition that the allegorical (in this reductive sense) is always capable of evolving into the symbolic. The difference between the seeming arbitrariness of the one and the authenticity of the other, moreover, is not just the difference between artistic contrivance and genuine perception but also a matter of degree. It is as natural to be "seized by fear" as it is to feel oneself intuitively aware of the deeper significance of an object or situation; what begins as an encounter with Fear personified can evolve into something more complex or profound as the source of the feeling assumes larger meanings and evolves toward the status of a symbol.

Indeed, it is just this ability to discover the relationship between such deeper levels of intuition and ordinary consciousness that constitutes the distinguishing characteristic of the best medieval allegories. Their focus is on the differing degrees of intensity with which reality is perceived by an experiencing subject, and it is often this emphasis on the subjective that accounts for the seeming arbitrariness of allegorical devices. What renders them arbitrary is their contingency on the hero's imperfect awareness of the nature of his situation. Virtually all of the "characters" in such works first appear, and in that sense originate, as projections of the imagination of the central figure, and this is as true in a poem like the *Divine Comedy*, where the majority of the characters have distinct historical identities, as it is in the *Romance*, where all are personifications.

The frequently disjointed quality of the imagery and setting, the isolation of major elements, and the seeming disregard for perspective and continuity can be seen to have a consistent purpose when viewed as a mirror of the hero's subjective preoccupations. Like the "mechanical" interactions of allegorical characters, which frequently serve to express the involuntary or compulsive nature of the hero's response to them, the "machinery" of the allegorical landscape makes best sense when viewed in terms of its sequential impact on the imagination.

We can better appreciate the distinctive character of fully developed psychological allegory, and the role of Guillaume's *Romance* in bringing its expressive powers to their full realization, if we give some consideration to the major elements of which it is composed and the different strands of literary tradition that the *Romance* brings together. Probably the most basic and certainly the most extensively used of all allegorical devices is personification. Nearly all the characters in Guillaume's *Romance* are personified abstractions, whose behavior defines the main areas of the poem's world and action: the social ambience and the values associated with it (Idleness, Sir Delight, Largess, Courtesy); the Lover's psychology (Reason, Hope); and the various forces that help and hinder his approach to the Rose (Jealousy, Evil Tongue, the lady's Fair Welcome, Shame), as well as the God of Love himself and many aspects of the experience of love.

The personification of moral and religious qualities (Fides, Virtus, Concordia) was a growing tendency in Roman poetry from the Augustan period forward, but the great prototype for medieval personification allegory is the *Psychomachia,* or *Soul-Battle,* of Aurelius Clemens Prudentius. This Latin poem of the early fifth century describes a series of seven combats, interspersed with speeches of heroic defiance, between Faith and the other virtues on the one hand and Cult-of-the-Old-Gods, Discord, and the vices on the other. While the poem has great historical interest as a document of the Christian polemic against pagan

culture, what is most interesting for our purposes, and the source of its great influence on the literature and iconography of the virtues and vices, is the involvement of its personae in a sustained dramatic action. Unfortunately, hand-to-hand combat, though it conveys the moral significance of the battle in an often powerful way, is extremely limited as a metaphor for internal processes. When the eyes of the fallen Cult-of-the-Old-Gods burst from her head and Faith crushes them with her foot, we gain a vivid sense of the Christian detestation of pagan idolatry but no insight into the psychology of belief. There are, of course, characters who cannot take the offensive: the enemy of Patience, Wrath, must destroy herself; Humility rather unconvincingly dispatches Pride, but only after Hope has instilled in her the love of Glory.

There is an occasional use of evocative detail, as when Sobriety puts to flight the forces of Luxuria (that is, dissipation or excess), whose trappings anticipate in a tentative way the more elaborately depicted personifications of medieval allegory. Luxuria has fought, not with weapons of war, but with flowers, whose "delicate poison" causes the virtues to grow weak and lay down their arms. When she falls at last, Jest, Sauciness *(Petulantia),* Ostentation, Allurement, Pleasure, and fugitive Love flee the field, leaving it littered with cymbals, garlands, necklaces, and other jewelry for Sobriety and her forces to trample underfoot. And Prudentius anticipates one of the most effective devices in all of medieval allegory when he has Avarice, thwarted repeatedly by Reason in her attempts to corrupt the Christian priesthood, adopt the stratagem of disguising herself as Frugality, in which role she successfully saps the morale of the virtues until she is seized and destroyed by Good Works. But the very breadth of the social comment in these episodes is a reflection of the lack of psychological concentration that limits the value of the *Psychomachia* as a model for allegorists like Guillaume. To the extent that Prudentius' battles are related to one another, the link between them is typological; the virtues never resolve themselves into a single psyche. His poem is not the story of a particular human experience, but a poetic tract on the virtues and vices in general.

The distinction is important, for the personification that by Guillaume's day had become an established technique of French vernacular poetry, though it owes much to the tradition of the *Psychomachia*, was largely the product of a desire to dramatize psychological processes. The development of narrative romance is the great achievement of northern French poets of the twelfth century, as the development of the "grand chant courtois" is the great achievement of the poets of the Languedoc region; and a striking feature of this new genre, from early adaptations of classical epic to the full-blown Arthurian *roman* of Chrétien de Troyes, is a new concern with the psychology of love. The troubadour poets, of course, subject the emotion of *fin amor* to a profound and subtle analysis, and they often describe their feelings in terms of the interaction of such quasi-personified qualities as Joy, Valor, and tyrannous Love, but the presence of these qualities is limited to their being named (and, in the case of Love, sometimes addressed directly). They never speak, and their actions are described only at second hand. Their existence, moreover, is confined to the closed world of the poem, and we can never translate the emotional crises they represent into social terms. The love with which the romances deal, by contrast, is set in a definite relation to the external world, and the psychological conflicts to which it gives rise involve concrete alternatives.

Here, as so often in medieval poetry, the influence of Ovid is extremely important. I have already mentioned the deep interest of the poets of the period in the codified view of love presented in Ovid's amatory poems. The other side of the coin is their fascination with his treatment of traditional stories of love in the *Heroides* and *Metamorphoses*, particularly the attempts of his romantic heroines to articulate and rationalize the sorrows and contradictions of love. The *Heroides*, a series of imaginary letters attributed to famous women of classical legend, offers a procession of abandoned wives and lovers whose soliloquies express indignation, helplessness, or despair in the face of the betrayal of their love; but it is the innocent victims of incipient (and often unnatural) passion in the *Metamorphoses*, youthful figures like Iphys, Myrrha, Canace, and Byblis, who seem to have had the greatest influence. As these figures are shown discovering, analyzing, and inveighing against their mysterious impulses, so twelfth-century romance abounds in soliloquies on the phenomenon of desire, the mystery of its origin, and the tension it creates between reason and passion. Among the earliest French vernacular adaptations of classical material are short narrative poems on Narcissus, Philomela, and Pyramus. The *Eneas* departs readily from the plot of Vergil's *Aeneid* to incorporate a lengthy account of the growth of love between Eneas and Lavine—who in Vergil's poem do not even meet—in which each of the lovers is made to "discover" the effects of love in a long soliloquy and to debate inwardly the pros and cons of responding to its urgings. The speeches are far more diffuse than Ovid's, and they lack the terrible urgency with which Scylla contemplates the betrayal of her father and his city or Byblis and Myrrha seek to control their incestuous desires, but they have a dramatic character of their own that expresses itself as a tendency of the lovers' self-recriminations to take the form of dialogue. Thus in the *Eneas*, Lavine reacts to seeing Eneas for the first time in a soliloquy:

> "Alas, sorrowful girl, what is he doing? Is he going away? In faith, yes, and he did not speak to me; he took no care for that. I do not think that he will come back."
> "Wretched fool, what does it matter to you?"
> "It matters much, since he has killed me."
> "How?"
> "He is carrying off my heart."
> (*Eneas*, John A. Yunck trans., p. 221)

Such internal dialogue became an extremely popular device in romances of the later twelfth century, and there is a marked tendency to personify the voices that oppose one another as Love on the one hand and Knowledge or Reason on the other. These speaking figures are accompanied by an increasingly elaborate array of attendant powers, whose behavior is described in ways that came to sound strikingly like the action of the *Romance;* thus in *Amadas and Ydoine,* the heroine's inclination toward love first appears when "at the command of Love, Pity, Franchise, and Anxiety quickly forge a keen arrow and, joining their powers together, thrust it within her heart" (1102–1106). But such moments never flower into full-scale allegory. Even at its most elaborate, the psychological analysis that takes place in such passages never becomes wholly a part of the central action of the poem but remains a gloss, or supplement, to the narrative. It was left to Guillaume de Lorris to realize the full possibilities of personification allegory as a device capable of sustaining a narrative of its own, and in so doing to bring the abstractions of earlier poetry fully to life as actors in a coherent psychological drama.

The achievement of narrative coherence is not, of course, an end in itself, and what enables Guillaume's psychological allegory to develop its full meaning is its placement within a setting in which traditional motifs are treated with a new flexibility. The great prototype for the Garden of Delight in Guillaume's *Romance* is the *locus amoenus,* or natural paradise, of late-classical Latin epithalamia, the garden of love where Venus, Cupid, and their attendant powers dwell amid boundless fertility and beauty. The poem that Claudian, a near contemporary of Prudentius, wrote for the marriage of the emperor Honorius shows us a meadow surrounded by a hedge, which contains countless birds singing among its beautiful trees, two fountains from which flow the sweet and the bitter experiences of lovers, and such inhabitants as Li-cense, Pleasure, Fear, Boldness, and wanton Youth (who is said to have excluded Old Age from the place). It is easy to see here an anticipation of certain essential features of Guillaume's garden, and such tableaux are the basis for a host of medieval visions of the "court of love." But Guillaume's garden, though his account of it abounds in long passages of description and enumeration, is a far less static place than Claudian's; its details are presented to us as they present themselves to the Lover-Narrator, and this emphasis on the serial nature of his experience enhances the suggestion of an initiatory process. Here, too, Guillaume seems to reveal an appreciation of the achievements of twelfth-century narrative poetry, and we may see the wounds the Lover receives and the obstacles he encounters not simply as representing the pains of love but as endowing these pains with something of the significance of the hero's ordeal in Arthurian romance. The paradisal beauty and archetypal implications of the garden and the fountain within it are set in opposition to the menace implicit in Danger's monstrous ugliness and the ramparts and weaponry of the castle of Jealousy, as the court of Arthur and the civilizing power of the chivalric ideal tentatively embodied in it are set against the complexities of the surrounding and encroaching wilderness and the perpetual challenge of mysterious and malign forces. The overpowering love that dominates Guillaume's hero, wholly eliminating his own will by its authority and becoming the sole source of the courage and resolution with which he pursues his quest, recalls the love of Chrétien's Lancelot, who undergoes loneliness, humiliation, and intense suffering in his journey to redeem Guinevere from "the kingdom whence none escapes," to the point at which his mission of redemption and the love that inspires it are made to assume a quasi-religious significance. Like Chrétien's Yvain, Guillaume's Lover is introduced to love through his encounter with a magical fountain, which both renders him subject to the all-consuming rage of a love without sense or restraint and grants him his initial idyllic vision of the Rose. The contrast between the maddening and idyllic aspects of the experience recalls in several ways the sequence of events that follows Yvain's ritual pouring out of the water of the fountain at which his adventure begins, a violent storm followed by an idyllic spring morning. Though other things are in question as well, we may see foreshadowed in this juxtaposition of violence with ideal beauty the emotional extremes that Yvain will undergo in his love of Laudine, and the sharply opposed significances with which, in Guillaume's *Romance,* the quest of the Rose will be endowed.

It would plainly be wrong to read any of Chrétien's romances exclusively as an allegory or to isolate the religious or philosophical aspect of his treatment of love from his equally evident concern with its moral and social implications. It is clear, however, that one function of love in his romances is to suggest the larger spiritual possibilities implicit in the questing hero's experience. In the *Romance,* love and its significance are far more explicitly and exclusively the central concern, but the larger meaning to which Guillaume's narrative repeatedly calls attention remains curiously enigmatic, hermetically closed off from natural and social reality. And this is not just a consequence of the unfinished state of Guillaume's poem. From the beginning love is so dominant, so utterly the raison d'etre of Guillaume's allegorical world, that this world is necessarily self-referential in character. Guillaume's *Romance* is a romance of a new kind. The society that defines the hero's values is an idealized vision of the life of courtly leisure. The hero himself never acts decisively, never overcomes an obstacle; rather, his actions seem continually to generate new obstacles, leaving him progressively more "abashed" (*esbahi*) as the complexity of his situation mounts. Indeed, perhaps the most curious feature of the poem considered as romance is the anticlimactic nature of its action. Each new

advance leads to a more decisive setback, and there is little evidence to account for the Narrator's insistence on the happy issue of his dream. The Lover's failures on the practical level seem to debilitate as well the imaginative resources that sustain his idealism, and as the poem proceeds, the prevailing note is nostalgia for an impossible joy, something that in Guillaume's world, contaminated by eroticism and at the same time menaced by the social realities of Evil Tongue and Jealousy, can amount to no more than a desperate wish. In the absence of a clear resolution, we may well wonder if Guillaume has not simply found in his fountain of Narcissus a new and equally insidious form of its original power to deceive and betray.

Here we must face the problem posed by the poet's continual insistence on the truth and importance of his dream experience. Other poets had used dream settings for allegorical visions, and Raoul de Houdenc had anticipated Guillaume's prefatory claim in his *Songe d'Enfer (Dream of Hell),* asserting that although dreams are often false, they may also come true. But Raoul's poem is a parody of the other-world journey and uses the mechanics of the revelatory dream vision only for satirical purposes. Guillaume's claim is bolder, and some have seen his opening lines, which explicitly contrast his own dream *(songe)* with falsehood *(menconge),* as a deliberate answer to the author of another dream vision, the *Voie de Paradis (Road to Paradise),* who had dismissed his dream in the end as falsehood and concluded his poem with a commentary on the afterlife and Last Judgment. Guillaume, moreover, supports his claim to significance by citing the late-classical encyclopedist Ambrosius Theodosius Macrobius, whose commentary on the visionary conclusion to Cicero's treatise "On the Republic," the famous "Dream of Scipio," was the source par excellence for medieval dream theory. We can probably assume that he wants his dream to be read as a *somnium,* a type of dream that, according to Macrobius, "conceals with strange shapes and veils with ambiguity'' a truth that must then be brought to light by interpretation. But the *Romance* is not, like Cicero's "Dream," a statesman's vision of the moral significance of cosmic order, and it claims no higher theme than love. The conclusion the *Romance* promises is not, as for Scipio, a vision of the origins and destiny of the soul or of some higher truth for which the Rose is a mere figure, but only the capture by Love of the castle of Jealousy. And there are good reasons for questioning the likelihood even of this worldly resolution. How can we reconcile the evident limitations of the story with Guillaume's repeated insistence on the truth that underlies it?

The beginning of an answer must lie, I think, in the terms on which the Dreamer encounters Love. If the Garden of Delight is in one aspect no more than a naively idealized vision of the world of courtly society, it is nonetheless described in terms of Edenic beauty and seems to the Dreamer himself to be a terrestrial Paradise. The fountain of Narcissus, the point at which the Dreamer's innocently subjective vision is brought irrevocably under the influence of desire, is in one aspect his link with the natural order and mirrors what may be seen as the plenitude of natural life. And the Rose, private meaning aside, may be seen to express the essential purity of nature thus envisioned. The point is not in the precise significance of the terms of the Lover's vision, but in the intuition that somehow leads him to this pure perception. The perception is, of course, only momentary. No sooner has his desire become focused on his chosen Rose than he becomes aware of the encroaching presence of the civilized world represented by the God of Love and his "laws." His initial spontaneous responsiveness becomes contaminated by the blending of conventional idealism and practical advice in these commandments, and his desire becomes self-conscious and euphemistic in its expression. But beneath this overlay of sophistication, there

exists inherent in the scene a sense of mystery, a suggestion that the Lover has been brought into contact with a divine source, and so to the threshold of a vision capable of transforming the garden, the Rose, and the significance of the Lover's quest. I would suggest that this momentary confrontation with the archetypal purity that the garden vision evokes is to be understood as informing the confused erotic idealism that motivates the Dreamer, and that the same vague intuition is also the justification for the Narrator's seemingly excessive claims for his poem. Though the pure beauty of the garden is disguised and distorted by the worldly ceremonial of courtly love, it remains alive, and its constant presence accounts in large measure for the apparent irresolution, the tendency to reflection and awe, that hinders the Lover's practical progress. It is the seemingly divine quality of this beauty that accounts for those moments when the Narrator seems to focus on two quests at once, viewing the pursuit of the Rose against the background of a deeper search for union and reward that the terms of the courtly allegory are somehow inadequate to express.

In the end, Guillaume's Lover is left suspended between spiritual and sexual objectives that seem equally unobtainable. The dream of Paradise is at best a subliminal element in his awareness, and the object of his erotic quest seems to recede before him. It is as if the original dream had been replaced— after affording a momentary intuition of the possibility of fulfillment, transformation, revelation—by a dream of a very different kind, expressive not of hope and promise but of dislocation and unconscious fears.

A focal point for considering the final stages of the Lover's experience is his relationship to Danger, who appears as he is about to touch the Rose. From the first, Danger is *vilains*, uncourtly, and his coarse, menacing aspect is itself enough to demoralize the Lover. He is usually read as the Rose-lady's resistance to undue familiarity; thus, he says at one point that the Lover is free to love so long as he keeps his distance, and it is he whom Franchise and Pity must lull in order to enable the Lover to reapproach and actually kiss the Rose.

But it is hard to reconcile a reading of Danger as wholly an aspect of the lady with the emphasis placed on his grotesque *vilainie;* he is better viewed in more general terms, as a threat of which the Lover becomes aware at moments when his desire for physical contact with the lady expresses itself too openly. And when examined closely, he seems as much an aspect of the Lover's own psychology as of the lady's. He first appears just after the too impetuous Lover has been called *vilains* by Fair Welcome. I think it is largely the shock of this accusation that triggers the sudden appearance of *Dangier li vilains* and accounts for his devastating psychological effect on the Lover. If Danger manifests the lady's wariness or resistance, his effectiveness is surely due in part to his providing the Lover with a mirror in which his own latent sexual aggressiveness appears in a particularly "villainous" form, reminding him with daunting clarity that courtly blandishments alone will not prevail, that he must declare his desire in a more active way and take possession of the object of his love. A similarly reflexive response occurs when Danger appears a second time to punish the Lover for stealing a kiss. Danger's wrath is described in terms identical to those that express the Lover's chagrin at being separated from Fair Welcome a few lines later ("so deeply angered is my heart": 3724 and 3749), suggesting that the tension and anxiety that are Danger's ambience are to some extent, at least, of the Lover's own making. Interposed between the Lover and the Rose, Danger's role may be seen as a prohibitory antitype to the initiatory function of the fountain, his power to mirror the Lover's inner misgivings a new and distorted version of the threat of a narcissistic self-mirroring that the fountain had only seemed to present. Some critics have seen in Danger's role and appearance reminiscences of the grotesque guardian of a supernatural barrier common in Celtic legend, recalled also by "Caro" (Charon), the infernal ferryman of *Eneas*, and the grotesque churl who guards the fountain in Chrétien's *Yvain*.

Carrying this approach to the Lover's condition a little further, I think it is possible to see a similar collaboration between his inner insecurity and the nightmarish suddenness with which the castle of Jealousy arises before his eyes. In the wake of Danger's second attack, the Lover retreats into his own unhappy thoughts, longing for death and feeling himself already "cast into hell." The castle that immures the Rose is a projection of this sense of inner bondage, an image of the Lover's despair that constitutes the antithesis to the rose garden that had focused his initial innocent desire.

From this point the Lover gradually succumbs to a sense of helplessness that leaves him, at the moment when Guillaume's poem breaks off, entertaining thoughts of death. The uninterrupted progress of his demoralization has the same dreamlike consistency as his original advance toward the discovery of the Rose, and the opposition between these two movements suggests a fundamental lack of psychological integration. It may be that the delineation of this inner failure of the Lover, his inability to realize either the sexual or the spiritual possibilities of his situation, is the poem's "point," and given the incomplete state of Guillaume's poem, there is little more we can say. One anonymous continuator found it possible to bring the Lover's quest to a happy conclusion in a mere seventy-eight additional lines, but the somber tone of the final soliloquy suggests other possibilities. One can imagine a second interview with Reason or the intervention of some new figure of authority by whom the Lover might be led to a reconsideration of his experience, perhaps in the light of a symbolic reading of the terms of his initial encounter with the fountain and the Rose, perhaps through a reexamination of his moral and psychological fitness to experience *fin amor.*

The Lover's psychological condition is the starting point for Jean de Meun's continuation of the *Romance*, though the focus is exclusively on his fitness to pursue the Rose as a concretely sexual objective. From the point of view Jean provides, all the refinements and suggestive nuances of the courtly world come to seem mere immaturity and self-deception. The bulk of his continuation takes the form of a series of long discourses in which a variety of characters undertake to explain how life and love are carried on in the real world.

Jean begins by bringing the final despairing soliloquy of Guillaume's Lover to a conclusion in which, resolving to die rather than renounce his love, he bequeaths his heart to Fair Welcome. Reason then reappears and, over the course of some 3,000 lines, attempts to argue him into recognizing the folly of that "sickness of mind" which he has been led to mistake for love. Reason is clear in her own mind about what love should be: she draws an absolute contrast between the irrational pursuit of lust and the office of generation, which seeks something beyond mere pleasure, and then enlarges on the value of a nobler, rational love that expresses itself in charity and largess, love of the community. Not only does love of this kind guard against the overvaluing of worldly things that subjects men to Fortune, but its informing presence is necessary to ensure that law and justice play a positive role in human life, rather than a destructive one. It was such a harmony of love and justice that sustained mankind in the Golden Age, before Jupiter introduced a new, harsher order by castrating his father, Saturn, and usurping his kingship. This temperate, beneficent love, which sustains justice and values the things of this world at their proper worth, is nothing more or less than the love of Reason herself, and this she now offers to the Lover.

But in describing Jupiter's castration of Sat-

urn, Reason had used the term *coilles* (balls), and the Lover declares himself offended by this indelicacy. Reason claims the right to call things by their proper names, which are *only* names (if testicles were called "relics," she says, they would still be what they are), and then explains that in any case her use of the word has an underlying meaning, for she has used the myth of Saturn and Jupiter to express a philosophical truth. But the Lover is not interested in philosophy, and when Reason cannot dissuade him from his service to the God of Love, she withdraws.

This long interview may seem to contribute little to the poem, for it does not advance the plot and only reemphasizes the impasse between Reason and the Lover already shown by Guillaume. But in bringing their differences to bear on a question of sexual terminology, Jean is offering his own forcefully reductive comment on the veiled significances of Guillaume's courtly garden and the Lover's experience within it. Courtly idealism that will not call things by their proper names is made to seem mere effeteness, an inability to deal with sexual reality. But Reason, too, contributes to the difficulty of the situation, for in flatly opposing an enlightened, procreative love to the folly that pursues mere delight, she fails to recognize that an element of such folly is a necessary ingredient in all sexual love, however noble the ends for which it is undertaken. She speaks as though it were possible for humankind to conduct their sexual lives in a wholly rational way.

The key to the misunderstanding between Reason and the Lover is the "hidden meaning" of the story of Saturn and Jupiter, a meaning that Reason alludes to but does not offer to explain. (Medieval tradition commonly conflates two separate myths, that of the castration of Ouranos the sky-god by his son Kronos, or Saturn, and that of the subsequent overthrow of Saturn, whose reign constituted the Golden Age, by his son Zeus, or Jupiter.) As interpreted by medieval mythographers, this myth of the destruction of the Golden Age illustrated the imposition of a finite, temporal existence on the abundance of life in the universe, the channeling of a primordial plenitude into cycles of life and death whose terms are fixed. When Saturn's testicles were cast into the ocean, the mingling of his seed with the sea-foam gave birth to Venus, under whose influence man engages in sexual procreation, his portion of the burden of resistance to death borne by all temporal life. The story is in effect a version of the Fall of Man, for it means among other things the destruction of a primal continuity between human life and the harmony of nature, and its replacement by an uncertain dependency on the irrational force, capable of both creation and destruction, represented by Venus. And it is this "fall" that accounts for the failure of communication between Reason, who does not recognize that sexual love cannot exist apart from Venus, and the Lover, who is anxiously aware of the necessity of coming to terms with Venus and sexual reality if his quest for the Rose is to succeed.

Thus the Lover's inability to understand Reason's straightforward approach to sexual love and its function is more than Jean's way of mocking the niceties of courtliness. It is a way of illustrating the dislocation suffered by man's nature with the loss of Paradise, and it provides a context in which we may view the tensions in the Lover's outlook, the almost schizophrenic division between his aesthetic idealism and his fear of the menace of practical reality, in a new perspective. The artifice and euphemism of the courtly drama of love, absurd and inadequate as Jean makes them seem, are a consequence of man's divorce from Reason, and they are no more absurd than the conviction that a rational alternative is available. Neither approach to love is adequate to counter or domesticate the irrational force of desire.

Jean's ironic resolution of the impasse between Reason and courtly idealism is to subject both to a debasing transformation, to reduce the former to the level of strategy and dialectical subtlety and to exploit the latter's Ovidian capacity for disguising and prettifying the realities of sexual intrigue. By this means, he introduces the Lover to the politics of love in an imperfect world. The result is a resolution of the Lover's quest vastly different from what Guillaume's delicate suggestions had seemed to promise, and at its climactic moment, the Lover explicitly repudiates Reason and her teachings. Yet there is a sense in which this resolution confirms Reason's convictions and the Lover's wavering idealism even as it mocks them. One effect of Reason's discourse is to remind us that there is, after all, a purpose in human sexual love, that procreation is a means whereby man can participate in a larger order, albeit sporadically and imperfectly. Reason's idealization of that "rightly directed" love that fulfills man's role in the natural order thus serves to define a standard to which, as to the paradisal promise of Guillaume's fountain, the Lover will instinctively respond. In the end, this correspondence between Reason's view of love and the deepest intuitions of courtliness proves central to Jean's view of human love, and it becomes the basis for a reorientation of the allegory of the *Romance* as a whole whereby Guillaume's garden is shown, in a comparison both ironic and significant, in its true relation to Paradise.

The 12,000 lines that intervene between the departure of Reason and the climax of the *Romance* take us far afield and must be very briefly summarized here. The Lover's Friend reappears to advise him on the importance of bribery, flattery, and other stratagems. The Lover is at first offended but is then lulled by the Friend's dazzling, erotic account of the Golden Age, which parodies both Guillaume's garden and Reason's ideal union of love and justice:

Without selfishness or violence they who took pleasure in love-play would embrace and kiss. The green trees of the groves stretched the pavilions and curtains of their boughs above them to protect them from the sun. There these simple, untroubled people carried on their dances, games, and leisurely amusements free from all care except to live pleasurably. . . . Not yet had king or prince done them wrong.

(8402–8416)

The God of Love summons his followers, proposes to lay siege to the castle of Jealousy, and sends False Seeming (an embodiment of corruption in religious life whose greed and hypocrisy are described at length) to negotiate with Evil Tongue. Disguised as a friar, False Seeming agrees to hear Evil Tongue's confession but then strangles him and introduces Largess and Courtesy into the castle. They encounter Fair Welcome's guardian, a worldly old woman who agrees to serve as go-between and who, after giving Fair Welcome a long account of her own experience of the game of love and its deceitful arts, persuades him to give the Lover an audience. They enjoy a brief interview but are discovered by Danger, Fear, and Shame. At this point, war breaks out in the form of a *psychomachia* in which Love's army, led by Franchise, Pity, and Delight, battles the defenders of the castle. After a truce, Venus appears to rally the forces of Love, and as they prepare to renew the struggle, the poet shifts abruptly to a long account of the powerful and beautiful goddess Nature and then describes her confession to her priest, Genius. With the introduction of these figures, who come into play at the moment when Venus' arrival on the battlefield introduces a new note of urgency into the sexual campaign, the poem once again ascends to a philosophical plane that needs a little explanation.

Nature and Genius have a complex history in late-classical and medieval thought and poetry, but the roles in which they appear in the *Romance* are determined by a group of twelfth-century Latin poets whose work reflects the influence of Platonist philosophy and humanist curriculum generally associated with the cathedral school at Chartres. The most famous of these poets, Alan of Lille, wrote a "Complaint of Nature" in which the goddess is presented as lamenting the flaw in her order caused by human sin, which is depicted metaphorically as sodomy, an abrogation of natural responsibility reflecting a deformity of will and reason. Alan's "Complaint" ends with the appearance of Genius, Nature's priest, who pronounces a solemn anathema on all who fail to fulfill their duty as creatures, excommunicating them from the "church" of Nature.

Jean's Nature and Genius bear essentially the same relation to mankind and to one another as in Alan's poem, though Jean takes a more literal view of Alan's sexual metaphors. For the purpose of the *Romance*, Nature's chief function is to ensure continuity in the universe by requiring that all creatures perform the duty of procreation. Genius, her priest, is the guiding principle of individual natures, that which makes them behave in accordance with Nature. Originally a tutelary spirit, an instinctive source of moral guidance and self-determination, he is here identifiable with man's sexual instinct, operating subliminally to transmit Nature's will by guiding sexual desire into the channels of procreation. It is in this sense, as solemnizer of the bond between man and Nature, that he can be called her priest.

Though Nature's long confession covers a range of topics, from destiny and free will to the nature of dreams and the properties of reflective and refracting mirrors, its gist, as in Alan's "Complaint," is a condemnation of man's abrogation of his duty to renew his kind, building to an angry enumeration of the infernal punishments such laxity deserves. Nature ends by sending Genius to convey her will to the army of Love. Arrayed by Cupid with a new miter and chasuble and bearing in his hand a torch provided by Venus, Genius launches into a long exhortation to fecundity, extolling it not only as man's duty and his means of resisting death but as the means of entry to the true Paradise, the Park of the Good Shepherd, a place far superior even to the world of the Golden Age.

Here Genius digresses to recall the destruction of the Golden Age through the castration of Saturn and explains at length how its loss required mankind to seek out arts and establish laws to maintain itself. He then returns to his theme and concludes with an extended comparison between the garden of Guillaume's portion of the *Romance* (which in Jean's continuation has virtually disappeared) and the Shepherd's Park, contrasting the selective and artificial character of the world of Sir Delight with the rich, natural abundance of Paradise, and the treacherous fountain of Narcissus with the purity and beneficence of the Fountain of Life.

The effect of Genius' discourse is to inspire a final assault that routs the defenders of the castle. The Lover makes his way into the ivory tower where the Rose has been hidden, and the final lines of the poem describe their physical union and the impregnation of the Rose. But it is clear that this straightforward result is not a simple triumph of natural desire over intrigue and suspicion. For Nature's will is obeyed only after Genius' authority has been reconfirmed by Venus and Cupid on their own terms, and it is they as much as Genius himself who mediate between her commandment and the Lover's fulfillment of his natural mission. In his final exhilaration, the Lover expresses gratitude to Venus, the God of Love, and his Friend, but says nothing of Nature, and expressly mocks Reason for wasting her time with him. Nature and Genius, it appears, are as little able as Reason to understand the realities of desire in a world cut off from its paradisal origins; their view of sexuality is wholly natural, unaffected by sin, and so their standard is the perfectly integrated life of prelapsarian man. Their condemnation of the idolatry and artifice of the garden and the absolute contrast Genius draws between Narcissus' fountain and that found in the Shepherd's Park ("the one makes the living drink of death, the other brings the dead to life") ignores the role that courtliness has played in introducing the Lover to the love that issues at last in procreation.

From one point of view, then, the conclusion of Jean's poem is an utter reversal of the relationship between idealism and physical desire in Guillaume's garden. The practicality and cynicism of the Friend, False Seeming, and the old woman who guards Fair Welcome compel us to focus on the material objective of the Lover's quest, and the emphasis on simple lust in the final lines is sufficient to overwhelm any hint of transformation. This latter point, in fact, is carefully underscored by a coarsely parodic use of religious imagery to describe the Lover's "veneration" of the Rose as physical object and by the fact that the Rose remains, throughout the graphic account of her deflowering and impregnation, a rose on a rosebush.

But viewed in a different way, the realization of the dictates of Reason, Nature, and Genius through the imperfect medium of the Lover's dislocated and unstable sexuality assumes a significance of its own, suggesting that a vestigial continuity of purpose has survived the corruption of human life to maintain a link between fallen man and his paradisal origins. In this light, the relation of Guillaume's garden to the higher level of reality on which Nature operates is also significantly altered, for the discovery of a love that leads ultimately to natural fulfillment confirms, albeit tentatively, the promise of the garden's paradisal imagery.

That Jean is acutely aware of the radically opposite meanings his conclusion can be made to yield is confirmed by the last of his many digressions, which occurs in the poem's final thousand lines and at the moment when the castle is on the point of yielding. As Venus is about to set fire to the ivory tower that enshrines the image of virgin purity, the poet withdraws abruptly to devote 400 lines to the story of Pygmalion—how he created a beautiful ivory statue and fell in love with it, his horror of his own idolatry, his desperate prayer to Venus, and the miracle of the statue's coming to life. Jean offers no comment on the story and proceeds to his conclusion without a backward glance, but the point of the interruption seems clear enough: from one point of view, Pygmalion's story is an image of the Lover's hapless and idolatrous pursuit of an image of his own desire to a purely fortuitous fulfillment; from another, it is a miracle, an affirmation of the higher meaning of human love. Pygmalion's story thus embodies in miniature the contradiction that pervades Jean's treatment of Guillaume's original story, and it may be said to constitute Jean's last word on the significance of the *Romance* as a whole.

Not all readers have been willing to accept Jean's technique, the balancing against one another of a range of incomplete views of the purpose and meaning of love, as a matter of conscious artistry. A number of modern critics have suggested that what I see as a deliberately unresolved conclusion, a presentation of alternative possibilities for interpretation, is actually a reflection of the inconsistency or simple incoherence of Jean's own attitude. And in the century following Jean's death, readers seem to have found it difficult to isolate Jean's own authorial perspective from the conflicting voices of his characters. In 1277, during the very period when we assume Jean to have been at work on the poem, the bishop of Paris, Étienne Tempier, issued a list of over 200 propositions circulating in the schools that were to be condemned as heretical. Though the condemnation was sweeping enough to include the work of the amiable Andreas Capellanus, it also included a number of "naturalist" ideas that seemed to promote sexual indulgence as a natural good at the expense of traditional virtues like continence and abstinence. The ideas in question are often close to the views on procreation and sexuality expressed by Reason, Nature, and Genius. There is no clear basis for supposing that Jean himself was one of those at whom the condemnation was aimed, but the indictment of Andreas suggests an insensitivity to irony that was to recur among Jean's medieval critics. A generation after Jean's death, Guillaume Deguileville produced an allegorical poem, the "Pilgrimage of the Life of Man," modeled in many respects upon the *Romance* but largely an answer to what Deguileville seems to have viewed as Jean's deliberate promotion of the cause of Venus. And at the end of the fourteenth century, Jean's work again became the subject of controversy in a debate that involved such famous figures as Christine de Pisan and Jean Gerson, chancellor of the University of Paris, both of whom found the *Romance* objectionable on the grounds of its sexual explicitness, its encouragement of lechery, and its harsh treatment of women and marriage. They were charged in turn with taking the arguments of Jean's various characters out of context and with failing to answer these arguments. The controversy as a whole is in many ways hard to understand at this distance, though it was evidently taken with some seriousness at the time and led to the formation of two courtly societies committed to upholding the honor of women. It is possible that the *Romance* was not so much an enemy in itself as a convenient occasion for promoting a reform of contemporary manners.

For Guillaume de Machaut, probably the major French poet of the fourteenth century, and for the numerous anonymous authors of love visions and other poetry in the courtly tradition, Jean is only an incidental source of moral philosophy, proverbial wisdom, and mythological exempla. Their concern is to create new variations on the form and the psychology provided by Guillaume, and the same emphasis is evident in the use made of the *Romance* by Dante, who was evidently the first major poet and certainly the first non-French author to give serious attention to the poem. Whether or not Dante was, as now seems probable, the author of *Il fiore* (*The Flower*), which tells the story of the *Romance* in a series of 232 sonnets, he certainly knew the poem well from early in his career. Its influence is evident in the portions of the *Vita nuova* describing his behavior under the influence of love and in the presence of Beatrice, which recall the God of Love's long account of the pains of love. And I think the larger thematic movement of the *Vita*, the withdrawal of Beatrice from the world and her ascent to a level of meaning at which Love in the courtly sense is inadequate to comprehend her, shows Dante attentive to the various ways in which Guillaume had opposed the ideal and the earthly levels of his love quest.

The *Divine Comedy*, too, is full of reminiscences of Guillaume, but by far the most striking is Dante's account of the earthly Paradise at the summit of Purgatory. Here the garden of Guillaume's allegory is re-created and endowed with new attributes. During his final night on the slopes of Purgatory, Dante dreams of Leah, a beautiful lady who moves singing through a meadow, gathering flowers with which to adorn herself, while her sister, Rachel, sits perpetually before her mirror, contemplating her own beautiful eyes. The two ladies are traditional types of the active and the contemplative life; their self-adornment represents the fulfillment of these roles, the realization of spiritual beauty. They serve to introduce the life of Paradise, just as Idleness, who has her mirror perpetually at hand and has no other task than to dress and adorn herself, represents the life of the Garden of Delight.

Upon entering Paradise itself and approaching a spring whose pure waters "hide nothing," Dante encounters a new counterpart to Idleness in the figure of Matelda, who, like Leah, is singing and gathering flowers. Like Idleness, she explains the nature of the place to the newcomer: the Supreme Good created the place for man; the spring is sustained by the will of God, infuses virtue, and cleanses the memory of sin; and the place itself is that true Paradise of which poets once dreamed in

their songs of the Golden Age. It is thus a synthesis of Guillaume's garden with Genius' Park of the Good Shepherd, a living confirmation of the "dreams" and intuitions of natural philosophy and courtly poetry, and a resolution of the imaginative schism that runs through the *Romance*. Dante recalls Guillaume again at the moment when, challenged by Beatrice to look upon her beauty, he looks down at the clear stream and is revolted by the sight of himself. Here the consciousness of sin has become a "narcissistic" subjection to the burden of self, and Dante is freed from this burden only by the purifying ritual of immersion in the waters of the stream. He is then drawn into the dance of the Cardinal Virtues, beautiful ladies whose behavior recalls that of Courtesy, who draws Guillaume's Lover into the dancing company of Delight. Then at last Dante is shown not the magical stones of Guillaume's fountain but the eyes of Beatrice, "the emeralds from which Love once shot his darts at you," in which he sees reflected a symbolic manifestation of the twofold nature of Christ.

If Dante brings the archetypal implications of the Garden of Delight to realization in a brilliant crescendo, it is Chaucer who of all poets shows the broadest and deepest appreciation of the *Romance* as a whole. The Middle English translation of which parts are usually attributed to him is likely to have been among his earliest exercises in poetry; *The Book of the Duchess*, his earliest datable poem, mentions the *Romance* by name, and all his major works reflect an ongoing fascination with the dialectics of its hybrid structure. *The Parliament of Fowls* somehow succeeds in achieving a thorough restatement of the major themes of the *Romance* in less than 700 lines, and its treatment of the relations between the natural order, human sexuality, and the civilizing graces of courtly love reflects a deeply insightful reading of the earlier poem. The *Troilus and Criseyde* centers on the relations between Troilus, a lover so pure in his courtly devotion that at moments only the language of Dante suffices to express his love, and Pandarus, a counselor whose pragmatic concern with bringing Troilus' love to a sexual fulfillment provides a sustained and consistently reductive gloss on the other's idealism. Like the God of Love, whose role his own behavior strongly recalls at a number of points, Pandarus succeeds in his campaign, but Troilus' idealism somehow survives his seduction, as Genius in the *Romance* adheres to his vision of the Shepherd's Park even as his powers are being appropriated by Venus. The effect of this interplay, in the *Troilus* as in the *Romance*, is to set the literal and visionary worlds in a balanced relation such that the reality and meaning of each are both enhanced and qualified. Chaucer, unlike Jean de Meun, finally goes beyond this opposition to extrapolate from the experience of Troilus a meaning that transcends the world of the poem, but his resolution becomes possible only after the interplay of Troilus and Pandarus, whose imaginative worlds are effectively those of Guillaume and Jean, has run its course.

The Canterbury Tales, too, though its overall structure has never been adequately defined, can be seen to conform in important respects to the pattern of the *Romance*. The setting provided by the general prologue, with its spring motif and evocations of love introducing the journey theme and the sequence of pilgrim portraits, has a marked resemblance to the opening of Guillaume's allegory, and the affinity becomes significant in relation to the recurring movement of the tales, which repeatedly move outward from a formal starting point and a strong assertion of traditional authority into a world of stress and cross-purposes, where one character after another moves to center stage and discourses at length on the relations of the sexes, happy and unhappy, or on the nature and truth of dreams. The ideal and the pragmatic interact in strange ways in the tales: aggressive assertions of sexual combativeness mask romantic yearnings, and real toads are discovered to harbor visions of imaginary gardens. Such paradoxes are Chaucer's version of the unwitting collaborations in the *Romance* between cosmic powers, human instincts, and social conventions. In *The Canterbury Tales* the elements of the great allegory become refracted and diffused into the fragmentary waking dream lives of ordinary human beings.

Selected Bibliography

EDITIONS

Amadas et Ydoine. Edited by John Reinhard. Paris, 1926.

Bernart von Ventadorn: Seine Lieder. Edited by Carl Appel. Halle, 1915. The poems of Bernart de Ventadour.

Eneas. Edited by J.-J. Salverda de Grave. 2 vols. Paris, 1925–1929.

Le Roman de la Rose. Edited by Ernest Langlois. 5 vols. Paris, 1914–1924. A critical edition based on a thorough survey of surviving manuscripts.

Le Roman de la Rose. Edited by Felix Lecoy. 3 vols. Paris, 1965–1970. A diplomatic edition based on a single carefully chosen manuscript and drawing on several others. My translations are based on the Lecoy edition.

TRANSLATIONS

The Romance of the Rose. Translated by Harry W. Robbins. Edited by Charles W. Dunn. New York, 1962. Generally accurate but occasionally wordy; in English blank verse with minimal introduction and notes.

The Romance of the Rose. Translated by Charles Dahlberg. Princeton, N.J., 1969. A good prose translation, though both translation and commentary are occasionally flawed by a tendency to force the poem's meaning into conformity with Christian ideas. Includes a generous selection of illustrations from manuscripts of the *Romance*.

Eneas. A Twelfth-Century French Romance. Translated by John A. Yunck. New York, 1974. The passage quoted in this essay is from this edition.

THE *ROMANCE OF THE ROSE* AND MEDIEVAL ALLEGORY

GENERAL WORKS AND SPECIAL STUDIES

Economou, George D. *The Goddess Natura in Medieval Literature.* Cambridge, Mass., 1972. A study of the role of this important allegorical figure in poetry from the late classical period through Chaucer.

Fleming, John V. *The "Roman de la Rose." A Study in Allegory and Iconography.* Princeton, N.J., 1969. A moral reading of the poem, forcefully argued but requiring the same sort of caution as Dahlberg's. Largely concerned with the significance of manuscript illustrations; contains a large selection of reproductions.

Fletcher, Angus. *Allegory: The Theory of a Symbolic Mode.* Ithaca, N.Y., 1964. A brilliant theoretical study.

Gunn, Alan M. F. *The Mirror of Love. A Reinterpretation of "The Romance of the Rose."* Lubbock, Tex., 1952. The fullest study of the poem; full of useful information and often very acute on problems of structure, but occasionally hard to follow.

Honig, Edwin. *Dark Conceit. A Study of Allegory.* Evanston, Ill., 1959. Concerned mainly with postmedieval literature.

Huizinga, Johan. *The Waning of the Middle Ages.* Translated by F. Hopman. London, 1924. Classic study of late-medieval cultural values.

Lewis, C. S. *The Allegory of Love.* Oxford, 1936. Beautifully written and provocative survey of allegorical treatments of courtly love through Spenser's *Faerie Queene.*

Muscatine, Charles. *Chaucer and the French Tradition.* Berkeley and Los Angeles, 1957. Contains excellent chapters on Guillaume de Lorris and Jean de Meun.

Piehler, Paul H. T. *The Visionary Landscape. A Study in Medieval Allegory.* London, 1971. Provides valuable insights into the psychology of the reader's experience of allegory and the archetypal implications of the imagery of medieval allegorical poems.

Poirion, Daniel. *Le Roman de la Rose.* Paris, 1973. Primarily a critical reading of the poem, but informative about sources and background; best book-length study of the *Romance.* (In French.)

Spearing, A. C. *Medieval Dream Poetry.* Cambridge, 1976. Almost entirely concerned with English material, but the first chapter is devoted to the *Romance* and its background.

Tuve, Rosemund. *Allegorical Imagery. Some Medieval Books and Their Posterity.* Princeton, N.J., 1966. An astute reading of Jean de Meun and valuable information about later medieval allegory.

Wetherbee, Winthrop. *Platonism and Poetry in the Twelfth Century.* Princeton, N.J., 1972. The background of the *Romance* in Latin poetry and philosophy.

WINTHROP WETHERBEE

JEAN JACQUES ROUSSEAU
(1712–1778)

JEAN JACQUES ROUSSEAU was a genius, but he was also a typically talented person of his time, which is to say, a dabbler in pastimes: he was a fitfully inspired musician and operatic composer, an amateur botanist, the author of a drawing-room comedy, a mediocre poet, and on two occasions a consultant in the planning of political constitutions. For all these accomplishments he would have earned at most a paragraph (for the music) and a few footnotes (for the rest of it) in the history of our culture. But he had still other callings, and in these he has had a more lasting and varied influence than any other eighteenth-century writer.

Our inheritance from Benjamin Franklin is more diverse but not as fundamentally important; if David Hume and Immanuel Kant founded the two main currents of modern philosophy, there is still little in what they have left us that pervades our social thought; if we are more deeply moved by the moral intelligence of Samuel Johnson than by any other phenomenon of his day, we find our world so much changed that we cannot hope to emulate him; and if the mercurial mind of Rousseau's great contemporary and enemy Voltaire more perfectly represents the best qualities of his period, we gain little from our exposure to it except the habit of skeptical curiosity, which we owe as much to Michel de Montaigne as to the spirit of the Enlightenment. Rousseau, however, has played an important role in shaping nearly every aspect—even seemingly incompatible aspects—of the modern world view. We owe our best and worst traits alike as much to Rousseau as to anyone.

As a political philosopher he has been nearly as instrumental as Karl Marx and Arthur Schopenhauer in forming the ideology of totalitarianism. Even "social historians," who often play down the role of individuals in events, freely admit that the reading of Rousseau inspired the French Revolution—just as the rereading of him helped carry it toward its late extremes. As an educational writer, on the other hand, he has influenced the most libertarian trends in what we call progressive education. As a metaphysician, albeit a reluctant and unsystematic one, he greatly influenced the philosophy of Kant and its aftermath by emphasizing man's innate moral sense and his capacity for disinterested thought and action. As a novelist, autobiographer, and theorist of cultural origins, Rousseau pioneered the special kind of preoccupation with the self that prevails everywhere today. In all these ways, and more than any other figure, he influenced the subsequent romantic revolt against both Enlightenment rationalism and the orthodoxy of established institutions. As the reader will notice in looking over this summary, Rousseau is remarkable for having exalted both the impersonally collective and the individualistic extremes of the human temperament. What is yet more remarkable is his having done so without seriously contradicting himself.

He was born in Geneva on 28 June 1712. The death of his mother a few days later accounted for much of his free-floating guilt in adulthood and also left an emptiness that none of the maternal women in his later life could ever quite fill. His father, Isaac, was a watchmaker who disliked his trade, apparently because he thought it was beneath him. He prefered the life of a nomad, though he did not always choose it freely: he had to flee from Geneva when Jean Jacques was ten, in consequence of a street quarrel. He did not trouble himself to return for years. Despite Rousseau's many studied eulogies of his father, and despite his cozy memories of being read to from Plutarch's fables amid the tools of the workshop, we have no reason to believe that his father felt any great affection for him. In these paternal traits many students have seen the adult behavior of Jean Jacques foreshadowed—especially the abandonment of his own children. Be that as it may, after his father went away Rousseau had to put his trust in extended families of the sort that he tried to create for the rest of his life, both for himself and for the brotherhood of man.

He and a cousin were first sent to live with a local pastor, M. Lambercier, and his sister. Beatings at their hands, in one case unjustly, startled Rousseau into his first experiences of sensual pleasure. He later put his undoubted masochism to constructive use in the motto that he chose for himself and sometimes tested to the full, *Vitam impendere vero:* To risk life for the truth. He next went to live with his uncle, and after a sojourn there he was apprenticed at thirteen to an engraver, in whose house he roomed. It is at this point that his autobiography most resembles that of his American contemporary Benjamin Franklin. Never at ease with authority, Rousseau was a bad worker and worse guest. He even began to steal. All the same, when he was fifteen his civic pride flared up long enough for him to inscribe on a gate the signature for which he became famous: "Jean Jacques Rousseau: Citizen of Geneva, 1727." One evening in the following year he returned from a country outing so late that he found the city gates closed. He had been punished more than once for missing the curfew, and this time, on an impulse, he simply walked off into Savoy. Like his father, he did not return for many years.

His road took him to a village where the Catholic curate gave him a lavish dinner and sent him on to see a woman in Annecy named Mme. de Warens, who supported herself in part by taking in and encouraging Catholic converts. She sent Rousseau to a hospice in Turin, where he was kept virtually a prisoner—so he tells us—and was much distressed to be the object of homosexual advances. During his stay at the hospice, whether because he was brainwashed or simply because he needed approval we cannot say, he allowed himself to become a Catholic. With the help of a friend, the abbé Gaîme (one of the models for the Savoyard Vicar in *Émile*), he eventually "escaped."

Then followed a period of service in the livery of several gentlepersons. Rousseau behaved badly as usual in such offices, and soon he drifted back to Mme. de Warens, in whose household at Chambéry he came to be installed. After a period when both he and she came and went unpredictably (we know, as Rousseau never did, that she carried messages for a rather seedy group of international spies), Rousseau and his "Maman" became more intimate, and when he was nineteen she made him her steward and her lover. In both these capacities he supplanted Claude Anet, who soon after committed suicide.

Having failed at various other trades, Rousseau was now urged by Maman to become a music teacher. Over the next few years he gained a degree of competence in music, in which at first he had been a complete charlatan without being very much hindered, sad to say, in his teaching. He now also developed a passion for learning. In reading Voltaire and others he augmented his childhood memories of Plutarch and the Roman historians and stored up the "reservoir of ideas" he was later to draw upon. All this came about in a country cottage that Maman had leased in the valley of Les Charmettes, near Chambéry. It was this place and period—the late 1730's—that grew to become the most important of the idylls that color Rousseau's later writings. Les Charmettes animates nearly all of the great fifth and sixth books of the *Confessions*.

At the turn of the decade the idyll began to fade. A growing uneasiness with himself that had to do in part with his impatience to succeed, and in part perhaps with a coolness between him and Maman, brought on an alarming nervous ailment. After several aimless excursions he decided to go to Montpellier to consult about his health. On the road there, however, he met an older woman, a Mme. Larnage, who turned out to be "the doctor I needed." His brief affair with her was probably the only uninhibited sensual interlude of his life. (A kind of incest taboo had very much chastened his attachment to Maman.) In Montpellier Rousseau idled for a while, putting off a visit to the home of Mme. Larnage partly because on the road he had masqueraded as an Englishman, "M. Dudding," and he now feared that his total ignorance of English would expose him. Finally he returned instead to Chambéry, only to find that he had been supplanted, like the unfortunate Claude Anet before him. The interloper was a Swiss named Winzenried. Rousseau lingered on for some time nevertheless. All his life he was inclined, like the Tutor in the final pages of *Émile*, to enjoy being the passive party, the mentor, in three-way affairs of the heart.

At length he tore himself away from Les Charmettes and made his way to Lyon, where he became a tutor in the household of M. de Mably, brother of the abbé de Mably, an author and an acquaintance of the future *philosophes*—as the writers came to be called who were soon to begin work on the great *Encyclopedia*. After a brief return to Les Charmettes, Rousseau at last determined to go to Paris, armed with letters of introduction from Mably, a sheaf of verses, a comedy entitled *Narcissus* that was to be performed ten years later, and a new system of musical notation that he hoped to place before the Academy. He was thirty and the published author of a long poem, "The Gardener of Mme. la Baronne de Warens," which sank without a ripple. His system of notation caused a stir, but the Academy exposed a flaw in it. Rousseau persisted in its defense, and to that end he published, in 1743, his *Dissertation on Modern Music*. Although he had studied and taught music and was already the author of an opera, *Les muses galantes* (*The Gallant Muses*), Rousseau never quite overcame the haphazardness of his musical training, and for this reason despite his talent he was bested repeatedly in controversy with the leading—and most acerbic—professional musician of his day, Jean Philippe Rameau.

In Parisian society Rousseau cut an awkward figure. Because he had no ready conversation, he blurted out nonsense whenever he felt called on to speak. Even so, he had a compelling presence; the intensity of his feelings could not but be felt, and he spoke with eloquence whenever he warmed to a topic. All this should be borne in mind if one is to understand his behavior during his years of fame. The clumsy fool he compulsively portrays in his autobiographies, a fool who in the hands of his biographers becomes a great bore and an appalling cad as well, could scarcely have inspired the mixed affection, reverence, and fear of literate Europe had he not made himself a presence to be reckoned with in Paris. He was often laughable, and in the long run he acted like the madman he in fact intermittently became; but in the meantime he was lionized by all the lions of his day. One of his first friends in Paris, and certainly his closest for the next few years, was the gregarious and many-talented Denis Diderot, who included a warm tribute to Rousseau in his first book. Through Diderot, Rousseau came to know the *philosophes*. He meanwhile made himself pleasing enough to Mme. Dupin, one of the most formidable women in Paris, to become her private secretary.

Partly through her influence, in 1743 he became secretary to the ambassador to Venice. This personage, M. de Montaigu, was an ill-natured aristocrat who was largely indifferent to his job. He was willing enough to have Rousseau take over the work as long as he made no attempt to stand on privilege. Rousseau had had enough of being treated like a valet, and he soon quarreled violently with Montaigu and left Venice—not, however, before having trysted with a courtesan who advised him to "give up the ladies, and study mathematics." During his stay he had also thought much about politics, with no little spiteful attention, one imagines, to the claims of political equality. From that time forward Rousseau planned some day to write a treatise on political institutions, of which we have only a series of famous subsections.

He returned to Paris more certain than ever that he could not have dignity without independence. He lived first with a Spanish friend, then moved to the Hôtel Saint-Quentin. There he found himself pitying a serving woman named Thérèse LeVasseur who was treated rudely by the other boarders. She was grateful to him, and so began an attachment that lasted until Rousseau died. Thérèse was a shrew, and she was practically illiterate. She may have shared more than Rousseau ever realized in the schemes of her mother and other relatives to siphon off his earnings. Certainly she was more calculating and more sexually adventurous than Rousseau ever knew—or admitted. Despite all this, though, the biographers who attempt to discredit her completely cannot quite succeed. For thirty-three years she followed him doggedly from hardship to hardship. She was often bored and knew how to infect others with her misery, but for some reason that no one has been able to discover, she never left Rousseau. Most of the time he treated her as a servant, and she rarely ate at table with him except when they were alone.

She was hated by some of his friends, laughed at by others, seduced by still others, and manipulated by those who needed leverage in their attempts to manage Rousseau's affairs.

By far the worst result of this strange relationship, however, was the birth of five children, all of whom, Rousseau confesses in a rush and with no attention to chronology, he gave immediately to a foundling hospital with no prospect of seeing them again. No one is sure why; perhaps he was afraid the children would inherit the "criminal tendencies" of Thérèse's family (one of her brothers once stole all his shirts); perhaps he thought that he was not their father; or perhaps he simply felt that he had no time for children. With his usual genius for sophistry, he made many excuses for what he had done, the chief of them being that Plato had advocated the separation of children from their parents in his *Republic.* But he never stopped feeling guilty. He considered the writing of *Émile*, as he nearly admitted in a note, to be an atonement of sorts, and in 1761, when he thought he was dying, he told his secret to Mme. de Luxembourg and prevailed upon her to start a search for the children. None was found.

The failure of his opera, *The Gallant Muses*, reminded Rousseau of his need for a livelihood, and reluctantly he took up in earnest the job of private secretary to Mme. Dupin. He also formed a friendship with the literary journalist Friedrich Melchior Grimm, whom he introduced to Diderot and who was more than once to play the villain later in his life. It was a time of great intellectual excitement in Paris, and Rousseau was to be affected in his own way. In July 1749 Diderot was arrested for writing in defense of atheism and imprisoned at Vincennes; one day in October, Rousseau went to visit him, reading a copy of the newspaper *Mercure de France* on the way. He noticed an advertisement for the Dijon essay competition, for which the year's question was: Has the renascence of the sciences and the arts contributed to the improvement of morals? Rousseau was suddenly flooded with inspiration, so overwhelmed in fact that he had to lie recovering under a tree for half an hour. His career—and his vision—were decided.

He took the negative side of the question, insisting that all human ills stem from acculturation: idleness, decadence, skepticism, ostentation, and, perhaps worst of all, the contempt for humanity that is inevitably bred by the self-consciousness of "philosophy." Although Rousseau said later that this "First Discourse," the *Discours sur les sciences et les arts* (*Discourse on the Sciences and the Arts*), was one of his "slightest" productions, it did win him the prize, and it made him famous. It prompted countless refutations, a few of which he answered. Slight as it was, it contained much of his mature thought in its early form. The austere Spartan state that he pointedly prefers to the cultivated Athenian one prefigures the political utopia that was to appear in all his later writings.

In the following years Rousseau's position in the literary world was established, but in 1753 he detoured somewhat from his main path. His comedy, *Narcissus*, was performed and published. For this occasion he wrote a preface that was, he says in the *Confessions,* "one of my best pieces of writing." In it, he goes on, "I began to set out my principles a little more fully than I had done hitherto."* He answers the obvious charge that an enemy of the arts and sciences has little business writing comedies, and in so doing for the first time he displays his skill as a dialectician (or as a sophist, his opponents might say): in a decadent society, he argues, the arts and sciences may serve in some measure to repair the damage they have caused. At about this time Rousseau's operetta, *Le devin du village* (The Village Soothsayer), was also performed—before the king, in fact, and with great success. It is typical at once of his social anxiety and of his reasoned distaste for convention that he refused an audience with the king on the day following this performance. The Encyclopedists thought this gesture merely obstinate. Charges of insincerity flew back and forth between Rousseau and his friends. They were signs, as it turned out, of the more violent misunderstandings that arose later.

It was at this period that Rousseau, no doubt goaded by all these occurrences, carried out a revolution in his own life. He gave up wearing a dress sword and modish clothes, he refused to wear a wig, and he established himself in the humble trade of music copyist. By this choice of livelihood, to which he adhered for the rest of his life, he intended to get bread from work that could never be imputed to or affected by vanity, whether social or intellectual. He was later to admit sheepishly, however, that "one must be thought a good author to make himself a bad copyist with impunity." A final result of his musical activities was his 1753 "Letter on French Music," in which he expressed a preference for Italian over French opera. This pamphlet aroused the anger of all Paris, especially of Rameau, who now claimed that nearly everything in Rousseau's music was plagiarized from the Italians.

Another Dijon competition having been announced for 1754, Rousseau wrote and entered his first masterpiece (which did not win the prize), the *Discours sur l'origine de l'inégalité parmi les hommes* (*Discourse on the Origin of Inequality*). The first part is a brilliant sketch of a hypothetical "state of nature . . . a state which no longer exists, which perhaps never existed, which probably never will exist." In this state, a condition of happy ignorance free from all the sources of competition (those being the various kinds of property: material, amorous, and ultimately even moral and intellectual), man may be thought to have existed in harmless stagnation. Rousseau argues that not even "natural" or biological inequality matters very much in a state of nature, because the experience of winning or losing in a dispute has little effect on the mind when it is not compounded by vanity or extreme want. Eventually there arises the need to confederate for reasons of mutual benefit

*In the Selected Bibliography, an asterisk appears next to all translations quoted in this essay.

(Rousseau does not clearly explain what causes this hitherto unfelt need suddenly to arise), and in the first stages of his cooperation man passes through what Rousseau judges to be his happiest condition, one roughly equivalent, he says, to that of contemporary savages like the Caribs. But socialization once begun can only grow more complex; subjugation and hoarding come into existence, and from the pursuit of property the condition of inequality in a state of society takes its origin.

Rousseau prefaced this work with a proud address "To the Republic of Geneva," in which he declared that the state of society is least burdened with inequality in his native land. Ever conscious of being a "citizen," he traveled to Geneva after the "Second Discourse" was published to accept the grateful praises of his fatherland and perhaps even to live there. The "Republic," however, was for the most part haughtily unmoved. Geneva was ruled, in fact, by what was nearly a hereditary aristocracy, and these persons did not covet the sermonizing—tinged with demagoguery—of a quarrelsome watchmaker's quarrelsome son. Rousseau returned to Paris in a few months. Over the past years he had written many articles for the *Encyclopedia,* most of them on music, and now he wrote his last, "Political Economy," which was based on notes for his planned "Political Institutions."

"I began to live on April 9, 1756," Rousseau wrote with his usual extravagance several years thereafter. On that date he moved with Thérèse and her mother into the Hermitage, a picturesque cottage on the estate of Mme. d'Epinay in the country suburb of Montmorency. It was here that his forest wanderings in the company of "imaginary beings" were to inspire his most fanciful work, including the first letters of Julie and Saint-Preux, the star-crossed lovers of *Julie, ou la nouvelle Héloïse* (Julie, or the New Heloise). Rousseau had known Mme. d'Epinay for nearly ten years, and had long since established with her, as he often did with elegant women, the role of mentor. Just before he moved to the Hermitage we find him writing formal letters to her on the education of her son and daughter. These were to comprise, as it turned out, a rough draft for *Émile* (1762).

Rousseau was highly sensitive on the subject of his independence, yet he was almost continually indebted, as his enemies never failed to remark, to the hospitality of the rich. He would accept no gifts of a conventional sort (wine, game, and the like), nor did he intend ever to enter any formal relation of dependency ("inequality") with his hosts. He realized, however, that he could hardly refuse summonses from the Mme. d'Epinays of his life, and he always resented their importunity. Other causes of tension in the Hermitage idyll were the conspicuous absence of the *philosophe* Rousseau wanted to see, Diderot, who was piqued at the implied censure of himself in Rousseau's flight from the literary whirl in Paris, and the conspicuous presence of the *philosophe* Rousseau did not much want to see, Grimm, who did visit and soon established himself as Mme. d'Epinay's lover.

In 1756 Voltaire, who now lived near Geneva and whose glittering cynicism Rousseau more and more disapproved of, sent him two poems written in consequence of the earthquake at Lisbon. This event had set all Europe gloomily reconsidering the providential optimism of Gottfried Leibniz and Alexander Pope, who had maintained that ours is the best of all possible worlds. Voltaire retorted, in his poem "On the Disaster of Lisbon," quite simply that it is not: whatever is, he complained, may very well be wrong. Rousseau, whom Voltaire had already called an "enemy of mankind," rose indignantly to the defense of what he always thought of as "the Supreme Intelligence" in his *Lettre sur la providence* (*Letter on Providence,* 1756). In this work he ingeniously maintains that even natural catastrophes are the fault not of God, but of socialized men: if we had not congregated in cities we would not fear falling tiles, and if we had not grown covetous, we would not risk our lives by lingering after the first tremors of an earthquake to salvage our goods. In short, as Rousseau's English contemporary William Cowper put it, God made the country but man made the town. Rousseau concludes this *Letter* with his well-known contrast ("I cannot help remarking, Sir . . .") between his own optimism despite personal misery and Voltaire's pessimism despite the perfect happiness of his life. In later years Rousseau often expressed the belief that Voltaire's *Candide: or Optimism* (1759) had been written in response to his *Letter*. At this period Rousseau also started many other projects: the fictitious love letters that were beginning to tell a story; the plan for a treatise on the conditioning of emotional responses (the *Morale sensitive*); and also a work that he soon completed, the edition (much modified by his own opinions) and accompanying criticism of the political writings of the abbé de Saint-Pierre (1756).

An admiring acquaintance of Rousseau's named Saint-Lambert, who was away in the army, urged his mistress, Mme. d'Houdetot, to introduce herself to the famous hermit. This she did, arriving unannounced at the Hermitage dressed as a man. Thus began Rousseau's most passionate and futile love affair. Every day he visited "Sophie," who admired him and was flattered by his homage—but loved Saint-Lambert. Rousseau tried to remain satisfied in his usual role of mentor and accordingly wrote the *Moral Letters to Sophie* (1757–1758), in which he encourages her and Saint-Lambert to give up passion and embrace virtue. Meanwhile, the growing malice of Grimm and the resentment of Mme. d'Epinay at her lodger's inattentiveness, together with the need taken for granted by all parties to keep Rousseau's infatuation from the notice of Saint-Lambert, who had been very ill—all these factors together resulted in a foolish but bitter quarrel that estranged Rousseau from nearly every friend he had.

He left the Hermitage in December of 1757, rented a drafty house in Montmorency, and moved himself into it along with Thérèse and her mother. Now came the final break with the editors of the *Encyclopedia*. He split with Diderot over a passing remark in one of the latter's novels, and with Jean d'Alembert, though there was no open hostility, over his *Encyclopedia* article on Geneva, which Rousseau judged rightly to have been written at the urging of Voltaire with the aim of establishing a Genevan theater. If this happy event were to occur, d'Alembert wrote, "Geneva would join the prudence of Lacedaemon to the urbanity of Athens." Now, Rousseau's whole message to date had been that "prudence" (read rather "virtue") and urbanity cannot coexist; Sparta and Athens were his favorite examples of upright and decadent cultures, respectively; Geneva was both his birthplace and his ideal republic; and he had already written that the theater is suitable only for those populations whose morals have already been sacrificed to refinement. He repeats these assertions in his fascinating *Lettre à M. d'Alembert*, commonly known as the *Lettre sur les spectacles* (*Letter to d'Alembert on the Theatre*, 1758), and dignifies them further by borrowing liberally from the arguments against artistic imitation in the tenth book of Plato's *Republic*. He relies most on Plato's claim that the necessarily unstable emotions and conflicting goals of dramatic characters cannot reflect the proper steadfastness of virtue, and that the drama will therefore "feed and water the passions." Not even Alceste, the virtuous hero of Molière's *Misanthrope*, is free enough from the foibles that invite laughter to be a satisfactory model for a man and citizen. In the *Confessions* (1766–1770) Rousseau writes of the *Letter to d'Alembert*: "This was the first of my works—for *Julie* was not then half finished—which I found any delight in writing." Presumably this was because he felt that its purpose was more disinterested, more benevolently practical than anything he had written before. The *Letter* has been widely and justly admired. It is marred, though, by a long digression on the intrinsic inferiority of women (a subject to which he turned again in *Émile*) that exhibits Rousseau at his most canting and mindless. In this respect as in few others he supports a commonplace view, forgetting that his key premise—man is corrupted and weakened by culture and not by nature—should also logically apply to women.

In 1758 Rousseau finished *Julie,* having earlier written a draft in four parts that was more or less completed before he met Mme. d'Houdetot. Her influence, or rather Rousseau's idealization of her, considerably altered the character of Julie, and it was in part Rousseau's longing for order and rationality during his infatuation that prolonged the novel through its treatment of the admirable but passionless utopian household of Julie's eventual husband, Wolmar. We cannot doubt the earnestness of the errant Saint-Preux's "I want to be what I should be." Rousseau's novel belongs to the already rich tradition of the epistolary novel developed by Samuel Richardson and Pierre Marivaux. As a narrative achievement it cannot be ranked as high as the work of Henry Fielding, Laurence Sterne, or perhaps even Tobias Smollett. It lacks the speed and verve of Johann Wolfgang von Goethe's *The Sorrows of Young Werther* (which it anticipates in theme, mood, and plot), and it certainly lacks the keen worldliness of Pierre Laclos and the marquis de Sade. But in the balance and richness of its psychological insight it ranks supreme in the eighteenth century with Richardson's *Clarissa,* with which Rousseau proudly compared it in the *Confessions.* From the day of its publication in 1761 it was immensely successful in Europe, and it went through seventy-two editions by 1800.

The plot is roughly as follows. At Clarens in Vevey, Switzerland (Mme. de Warens's birthplace), the seventeen-year-old Julie d'Étange lives chiefly in the company of her nineteen-year-old tutor, Saint-Preux (Voltaire understandably declared that Julie's parents were "idiots"), who attempts to seduce her and himself as well by preaching a confused gospel of virtue in the service of passion. Each has a confidant, Julie a neighbor named Claire and Saint-Preux an irrepressible Englishman, Milord Bomston (shades of "M. Dudding"!); but most of their letters are written not to these friends but to each other in the early books. Though they live in the same house, their love is too shyly profound to permit amorous interviews. At length Saint-Preux, who is by no means a forward lover, has his way. He and Julie then go on urging each other to flout conventional opinion, and Julie even decides to get pregnant. Her father now returns from a journey, repeating his longstanding wish that Julie might marry his fifty-year-old friend Wolmar. At the insistence of everyone, including Julie herself—who has miscarried—Saint-Preux is sent away. He threatens suicide and Julie wavers. Milord Bomston offers an estate in England, should they wish to elope. But there is growing in Julie an ever greater love of self-sacrifice. She discovers the calm and sublime majesty of a pure life. On the day she marries Wolmar she has a kind of conversion experience, conceives a still deeper passion for "virtue," and writes Saint-Preux that even if she were now wholly free to choose she would still prefer her husband to him. After this news Saint-Preux goes off to sea and disappears for three years, while Julie and Wolmar, whose cool capability resembles that of the Tutor and the Lawgiver in Rousseau's other works of this period, establish a utopian commune at Clarens modeled on the principles—to be discussed below—of Rousseau's "social contract." Saint-Preux returns at length, and Wolmar undertakes to make a communard of him. He arranges a series of tests to see whether Julie and Saint-Preux can suppress their passion for each other. Technically they pass these tests, and life at Clarens continues outwardly happy, with all parties claiming to delight in their "perfect communion" with each other. In the long run, however, Julie's imperfectly muffled passion proves her undoing; unable fully to reconcile heart and mind, she goes into a decline. Her serene yet rapturous deathbed "profession of faith" in a rather indeterminate God anticipates that of the Savoyard Vicar in *Émile*. It is tame reading today, but it shocked the orthodox in Rousseau's time and contributed in the long run to the prosecution of his work.

As his novel neared completion Rousseau became intimate with the maréchal and Mme. de Luxembourg, who were to be his next and most estimable hosts. At their insistence he began to make extensive use of the Petit Château on their Montmorency estate. He was more in their company than out of it for the next three years. During this time he worked on *Émile* and *Du contrat social* (*The Social Contract*), both of which he was soon after to describe as forming "one whole" with *Julie*. A fuller examination of this alleged unity may be postponed for later discussion. Briefly, *Émile* can be described here as the record of the training and growth of a sensibility. At first the text is nearly all generalized advice; later, as the pupil's personality becomes distinct and his tutor must take more specific action with him, a kind of narrative develops, culminating in the introduction of a third character, Sophie, whose education "as a woman" is described. Her family and home are also vividly described and placed in an idyllic setting not unlike parts of Oliver Goldsmith's *Vicar of Wakefield*. The "Profession of Faith" that is interpolated midway through the text of *Émile*, not so much to teach religion to Émile as to show how the author came to view the universe as he does, attracted nearly all the attention that the book was to receive in its own time.

The influence of *Émile* today, however, is widespread if not always fully or even consciously comprehended. Rousseau's insistence that the pupil learn by experiment, not rote, that he not be taught to reason or even to cultivate feelings prematurely—that he be left, in short, in a condition approaching the "state of nature"—all this in its general tendency can be said to have changed the course of education. Rousseau can also be credited with making breast feeding by mothers respectable among the well-to-do, who had formerly hired wet nurses, and with putting an end to the practice of tightly swaddling infants.

In all, though, *Émile* remains the strangest of Rousseau's works for the modern reader, not so much because we sense an unhealthiness—a *denial* of freedom—in the Tutor's round-the-clock zeal or because we sense that even the freshest aspects of Émile's upbringing themselves quickly become rote exercises, but because the work itself is so uncertain as to its own identity; it teeters between the genres of manifesto, handbook, and novel for no apparent reason, unless it be that its subject makes the author nervous. *Émile* is, after all, his attempt to atone for having abandoned his children, and even more importantly it is an attempt by Rousseau to start from the beginning and re-create himself, to imagine his own childhood as it might better have been if the adult Rousseau were to be "as he should be."

The Social Contract (1762) is a society made up of Émiles. They are "natural," sturdy, and open-hearted people, yet they are also "docile" and contented in their "yoke," these being some of Wolmar's favorite terms in *Julie*. Behind these compatriots, shaping their attitudes, stands a sublimely shadowy figure in the role of the Tutor, namely, the Lawgiver. His task is to create laws that will permanently mold the will of a populace into unanimity, taking into account their numbers, their collective temperament, their climate, and so on. This unanimity Rousseau calls the General Will, an absolute consensus of all citizens on all matters to which even the Sovereign—the executive branch of government—must submit. We shall return later to the crucial concept of the General Will, which is carefully defined by Rousseau in *The Social Contract*, and which preconditions all the more specific comparisons in later chapters of the various forms of government. It is Rousseau's most seminal concept and also his most dangerous. It breathes through the French Revolution, especially during the Terror. It justifies the punishment of all dissidence and requires that every citizen become a public informer. It is chilling to read such passages as this one: "Whoever refuses to obey the general will shall be constrained to do so by the whole body, which means nothing other than that he shall be forced to be free" (p. 64). *The Social Contract* was burned in several countries when it appeared in 1762, but not because of its politics. Its chief offense was having been written by the infidel author of the "Profession of Faith."

In 1762 the main business before the Parlement of Paris was to find ways of curbing the influence of the Jansenists. It seems likely, then, that the proceedings brought against *Émile* were meant to show the world that the parlement could also be stern with freethinkers. Whatever the motive, these proceedings led to Rousseau's flight from France, the circumstances of which remain obscure in other respects as well. The Luxembourgs were intimate with the prince de Conti, who often acted like a royal opposition of one, and also with the censor, Malesherbes; they all admired Rousseau and underestimated the seriousness of his opponents. Largely as a favor to Rousseau, they sped up the publication of *Émile* by having it published in Paris, not in Holland as planned. There were still delays, which enraged Rousseau and brought on symptoms of the paranoia to come. When he learned how unjustified his suspicions of Malesherbes in particular had been, he wrote him four apologetic and self-explanatory letters that we read today as a rehearsal for the *Confessions*. Unfortunately for Rousseau, the support of his powerful friends jeopardized their own position and necessitated their eventual treachery. When it became clear that *Émile* would be prosecuted, they all stood liable to the charge of sedition if their arrangements for the French printing came to be known, and they were not encouraged to rely on Rousseau's discretion in view of his deter-

mination to plead his case before the parlement, like Alceste, in the teeth of all protocol. In any case, we know that the Luxembourgs, in their effort to get him out of France, played up the rumor that the author as well as the book was to be tried and punished. Rousseau consented to flee, persuaded only, as he swore, by the knowledge that Mme. de Luxembourg might be compromised if he stayed on.

He arrived at Iverdun in June of 1762, hoping to find asylum among the Genevans, for whom he thought he had done so much. Four days later the news arrived that both *Émile* and *The Social Contract* had been burned in Geneva. Like the French, the Protestant aristocrats of Geneva wanted nothing to do with sedition or "theism." Rousseau went on to the canton of Berne, but he was denounced by the magistrates there as well. He continued into Neuchâtel, a Prussian territory, and settled in the town of Môtiers.

His first act was to write a haughty letter to Voltaire's patron, Frederick the Great, brusquely affirming that he cared neither for Frederick nor for his policies, but requesting nevertheless to be allowed to live in his dominions. The urbane Frederick was doubtless amused at this missive; one imagines that he counted it an honor to have another luminary on Prussian soil. The marshal in Rousseau's region, a Scottish expatriate named Keith, both appreciated and humored his visitor. He is one of Rousseau's most attractive "fathers," and his friendship was a consolation throughout the humiliations to come. Rousseau now sent for Thérèse, warning her that she might not find it pleasant to follow him into exile. But follow she did. At this time Rousseau adopted as his daily costume an Armenian robe, partly out of singularity and partly for the quicker relief of a urinary disorder that had tormented him for years. Still another gesture as he settled in was to petition the local minister, one Montmollin, to be allowed to take Communion in his congregation. His petition was granted, but with misgivings that were to deepen.

Rousseau answered only one of the tirades against *Émile;* his respectful and eloquent *Letter to the Archbishop of Paris* was his first work completed in exile. During this period he also began the "life" of himself that had been requested by his publisher in Holland. It quickly became the first six books of the *Confessions.* In 1763, after many insults and rebuffs, Rousseau abdicated from his Genevan citizenship, a gesture that, in the sheer pathos of its ineffectuality, rivals that of Shakespeare's Coriolanus ("I banish *you!*"). In September there appeared in Geneva an anonymous, well-written treatise, *Letters Written from the Country,* against "Rousseauistic" tendencies in politics and religion. Rousseau spent the winter replying to this work in his *Letters Written from the Mountain.* He begins with yet another vindication of himself from all charges of sedition and irreligion, then proceeds to the strongest attack he ever wrote on the intolerance of the Genevan pastors and the elitism of Genevan politics.

During the lull before this work was published in 1764, Rousseau received a flattering request from a Corsican emissary. He had said in *The Social Contract* that of all the European states only Corsica was "youthful" enough to be given a new constitution, and now he found himself being asked to write it. The result was his "Project for the Constitution of Corsica," but nothing practical came of it because, as Rousseau had feared, the Corsicans had to go on fighting for their independence from Genoa and France. When *Letters Written from the Mountain* was published, all Switzerland fell upon its author. The furor reached Neuchâtel for the first time; Montmollin tried to keep Rousseau out of his church, wrote pamphlets against him, and finally even preached against him. On two occasions Rousseau's house was stoned; the second time he was nearly struck by a rock that flew into his bedroom. Another cause of this redoubled hatred was the publication of a pamphlet, almost certainly by Voltaire (though Rousseau never guessed it), called *The Sentiment of the Citizens.* It was a slander, but it contained one truth: the author of *Émile* had gotten rid of his children. Rousseau henceforth felt that his *Confessions* were no longer an avocation but a necessity. He had no other forum. From then on one of the main topics of his paranoia was the *Confessions* manuscript, which he copied again and again and sent to various friends, only to suspect them afterward of tampering with it.

Once more Rousseau was obliged to steal away. He entered upon one of his happiest idylls, on the island of Saint-Pierre in the Lake of Bienne, which he rendered exquisitely in the fifth Promenade of his *Reveries.* Here he wandered daily, indulged his new passion for botany, and rowed on the lake. One day he rowed a few rabbits to a nearby island and "founded," as he put it, "a small colony." The island of Saint-Pierre could not be a permanent refuge, however, because it was in Berne. Rousseau was driven away after two months. He proceeded to Strasbourg, where he lingered uncertainly. At last he decided to accept the longstanding invitation of the philosopher David Hume to come to England, and accordingly he went ahead to Paris. He reentered the city without hindrance in December of 1765 and stayed for a few days, then journeyed to London in the company of Hume, who made a very favorable first impression on him.

Rousseau still knew no English, and for that reason Hume wanted him to stay in London, fearing that in the countryside, where Rousseau wanted to settle, he would not be able to make his wants known. This conflict of purpose, together with Rousseau's inability to understand how Hume could remain on friendly terms both with the Paris *philosophes* and with himself, colored his view of his host almost from the beginning. Matters were made worse by the fact that even before Rousseau arrived there was circulated in London a satiric "Letter from Frederick II to Rousseau," requesting him to "come and live with me" on condition that he give up his love of being persecuted. It was written by the wit and litterateur Horace Walpole. Rousseau never found out the secret and rightly suspected Hume of being unwilling to divulge it.

At length Rousseau found a country residence with Richard Davenport at Wootton in Derbyshire. He lived there for a year and seemed—not for the first time—to be as much loved by the local gentry as he was reviled everywhere else. Thérèse had long since arrived in the escort of an acquaintance from the Môtiers period. This was one of Europe's most accomplished autograph hunters and rakehells, Dr. Johnson's biographer James Boswell, who seduced Thérèse (or was seduced by her) as soon as they were alone together. Most of the pages relating to the feats they performed on their journey have been discreetly torn out of Boswell's famous *Journal.* Thérèse arrived, found that she hated England, and set about making life difficult for everyone, especially Davenport's servants.

One hesitates to call anyone paranoid who had been as often and as diversely tormented as Rousseau was, but it is indeed true that he imagined even worse persecutions than he suffered. Soon enough convinced that Hume was and always had been in league with the Grimm circle, Rousseau wrote him in July of 1766 an absolutely crazed twenty-five-page letter of accusation. Hume was gravely offended, though even at the time he pitied Rousseau's mental plight. The contents of this letter and of similar ones to others were noised abroad. Hume hesitated for a long time before defending himself publicly, but finally he was driven by fear of what Rousseau might say about him in the *Confessions* to publish his *Succinct Exposé* of his dealings with his guest.

In May of 1767 Rousseau "escaped" back to France in a condition near lunacy. Still fortunate in finding eminent hosts, he went first to stay on the estate of the marquis de Mirabeau. The prince de Conti wished, however, to control Rousseau's movements more carefully than Mirabeau's patronage would permit. The prince still wanted at all costs to keep Rous-

seau away from Paris; to this end he took him in hand, painted lurid pictures of his probable condemnation without a hearing, and whisked him off to his own estate, Trye-le-Château. There Rousseau remained for a time, taking an assumed name, Renou. Early in 1768, the old concierge of the château died, and Rousseau was suspected locally of having poisoned him. Under this shadow Rousseau departed for Lyon, where he had old friends, and settled nearby. At this point, after twenty-three years, "Renou" married Thérèse, perhaps in order to lend respectability to his impersonation. Then a man came forward with a complicated story about a debt, embroiling Rousseau in yet further scandal. He moved on to the village of Monquin, still in the vicinity of Lyon.

By 1770 Rousseau had had enough of concealment and determined to go to Paris at whatever cost. He resumed his name and traveled through Lyon, where he had the pleasure of seeing his operas staged. It was then also that he had his most important poem (or "lyric scene"), *Pygmalion,* set to music. This is the poem of a person who feels, as Rousseau did in 1762 when he wrote it, that he has completed his work and has fallen in love with it, like the unfortunate sculptor in the myth. In the cold form of his creation Pygmalion sees himself reflected. Just so Rousseau, with his sense of selfhood resurgent, now goes to Paris intending to bring his Galatea to life by reading the recently completed *Confessions* aloud in the salons.

The story we have been sketching is essentially that of the *Confessions,* though we have had to redress some imbalances and fill in some blank spots. But obviously to sketch Rousseau's story is not enough. Though not quite "without precedent," as Rousseau boasted in the first paragraph (there had been Saint Augustine, of course, and there were other related works), the *Confessions* is certainly "unique," and it remains one of the three or four greatest autobiographies ever written. The early books are marked especially by two conflicting qualities: first, by their painful candor, as when Rousseau makes a clean breast of having once accused a fellow servant of stealing a ribbon he himself had stolen to give to her; and second, by their idyllic evocation of rural Savoy, so clearly inspired by the need to reconstruct the past by purifying its images in the memory. Of course, this conflict between confession and idealization plays havoc with the facts; at the same time, however, the text probably owes its power to that very tension. The second six books, written long after the first six, are much darker. At times, like a typical madman in fiction, Rousseau pauses in his narrative to peer out the window, hoping to descry the "enemies" in the bushes who lie plotting to snatch his manuscript from him. The closer to the present he gets, the less he professes to understand his plight, and so book 12 pathetically opens: "Here begins the work of darkness in which I have been entombed for eight years [since 1762], without ever having been able, try as I might, to pierce its hideous obscurity."

Rousseau had another flattering invitation to play the Lawgiver in 1772, one that resulted in his posthumous *Considerations on the Government of Poland*. But he was mainly concerned now to consider and reconsider himself. His public readings of the *Confessions* were not as satisfying as he had hoped they would be: people flocked to hear them, but their motive was too obviously curiosity and not the wish to render justice to the author. For the next four years, from 1772 to 1776, Rousseau worked on his endless *Dialogues: Rousseau juge de Jean-Jacques*. This work appears in three parts, each of them cast as a conversation between Rousseau and an initially hostile "Frenchman" whom he converts to his cause. The first dialogue rehearses the plot against him, the second presents the "true Jean-Jacques," and the third examines and vindicates his writings. In the summer of 1776 Rousseau's madness worsened. First he tried to put a copy of the *Dialogues* on the altar at Notre Dame cathedral, then he wrote yet another self-defense called "To Every Frenchman Who Still Loves Justice and Truth" and tried to hand it out to passersby in the Tuileries.

In the fall he grew calmer and began to work intermittently on his last confession, a minor and grotesquely flawed masterpiece entitled *The Reveries of a Solitary Walker* (1776–1778). This text consists of ten Promenades, the last being an unfinished tribute to Maman and Les Charmettes. The others are nearly all filled with the tedious refrain that he never thinks about his enemies anymore; yet there is a truly meditative freedom of movement in these essays—from apostrophe to analysis, from dialectic to description—that creates a charged atmosphere despite the vituperative digressions. In the spring of 1778, with this manuscript in hand, Rousseau went to live with his last host, the marquis de Girardin, at Ermenonville, where he died two months later of uremic poisoning. At his own request, or so Girardin claimed, he was buried on the Isle of Poplars at Ermenonville. Biographers have suspected Girardin of wishing to hoard Rousseau's reputation, his ashes, and especially his *Confessions* manuscript for profit; hence they welcomed the transfer of Rousseau's remains to the Panthéon in Paris during the Revolution that his writings had helped to inspire. Thérèse lived through the Revolution and was much fêted by its leaders. She somehow managed to blackmail Girardin into giving up the *Confessions* manuscript, which she then presented to the French nation. Until her death she regaled listeners with drunken accounts of the genius she had coped with for so long.

As we have seen, most of Rousseau's writings hover near the border between fiction and nonfiction. Though sometimes he seems to be describing an actual state of things, he rarely does so. Nearly all of his works include an idyllic interlude, often only vaguely connected to the main argument, which is designed in part to signal the close neighborhood of the fabulous to the real. All is hypothetical: a conceivable "state of nature" (Second Discourse); an ideal society free from the effects of civilization (First Discourse, "Preface to Narcissus," Letter to d'Alembert); a society of "true Christians" ("Profession of Faith," Letters Written from the Mountain); a society properly confederated (The Social Contract); a "natural" childhood (Émile). We laugh when somebody says: "My mind's made up; don't confuse me with facts." Rousseau was very serious, though, when he wrote in the Second Discourse: "Let us begin by setting the facts aside, for they do not affect the question." What does affect the question, then? A first clue may appear in his insistence, in the Reveries, that the distortions of fact in the Confessions are in no sense lies: "to lie without prejudice to oneself or another is not to lie; it is not a deceit, it is fiction." We know that Rousseau assumes the Confessions before all else to be "true"; hence we seem to have arrived at the paradox that the truth may reside, may even most properly reside, in fiction. If we are to understand Rousseau we must understand this paradox, and also try to see how and why it makes sense.

Rousseau loved to support his arguments with anecdotes from "history," usually from the annals of Livy, Tacitus, or Plutarch. However, he did not relish history as a source of facts. For him it was a form of instructive fiction. As he put it in a note to Émile: "A wise man should consider history a tissue of fables whose morals are well adapted to the human heart." All knowledge, all stored knowledge, that is, turns stale for Rousseau simply from being too commonly and inertly "known," in being the object of that "study" which is too often a form of ostentatious idleness and corrupts spontaneous feeling. At its best knowledge remains vitally present in "fables."

Such fables are "adapted" to the heart but by no means necessarily adapted to circumstances in the external world. Hence in 1764 the author of The Social Contract can honestly remind a correspondent that "fanciful ideas are very good in books, but when it is a ques-

tion of forming a body-politic one must begin by knowing men well and taking them as they are." Thus, despite their uncompromising manner, Rousseau's writings still allow for actuality, which is most often precisely opposite in its nature and its requisites to the ideal. Whenever he confronts the actual, Rousseau is no longer an innovative thinker; he follows the lead of Montesquieu in The Spirit of the Laws, who says that the mores of a people will always depend on their climate, geography, and racial or national character.

In treating the real and the ideal Rousseau entertains a double standard, then, which has caused a great deal of misunderstanding among readers. For example, he often argues that what is pernicious when virtue flourishes in youthful societies is actually beneficial when societies have already been corrupted by the influence in question. The same theater that would destroy the Spartan virtues of Geneva is needed in Paris to divert idlers and rogues from worse mischief. This tendency of Rousseau to overturn his most heartfelt maxims under the pressure of reality extends even to his condescending estimate of women. In his published work he often says that by nature women are meant solely for childbirth and household economy—and that they should never cultivate talents that would draw them away from the home. He turns rather finely against these bromides, however— without contradicting them—in his correspondence with a Mlle. Henriette, who wished to become a philosopher: "Though my ideas on these things differ much from yours, we are approximately in agreement as to what you ought to do. Study is from now on the lance of Achilles for you, which should heal the wound it has made."

When he appeals to ideal standards, Rousseau typically applies the lash by reminding us of what we are not. And not just "we": in certain moods it is his singular genius, developed almost to the point of morbid self-loathing, to assume that whatever he himself is not is better than what he is. He rarely recommends, however, what the hapless Saint-Preux recommends for himself—namely, that we attempt belatedly to become what we might have been. Like so many other theoreticians of change, Rousseau disappointed his disciples by preferring the status quo in practical affairs: "Once customs are established and prejudices rooted, reform is a dangerous and fruitless enterprise" (*The Social Contract*, pp. 88–89). Just how, then, is Rousseau's critique of life in society from an ideal standpoint to be "adapted" to things as they are? How *do* we make use of a maxim, historical or otherwise, if it is nothing more than the moral of a "fable" for the heart?

The answer, for Rousseau, is that underneath all the veneers and rouges of society the heart itself is unchanging. He writes for no other purpose than to repeat, as he insists over and over, that "man is born good." In each succeeding text he tries to prove this assertion by reconstructing possible moments and environments in which the innate goodness of man can shine forth. "Reconstruct" is a useful word here, because Rousseau always proceeds to his point by tracing his subject back to its origin or essence and then drawing it toward the present along essential rather than accidental lines. Thus the fact that the Tutor begins to train Émile when he is an infant is a result, perhaps, of Rousseau's having realized that by the time Wolmar began training the adult Saint-Preux it was already too late. And thus also the *Confessions* can have an expiatory, cleansing function only if they begin not by merely recording the birth of the hero but by "remounting" (*remontant*) toward the sources of the hero's character.

The presupposition behind this habit of *remontage* in Rousseau is a large one. He assumes that the heart, as the source of our moral sense, is inalienable, on the grounds that what is original is also what is authentic. At our origin, if we can recover it, we will find that we are fully present to ourselves, whole and self-confirming, without the need for reflection or relationship. However unappealing

Rousseau's portrayal of the state of nature may sometimes be (in *The Social Contract* he stresses its Hobbesian bestiality far more than in the *Discourse on Inequality*), it remains, in both his autobiographical and social writings, a paradise from which man is expelled by falling into the interdependencies of culture. "Man is born free," *The Social Contract* begins, "but everywhere he is in chains." The aim of *remontage* is to remind man of his original freedom, which is to say his authenticity. In the *Discourse on Inequality* Rousseau puts this aspect of the contrast between the states of nature and culture very clearly: "The savage lives within himself; the sociable man, always outside of himself, knows how to live only in the opinion of others; and it is, so to speak, from their judgment alone that he draws the sentiment of his existence" (p. 179). If there is a single continuous topic in Rousseau, it concerns the misfortune of "living outside oneself." The whole of his critical armory is discharged against the inauthenticity fostered by society.

In his very first work, the trivial comedy *Narcissus, or the Self-Lover,* this theme already appears in the treatment of the two male characters. Valère, a vain fop, would seem immediately to urge the objection of Rousseau's detractors that "authenticity" is really anti-social narcissism, but this is not quite the point of his characterization. He falls in love not with himself absolutely, but with a picture of himself in woman's clothes—with a mirror image of himself as another. To echo this theme, Léandre has needlessly complicated the feelings of his betrothed by having wooed her in another city under an assumed name. Both are determined by another: Valère loves himself as another, Léandre misrepresents himself to another. In Rousseau's last work, the *Reveries,* we find his profoundest treatment of this same theme. In the Fourth Promenade he meditates on what it means to be "good," and more specifically he reviews the reasons why he has stubbornly maintained all his life that his true character is virtuous, whatever his behavior may have been. In the serene return to the self in absolute solitude that occasions and informs the *Reveries,* Rousseau insists that goodness can have no other measure than that of sincerity, and that it must therefore constantly elude the moral estimates of society: I, Jean Jacques, than whom no one has ever been more remorselessly banished from society, have never yet been banished, even by my cleverest enemies, from myself; I am proof, then, that the heart is unchanging and can be recalled to itself. Thus Rousseau's fables, "adapted to the heart," however fabulous they may be, can still be realized.

Rousseau's distinction between the alienated and the authentic self in his autobiographies has its equivalent, in his social thought, in the distinction between "men" and "man." *Émile,* he writes to a Genevan correspondent, "is a philosophical work on the principle advanced by the author in other writings, *that man is naturally good.* To reconcile this principle with the other truth, that men are bad, it would be necessary to show in the history of the human heart the origin of all the vices." In the *Discourse on Inequality* he clearly shows what he thinks this origin is: it is property. In the state of nature no one owns anything because things are used simply as they are needed. Nothing is desired, because the imagination is still dormant, and savage man is therefore free from the torments of recollection and anticipation. If the stronger bullies the weaker over some passing matter, there are no jealousies to prolong the quarrel. Then, after many changes have occurred, the imagination comes into being, with its power of retaining images on the memory and projecting them into the future. Once duration has been experienced, preference and attachment will arise of themselves. Need becomes desire, and possession becomes proprietary: "The first person who, having fenced off a plot of ground, took it into his head to say *this is mine* and found people simple enough to be-

lieve him, was the founder of civil society." He was also the founder of inauthenticity, because the people who believed him began from then on to value themselves by his standard.

Imagination, as we know from all of Rousseau's personal writings (starting with the letters to Malesherbes), is the downfall of natural man but the salvation of social man. Through imagination man in society can "remount" to discover the inner worth from which the debasements of imagination (ambition, avarice, envy, lust) have hitherto alienated him. Here is the paradox in Rousseau that has most deeply influenced the course of romanticism: through desire we can transcend desire. It is in the *Reveries* that, left solely to "the sweetness of speaking with my own soul," Rousseau is for the first time able to forget Jean Jacques, to obliterate his identity among men and recover his identity as man. The function of desire in this sort of reverie is that it carries Rousseau back to the embrace of nature.

That nature can be the vehicle or medium of man's self-recovery is a possibility we should infer from Rousseau's avowal that man is born *naturally* good. It remains, then, to ask what "nature" is, and how we can return to it. This is an important question, because if no recovery of nature is possible, then we still have not found a bridge from fable to the external world and remain imprisoned in ourselves while living only in the eyes of others. Rousseau's work indicates two opposite paths toward reintegration, two sorts of liaison between self and world, which may not amount to the same thing but are closely related and may serve their turn alternately.

Along one of these paths, nature is a landscape without figures, a space where society is not and that the individual may then fill with himself, as it were, through a soothing act of identification. So it is when nature seems to reflect or second one's emotional state, as in the wintry *Reveries:* "The country, still green

1534

and smiling, but unleafed in part, and already almost desert, offered everywhere the image of solitude and of the approach of winter" (p. 46). This form of identification with nature does not work, however, when at the same time there exists a need for conformity to the will of others; when man is too far socialized, in other words, for the luxury of isolation to be possible. Thus, in *La nouvelle Héloïse*, Saint-Preux and Julie, who is now married to another and deeply committed to the idea of social virtue, find themselves alone together in a landscape that invites them to reject society and recover their natural affinity for each other. In this "solitary place," which is "wild and lonely, but replete with beauties of the sort that please only sensitive spirits and seem horrible to others," Julie and Saint-Preux *renounce* the mirror of themselves they find in nature and return to their sheltered utopia, within which anything "wild and lonely" would indeed seem "horrible."

In the long run this renunciation will prove tragic for Julie, who cannot be reconciled emotionally to the socialization for which she has volunteered. Even so, what Julie fails to do is possible to do in theory. If at one extreme man can be restored to nature in solitude, at the other extreme he can recover his "natural" authenticity, as Julie attempts to do, through an absolute commitment to the social order. What then can "nature" possibly mean in this case? Julie's famous garden may provide an emblem for it. Saint-Preux visits the enclosure where her "garden" is planted and remarks, true to his "wild and lonely" instincts: "You did nothing but leave nature alone. . . . I see no trace of human design." To which Julie responds: "It is true that nature has done everything, but she has done it at my behest, and there is nothing that I have not planned." Thus we arrive at still another important paradox in Rousseau, the one that most concerns students of his political philosophy: The utmost *artifice* must be used in the re-creation of "nature" for social ends.

For Julie, who cannot finally harmonize the moral order (as represented by the guidance of Wolmar) with the passionate "disorder" of her nature (as reflected in Saint-Preux), this experiment in the re-creation of nature must be said to fail. In general, though, it is an essential tenet of Rousseau's regenerative fable that the experiment may succeed. "Much art is required," he says in *Émile*, "to prevent man in society from becoming altogether artificial" (p. 282). What is needed is a guiding hand that combines the skill of a savant (even in his polemics against the arts and sciences Rousseau admitted that in every era there are a few persons suited for "study") with the disinterestedness of man without desire or acquisitiveness in the state of nature. In this figure, that of the guide whose hand, like Wolmar's, controls all things, Rousseau invests his identity as a moral teacher, just as he invests his identity as a "sensitive spirit" in figures like Saint-Preux. We find the guide present in nearly all of Rousseau's work, beginning with the Soothsayer in *Le devin du village*. In this early operetta, because Rousseau has not yet determined that disinterestedness alone can lend dignity to wisdom, he gives the Soothsayer a personal motive—to avenge himself on the Lady of the Manor—for his benevolence toward his pastoral charges. Already, though, the Soothsayer manifests a strange attribute of all the guides in Rousseau: he needs to use duplicity in order to enforce sincerity among men—to promote nature, in short, by means of art. Thus the Soothsayer sways the affections and actions of the artless couple he advises by pretending to have magical powers, by presenting ordinary good sense in the guise of supernatural knowledge. This same trick will be used by the Lawgiver in *The Social Contract*. Admitting that the work of the Lawgiver is "a task which is beyond human powers," Rousseau then explains why the pretense of divination is needed to make the task feasible. In order to accept law, "men would have to have become before the advent of law that which they become as a result of law. . . . It is this which has obliged the founders of nations throughout history [for example, Moses] to appeal to divine intervention and to attribute their own wisdom to the gods" (p. 89).

"The greatest art," Horace had written long before, "is to conceal art," and this is the central maxim of the ultimate Rousseauian preceptor, the Tutor in *Émile*. It is odd to find Rousseau speaking repeatedly in that strange text of "the great art of the master," and yet saying, often in nearly the same breath, that Émile "is a man of nature's making, not man's." Possibly it is too much to claim that there is no contradiction at all here, but the sympathetic reader may feel the contradiction less by recalling the way sculptors have of saying that their work "simply brings out the natural potential of the material." If the Tutor in *Émile* were to handle his pupil against the grain, as it were, the pupil would resist and refuse in the long run to be shaped at all. Hence it is necessary for the guiding hand to be hidden, a *main cachée*. Not without reason, this recurrent phrase in Rousseau has raised many specters in the minds of later readers: thought control, subliminal advertising, stock responses, all are products of the hidden hand. In fact, it had been Rousseau's plan, in a project to be called the *Morale sensitive*, to study the way in which feelings arise from sensations and to recommend alterations in the human environment, based on his findings, that would make feelings predictable and uniform. Whatever the unpleasant consequences of this notion might be, it should be added in fairness that it is the brainstorm of one who had reason enough to know the anarchy of untutored feeling. Perhaps it is reserved more properly for the "romantic" Rousseau than for T. S. Eliot to remark that "only those who have personality and emotions know what it means to want to get away from these things."

Within the individual, there is a tutorial presence in addition to the one that is placed above him. Rousseau calls it "conscience" or the "inner voice." We can appreciate the sincerity of his belief in the need for a "hidden hand" by making note again of his conviction that he needs it most for himself. First in the letters to Malesherbes and later in the *Reveries*, Rousseau admits that for him, as for the child Émile and for the common citizen, all duty understood merely as duty is onerous: "The least duties of civil life are unbearable," he tells Malesherbes, and in the *Reveries* he recalls how he once had to change the route of his daily walk in order to avoid giving alms to a certain mendicant child, alms formerly a pleasure to dispense but later a mere routine. For duty to be tolerable, in other words, it must be indistinguishable from the spontaneous dictates of the "inner voice"; the art of smooth government consists in bringing about a perfect congruence of this kind between conscience and duty. In the possibility of this congruence we find the key doctrine of *The Social Contract*, that of the General Will.

"My dog himself was my friend, not my slave," writes Rousseau, referring to his idyllic walks in the country; "we always had the same will, but it was not because he obeyed me." This relation between dog and master is the same as the relation between man as an individual and man as a citizen in *The Social Contract*. The selfish side of me, subject to every sort of passion and private interest, is the *moi humain*; the disinterested side, the *moi commun*, is the part of me that reason bids to enter into a contract with others for the purpose of mutual protection from all selfish interests whatsoever, including my own. Notice that in this contractual sacrifice my selfishness is not somehow magically rooted out. It is given that I cannot prefer "that which is external to me" (1764 letter to the abbé de Carondelet) to my own interests. On the contrary, my deference to the *moi commun* is in my interest—"the ordering of things is all done with reference to myself," because I am the one who is to be protected from (among others) myself.

This union of all men against their own caprices, then, constitutes the General Will.

Whenever the individual loses himself in the citizen (again, "men" are lost in "man"), it is impossible that his will should then be in conflict with the General Will because in fact as an individual—as one whose interests and desires differ from those of others—he no longer exists. The General Will is the emergence of a single "nature," stripped of all accident and idiosyncrasy, which comprises man. Hence, at the opposite extreme from the solitary communion with nature that is engaged in by the "unique" Rousseau of the confessional writings, this political entity is, in itself, the second solution we mentioned earlier to the problem of human inauthenticity. Man cannot "live outside of himself," authenticated only in the parading of his personality for the approval of others, if in fact he has no distinct personality or *moi humain* to live outside of. The "solitary walker" merges himself with the natural world and thus finds himself, whereas the "citizen" finds himself through his merger with human "nature," an indivisible and undifferentiated entity, in the social world.

Perhaps this identification with others is made easier for Rousseau by the vividness with which he can imagine society as a single body, a body politic. The metaphor is of course nearly as old as political thought itself, and is implicit in the title of Thomas Hobbes's *Leviathan*. But if Hobbes thought of the social body as a brutishly demoniacal thing like the biblical monster, Rousseau by contrast thought of this body as a happily intertwined family. The relations of husband and wife, father and son, tutor and pupil—all are clearly present in it, as are other more remote relations that Rousseau's personal longing for a family familiarizes even to the point of incest. Mme. de Warens is "Maman," Thérèse is "Tante," older friends are "fathers," and younger friends are "sons" and "daughters." Thus in Rousseau's life as well as in his work, society is joined together, and the *moi humain* can be lost in the *moi commun* as the head is lost in the heart.

The obverse of this tendency to unify human relations is Rousseau's heightened sense of the fragility of society. If for other observers society is never perfect but always muddles through, for Rousseau society is theoretically perfectible but actually on the brink of catastrophe, riven as it is by dangerous family quarrels. Just so, there is no middle ground between intimate friendship and inveterate enmity. This attitude is partly rhetorical; it can be traced back to the exaggerations of neoclassical tragedy, in which speakers are either confidants or traitors. But it stems also from the unusual intensity with which Rousseau experienced friendship. Even for the "imaginary beings" he often said he preferred to real ones, he could experience perfect ecstasies of feeling. He viewed love as a "terrible passion" fraught with "its perplexity, its frenzies, its palpitations" (*Letter to D'Alembert*). During his walks to visit Mme. d'Houdetot he would be seized with paroxysms of longing that would leave him trembling and weak. A temperament this high-strung is also bound to suffer transports of revulsion or, worse, to assume that others do. For others the experience of friendship is calmer, less all-consuming than it is for him. How then can it be sincere? Is it not likely that the lukewarm attentions of friends are but cunning masks for their treachery?

There is only one way to be sure, and that is to eliminate privacy from the lives of all those who have entered into the social contract. Like most political theorists, Rousseau declares that the ideal state must be a small one, but for him this assertion has a personal twist. He requires:

a state where, all the individuals knowing one another, neither the obscure maneuvers of vice nor the modesty of virtue could be hidden from the notice and judgment of the public, and where the sweet habit of seeing and knowing one another turned love of the fatherland into love of the citizens rather than love of the soil.

("To the Republic of Geneva," p. 79)

In this view, it is a noble calling to be a public informer. Rousseau, who was more afraid of the dark than most, associates privacy with darkness and dark deeds: "Innocent joy is likely to evaporate in the full light of day; but vice is a friend of shadows, and never have innocence and mystery lived long together." Émile reaches the age of twenty, yet the Tutor still sleeps in the same room with him so that he will not form the habit of masturbation. Privacy is antisocial and weakens the bonds of love, perhaps even cheats them, as the Tutor's fears would suggest. Any aloofness from others in society is likewise a sign of bad faith.

Certainly it is so in the case of Rousseau himself. The conflict between hypothesis and reality is clearest at this juncture in his thought. Whereas in his fable of the good society all inwardness is assumed to be criminal, in actual society Rousseau himself was withdrawn and solitary by choice. His sociable friends of the Parisian 1840's, Diderot and the others, were quick to tax him with what they took to be an inconsistency in this regard. Rousseau's final break with Diderot came when he rightly understood a line in Diderot's play *The Natural Son*, "only those who are evil live alone," to refer to himself in his retreat at the Hermitage. After announcing this estrangement in the preface to the *Letter to D'Alembert* ("I had an Aristarchus, severe and judicious. I have him no more"), Rousseau immediately goes on to defend himself against Diderot's charge: "Solitude," he says, "calms the soul and appeases the passions born of the disorder of the world. Far from the vices which irritate us, we speak of them with less indignation. . . . Since I see men no more, I have almost stopped hating the wicked." It is later in this same text that Rousseau seems deliberately to contradict this passage and to agree with Diderot after all. But he does not. Here he is discussing an ideal society in contrast to the one that appears on the tragic stage: "The most vicious of men is he who isolates himself the most, who most concentrates his heart in himself; the best is he who shares his affections equally with all his kind." This last phrase is a signal to the attentive reader that the equality in question is that of the fabulous *moi commun,* and that the viciousness of solitude is thus asserted only as part of a corrective fiction, one that is preferable to the enervating fictions of the French stage.

Privacy is a dangerous thing, because, as Rousseau everywhere complains, it allows secrets to spring up between people who should be completely candid and sincere with each other. In politics there should be no secrets because in theory there *can* be none between persons whose interests are the same. In education the pupil can have no secrets from his tutor because any instance of bad faith, however trivial, bespeaks the wish of the pupil to shake off the tutor's "gentle yoke." In each case and also, of course, in friendship and in love, there can be no distance between parties, no opacity; they should be able to read each other (in Rousseau's frequent metaphor) like an open book. Hence there is only one relationship in which man need not be physically present to the others, in which, that is, he may indeed remain solitary. That is the relationship with God as it is described by the Savoyard Vicar in *Émile:* "If I do a good deed in secret," he says, "I know that it is seen." In other words, if a secret act is performed in good faith, it is really not a secret because it is published in the divine ledger.

Hence one's relations with God in private and also with other persons in public should approach the condition that has been stressed by one of Rousseau's best interpreters, Jean Starobinski, namely the condition of "transparency." In the "Profession of Faith," other men, who at best will be transparent to each other, are so many barriers betweeen the worshiper and God: "What! Nothing but human testimony! Nothing but men who tell me what others told them! How many men between God and me!" Clearly in such passages Rousseau is scarcely a creditable Catholic, nor even Protestant enough to suit the prelates of Switzerland, because he stands opposed to all mediation in religious matters. Human interpretations of the divine, even the human transcription of the divine Word in the Bible, are necessarily distortions of the transparent Word itself, and Rousseau wants none of them. Except, of course, his own—which is based, predictably enough, on an idea of Divine Intelligence as thought that has no need for interpretation: "Man is intelligent when he reasons, but the Supreme Intelligence does not need to reason; there is neither premise nor conclusion for him, there is not even a proposition. The Supreme Intelligence is wholly intuitive." To be present to the divine mind, then, is to participate in a paradise of mental repose in which one's need to interpret can be set aside; in the presence of God there is no longer any need to interpret the ambiguous gesture of a friend or the doubtful meaning of words.

The profoundest moments for Rousseau are always wordless, and one of the sadder paradoxes of "authorship" (his contempt for this trade was only partly affectation) is that torrents of words must be poured out in the service of truths that are in themselves, like the Ideas of Plato, properly inexpressible. One troublesome feature of the famous first sentences of the Confessions is that the book he promises is certainly needed to explain the author to other men but should not be required reading for God, from whom we can keep no secrets: "I have bared my secret soul as thou thyself hast seen it, Eternal Being! So let the numberless legion of my fellow men gather round me, and hear my confessions." Well and good, but nothing shows how word-bound Rousseau actually is more than the fantasy that precedes this passage: "Let the last trump sound when it will, I shall come forward with this work in my hand, to present myself before my Sovereign Judge." Perhaps it is a sign not so much of contradiction as of insecurity that Rousseau doubts the transparency of his tangled life even in the eyes of God.

The theme of the Confessions is, after all, the loss of transparency. With the sustained beauty of its idyllic interludes and the pathos of its regretful wanderings over the face of the earth—as much Cain's as Adam's—the Confessions even more than, say, the Discourse on Inequality is Rousseau's Paradise Lost. If he is to witness the calamity of man's fall through his own fault, as Milton's Adam does, Rousseau's record of motives and events must be thorough; he must leave nothing unspoken and "tell the whole truth" (tout dire), or else he will not have restored himself to transparency. He will stand accused, instead, of harboring a reserve of privacy, like a bad citizen or a rebellious pupil: "Since I have undertaken to reveal myself absolutely to the public, nothing about me must remain hidden or obscure. I must remain incessantly beneath [the reader's] gaze, so that he may follow me in all the extravagances of my heart and into every least corner of my life." And so he does, at least up to the limits of his ability to endure self-loathing.

He believes that all his errors stem from his having entered into false relations with a corrupt society, but that he remains, in spite of all the actual harm he has done, essentially good, like "man" in his treatises. If it be said that this reserve clause in his own praise makes it easier for him to catalog his sins of omission and commission toward others, it should also be said that he has entered no plea in his own behalf that he has not entered elsewhere in behalf of mankind. It is fruitless to place him in a double bind wherein his self-praise is conceit and his self-humbling is masochistic exhibitionism. There can be no harm in admitting that, for whatever reason, Rousseau is more candid about even his most sordid failings than most of us could be.

The Confessions must be taken, at least in part, as an exception to our notion that all of Rousseau's works are "a tissue of fables whose morals are well adapted to the human heart." He has no intention of making his confessions fabulous; rather, he says that if they are not unflinchingly accurate they are useless. We have seen, though, that in the Reveries he says defensively that his mode of accuracy is moral rather than factual. He must concede in any case, however, that his medium, language, is scarcely ideal for the achievement of his desired "transparency." It is not really "men," after all, who distort truths, but rather their language distorts them by interpreting them. Language can have only a conventional connection with whatever it signifies: "Let us be in no hurry," Rousseau pleads in *Émile*, to turn the mind of the pupil "towards conventional signs." After all, part of the paradisiacal bliss of childhood is to experience all things firsthand, both in their concreteness and in their closeness—their seeming affinity—to the self.

When the child enters adolescence and becomes subject to "all the vices of our years," even nature itself, which Rousseau often describes as an open book for those willing to read it, loses its immediacy: "The country no longer had for us those sweet and simple charms that touch the heart; it seemed to our eyes depressing and empty, as if it had been covered up by a veil that cloaked its beauties" (*Confessions*, p. 31). So it is also with language, the use of which becomes a token of the loss of innocence in *Émile*. Language is a currency or system of exchange between its users. That is, it is *property*, which is the "origin," we recall, of inequality, and becomes necessary, like money, only in a fallen state. Thus in one sentence Rousseau can write: "The sign has led to the neglect of the thing signified, [and] money is the source of all the false ideas of society." Émile at first "will use speech with all the simplicity of its first beginnings." Even the simplest way of speaking, however, as Rousseau makes clear in his "Essay on the Origin of Languages" (1754), is wildly inaccurate in its first beginnings because at that point it is most figurative, animistic, and subject in general to the whims of the primitive imagination. "Figurative language was the first to be born," Rousseau writes. "Proper meaning was discovered last."

Thus language in its first beginnings is to be preferred for Émile, not because it represents reality more faithfully than the worn-out abstractions and idioms of later times (as many of Rousseau's contemporaries thought), but because it is spontaneous and sincere. The power of generalization needed to fix the "proper meaning" of words takes place at so great a distance from things in themselves that duplicity and bad faith are almost certain to intervene, alienating the mind from reality and filling it with words alone: "Never substitute the symbol for the thing signified, unless it is impossible to show the thing itself; for the child's attention is so taken up with the symbol that he will forget what it signifies."

Rousseau alleges the existence of an intermediate virtue, neither primitive nor sophisticated, in the use of language, one that the Tutor encourages when Émile becomes a young man: "His language will be on the whole simple and literal. He usually speaks to the point and only to make himself understood. He is not sententious, for he has not learnt to generalize; he does not speak in figures, for he is rarely impassioned." This notion of a "literal" language would seem to violate Rousseau's usual understanding of the conventionality of linguistic signs. He had noted in the "Essay" that language is "literal" only when it uses hieroglyphic signs in writing; hence the wish for a literal speech cannot be fulfilled. The ambition to speak literally, without the distortion of figure or abstraction, had already been ridiculed by Jonathan Swift, whose "Projectors" in *Gulliver's Travels* abolish speech altogether and communicate with sacks of objects they carry on their backs and show to one another as the need arises.

Even if a "literal" language were possible, however, it would hardly suit Rousseau's own purposes as a stylist. His style is *always* either "figurative" or "generalized," and derives its power from the way it swings back and forth between these extremes. When Rousseau is most inward, most passionately committed to the authenticity of personal experience, his language is figurative, rich in metaphors and apostrophes and outbursts of lyricism. Typically at the opposite extreme, which is no less rhetorical in its purpose and effect, Rousseau speaks in breathtakingly compressed and abstract sentences, or "maxims," as he often calls them. An example from *The Social Contract* may suffice: "In this inquiry I shall try always to bring together what right permits with what interest prescribes so that justice and utility are in no way divided." A sentence this abstract is so sweeping that it can anticipate the whole course of an argument; each conceptual term is so heavily freighted with implication that the sentence almost seems to contain a drama. It is really as animated and "figurative" as the kind of language that is openly so. It is this second style, which Rousseau learned in large part from the terseness of the Roman historians and moralists, that constitutes his most audible influence on the French Revolution. With the passage just quoted one may compare this brilliant, frightening sentence by the greatest orator of the Terror, Saint-Just: "A republican government has virtue for its principle; if not, terror."

"Force till right is ready," said Joseph Joubert. This principle, couched in language of this kind, is the byword of revolutionary utopianism and becomes an excuse for political enormities. The abstractness of the utopian Rousseau is also the abstractness of the General Will itself—so sweepingly valid, we are meant to feel, that to differ from it in any way can be considered criminal. The reader who feels merely indifferent in the face of these totalizing and totalitarian tendencies of style will probably feel indifferent likewise to utopian thought. This style is meant to induce a kind of breathlessness, even vertigo (in crossing the chasm, for example, between "virtue" and "terror," "right" and "interest"), that weakens resistance. The reader who feels any trace of that sensation—who would "rather be dead than red," or who feels that "if one is not part of the solution one is part of the problem"—will also feel the pull of Rousseau's mind.

His equally compelling power of seeing things concretely and vividly, if no less fancifully, may furnish an antidote to his utopian austerity. He could imagine the lives of beings who never existed, as he often sheepishly admitted, even more vividly than those of real people. Here, for instance, are those conjectural forest beings in the *Discourse on Inequality*, attempting a cooperative hunt for the first time:

> Was it a matter of catching a deer, everyone clearly felt that for this purpose he ought faithfully to keep his post; but if a hare happened to pass within reach of one of them, there can be no doubt that he pursued it without scruple, and that having obtained his prey, he cared very little about having caused his companions to miss theirs.

We can indeed have "no doubt" of it, nor is it possible not to feel the deliciously vacuous laziness of an existence in which "if someone chases me from one tree, I am at liberty to go to another." More often than not we can say of Rousseau's fables what his contemporary Samuel Johnson said of Shakespeare's: "The event which he represents will not happen, but if it were possible, its effects would probably be such as he assigned."

But perhaps the reader will end by preferring above all other moments in Rousseau those few, chiefly in his letters, when he seems not to be writing for effect at all and suddenly hits upon a thought that is neither parable nor maxim but simply apperception. Ordinarily, for example, he is condescending toward the advantages of fame, but on one occasion he admits to enjoying one of them with a cogency that anyone who has ever felt nervous in company will appreciate: "I had done some scribbling and was quite sure of not being taken for a fool, even though guilty of some nonsense in conversation." Or, again, here is Rousseau beseeching Mme. de Verdelin to look after his cat and to "see . . . that no dog bothers her, for she is gentle, timid, and very easy to scare." Sometimes what is most moving, not to say reassuring, in this apostle of Spartan firmness is his irrepressible sympathy for the weak. To the rhapsody of one correspondent about an ideal state in which every citizen would have an "exquisite delicacy" of virtue simply in being a Christian, Rousseau stunningly retorts: "What was our Master thinking of, then, when he blessed the poor in spirit?"

It is even more reassuring when he confesses to a certain spiritual poverty of his own, as in this note to the marshal Keith: "No, Milord, I am not in good health nor am I content. . . . I have a downcast spirit and I derive less courage from my philosophy than from your wine of Spain." The marshal's gift, supposing it to have been a case of Malaga, is the same wine that Julie counterfeits from local grapes in *La nouvelle Héloïse* because, she says, "everything that comes from afar is likely to be disguised or falsified." This may well be true; and it touches upon an important theme in Rousseau's work, as we have seen. But the reader is still free to choose between his confession, which speaks for itself, and his fable with its maxim, which gives preference, as Rousseau's programmatic writings always do, to one kind of falsification over another.

Selected Bibliography

EDITIONS

Correspondance complète de Jean-Jacques Rousseau. Edited by R. A. Leigh. Geneva, 1965– .

Correspondance générale de Jean-Jacques Rousseau. Edited by T. Dufour and P.-P. Plan. 20 vols. Paris, 1924–1934.

Oeuvres complètes. 13 vols. Paris, 1884–1887.

Oeuvres complètes. Edited by Bernard Gagnebin and Marcel Raymond. Paris, 1959– .

The Political Writings of Rousseau. Edited by C. E. Vaughan. 2 vols. Cambridge, 1915.

TRANSLATIONS

*Citizen of Geneva: Selections from the Letters of Jean-Jacques Rousseau. Translated by Charles W. Hendel. New York, 1937.

A Complete Dictionary of Music. Translated by W. Waring. London, 1779.

*Confessions. Translated by J. M. Cohen. Harmondsworth, 1965.

Considerations on the Government of Poland. Translated by W. Kendall. Minneapolis, 1947.

Eloisa; or, A Series of Original Letters. Translated by W. Kenrick. 4 vols. London, 1776.

*Émile. Translated by P. D. Jimack. New York, 1977.

Emilius and Sophia. London, 1783. Sequel to *Émile.*

*The First and Second Discourses. Translated by Roger D. Masters. New York, 1964.

Julie; or, The New Eloise. Translated and abridged by Judith H. McDowell. University Park, Pa., 1968.

Letters on the Elements of Botany. Translated by T. Martyn. London, 1787.

*The Miscellaneous Works of Mr. J. J. Rousseau. 5 vols. London, 1767.

*On the Origin of Language. Translated by John H. Moran and A. Gode. New York, 1966. Essays by Rousseau and Herder.

*Politics and the Arts: Letter to M. D'Alembert on the Theatre. Translated by Allan Bloom. Ithaca, N.Y., 1977.

Pygmalion, a Poem. London, 1779.

*The Reveries of a Solitary. Translated by John Gould Fletcher. London, 1927.

*The Social Contract. Translated by Maurice Cranston. Harmondsworth, 1974.

BIOGRAPHICAL STUDIES

Crocker, Lester G. *Jean-Jacques Rousseau.* 2 vols. New York, 1968–1973. A standard work.

Guéhenno, Jean. *Jean-Jacques.* Translated by John Weightman and Doreen Weightman. 3 vols. London, 1966.

Guillemin, Henri. *"Cette affaire infernale": L'Affaire Jean-Jacques Rousseau–David Hume, 1766.* Paris, 1942.

Marty, Olivier. *Rousseau de l'enfance à quarante ans.* Paris, 1974.

Mornet, Daniel. *Rousseau, l'homme et l'oeuvre.* Paris, 1950.

JEAN JACQUES ROUSSEAU

CRITICAL STUDIES

Althusser, Louis. *Politics and History*. London, 1972.

Amiel, Henri F. *Jean-Jacques Rousseau*. Translated by Van Wyck Brooks. New York, 1922.

Babbitt, Irving. *Rousseau and Romanticism*. Boston, 1919. New edition, with a foreword by Harry Levin. Austin, Tex., 1977.

Barish, Jonas, "The Anti-Theatricalism of Jean-Jacques Rousseau." *Stanford French Review* 1: 167–190 (1976).

Barth, Karl. *Images du XVIIIe siècle*. Neuchâtel, 1949.

Blanchard, W. H. *Rousseau and the Spirit of the Age*. Ann Arbor, Mich., 1967.

Brookner, Anita. "Rousseau and the Social Contract." *Times Literary Supplement* 4011:149–151 (8 Feb. 1980).

Brooks, Peter. "Romantic Antipastoral and Urban Allegory." *Yale Review* 64:11–26 (1974).

Brown, Marshall. "The Pre-Romantic Discovery of Consciousness." *Studies in Romanticism* 17: 387–412 (1977).

Burgelin, Pierre. *La philosophie de l'existence de Jean-Jacques Rousseau*. Paris, 1952.

Cassirer, Ernst. *Rousseau, Kant, Goethe*. Princeton, N.J., 1945.

————. *The Question of Jean-Jacques Rousseau*. Princeton, N.J., 1951.

Cobban, Alfred. *Rousseau and the Modern State*. Hamden, Conn., 1964.

Coleman, Patrick. "Characterizing Rousseau's *Émile*." *MLN* 92:761–778 (1976).

Daedalus 107, 3 (1977). A special Rousseau issue.

De Beer, Gavin R. *Rousseau and His World*. London, 1972. Illustrated.

della Volpe, Galvano. *Rousseau and Marx*. Translated by John Fraser. London, 1978.

de Man, Paul. *Allegories of Reading*. New Haven, Conn., 1979.

Derrida, Jacques. *Of Grammatology*. Translated by Gayatri C. Spivak. Baltimore, 1976.

Dickstein, Morris. "The Faith of a Vicar." *Yale French Studies* 28:48–54 (1961–1962).

Duchet, Michèle, and Michel Launay. "Synchronie et diachronie: *L'Essai sur l'origine des langages* et le second *Discours*." *Revue Internationale de la Philosophie* 82:421–442 (1967).

Durkheim, Emile. *Montesquieu and Rousseau*. Ann Arbor, Mich., 1960.

Ellensburg, Stephen. *Rousseau's Political Philosophy*. Ithaca, N.Y., 1976.

Gay, Peter. *The Enlightenment: An Interpretation*. 2 vols. New York, 1967.

Gouhier, Henri. *Les méditations métaphysiques de Jean-Jacques Rousseau*. Paris, 1970.

Green, F. C. *Jean-Jacques Rousseau*. Cambridge, 1956.

Greene, Liliane. "Landscape in Rousseau." In *Symposium on Romanticism*, edited by Pierre Deguise and Rita Terras. New London, Conn., 1975.

Grimsley, Ronald. *Jean-Jacques Rousseau: A Study in Self-Awareness*. Cardiff, 1961.

————. *Rousseau and the Religious Quest*. Oxford, 1968.

————. *The Philosophy of Rousseau*. New York, 1973.

Hazlitt, William. *The Round Table*. London, 1817.

Huizinga, J. H. *Rousseau: The Self-Made Saint*. New York, 1975.

Jauss, Hans Robert. "Vorselektion der Welt, im Blick auf Rousseau." In *Positionen der Negativität*, edited by H. Weinrich. Munich, 1974.

Jimack, P. D. "Rousseau and the Primacy of the Self." *Studies on Voltaire and the Eighteenth Century* 32:73–90 (1965).

Josephson, Matthew. *Jean-Jacques Rousseau*. New York, 1931.

Launay, Michel. *Jean-Jacques Rousseau, écrivain politique*. Cannes, 1971.

————. *Rousseau*. Paris, 1968.

Lecercle, Jean-Louis. *Jean-Jacques Rousseau, modernité d'un classique*. Paris, 1973.

————. *Rousseau et l'art du roman*. Paris, 1969.

Lejeune, Philippe. *Le pacte autobiographique*. Paris, 1976.

————. "Le peigne cassé." *Poétique* 25:1–30 (1976). On the *Confessions*.

"L'impensé de Jean-Jacques Rousseau." *Cahiers pour l'analyse 8* (Paris, 1970). Special Rousseau issue: see articles by Louis Althusser and Alain Grosrichard.

Lovejoy, Arthur O. *Essays in the History of Ideas*. Baltimore, 1948.

Lowell, James Russell. *Among My Books*. Boston, 1892.

MacCannell, Juliet F. "History and Self-Portrait in Rousseau's Autobiography." *Studies in Romanticism* 13:279–298 (1973).

————. "Nature and Self-Love: A Reinterpretation of Rousseau's 'Passion Primitive.'" *PMLA* 92:890–902 (1976).

————. "The Post-Fictional Self." *Modern Language Notes* 89:580–599 (1973).

Manuel, Frank E., and Fritzie P. Manuel. "Sketch for a Natural History of Paradise." *Daedalus* 101:83–128 (Winter 1972).

Maritain, Jacques. *Three Reformers: Luther-Descartes-Rousseau.* New York, 1929.

Mauriac, François. *Trois grands hommes devant Dieu.* Paris, 1947.

May, Georges. *Rousseau par lui-même.* Paris, 1961.

Monglond, André. *Le préromantisme français.* Grenoble, 1930.

Moreau, Joseph. *Jean-Jacques Rousseau.* Paris, 1973.

Morley, John. *Rousseau.* London, 1873.

Perkins, Jean. *The Concept of Self in the French Enlightenment.* Geneva, 1969.

Poulet, Georges. *Études sur le temps humain.* Paris, 1949.

————. *Les métamorphoses du cercle.* Paris, 1961.

Raymond, Marcel. *Jean-Jacques Rousseau: La quête de soi et la rêverie.* Paris, 1962.

Roche, Kennedy F. *Rousseau: Stoic and Romantic.* London, 1973.

"Rousseau et la philosophie politique." *Annales de philosophie politique* 5 (Paris, 1965). Special issue.

Sainte-Beuve, C. A. *Nouveaux lundis.* Vol. 9. Paris, 1884.

Shell, Marc. *The Economy of Literature.* Baltimore, 1977.

Shklar, Judith. *Men and Citizens: A Study of Rousseau's Social Theory.* London, 1969.

Spink, J. S. *Jean-Jacques Rousseau and Geneva.* Paris, 1934.

Staël-Holstein, A. L. G. (N.), baronne le (Mme. de Staël). *Letters on the Works and Character of Rousseau.* London, 1789.

Starobinski, Jean. *Jean-Jacques Rousseau: Le transparence et l'obstacle.* Paris, 1957.

————. *Le relation critique.* Paris, 1970. Pp. 82–173.

Trilling, Lionel. *Beyond Culture.* New York, 1955.

Wahl, Jean. "La bipolarité de Rousseau." *Annales Jean-Jacques Rousseau* 33:49–55 (1953–1955).

Weil, Eric. "Jean-Jacques Rousseau et sa politique." *Critique* 56:3–28 (January 1952).

BIBLIOGRAPHY

Together with the annual Modern Language Association's *International Bibliography,* see *Annales Jean-Jacques Rousseau,* Geneva, 1974 (pp. 291–389), and Jean Sénelier, *Bibliographie générale des oeuvres de Jean-Jacques Rousseau,* Paris, 1950.

PAUL H. FRY

ANTOINE DE SAINT-EXUPÉRY

(1900–1944)

FOR MANY READERS, Saint-Exupéry is the quintessential "heroic" writer of the first half of the twentieth century, a novelist who, as Germaine Brée has remarked, looks more like the hero of a novel. As a pilot, he participated in the new age of aviation during those pioneer days when to fly was an adventure, and again in wartime as a fighter against the invaders of his country. As a writer he set down in a spare, lyrical prose that would become the hallmark of his style his compassionate view of mankind and the record of his adventures, discoveries, and reflections. Not surprisingly, these have more to do with the psychological and moral nature of man than with geography or technology, because for Saint-Exupéry a man's chosen *métier*—his craft in life—was above all an instrument for achieving an awareness of the self and of the world. The two facets of his life—the active and the reflective, the adventurous and the literary—together constitute something more than a man: they make up a legend that continues to attract modern readers through the impact of its unique humanistic perspective.

Antoine Jean-Baptiste Marie Roger de Saint-Exupéry was born in Lyons on 29 June 1900. His parents could trace their aristocratic origins on both sides far back into the proud traditions of France; the town of Saint-Exupéry, which lent its name to his father's family, is in the department of the Corrèze. His father died when Antoine was barely four years old, leaving his mother to raise her five children as best she could: Antoine, his two older sisters, Marie-Magdeleine and Simone, a younger brother, François, and a younger sister, Gabrielle.

His mother, Marie de Fonscolombe, herself of the Provençal aristocracy, managed to provide a beautifully warm and secure environment for her "tribe," as Antoine would refer to his family, despite the heaviness of her burden. Saint-Exupéry would retain virtually no memory of his father, but his abundant references to his family and to childhood are thoroughly imbued with the dreamy, romantic tinges of a golden age. His maternal grandmother and great-aunt each owned an estate, one not far from Lyons, at Saint-Maurice-de-Rémens, the other at La Môle, inland from Saint-Tropez. Antoine spent much of his childhood in these two family châteaus, playing with his sisters and brother, exploring the gardens, becoming familiar with plants and animals, and enjoying the security furnished by the gentle presence of his mother and the governesses who helped look after them.

His mother, who held a diploma in nursing and could write poetry, paint, sing, and play the guitar, provided an atmosphere that fostered creativity in the family. Antoine, or the "Roi Soleil," as he was called because of his blond curls, flourished here; he wrote bits of poetry, dabbled at the violin, and joined his brother in devising mechanical inventions, including an attempt to create a flying machine by attaching wings to a bicycle.

In 1909, Antoine's mother moved her family to Le Mans and enrolled her two sons in the Jesuit school that their father had attended. Antoine would remain here until 1914, enduring, as best as might be expected for a somewhat restless and easily distracted boy, a kind of discipline for which he had not been prepared. He wrote poetry and won recognition from his teachers for his literary talents. On vacation at Saint-Maurice, in 1912, he was given his first airplane ride at the Ambérieu aerodrome and wrote his first aeronautical poem (of which three verses are still extant).

When war broke out in 1914, Antoine's mother moved her family to Ambérieu to take on the post of head nurse in the local hospital. Her sons adjusted poorly to the local school and so were sent back to Le Mans to finish out the year. The following year they were sent to a Marist college in Fribourg, Switzerland. While Antoine would reject the teachings of church dogma, the emphasis placed on the cultivation of individual responsibility was one that suited his own temperament and would serve him well for the rest of his life. He later remembered his two years spent there with a sense of satisfaction that his teachers had communicated the right ideals of heroism. Indeed, he was called upon to put those ideals to the test sooner than expected. His brother, François, developed a serious case of rheumatic fever. Antoine had barely passed his *baccalauréat* examinations in June 1917 when François died, leaving Antoine the only remaining male member of the family.

In the fall of 1917, Antoine left for Paris to begin his preparatory studies for entrance into the naval academy in Brest. He passed his written exams in 1919, only to fail the orals that June. Having exceeded the age limit for taking the exam, he was effectively excluded from entering the navy. For the next two years he essentially marked time as a student in the architecture department at the École des Beaux-Arts. Meanwhile he had developed strong friendships that would last him a lifetime, and benefited from the excellent contacts opened to him by his aristocratic Parisian relatives.

In April 1921 he was called up for his two years of military service. In a fateful act that would determine his future career and the shape of his life, he chose the Second Air Force Regiment in Strasbourg. Assigned to the ground crew to work in the repair shops and to teach aerodynamics, he began almost immediately to yearn to fly, and so he took private lessons at a civilian station that shared the Strasbourg airfield with the military. Events moved in a rapid, decisive manner from this point on. By early summer he had completed his first solo flight and, despite a dramatic landing with full engines smoking, was granted his civilian license. His unit sent him to Morocco to continue flight training, and by December he had received his military pilot's license. Back in France, he was sent to the pilots' school in Avord in April 1922. By October, Corporal Saint-Exupéry had completed his training, been promoted to second lieutenant, and given his choice of assignments. In the brief interim from April 1921 to October 1922 he had thus had his first taste of the desert—a setting for which he would develop a deep and abiding attachment—and had made strong friendships with several fellow pilots: Marcel Migéo, Jean Escot, Marcel Reine, and, most notably, Henri Guillaumet. He had also developed an art form that gave him much pleasure, the pencil sketches with which he now illustrated his letters; they would finally be given official status in *Le petit prince* (*The Little Prince*, 1943/1946).

Saint-Exupéry completed his tour of duty at Le Bourget. The proximity to Paris allowed him many social pleasures, not least of which was the company of Louise de Vilmorin, later to become a well-known writer and social figure. The Vilmorin family was not pleased with the prospect of this match, however, and even less so after he suffered a fractured skull in a crash early in 1923. He would clearly have to choose between a career in aviation and marriage to

Louise. Upon leaving the military, he chose Louise.

The period from June 1923 to the fall of 1926 forms a bleak interlude in the life of Saint-Exupéry. Blessed with an essentially optimistic nature, he nonetheless made choices that turned out to be the wrong ones for him. The Vilmorin family had found him an office job at a tile factory. When that left him unsatisfied he turned to a job selling trucks, but managed to sell only one truck in his eighteen months there. His engagement to Louise, further, did not last long. Sensing that the relationship did not hold great promise, or perhaps conceding to her family that he was not her best choice, Louise simply stopped seeing him. Finally, in 1926 his life was once again touched by a tragic loss with the death of his sister Marie-Magdeleine.

His time in Paris was relieved, however, by some important consolations. He would fly as often as he could at Orly, for that had become a joy upon which he could always rely, but increasingly his thoughts turned to another serious preoccupation: writing. In his letters to family and friends he made references to a novel he was working on, and began giving thoughtful critical judgments on contemporary writers and on the art of writing. The twenty-five-year-old Saint-Exupéry, in a classic example of a visible maturation process, expresses his distrust for the superficial and for mere verbal trickery; he identifies good writing with the honest attempt to come to grips with oneself, with real experience as transformed by studious reflection. Finally, in the April 1926 issue of Jean Prévost's short-lived journal *Le navire d'argent,* Saint-Exupéry's first published effort appeared. Entitled "L'aviateur" ("The Aviator," published in *A Sense of Life*), it is a short story describing episodes in the life of a pilot, Jacques Bernis.

Saint-Exupéry's time of floundering eventually came to an end when he was introduced to the head of the newly founded Latécoère Aviation Company. Offered an office position in Madrid, he would settle for nothing less than a flying job. His persistence paid off, as it would many times again in his life: he was assigned to the main operations station in Toulouse.

He began his new job in October 1926. His supervisor, Didier Daurat, was probably the single most influential shaping force in Saint-Exupéry's life as a pilot, and undoubtedly the model for the imposing character Rivière in the novel *Vol de nuit* (*Night Flight,* 1931). Daurat immediately put the novice to work on airplane engines so that, like any other pilot of the time, he would be able to serve as his own mechanic in case of trouble. Within a few months' time Saint-Exupéry was flying the regular company flights from Toulouse to Spain and on to Morocco and Dakar. In his letters he now expressed a sense of profound personal satisfaction in being joined with his pioneering comrades on the line.

Later in 1927, Daurat assigned him to direct the airport at Cape Juby, in the Spanish Sahara colony of Río de Oro. This was one of the ten regular stops between Casablanca and Dakar, but it was a particularly difficult post (as even Daurat was well aware), for the French company had to deal with Spanish military personnel who were frequently at odds with rebellious desert tribes just inland from the coast. Nevertheless, with his considerable personal charm and naturally outgoing manner, Saint-Exupéry had soon befriended the Spaniards as well as a number of Muslim tribesmen in the area, from whom he even learned some Arabic. He gained their respect by himself respecting their culture, and developed enough of a following among them to carry off several rescue missions of French and Spanish pilots who had been forced down in rebel country and taken hostage in exchange for an anticipated ransom. His extraordinary feats at Cape Juby were sufficient to win him the Legion of Honor award in 1930.

The strong impact of this desert mission on Saint-Exupéry's sensibilities would be revealed in his writings. He discovered his talents for diplomacy in dealing with people and their problems, a natural outgrowth of his feelings of respect and affection for people of all cultures. The sense of danger that came not only from his sporadic dealings with hostile tribesmen but—more regularly—from the ever-present menace of airplane accidents sharpened his appreciation for the things he valued most in life. Finally, the life of severe simplicity and monastic poverty that he and his men were obliged to lead in the desert opened him up to the spiritual wealth hidden in the emptiness of wind, sand, and stars. Where other Westerners might have discovered frustration and suffering, Saint-Exupéry found the necessary distance for reflection and a fertile terrain in which his affectionate curiosity for mankind and nature could grow. It was during these eighteen months that he wrote *Courrier sud* (*Southern Mail,* 1929).

This first novel was the fruit of a talent that had slowly been maturing in the young man's mind. That he was gifted in the use of language had already been demonstrated in his school years. That he had a strong need to express his thoughts and attitudes through the written word was also made clear in his abundant correspondence over the years with his mother (published as *Lettres à sa mère* [Letters to His Mother], 1955) and to Renée de Saussine, sister of his friend Bertrand (published in 1953 in two versions, *Lettres de jeunesse* [Letters of Youth] and *Lettres à l'amie inventée* [Letters to the Invented Friend]). These letters contain statements of literary attitudes that perhaps only someone who is thinking of becoming a writer would make, in preparation for establishing his own models of literary style and worth. Meanwhile, Saint-Exupéry had already published a sort of trial version of his novel in the story "L'aviateur," consisting of eight fragments recounting "L'évasion de Jacques Bernis" (The Escape of Jacques Bernis). More recently, Saint-Exupéry's friend and admirer Jean Prévost had introduced him to the publisher of the *Nouvelle revue française,* Gaston Gallimard, who published *Southern Mail* in 1929.

This novel weaves two narrative threads in

the life of Jacques Bernis: his experiences as a pilot delivering the mails from Toulouse southward along the line, and his love affair with Genevieve, a childhood playmate now married and living in Paris. The narrator, an old friend and fellow pilot, awaits Jacques's arrival at Cape Juby. He possesses the omniscience that will allow him to tell us what Jacques has done, thought, and felt, either through a real knowledge of the facts or through a kind of sympathetic imagination that allows him to identify with Jacques.

The image we have of Jacques is that of a dreamer who has not given up his childhood love of exploration. Having chosen the world of aviation, he has simply exchanged the childhood mysteries of garden and house for the adventurous world of a pioneer airman. His state of mind is that of a young man dissatisfied with ordinary people and restlessly seeking some undefined realm beyond. Both the narrator and Jacques can be seen as projections of the author himself, who takes the two roles of observing subject—the sympathetic, rational commentator—and his observed object, the rather romantic seeker of something not yet fully grasped.

The story is divided into three sections. The first is supported by a number of details drawn from Saint-Exupéry's personal experiences. The narrator, awaiting the arrival of Jacques's flight, describes the sensuous pleasures of night in the desert at Cape Juby and focuses our attention on the stages in Jacques's journey: dressing for flight, taking orders from the chief, takeoff, meditation during flight, and landing at his first stop in Spain. In the course of his meditations he recalls his most recent trip to Paris, two months earlier. These last recollections—a flashback recounting his affair with Genevieve—constitute the second part, the core of the story.

If Genevieve bears a special significance for Jacques now, it is essentially because she played an important part in his childhood. Earlier he had described himself to the narrator as "the water-diviner whose rod trembles and who moves it over the world to the treasure"—though a treasure unknown, in a quest not yet understood—until he finds Genevieve again: "I have found the spring. Do you remember her? Genevieve. . . ." During their play as children Genevieve seemed to possess a key that allowed her to unlock the secret meaning of things. Upon Jacques's return to Paris, on leave from his duties at Cape Juby, he will rediscover Genevieve and find in her an antidote to his dissatisfaction with the ordinary people he finds there, whose lives seem devoid of meaning to him.

Genevieve, too, is dissatisfied with the way her life has turned out. Married to a man who is the stereotype of the insensitive and uncaring husband, she finds in Jacques a renewed hope for emotional fulfillment. After her child falls ill and dies, she goes off with Jacques hoping to find a new meaning in life with him. But she suffers from her separation with the familiar world she had organized for herself, and Jacques, realizing she needs that stability to be happy, lets her go. Once alone, Jacques attempts to find consolation for his unhappiness. A visit to the cathedral of Notre-Dame convinces him that religion will not furnish him the answers he needs. His Paris leave now over, he takes the train to return to his post at Toulouse.

In the last part of the novel, the two narrative threads come together. Arriving finally at Cape Juby, Jacques recounts to the narrator his last sight of Genevieve, but in the altogether different mode of a tragic fairy tale. Stopping on his way to Toulouse at the town where Genevieve is staying, he is guided along to her place by dreamlike guardian figures who recognize in him the necessary qualities that allowed Orpheus to pursue his search for the woman he loved. When he arrives Genevieve barely recognizes him, as she is now on the threshold of death. Leaving her for the last time, he understands that he has lost that precious gift by which meaning was bestowed upon things.

When he finishes this strange story, Jacques then flies on to another stop on the company line, and at one point his plane disappears over the desert. The narrator sets off after him and finds him alone on the desert dunes, his arms stretched out as though crucified, his face turned toward the stars. The narrator laments the death of his companion in a poetic ending that prefigures the pilot's lament in *The Little Prince* upon the death of the boy. By contrast, the official wire message tells us simply, "Pilot killed plane broken mail intact. Stop."

In examining how Saint-Exupéry has structured the story of the love affair in such a way as to doom it to failure, it is not difficult to find the deeper explanation of his attitude toward domestic happiness as opposed to his growing attachment to the extraordinary world of aviation. Jacques's love for Genevieve is clearly grounded on something that will not work. In endowing Genevieve with her mystical gift, Saint-Exupéry appears to be stressing not so much her understanding of the natural world as the joys of the past. For Genevieve is the person who allows Jacques to rediscover the precious world of his childhood. To pursue his affair with Genevieve would in a sense be to revert to that protected world, and, like the character Franz de Galais in Alain-Fournier's classic neoromantic tale *Le Grand Meaulnes* (*The Wanderer,* 1913), to live out his life in a perpetual state of childhood. By having Genevieve's child die, Saint-Exupéry has given us the real reason why the affair cannot go on. It is as though the death of the literal child signals the necessary death of childhood for Genevieve and Jacques. They cannot continue their affair because they are no longer children, and they must somehow reorder their lives in conformity with a framework of meanings that pertain to the adult world.

The final depiction of Genevieve dying in the manner of some romantic heroine strengthens the reader's reluctance to give her serious consideration as a real character in her own right. Genevieve is Saint-Exupéry's only attempt at developing a female character in some depth, and she no doubt demonstrates his limitations in this respect. In bestowing mystical powers upon her, and in casting her story in a legendary mode, he has deprived her of the opportunity to become a flesh-and-blood character. She is a foil for Jacques, existing above all as an object of Jacques's spiritual needs. She is a symbol, and to the extent that her significance is based on Jacques's perception and understanding of that symbol, her death simply duplicates the death of her own child. It will confirm the message that Jacques must not count on reliving the comforts of his childhood; the precious qualities of childhood must somehow be metamorphosed into a state that can exist comfortably within the adult.

Like other first principal works of blossoming writers, this novel should be judged on the basis of what it gives us of the future writer at his best. Saint-Exupéry never repeated his attempt to write a love story, and on the whole reduced the sentimental element in his future work. His interest in childhood was henceforth focused on children, whether real or imaginary, and not on recollections of past childhood. But many of the qualities and themes upon which his reputation later rested are already here. *Southern Mail* depicts in subtle detail the process by which an ordinary man is transformed into a special being through his chosen field of aviation, and it documents the heightened state of awareness that aviation bestows upon him. It describes the particularly close bonds of comradeship of men who participate in the same heroic enterprise. And it makes consistent references to those elements of the natural world that become part of the central poetic stock of language found in all his work: wind, sand, stars, water, and the night.

Back in France after his successful eighteen-month period on the Africa line, Saint-Exupéry took an advanced aerial navigation course in Brest. He had a strong aptitude for mathematics and science, and would invent and even patent a number of mechanical devices for the airplane over the next few years. Yet despite this practical streak, at Brest he developed something of a reputation for being absent-minded, and made a poor showing on his final examinations. Daurat took him back without reservations, however, to serve the recently formed Compagnie Générale Aéropostale, another pioneering venture in commercial aviation—this one linking France with a new aerial network in South America. Within two weeks of his arrival in Buenos Aires, in October 1929, Saint-Exupéry was named director of the Aeroposta Argentina, a subsidiary of the main company. There he established a number of new airfields linking Buenos Aires with towns toward the west and the south, so that by April 1930 the mail could be flown the entire length of the region of Patagonia. But his domain was only a small part of the greater pioneering adventure that was taking place and that he would soon consecrate in *Night Flight*. His old friend Jean Mermoz had already developed night flights as the chief means to gain time in the delivery of the mails. Mermoz now accepted Daurat's request to run the first transatlantic crossing from Dakar, on the western tip of Africa, to Natal, at the eastern tip of Brazil. From there a relief race run by Saint-Exupéry's fellow pilots took the mail onward, to Rio, to Buenos Aires, and to Santiago. By 15 May 1930, the complete circuit from Paris to the Pacific was down to four and a half days.

It is no exaggeration to say that these men were continually risking their lives. To cross great expanses of land, sea, and mountain ranges in the fragile flying machines of the 1920's, subject to the storms and powerful gusts of wind that could come up unpredictably, and without the benefit of visual contact with any land objects other than occasional lights at night—these were truly death-defying feats that tested the courage of the men Saint-Exupéry writes of in the collection *Terre des hommes* (*Wind, Sand, and Stars*, 1939), which relates several such episodes. The best depiction of the struggle between man and the elements, however, and the meanings that can be derived from engaging in this struggle, come across most clearly and dramatically in his second novel, *Night Flight*, which he began during the summer of 1930. In a severe attempt to reduce the lyrical element—perhaps in acknowledgment of some of the criticism *Southern Mail* had received—he cut the final version from over four hundred pages to less than two hundred. The result is a spare and sober novel, very much in the French "classical" style of elegant simplicity, with a sharp focus on the central element: the moral drama taking place within the mind of the chief character, Rivière.

The story is told through the progress of three mail planes flying toward Buenos Aires: one from Chile, another from Paraguay, the last from Patagonia. Upon arrival, their various cargoes will be transferred to a plane bound for Europe. The movements of the three planes are being monitored by the French team at the airport, presided over by Rivière, who runs the entire operation as though it were his personal empire. This empire is essentially a commercial one: by cutting mail delivery to the shortest possible time, the company hopes to maintain its advantage over other, competing means of transport. Yet at no point do commercial preoccupations come to the fore. This is a story about the courageous struggle of pilots and their director to win a race against time, in a combat pitting human determination against a multitude of hostile natural forces.

Saint-Exupéry weaves his plot in such a way as to create a strong dramatic tension. Suspense is heightened through the constant forewarnings of the dangers of flying, especially stormy weather, which requires the total concentration of a pilot's resources to keep control over his machine, and flying at night, when his only sense of security is provided by the lights down below. The pilot coming in from Chile flies through the forbidding, snow-covered peaks and crags of the Andes without incident, only to have to contend with a storm on the other side. Nonetheless he arrives safely, as does the pilot flying in from Paraguay. It is Fabien, the pilot advancing northward from Patagonia, who serves as the tragic focus of the reader's attention. Flying through calm skies, he suddenly comes upon a storm that has ap-

peared without warning. Unable to maintain control of his craft against the powerful buffeting, he catches a sight of a star overhead and allows his plane to rise up over the cloud cover. Now hopelessly lost and with little gas left in his tank, he is doomed.

The point at which it becomes clear that Fabien cannot be saved would appear to be the climax of the story, but in fact is not. For the narrator now shifts our view away from the final moments of Fabien to the thoughts of Rivière. As head of the operation he is ultimately responsible for this loss; hence he will have to reevaluate the goals of his enterprise. He is also the one who will have to deal with the grief of Fabien's wife. It is therefore not so much the pilot who demands our attention but rather Rivière, who must bear the consequences of the enormity of this event. In like fashion, the personal drama of each of the pilots pales before the much greater drama that is at stake in Rivière's attempt to create a special order over and beyond the demands of human happiness, represented here through the pilots' wives. In short, character parts in this drama can be reduced to three main roles: the pilots—all the pilots, whether specifically named or not; their wives—again, all their wives, representing that other existence of pilots when they are merely ordinary men seeking unheroic happiness; and finally Rivière, who must bear the drama of these differences and find a satisfactory justification for the superhuman endeavor he is promoting.

The pilots are clearly men who are set apart. While not arrogant, they are keenly aware of their special calling in forgoing the pleasures of ordinary men in order to exercise their taste and talent for risk-taking beyond the ordinary. A pilot in his plane is depicted as a sort of knight on his steed, so that pilots together form a new sort of knight-errantry for the modern age. What these men hold in common is a particular myth—"myth" taken in the sense of a shared set of beliefs that validate life: the myth of the *métier*. This French word suggests at the same time the notion of profession, vocation, craft, or, more simply, a job taken seriously. The myth applies to men at lower levels as well. Among the ground crew, for example, Rivière admires Leroux, an old-timer who looks back on his life with "the happy tranquillity of a woodworker who has just smoothed a good board."

These men are joined in a brotherhood of shared work. As in any mythic system, the rewards may be considered in both personal and universal terms. At the personal level, the common goal provides them with a ready-made path of achievement that has been socially validated, allowing each to direct his energies toward a well-defined goal. When well accomplished, the job will bring satisfaction and even the sense of exaltation found in victory. This state of spiritual well-being is such that individuals may be willing to pay the price of suffering and even to risk death along the way. At the universal level, the myth demands of each member his obedience and his honest and generous service for the good of all. These men do not often speak; they do not need to: "A strong sense of brotherhood allowed them to do without words."

An important motif illustrating this expectation of common service runs throughout the novel. The pilots are essentially participants in a relay race. When one lands, it is so that another may take his place to cover the next lap, and so on. This continuity exists on earth as well: "A man was at work somewhere so that life could remain continuous, so that human will could remain continuous, and in this way, from one stop to the next, so that the chain stretching from Toulouse to Buenos Aires should never be broken." Lights on earth serve as guideposts provided for the pilots' benefit to show them the way. Likewise, radio operators pass on information about the weather in chain fashion to guide them safely home. Shared work thus provides personal satisfaction and social usefulness: it creates human bonds and provides a vehicle for justifying an individual human being's existence.

The second role is played by the wives of the pilots. They are relatively minor characters (only two are shown in some detail: the wife of the pilot who must be awakened to prepare for his flying mission, and Simone, the wife of the doomed pilot). Together they portray a universal condition. Taken as realistic depictions of women they appear superficially weak, destined to lead a life of eternal sacrifice because their husbands will always go off to face untold dangers. But woman for Saint-Exupéry also incarnates an age-old archetype, the provider of comfort, and therein lies her real strength. She is the keeper of the hearth and the port of refuge to which her loved one can come home when the dangers of the day are over. Underneath this stereotypical depiction of woman we can glimpse the archetype of the protective mother threatened with imminent bereavement; one cannot help but suspect that the true model here is Saint-Exupéry's conception of his own mother. If this model is present here, it is to represent a view opposed to Rivière's notion of heroic action. But if these women cannot be said to have fully developed personalities, the same can be said of the pilots as well. The important thing is to demonstrate two differing notions of what life is supposed to mean, and to furnish Rivière with intellectual justification for espousing one view over the other.

The likely model for Rivière was Saint-Exupéry's own supervisor, Didier Daurat, and once again what is important in this character sketch are not his specific qualities but the typical qualities of a leader of men. He is a solitary figure who chooses not to show his love for his men and the pity he often feels for their human frailties, so that the will required to maintain the spirit of his group enterprise will not be weakened. The chief frailties are carelessness and fear. Rivière will go so far as to cast shame on his men when that is what is necessary to get them to shake off their fear and self-pity, or to avoid mistakes. To underscore this point, Saint-Exupéry has created a foil for Rivière in the character of Inspector Robineau, a frankly mediocre man who admires Rivière but does not seem to have learned any of the duties of leadership from him. His hunger for friendship is so great that he invites a pilot to have dinner with him, blind to the fact that fraternizing will only create expectations that can interfere with the efficacy of his authority. Rivière will make Robineau find some pretext by which to punish the pilot so as to restore the necessary relationship.

Rivière recognizes that the task of organizing his men will always be a Sisyphean struggle against forces exceedingly more powerful than man. He expresses these as "events" that must be controlled, associating with them two types of metaphor. When human frailty shows itself, he thinks of it as a *mal,* a sickness or evil that must be eradicated. After he fires a workman for having performed a dangerously careless piece of work he thinks:

> If I fired him in such a brutal way, it is not because of him but because of the evil—for which he may not even have been responsible—that was passing through him. Events *have* to be controlled . . . and then they obey, and one can create. And men are pitiful things, and one can create them too. Or else you move them out of the way when evil passes through them.
>
> (p. 83)

This metaphor expresses an internal danger; Rivière uses another type of metaphor to express the external danger as well. When men let go, events take over, like jungle growth swiftly reclaiming its rights over great monuments that have been abandoned. Even a gardener working his lawn, for example, is engaged in a perpetual struggle to prevent the soil from producing the primitive forest it contains within itself.

Readers may be tempted to see in Rivière something of a sadistic martinet or, in view of the fact that Saint-Exupéry was an enthusiastic reader of Nietzsche, some tyrant of the Will; but this is not what the author means to convey. Rivière is a fifty-year-old man obsessed by the fragility of human life in the face of those enemies that consume life: time and death. Man's dream, for Rivière, is "to endure, to create, to exchange his perishable body." The only way to overcome his human condition is through a transcending of his individual life in the name of something greater: the human race, which will continue to exist beyond his individual death. He recalls that an engineer once told him that people continue to build bridges over rivers despite the inevitable construction accidents that occur. Rivière had answered: "If human life is priceless, we always act as though something surpassed human life in value. . . . But what?" This quality, whatever it may be, must be worth the price of snatching men away from their lives of simple happiness.

In the final analysis, the question of human happiness in this novel is focused on the pilots, who are offered two separate and competing paths to follow. Their wives offer warmth, comfort, and love—but nothing that can stand up against the natural fear of death. Rivière offers a heroic, dynamic value that is higher than happiness—higher because it involves more than individual men and projects the meaning of their existence into the future. In Rivière's empire some men must die, but in the system of domestic happiness represented by the wives all men will eventually die anyway. At least in Rivière's system the notion of a heroic humanity transcending individual death will live on.

Rivière virtually admits that his system is a blind gamble when he thinks to himself, "We don't ask to be eternal but, rather, not to see our acts and things suddenly lose their meaning." And again: "Our goal may not justify anything, but action frees us from death. These men endured through their machines." Perhaps, then, the illusion of an eternal meaning is sufficient if it allows his men to achieve an unsuspected height of human potential. But so far as the pilots are concerned, the conflict over two opposing systems is not really an issue. They do not have to choose sides, but rather profit both from the benefits of domestic happiness as provided by their wives and from the heroic action of their knightly brotherhood as organized for them by Rivière. At the end of the novel, Rivière's ideology will hold sway. In spite of death and grief, the flights will go on.

Saint-Exupéry brought the manuscript for the novel back to France with him in 1931, and Gallimard published it later that year. It became an immediate success. André Gide read it and was sufficiently impressed to contribute a preface extolling the nobility of human achievement represented within its pages, the spirit of self-sacrifice, and the important moral lesson it gave on the need to accept responsibility as a duty. By the end of the year the novel had won one of France's most prestigious literary awards, the Prix Fémina, and henceforth Saint-Exupéry was assigned to the ranks of the most important current authors.

The manuscript was not all Saint-Exupéry had brought back to France from Argentina, however. At a reception of the Alliance Française, he had met Consuelo Suncín, the widow of an Argentine journalist. With her vivacious Latin charm and somewhat temperamental personality, she was not exactly the type of woman one would have expected him to marry, yet they were indeed wed shortly after his return to France. Relatively little has been written of their relationship, but it is known that they frequently broke up and lived apart despite the obvious signs of mutual attachment and affection they shared.

Meanwhile, changes were taking place in Saint-Exupéry's world of aviation, some of which had begun to make themselves painfully evident to him at about the same time *Night Flight* was published. During a dispute between the Aéropostale and the French government, Daurat had been called upon by the government to keep the flights going, and he accepted. As the dispute developed, some of Saint-Exupéry's comrades turned against Daurat, Saint-Exupéry's subsidiary company was abolished, and Daurat himself was fired. The company was merged with others into a larger one: the movement toward commercial efficiency was accelerating, and the pioneer spirit

seemed to be fading into the past. Meanwhile, Saint-Exupéry was distressed to learn of the reaction of a number of pilots to the success of his recent book: he was now being looked upon as an amateur aviator who had somehow broken the brotherhood's code of honor by writing of it for outsiders.

Finding himself without his old job, he was obliged to take on various piloting positions and for a while became a test pilot for seaplanes being produced by Latécoère. On one testing mission at Saint-Raphaël, in 1932, he crashed into the sea and very nearly drowned. In 1934 he joined the recently formed company Air France to serve as a publicity specialist, making a number of lecture trips within France and abroad, and traveling as far as Indochina.

In view of the rapid strides taking place in the field of aviation, he was determined not to abandon the heroic spirit of adventure of the earlier days. When Pierre Billon decided to make *Southern Mail* into a movie in 1934, Saint-Exupéry joined his team on location in Morocco and performed the stunt-flying for the actor playing the role of Bernis. Soon after, he secured a plane for himself, a Simoun model, and on 29 December 1935 set off together with his mechanic Prévot on a Paris-to-Saigon long-distance run in an attempt to beat the record. At one stage of their North Africa leg, they set off from Benghazi eastward to fly over the desert, without the benefit of lights or radio contact. They were soon lost and through a fatal judgment of altitude crashed into the heart of the desert, about two hundred kilometers west of Cairo. The ordeal of survival in this unforgiving landscape, the men's fateful decision to walk eastward despite their mistaken belief that they were already east of Cairo, and the miraculous encounter with the Bedouin caravan that would save them—all these adventures were later recounted in detail in *Wind, Sand, and Stars*. In 1935 he proposed a race to set a new world record, this time from New York to Punta Arenas, at the southern tip of South America. Together with Prévot, in his Simoun, Saint-Exupéry sailed for New York in

January 1938 and in February began his race southward. Upon takeoff from Guatemala City, the two men experienced their worst accident yet. Prévot suffered a broken leg, and Saint-Exupéry a brain concussion and multiple fractures from which he would never fully recover. After spending a month in a Guatemalan hospital, he was taken back to New York for a long convalescence. There, in a borrowed apartment with a view of the East River, he began organizing his texts for *Wind, Sand, and Stars.*

Some of these texts were pieces Saint-Exupéry had written earlier. Since publishing *Night Flight* he had not tried his hand at fiction other than to complete a filmscript begun in Argentina. Rather, he had become increasingly interested in developing his skills as a writer of articles and short essays, eyewitness accounts, character profiles of friends, personal reminiscences, and similar types of anecdotal sketches that permitted him to elaborate a personal journalistic style, whereby he could blend moral observation with philosophical meditation, and employ a spare prose with poetic sensitivity. As a publicity agent for Air France, he contributed several pieces to their official flight magazine. In 1935 he was asked by the newspaper *Paris-Soir* to go to Moscow to give an account of the new Russia from a human perspective. In 1936 another Paris journal, *L'Intransigeant,* published his account of his crash in the Libyan desert, and sent him to Spain to report on the fighting there. More articles were commissioned by *Paris-Soir* in 1937 and 1938, before and after his crash in Guatemala, and meanwhile he was being asked to write prefaces and introductions to works relating to the aviation world, including Anne Morrow Lindbergh's *Listen! the Wind* (1938). Some of these pieces found their way, faithfully reproduced or in somewhat revised form, into *Wind, Sand, and Stars.* Others eventually appeared, posthumously, in *Un sens à la vie* (*A Sense of Life,* 1956), an anthology of diverse pieces. Still others appeared periodically in the French aviation magazine *Icare,* and have never been anthologized.

Of all these pieces, the collection to which Saint-Exupéry attempted to give a unified form was *Wind, Sand, and Stars.* Even here we face the problem of having to deal with two different versions, the American and the French. While in New York he gave the manuscript of some of the pieces to his translator, Lewis Galantière, for preparation of the American edition. Back in France, however, he continued editing the work, adding a few passages not found in the American edition and cutting others. The French version begins with a brief statement that provides the unifying message of the book: Man can discover himself only when he measures himself against an obstacle. For this he needs a tool, and herein lies the significance of the *métier.* Although the texts do not stress the superiority of the airplane as a tool, they make it clear that the plane can offer an original and particularly instructive vantage point: the view of all mankind down below. What that view reveals to Saint-Exupéry is the essential unity of all men, but also one's obligation to speak to others, in the face of so much mutual hatred and hostility, of the need for unity.

The first chapter describes the metamorphosis of an ordinary young man into a new type of human being when he becomes a pilot. The pilot is an exemplary man because he lives in a state of awareness that will allow him to fulfill his own potential while serving the needs of mankind. The second chapter then gives us profiles of two such exemplary figures, chosen from among the great veterans of the early days that he knew personally. The first is Mermoz. After surviving incredible feats of flight-pioneering on so many fronts—across the ocean, over mountain ranges and deserts, and through the night—one day he does not return from one of his flights. What we consider heroism is simply acting as though the odds did not exist, until one day one can act no more. The second is Guillaumet. Crash-landing in the Andes, he survives his ordeal by simply going on, oblivious to what everyone had said to be impossible, and goes through—as he puts it—what no animal would ever have gone through.

In the chapters following, Saint-Exupéry takes up the theme of the airplane as an instrument of individual self-knowledge and also of knowledge of the human experience in the cosmos. Having once seen the earth from above, when the pilot lies on the desert sands below he understands that the earth is like a ship, bearing each of us with the force of its gravity. The distances the plane allows man to cover reveal the exotic differences among people and also their essential similarities. In "Oasis," for example, he tells of the peasant family who take him in when he is forced to land on a stretch in Patagonia. The two daughters who sit shyly judging him over dinner test his reactions by announcing that the strange movements coming from below the table are caused by snakes that live in a hole there. These girls behave like his own sisters, who, he recalls, would call out mysterious numbers to each other when young male guests were invited, making use of a secret code that summarily ranked the worth of the guest on a scale from one to twenty.

In the chapter "Dans le désert" ("Men of the Desert") Saint-Exupéry gives us glimpses of cultural exchange between two groups considered alien to each other: Europeans and Muslim tribesmen of the desert. The latter are truly scornful of the French, no matter what their material accomplishments, because they are Christians who do not have God on their side. Those Muslims who have been to France (according to the American edition) are unimpressed by buildings, radios, locomotives, or even the Eiffel Tower. But they do admit to their great attraction for circus women who can jump standing from one galloping horse to another. Above all they are impressed by the forests, the waterfalls, and greenery. These men who have made their religion "out of a fountain" are puzzled by the irony of a mysterious God who has been so much more generous to the French than to the Moors.

But even desert tribesmen share our essential brotherhood, as Saint-Exupéry demonstrates at the end of the next chapter, "Au centre du désert" ("In the Center of the Desert"). Here he describes his accident in Libya according to the classic formula of the adventure tale. Beginning with his original desire to prove his own valor to himself by means of a record-breaking race, the text moves through the early stages of the trip to the central terrain of hardship, the fateful event, the ordeal in the desert, the discovery in the wreckage of the plane of an orange that provides a miraculous respite from hunger and thirst, and finally the unhoped-for encounter with the desert caravan. Here is the embodiment of a human society forever vigilant to come to the rescue of fellow men. He thinks of the Arab who first sees him: "You are Man and you appear before me with the face of all men at once."

By this point the thematic emphasis of the book has shifted from the privileged insights of the pilot to the pressing need for human unity and brotherhood. The final chapter, "Les Hommes" ("The Men"), gives us Saint-Exupéry's views on the Spanish Civil War. What is important here is not the description of battles or the temporary victories of one side over the other, but the impassioned plea to men to stop fighting each other and move together toward a common goal. The profile sketch of an old army sergeant serves as the example of a man discovering his need to find a truth he is willing to die for, so long as he shares the fight with his companions. The only problem is that he and his companions are eager to fight and kill other men who are fighting for *their* truth. Saint-Exupéry therefore calls for the abandonment of political ideology. Both sides have a truth, and in the ultimate sense that a truth is what gives meaning to life, their truths are identical (the author would, of course, receive some sharp attacks for failing to distinguish the nature of the respective truths). In an uncharacteristic foray into sociohistorical analysis, he explains that if the Europe of the 1930's is suffering such widespread anguish, it is because the industrial age has stripped men of their peasant identities and thrown them into ghettoes, and because they are made to learn the narrowest of trades instead of human culture. Meanwhile hope is fading for the bulk of humanity. The book ends on a memory that comes back to him from a train trip he once took through Poland: the scene of a beautiful young boy sleeping between his working-class parents, and doomed to spend the rest of his life in the same sort of misery as they, despite all the promise he carries within him of a future Mozart. He is the image of a Mozart murdered in the bud, a new rose that will not be cultivated because there is no gardener for mankind. He is a symbol of what must not be allowed to happen to modern man.

Wind, Sand, and Stars was released virtually simultaneously in France and America early in 1939 and achieved instant success in both countries. In France it received the Grand prix du roman de l'Académie française; in America it was chosen as the Book-of-the-Month Club selection for June and received the National Book Award and other honors as well. Saint-Exupéry had clearly become something of a national—and increasingly international—celebrity. In May he was awarded the rosette of the Legion of Honor, in a ceremony at which Guillaumet also received the Legion award. As though to underscore the worthiness of the message of his book, Saint-Exupéry and Guillaumet broke the transatlantic record returning from New York to France on Bastille Day. He returned almost immediately to New York to participate in the honors being bestowed upon him by his American public.

But amidst these personal glories he had begun to turn his mind to the signs of war, which were growing increasingly ominous late that summer. He returned to France in August and reported for military duty at Toulouse as a captain assigned to flight training. Pressing his request for reassignment to active flight duty, he attained his goal in short order. Despite the fact that he was technically over the age limit, and against the advice that he was not medically in shape as a result of his Guatemalan accident, by early November he was transferred to Reconnaissance Group 2/33, sta-

tioned north of Paris at Orconte. Here he recapitulated the earlier pattern of his life by developing a tight network of emotional ties with a brotherhood of men serving a common cause, and sharing life in the monastic ambiance of a military barracks. The group was involved in carrying out dangerous missions over enemy-held territory to photograph military operations. One such mission, over Arras on 22 May 1940, was to become the subject of his next book, *Pilote de guerre* (*Flight to Arras,* 1942); but he would not write that book until France had lost the fight and he was in America.

With the defeat of the French military in June 1940, the officers of Saint-Exupéry's group were sent to Algiers to carry on the struggle from North Africa. With the signing of the armistice later that month, resistance collapsed, and by the end of July his group had been demobilized. Sharing the shock and bewilderment of so many of his countrymen, he spent the next few months deciding what his best course of action should be in view of the fall of the Paris government and the installation of the puppet regime in Vichy. Friends had been urging him to go to the United States to represent the voice of free France. Opposed to working with the Vichy government, not sufficiently attracted to de Gaulle to cast his lot with the general, and encouraged by his American publishers to come to New York, he made his decision to go to the United States.

At no point did Saint-Exupéry think of himself as either an emigrant or an immigrant, but rather as a traveler whose duty was to represent his country in the best light while waiting to return home. He was happy to have occasion to come in contact with the French community living in exile, a number of whose members he had personally known in France, but he was dispirited by their tendency to indulge in partisan politics. Some were for Vichy, others for de Gaulle, and both camps solicited his allegiance. This factionalism did not diminish the ordeal of France, which was uppermost in his mind, rendered all the more painful for him by the widespread public view that France had somehow been shamed by not having fought harder against the Germans. His American publishers pressed him to write a book that would speak for France. He therefore decided to interrupt his efforts to get on with the book he had long projected as his major work, *Citadelle* (*The Wisdom of the Sands,* 1948), to write *Flight to Arras.*

It would be difficult to classify this work by literary genre. It clearly combines the two major types of writing that Saint-Exupéry had thus far elaborated in his career as an author—autobiographical reminiscences and the novel form. The main story line gives an account of his reconnaissance flight to Arras in the north of France, now occupied by the Germans, culminating with the arrival of his plane over that town in a hail of shellfire. Hence there is a strong element of suspense as the reader is left wondering whether the plane will reach its destination without incident, take the aerial photographs it has been sent to get, and make it back safely. Although based entirely on fact, the story has been shaped into a dramatic tale and given a universal perspective by the personal memories and reflections that come to the narrator's mind during and after his flight.

The fighting group to which Saint-Exupéry belongs bears an unmistakable resemblance to the brotherhood of knights he had described earlier in *Night Flight.* Daurat, now dead, has been replaced by Major Alias, playing the set role of commanding officer. Each of Saint-Exupéry's comrades-in-arms (to whom the book is dedicated) is each given a distinctive character sketch that brings him to life for the reader: Dutertre, Israel, Gavoille, and a cowardly gunner referred to simply as T., who dies while trying to parachute out of a plane headed into enemy territory. Given the overwhelming military superiority of the Germans, the French effort to resist invasion remains hopeless. The question keeps recurring like a refrain: Why are the men of Saint-Exupéry's unit being called upon to risk their lives conducting reconnaissance flights when it is understood by everyone that the photographs they bring back

are absolutely useless? The answer is that such are "the rules of the game." An overpowered army must continue to fight on, and men must continue to perform their duties even in the face of defeat. The absurdity of their gesture is never felt more keenly than when their planes must fly directly into the path of antiaircraft batteries determined to do them in. But the rules of the game are still good rules because they spring from the need to give meaning to life. These men are united in the common cause of saving France, and even when their goal is doomed to failure they are still engaged in an endeavor that gives their own lives meaning. In trying to save France they are therefore affirming a transcendental value that nourishes them all.

To view this attitude merely as blind patriotism would constitute a serious misreading of the text. Taking to heart his role as spokesman for France, Saint-Exupéry's purpose will be to justify her in defeat. When the critics of France say that French military resistance was insufficient, they have overlooked the very real differences between, as he points out in a hyperbolic example, a nation of 80 million industrial workers and a nation of 40 million farmers. And yet, as France's critics have apparently not understood, the French have continued to play by the rules of the game by fighting on. Of the twenty-three air reconnaissance crews in Saint-Exupéry's unit, seventeen were shot down in what could, in the cold light of reason, be judged to have been a totally absurd sacrifice. To counter the critics who say the French gave in too quickly in order to avoid suffering, Saint-Exupéry gives us a picture of a France rapidly disintegrating before his weary eyes. Villages are burning and people streaming southward by the millions, sporadically bombed and strafed by the enemy for no apparent reason. Roads are hopelessly blocked; order has broken down. France has not avoided suffering.

Given the chaos and the tragic turn of events, who can sit in judgment of France? It is clear that Saint-Exupéry has summoned his arguments in defense of France to persuade the Americans in particular. In a section containing some of his most strongly polemical language he writes that if France is fighting for democracy, then it is the duty of the democracies, and in particular the most powerful one, to join the fray. In preaching democracy, he has in mind not so much a set of principles as a set of desires: that men be brotherly, free, and happy. His "patriotism" is in fact a form of humanism. He may love France, where people are free and happy to be French, but he loves men of other nations as well and respects their right to be free and happy within their own national identities.

Never before had Saint-Exupéry developed his arguments on the spiritual dimensions of the human adventure—everything that would constitute his humanistic message in all his subsequent works—in such ample detail and with such assurance. What defines man, in his view, is his spirit, and the key to understanding him is the action that he brings to bear in a social context. Saint-Exupéry speaks often here of the web of human relationships that together form a "civilization," giving a "density" to individual lives. A Dominican friar at prayer, Pasteur looking into his microscope, Cézanne motionless before his easel, or Saint-Exupéry in his room at Orconte—these are all examples of men imbued with a culture that gives their lives meaning, much as the *métier* gives meaning to men. Further, to be a human being is to be a participant and not a spectator. Because he is woven in a web of relationships with his comrades, Saint-Exupéry achieves his own density through fulfilling his obligations toward them; for he is a part of his men, just as they are a part of their country.

While flying through fire over Arras, Saint-Exupéry relates, his plane is struck but, miraculously, does not go down. He then joyfully anticipates returning home to his web of relationships, which must forever be cultivated and renewed. Upon his return he goes to have dinner with a farmer's family, and feels he has reestablished his ties with all humanity.

When the farmer's niece smiles, "her smile was transparent for me and, through it, I saw my village. Through my village, I saw my country. Through my country, I saw other countries. For I am of a civilization that has chosen man as its keystone."

At the end of the book Saint-Exupéry offers his Credo, an extraordinary document of religious humanism that marks the transition to a new, more didactic and consciously rhetorical style, one that will characterize much of his subsequent work. Individual men have no meaning except through a transcendental notion of Man, just as a pile of stones does not take on meaning until it is formed into a cathedral. While Saint-Exupéry was never a particularly observant Christian, his humanism is clearly founded on a respect for the values espoused by the Western Christian tradition. Modern democracy is the heir of that tradition. Men cannot be brothers nor can they be equal except *in* something, and that something is essentially Saint-Exupéry's definition of God. The notion of responsibility is the heir of the traditional value of bearing the sins of others, and what is called charity is the sacrifice granted to man in order that he may find personal fulfillment.

Flight to Arras appeared in New York early in 1942. It was greeted by critics in America as one of the great testaments to the abiding spirit of hope for a liberated France. Henri Peyre wrote that it was "the finest prose work that World War II seems as yet to have produced." Through some curious misreading of the text, permission was granted for its publication in Vichy France later that year, with only four words censored. That error was caught soon after and the book was banned, but clandestine versions continued to circulate. Meanwhile Saint-Exupéry, now joined by his wife, Consuelo, in New York, continued to write at a rapid pace. He prepared an article, "Message to Young Americans," for a national high school magazine, sharing his message that war requires the best of each individual. His "An Open Letter to Frenchmen Everywhere" appeared in the *New York Times Magazine* soon after the Allied invasion of North Africa, late in 1942, and was broadcast to France as "Lettre aux Français." Here he formally recognized de Gaulle—somewhat belatedly, in the view of the general's followers—as a figure fully capable of leading the French cause.

By early 1943, Saint-Exupéry had completed and published two additional works in New York, *Lettre à un otage* (*Letter to a Hostage*) and *Le petit prince* (*The Little Prince*). The first takes up the ideological threads of *Flight to Arras* in a renewed call for the urgent defeat of the Nazis. The second, variously known as a whimsical fairy tale for adults or a hauntingly sad story on the loss of childhood, remains by far the work upon which the author's popularity is most firmly established. Despite their apparent differences in structure, tone, and intent, at a deeper level the two works reflect elements of kinship, for in both we find the tone of loss, nostalgia, and tenderness expressive of a man whose emotional roots have been violently wrenched from their nourishing earth.

This nourishing earth, in *Letter to a Hostage,* is France and the friends he has left behind as hostages of the German occupation. He writes in particular to one of his very close friends, Léon Werth, who as a Jew bears the brunt of the tragedy in a particularly poignant way. There are six sections in the letter, each intricately woven of memories and feelings expressed in a spare, elegiac manner.

The book begins by portraying Saint-Exupéry as a reluctant voyager as he is about to set sail from Lisbon to New York, surrounded by refugees—for the most part well-to-do—who instill in him a sense of guilt at leaving his friends behind. But the memories of these friends move him to begin preparing his return even as he is about to depart. He compares exile to a magnetic field: his friends, his memories, and his loyalties are the poles, pulling so strongly at him that he can think of himself only as a temporary voyager. One of those memories then comes to life. One day when he

and Léon Werth were picnicking by the river, they invited two nearby boatmen, one Dutch, the other German, to join them in a drink. The smile that they all shared became a bond of friendship, uniting them in a sort of mystical communion. He then takes up the smile as the motif of universal fellowship. He recalls how, in Spain, his situation was saved one day when, caught by militants who thought he was one of the enemy, he asked one of them for a cigarette, gave a smile, and received a smile in return. And he also remembers the smile of the Arab whose caravan party rescued him and his mechanic from certain death in the Libyan desert.

Saint-Exupéry then turns to the more immediate matter of why the Nazi enemies must be defeated. The war can be reduced to a struggle between two fundamentally different attitudes: one that respects individual persons and allows them to find their own path of "ascension," the other that refuses "creative contradictions" and forces all men to fit the totalitarian model. Saint-Exupéry's political idealism shows through: as long as men maintain a fundamental respect for the notion of Man, it does not matter which political system dominates. What matters in a civilization is not its form but its substance. Reflecting on his friend Léon Werth, in the last section, he affirms his belief that their friendship is all the stronger because each is different, while respecting the differences of the other. If he fights again, he promises to fight for Werth's truth as well as his own, to recover the smile he needs from his friend. All Frenchmen, being of the same tree, must be free to sink their roots into the same land. As a testimony to friendship as a fundamental value in a free society, Saint-Exupéry's little book thus turns the expression of personal feeling into a political statement.

As for *The Little Prince*, one is tempted to ascribe its popular success in no small part to the fact that for years it was used as a reader for teaching French in American schools; but of course it has been read widely in many other countries and other contexts as well, and its charm has been universally acclaimed. It is the only book of its sort that Saint-Exupéry wrote, and the only one in which he finally put his talents as an illustrator to the test. The combination of text and illustrations proved to be a winning one, and Saint-Exupéry was himself very fond of the book. He had begun making sketches of the Little Prince as early as 1939, but began to write the book only in 1942 in response to his New York publisher, who encouraged him to produce a children's book after seeing one of his little drawings.

The story tells of a small boy who lives alone on a tiny planet, to which the narrator assigns an asteroid number to satisfy his adult readers' impatience for scientific classifications. The boy performs regular chores: he sweeps out the three volcanic chimneys of his planet and uproots the baobab-tree seedlings that could overrun the planet's surface if allowed to take hold. When he feels melancholy he turns his chair to watch a rapid series of sunsets. He would be happy if he could count on the love of a rose that grows there, but she is not reliable in her affection and makes unreasonable demands upon him until, one day, unable to bear the emotional strain any longer, he decides to leave his planet by latching onto a flock of migratory birds traveling through space.

He then stops briefly at six tiny planets, each of which is inhabited by a single human being caught in some characteristic act. The King is delighted by the boy's arrival, as it provides him with a subject for him to rule over; the Vain Man, eager for an audience, asks that that the boy applaud him in his various posturings; the Drunkard cannot escape from the vicious circle in which he is trapped, feeling shame for his drinking and then drinking in order to forget his shame. The fourth planet is the home of the Businessman (Saint-Exupéry uses the English term), who sits at his desk counting stars in the belief that he owns everything he counts. The Lamplighter, whose job it is to light his planet's lamp each night and extinguish it the following morning, finds himself growing increasingly weary as his planet rotates faster and faster. The Geographer does not go off on explorations himself but sits at his desk taking notes on the discoveries reported to him by others.

All of these figures may be presumed to be allegories of human types based on the author's experience with men. Essentially they give a critique of false values in the modern world. The common denominator for establishing a scale of moral values here would appear to be the quality of human relationships toward other men and the world. At the negative pole one would find the Vain Man, the Drunkard, and particularly the Businessman, who represents the extreme perversion of relationship as quantifiable possession. At the positive extreme the Lamplighter performs his duties—his *métier*—with admirable faithfulness, despite his perception that the task has become absurd; moreover he actually *does* something, and does not scribble at a desk. But we must not forget that these views are supposed to be those of a child looking at "serious" adults, as imagined by an adult who has great sympathy for the way children see the world. A reader who goes much further in pressing meanings out of types created with such playful whimsy runs the risk of being taken for a "serious" adult himself.

The Little Prince finally arrives on the seventh planet, Earth, and meets the narrator, Saint-Exupéry playing himself in a somewhat altered account of his crash in the Libyan desert. Working hard at his plane repairs like any serious adult, he is challenged by the boy to reconsider his notions of what is truly serious in life. One of the major themes of the book, then, is that adults are impoverished by having lost their capacity to view the world through a child's eyes. The pilot prides himself in his belief that he is exempt from that charge; he understands, for example, that a particular drawing illustrated in the book represents not a man's hat lying on the floor but rather a boa constrictor that has swallowed an elephant. He also succeeds in calming the boy's anxieties about a certain sheep on his planet that might very well eat his beloved rose, by drawing a container in which to safely pen the sheep. The narrator is thus here to partake of the boy's experience and to communicate it to the reader in a manner that is affectionate and lighthearted, but at the same time grave and profound. Above all he accepts the responsibility to speak to adults of the benefits of looking at the world, and themselves, through the fresh perspective of a child.

While he is on Earth, the Little Prince makes many discoveries, and eventually attains the wisdom that allows him to understand that what he truly desires is to return to his rose. In one way or another, all the lessons he learns have to do with love. On his planet the Little Prince's rose was unique, and so he is astonished to find on Earth a garden filled with roses, all alike, that make his own rose seem merely ordinary. Weeping in the grass, he is approached by a desert fox who will serve as his mentor figure (Saint-Exupéry had himself described an encounter with a desert fox in *Wind, Sand, and Stars*). The Little Prince would like to be his friend, but the fox explains that they must first "tame" each other (the French word *apprivoiser* carries the sense "to make more sociable"). People who tame each other come to need each other; they become unique for each other. This process is slow, requiring patience and ritualized gestures rather than words. The fox also teaches him to strengthen the ties of love through sensuous and poetic associations, to see with his heart rather than his eyes, and to understand that the object thus tamed—that is, the loved one—is also the object for which one becomes responsible.

The Little Prince shares these lessons with the narrator, and teaches him to see the special beauty of an object that is needed. The narrator then understands, for example, the true value of water found in a desert well: "This water was much more than nourishment. It was born of my walk beneath the stars, of the song of the pulley, of the efforts of my arms. It was, like a gift, good for the heart." Indeed, the Little Prince becomes both the tamer of the narrator and his mentor, offering him one aphoristic truth after another, each a variation on the same essential cluster of themes: men rush about but do not know what they are looking for; the most important things in life are invisible, and to find them requires the patience of indirect action and vision.

Finally, understanding that to return to his planet he must dispossess himself of his physical body, the Little Prince goes out to meet the serpent who had earlier promised to help him die. Before he goes, however, he bestows a farewell gift. The pilot had loved to hear the boy's laughter; now, through the magic powers of association, that laughter will sound like the tinkling of bells emanating from the Little Prince's planet and stretching across the vast expanses of space. And so it comes to pass. Six years later the narrator can see stars, "hear" their tinkling and the boy's laughter beyond; but he also wonders if the Little Prince has managed to save his rose from the sheep.

One cannot dismiss the claim that this book is a fairy tale of sorts, but it clearly has a density of thought that goes beyond the ordinary children's tale, and a melancholy tone that may not even be understood by children. Some readers will be tempted to see the book as a roman à clef and look for biographical clues: the rose refers to Saint-Exupéry's wife, or perhaps to Louise de Vilmorin; the Little Prince is the son the author never had; the death of the boy alludes to the death of Saint-Exupéry's young brother; the dispossession of the physical body is an allusion to the Christian notion of resurrection, which had an appeal for the writer; and so on. In one sense the visit of the Little Prince as an extraterrestrial traveler can be seen as a pretext for social observation and satire, albeit of a very elementary and playful sort. But all critics seem agreed that the Little Prince is considerably more than a pretext for satire; as an externalized projection of the author's psyche, the boy embodies Saint-Exupéry's profoundest attitudes toward childhood, affection, love, and death. It is no doubt this very richness of interpretive potential, in addition to its undeniable charm for children and adults alike, that has guaranteed the work a place as a classic of modern literature.

During the few months between the publication of *Letter to a Hostage* and *The Little Prince,* Saint-Exupéry found his chance to end the melancholy burden of his passive exile and to return to active duty. The Allies had debarked in North Africa in November 1942; by April 1943, Saint-Exupéry found himself passage on an American troop ship headed for Algiers. Despite his age, his persistence in pursuing his goal led to success. He was given the rank of major and was assigned to the unit of his choice, his old Reconnaissance Group 2/33, now stationed at an American base in North Africa. Henceforth he would fly the Lockheed Lightning, which was considerably larger and more sophisticated than the planes he had known before the war. Within a few weeks he had made his first reconnaissance flight over France and was overjoyed finally to see his land once again, even from such a great height. But at the end of July, returning from his second mission, he made a bad landing, damaged his craft, and was grounded by the American commander. He spent the next several months in Algiers at the home of his friend Dr. Georges Pélissier, in a state of profound gloom as a result of having lost his chance to fight with his comrades so soon after reentering the fray.

During this period he continued working on the manuscript of *Citadelle* (*The Wisdom of the Sands*). It was also then that he very likely wrote his "Lettre au Général X" ("Letter to General X"), discovered among his papers after his death. This manuscript contains statements astonishing in their pessimism for someone who had so consistently expressed his hope in man: the airplane has become merely a transportation device; while improvements in our material existence have become increasingly visible, man's spiritual life has been impoverished to an extent hitherto unknown; totalitarian governments, whether fascist or Marxist,

have become propaganda machines transforming individual citizens into robots and cattle; once the Germans have been defeated, the fundamental question of the meaning of man will still remain unanswered; and so forth. Saint-Exupéry's demoralized state can certainly be understood in view of his gnawing anxieties over the fate of relatives and friends still living under the heel of the Nazi occupation. The fact that some of de Gaulle's advisers were still harboring a grudge against him for not having sided with the general while in New York did not help matters. The only antidote to his depressed state was active service and not a desk job as a reservist in Algiers.

He finally saw another chance in April 1944, when he was given a new assignment as commander of a bombing squadron stationed in Sardinia. Again, after incessant pleadings to carry out reconnaissance missions himself, and despite the maximum age limit of thirty-six for piloting fighter planes, he was granted permission by his American commander to rejoin his old group, now stationed in Corsica, and to conduct five additional missions. Only then was Saint-Exupéry satisfied, sharing the rigors of military life with his old friends and flying over his native land, particularly the Alpine corridor leading north to the Annecy region that he knew so well. Only then, when risking his life under extremely dangerous circumstances, did he feel truly fulfilled.

And so he went on beyond the five missions he had been allotted, over the anxious objections of his friends. They finally managed to work out a discreet scheme with the American authorities to ground him for his own good. Their plan would have taken effect on the evening of 31 July. Meanwhile, Saint-Exupéry had been granted permission to fly a mission—his ninth—on the morning of 31 July. This did, indeed, prove to be his last mission, for he flew off and was never heard of again. The official military report would record simply: "Mapping east of Lyon . . . No pictures. . . . Pilot did not return and is presumed lost." The most plausible theory was that he had been shot down by

German fighter planes off the coast of Corsica on his way northward to the Annecy area. His comrades waited for his return for a long while. They continued to wait for news that he had somehow survived a crash over France, as though in fulfillment of the romantic legend of a charmed existence that had come to be associated with him. But this time he did not return; he had disappeared without leaving a trace. In November of that year Saint-Exupéry was awarded a posthumous military citation for his qualities of daring and skill, signed by de Gaulle. On 12 March 1950, he was again awarded a citation, carrying the Croix de Guerre, with palm, for having made "French wings shine with a new brilliance" and for having expressed "his taste for action and the generosity of his ideals in literary works ranking among the most important of our time and celebrating the spiritual mission of France."

Among the writer's papers was found a short piece that would be published in 1948 as "Seigneur berbère" (not translated into English), telling of an old Berber chieftain and his stronghold empire in the desert—a subject that was perhaps surprising in its exoticism and certainly quite different from the sort of thing Saint-Exupéry had written up to that point. His immense attraction to the desert dated back, of course, to his earliest years as a pilot in North Africa, and he considered himself reasonably well-informed on the customs and beliefs of the Muslim tribesmen of the region. The Berber lord examines his power over his subjects; he is a despot, but a benevolent one, caring for the well-being of each individual through the creation of bonds of responsibility, a unified state, and subservience to a silent God. In its broad outline, then, this text of about ten pages can be seen as a trial version of Saint-Exupéry's last great work, where he would again place his ideas on political leadership, man's moral nature, God, and other themes in the mouth of a desert chieftain rather than in that of a Rivière type of Westerner.

The most voluminous packet of manuscripts found among his papers was the work that was published posthumously as *The Wisdom of the Sands*. There is some irony in the notion that it is a "posthumous work"; Saint-Exupéry himself jokingly referred to it as such, claiming it would need another ten years for completion. He had begun in 1936 to take notes for it in his notebook, later published in French as *Carnets* (1953). The bulk of its typewritten pages were probably composed in New York. He carried it with him to North Africa, where he continued working on it up to two months before his death; a separate folder containing a thick sheaf of handwritten pages was found together with the typescripts.

Saint-Exupéry often spoke to his friends about his book in progress and thought of it as his most significant literary achievement; indeed, he is quoted as having stated that next to this work all his other books were "mere exercises." The problem of editing the work according to the presumed intention of the author would therefore appear to have been a crucial one. We must remain content with the resulting close approximation, however, for the editors had little way of knowing where the supplementary pages were to be added or what the precise order of the chapters should be; moreover, some the handwriting was virtually illegible. Further, given our knowledge that Saint-Exupéry had cut out more than half the bulk of his draft of *Night Flight* in its final editing, in order to achieve the succinctness and tightly knit structure for which it is justly famous, the question remains as to what the total length of the work would have been. Even after final excisions of obvious redundancies, the French version still contains 219 chapters and 527 pages. The American version, with its 123 chapters and 350 pages, presents a distinctly more manageable text.

Critics frequently choose to refer to *The Wisdom of the Sands* as a "work," as though hesitant to call the book a novel. At least in the formal sense, however, it can be considered a novel of the fictional-memoir type. A desert chieftain, the Great Caid, delivers his meditations to the reader in a prose style reminiscent of certain portions of the Bible where a universal perspective of human society is stated with simple grandeur and rolling cadences, with fervor and feeling. (The true model may in fact have been Nietzsche's *Also sprach Zarathustra*.) There are virtually no characters and no plot in the usual sense. The narrator is a relatively young man who tells of the lessons he has learned from his recently assassinated father and the lessons he has himself mastered from the practice of ruling over his empire. Specific events are recounted and particular persons described as examples of the way people behave, and these in turn become pretexts for explaining and justifying how a ruler should use his knowledge to shape the state in the name of the common good. Thus, despite the exotic setting and the very different format chosen, the work contains many of the major themes that Saint-Exupéry elaborated over the years.

Saint-Exupéry was not a "philosopher" in any formal sense, and it is clear that he distrusted any logical system not tempered by the heart. One is reminded of the seventeenth-century writer whom he greatly admired, Blaise Pascal, who eventually came to the realization that logic and reason could carry man only so far in his search for truth, beyond which only the heart and faith could serve as satisfactory guides. In choosing to communicate his ideas through parables rather than logical demonstrations, Saint-Exupéry ran the risk of structuring contradictions into his work, and these may well puzzle the reader. As a desert patriarch—presumably Muslim—the chieftain combines qualities that may appear contradictory: the leadership ability of a King David, the wisdom of a King Solomon, the thirst for adventure and the aloofness of a legendary Alexander or Cyrus, but also the ruthlessness of a tyrant. Like his father, the chieftain metes out punishments that are harsh and cruel, but he also performs acts of charity and speaks of his subjects with fraternal tenderness. For, while authoritarian, he is aware of his own imperfections, and while noble, he is not arrogant. Punishments carried out for the good of the culprit, or as an example to society, are reminiscent of Rivière's methods in *Night Flight* and, as critics have often noted, demonstrate a Nietzschean influence in Saint-Exupéry that is difficult to reconcile with the Christian notions of humaneness that he also espouses. Would he have clarified these ambiguities in a final editing, or would he have left them as an integral part of the fabric of the book? To use one of his recurring images, the work is still imbedded in its *gangue*—its matrix—like a sculpture only partially released from the marble in which it is imprisoned.

The "citadel" of the French title suggests a city that must be safeguarded. In its wider sense it represents a total civilization composed of the sum of relationships of all its citizens: relationships with one another, with their material world, with their past history and traditions and with their future as well, as the civilization itself takes on a transcendental value that gives meaning to the life of each individual and to all those yet to come. The role of a political leader is to promote the defense and development of this citadel, and to "found" it in the heart of each citizen.

In its broad outline, the Caid's "wisdom of the sands" constitutes nothing less than the sum of Saint-Exupéry's humanistic philosophy. Man is not simply a physical presence on earth but a sum of values—values that must be constructed, then strengthened, and finally defended against the internal and external forces that are disposed to weaken and demolish the structure. In this struggle, authority of a paternalistic or feudal type is essential to impose constraints on the people for their own good. While such notions as justice, equality, and individual freedom are important and have their place, the notions of discipline, fraternity, and responsibility hold a higher rank in the hierarchical value system of this empire; for whatever *creates* Man must take precedence over that which merely allows an individual to enjoy life, since to create Man is to give him spiritual meaning. Human beings find their greatest fulfillment when they "barter" their ephemeral existence on earth for eternity by performing acts that will outlast them and become part of the heritage of the civilization itself. As the Caid says:

> For I respect above all that which endures longer than man, and thereby saves the meaning of their barter, and constitutes the great tabernacle to which they entrust everything of themselves. . . . They shall gladly barter themselves for that which is more precious than themselves. Thus are born painters, sculptors, engravers and carvers. But hope not for man if he work for his own life and not his eternity.

(p. 38)

The material, utilitarian world may serve as a means to attain that end, like steps leading to a temple, but the ultimate goal of a civilization is to create and strengthen a knot of relationships. In this system God is defined as the "essential knot of diverse acts," or—to use Saint-Exupéry's architectural analogy—the keystone in the arch supporting the entire structure. But this God is beyond our reach. By his very nature—one might say his noble nature, for Saint-Exupéry often reveals an aristocratic bias—God will not respond to prayer, nor should our turn of mind be so utilitarian as to expect him to do so. Throughout *The Wisdom of the Sands,* Saint-Exupéry appears ripe for a mystical experience leading to true faith, but that faith never fully asserts itself. He undoubtedly felt nostalgia for his early Catholic upbringing; what he retains of it primarily, however, is a respect for ritual, authority, and the "Christian" values of Western civilization, but where Christ is only the palest of shadows. Ultimately, his God is an ideal deistic notion that imbues human life with the spiritual meaning necessary to foster creative acts, ties of love, and the steadfast acceptance of social duty.

Saint-Exupéry read the first few pages of the work to Drieu La Rochelle and Benjamin Crémieux, two friends whose judgment he re-

spected. They did not hide their disappointment. For them, he was the poet of action, an enthusiastic, virile writer of whom they were expecting new stories of adventure. Their reservations undoubtedly stemmed from the marked abstractness of the ideas expressed in the book and its immense distance from the concrete world to which they had become accustomed in their friend's work—the world of the pilot, of discovery, of courage, and of warm friendships. While *The Wisdom of the Sands* can count several strong supporters among Saint-Exupéry's critics, others tend to view it as ponderous or as an anomaly in the canon of his works, occupying a questionable place in that canon because it does not bear the author's final imprimatur.

A summary glance at Saint-Exupéry's total literary production will show that there is a gradual evolution in the writer's choice of literary forms, paralleling his search for a personally satisfying ideological base. This evolution is marked by three phases. In the first, his attraction to the novel form of a traditionally realistic type gives us two very different kinds of thematic material. In pursuing its focus on the past—childhood, love, consolation—his first novel, *Southern Mail,* depicts a quest for something not yet known; the meanings are uncertain, and the reader is left with the impression of a romantic longing that cannot be satisfied. In *Night Flight,* the goal is clearly sighted: civilization itself is a value system that will allow men to fulfill themselves through giving their best. What is important, then, is to barter the ephemeral nature of an individual life for the enduring values of human structures; and the right path is that of duty, responsibility, courage, and a Nietzschean shaping of the self through the agency of a *métier.*

The principal literary form of the second phase is a type of eyewitness journalistic reporting that becomes increasingly autobiographical (*Wind, Sand, and Stars; Flight to Arras; Letter to a Hostage*). Here Saint-Exupéry focuses on what he perceives to have gone wrong in the modern world. Materialism has triumphed over the spiritual and brought on a reign of mediocrity, efficiency has replaced courage, political hostilities have corrupted friendship and love, state-sponsored conformism has obliterated the diversity that fosters creativity, and young Mozarts are being murdered in the bud. His response is to hold up images of Man's unending potential through examples of courageous men he has known; to cultivate the smile of friendship among men of all nations and cultures; to deny victory to the Nazi invaders despite their overwhelming strength, by stubbornly fighting on in the name of civilization itself, which will ultimately triumph.

In his third phase, he returns to fiction, but in the nonrealistic tradition of fable and parable (*The Little Prince, The Wisdom of the Sands*). Here the author has moved still further in the direction of giving sharp definition to the spiritual insights and rules of moral conduct that he had slowly been formulating from his earliest period onward. His writing is never so frankly didactic as in this last phase. The aphoristic lessons of *The Little Prince* and the codification of ethical and political rules in *The Wisdom of the Sands* bespeak a writer who not only has found the right spiritual path to follow but now accepts the responsibility of bringing his message to the readers of his troubled times.

On balance, however, the relative artistic success or failure of each of his works does not depend so much on the choice of literary form or the elaboration of philosophical ideas as on certain distinct characteristics of his style. One is the concreteness of his inspiration. Saint-Exupéry is probably never better than when he writes of the joy of the pilot in his plane, fully aware of his existence and in a privileged position to cast new perspectives on the meaning of the human adventure taking place on earth. At the other extreme we sense that the representation of certain types of point of view—that of a woman, or of a desert chieftain, or of men choosing sides in a political battle that is not their own—may be too remote from the au-

thor's own experience to allow his text to come to life with the same vigor or his arguments to be made with the same conviction. When Saint-Exupéry deals with what is most familiar to him, his gift for bringing thematic material to life through simple and striking imagery is at its most impressive. His vocabulary is studded with a number of concrete poetic images, key words radiating symbolic ideas relatively complex in their meaning yet easily graspable: *to tie, to tame, to barter, bonds, thirst, métier, cathedral, tree, fountain, smile, house, ship, stars,* and so forth. By contrast, some of the terms found primarily in his last work have a decidedly more abstract cast: *to found, slope, matrix, empire, domain.*

Finally, there are opposing tensions in much of Saint-Exupéry's work, and these work to greatest advantage when they are clearly identified and then left in an unresolved state. The power of *Night Flight* is attributable in large measure to the fact that each of the opposing sides in the debate is recognized as having a value that should not be canceled by the other. A woman's love and a pilot's right to private happiness are too important for a Rivière to achieve a final and definitive triumph—as Rivière is himself aware. We may admire Rivière's strength of character and the ultimate societal benefits of his ideology while fully recognizing, as he does, that his victory must remain a provisional one; the debate remains in a state of creative nonresolution. Similarly, the Little Prince's decision to return to his beloved rose signals the beginning of his metamorphosis into a "serious," responsible adult, a shift that is further dramatized by the death and disappearance of the child; but the fact that Saint-Exupéry wrote the story proves the adult author's need to remain in a situation of creative dialogue with the vulnerable child he would always carry within.

To reduce Saint-Exupéry's search to a few ideological formulas, or even to think of him principally as a purveyor of philosophical ideas, is to ignore the true value of his writing as the expression of a vigorously affirmative attitude toward life—the attitude that life itself is a never-ending adventure. First and foremost, he was a poet with an unflagging passion to live life to the fullest in the company and service of his comrades. His talents of observation served as the vehicle for expressing his vitally curious and compassionate attitudes toward men and the world, with a sense of wonder and spiritual concern, but also with deep affection and gentle humor. Critics are correct in viewing his career, both as writer and as adventurer, as a quest; for the notion of "quest" assumes a forward-looking orientation and a positive, even heroic, turn of mind that readily applies to Saint-Exupéry. In his works, life is seen less as a problem than as a mystery. His message to us today is that the spiritual meaning is there, but that it is not visible because it has been obscured by the dehumanizing materialism of our age. Given this outlook, the task of the writer is to pursue paths that will lead to a perception of spiritual meanings. In this endeavor it is not so much the ultimate answer that matters as the search itself, which will allow human beings to be joined to something greater than their individual selves.

Selected Bibliography

EDITIONS

INDIVIDUAL WORKS

Courrier sud. Paris, 1929.
Vol de nuit. Paris, 1931.
Terre des hommes. Paris, 1939.
Pilote de guerre. New York, 1942; Paris, 1942.
Lettre à un otage. New York, 1943; Paris, 1945.
Le petit prince. New York, 1943; Paris, 1946.
Citadelle. Paris, 1948.
"Seigneur berbère." *Table ronde* (July 1948): 1091–1101.
Un sens à la vie. Paris, 1956.
Écrits de guerre, 1939–1944. Paris, 1982.

COLLECTED WORKS

Oeuvres. Paris, 1959.

NOTEBOOKS

Carnets. Paris, 1953.

CORRESPONDENCE

Lettres de jeunesse, 1923–1931. Paris, 1953.
Lettres à l'amie inventée. Paris, 1953. (Same letters as above, with illustrations by Saint-Exupéry.)
Lettres à sa mère. Introduction by Saint-Exupéry's mother. Paris, 1955.

TRANSLATIONS

Airman's Odyssey. New York, 1942. (A trilogy comprising *Wind, Sand, and Stars*; *Night Flight*; and *Flight to Arras.*)
Flight to Arras. Translated by Lewis Galantière. New York, 1939.
Letter to a Hostage. Translated by John Rodker. In *French Short Stories.* New York, 1948.
The Little Prince. Translated by Katherine Woods. New York, 1943.
Night Flight. Translated by Stuart Gilbert. New York, 1932.
A Sense of Life. Translated by Adrienne Foulke. New York, 1965. (Includes "The Aviator," "An Open Letter to Frenchmen Everywhere," "Letter to General X," and other pieces.)
Southern Mail. Translated by Stuart Gilbert. New York, 1933.
Wartime Writings, 1939–1944. Translated by Norah Purcell, with an introduction by Anne Morrow Lindbergh. New York, 1986.
Wind, Sand, and Stars. Translated by Lewis Galantière. New York, 1939.
The Wisdom of the Sands. Translated by Stuart Gilbert. New York, 1949.

BIOGRAPHICAL AND CRITICAL STUDIES

Berghe, Christian van den. *La pensée de Saint-Exupéry.* New York, 1985.
Bréaux, Adèle. *Saint-Exupéry in America, 1942–1943.* Rutherford, N.J., 1971.
Brée, Germaine, and Margaret Guiton. *The French Novel from Gide to Camus.* New York, 1962.
Cate, Curtis. *Antoine de Saint-Exupéry: His Life and Times.* New York, 1970.
Chevrier, Pierre. *Antoine de Saint-Exupéry.* Paris, 1959.

ANTOINE DE SAINT-EXUPÉRY

Delange, René. *La vie de Saint-Exupéry,* followed by Léon Werth, *Tel que je l'ai connu.* Paris, 1948.

Estang, Luc. *Saint-Exupéry par lui-même.* Paris, 1956.

Forsberg, Roberta J. *Antoine de Saint-Exupéry and David Beaty: Poets of a New Dimension.* New York, 1974.

Ibert, Jean-Claude. *Antoine de Saint-Exupéry.* Paris, 1960.

Knight, Everett W. *Literature Considered as Philosophy: The French Example.* London, 1957.

Major, Jean-Louise. *Saint-Exupéry: L'Écriture et la pensée.* Ottawa, 1968.

Monin, Yves. *L'esotérisme du Petit Prince de Saint-Exupéry.* Paris, 1984.

Ouellet, Réal. *Les relations humaines dans l'oeuvre de Saint-Exupéry.* Paris, 1971.

Pélissier, Georges. *Les cinq visages de Saint-Exupéry.* Paris, 1951.

Peyre, Henri. *French Novelists of Today.* New York, 1967.

Quesnel, Michel. *Saint-Exupéry; ou, La vérité de la poésie.* Paris, 1964.

Robinson, Joy D. Marie. *Antoine de Saint-Exupéry.* Boston, 1984.

Rumbold, Richard, and Margaret Stewart. *The Winged Life: A Portrait of Antoine de Saint-Exupéry, Poet and Airman.* London, 1954.

Simon, Pierre-Henri. *L'Homme en procès: Malraux, Sartre, Camus, Saint-Exupéry.* Neuchâtel, 1949.

Smith, Maxwell A. *Knight of the Air: The Life and Works of Antoine de Saint-Exupéry.* New York, 1956.

Vercier, Bruno. *Les critiques de notre temps et Saint-Exupéry.* Paris, 1971.

RALPH TARICA

GEORGE SAND
(1804–1876)

INTRODUCTION

TO THOSE WHO have been brought up in a French environment, George Sand is generally associated with such pastoral novels as *La petite Fadette*, (*Little Fadette*, 1848–1849) and *François le champi* (*François the Waif*, 1847–1848). Marcel Proust's case, in this respect, is typical. George Sand's rustic novels, which Proust received as gifts from his mother and grandmother, enriched and brightened his boyhood; and he always spoke of their author with affection and admiration.

Despite her controversial reputation, George Sand was greatly respected and admired by writers, painters, and composers, who did not hesitate to turn to her for advice and moral support. One of the few dissenting voices in this chorus of praise was that of Charles Baudelaire, whose animosity toward her was not without envy of her literary success and abundant creativity. While Proust saw in George Sand's prose the very essence of human generosity and moral goodness, Baudelaire regarded her as a dangerous and seductive apologist for romantic socialism. To be sure, he himself had flirted with revolutionary politics in 1848, a heady but brief escapade he later bitterly disavowed. For Baudelaire, George Sand became the living embodiment of the kind of romantic utopianism he had originally enthusiastically endorsed and eventually repudiated. That works poured forth from her pen with extraordinary ease while he labored painfully over every line of prose or poetry only heightened his hostility toward what he viewed as her facile sincerity, her gushing sentimentality, and her naive and idealized notion of human nature.

George Sand's position among French romantics is crucial by virtue of several factors: her life span embraced an era marked by momentous changes; she welcomed, indeed thrived on, conflict and strife; in both her fictional and nonfictional works she showed a keen awareness of the importance of the historical context in the life of every individual. History, as she saw it, is determined both by events of a cataclysmic nature—such as wars and revolutions—and by the slow, sometimes imperceptible impact of ideas. She recognized that the interrelation between these two sets of events is at once crucial and immensely complex. Events of an immediately portentous nature certainly played a decisive role in shaping George Sand's political and social attitudes and beliefs, as her autobiography, *Histoire de ma vie* (*Story of My Life*, 1854–1855), makes clear.

George Sand dealt more boldly than any of her female predecessors (including Madame de Staël) with such themes as passion, marriage, and the painful conflicts between love and duty. That she flouted social conventions openly in her own life, and lived her romances fully and intensively, added to her notoriety, but also obscured the seriousness of her commitment as a writer. Furthermore, her generous, compassionate nature caused her to identify with the weak, the poor, and the oppressed; she maintained strong ideological ties with the ideals of the Enlightenment and the French Revolution and remained a steadfast admirer and disciple of Jean Jacques Rousseau.

An uncommonly prolific output—owing partly to her longevity and partly to her industriousness—may well have contributed to a basic misunderstanding of George Sand's rightful place among great writers of the nineteenth century. The general reproach has been that she was too facile and unselfconscious to be ranked with such giants as Stendhal, Balzac, and Flaubert. She could not be a true artist because her easy, flowing style showed no obvious traces of self-torment or self-doubt. While far from unaware of this criticism, George Sand remained convinced that as an author she had the right, indeed the duty, to give free rein to her thoughts and feelings without undue concern for formal niceties. Hence her espousal of a direct, unambiguous, even improvisatory style of writing. Yet in spite of, or perhaps precisely because of, this absence of lengthy premeditation or painful revision, George Sand's style retains a freshness and richness that are only now being fully appreciated.

Not content to cultivate and nurture her own exceptional talents, George Sand did everything she could to encourage those she loved or admired: Alfred de Musset, Franz Liszt, Frédéric Chopin, Alexandre Dumas *fils,* Flaubert. She was, moreover, at the center of the cultural, artistic, and political life of her age. She regularly contributed to some of the most popular and influential periodicals of her time: the *Revue des deux mondes,* the *Revue de Paris,* and the *Figaro,* among others. She founded two reviews of her own, the *Revue indépendante* and the *Cause du peuple.* She not only enjoyed close friendships with such great

French writers, artists, and composers as Chateaubriand, Balzac, Musset, Hugo, Sainte-Beuve, Flaubert (whose talent she was among the first to recognize), Delacroix, Berlioz, Chopin, and Liszt; her renown extended beyond France, and among her foreign admirers were such diverse personalities as Mickiewicz, Turgenev, Dostoevsky, Heine, George Eliot, Henry James, and Whitman.

She was also a passionate pacifist and a writer with a profound sense of political commitment; she took an active part in the Revolution of 1848 and untiringly fought against social injustice and, of course, inequality of the sexes. In a society hostile to independent women with literary or artistic ambitions, she managed to gain the respect of the men who dominated the cultural scene as writers and as publishers. And in her own works, she expressed her rich and often painful experience as a woman who, against all odds, had determined to realize her full potential as a human being and as an artist.

George Sand in a mannish outfit and with a man's name created a titillating legend of assumed masculinity. But these idiosyncrasies were only the outward manifestations of a deep-seated uneasiness. Insinuations were made about her sexual identity and about lesbian tendencies. Her complex and at times contradictory personality, and of course her numerous love affairs, have continued to intrigue biographers and literary critics.

There was a high price to pay for the boldness with which George Sand transgressed the rules of society. Because she refused to accept the role expected of her, because she openly proclaimed equality of the sexes—at the very least in such social institutions as marriage—she was widely vilified and calumniated. Her social radicalism, and especially her novels with political messages, hardly helped to make her a "respectable" figure among the conservatives of her time. In effect, she was a woman and writer who came to embody all the liberal causes and struggles of her age.

GEORGE SAND

A CHILD OF TWO WORLDS

On the evening of 16 September 1808, a horseman returning home in the small town of La Châtre, in central France, was suddenly thrown and his neck broken as his mount unexpectedly reared at a pile of stones. Thus died, at the age of thirty, Maurice Dupin, a handsome officer in the French army who had distinguished himself on the battlefield. He bore the name of his famed grandfather, Maurice, count of Saxe and, under Louis XV, marshal of France, who had been equally renowned for his military and amorous conquests. The Dupins were also descendants of King Augustus II of Poland, one of the most notorious womanizers of his time.

In 1800 Maurice Dupin, serving as first lieutenant in Milan under Napoleon, had met and fallen in love with the vivacious Sophie-Victoire Delaborde, mistress of General Claude-Antoine Collin. That Sophie was the daughter of a bird-seller on the quai de la Mégisserie in Paris, that she had led a most irregular life and given birth to two illegitimate children of different fathers, did not deter him from marrying her in a civil ceremony on 5 June 1804. Hardly a month later, on 1 July, a daughter, named Amantine-Aurore-Lucile Dupin, the future George Sand, was born in Paris. The father was twenty-six, the mother thirty-one, at the time. Whether Maurice Dupin contracted these marriage vows out of passion or a sense of compassion and duty will never be known. What is certain is that his doting mother, the aristocratic and highly cultured Marie-Aurore Dupin de Francueil, chatelaine of the handsome country estate of Nohant, in Berry, where George Sand was to spend her childhood and many years of her life, was profoundly dismayed by this "misalliance." In her eyes the woman selected by her son would always remain little more than a camp follower.

In her compelling autobiography, *Story of My Life,* George Sand makes much of the fact that in her veins coursed the blood of both kings and paupers, patricians and plebeians:

> My ancestry, for which I have been so frequently and curiously reproached on both sides of my family, is indeed a rather curious fact, which has caused me to devote some thought to the question of genetics. I especially suspect my foreign biographers of being rather aristocratic, for they have all granted me an illustrious origin without taking into consideration (well-informed though they must have been) a rather glaring stain on my coat of arms. One is not only the child of the father, one is also a bit, I think, the child of the mother. It seems to me even more so, for we are connected to the womb that has carried us by the most direct, the most powerful, the most sacred bond. Thus while my father was a great grandson of Augustus II, King of Poland, and I am indeed a near if illegitimate relative of Charles X and Louis XVIII, it is no less true that I am just as intimately and directly related to ordinary people; moreover, there is no bastardy on that side of my bloodline.
>
> (*Histoire de ma vie*, G. Lubin ed., 1.15–16)

The premature death of her father left Sand, at an early age, in the care of two women, her mother and grandmother, who heartily disliked each other and who could not have been more dissimilar in upbringing, social background, and temperament. Poles apart in nature and rank, they had reluctantly accepted each other. Grief drew them together, but not for long.

High-born, cultivated, and well-read, Madame Dupin de Francueil was a disciple of the Encyclopedists, and wholeheartedly subscribed to their intellectual and moral principles. She was also talented and could sing beautifully, even in old age, the principal parts of the operas of Modeste Grétry as well as the part of Colette in Rousseau's *Devin du village* (*The Village Soothsayer*, 1752). Rousseau was an author she especially admired, and a charming anecdote related in Sand's autobiography tells how her grandmother had been so deeply moved by Rousseau's novel *La nouvelle Héloïse* (1761) and had wept so bitterly over the tragic fate of its heroine, Julie, that her sympathetic husband had managed to get the misanthropic Rousseau, then living in Paris, to dine at their home. The actual encounter turned out to be both embarrassing and touching for the shy, wary author and his worshiping disciple:

> Having completed my toilette, and with my eyes still red and swollen [from reading *La nouvelle Héloïse*], I go to the salon; I see a small man rather badly dressed and with a sullen expression. He rises rather heavily and mumbles a few unintelligible words. I look at him, and guessing who he is I want to speak and break into sobs. Stunned by this reception, Jean Jacques wants to thank me and breaks into sobs. . . . Rousseau shook my hand without saying a word to me. We tried to dine to put an end to all this sobbing. But I was unable to eat anything . . . and Rousseau sneaked out after dinner without having said a word.
>
> (*Histoire de ma vie* 1.49)

Madame Dupin de Francueil had also corresponded with Voltaire, and Buffon was another famous man she had known personally. At the age of thirty, she had married the sixty-two-year-old Dupin de Francueil, a cultured, worldly tax collector, in a marriage of reason that turned out to be a good one for the ten years before she was widowed. She then discovered, to her dismay, that her husband had left his financial affairs in disarray. The Revolution was to make further inroads into the estate. As an admirer of the Enlightenment, she had greeted the Revolution with enthusiastic approval; but she found herself imprisoned as an "ex-noble" and was released only after the fall of Robespierre.

On the other hand, George Sand's mother, in the writer's own words, was "a poor child of the old streets of Paris" about whose ancestry she knew next to nothing. Yet she managed to dig up whatever information she could about this branch of her family, for she took great pride in being the offspring not only of

aristocrats but also of ordinary folk. For three years after the premature death of her husband, Sophie (Sand's mother) stayed at Nohant as her mother-in-law's guest. Madame Dupin de Francueil, however, was determined to become the guardian of her granddaughter and to take charge of her education. Sophie for her part loved her daughter dearly, but was too much of a realist not to see the clear advantages of this arrangement for the child's future. Thus in 1809 she reluctantly agreed to entrust Aurore to Madame Dupin. If Sophie was not a formally educated women, she was far from stupid and had artistic talents, notably for singing, embroidery, and drawing.

Young Aurore found herself torn between two women she loved for different reasons. Her natural affection for her mother had been considerably heightened by the latter's profound despair and loneliness upon her father's untimely death. Her grandmother never displayed her emotions, for she was a rational person who especially appreciated wit, good manners, graciousness, and self-possession. She was fair-haired, white-skinned, with delicate features, and she was unfailingly dignified and courteous in demeanor. Her mother, for her part, was a tempestuous, dark-skinned brunette, with an unpredictable streak in her nature and given to great outbursts of affection or rage. To be sure, the tragic death of the man both women adored brought about a rapprochement; but it could be only temporary. As for Aurore, she fondly loved her grandmother but worshiped her mother with a fierce passion that separation made even more intense.

Madame Dupin maintained an attractive apartment in Paris, where she settled with her granddaughter so that she could closely supervise her upbringing. But Aurore lived only for her mother's visits and hardly appreciated the elegant amenities and refined style of life that graced her new home. She obeyed her mother blindly, never questioning her most arbitrary or capricious demands, and eagerly shared her likes, dislikes, and prejudices. For example,

Sophie, like most people of her class, fervently admired Napoleon. Madame Dupin, on the other hand, regarded the emperor as an ambitious, ruthless, unscrupulous individual who had caused untold suffering through his wars of conquest. Aurore, like her mother, looked on Napoleon as a hero and great leader. Madame Dupin socialized with elderly men and women who nostalgically clung to the refined ways of the Old Regime, and young Aurore observed this circle with bemused curiosity.

In preparation for a suitable marriage, Aurore was duly tutored in the customary subjects: a smattering of history, Latin, mathematics, literature, music, and dancing. Madame Dupin and her charge divided their time between Paris and Nohant. In the spring of 1813 came the news of the disastrous Russian campaign, of the burning of Moscow, and of the retreat of Napoleon's legendary Grand Army. Sophie had in the meantime sparingly spaced her visits to her daughter, realizing that these only caused greater suffering and aggravated her own conflicts with her mother-in-law. In her loneliness, Aurore developed a passion for music and reading. She was not content, however, to play the piano and to read voraciously; she also composed musical pieces and tirelessly invented stories.

Madame Dupin found her charge increasingly difficult to handle, for the young girl had turned into a defiant, sullen rebel. That Aurore had in the meantime become deeply religious convinced Madame Dupin, against her own eighteenth-century anticlerical notions, that a convent would be the best solution to the problem. Thus Aurore spent two years in the convent of the Dames Augustines Anglaises, an English establishment in Paris, from 1818 to 1820. The summer of 1819 was a period of particularly intense devotion. Aurore eagerly welcomed the quietude and tranquillity of the convent, for she was weary, as she tells us in her autobiography, of being the perpetual "apple of discord" between her mother and grandmother. The rigors of claustral life held no terrors for her. Her grandmother became more alarmed by the extent of her religious fervor than she had been by her mutinous behavior as a temperamental child.

MARRIAGE

After leaving the convent Aurore was besieged with marriage proposals and projects. Her greatest fear at this time was that she would have to submit to an arranged marriage. In early 1821 her grandmother was stricken by apoplexy, and Aurore became her devoted nursemaid, staying up nights and helplessly observing the ineluctable progress of the malady. After many ups and downs, Madame Dupin de Francueil died on 26 December 1821.

Aurore was then seventeen years of age. She had inherited from her mother her dark hair and olive complexion. With her lively features, expressive eyes, and lithesome figure, she was an attractive if not beautiful young woman. She was also an accomplished one, for she had read widely, could play on the piano and harp as well as sing, knew how to draw, and was an excellent dancer and good horsewoman. A not inconsiderable fortune, including the Nohant estate in Berry and a sizable dowry inherited from her grandmother, would under normal circumstances have made her a most desirable match for a well-born young man. But her near-illegitimate birth and, more importantly, her mother's obscure origins and less than irreproachable past cast a shadow on her pedigree. Most of the suitors who presented themselves were therefore men well past their prime. Against repeated attempts at matchmaking on the part of well-meaning relatives and friends, Aurore fortified herself by reading Montaigne, Rousseau, and Chateaubriand. And since her grandmother's death, her relationship with her mother had been sorely tested by the latter's volatile, unpredictable temperament.

On 19 April 1822, Aurore was introduced to a tall young sublieutenant, Casimir-François

Dudevant. He was a worldly twenty-six to her innocent eighteen. He was the illegitimate but acknowledged son of a baron of the empire and a servant girl, Augustine Soulès. His family owned an estate at Guillery, in the Gascon country, and was financially independent.

Although Aurore had read many books, she had very little experience of the realities of life. She quickly succumbed to Casimir's easy charm and warm camaraderie. When he formally proposed on 2 June 1822, she gave her consent, and on 17 September the marriage took place in Paris. Soon thereafter the couple left for Nohant. At first Aurore was very happy, and on 30 June 1823 she gave birth to a son, Maurice. Her bliss, however, was short-lived. She had tried very hard to find fulfillment in domesticity; but she soon had to admit that, in her eagerness to escape from her mother's temperamental and overbearing ways and to assert her independence, she had succeeded only in exchanging masters. Casimir shared none of her intellectual interests, and he was an inept manager of the family estate. Hunting, drinking, and womanizing were his main passions. No wonder, therefore, that in 1825, Aurore, during a stay in the Pyrenees, should have fallen in love with Aurélien de Sèze, a young gentleman from Bordeaux with handsome, dark good looks and aristocratic bearing. On 15 November 1825, Aurore wrote her husband a long confessional letter. To be sure, her liaison with Aurélien had remained on a lofty, chaste, idealized level. A reconciliation of some sort took place.

Aurore's first real lover was Stéphane de Grandsagne, the impecunious tenth child of an aristocratic family. A student of medicine and natural history, he greatly impressed her with his scholarship and serious demeanor, and she saw much of him in the fall of 1827. She had known him since 1820, for she had been his pupil, and it was he who first encouraged her to wear men's outfits when riding so as not to be hampered by the tight-fitting women's clothes then in fashion.

When Aurore gave birth to a daughter, So-lange, on 13 September 1828, it was rumored that Stéphane was her father, a matter that has never been fully clarified. Casimir Dudevant, however, kept up a brave front, not only out of apathy and passivity, but also because he too had been unfaithful, and his taste in such matters was of a rather coarse nature.

THE METAMORPHOSIS OF J. SANDEAU INTO GEORGE SAND

Out of the disappointments she had encountered in life, Aurore began sketching plots of novels. She had always had a powerful need to express her thoughts and feelings in writing, and thus far had found her main outlet in long, effusive letters to friends and confidantes, as well as in novelettes, such as *Le voyage en Auvergne* (Travels in Auvergne) and *Le voyage en Espagne* (Travels in Spain) both penned in 1829 but published posthumously.

On 30 July 1830, Aurore met in Paris Jules Sandeau, a young lawyer of modest origins turned journalist and playwright. The events of the July Revolution had profoundly stirred her and coincided with her dreams of freedom and independence. She enthusiastically sided with the republican cause, and felt that the revolution had been betrayed when Louis-Philippe and the citizen-king's bourgeois monarchy gained the upper hand. She refused to keep her love affair with Sandeau secret in order to conform to the hypocritical dictates of respectability. In November 1830, Aurore, finding her relationship with her husband no longer tolerable, decided to make a clean break. She would spend half of the year in Paris and the other half in Nohant. She would have custody of Solange, and Maurice would stay in Nohant; and she would have an annual allowance of three thousand francs.

Aurore left Nohant for Paris in January 1831. She was then twenty-seven. She found herself the sole woman in a circle of young writers and artists. In order to move about more freely, especially in the evening, she donned a man's trousers, long frock coat, and hat. In such garb she could frequent restaurants and theaters, and circulate freely in the streets. What gave her special pleasure was that this outfit enabled her to flout bourgeois conventions regarding the proper role of woman in society.

Aurore's allowance from her estranged husband did not suffice for her financial needs. She decided to try to support herself with her pen. Sandeau, for his part, also had literary ambitions. They therefore agreed to join efforts, signing their productions, mostly short stories, J. Sandeau. Most noteworthy from this collaboration is the long novel *Rose et Blanche* (1831), the melodramatic story of an actress and a nun, which was quite favorably received by the public and critics.

Indiana appeared in 1832, under the pseudonym "G. Sand." Under the guise of a masculine narrator, *Indiana* tells the story, set during the last years of the Restoration and the 1830 Revolution, of a Spanish creole, Indiana, unhappily married to an elderly, unfeeling officer, Colonel Delmare. When she eventually escapes the bonds of matrimony in order to rejoin her lover, Raymon de Ramière, an egotistical nobleman who is also a self-indulgent womanizer and a political conservative, he rejects her in favor of a socially advantageous marriage. In her humiliation and despair, Indiana contemplates suicide; but fortunately she finds happiness with her loyal cousin, Sir Ralph Brown, a calm, noble Englishman. The main impact of the book lies in its eloquent and bold treatment of the "woman question." In her preface Sand clearly states the novel's intentions:

> Indiana is a type. She stands for *Woman*, a weak creature representing those passions that have been compressed, or, if you will, suppressed by human laws. She is Choice at odds with Necessity; she is Love blindly butting its head against all the obstacles set in its path by civilization.

Indiana is artistically transposed autobiography, and its heroine, like George Sand herself, finds disappointment in both marriage and passionate love. The artificially happy ending lacks plausibility but hardly detracts from the main thrust of the novel, which powerfully contrasts woman's quest for fulfillment in an authentic and passionate relationship with man's selfish vanity and sensuality.

Just as Aurore Dudevant had wished to escape from the narrowness of a woman's life by wearing male apparel, George Sand deliberately assumed a male identity as a writer, thereby setting an example followed by George Eliot, among others. The obstacles to her career as a novelist continued to be formidable. She submitted the manuscript of a novelette, *Aimée*, to an established author, Auguste de Kératry; he advised her to produce children rather than books. She was luckier with Hyacinthe de Latouche, a successful novelist and publisher of the *Figaro*, at that time a satirical journal with an antimonarchical viewpoint. Latouche perceived literary promise in the young woman's novel, and while sternly criticizing its weaknesses, he also invited her to join his team of journalists. Her debut proved an immediate success, albeit of a controversial nature, when one of her first articles, a sharp satirical piece directed against Louis-Philippe, caused the *Figaro* to be closed. She introduced Sandeau to Latouche, and the latter enlisted his services for the paper.

Although intoxicated with her newfound independence, Aurore needed to escape from the frantic pace of Parisian life. Since she had maintained cordial relations with her estranged husband, the latter, who lived at Nohant, easily accommodated himself to her presence whenever she felt the urge to breathe fresh air, replenish her strength, and write in the tranquillity of the country.

In the meantime her love for Sandeau had considerably cooled. With her active, energetic nature, she had found it increasingly irritating and disconcerting to put up with

Jules's indolence and bouts of depression, and she carried the main burden of their collaboration. For some years, however, she would continue to help him financially. Her own literary success, confirmed with the publication of *Indiana,* warmly praised by the most influential critics and admired by Balzac, only deepened the crisis in their relationship, for Jules greatly resented being relegated to a secondary position. A break became inevitable; it took place in March 1833.

By now George Sand had gained the admiration and interest not only of Balzac, but also of the critic Sainte-Beuve. Famous for the sharpness of his literary judgments, he had written a laudatory review of *Indiana* in the weekly *National* and soon became a trusted personal confidant and literary counselor. In 1832 George Sand published *Valentine,* another story of an unhappy woman torn between her husband and her lover. The denouement is excessively melodramatic in the most morbidly romantic tradition: the lover dies, impaled by the jealous husband on a pitchfork. But the novel is redeemed by its idyllic and rustic setting and its lively portraits of peasant types. In this respect it prefigures Sand's rural novels.

Lélia, published in 1833, is George Sand's boldest and most confessional novel. It owed a great deal to Balzac's recently published *Peau de chagrin* (*The Magic Skin,* 1831), which features a gifted but penniless young writer, Raphaël de Valentin, who throws himself into reckless orgies after being rejected by the beautiful but unfeeling countess with whom he has fallen in love. *Lélia,* on the other hand, depicts a young poet, Sténio, who is driven to despair and a life of debauchery after being repulsed by a seductive but unmerciful woman named Lélia. Lélia is a woman who, not unlike George Sand, finds disappointment in love and pursues her ideal of perfect, all-consuming passion by going from man to man. She might thus be looked on as a female counterpart of the romantic conception of Don Juan. The novel's bold, erotic scenes of physical passion made a tremendous impact on the contemporary reading public. No wonder, therefore, that *Lélia* should have been characterized by Curtis Cate as a "pre-Freudian novel."

Among George Sand's new friendships was that with Marie Dorval, the famous actress whose fiery performances had done so much to gain acceptance for such romantic playwrights as Hugo, Alfred de Vigny, and Dumas *père.* The intense, emotional nature of their intimacy gave rise to rumors of a lesbian relationship. In general, however, Sand, as she herself readily admitted, preferred the company of men to that of women, not because she considered herself superior to most members of her sex, but rather because, aside from sexual attraction, she felt that each gender is complementary to the other. She herself was volatile and high-strung; she therefore derived little pleasure or solace from women whose eagerness to confide in her their problems, insecurities, and frustrations only heightened her own disquietude and restlessness. Marie Dorval, despite her passionate, nervous temperament, remained the exception to that rule.

It was also in early 1833 that George Sand met and became fascinated by Prosper Mérimée, a great friend of Stendhal, Musset, Sainte-Beuve, and Delacroix. At that time Mérimée was primarily known for his plays in the tradition of the Spanish drama. A young, handsome, scholarly, and cynical dandy, Mérimée nevertheless soon became greatly intrigued by George Sand. They had a brief and unsatisfactory affair, the details of which she naturally confided to Marie Dorval.

ALFRED DE MUSSET

In June 1833, at a dinner for the contributors of the *Revue des deux mondes,* George Sand and Alfred de Musset found themselves seated next to each other. Musset was then twenty-three, six years younger than George

Sand. She was at first reserved toward this dangerously seductive, Byronic dandy with a notorious reputation for dissoluteness and debauchery. For his part, however, Musset was immediately conquered, and he soon declared his passion. Sand was touched by the ardent yet respectful courtship of this dazzling young poet. They exchanged letters, as well as elaborate compliments on each other's works. Musset wrote a poem inspired by *Indiana*, and also expressed enthusiastic admiration for *Lélia*.

George Sand was all the more sensitive to Musset's charm and flattering attentions since her recent amorous disappointments had left her in a depressed frame of mind. In the company of Musset she regained her natural cheerfulness and joie de vivre. He brought into her life enthusiasm, mischievousness, poetic imagination; she felt renewed and rejuvenated. By the end of July 1833 they were lovers, Musset was settled in her apartment on the quai Malaquais, and they were excitedly devising a plan to spend the winter in Italy.

On 12 December 1833 the couple set off on their journey, proceeding by steamship down the Rhône river in the company of Stendhal, who was reluctantly returning to Civitavecchia in order to resume his duties as French consul. At Marseilles, they went their separate ways. Two humorous sketches of the portly Stendhal by Musset record this encounter. One of the drawings shows a jolly Stendhal dancing a jig in his ample winter overcoat, top hat, and boots while George Sand observes him with a bemused smile.

The myth of the romantic couple had of course enormous appeal for the popular imagination, and it was fed in great part by the glamorous vision of the lovers in Venice, silently gliding in a gondola in the moonlight. Reality, despite ecstatic moments, never quite lived up to this exalted legend. The two temperamental travelers quarreled, and Musset ran after other women. He drank heavily and fell gravely ill. The stress of dealing with Musset's infidelities and sickness affected Sand's

own health, and she soon had bouts of fever. They were attended by a young physician, Dr. Pietro Pagello, who had literary aspirations and promptly fell in love with George Sand. By the end of February 1834, she had yielded to his pressing advances, perhaps partly to get back at Musset for his philandering. Musset and George Sand returned to France separately. To be sure, there was to be a reconciliation in January 1835, but continuous quarrels prompted a final break in March 1835.

This stormy relationship lasted less than two years but was to have endless literary repercussions in George Sand's writings, notably in her correspondence, in her *Journal intime* (*Intimate Journal*, published posthumously), in her *Lettres d'un voyageur* (*Letters of a Voyager*, 1834–1836), and in her novel *Elle et lui* (*She and He*), published two years after Musset's death in 1857.

In this thinly disguised fiction Musset is easily recognizable in the portrayal of the painter Laurent, with his unpredictable moodiness, his erratic ways, and his fits of rage. Thérèse, on the other hand, is given an idealized treatment; she becomes Laurent's mistress more out of maternal compassion than sexual attraction. The parallel with George Sand is inescapable. As for Musset, his fictionalized autobiography, *Confession d'un enfant du siècle* (*Confessions of a Child of the Century*, 1836), presents his own highly colored version of their notorious affair. Musset's power and skill as a narrator are a good match for George Sand's passionate prose, and in his *Confession* one finds all the major romantic themes: melancholy and restlessness, generosity and suspiciousness, enthusiasm and nihilism, and above all else the pervasive ailment of the soul characterized as *mal du siècle*.

Mutual recriminations, allegations, and justifications between George Sand and Musset were plentiful. Even interested third parties did not hesitate to offer their say on the subject, among others Musset's brother, Paul, and Dr. Pagello. In this contest, however,

George Sand was bound to gain the upper hand, thanks to both her prolific pen and her longevity.

After Musset's early death, George Sand went on giving her side of the relationship. That her intimate revelations served only to fuel the accusations and denunciations directed at her unconventional behavior and ''immorality'' did not deter her from telling all, either directly in her works of a personal nature (letters, journals, autobiography), or in barely transposed form in her novels. It is probably in the correspondence between the two lovers that one can find the most authentic and moving expression of their passion, happiness, and eventual estrangement. A letter to Musset dated November 1834, written at night following a quarrel, will perhaps give an idea of George Sand's anguished frame of mind at that time:

> You do not love me. You do not love me any more. I cannot blind myself to the truth. Last evening while we were together I was feeling very ill. As soon as you noticed it you went away. No doubt it was right to leave me, because you were tired last night. But today, not one word. You have not even sent to inquire about me. I hoped for you, waited for you, minute by minute, from eleven in the morning until midnight. What a day! Every ring of the bell made me leap to my feet. . . . I wrote to you early this evening. You have not answered my note. They told my messenger you had gone out; yet you did not come to see me for even five minutes. You must have returned very late. Great heavens! Where were you all evening? Alas, all is over between us. You no longer love me at all.
>
> (*The Intimate Journal of George Sand,*
> Howe trans., p. 19)

Whenever powerful emotions upset her inner equilibrium, George Sand turned to letter writing or the diary form to seek an outlet for her spiritual turmoil. She was also fully aware that a woman, especially a famous one, is vulnerable to calumny. She had paid an excessively high price for her legal separation from her husband and for her freedom and independence. She had therefore learned that to love and forgive is not enough. She met slander and criticism with her usual fearless honesty and frankness. She had learned by now that her best therapy and cure for suffering and loneliness was to take refuge in writing. The written word somehow exorcised her inner demons.

During her stay in Venice, George Sand finished the novel *Jacques* (1834), which may not rank among her best but created a sensation. It is another story of adultery in which a married woman leaves her husband for a young dandy. She also completed the first four letters of the *Lettres d'un voyageur*. The letters, of which there would be twelve, enabled her to express her views on a wide range of topics in an informal manner that mingles observations on customs, manners, politics, and the arts with more introspective reflections on love and friendship. Unlike *Jacques*, which received unfavorable criticism from such connoisseurs as Balzac and Stendhal, the *Lettres d'un voyageur* were widely admired and contributed to the vogue of the personal kind of travel literature favored by the romantics.

What is it that attracted George Sand and the romantics to the travel journal or travel account as a literary genre? Their personal restlessness and love of travel, the delight they took in comparing cultures and civilizations, and the pleasure they derived from discovering new places and customs certainly had a great deal to do with this fascination. But traveling for the romantics was no mere search for novel sensations and pleasurable impressions. Their quest was of a more profound nature. They sensed intuitively that one of the deepest yearnings of the human spirit is for the unknown, the strange, the exotic.

It was also while in Venice, partly in order to seek escape from her emotional turmoil, that George Sand dashed off in a week *Leone Leoni* (1834), a novel inspired by the abbé Prévost's famous *Manon Lescaut* (1732), the last book she had read before leaving Paris.

She transposed the characters and reversed the situation by endowing the man, Leoni, with Manon's fatal seductiveness and amorality. Like Manon, Leoni is eventually redeemed through love for his adoring, forgiving mistress, Juliette, who like Prévost's Des Grieux yearns for a quiet existence in some rustic retreat, yet succumbs to passion and adventure. In both novels the story is recounted in the first person, and the main protagonist remains mysteriously elusive. As was the case with *Manon Lescaut* a century earlier, *Leone Leoni* was denounced as a dangerous, immoral work by conservative critics. And that Leoni should have been identified with Musset is no mere coincidence. He is a figure of larger-than-life dimensions, and he embodies at once the highest virtues as well as the basest vices of human nature. The personal tone of the narrative has led commentators to regard *Leone Leoni* as a barely disguised fictionalized autobiography.

George Sand's disastrous Venetian experience also found expression in such tales of passion and mystery as *La dernière Aldini* (*The Last Aldini*, 1838), the dramatic story of a patrician Venetian woman enamored of a gondolier; *L'Orco* (1838), a symbolic novella with fantastic overtones; and *L'Uscoque* (1838), a romance with Byronic strains greatly admired by Dostoevsky.

THE HUMANITARIAN AND SOCIAL REFORMER

George Sand's return to France in October 1834 inaugurated a difficult period of readjustment. As always when she needed to restore her inner equilibrium, she spent some time in Nohant. In November she posed for the painter Delacroix, whom she had long admired, and the resulting powerfully expressive portrait shows a youthful-looking woman mannishly dressed in a frock coat, with a kerchief around her neck and short hair framing her face. Her melancholy, serious demeanor is heightened by large, dark, expressive eyes, a longish nose, and sensitive yet unsmiling lips.

George Sand's concern for the poor and for political and social reform, as well as her passionate preoccupation with the cause of women's rights, took on new importance at this time. Musset's indifference to such issues could only contribute to her estrangement from him. She was ready to invest her enormous energies in activities that would have a broader scope than the dream of finding happiness through perfect love.

To assert her independence and freedom was now uppermost in George Sand's mind. She therefore wished to legally finalize her separation from her husband. Divorce, approved in 1792 during the Revolution, had been abrogated in 1816 under the Restoration. The only recourse for a woman in George Sand's position was legal separation of person and property. This she was able to obtain in July 1836, but not without much wrangling and a court trial, which she had tried in vain to avoid. She was at least able to remain sole mistress of her beloved Nohant, although Casimir got, for his part, the Hôtel de Narbonne on the rue de la Harpe, with its handsome annual revenue in rent. Sand gained custody of Solange, and Casimir of Maurice; but in fact she was able to keep both children.

The lawyer recommended to George Sand during her legal struggle with her husband was Michel de Bourges, a political activist in the cause of republicanism. Unlike the aristocratic Musset, he was of peasant stock and passionately committed to the social betterment of the downtrodden. George Sand herself was deeply preoccupied with social issues, and she and Bourges became more than partners during the legal entanglements with Casimir.

More than his personal attractiveness, Bourges's fiery speeches against an unjust society appealed to George Sand and reinforced her desire to revoke her conjugal vows. Through him she met a number of republican, revolutionary, and radical thinkers and familiarized herself more directly with socialist doctrines. Their relationship came to an end in July 1837, for he was not only a married man but also one who had a far greater understanding of social inequality than of the inequality of the sexes.

In 1835 George Sand met Robert Lamennais, the fiery and controversial French cleric whose *Paroles d'un croyant (Words of a Believer)* had appeared in 1834, and she turned to him for guidance and inspiration. She was profoundly affected by his socially minded zeal, which had alienated him from the ecclesiastical hierarchy. Herself estranged from Catholicism, she nevertheless retained strong religious feelings, and therefore thought at first that Lamennais's reforming fervor offered the best solution to her own dilemma.

For his part, Lamennais remained wary of this notorious woman who so insistently wished to become his disciple, and he kept her at arm's length. Her initial enthusiasm for him cooled considerably when she realized that he was not willing to endorse her bold ideas on marriage and divorce, as set forth in the "Lettres à Marcie" (Letters to Marcy), which appeared in 1837 in the *Monde*, Lamennais's own newspaper. Lamennais himself suspended these letters after the appearance of the sixth in the series—clear proof of his misgivings on this explosive subject.

It was Pierre Leroux, whose books and journalistic writings eloquently denounced social inequities, who had the most powerful impact on George Sand's political orientation. Introduced to him by Sainte-Beuve, she did not hesitate to hail him as an authentic speaker for the oppressed and to place his political theories alongside Rousseau's. Leroux, a widower in his forties with several children to support, eked out a meager living as a printer and compositor. As a brilliant young student, he had to give up scholarly aspirations and a promising career in order to go to work, for he came from a poor family.

Leroux's experience as a typesetter led him to become one of the founders of the *Globe*, a periodical that advocated Saint-Simonianism, which called for public control of the means of production and a more equal distribution of wealth; it was through the *Globe* that he met Sainte-Beuve, who in the early 1830's contributed to the publication. Leroux was also involved in the enormous enterprise of publishing a *Nouvelle encyclopédie* (New Encyclopedia), which was to follow the example of Diderot's famous compendium in making knowledge serve an ideology of general enlightenment and social betterment. Unlike the Encyclopedists, however, Leroux was a fervent if unorthodox Christian. But what especially appealed to Sand was that Leroux propounded emancipation of women and equality of the sexes. Immensely impressed by his idealism, yet aware of the utopian nature of many of his theories, she helped him in every way she could, making valiant efforts to spread his political doctrines as well as his Christian brand of socialism.

In her *Story of My Life*, George Sand describes her religious evolution in some detail. Under the influence of her grandmother's Voltairean deism, she chafed at having to learn her catechism by rote "like a parrot, without seeking to understand it" (1.840). She found herself facing a dilemma, for while her grandmother's example had led her to question the basic articles of Catholic faith, the same grandmother insisted on the importance of her making first communion. And when the day arrived, on 23 March 1817, Madame Dupin made it a point to be present at the ceremony, although "she had not set foot in a church since my father's marriage" (1.842).

This early skepticism gave way to a period of profound mysticism that corresponded with George Sand's two-year stay at the convent of the Dames Augustines Anglaises, from 1818 to 1820. Everything in the convent conspired to enhance the young girl's religious fervor, and she even became convinced that she was destined to be a nun. After leaving the convent, however, she found herself once more in a state of painful uncertainty; and she was a

Catholic in name only when, after reading widely and voraciously philosophers, moralists, and poets, she at last came upon Rousseau:

> While continuing to practice this religion, I had abandoned, without quite realizing it, the narrow path of its doctrine. . . . The spirit of the Church was no longer in me.
>
> (1.1053)

It was through Rousseau that George Sand had the revelation of a natural religion, freed from doctrine and dogma. She rejected the doctrines of original sin and eternal punishment for one's sins in the afterlife, and she argued against celibacy for priests. But she would never waver from her Rousseauistic faith in a benevolent God, and she continued to believe in the immortality of the soul. This religious faith based on individual feeling suited her temperament, for she was, as she proudly proclaims, "a being of sentiment," for whom sentiment alone settled the most portentous problems. This personal creed would coincide perfectly with her later militant political and social activism.

The Profession of Faith of the Savoyard Vicar in Rousseau's *Émile* (1762) became George Sand's own creed. Evoking this crucial revelation, she says: "As for religion, he seemed to me the most Christian of the writers of his time" (1.1061). And like Rousseau, she would always disapprove strongly of atheism and materialism while disdaining ontological and theological arguments. Her religious faith remained founded on a spontaneous impulse of the heart, a communion with God through social humanitarianism. She therefore had no difficulty endorsing Lamennais's unorthodox Catholicism and especially Leroux's messianic socialism. At the same time she never repudiated her anticlerical stance; on the contrary, she was especially hostile to the French clergy of her time. With increasing vigor and boldness she openly opposed the temporal power of the church, for she was convinced that it had failed in its mission to protect the poor and the powerless.

Some of the novels George Sand wrote after her association with Lamennais and Leroux—notably the mystical allegory *Spiridion* (1838–1839), the philosophically ambitious *Les sept cordes de la lyre* (*The Seven Strings of the Lyre*, 1839), the religio-socialist *Le compagnon du tour de France* (*Journeyman-Joiner*, rejected by the *Revue des deux mondes* in 1840), and the sweeping *Consuelo* (1842–1843), with its sequel, *La comtesse de Rudolstadt* (*Countess Rudolstadt*, 1843–1844), reflect her spiritual quest and evolution from orthodox Catholicism to Christian socialism. Her publisher, François Buloz, was not too happy with these metaphysical and ideological works and preferred, for obvious reasons, her best-selling novels of amorous conflicts and unhappy marriages. Sainte-Beuve also expressed strong reservations, and among more modern critics André Maurois has harshly characterized *The Seven Strings of the Lyre* as a "detestable pastiche of Goethe's *Faust*." On the other hand Ernest Renan, the religious historian and author of the famous *Vie de Jésus* (*Life of Jesus*, 1861), was a great admirer of *Spiridion*, and *Consuelo* was the favorite novel by George Sand of Dostoevsky and Whitman. Henry James considered *Consuelo* her masterpiece and the philosopher Alain ranked it with Goethe's *Wilhelm Meister*.

Consuelo is a novel of great sweep and scope, what the French call a *roman-fleuve*, and one for which George Sand did extensive research. Her heroine, Consuelo, is a Spanish-born singer and adventurous female Don Juan in quest of perfect love. More significantly, however, she is the artist searching for truthful self-expression. In many ways she is reminiscent of Madame de Staël's touching heroine Corinne, in the novel by the same name (1807). Her wanderings take Consuelo from Venice to the courts of Maria Theresa in Vienna and Frederick the Great in Potsdam; they also bring her into contact with the great composers of her day, for music plays an important part in the novel. In *Consuelo* George Sand expressed all her personal and artistic aspirations; with *Countess Rudolstadt,* it constitutes her most ambitious work. Above all else, the life of the heroine, a singer-composer like Madame de Staël's Corinne, represents, through her many trials and tribulations, a woman's odyssey, a female quest for creativity and spiritual transcendence. Unlike Madame de Staël, who had given *Corinne* a tragic ending by making her heroine the lonely victim of society's prejudices and her timorous lover's pusillanimity, George Sand ends *Consuelo* on a hopeful note. The heroine not only survives misfortunes and persecutions—she even manages to find happiness and serenity. Electing to live among simple, ordinary people, she offers them music in exchange for their hospitality, according to a communal system reminiscent of Leroux's philosophy of a propertyless society that resorts to barter rather than money as a means for the exchange of goods.

Having broken with Buloz as a result of his reluctance to publish her more ideologically oriented writings, George Sand founded the *Revue indépendante* with her friend Leroux (1841). To this journal she contributed articles and such works of fiction as *Horace* (1841–1842), a novel with strong socialist tendencies and an equivocal young hero, the charming but unpredictable Horace. Drawing on her own experience following her initial arrival in Paris and her introduction to a bohemian milieu, she gives a vivid and sympathetic depiction of rebellious young intellectuals and students. Horace is a kind of antihero whose personal seductiveness is a mixture of narcissistic affectation and lackadaisical languor. That he shares many traits with Jules Sandeau, George Sand's lover and first literary collaborator, is no mere coincidence. Sandeau, for his part, had recently published a fictionalized account of his liaison with George Sand, entitled *Marianna* (1839), which lacked gentlemanly discretion. No doubt a desire, conscious or unconscious, to

even the score had something to do with the creation of the charming but feckless and unpredictable Horace. But Horace is also reminiscent of some of George Sand's other lovers, notably Musset, with his ambiguity toward women and his violent outbursts of rage. *Horace* is one of George Sand's most colorful and engrossing works, and it deserves more attention than it has received thus far from critics and commentators.

After her return from Venice, George Sand managed, despite her absorbing activities and preoccupations, to make a number of new friends. In addition to Lamennais and Leroux, she singled out two intimates, Heinrich Heine, the German poet and journalist, who had been living in Paris since 1831, and Franz Liszt, the keyboard virtuoso. That both men had a strong concern for social justice could only endear them to her. Heine playfully called George Sand his cousin, and she in turn was very fond of him. Music had always been one of her great passions, so it was no wonder that she should be especially drawn to Liszt, an attraction that was mutual. But Liszt already had a romantic mate in the person of the countess Marie d'Agoult, who like George Sand had forsaken respectability for personal freedom. At the end of August 1836, George Sand with her two children joined Liszt and Marie d'Agoult in Geneva, where she pleasantly vacationed until October; in February and May 1837 she was in turn their hostess at Nohant, where one of her great joys was to listen to Liszt playing passages of his own composition on the piano.

Following her break with Musset, George Sand had been working on a new novel, *Mauprat,* which was published in 1837. Despite the cool reception accorded to it by such influential critics as Sainte-Beuve, it was one of her best works and continues to be highly readable to this day. Similarities between this novel and Emily Brontë's *Wuthering Heights,* which appeared ten years later, have been noted by subsequent critics. In both cases, love transforms and ennobles a rough-hewn, primitive man. But whereas Brontë's story ends in tragedy, George Sand's concludes on a note of hope and affirmation of the redeeming value of marriage.

Mauprat is set in the period immediately preceding the French Revolution. In the orphaned, mistreated young hero, Bernard de Mauprat, George Sand presents a compelling picture of an illiterate, brutish youth, all instinctual impulsiveness, who like Heathcliff rises above his stormy, unrestrained nature through suffering and a great love. Just as in *Wuthering Heights*, the brooding, somber atmosphere of an untamed natural setting blends with the violent emotions that rule Mauprat's life.

It is also worth noting that *Mauprat* is reminiscent of the eighteenth-century memoir novel, since Bernard is both protagonist and narrator. In this respect, the confessional tale of the old Mauprat follows a model that had already been well established in various guises by the great novelists of the preceding era. From his rich human experience the aging hero has acquired wisdom and a clear understanding of his flaws and limitations of character, and it is with unflinching honesty and forthrightness that he looks back on his life. *Mauprat* is a novel of experience, a bildungsroman with a strong didactic component. Its main attraction for the modern reader, however, lies in its mysterious, Gothic-like setting and its romantic duel between the near-savage young Bernard and Edmée, the exceptional young woman who will lead him toward greater spiritual and moral self-awareness and sensitivity. It is hardly surprising that, once more, George Sand should have endowed her female protagonist with a nobler character than her imperfect lover.

Marriage plays an important role in Bernard de Mauprat's redemption; as George Sand points out in the preface to her novel, it was precisely while suing for final separation from her husband that she felt the greatest need to extol the sanctity of this bond and its irreplaceable value as a social institution:

> While writing a novel as an occupation and distraction for my mind, I conceived the idea of portraying an exclusive and undying love, before, during, and after marriage. Thus I drew the hero of my book proclaiming, at the age of eighty, his fidelity to the one woman he had ever loved.

George Sand had written *Mauprat* laboriously and without deriving pleasure from the effort; yet it remains one of her most absorbing and original fictional creations.

FRÉDÉRIC CHOPIN

It was through Liszt that George Sand met Frédéric Chopin in the autumn of 1836. Chopin had been living in Paris since 1831. On their first meeting, impressions were mutually unfavorable. At twenty-six, Chopin found the thirty-two-year-old writer overly assertive and mannish, whereas she was struck by his frailty and almost girlish looks and demeanor. Despite his professed aversion to the controversial author, Chopin invited her to a soirée in his apartment in November 1836. In December he gave a musicale attended by such notables as Delacroix, Liszt and d'Agoult, Eugène Sue, Mickiewicz, and George Sand, who brought along Heine. Liszt and Chopin each played the piano. Seated in an armchair and smoking a cigar, George Sand was enraptured.

But it was not until June 1838 that the liaison between George Sand and Chopin began in earnest. In the meantime the composer had had an unhappy love affair with a young Polish compatriot, Maria Wodzinska. The year 1837 had also been a difficult one for George Sand, for it marked the final illness and death of her mother, as well as renewed legal difficulties with her estranged husband. During the winter of 1837–1838 her health suffered as a result of all these stresses, and she had severe attacks of rheumatism. By the end of February 1838, however, she was well enough to have Balzac as a guest at Nohant.

The spring of 1838 found George Sand again in Paris, where her lawsuit with Casimir Dudevant required her presence. She had sufficiently recovered from her ailment to appear at brilliant soirées attended by the leading writers and artists of the day. Listening to Chopin's piano improvisations at one such concert-dinner she was again enthralled. As in the case of Musset, her amorous feelings were inextricably intertwined with a maternal desire to protect and nurture a fragile, child-like genius.

Because of Chopin's weak lungs and her own recent bouts with rheumatism, George Sand was determined to spend the winter in a warm climate, and she persuaded him to disregard scandalmongers and escape Paris with her. In October 1838 the lovers departed for Majorca, taking with them George Sand's two children, the fifteen-year-old Maurice and the ten-year-old Solange.

After some searching they rented a sparsely furnished villa a short distance from Palma. The house, named *Son Vent* (House of Wind in the Majorcan dialect), lived up to its designation only too well. George Sand also made arrangements to rent several rooms in an abandoned monastery, the charterhouse of Valdemosa, a village farther to the north of Palma.

At first George Sand and Chopin were ecstatic and duly admired the beauties of the surrounding countryside. But they could not long remain oblivious to the total absence of the most elementary physical comforts in their picturesque but hardly livable dwellings. To attempt to either write or compose in such circumstances was a frustrating task, especially in the fall season, with its torrential rains and incessant gales, followed by even more trying winter storms.

Chopin fell ill, and George Sand had to cope with an invalid and two children. In February 1839, they slowly made their way back to France. By the time they reached Marseilles, Chopin's alarming condition had considerably improved. At the end of May they were back in Nohant, where Chopin could complete his recuperation.

The winter in Majorca had been a sobering experience, especially for George Sand. Devotedly nursing the ailing and frequently moody Chopin, she had come to regard him as a son rather than a lover. But her admiration for his genius and fondness for him remained undiminished. In the *Story of My Life* she paid him this homage:

> Chopin's genius is the most profound and the richest in feelings and emotions that ever existed. He has made a single instrument speak the language of infinitude; he was able to summarize, in ten lines that a child could play, poems of an immense elevation, dramas of an unequaled energy. He never needed great material means in order to give full expression to his genius. . . . His individuality is even more exquisite than that of Sebastian Bach, more powerful than that of Beethoven, more dramatic than that of Weber. . . . Only Mozart is superior to him.
>
> (2.421)

On returning from Majorca, George Sand settled down to a more tranquil routine. Realizing that Chopin needed a quiet, orderly life to survive and compose, she spent the summer months in Nohant and the winters in Paris. Chopin became a permanent host and fixture in Nohant, but he found country life rather monotonous and dull. George Sand did her best to distract him by inviting her Berry friends as well as Parisian luminaries. Disregarding his fastidiousness and bouts of temper and melancholy, she continued to assume responsibility for his health and well-being until 1847 (two years before his death), when in a bitter quarrel with her daughter, Solange, and the latter's husband, she discovered to her dismay that Chopin had sided against her. After the many years of loving solicitude, she felt deeply hurt and betrayed. That Chopin had been able, despite his precarious health and frequent bouts of depression, to write some of his finest compositions is in no small measure due to George Sand's attentiveness to his physical and spiritual needs.

THE FAILED REVOLUTION (1848)

After the Majorca disaster, George Sand came to the realization that she was past the age for passionate love affairs. She now threw her considerable energies into her work as a novelist and assumed, more then ever, the militant activist role of speaker for the downtrodden and the oppressed. Chopin, however, had this much in common with Musset: the plight of the poor was of only slight interest to him.

While eagerly pursuing her political activities, George Sand took a lively interest in popular poetry, for she came to look upon this generally neglected form of expression as a harbinger of the liberation and enlightenment of the masses. Hence her "Dialogues familiers sur la poésie des prolétaires" ("Familiar Dialogues on the Poetry of the Proletarians"), published in 1842 in the *Revue indépendante*. Parallel to her growing involvement in social issues was her heightened interest in the life and concerns of the peasants of her hamlet of Nohant and the Berry region. She eagerly took part in rustic weddings, feasts, and celebrations. She studied the local dialect and traditions, realizing that industrialization and the railways would soon do away with a provincial culture dear to her heart. And in the wintertime, when she was in Paris, she sorely missed the sounds and smells of Nohant.

No wonder, therefore, that she should have turned to the life of country folk as a theme for novels as well as crusading journalism. Hence

a cycle of works with rustic settings and characters, such as *Jeanne* (1844), which incorporates Berry legends and speech patterns : *Le meunier d'Angibault* (*The Miller of Angibault*, 1845), the story of a simple peasant girl (a novel admired by Balzac); *La mare au diable* (*The Devil's Pool,* 1846), dedicated to Chopin, a rural love story that was to become one of her most popular novels; *François the Waif*, which treats the theme of bastardy in provincial France and out of which Sand constructed a highly successful play (1849); *Little Fadette,* the touching story of a persecuted and eventually vindicated peasant girl; and *Les maîtres sonneurs* (*The Master Bellringers,* also translated as *The Bagpipers,* 1853), her most ambitious tale of rustic life.

George Sand's preface to *The Master Bellringers* is indicative of what she tried to achieve in her cycle of rural novels:

> The peasantry guess or comprehend much more than we believe them capable of understanding. . . . Therefore it is not, as some have reproachfully pointed out, for the mere pleasure of reproducing a style hitherto unused in literature . . . that I have assumed the humble task of preserving the local color of Étienne Depardieu's tale [Depardieu is the narrator and hero of the novel]. If, in spite of the care and conscientiousness which I bring to my task, you find that my narrator sometimes sees too clearly or too deeply into his subject matter, you must blame my faulty presentation.

George Sand was intent on reproducing in these novels the manners, mores, and speech of the countryfolk of the Berry region that she knew so well from personal experience. But while she was fascinated by the traditions, values, and even superstitions of the local peasantry, she wanted to combine this local color with her political and humanitarian ideology. And she eminently succeeded in depicting the suffering and aspirations of the most humble rustics in these Vergilian idylls, for she had learned to respect their good sense and dignity in her frequent dealings with them. Her strong empathy for the plight of the French peasantry led her to make such revolutionary statements as this one, which highlights her preface to *The Devil's Pool:* "These riches that cover the soil are the property of the few and the cause of enslavement and exhaustion of the largest number."

In these folk tales with a rustic setting George Sand inaugurated a novelistic tradition that continues to thrive to this day. To be sure, to depict French peasantry with authenticity and truthfulness also tempted such nineteenth-century masters of the novel as Balzac, in *Les paysans* (*The Peasants,* 1844), and Émile Zola, in *La terre* (*The Earth,* 1887); and vivid glimpses of peasant mentality and mores are afforded in Flaubert's *Madame Bovary* (1857) and "Un coeur simple" ("A Simple Heart," 1877). But unlike Balzac, Flaubert, and Zola, who presented their peasant characters in a relentlessly harsh, even at times odious, light, and insistently underscored the ugliness, meanness, and quasi-bestiality of peasant life, George Sand put her talent as a writer in the service of her crusading humanitarian cause by elaborating a poetic, lyrical conception of this genre.

George Sand's uncommon capacity to identify with others enabled her to endow the most primitive and simpleminded peasant types with considerable nobility and dignity. Her romantic utopianism offers us an idealized and sentimentalized panorama of country manners and mores. Yet she knows how to spin a tale, set a scene, present believable and appealing characters, incorporate authentic-sounding dialogues into her narration, and create suspense. Her intense involvement with country men and women, their daily cares and preoccupations, their prejudices and superstitions, are apparent throughout these engrossing tales. It is therefore hardly surprising that their popularity should have been so enduring and that they should have delighted generations of French children and young adults. Proust's experience in this respect is

eminently representative of that of his compatriots.

The year 1847 was a painful one for George Sand; she quarreled with her daughter, Solange, and broke with Chopin. Solange had married the sculptor Auguste Clésinger that year. Clésinger, as things turned out, was heavily in debt, and George Sand, deeply worried by her daughter's financial plight, tried her best to salvage her dowry. As always, however, she found her best revenge against the realities of existence in her creative work; she embarked on the ambitious enterprise *The Story of My Life.*

As a loyal disciple of Rousseau, George Sand endeavored to be fearlessly frank and truthful in recounting the main events of her life. But she differed from her master on some essential points. While truthfulness was her goal, she remained wary of the compulsion to tell all in the name of veracity. Her concept of autobiography, unlike that of Rousseau, was that a personal memoir need not be confessional. As a woman with a highly controversial reputation, she was determined not to feed the public's morbid curiosity for sensational revelations, and she was convinced that to dwell on one's failings and shortcomings would be both counterproductive and masochistic. One does not disarm one's readers through total and indiscriminate self-revelation. George Sand was of course keenly aware of the exigencies of the autobiographer and of the dangers that lurk in the writer's natural tendency to dramatize and color facts. In the opening pages of *The Story of My Life,* she gently takes Rousseau to task for being guilty of this kind of self-indulgence: "He accuses himself in order to have the opportunity of exonerating himself; he reveals secret misdeeds in order to have the right to reject public calumnies." And again: "I am deeply mortified when I see the great Rousseau humiliate himself in this manner."

George Sand's strategy as an autobiographer combines both revelation and reticence. A great deal of space is devoted to her ancestors and especially to the relationship between her father and mother before her birth. Having reached the fourteenth chapter before making her own appearance on the scene, George Sand realized her reader might be justified in becoming somewhat impatient at the slowness of her pace:

> If I pursue the story of my father, I will probably be told that I greatly delay keeping my promise of telling my own story. Must I repeat here what I said in the beginning of my book? . . . All human lives are interdependent, and the person who would present his story in isolation without relating it to that of his fellow man would only end up with an undecipherable enigma. This interdependence is even more evident when it is immediate and involves parents and children.
>
> (1.307)

George Sand also knew that many of her readers would be disappointed by her cautious reserve regarding intimate details of her love affairs, but she was willing to take this risk:

> The sorrows I would have to relate about purely personal events would have no general application. I will only deal with those that may have meaning for all humankind. Once more, therefore, scandalmongers, shut my book after reading the first page; it was not written for you.
>
> (1.15)

For George Sand autobiography becomes truly meaningful only if it is closely related to the broad historical context. Each individual destiny is significant insofar as it is part of the vast panorama of human events. The collective experience is what matters. George Sand's autobiography ranks among her most original and powerful works. Besides offering a sweeping and lively tableau of French society from the last decades of the Old Regime until the middle of the nineteenth century, she recounts her own saga with great gusto and unflinching honesty, and without any kind of self-pity.

When the Revolution of 1848 broke out, Sand was well prepared for it. Her political involvement in this momentous event was enthusiastic and from the outset she eagerly put her talents as a writer in its service. In addition to founding the journal *La cause du peuple*, she wrote political articles and exulted in the triumph of the republic. Her joy, however, was of short duration. While she wholeheartedly sympathized with the most radical elements of the revolution, she shied away from the use of force and illegal coercion as a means to achieving success for the right cause. The precedent of 1793 was too vivid in her mind to follow that radical course. To institute another Reign of Terror was not what she wanted, and she tried her best to combat the intransigence of her most uncompromising friends. Yet she also realistically anticipated the results of the elections. And, to be sure, her pessimistic expectations were entirely fulfilled.

When it was all over, George Sand was left with a feeling of profound disappointment. She had committed herself wholeheartedly to the revolution, notwithstanding the risks involved. Yet she did not regret her political involvement; far from it. That her ideal of a successful and bloodless revolution had not come about in her lifetime did not dishearten her for very long. A romantic in matters of the heart, she tended to be more pragmatic and realistic in her politics.

The 1848 disaster enabled George Sand to fortify and renew her sense of social commitment. More than ever she subscribed to such simple virtues as goodness, friendship, and generosity. Her last years were increasingly marked by an attempt to reconcile her political involvement with her personal need for retirement, and more and more she identified with the aging Rousseau of the *Rêveries du promeneur solitaire* (1782).

George Sand remained steadfast in her beliefs through the double tragedy of the war of 1870 and the Commune. By then, however, she had learned the hard lessons of serenity and detachment. Yet this newly acquired tranquillity was linked with a sense of sadness and melancholy, best reflected in her novel *Monsieur Sylvestre* (1865). She was now increasingly preoccupied with illness, old age, and death. But while she sought peace and repose, she was not yet quite prepared to renounce entirely the pleasures and challenges of human relationships. Her friendship and correspondence with Flaubert are perhaps the best case of a relationship based on opposites rather than affinities in character and literary inspiration.

THE GOOD LADY OF NOHANT

More than ever George Sand found renewed sources of energy and inspiration in her beloved Nohant, where she came to be known as "la bonne dame de Nohant" (the good lady of Nohant) because of her personal involvement in the well-being of the farmers of the locality. Her benevolence extended to animals and birds, and botany became one of her favorite hobbies. By now, thanks to her considerable productivity as a writer, her activism as a social propagandist, and her controversial personal reputation, she had become something of a living legend. Visitors from all corners of Europe flocked to Nohant.

Yet the conservative climate under the Second Empire hardly favored George Sand's political views, and some of the most noteworthy writers of the new generation, notably Baudelaire, the Goncourt brothers, and even Flaubert, had ambivalent attitudes toward women in general and little fellow feeling for women authors in particular. George Sand tried her best to adapt herself to the new aesthetic credo of realism. Her novel *Le dernier amour* (*The Last Love*, 1866) is dedicated to Flaubert and obviously influenced by *Madame Bovary.* Flaubert was one of George Sand's privileged houseguests at Nohant, and she in turn visited Croisset, Flaubert's home near Rouen. They delighted in corresponding with each other, and in his uninhibited letters to her Flaubert revealed his innermost thoughts and feelings. Their friendship had begun in 1863, when George Sand wrote an appreciative review of his novel *Salammbô,* and endured until her death. Flaubert, whose sexuality and relationships with women had always been fraught with torment and contradictions, was willing to make an exception to his general condescension toward women in favor of George Sand. He especially admired her courage and serenity as she faced the ailments and disabilities of old age.

George Sand worked hard and lived fully until her death, and as ever enjoyed gathering at Nohant old friends and their families. She also welcomed newer associates, such as the Russian novelist Ivan Turgenev, who visited in the spring of 1873. And she traveled quite extensively, visiting different parts of France. She was about to celebrate her seventy-second birthday when she began feeling constant and acute abdominal pain. When death came on 8 June 1876, despite the ministrations of hastily summoned doctors, she met it without fear or regret, with her children at her bedside.

The simple funeral service took place in the church of Nohant, and afterward the peasants carried the coffin to the small cemetery adjoining George Sand's estate, where she was buried next to her grandmother and her parents. There was a Catholic service, and Flaubert, who attended, noted that the country folk kneeling on the grass wept a great deal during the ceremony. He too, for that matter, shed copious tears, as he confided to Turgenev in a letter dated 25 June 1876:

The death of poor old Sand has caused me infinite pain. I wept like a babe at her funeral, and twice: the first time when I kissed her granddaughter Aurore (whose eyes that day so closely resembled hers that it was as though she had risen from the grave), and the second time when the coffin was borne past me.

Flaubert was not the only friend who made the trip to Nohant to pay his last respects to George Sand. The score of mourners who stood at the graveside included the historian and critic Ernest Renan, the dramatist and novelist Dumas *fils,* the publisher Calmann Lévy, and the actor Paul Meurice, who had appeared in her plays and who read the funeral oration, which was written by Victor Hugo. Flaubert also noted in his letter to Turgenev that a gentle rain kept falling throughout the service. The rustic burial scene—a small country graveyard under an overcast sky and a steady drizzle, with an old priest muttering the prayer for the dead and peasant women with rosaries hanging from their gnarled fingers, the somber group of intimates forlornly huddling against the wind and rain—would not have displeased George Sand, for it might have fitted quite easily in a chapter from one of her novels.

CONCLUSION

George Sand's reputation has been greatly enhanced by the feminist movement. She has by now fully earned her niche in the pantheon of women of exceptional talent and generous commitment to the betterment of humankind. That she did not merely touch upon the popular chords of her time is now fully attested by the numerous editions of her works, translations into English and other languages, international societies and symposia in her honor.

George Sand's works do not easily lend themselves to classification. She was a romantic, but this classification hardly suffices to characterize the vast corpus of her works. Her novels are in turn historical, autobiographical, rustic. Her ideology, on the other hand, reflects her innermost political preoccupations. Yet her own rich and variegated personality is at the core of all of her writing. Her willingness to take chances with new forms and especially to renovate older genres is one of the keys to her great success as a writer. Granted, her faith in improvisation and spontaneity was sometimes greater than her technical ability. But it is this faith in renewal that endows her work, to a great extent, with a unique aura of freshness and authenticity. Familiar though she was with literary traditions, George Sand preferred to rely on her own inspiration. And in this she was not mistaken. Among her considerable talents was that of the accomplished storyteller. And her descriptive powers are far from negligible. On the other hand, her political involvement, culminating in the active role she played during the Revolution of 1848, should not be overlooked in assessing her contribution to French letters.

From the outset and in her own lifetime, George Sand has had her passionate apologists and vociferous detractors. As a result she has been excessively idealized by some and violently denounced by others. The feminist movement, however, has not only rekindled interest in George Sand; it has also vigorously fostered a serious reexamination of each of her works. Recent critical editions of her novels as well as of her autobiography and correspondence amply testify to this resurgence of interest. But in view of her voluminous output, much work remains to be done. Assessments of her writing and her personality are now being revised. She is a far more complex author and personality than had for long been believed. Above all, the diversity of her work attests to an exuberant affirmation of the values of generosity, courage, and love of life.

Selected Bibliography

FIRST EDITIONS

INDIVIDUAL WORKS
Rose et Blanche. Paris, 1831.
Indiana. Paris, 1832.
Valentine. Paris, 1832.

GEORGE SAND

Lélia. Paris, 1833.

Jacques. Paris, 1834.

Leone Leoni. Paris, 1834.

Lettres d'un voyageur. Paris, 1834–1836.

Mauprat. Paris, 1837.

L'Uscoque. Paris, 1838.

L'Orco. Paris, 1838.

Spiridion. Paris, 1838–1839.

Les sept cordes de la lyre. Paris, 1839.

Le compagnon du tour de France. Paris, 1840.

Horace. Paris, 1841–1842.

"Dialogues familiers sur la poésie de prolétaires." In *Questions d'art et de littérature.* Paris, 1842.

Un hiver à Majorque. Paris, 1842.

Consuelo. Paris, 1842–1843.

La comtesse de Rudolstadt. Paris, 1843–1844.

Jeanne. Paris, 1844.

Le meunier d'Angibault. Paris, 1845.

La mare au diable. Paris, 1846.

François le champi. Paris, 1847–1848.

La petite Fadette. Paris, 1848–1849.

Les maîtres sonneurs. Paris, 1853.

Histoire de ma vie. Paris, 1854–1855.

Elle et lui. Paris, 1859.

La ville noire. Paris, 1860.

Monsieur Sylvestre. Paris, 1865.

Le dernier amour. Paris, 1866.

Journal intime. Edited by Aurore Sand. Paris, 1926.

COLLECTED WORKS

Oeuvres de George Sand. 16 vols. Paris, 1842–1844.

Oeuvres choisies de George Sand. 3 vols. Brussels, 1851.

Oeuvres illustrées de George Sand. 9 vols. Paris, 1851–1856.

Oeuvres complètes de George Sand. 115 vols. Paris, 1852–1926.

Théâtre complète de George Sand. 4 vols. Paris, 1866–1867.

Correspondance de George Sand et d'Alfred Musset. Edited by F. Decori. Brussels, 1904.

George Sand–Marie Dorval: Correspondance inédite. Edited by Simone André-Maurois. Paris, 1953.

Correspondance. 16 vols. Edited by Georges Lubin. Paris, 1964–1981.

Les lettres de George Sand à Sainte-Beuve. Edited by Osten Södergard. Geneva, 1964.

Lettres de George Sand à Alfred de Musset et Gustave Flaubert. Edited by Jean-Luc Benoziglio. Paris, 1970.

Oeuvres autobiographiques. Edited by Georges Lubin. 2 vols. Paris, 1970–1971.

MODERN EDITIONS

La comtesse de Rudolstadt. Edited by L. Cellier and L. Guichard. Paris, 1959.

Consuelo. Edited by L. Cellier and L. Guichard. 3 vols. Paris, 1959.

Elle et lui. Edited by M. Guillemin. Neuchâtel, 1963.

François le champi. Edited by P. Salomon and J. Mallion. Paris, 1962.

Indiana. Edited by Georges Lubin. Paris, 1976.

Un hiver à Majorque. Edited by B. Didier. Paris, 1984.

Lélia. Edited by P. Reboul. Paris, 1960.

Les maîtres sonneurs. Edited by P. Salomon and J. Mallion. Paris, 1968.

La mare au diable. Edited by P. Salomon and J. Mallion. Paris, 1962.

Mauprat. Edited by C. Sicard. Paris, 1969.

La petite Fadette. Edited by P. Salomon and J. Mallion. Paris, 1958.

Les sept cordes de la lyre. Edited by R. Bourgois. Paris, 1973.

Spiridion. Edited by Georges Lubin. Paris, 1976.

La ville noire. Edited by J. Courrier. Echirolles, 1978.

TRANSLATIONS

The Bagpipers. Chicago, 1977.

The Compagnon of the Tour of France. Translated by Francis Shaw. New York, 1976.

Consuelo: A Romance of Venice. New York, 1979.

The Country Waif. Translated by Eirene Collis. Lincoln, Neb., 1977.

The Devil's Pool. Translated by Hamish Miles. London, 1929.

Fanchon the Cricket. Chicago, 1977.

François the Waif. Translated by Jane M. Sedgwick. New York, 1894.

George Sand in Her Own Words. Translated by Joseph Barry. New York, 1979.

The George Sand–Gustave Flaubert Letters. Translated by Aimée L. McKenzie. Chicago, 1979.

Indiana. Translated by G. Burnham Ives. Chicago, 1978.

The Intimate Journal of George Sand. Translated by Marie Jenney Howe. Chicago, 1978.

Lélia. Translated by Maria Espinosa, with foreword by Ellen Moers. Bloomington, Ind., 1978.

Leon Leoni. Translated by G. Burnham Ives. Chicago, 1978.

Little Fadette. Translated by Hamish Miles. London, 1928.

The Masterpieces of George Sand. Translated by G. Burnham Ives. 18 vols. Philadelphia, 1900.

Mauprat. Translated by Stanley Young. New York, 1902. Republished Chicago, 1977.

My Convent Life. Translated by Maria Ellery McKay. Chicago, 1977. From the first book of Sand's *Histoire de ma vie.*

My Life. Translated and adapted by Dan Hofstadter. New York, 1979.

She and He. Translated by G. Burnham Ives. Chicago, 1978.

Valentine. Translated by G. Burnham Ives. Chicago, 1978.

Winter in Majorca. Translated by Robert Graves. Chicago, 1978.

BIOGRAPHICAL AND CRITICAL STUDIES

Atwood, William G. *The Lioness and the Little One: The Liaison of George Sand and Frédéric Chopin.* New York, 1980.

Barry, Joseph. *Infamous Woman: The Life of George Sand.* New York, 1977.

Blount, Paul G. *George Sand and the Victorian World.* Athens, Ga., 1979.

Brée, Germaine. "George Sand: The Fictions of Autobiography." *Nineteenth-Century French Studies* 4:438–449 (1976).

Carrère, Casimir. *George Sand amoureuse.* Paris, 1967.

Cate, Curtis. *George Sand: A Biography.* New York, 1976.

Cellier, Léon, ed. *Hommage à George Sand.* Paris, 1969.

Chonez, Claudine. *George Sand.* Paris, 1973.

Didier, Beatrice. "l'Image de Voltaire et de Rousseau chez George Sand." *Revue d'histoire littéraire de la France* 79:251–264 (1979).

————. "Femme/Identité/Écriture: À propos de l'*Histoire de ma vie* de George Sand." *Revue des sciences humaines* 168:577–588 (1977).

————. "Le souvenir musical dans *Histoire de ma vie.*" *Présence de George Sand* 8:48–52 (1980).

Doumic, René. *George Sand.* Paris, 1909.

————. *George Sand.* Translated by Álys Hallard. New York, 1910.

Dussault, Louis. *George Sand: Étude d'une éducation.* Montreal, 1970.

Greene, Tatiana. "De J. Sand à George Sand: *Rose et Blanche* de Sand et Sandeau et leur descendance." *Nineteenth-Century French Studies* 4:169–182 (1976).

Hovey, Tamara. *A Mind of Her Own: A Life of the Writer George Sand.* New York, 1977.

Howe, Marie Jenney. *George Sand: The Search for Love.* Garden City, N.Y., 1929.

Jordan, Ruth. *George Sand: A Biography.* London, 1976.

Larnac, Jean. *George Sand Révolutionnaire.* Paris, 1947.

Lubin, Georges. *Album Sand.* Paris, 1973.

————. *George Sand en Berry.* Paris, 1967.

————. "George Sand et l'éducation." *Nineteenth-Century French Studies* 4:450–468 (1976).

Mallet, Francine. *George Sand.* Paris, 1976.

Maurois, André. *Lélia ou la vie de George Sand.* Paris, 1952.

————. *Lélia: The Life of George Sand.* Translated by Gerard Hopkins. New York, 1953.

Maurras, Charles. *Les amants de Venise.* Paris, 1903.

May, Gita. "Des *Confessions* à l'*Histoire de ma vie*: Deux auteurs à la recherche de leur moi." *Présence de George Sand* 8:40–47 (1980).

Moers, Ellen. *Literary Women.* New York, 1973.

Paillou, Paul. *La vie émouvante de George Sand.* Paris, 1946.

Poli, Annarosa. *L'Italie dans la vie et dans l'oeuvre de George Sand.* Paris, 1960.

————. *George Sand et les années terribles.* Paris, 1975.

Salomon, Pierre. *George Sand.* Paris, 1953.

Séché, Alphonse, and Jules Bertaut. *George Sand.* Paris, 1909.

GEORGE SAND

Seilliere, Ernest. *George Sand, mystique de la passion, de la politique et de l'art.* Paris, 1920.

Seyd, Felizia. *Romantic Rebel: The Life and Times of George Sand.* New York, 1940.

Thomas, Edith. *George Sand.* Paris, 1959.

Thomson, Patricia. *George Sand and the Victorians.* New York, 1977.

Waddington, Patrick. *Turgenev and George Sand: An Improbable Entente.* Wellington, N.Z., 1980.

Winegarten, Renée. *The Double Life of George Sand: Woman and Writer.* New York, 1978.

Winwar, Frances. *The Life of the Heart: George Sand and Her Times.* London, 1946.

GITA MAY

JEAN-PAUL SARTRE

(1905–1980)

I'm not at ease except in Nothingness—I'm a true Nothingness, drunk with pride and translucid.
                    —*The War Diaries,* 1940

SHORTLY AFTER THE end of World War II the streets of Paris were once again occupied, this time with the *offensive existentialiste.* In newsreels from the time existentialism is portrayed as a fashionable attitude and life-style, an intoxicating ideology of freedom that promises a release from convention and authority. In its popular form existentialism maintains that human beings, regardless of circumstances, choose their own actions and are therefore responsible for their own fates. And yet there are no objective authorities to dictate which choices are right and which are wrong; those standards are also a matter of choice. Although one can discern the heady implications of such a radical defense of freedom, one can perhaps also sense the dislocation and despair of living in a world where one must choose one's course of action without recourse to any legitimating authority. This quandary is doubtless intensified if the situation in which one must choose is that of war and the consequences involve the fate of other people's lives. Far from a naive defense of freedom, Sartre's existential philosophy acknowledged the difficulty of making choices in a world that is largely beyond one's control, one where the consequences of such choices are grave. Indeed, the tragic brilliance to be found in Sartre's literary and philosophical work attests to the inherent ambivalence of human choices.

Is it fair, then, to characterize Sartre as a philosopher of freedom, a writer in defense of liberty? From the outset of his intellectual career, he recognized the intransigent character of the world, its opacity, its resistance to alteration by the human will. One may well be free, but what does freedom mean in a world characterized by disorder, irrationality, and catastrophe? Freedom is thus always a tragic mode of being related to a resistant world. And the world's hostility to freedom is not merely the consequence of the historical moment. This tragic relationship is to be found in the very structure of consciousness. An object appears only partially; it resists consciousness. Another human being appears inscrutable; he reminds us of our limits. In 1939 Sartre wrote, "This world is *difficult.* . . . [Difficulty] is there, on the world." The field of objects and other individuals remains strange, opaque, hostile, and inapprehensible until consciousness can find itself expressed in the world that it encounters. In everyday perception, consciousness designates objects and others through negation, through the act that posits things as *not* consciousness. But this antagonism between consciousness and its world does not result in a thoroughly pessimistic conclusion. A consciousness thoroughly knowledgeable about the world, a freedom that finds its limits nowhere—these cannot be produced by everyday perception, but they can be the fruits of a thoroughly imaginary world.

Evident in Sartre's earliest philosophical and literary works is the conviction that the imagination is an experience of freedom unfettered by "difficulty," released from the usual material constraints. Sartre identified the imagination and imaginary works as the locus of a temporary reconciliation between consciousness and world in the two early tracts on the imagination, *L'Imagination* (*Imagination: A Psychological Critique,* 1936) and *L'Imaginaire* (*The Psychology of the Imagination,* 1940). That Sartre never fully forfeited this view becomes clear in his last great work, published in 1971 and 1972, *L'Idiot de la famille: Gustave Flaubert de 1821 à 1857* (*The Family Idiot*).

Indeed, Sartre is not only a philosopher of freedom but, perhaps more descriptively, a philosopher of the imaginary. In an important sense the imaginary—the world of dreams, of images, of fictional works, of visions of the future—attests to the impossibility of fulfillment in a present that is hostile to freedom. The imaginary is freedom postponed and deferred, the vestige of freedom in the face of intransigence. For Sartre, then, to be free is to be caught in a tragic bind: to be unsuited for the world in which one finds oneself, exiled by virtue of one's constitution, as a free being. And yet this sense of existence as rife with irresolution may be either the source of anguish or, significantly, the source of creativity. To create an imaginary world that can suppress the "difficulty" of the world, to create a well-carved reflection of a freedom that endures—this is the task of the imagination caught in existential impasse. Hence, if we are to discover the concrete meaning of freedom in a hostile world, we must look for the capacity to imagine.

It is always questionable to maintain that a writer has only one central insight, and that is not my purpose here. A prolific and diverse writer, Sartre immediately escapes any effort to categorize him in definitive terms. Is he primarily a philosopher? After all, he wrote *L'Être et le néant: Essai d'ontologie phénoménologique* (*Being and Nothingness: An Essay on Phenomenological Ontology,* 1943), which was received internationally as one of the most significant philosophical works of the twentieth century. But perhaps he is more appropriately considered a novelist. Awarded the Nobel Prize for literature in 1964, Sartre was acclaimed as having introduced an absurdist literary genre that typified the modern experience of displacement and solitude. And yet not long after these philosophical and literary triumphs, Sartre embarked upon a career as a political spokesman and essayist, first in his capacity as editor of *Les temps modernes* (a progressive journal that examined the role of the intellectual in French political life), then as a self-identified Communist, and finally as a socialist humanist sympathetic to Maoism.

Reflecting upon this varied and colorful career, one might be tempted to see nothing but discontinuity, sudden shifts, conversions, and changes of directions, and conclude that Sartre was a man of multiple identities for whom no simple categorization would suffice. In a sense that conclusion would be right. Sartre detested categorization in general, fearing that being placed in a category would deprive him of his freedom as an active and changing thinker. And we may understand his sudden shifts of direction and allegiance as so many efforts to escape the rigid categories that others were ready to prepare for him. In a dramatic gesture Sartre refused to accept the Nobel Prize, informing the Swedish Academy that he did not want to become "an institution."

So what are we to make of this elusive Sartre? My suggestion is that we consider his slipperiness as the very attribute that needs to be explained. Even through the shifts of position and politics, Sartre was a thinker and writer who sought to free his thought from the reifying categories of institutionalized academe. Rather than become a thinglike entity, a category or institution, Sartre exemplified his theory of consciousness in his own person, in the career of his own consciousness as an irreducible spontaneity, the manifestation of freedom and individuality. Let us then consider this career as a sustained effort to safeguard freedom in the face of intransigence, to elude the rigid categories of the institutionalized intellect, and to imagine possible ways of transfiguring a hostile world.

Before we can ask who Sartre is, we must, in Sartrian terms, reflect upon the more general problem of how it is possible to understand another human being. In a sense this was the question that preoccupied Sartre, first as a novelist in his efforts to create plausible characters, then as an "existential psychoanalyst" who sought to understand the general structure of the individual in terms of his abiding projects, and then, quite obviously, as a biographer who sought to reconstruct the lives of other human beings through the written remnants of their lives. We cannot attempt a biography of Sartre, but we can perhaps discern the fundamental projects that structured his life. And we can take as our guideline the various inquiries into "self" and "others" that Sartre himself accomplished.

THE NOTHINGNESS OF THE SELF

The hero of *La nausée* (*Nausea*, 1938), Roquentin, discovers in himself a growing awareness of death. Every moment threatens to bring him closer to that inevitable fatality; indeed, every moment promises that death will arrive just that much sooner. And objects, too, appear as so many lifeless things, inanimate and impenetrable, without any reason for existing. This sudden recognition of purposelessness and mortality plunges Roquentin into a series of internal monologues in which he questions the justification for his own existence and concludes that existence is that which has no justification, no intrinsic meaning or necessity. For the duration of the novel, this recognition produces only nausea and dread, the feeling

that everything that exists is superfluous, both "too much" and "unnecessary." Indeed, the material world, including his own body, offends Roquentin, and he recoils at the thought that he is, like an animal or a plant, yet another piece of material subject to the transience of life on earth.

As Roquentin surveys the world of objects about him, he is struck by their contingency. In other words, there is no reason why they should exist rather than not exist. This insight fills him with nausea, the felt sense of endless possibilities. Among the contingent objects he encounters is his own existence, although he is clear that he differs drastically from the objects that surround him. They are dense and solid, material yet contingent, and although his body shares certain material features with theirs, he is distinguished by his consciousness. He *sees* the trees, the garden, the face of the woman he meets on the street; but this seeing, this consciousness, is not a thing among things. Indeed, it is nothing, for it has neither substance nor materiality of its own.

Written in 1938, *Nausea* marks a significant development in Sartre's literary and philosophical career. Roquentin is divided against himself—a material object, mortal, yet also a nothingness, a consciousness, that appears to persist in its own manner as a nonmaterial existence. As a novel *Nausea* is a drama of consciousness not unlike the novels of William Faulkner, Marcel Proust, or James Joyce. As a means of investigating consciousness, *Nausea* is a modernist text, and its hero is an antihero. Roquentin constantly discovers his own limits, and his is the agony of a thoroughly secular vision, one that is, however, not so distanced from the illusions of redemption as not to long for their re-emergence.

At the close of *Nausea*, Roquentin longs for a world of pure forms, a philosophical redemption from transience, in which perfect shapes, like circles, abound. He imagines pure nonmaterial circles, figures with a fully imaginary existence, figures at once complete and infinite, transcending the fatal linearity of human life. But finally Roquentin settles on a slightly different solution and resolves to write the story of consciousness that he has lived, to give it form and hence a second life. In the final pages of *Nausea,* Sartre gives us a theory of literary forms as secular miracles, as if the writing of experience were its redemption from transience. As we shall see, this theory of literature will undergo a number of revisions throughout Sartre's career.

Before writing *Nausea* in the mid 1930's, Sartre traveled to Berlin in the period 1933–1934 to study the work of Edmund Husserl, the leading German phenomenologist. Sartre was interested in an investigation of consciousness, but he sought to avoid idealist theories that would cast doubt on the capacity of consciousness directly to apprehend the reality of things. Tired of philosophical positions that claimed that human beings could know their own representations of objects but never the objects themselves, Sartre understood that phenomenology resolved to return to "the things themselves." Before hearing of Husserl, Sartre had discussed his philosophical notions in private with Simone de Beauvoir, his lover and companion, and Paul Nizan during his studies at the École Normale Supérieure in the period 1924–1929, when he was in his early twenties.

After serving as a meteorologist in the army from 1929 to 1931, he returned to Le Havre to teach philosophy; he was considered a tough and enthusiastic teacher. During that time a famous encounter with Raymond Aron occurred that in some ways resulted both in the writing of *Nausea* and in the early writings on phenomenology. Despite Roquentin's momentary hankering after Platonic solutions, Sartre himself sought a philosophical perspective that would at once resist the conflation of consciousness and world, and yet endow consciousness with the power really to know that which is utterly different from itself. In her memoir *La force de l'age* (*The Prime of Life*), Simone de Beauvoir records the encounter with Aron that eventually propelled Sartre to Berlin:

Raymond Aron was spending a year at the French institute in Berlin and studying Husserl simultaneously with preparing a historical thesis. When he came to Paris he spoke of Husserl to Sartre. We spent an evening together at the Bec de Gaz in the Rue Montparnasse. We ordered the specialty of the house, apricot cocktails; Aron said, pointing to his glass: "You see, my dear fellow, if you are a phenomenologist, you can talk about this cocktail and make philosophy out of it!" Sartre turned pale with emotion at this. Here was just the thing he had been longing to achieve for years—to describe objects just as he saw and touched them, and extract philosophy from the process.

(Peter Green trans., p. 112)

Husserl's phenomenological philosophy disrupted the terms of the usual philosophical debates of the time in France. Because philosophy was taught in universities governed by the state ministry of education, certain philosophical courses of study were required and these tended to support certain kinds of philosophical positions rather than others. The philosophy most acceptable to the state university system appeared to be a kind of neo-Kantianism that centered on the idealist theory of representationalism. According to this theory, one could never get beyond one's own thinking to reach an exterior world. The discovery of German philosophers like Georg W. F. Hegel and Husserl during the 1930's and 1940's permitted philosophers to relate their discipline to concrete historical and personal experiences in the world. In Husserl, Sartre discovered a liberation from representationalism. Objects were no longer mental pictures that were "in" the mind; indeed, the mind was not a repository at all, but rather a relationship to the world. Preferring to call this relationship "consciousness," Sartre learned from Husserl that consciousness was necessarily related to the world, that consciousness had no "being" of its own but was always a consciousness "of" the world.

Roquentin makes a similar discovery in *Nausea.* Nowhere can he find the consciousness that takes in the world, and yet it does effectively apprehend objects and others outside itself. Operating incessantly, an impulsively referential activity, it is not itself a substance. Sartre makes use of imagery to describe the phenomenon of consciousness: it is the "quick, obscure image of a burst," "clear as strong wind," "a sliding beyond itself." Although it is not the same as the objects and the others that it apprehends, consciousness is always related to them. The structure of this relationship is, in phenomenological terms, called intentionality.

In *The Psychology of Imagination,* published in 1940, Sartre suggests that this intentional relation to the world is present in a variety of forms of consciousness: in the imagination, in the emotions, and in perception. These modes of consciousness are not stable, interior structures or faculties of the mind; indeed, they are not interior to anything. They are various modes of being related to the world, spontaneous outbursts toward the world. Loving something, fearing it, loathing it, or needing it—these are all intentional relations to something real. The consequences of this view of intentionality were significant for Sartre. His work on the imagination disputed those theories that held imagination to be nonreferential. In their place Sartre suggested that imagining a thing was a way of being related to it in the mode of de-realization. Images could no longer be understood as meaningless, bearing no relationship to reality; images transfigured reality, and this transfiguration was the very mode of their relatedness.

In 1939 Sartre published *Esquisse d'une théorie des émotions* (*The Emotions: Outline of a Theory*), which argued that emotions, rather than interior disturbances or confusions of some kind, were ways of being related to the world. To be angry is not merely to suffer some chemically induced agitation, but to be angry at something exterior to oneself, or perhaps at oneself. In any case, anger has an object, and the effect of anger is to saturate consciousness with itself in order temporarily to blot out the

offensive object. Hence, anger is related to its object in the mode of negation, although the negating is less real than magical. Indeed, for Sartre all emotion has a magical quality. The joyous person waiting for the beloved to arrive on the train jumps up and down in a kind of dance of joy. The dance both anticipates the arrival of the beloved and preempts it—it is as if the time between waiting and the arrival is magically eclipsed by the dance, which magically instates the other person even in his or her absence.

As in Roquentin's quest for an aesthetic redemption of experience, in the structure of the imagination and emotions Sartre pursues a temporary relief from the purely perceptual experience of the world. Although objects appear to us in perception as only partial (they cannot show all of their dimensions at once), they appear complete to the imagination. And although we are powerless to force the train to arrive earlier than it will, we can imagine its presence and effect an emotional incantation of its arrival.

Sartre's novelistic and philosophical pursuits in the 1930's centered on the problem of consciousness, its status as an intentional relationship, its power to transfigure the world through emotional, imaginative, and literary means. But these primarily epistemological studies were restricted to the problems of knowing and apprehending exterior objects. And although Sartre expanded the meaning and scope of consciousness, he was moved to consider an even deeper set of problems. Can we speak about the emotions without first asking who experiences these emotions? Who imagines and who writes? Is there perhaps a single project that is expressed in the intentional structure of consciousness? What kind of being is a human being such that it is constantly apprehending and transfiguring that which is exterior to itself? And what about the apprehension of other human beings? Does that not perhaps have a distinctive structure? Sartre's investigations of epistemology thus turned to more fundamental questions of ontology, and the question of how and what we know gradually became subordinated to the question of who and what we are.

If *Nausea* was a documentation of consciousness, Sartre's ensuing novelistic enterprises tended to be more concerned with character and plot. Just as Husserl's phenomenology offered Sartre a philosophic route into the world of mundane affairs, so his novels expanded their scope and became increasingly concerned with the choices and actions of individuals in complex historical situations. As World War II threatened to become reality in 1938, Sartre began work on *Les chemins de la liberté* (The Roads to Freedom), a trilogy of historical novels situated in France during the advent of war, the experience of occupation, and the drama of liberation. *L'Âge de raison* (*The Age of Reason*), the first novel of the trilogy, published in 1945, depicts a philosophy instructor, Mathieu, who finds that his philosophical defense of freedom is increasingly difficult to realize in his complex personal and political situation. Also published in 1945, the second novel of the trilogy, *Le sursis* (*The Reprieve*), depicts a world more dramatically out of control as the Munich Pact appeared to consolidate the Stalin-Hitler offensive.

Although the first volume treated the characters as individuals faced with the possibility of forfeiting their separate lives for a more collective identity, the second volume attempted to identify the individual fates of the characters with that of France as a nation. Sartre intended the works to be a continuation of *Nausea* and wanted to encourage his readership to consider Mathieu as a Roquentin faced with the prospect of war. If Roquentin discovered himself as a free and contingent consciousness, Mathieu continues that discovery, learning that he is free to lie, cheat, and steal in order to protect himself. As a figure for the French public under occupation, Mathieu presented a contemptible image for the French to ponder. Unsurprisingly, the publication of the novels produced an outraged reaction.

Between the first and second volumes, Sar-

tre worked on *Being and Nothingness*, a philosophical inquiry that brought Husserl's phenomenological method to bear on a theory of freedom and, most significantly, a vision of human beings as a product of their own choices. Written first in a series of notebooks that Sartre kept in the military during the period 1939–1940, *Being and Nothingness* sought to identify the nothingness of consciousness (Sartre's phenomenological insight) with the nothingness of the self (Roquentin's self-discovery). The result was an utterly original philosophical vision—what Sartre termed "phenomenological ontology"—that later became existentialism. As consciousness was a spontaneous outburst toward the world, an incessant referentiality, so human beings could be understood, like Mathieu, as compelled to situate themselves in the world, to be projected toward the world—indeed, to "exist" only to the extent that they commit themselves to various actions.

The doctrine of intentionality was thus replaced by the notion of "a project." Significantly, human beings have no identity—they are nothing—except to the extent that they create an identity through sustained relationships with objects and others outside themselves. Moreover, the only way to sustain these relationships is through the effort of making choices. Hence, the spontaneity of consciousness, its relentless directedness toward exterior objects and others, becomes identified as the choice at the foundation of every human individual; and from now on, consciousness is understood as a manifestation of freedom, and Sartre's epistemological concerns are subordinated to his inquiry into human beings in their primary characterization as free.

How, then, are we to conceive of human beings? What kind of "being" is a human being? Sartre makes clear in *Being and Nothingness* that human reality is not a kind of being but a lack, a void, a nothingness. To be human means not to "be" in any stable sense. Whereas in the case of material objects it is possible to assume a relationship of self-identity (a thing is what it is and, for that reason, not some other thing), human reality poses a quite different ontological situation. As Sartre would put it, human reality signifies a "rift" in being, an ontological scandal. In distinction from self-subsisting, fully actualized beings, human beings are fields of open possibility. Born into a world without a fixed identity or value, human beings must construct themselves, realizing certain possibilities and letting others remain unrealized. The self that emerges in the course of experience is constructed through the series of choices and actions that only retrospectively confer a characteristic meaning upon the agency of those actions. No longer can we refer to a silent, essential self buried in the depths of the soul, as yet unrealized. There is no necessity that we become the kinds of individuals that we eventually do become; in principle, we could become some other kind of individual. There is no mystery to the self that we have; it is our creation and, for that reason, our burden. Nothing is predetermined about our individual existence except that we must choose it in some way; there is no freedom not to choose, for that refusal becomes its own kind of choice. Inasmuch as choice is the realization of possibilities, it is the modality by which an agent brings himself into existence, and yet this choice is not a single event, a self-inception that, once effected, becomes a fact of the past. In a daily sense we choose ourselves again and again; this constitutes the openness and malleability of our existence, but also what Sartre terms "the burden of freedom."

Opposing Freudian psychoanalysis on the grounds that it misunderstood the complexity of consciousness and tended to reduce the individual to primary drives, Sartre developed his own alternative, existential psychoanalysis, which made the notion of choice into its primary explanatory tool. What Freud termed "unconscious," Sartre interpreted as pre-reflective consciousness. Sartre argued that individuals may not always have a lucid understanding of why they are acting in the ways that they do, but that, upon reflective scrutiny, they can realize that they have chosen to act in this way, although the choice may not have been deliberate. In maintaining that there was a significant meaning to a non-deliberate choice, Sartre hoped to account for the occasional opacity of human actions within the terms of consciousness. At stake for Sartre was the autonomy of the individual, something that Freudian psychoanalysis in its bifurcation of the psyche into conscious and unconscious processes appeared to discourage. Moreover, the autonomy of the individual was crucial to the theory of responsibility at the core of Sartre's philosophical program. Only human beings who could recover and appropriate their own motivations in toto could be held fully responsible for their actions.

Sartre insisted that every individual can be understood as a unity of choices. Acts can be traced back to prior choices, and these choices are unified or internally consistent in that collectively they express a unitary project of the individual. This individual project is not identical with the myriad specific choices that an individual makes, although the project is manifest in those choices and only in those choices. As a coherent style or pattern of choice, the project constitutes the specific choices as a unified set. Moreover, in an important sense, the individual's project, what Sartre terms "the fundamental project," is not exclusively his or her own. Every individual, in virtue of being human, strives for the same goal, "the desire to be," which Sartre calls "the original project." Because human reality is nothing save what it makes of itself, it is always craving a substantial identity that it cannot have.

But why should this be the case? Why should individuals wish to resolve their freedom into a substantial, self-identical, objectified reality? Why don't they simply rejoice in their freedom and go on about the business of daily life? Being free, individuals are without a necessary ground or reason to exist; indeed, being free, they are compelled to endow themselves with a reason for existing. This groundlessness produces anxiety that, in turn, gives rise to the desire to achieve fixity, stability, and necessity. Because freedom is burdensome, human beings desire to throw off this burden by assuming a thinglike posture. The conservative moment of all desire, this is the resolve to relinquish desire, to be finally what one is and nothing more, the Sartrian transcription of Thanatos.

Sartre examines this tendency under the rubric of "bad faith." One example he gives is of Pierre the waiter, Pierre who has become a waiter, whose every act and gesture exude his essence as a waiter. One cannot separate him from his identity; he has embodied it with a vengeance, as if it were dictated from birth. Originally a role that Pierre must have practiced, being-a-waiter has become a fixed identity, a necessary existence. Pierre has not stopped choosing his role, but he has also chosen to conceal the reality of that choice. Assuming the role as a necessity, he is, in Sartrian terms, acting in bad faith.

Bad faith, then, is precisely the pretense of being a thing, the transformation of a choosing and dynamic human existence into the semblance of a material object. And yet, bad faith is bound to fail. Because freedom can be concealed but never effectively negated, bad faith is bound to become a dissatisfying project. As much as human beings experience freedom as a burden, they are willing to sacrifice freedom only with ambivalence. Once they are entombed as a thing, ensconced in bad faith, anxiety persists, this time as the anxious desire to be free. Hence, coupled with the desire to be is the desire to be free, and these two desires coexist in continuous tension with one another. This paradox of freedom and necessity is only temporarily resolved through the strategies of bad faith, where bad faith designates either a posture of total necessity or a posture of total freedom (I am *not* a waiter, *not* a Frenchman, *not* any determinate thing, but a pure, elusive freedom). In the former case bad faith dramatizes the self as a self-identical being, a being who is what it is and nothing more, that is, a being who has resolved its

quarrel with freedom and has won. In the latter case bad faith is the posture of pure flight, the dramatization of the self as never being what it appears, a principle of negativity and escape, the triumph of freedom over necessity.

Sartre concludes in *Being and Nothingness* that every individual desires a resolution to this ontological paradox, a reconciliation of freedom and necessity. But this idealized synthesis remains an impossible dream, the purely imaginary object and telos of all human desire. In Sartrian terms this is the "desire to be God," and it is shared universally by every individual.

What would it mean to be "God" in the sense that Sartre intends and why is it impossible? In the first place, to be God would be to choose the facts of one's own situation, the material conditions into which one is born, one's own body, the history that precedes one's own birth. In point of fact, however, these factual dimensions of the world are not the product and expression of individual freedom, but appear instead as brute and resistant otherness, the absolute opposite of freedom. And yet, if human beings could be God, they would be able to ground facticity. Second, one's individual freedom would be the necessary result of one's material and historical station in the world; it would have a purpose and meaning that could be easily derived from the historical and material dimensions of one's existence. In other words, the world in all its facticity would be infused with the human will, its creation and expression.

If human beings are not God, and if they cannot hope to be God, why do they continue, against the odds, to entertain the desire to be God? As if freedom were the vestige of an anachronistic theological dream, the free individual aspires to a kind of efficacy impossible within the material constraints of the world. In a sense freedom acts as God in exile, but insofar as it is human freedom, it is a captive deity, trapped within a resistant material world. Not unlike Sartre's own position in German-occupied France in the early 1940's, the experience of being "outside" a world that one is invariably "in," existence is described as captivity and exile at the same time. But in *Being and Nothingness* the intransigence of the world is its brute facticity, conceived as an existentially invariant feature and not, as yet, a consequence of historical circumstance.

Because there can be no lasting reconciliation between a free consciousness and an intransigent world, there can only be a dream of reconciliation. One can imagine an efficacious transfiguration of the world of facts that would reflect the human will, but that is a vain imagining. Or is it? One who realizes the dream through expression, one who writes the dream and fashions it in aesthetic and communicable form, is an artist who transforms some aspect of the material world to reflect his or her own will. Later we shall see that Sartre considered praxis as a kind of politically informed transformation of facticity and, indeed, sought to subordinate his theory of art to that political program. But first, let us consider the optimism that Sartre entertained with regard to artistic work, especially literary ones, to realize the impossible dream of being God.

SARTRE'S SIDEWAYS EYE ON POSTERITY

One might conclude that Sartre's ontology of human exile is a pessimistic vision but still consider the rich aesthetic consequences of an ontology of human existence that necessitates human beings to be dreamers compelled to realize their dreams. Ontological exile thus becomes the condition of aesthetic creativity. In his biographical studies—*Baudelaire* (1946), *Saint Genet, comédien et martyr* (*Saint Genet: Actor and Martyr*, 1952) and *The Family Idiot*—Sartre combined an inquiry into the fundamental projects of these individuals with an analysis of the ontological sources of aesthetic creativity. In his autobiography *Les mots* (*The Words*, 1964) Sartre is similarly preoccupied with the fundamental project of the literary

writer, with the life that is propelled by the abiding desire to write. In all four cases the original project to be God is manifest in a fundamental project to be an author of compelling imaginary worlds. Intended as concrete examples of his own theory of existential psychoanalysis, Sartre's biographies also aim at uncovering the truth about their subjects. But, considered closely, they reveal traces of a self-analysis as well. What Sartre shares with his biographical subjects is a fundamental desire, an abiding project, to become necessary in and through the written word. After all, Sartre's autobiography is not entitled "Sartre's Life," "Sartre's Words," or even "My Words," but *The Words.* These are words that assume an autonomous and necessary status, eternal or divine words that surpass and sustain the life that creates them.

In 1947, however, Sartre proposed a radically different purpose for literature in his *Qu'est-ce que la littérature?* (*What Is Literature?*). He called for an engaged and committed literature that defended definite political positions and demanded a critical appraisal of contemporary political viewpoints from its readership. Although *Nausea* appeared to defend literature in virtue of its own formal and aesthetic qualities, *What Is Literature?* subordinates the aesthetic value of literature to its ethical or political purpose. The former version of literary works as secular miracles, ways of transcending the transience of life, contradicts the latter version of literary forms as political tools. If one writes in response to a contemporary situation, the relevance of the writing risks being circumscribed by the immediate situation. Indeed, it would be difficult to conceive of such writing as the literary equivalent of a Platonic form.

In *What Is Literature?* Sartre maintains that every writer must ask for whom he writes. But in the case of Sartre himself, the answer is not immediately clear. He was uncertain about his audience, at times directing his works to his contemporaries, and at others writing for the future readers who would guarantee the perpetuity of his name. As early as 1939 Sartre recorded this tension in his literary views; he questioned whether one wrote to escape or to transform one's life. In *Les carnets de la drôle de guerre: Novembre 1939–Mars 1940* (*The War Diaries,* 1983) he writes: "I don't think I'm being over-schematic if I say that the moral problem which has preoccupied me up till now is basically one of relations between art and life." As we shall see, this tension continued to characterize his entire career.

Consider the following dialogue between Sartre and Simone de Beauvoir in 1974, just six years before his death. (The short story "Pour un papillon" [For a Butterfly] was written by Sartre as a child.)

SARTRE: When I originally wrote "Pour un Papillon" (For a Butterfly), I wrote something absolute . . . which was, in short, myself. I carried myself over into an everlasting life. An artistic creation outlives mundane things. If I bring one into existence, it outlasts mundane things and therefore I, the author that it embodies, I outlast mundane things. Behind this there was the Christian idea of immortality—I passed from mortal to immortal life.

DE BEAUVOIR: And it was that notion which came to an end when you reached your committed writing?

SARTRE: It came to an end entirely.

DE BEAUVOIR: There was no idea of salvation anymore? It's never come again? I imagine the very notion has faded away? Not that that means you haven't kept an eye, a rather sideways eye [*un coup d'oeil, un peu en biais*], on posterity.

SARTRE: Until after *Nausea* I had only dreamed of genius, but after the war, in 1945, I'd proved myself—there was *No Exit* and there was *Nausea.* In 1944, when the Allies left Paris, I possessed genius and I set off for America as a writer of genius who was going for a tour in another country. At that point I was immortal and I was assured of my immortality. And that meant I no longer had to think about it.

(Quoted in Simone de Beauvoir, *Adieux: A Farewell to Sartre,* pp. 152–153)

In the same dialogue Sartre explained that once his immortality was assured, he could turn with ease to the mundane world of politics: ". . . it's better not to think of immortality, except out of the corner of your eye [*sauf du coin de l'oeil*], but rather to stake everything on life." And yet, "out of the corner of his eye," Sartre made sure posterity was his. De Beauvoir's playful references to Sartre's wall eye, including the suggestion that he might be able to look in two directions at once, suggest a serious framework for Sartre's dual identity as politician and aesthete. Just as peripheral vision may be said to enhance central vision, so Sartre's immortal sense of self enabled and illuminated his political career.

Sartre's reliance on visual metaphors for describing his relationship to his audience suggests a spectatorial (rather than an engaged) authorship. Indeed, Sartre was watchful of others, somewhat distanced and detached, and especially watchful of the gaze that might be turned on him. The section in *Being and Nothingness* titled "Concrete Relations with Others" argues that the primary relationship between individuals is a mixture of distrust and dependency. Because the self is an immaterial nothingness, it knows itself only when it becomes an object for itself. In rarefied instances it becomes an object when expressed in a literary work. But for the most part self-knowledge requires the presence of other selves who reflect the self in and through their "look." In a significant sense the look of the Other gives the self its objectivity, for the Other can see the self as an object, but the self can become an object for itself, and therefore knowable, only by taking on the point of view of the Other. Sartre capitalizes "the Other" in *Being and Nothingness* because it is a generalized Other, the point of view of anyone who views the self from the outside, anyone capable of this objectifying look.

Because we cannot wholly objectify ourselves, we remain inevitably opaque to ourselves, dependent on others to get a glimpse of how we appear. In *Huis clos* (*No Exit*), a play published in 1945, this point is dramatized through the hellish interaction of three characters, all of whom wield the authority of the "look" to objectify and possess each other. The viewpoint of the Other is, by definition, more comprehensive than that of the self, and the Other can pierce the bad faith of the self, exposing its characteristic ploys and strategies and reducing it to its appearance.

The "look" suggests that human beings stand at a spectatorial distance from each other, that they are separated by a necessary space across which they see one another more clearly than they can ever see themselves. Hence, the look suggests yet another constraint upon individual freedom, a way in which the self is socially constituted against its will. The self may give itself a meaning or value, but the Other, wielding the power of objectification, may refute that self-evaluation and expose that self-definition as a sham. Futile though it may be, the self desires a release from the look of the Other in order to be the source of its own objectivity. But here again, this Godlike project is impossible. Constrained by its own perspective, the self cannot exist fully except under the gaze of the Other, although the Other may not see the self as it would wish to be seen. In other words, the self needs the Other in order to exist, but existence is achieved at the price of freedom and self-definition. This struggle between autonomy and dependence constitutes the battlefield of interpersonal relations and leads Sartre to conclude that "Hell is other people."

But can this hell be transformed? The function of literature for Sartre is to objectify the author in a communicable, aesthetic form and, further, to command the recognition of others who will give that author an objective and enduring existence. In the case of politically committed literature, the author engages others to consider the bad faith in which they live: here the author is the Other whose look, transcribed in the text of the play or novel, exposes the audience for what they are. And yet, even in this version of political art as pedagogy and indictment, the audience still retains the power to "look at" Sartre. But where is he, and what does he show of himself? Does he participate in the world he describes and show himself as an actor in the scenes that he devises? Sartre is not there to be seen but is instead the ever-seeing eye, the pretense of omniscience that looks at everyone but is never seen. Can this grand spectator create an engaged literature and an effective political program? How will he fare as he enters the domain of everyday life?

In *War Diaries* Sartre maintained, "I think with my eyes." In a philosophical critique of Sartre, Maurice Merleau-Ponty suggested that the look was not an adequate concept for explaining interpersonal relations. In *Visible et l'invisible* (*The Visible and the Invisible* 1968), a late and incomplete work, Merleau-Ponty argues (against Sartre) that human beings are not born into the world in physical isolation from one another, that the first and primary mode of interrelatedness is that of touch, not sight. Elaborating on his critique of Sartrian premises, Merleau-Ponty suggests that Sartre overestimates the spectatorial point of view, and that he cannot see or comprehend the interrelations between individuals, or between social and natural existence, precisely because he has already, through the adoption of the spectator role, excluded himself from those domains. As one who watches the world, Sartre never discovers himself as a body among bodies, participating in a sensual universe that binds the individual to the world of others and material objects. In effect, Merleau-Ponty argues that a philosophy of engagement cannot be derived from Sartrian premises, that Sartre cannot relax his watchful eye long enough to enter and engage in the everyday world. In other words, through taking up the position of the spectator, Sartre has deprived himself of the very experience of the world that he wishes to describe. In what follows, we will watch this spectator in the midst of historical events and assess whether Merleau-Ponty was right.

"A STROLLER IN THE PARIS INSURRECTION"

Not until the age of thirty-six did Sartre begin to consider himself a political writer and actor. The year was 1941, and Sartre, on leave from his military post, vowed to Simone de Beauvoir that he must find a more active way to oppose the war. Although Sartre's life was surrounded by world events, he remained aloof from their consequences until the war appeared to impinge upon him directly. He first joined the military at the age of nineteen and learned meteorology. After two years of service, he taught philosophy at the lycée in Le Havre, and in 1933 traveled to Berlin to study Edmund Husserl and Martin Heidegger for a year. After returning to France in late 1934, he continued to teach sporadically, to work on *Nausea,* and to write phenomenological treatises on the emotions, the imagination, and the structure of consciousness. On 1 September 1939, Sartre's budding literary and philosophical career was interrupted by World War II; he was part of a military reserve force that was called up for duty. Assigned to Alsace during the winter of 1939–1940, Sartre enjoyed a prolonged term of leisure because Germany, which had already declared war, waited to invade France until May 1940. This inactive period was called the *drôle de guerre* (Phony War; literally, "joke of a war"), and it provided Sartre with time to write in his diary, which was eventually published as *The War Diaries.*

The diaries contained extensive notes for *Being and Nothingness* as well as early drafts of *The Words,* a project that was to take ten years to complete. Although Sartre wanted his diary to be a war diary, recording the experience of a man in the midst of war, he himself was nowhere near the center of action. Indeed, for him the war meant solitude, leisure, and the uninterrupted time to write. And yet, on leave in 1940, Sartre voiced to Simone de Beauvoir a fear of the impending consequences of European fascism and vowed to supplement his contemplative existence with some more active

form of resistance. Upon return to his post, he was imprisoned by the Germans for nine months and released in March 1941 because of ill health. While in prison he was given a copy of Heidegger's *Sein und Zeit* (*Being and Time,* 1927), and continued to have the time to write.

During the spring and early summer of 1941, Sartre traveled to the south of France to consult with André Malraux and other progressive intellectuals who had sought sanctuary far from occupied Paris. He helped to organize a resistance group called Socialisme et Liberté, which helped to distribute underground literature and participated in producing the underground journal *Les lettres françaises.* Toward the end of the war the group released a number of statements defending the sanctity of freedom, but it never became involved in acts of violence or sabotage.

Although antifascist in his sentiments, Sartre was not prepared to defend communism during the war years. Indeed, he remained committed to his own philosophy of freedom— what became existentialism in the postwar years. Determined to defend his status as a free intellectual and yet to maintain sympathy with antifascist ideologies, Sartre pursued a double course as a defender of freedom and a sympathizer with Communist aims.

Upon his release from the prison camp, Sartre had returned to Paris to find that the publishing houses were either under German control or had made compromising deals with the occupation forces in order to maintain some of their independence. Gallimard, a well-regarded publisher of contemporary philosophical and literary works, had agreed to cease publishing Jewish authors in return for its continued independence. Knowing that Gallimard had agreed to this restriction, Sartre nevertheless published *Being and Nothingness* with the firm in 1943. A year earlier Albert Camus had agreed, under the same conditions, to publish *L'Étranger* (*The Stranger*) with Gallimard. After the war there was some effort on the part of leftist writers to censure those publishers who had struck deals with the German forces. Sartre rose in defense of Gallimard, claiming that what mattered was that such houses were able to publish significant literature because of these deals.

Ironically, the years of the occupation were extremely lucrative for both Sartre and Simone de Beauvoir. Sartre's plays *Les mouches* (*The Flies*, 1943) and *No Exit* were produced without objections by the German censors, and de Beauvoir published *L'Invitée* (*She Came to Stay*). Jewish writers of the time were in prison, underground, or in exile, and other antifascist writers refused to publish or produce their work under the terms of Nazi-occupied France. Sartre agreed, on the other hand, to open *The Flies*, his existentialist version of the *Oresteia*, at the Théâtre de la Cité, which had been the Sarah Bernhardt Theatre before it was "purified" of that actress's Jewish name.

In November 1946 Sartre published *Réflexions sur la question juive* (*Anti-Semite and Jew*), which addressed the problem of anti-Semitism among the French. He argued that the Jew represented the Other for the French bourgeoisie, the projection of their fears and the locus of their bad faith. Clearly intended as a sequel to Marx's *Judenfrage* (*The Jewish Question*), *Anti-Semite and Jew* proposed a socialist democracy in which ethnic differences would be subordinated to the universal rights of human beings. Although the work was an often stunning exposé of the anti-Semite, Sartre's characterization of the Jew was less successful; indeed, his characterizations occasionally tended to affirm the anti-Semite rather than refute him. As a political defense of Judaism, the result was fairly ambivalent.

Sartre's efforts at political analysis more often than not seemed double-edged. While his intentions were invariably progressive (against fascism, against anti-Semitism, for principles of equality and freedom), his methods were less sure. As the war drew to a close, Camus organized a progressive journal, *Combat*, which included Sartre, Aron, Merleau-Ponty, and de Beauvoir on its editorial staff. In one of the first issues Sartre wrote an article

on his experience of the liberation. The title, "Un promeneur dans Paris insurgé" (A Stroller in the Paris Insurrection), expresses Sartre's paradoxical position as the leisurely spectator recounting the joy, the disbelief, and even the anguish of the French as the Allies arrived in Paris.

In the autumn of 1945, Sartre founded *Les temps modernes* with Aron and other leftist intellectuals. In the first few years the journal considered the question of whether independent intellectuals could work in tandem with the Communist party and whether culture and politics were autonomous domains. Often quarrels would erupt between *Les temps modernes* and the Communist newspaper *L'Humanité*. Indeed, at the time the official Communist party was skeptical of Sartre, his popularity after the war, and his defense of "bourgeois freedom." Accusing him of decadence and pseudo-Marxism, the Communist parties in France and in the Soviet Union were indifferent toward Sartre's highly deliberated relation to them. Indeed, a radical break between Sartre and the party occurred in 1949, when Sartre and Merleau-Ponty published reports on the existence of Soviet prison camps filled with political dissidents. They estimated that as many as 10 to 15 million individuals were coercively detained in such camps and further claimed that "there is no socialism when one citizen in twenty is in a camp."

The response was vehement. Sartre was denounced by both *L'Humanité* and *Les lettres françaises*, the latter the very journal that, in its earlier underground form, had been quite sympathetic to Sartre. The following two years saw a radical revision in Sartre's political thinking. Rather than maintain the double course of socialism and humanism, he began to reflect on the necessity of aligning himself unconditionally with the Communist party. In 1951 Sartre publicly accepted Stalinism. In the same year he published the play *Le Diable et le bon Dieu* (*The Devil and the Good Lord*), which rejected the posture of political neutrality and argued that the refusal of a political commitment was itself a commitment to reactionary forces. But, more important, the play showed the futility of purely individual action and suggested that atheism was the necessary ideology of class struggle. "Les communistes et la paix" (*The Communists and Peace*), published between July 1952 and April 1954, might well be read as the theoretical equivalent of *The Devil and the Good Lord.* Published first in *Les temps modernes,* Sartre's essay defends the Communist party as the legitimate representative of the proletariat and assails any position that questions the relationship between them. In an interesting twist of existential theory, Sartre maintains that the only authentic choice for anyone in Sartre's historical situation is the defense of communism.

Sartre's dogmatic defense of communism created a number of controversies at *Les temps modernes.* In October 1951 Camus published *Le revolté* (*The Rebel*), which received a damning review in *Les temps modernes* in July 1952. Clearly unwilling to accept either an unwavering Communist alliance or an uncritical defense of capitalism, Camus reserved a place for morality above the fray of political quarrels. In a sense *The Rebel* came to exactly the opposite conclusion of *The Devil and the Good Lord.* Camus satirized the Marxist notion of history, charging that there were abuses of human rights on both ends of the political spectrum. The review in *Les temps modernes,* written by Francis Jeanson, charged Camus with political and historical naïveté. Camus's reply appeared the following month, addressed to "Sartre, Monsieur le Directeur," suggesting that Jeanson was but a proxy for Sartre. Camus made it clear that he considered Sartre's new Communist identity to be laughable, especially in light of Sartre's long history of political inaction. Camus remarked that he would no longer receive "lessons in efficacy" from those who "never placed anything other than their armchairs in the direction of history. . . ."

Sartre's differences with Merleau-Ponty also were born of Sartre's increasingly dogmatic defense of communism, particularly in its Stalin-

ist form. Merleau-Ponty opposed the Soviet role in the Korean War in 1950 and remained disillusioned as a result of the prison camp revelations. Although he strongly defended Soviet communism in *Humanisme et terreur: Essai sur le problème communiste* (*Humanism and Terror: An Essay on the Communist Problem*) in 1947, Merleau-Ponty forfeited his allegiance to the party as its imperialist designs became more clear. As *Les temps modernes* became increasingly pro-Soviet, Merleau-Ponty and others decided that it was no longer desirable to remain on the editorial board.

In 1955 Merleau-Ponty published *Les aventures de la dialectique* (*Adventures of the Dialectic*), which included a long chapter on Sartre's *The Communists and Peace,* titled "Sartre and Ultra-bolshevism." Challenging Sartre on both philosophical and political grounds, Merleau-Ponty argued that Sartre's philosophy of freedom was incompatible with the social theory and political program that Sartre currently defended. In his defense of communism, Sartre was eager to show that the free subject, the choosing agent, was now embodied or represented by the Party. In response Merleau-Ponty charged that this was the thorough effacement of the existing individual and that the Party, conceived as the sole legitimate Subject, portends dangerous and totalitarian consequences. How, Merleau-Ponty asked, can the individual and his freedom become reconciled with a Party elite that acts as the proxy of the membership and presents itself as a unified collectivity? Is this not an instance of bad faith, consciousness resolving itself into a substance, relinquishing the burden of its own freedom?

Merleau-Ponty further charged that there was a missing link in Sartre's argument that was the inevitable consequence of his faulty ontology. Sartre cannot account for a collective subject (or he can only account for one in mistaken ways) because he has no vocabulary for understanding the social world. Because the individual subject is still an ontological priority, the "I" rather than the "we," Sartre can only imagine the Party as an individual subject writ large. The collectivity now becomes the locus of individual freedom and the real individual is effectively erased. Hence, the project to derive a social theory from Sartrian premises culminates in the denial of those very premises.

In 1955 Simone de Beauvoir entered the fray of political quarrels that *Les temps modernes* included among its pages. In her essay "Merleau-Ponty et le pseudo-Sartrisme" (Merleau-Ponty and Pseudo-Sartrianism), she denounced Merleau-Ponty's criticisms, charging that his theory of the social world was a derivation of Sartre's theory in *Being and Nothingness.* Moreover, Sartre's political positions, she reasoned, were an elaboration of the very theory of commitment that characterized his earlier work. From that point on, the break between Merleau-Ponty and Sartre was decisive, although cordial relations were resumed before Merleau-Ponty's tragic death in 1961. Paradoxically, by the time the first volume of his *Critique de la raison dialectique* (*Critique of Dialectical Reason*) appeared in 1960, Sartre had accepted a good many of Merleau-Ponty's criticisms; and after the latter's death Sartre dedicated a special volume of *Les temps modernes* to his work.

In 1956 the Soviet invasion of Hungary prompted a swift revision in Sartre's pro-Communist stance. He could no longer maintain that the party represented the proletariat when it was clearly the party that suppressed a worker-led insurrection in Hungary. Moreover, Sartre was forced to the conclusion that history was perhaps not as teleologically inclined as he had previously thought. The spirit of socialism was not necessarily embodied in official Communist doctrine or policy, and Sartre conceded that a socialist humanism independent of Soviet communism was necessary.

The period 1956–1957 saw the appearance of two important Sartrian documents, "Le fantôme de Staline" (*The Ghost of Stalin*), an elaborate description and denunciation of the Soviet invasion of Hungary, and "Questions de méthode" (*Search for a Method,* first published

in the Polish journal *Twórczosc* under the title "Marksizmi egzistencjalizm," 1957), reprinted in *Les temps modernes,* and published in 1960 as the introduction to the first volume of the *Critique of Dialectical Reason.* In the former essay Sartre maintained that the Communist party had failed its historical mission and regressed to an earlier stage of its development. Rather than contribute to the universal democratization of humankind, it had constructed a new form of oppressive hierarchy. In *Search for a Method* Sartre questioned the relationship between existentialism and Marxism and concluded that existentialism could only be a subsidiary ideology to Marxism, which was the necessary philosophy for the present historical epoch. While criticizing Marxism for not taking into account the individual's concrete situation, the felt experience of labor and alienation, his concrete choices, Sartre also argued that a purely existential framework could not provide a program for socialist emancipation. Incorporating Merleau-Ponty's criticisms and responding to historical events, Sartre undertook the project to examine the relation between individual actions and collective praxis, that is, between individual freedom and the creation of universal history.

This project was further elaborated in the *Critique of Dialectical Reason* as the theory of ensembles, seriality, the fused group, the function of scarcity and need, and the transformative action of collective praxis. Sartre maintained, however, even in *Search for a Method,* that there was a meaning and integrity to history that signified the achievement of universal socialism in the future. Although Sartre rejected a scientific Marxism that would predict historical change on the model of naturalistic processes, he remained committed to a theory of dialectical materialism that envisioned history as a set of successive, internally unified stages. The problem became twofold: What are the constituent actions of individuals that, executed in tandem, result in a revolutionary praxis, a progressive transformation of one historical state of affairs into another? Secondly, how do we account for the possibility of collective action without forfeiting the individual's freedom in the process? For Sartre the reconciliation of Marxism and existentialism hung in the balance. Moreover, he wanted an answer to questions that had concerned him since the inception of his *War Diaries:* What does freedom mean in the context of adverse historical circumstances, and how does the life of the individual express and recapitulate the historical circumstances in which he lives? In short, how are we to conceive the individual in history?

THE "SINGULAR UNIVERSAL": FROM MARXISM TO BIOGRAPHY

Apart from the few years in the early 1950's when he thought that a dogmatic fidelity to the Communist party was necessary, Sartre was always in tension with official ideologies and institutions, as if the tension itself was what attracted him—and perhaps it was. In *Search for a Method,* Sartre made it clear that he now viewed existentialism as an ideology both spawned and criticized by Marxism. But the Marxism that Sartre defended was hardly conventional. In 1975 Sartre was asked whether he preferred being called an "existentialist" or a "Marxist"; he replied that if a label were necessary, he would prefer to be called an existentialist. Later in that same interview Sartre referred to Marxism as a theory he needed to absorb, but that he now endeavored to go beyond.

The *Critique of Dialectical Reason* represents Sartre's most significant contribution to Marxist theory. The question he wanted to pose stems directly from his earlier philosophical and literary pursuits: How do individuals seize upon their historical circumstances and transform them? If this transformation requires collective action, how are these collectivities formed and how do they get to the stage where they can transform history? One might expect Sartre to answer these questions through a specific historical analysis of group formation and revolutionary collectivities, but instead he describes idealized groups in isolation from any given social context. In this sense Sartre claims a transcendental insight into the invariant structures of social reality—hardly a characteristic Marxist position. Indeed, Sartre poses as a phenomenologist who has wandered mistakenly onto Marxist terrain.

Sartre called for a Marxist method that would integrate the actions and political efforts of individuals with a collective, dialectically achieved historical destiny. That destiny would not be enforced or imposed through totalitarian means; it must be the autonomous commitment of every individual. From Marxism, Sartre accepted a notion of historical necessity, the development of history as both unified and dialectically progressive. Inasmuch as history was progressive, it was considered totalizing, engendering ever more integrated forms of social organization until a universal community of democratic socialism would be achieved. Although Sartre once had seen historical events as so much "contingency" and "arbitrariness," he now conceived this contingent and lawless character of historical events to be the product of an alienated consciousness, evidence of their reified status in a system that conceals the workings of its own interrelationships.

For the Sartre of 1960, then, the world remained "difficult," but this difficulty no longer constituted a limit to intellectual analysis. Indeed, the historical conditions of that difficulty, the historical means of its reproduction, are precisely what the Marxist theorist must examine. Moreover, it becomes impossible to decontextualize the life of the individual or to reduce that life to a set of fundamental and self-generated choices. On the other hand, it is crucial to avoid the reification of history, for no history can develop except through the composite effort of individuals. Hence, history retains its character as a progressively unified experience only inasmuch as individuals vow to create this unity, that is, to create a universal democracy. Sartre's metaphysical assertion of the "unity" of history, then, depends essentially on the successful integration of existential premises into Marxism:

> In short, if there is such a thing as the unity of History, the experimenter must see his own life as the Whole and the Part, as the bond between the Parts and the Whole, and as the relation between the Parts, in the dialectical movement of Unification. . . .
>
> (*Critique of Dialectical Reason*, vol. 1, p. 52)

The *Critique of Dialectical Reason* thus traces the careers of individuals as they assume first an identification with a historical group and then resolve to become part of a collective transformation of history. This journey from the particular to the universal undergoes a series of developmental stages, and the successive chapters of the *Critique* constitute a kind of *Bildungsroman* of the revolutionary.

Rife with examples from everyday life, the *Critique of Dialectical Reason* provides descriptions of how group allegiances are formed, how they are both acknowledged and denied, and how an explicit collective identity is forged. In his discussion of people waiting for the bus in the morning, Sartre describes isolated individuals who are nevertheless joined in their act of waiting, their weariness, their utter subjection to an anonymous transportation system that may or may not deliver a bus in time for any of them to get to work. Although their workplaces and occupations may differ radically, they are joined by the historical necessity that they work. Their anger at each other, their struggle to get first in line, their hostility in getting a seat, the way they look at each other without seeming to—all of this constitutes a negative bond of relatedness. Any one of these individuals is both irreducibly himself or herself and necessarily more than himself or herself, identical or interchangeable with an Other. Rendered interchangeable in virtue of the anonymity of the social system to which they are subject, these individuals also carry the specific anonymity of the Parisian bus system, the specific familiarity of being one of a group of Parisians waiting at the curb. The situation can thus be analyzed in terms of the concrete mediations of individual and general circumstances that constitute the socially specific experience of this "group" and that, theoretically, can be understood in terms of its potentially politicizing effects. Sartre asks not only how this negative bond is at once acknowledged and denied, but also under what conditions this negative bond can be transformed into a positive one. To put it another way, he seeks to know how alienation can produce a collective, self-conscious will.

In Sartre's defense of his own position as a Marxist theorist, he maintains that any given analysis must take place from a prospective point of view, the hypothetical future in which a true collectivity is possible. This is the only way to theorize with a view to change. Only from this point of view of an imagined future, a future dialectically extrapolated from the present, does the potential collectivity stand out in the present situation of waiting for the bus. Only through the adoption of the prospective point of view can the dialectical theorist imagine the individual acting through collective identification and action.

The imaginary thus re-emerges in the *Critique* as a fundamental feature of the theoretical attitude. For Sartre it is impossible to think dialectically without the imagination, for the imagination entertains possibilities and the future is precisely a matter of possibilities rather than realities. And yet, does his imaginary theorizing remain the lone musing of Sartre the individual theorist? Would his speculations on group formation aid the general public in their concrete efforts to form allegiances and act collectively? Can Sartre establish that the unified history, the universal community, that he imagines is a real future possibility for existing individuals and groups?

Sartre proposed to answer this question in

the second volume of the *Critique of Dialectical Reason,* a study he only partially completed. Published in 1985 by his adopted daughter, Arlette Elkaïm-Sartre, the second volume concentrates on an explanation of historical change as a result of conflict and strife. Left unanswered, however, is the question of why the various histories that exist cross-culturally and among different sociohistorical groups and traditions should come together into a single history in the way that Sartre imagines. Although Sartre promised to answer the question, it appears that other philosophical issues and failing health precluded the possibility of an answer. Another perspective, however, emerges in Raymond Aron's critique of Sartre's political philosophy. In his *Histoire et dialectique de la violence* (*History and the Dialectic of Violence,* 1973) Aron charged that there could be no justification for Sartre's postulation of a single, self-actualizing history. Suggesting that Sartre's argument rested on the transposition of a Spinozistic notion of compulsion and necessity onto historical experience, Aron called this doctrine indefensible. Although it can be shown, perhaps, that under certain conditions of conflict, a more unified social organization can emerge, such an argument cannot predict that it will, of necessity, emerge. And it was this claim that Sartre appeared to make. Moreover, this doctrine of historical "necessity" stands in stark contradiction to Sartre's defense of freedom and "contingency," the insight that Sartre once considered to be his greatest.

Sartre's unwillingness to finish the second volume of the *Critique* may well be related to the problematic character of history in that work. Perhaps with an understanding that proof of his dialectical views would require an analysis of a concrete situation, Sartre wrote the biography of Jean Genet, playwright and poet, thief, homosexual, and occasional prisoner. The biography of Genet was written simultaneously with the *Critique* and published in 1952. Although not a particularly Marxist study, *Saint Genet: Actor and Martyr* does take

up one of the *Critique*'s central questions: How do individuals appropriate and reproduce the conditions into which they are born and, through that appropriation, transform their material conditions into a reflection of their own freedom? Although Genet does not prove Sartre's point in the *Critique* that the individual manifests universal history, he does provide the occasion for Sartre to rework his theory of freedom and his view of the imaginary in light of his growing understanding of the effects of historical circumstance. Although unsystematic and highly speculative, *Saint Genet* exemplifies an individual career committed to the relentless transfiguration of historical circumstance. Born into the world without legitimate parentage, Genet seizes his illegitimacy as his identity and reappropriates its meaning in his own terms. Called a thief at an early age, Genet resolves to become a thief and then, later, to write about thieves—indeed, to make writing itself into a scandalous act. Genet is an artist of subversion and reversal, a slick strategist who escapes the definitions that others impose upon him by shifting the very meaning of the terms they use.

In Sartre's obvious fascination with Genet, one can discern his residual faith in the literary experience as the locus of human freedom, the domain of possibility. But Genet is not a hopeless dreamer; he is a writer who produces literary works that are circulated and performed. In other words, Genet institutionalizes his dreams and in that sense produces a new reality. Not unlike the Marxist theoretician who would institute new possibilities through the creation of new forms of praxis, Genet brings possibilities into existence and realizes them through unprecedented literary forms. His works, the labored products of his imagination, are seen by others and have the power to redirect their gaze. No longer a flight from reality, the imagination is the occasion for the realization of a new social experience, the disruption of social conventions, and the subversion of hierarchies.

Sartre's biographical studies of Genet and

Flaubert constitute a bridge between his theory of existential psychoanalysis, outlined in *Being and Nothingness,* and his promise in the *Critique* to display the dialectic in the context of an existence both singular and universal. If the *Critique* can be faulted for its failure to acknowledge contingency, the biographical studies demonstrate that the existential doctrine of choice retains wide-ranging explanatory power. At the close of *Being and Nothingness,* Sartre proposed to demonstrate his theory of existential psychoanalysis in the context of two biographical subjects: Flaubert and Dostoevsky. In 1946 he published a short biographical sketch of Baudelaire, a study that relied on the basic categories of *Being and Nothingness* but lacked a concrete historical dimension, thus raising the question of whether Sartre's interest was in Baudelaire the person and writer or in the demonstration of his own theoretical postulates. In 1954 Roger Garaudy, a Communist and onetime critic of Sartre's existentialism, suggested that he and Sartre both write a biography of the same subject; Garaudy would use a Marxist method while Sartre would employ an existential one. The one work that resulted was Sartre's: a three-volume study of the life and work of Flaubert, Sartre's longest work and his last major publication, which synthesized Marxist, existential, and psychoanalytical interpretive procedures. The final product was not completed until sixteen years later, after three separate efforts to do so: 1954–1955, 1963, and 1968–1970. Sartre proposed a fourth volume that he never completed, and interrupted his study several times to pursue other projects, including the biography of Genet. As an explicit effort to justify the method of existential psychoanalysis, the biography of Flaubert represented an idiosyncratic return to existential themes in 1954, a year in which Sartre's allegiance to communism was at its most firm.

Perhaps he abandoned the project in 1955 precisely because its publication would open him to criticism as a bourgeois thinker preoccupied with bourgeois literary productions.

When he returned to the manuscript, however, it became clear that the biographical study could demonstrate the central claim of the *Critique* that an individual existence could be seen to recapitulate universal history in its own singular way. But even in this last great work, Sartre was deflected from his defense of universal history in favor of a more limited set of historical claims. Flaubert's life and work can be seen to reproduce the particular epoch of French letters and bourgeois culture in which he lived, but there is no effort to link this epoch to a developmental notion of totalizing history. Indeed, that Sartre confidently refers to unified epochs is already cause for hesitation. How are we to decide the parameters of a given historical epoch? When does it begin and end, and from what perspective can its contours be perceived? Has Sartre forgotten the lesson he learned from reading Henri Bergson in the 1930's—that philosophers err when they impose spatial categories on time?

But Sartre's biographical studies are less interesting as philosophies of history than as studies in the historical and existential genesis of literary productions. After all, Sartre's biographical subjects are invariably authors, writers of the imaginary, whose plays, poems, and novels are at once an expression of a singular choice and a transfiguration of an existing situation. As such, they are both the obvious focus of an existential psychoanalysis and the exemplars of Sartre's developing notion of praxis. If there is a continuity between the early and the late Sartre, the existential theorist and the Marxist, it is most likely to be found in these biographical demonstrations, as it were, rather than in the long-awaited second volume of the *Critique of Dialectical Reason* or in the *Cahiers pour une morale* (Notebooks on Morality, 1983).

As late as 1969 Sartre spoke as if there had never been a significant break in his own intellectual project, affirming that the imaginary, the domain of possibility and its unprecedented realization, had always been his central theme. As he said in an interview in the *New*

Left Review that year, "The reason why I produced *Les Mots* is the reason why I have studied Genet or Flaubert: how does a man become someone who writes, who wants to speak of the imaginary?" Questioned why he chose Flaubert, Sartre answered in words that might also explain his choice of Genet: "Because [Flaubert] is the imaginary. With him, I am at the border, the barrier of dreams."

According to Sartre's early theory of existential psychoanalysis, the imaginary is an illusory experience of metaphysical plenitude, the temporary eclipse of freedom by a product of its own making, the concealment of contingency. In the production of a compelling image or a literary experience, consciousness is in the presence of a seamless experience, an uninterrupted presence that is at once its own creation and its manner of hiding its own "lack" from itself. In other words, in the experience of an imaginary world, consciousness is temporarily relieved of its experience of itself, and its ontological struggle to find a necessary ground for its own contingent existence is temporarily put out of play. In this sense the author, once fully established as narrator, assumes the God-like position that is otherwise denied human beings. He creates the world of his experience, transfigures the environment in his own image, and nowhere confronts his own negativity or contingency. As author he is the necessary ground of the world he creates, and as creator he is free.

Clearly, for the early Sartre authorship was one tactic in the struggle to overcome the ontological paradox of human reality. For the later Sartre this meaning of authorship is not wholly gone, but both the structure and the content of creativity are radically altered. Genet does not simply create his fictional worlds ex nihilo; rather, by fictionalizing an already existing situation, he challenges the meanings that the situation already has, releasing new meanings to alter the situation. In other words, the creative act is a reproduction of an existing situation and is, in that sense, always dependent upon an existing situation for its content.

In *Being and Nothingness* desire and choice emerge ex nihilo from the for-itself, but in *The Family Idiot* desire, choice, and the imagination reproduce the historical situation of the individual. And yet for Sartre there is choice in the manner and meaning of reproduction, that is, in the subversions and reversals that reproducing a situation can effect. In Sartre's words, however, "what is important here is to reject idealism—fundamental attitudes are not *adopted* unless they first exist. What is taken is what is at hand."

But how are we to delimit the "situation" of the author? Clearly it involves not only the present circumstances of his life but also his personal history and childhood, the various cultural factors that determine his language and literary history, his class, race, gender, historical location, and political affiliations. Here we can see that Sartre's "search for a method" is fulfilled in the biographical effort to delimit a relevant "situation"; the demonstration of a life as both singular and universal depends essentially on the capacity of the biographer to show the links between these various levels of existence. In *The Family Idiot,* Sartre begins with an examination of early childhood in order to identify those constitutive relations with others that are later reproduced in the characteristic actions of the individual and in his literary works. Choice, once considered an essential determinant of the self, is now understood as an expression and recapitulation of these early relations with others. Hence, Sartre turns to psychoanalysis because "without early childhood, it is obvious that the biographer is building on sand."

For both Genet and Flaubert early childhood was a scene of deprivation; Genet was excluded from legitimate society, while Flaubert was mishandled and poorly loved. Originally victimized by these negative relations with others, both Genet and Flaubert eventually reinterpreted their situations through an imaginary transvaluation of the scene. In Sartre's view these scenes of victimization and exile are invariably reproduced in the works of Genet and

Flaubert, but in reproducing these scenes both authors gain a certain mastery over them that they originally lacked. As a child Flaubert was afflicted with a passive sensibility. Deployed in the service of writing, this passivity constitutes an extraordinarily receptive sensibility, acutely sensitive to details, absorbing whole worlds of experience and recapitulating them in fictional form. The key, for Sartre, is in the act of recapitulation, which ought not to be interpreted as simple repetition or as a conditioned behavioral response. In the recapitulation of the scene is a latent decision or resolve to alter the terms of the scene, especially when the original scene is experienced as a source of suffering. Not unlike the Freudian account of fantasy as a strategy of compensation, Sartre's developed theory of the imagination involves the twofold project to re-enact and, thereby, reinvent the past. Hence, the imagination remains an expression of freedom, but freedom is no longer the unconditioned spontaneity described in *Being and Nothingness*. Still contingent and unjustified, freedom is nevertheless severely restricted in its efficacy. For the Sartre of *The Family Idiot,* one is certainly free, but only to choose one's past again and again, with the hope that the recapitulations will become more creative, more subversive, more promising of possibility.

Sartre delimits the situation of Flaubert in terms of his childhood and adolescence, but also in terms of the Industrial Revolution, the breakdown of feudal relations in France, the history of the bourgeoisie. In this regard Flaubert is the occasion for a dialectical social history of nineteenth-century France, and yet Sartre does not want to say that Flaubert simply represents this epoch in French social history. The epoch produces the career of the individual, but the products of the individual reproduce and alter the very structure of that epoch. Hence, Sartre does not ask what effects the epoch had on Flaubert but, rather, how Flaubert realized this epoch in his own person and work, how this epoch "lived" in the person of Flaubert, and how that singular existence conferred a new meaning on the epoch itself. Nowhere is this dialectical relation between individual and epoch more evident than in those cultural products (such as literary works) that are taken to be both emblematic and transformative. As Sartre states in *The Family Idiot,* "Summed up and for this reason universalized by his epoch, he [Flaubert] in turn resumes it by reproducing himself in it as singularity."

Although Sartre claimed that he gave up his quasi-religious illusions about the immortalizing possibilities of great literary works, it appears that even *The Family Idiot* reflects a fundamental optimism regarding the salutary effects of literary works. If words fail to guarantee immortality, they nevertheless carry the power of inversion that permits the temporary triumph of consciousness over the difficulty of the world. Flaubert may suffer, but by giving words to that suffering, he creates beauty and a temporary redemption. By naming his experience Genet makes himself into a social fact, a public presence, the permanent property of culture, thus reversing his fate as an illegitimate child in exile from society. These literary reversals of experience are not mere fantasies of reparation; as present facts they confer fresh meanings upon the past, carrying that past into the present in a new form. Moreover, the "irreality" of the fictional world allows the transformation of brute facts into fields of possibility; the abandoned or unloved child becomes God over his own past, re-creating it in the image of his desire. Literature thus becomes the occasion of a perpetual reinvention of experience.

As a biographer Sartre makes use of the personal and historical past of his subject in a highly nontraditional way. Rather than find in the past the causes or motivations for future behavior, Sartre understands the past only in terms of the future that the subject projects. In *Being and Nothingness* he made it clear that projects, those fundamental desires which are elaborated in sustained modes of actions, give unity to life. These commitments, which necessarily involve a vision of a future self, confer a retroactive meaning upon the past. Because the subject is always in the process of creating its meaning, the past continually takes on significance in terms of the projected unity of the future self. Hence, the personal and historical past has no intrinsic meaning but requires the project as its necessary context. In this sense the self is a locus of perpetual reinvention and continuous redemption. No single set of facts defines an individual, for those facts must be interpreted, and interpretation is effected through the appropriation of those facts in a current project.

In *The Family Idiot* Sartre is more clearly aware that the interpretation of the personal and historical past is not solely a subjective affair, that the projects which confer meaning upon the past are more often intersubjective in nature. Flaubert is not only what he makes of himself but also what others make of him as he makes himself. Although Sartre emphasized the constituting look of the Other in *Being and Nothingness,* he tended to reduce the complexity of the social construction of identity, the various cultural and linguistic factors that constitute signification and that signify the subject even before the subject interprets himself. The structuralist and poststructuralist critique of Sartre often centers on this problem. A self-reflexive interpretation must make use of language; and subjects do not determine the meanings of a language into which they are born, the language to which they are subject even as they attempt a radical self-definition. Occasionally this criticism is limited to the claim that the Sartrian subject, inasmuch as he does not choose the language that constitutes the possible field of meaning into which he is born, is less free than Sartre himself imagined.

A stronger criticism is sometimes made that the subject is a product of a specific historical system of meaning, a discourse, and is in that sense wholly determined from the outset. Although Sartre generally refused to engage such critics, he knew that they existed, and *The Family Idiot* might well be understood as an effort to defend the self-defining subject even

while acknowledging the complex historical and linguistic situation in which it is mired. After all, Flaubert is stuck with an enormous historical and cultural legacy, the history of letters, the Industrial Revolution, the crises of the bourgeois class. But does this situation have only an objective meaning, or does it also remain possible to ask what meaning this history takes on *for him*? Here we are referring not only to an attitude or reflective awareness of the situation but also to a mode of positioning himself in and through the terms of this situation.

The subject may well be constituted by a field of significations of which he himself is not the sole author, or even not the author at all. But this field must be experienced in some way; and that experience, lived as it is by a singular individual from a distinct perspective, a distinct location in space and time, is what constitutes the field as a situation *for him.* Surely it is a situation for others as well, but not in the same way. No one can share the lived experience of that field of significations, because no one can live in the place of anyone else. Moreover, a situation is not passively or contemplatively experienced but is, in Sartre's terms, "existed" in a transitive sense. In other words, experience requires a reflexive act of self-determination, a positioning of oneself, a taking-up of possibilities from that field of significations and a letting-go of others. To experience is to discriminate among possibilities, to act, and therefore to commit oneself in virtue of that act.

Despite the popular characterization of Sartre's philosophy as absurdist, portraying human actions as arbitrary and incoherent, Sartre was concerned with the intelligibility of human actions, their coherence within the life of the individual, and their implicit unity. In *Being and Nothingness* he refers to the reflexive style of the individual, the coherent pattern of choices that come to constitute the self. And in *The Family Idiot* Sartre maintains that Flaubert's life is a unity, a dialectical mediation of the singular and universal features of his experience. In the former work the unity of a life is self-constructed, a unity of desires and choices, and in the latter that unity is an effect of dialectical necessity. In both cases, however, the emphasis on internal coherence and consistency suggests that freedom is not an aimless and arbitrary activity, but retains within itself a normative ideal. This may sound strange as a characterization of an existential philosophy, for existentialism is commonly said to renounce the ascription of any intrinsic normative goals for existence, the latter being the freely chosen projects of each individual. But how then are we to contend with Sartre's insistence that each and every life maintains a unity structured by the desire or necessity to create itself as an internally consistent assemblage of actions? What dictates this unity as a desideratum?

As unified and complete, a given life takes form as a kind of being, a plenum of experience that is achieved through the gradual cultivation of an identifiable self. Being internally consistent, this life masks its own contingency, appearing as a series of choices and actions structured by a unifying theme. Unity is thus a normative ideal toward which any given life strives, but for Sartre it is also a theoretical a priori for the understanding of any given life. As a result the circularity of Sartre's argument precludes the possibility of its demonstration.

But are we to accept Sartre's thesis as true? Is completeness and unity the structure and telos of all human striving? And is Sartre himself clear on where he stands? In the early investigations of the imagination, in *Nausea* and even in *The Words,* literary experience was understood as a kind of vital plenum, a complete and unified experience that masked the contingency and negativity of ordinary experience. In that sense it was an escape from the real, the secularization of absolute presence. Sartre appeared to concur with Nietzsche's *Birth of Tragedy* that life could only be justified as an aesthetic phenomenon.

In *What Is Literature?* Sartre repudiated this version of literature as escape and called for a committed literature that would risk transience for the sake of political efficacy. But the continued insistence on the "unity" of a life in the later biographies suggests that he did not wholly rid himself of the desire for a completed existence, a life that would appear as a work of art, a well-carved reflection of a freedom that endures. At the end of *Nausea,* Roquentin considers that suffering is never transcended but is transformed into melody, a melancholy melody, and that this aesthetic transformation, in its simplicity and completeness, is a kind of temporary redemption. The biography of Genet pursues a similar kind of experience, the beauty of poetic utterance that, Genet says, "reduces the body to a speck of light."

Even though Sartre voiced antipathy for Flaubert, the latter's pursuit of a fully imaginary existence resonates with Sartre's own literary career. In *Critique of Dialectical Reason* Sartre asserts the unity of history but maintains that this unity can be dialectically imagined only in a future synthetically built from contemporary historical experience. Once again the promise of the plenum exists for an imagination that can project the future and then come to believe in the reality of that projection.

But consider the following: the second volume of the *Critique,* which was intended to prove this unity of history, remains incomplete, as does the final volume of *Flaubert,* in which the grand synthesis of singular and universal experience was expected to take place. What rhetorical meaning are we to discern in the incompleteness of these works that argue the case for completeness? It is as if Sartre refused to complete his works, or perhaps his life, by leaving these works open.

In a late interview with de Beauvoir, Sartre stated, "I didn't finish the Flaubert and I never shall." Although colored by a sense of failure, Sartre's penchant for nonclosure also has the air of defiance about it, as if the perfect text were a dangerous thing, inimical to life. Reflecting on his career, Sartre considered *Nausea* and *The Words* to be completed and perfected texts, and yet that kind of writing became increasingly less important to him. He conceded that he no longer wrote very well, and considered *The Family Idiot* to be clumsily composed. The prose is rushed, infused with the speed of experience, and in the *Critique* there is an indifference to beautiful language. Asked why he no longer wrote fiction by the time he took up *The Family Idiot,* Sartre replied that the problem with literary descriptions is that *they are not time.*

And yet, this "problem" was once considered by Sartre to be the source of literature's value, its redemptive power, its capacity to stay time and make the world appear in its absolute presence. The closure of experience seemed less desirable to him as his own life threatened to close. And despite his illness and failing sight, Sartre's uncompleted works suggest a final disenchantment with the imaginary pursuit of plenitude—this, at the threshold of its realization.

Selected Bibliography

EDITIONS

NOVELS
La nausée. Paris, 1938.
L'Âge de raison. Paris, 1945.
Le sursis. Paris, 1945.
La mort dans l'âme. Paris, 1949.

SHORT STORIES
Le mur. Paris, 1939. Includes "Le Mur," "La Chambre," "Erostrate," "Intimite," and "L'Enfance d'un chef."

DRAMA
Les mouches. Paris, 1943.
Huis clos. Paris, 1945.
Morts sans sépulture. Lausanne, 1946.
La putain respectueuse. Paris, 1946.
Les mains sales. Paris, 1948.

Le Diable et le bon Dieu. Paris, 1951.
Kean. Paris, 1954.
Nekrassov. Paris, 1955.
Les séquestrés d'Altona. Paris, 1960.
Les troyennes. Paris, 1966.

LITERARY CRITICISM
Situations. 10 vols. Paris, 1947–1976.
Un théâtre de situations. Edited by Michel Contat and Michel Rybalka. Paris, 1973.

AUTOBIOGRAPHY
Les mots. Paris, 1964.

BIOGRAPHY
Baudelaire. Paris, 1946.
Saint Genet, comédien et martyr. Paris, 1952.
L'Idiot de la famille: Gustave Flaubert de 1821 à 1857. 3 vols. Paris, 1971–1972.

PHILOSOPHY
L'Imagination. Paris, 1936.
La transcendance de l'égo. In *Recherches philosophiques,* vol. 6. Paris, 1937. Reprinted with introduction, notes, and appendixes by Sylvie Le Bon. Paris, 1965.
Esquisse d'une théorie des émotions. Paris, 1939.
L'Imaginaire: Psychologie phénoménologique de l'imagination. Paris, 1940.
L'Être et le néant: Essai d'ontologie phénoménologique. Paris, 1943.
L'Existentialisme est un humanisme. Paris, 1946.
Question de methode. In *Twórczosc* (as "Marksizm i egzistencjalizm"; 1957). Reprinted as introduction to *Critique de la raison dialectique,* vol. 1. Paris, 1960. Reprinted separately, Paris, 1967.
Critique de la raison dialectique. Vol. 1, *Théorie des ensembles pratiques.* Paris, 1960. The second volume, never completed, was published posthumously.

POLITICAL WORKS
Réflexions sur la question juive. Paris, 1946.
Entretiens sur la politique. Paris, 1949. With Gérard Rosenthal and David Rousset.
"Les communistes et la paix." In *Les temps modernes,* 81:1–50 (July 1952); 84–85:695–763 (Oc-

tober–November 1952); 101:1,731–1,819 (April 1954). Reprinted in *Situations,* vol. 6, pp. 80–384.

"Le fantôme de Staline." In *Les temps modernes,* 129–130:577–696 (November–December 1956) and 131: (January 1957). Reprinted in *Situations,* vol. 7, pp. 144–307.

"Le génocide." In *Les temps modernes,* 259:953–971 (December 1967). Reprinted in *Situations,* vol. 8, pp. 100–124; and in *Tribunal Russell.* Vol. 2, *Le jugement final.* Paris, 1968.

Plaidoyer pour les intellectuals. Paris, 1972.

On a raison de se revolter. Paris, 1974. With Philippe Gavi and Pierre Victor.

POSTHUMOUS PUBLICATIONS

Cahiers pour une morale. Paris, 1983.

Les carnets de la drôle de guerre: Novembre 1939–Mars 1940. Paris, 1983.

Critique de la raison dialectique. Vol. 2, *L'Intelligibilité de l'histoire.* Edited by Arlette Elkaïm-Sartre. Paris, 1985.

TRANSLATIONS

The Age of Reason. Translated by Eric Sutton. New York, 1947.

Anti-Semite and Jew. Translated by George J. Becker. New York, 1948.

Baudelaire. Translated by Martin Turnell. New York, 1950.

Being and Nothingness: An Essay on Phenomenological Ontology. Translated by Hazel E. Barnes. New York, 1956.

Between Existentialism and Marxism. Translated by John Mathews. New York, 1974. Originally *Situations,* vols. 8 and 9.

The Communists and Peace. Translated by Martha Fletcher. New York, 1968.

The Condemned of Altona. Translated by Sylvia Leeson and George Leeson. New York, 1961.

Critique of Dialectical Reason, vol. 1. Translated by Alan Sheridan-Smith. Edited by Jonathan Rée. London, 1976.

The Devil & the Good Lord. Translated by Kitty Black. In *The Devil & the Good Lord and Two Other Plays.* New York, 1960.

Dirty Hands. Translated by Lionel Abel. In *Three Plays.* New York, 1949.

The Emotions: Outline of a Theory. Translated by Bernard Frechtman. New York, 1948.

Existentialism and Humanism. Translated by Philip Mairet. London, 1948.

The Family Idiot. Translated by Carol Cosman. 2 vols. Chicago, 1981–1987.

The Flies. Translated by Stuart Gilbert. In *No Exit . . . The Flies.* New York, 1946.

The Ghost of Stalin. Translated by Martha Fletcher. New York, 1968.

Imagination: A Psychological Critique. Translated by Forrest Williams. Ann Arbor, Mich., 1962.

Kean. Translated by Kitty Black. London, 1954. Also in *The Devil & the Good Lord.* New York, 1960.

Life/Situations. Translated by Paul Auster and Lydia Davis. New York, 1974. Originally *Situations,* vol. 10.

Literary and Philosophical Essays. Translated by Annette Michelson. New York, 1955.

Nausea. Translated by Robert Baldick. Harmondsworth, England, 1965.

Nekrassov. Translated by Sylvia Leeson and George Leeson. London, 1956. Also in *The Devil & the Good Lord.* New York, 1960.

No Exit. Translated by Stuart Gilbert. In *No Exit . . . The Flies.* New York, 1946.

The Psychology of Imagination. New York, 1948.

The Reprieve. Translated by Eric Sutton. New York, 1947.

The Respectful Prostitute. Translated by Lionel Abel. In *Three Plays.* New York, 1949.

Saint Genet: Actor and Martyr. Translated by Bernard Frechtman. New York, 1963.

Sartre on Theatre. Translated by Frank Jellinek. Edited by Michel Contat and Michel Rybalka. New York, 1976.

Search for a Method. Translated by Hazel E. Barnes. New York, 1963, repr. 1968.

Situations. Translated by Benita Eisler and Maria Jolas. New York, 1965. Originally *Situations,* vol. 4.

The Transcendence of the Ego. Translated by Forrest Williams and Robert Kirkpatrick. New York, 1957, repr. 1972.

The Trojan Women. Translated by Ronald Duncan. New York, 1967.

Troubled Sleep. Translated by Gerard Hopkins. New York, 1951.

The Wall and Other Stories. Translated by Lloyd Alexander. New York, 1948.

The War Diaries, November 1939–March 1940. Translated by Quintin Hoare. New York, 1985.

What Is Literature? Translated by Bernard Frechtman. New York, 1949. Originally *Situations,* vol. 2, pp. 57–330.

The Words. Translated by Bernard Frechtman. New York, 1964, 1981.

BIOGRAPHICAL AND CRITICAL WORKS

Aron, Raymond. *History and the Dialectic of Violence: An Analysis of Sartre's Critique de la Raison Dialectique.* Translated by Barry Cooper. Oxford, 1975.

Aronson, Ronald. *Jean-Paul Sartre: Philosophy in the World.* London, 1980.

Barnes, Hazel E. *An Existentialist Ethics.* New York, 1967.

——— . *Sartre and Flaubert.* Chicago, 1981.

Beauvoir, Simone de. *The Prime of Life.* Translated by Peter Green. New York, 1962.

——— . *Force of Circumstance.* Translated by Richard Howard. New York, 1965.

——— . *Adieux: A Farewell to Sartre.* Translated by Patrick O'Brian. New York, 1984.

Caws, Peter. *Sartre: Arguments of the Philosophers.* London and Boston, 1979.

Cohen-Solel, Annie. *Sartre: A Life.* Translated by Anna Cancogni. Edited by Norman Macafee. New York, 1987.

Culler, Jonathan. *Flaubert: The Uses of Uncertainty.* Ithaca, N.Y., 1974.

Danto, Arthur. *Jean-Paul Sartre.* New York, 1975.

Grene, Marjorie. *Sartre.* New York, 1973.

Halpern, Joseph. *Critical Fictions: The Literary Criticism of Jean-Paul Sartre.* New Haven, 1976.

Jameson, Fredric R. *Sartre: The Origins of a Style.* New Haven, 1961.

Jeanson, Francis. *Sartre and the Problem of Morality.* Translated by Robert V. Stone. Bloomington, Ind., 1980.

LaCapra, Dominick. *A Preface to Sartre.* Ithaca, N.Y., 1978.

Merleau-Ponty, Maurice. *The Visible and the Invisible.* Translated by Alphonso Lingis. Edited by Claude Lefort. Evanston, Ill., 1968.

——— . *Adventures of the Dialectic.* Translated by Joseph Bien. Evanston, Ill., 1973.

Murdoch, Iris. *Sartre: Romantic Rationalist.* New Haven, 1953; London, 1961.

Natanson, Maurice. *A Critique of Jean-Paul Sartre's Ontology.* Lincoln, Nebr., 1951; repr. New York, 1972, and The Hague, 1973.

Poster, Mark. *Existential Marxism in Postwar France: From Sartre to Althusser.* Princeton, 1975.

Schilpp, Paul Arthur, ed. *The Philosophy of Jean-Paul Sartre.* La Salle, Ill., 1981.

Silverman, Hugh J., and Frederick A. Elliston, eds. *Jean-Paul Sartre: Contemporary Approaches to His Philosophy.* Pittsburgh, 1980.

Warnock, Mary, ed. *Sartre: A Collection of Critical Essays.* New York, 1971.

BIBLIOGRAPHIES

Contat, Michel, and Michel Rybalka, eds. *Les écrits de Sartre.* Paris, 1970. Translated by Richard McLeary as *The Writings of Jean-Paul Sartre,* 2 vols. Evanston, Ill., 1974.

Lapointe, François. *Jean-Paul Sartre and His Critics: An International Bibliography (1938–1980).* Annotated and revised 2nd ed. Bowling Green, Ohio, 1981. With Claire Lapointe.

JUDITH P. BUTLER

ALEKSANDR SOLZHENITSYN

(b. 1918)

LIFE

BY THE TIMING of his birth on 11 December, 1918, Aleksandr Solzhenitsyn automatically earned the designation of "October child." This was a Soviet term for youngsters born soon after the 1917 October Revolution who were expected, as members of an entirely new generation, to complete the glorious social structure projected by the architects of communism. These expectations proved completely inaccurate, and in Solzhenitsyn's case particularly so. He was destined to experience at first hand the nightmare reality lurking behind the facade of lofty slogans, and by the power of his pen to do more than any other human being to demolish the mendacious myths on which the Soviet system is based.

Aleksandr Isaevich Solzhenitsyn was born in Kislovodsk, a small town in the Caucasus mountains that was about to be engulfed in the Russian Civil War. Both parents were of peasant stock, but their ties to the traditional way of life had been loosened by extensive schooling. The future writer's father, Isaaki Solzhenitsyn, had left the family farm to pursue an education and was enrolled at Moscow University at the outbreak of World War I. Despite pacifist leanings inspired by the teachings of Tolstoy, he dropped out of college to enlist in the military, serving with distinction as an artillery officer. The writer's mother (née Taissia Shcherbak), the daughter of a prosperous Ukrainian farmer,

had graduated from an exclusive girls' school and was studying at an agricultural academy in Moscow when she met Isaaki Solzhenitsyn. The pair were married in 1917, but Solzhenitsyn's father did not live to see his firstborn: he died as a result of a hunting accident several months before Aleksandr's birth.

After the untimely death of her husband and the expropriation of her father's land and possessions by the Bolsheviks, Taissia Solzhenitsyn had no choice but to seek employment, a task made difficult by the new regime's policy of deliberate discrimination against relatives of former landowners and officers. The meager earnings brought in by sporadic work as typist and stenographer in Rostov-on-Don were barely enough to sustain mother and son, and Solzhenitsyn's childhood was a time of severe and continuous deprivation. Yet despite these hardships, and despite the lack of sympathy for the Soviet regime among the family's closest circle of friends, we have the writer's recollection that he soon began to be swayed by the ideological fervor of the time. Soviet education was winning him over, and by the late 1930's Solzhenitsyn had become a committed disciple of Marx and Lenin.

The same years also marked the beginning of persistent literary experimentation in both prose and verse. Solzhenitsyn dismissed these early writings as "the usual adolescent nonsense," but with one significant exception: during his last year in high school and first year at university, Solzhenitsyn had undertaken extensive research into the Russian army's ill-conceived invasion of Eastern Prussia in August of 1914, his ultimate purpose being to incorporate an account of the ensuing Russian defeat into a large epic devoted to the Russian Revolution. We can easily recognize Solzhenitsyn's *Avgust chetyrnadtsatogo* (*August 1914*, 1971; complete text, 1983) and its sequels in this early design, even though in the intervening decades the author's views of the Revolution itself were to undergo a radical transformation.

Solzhenitsyn entered Rostov University in 1937, specializing in mathematics and physics despite his growing interest in literature. His choice was in large part determined by concern for his ailing mother, who had developed tuberculosis and was by now too ill to move from Rostov or to be left behind if he were to enroll in an institution where literature was taught at a level more sophisticated than that available in Rostov. (In later years Solzhenitsyn came to regard this decision as providential, since it was precisely his diploma in mathematics that would bring about his removal from labor camp—at a time when his physical survival was at risk—to the relative security of a closed prison institute.)

In any event, Solzhenitsyn was outstandingly successful in his university career, an excellent academic record being matched by his enthusiastic involvement in activities such as the editorship of a student newspaper. He also managed to undertake a systematic study of literature through a correspondence course offered by the prestigious Moscow Institute of Philosophy, Literature, and History (MIFLI). His manifold activities did not prevent him from striking out in other directions as well. He met and courted Natalia Reshetovskaia, a fellow student at the university who, just like himself, was studying science but in addition had extensive interests in music. They were married in 1940.

Solzhenitsyn graduated with distinction in the spring of 1941, but instead of looking for a position in science or mathematics, he resolved to take up the full-time study of literature in Moscow. As he arrived in the capital in June of that year, the Nazi attack on the Soviet Union made shambles of all his plans. Solzhenitsyn immediately tried to enlist, but to his great chagrin was disqualified on medical grounds. Four months later, however, he was called up for service in a horse-drawn transport unit. Frustrated by the unfamiliar task of dealing with horses, Solzhenitsyn wrote incessant appeals to be transferred to the front. At last his luck changed and he was admitted to a wartime training course for artillery officers. His skill in mathematics determined the rest: Solzhenitsyn came to specialize in sound ranging, a technique whereby the location of an enemy battery is determined by means of dispersed microphones.

Commissioned in 1942, Solzhenitsyn soon received command of his own battery, and from mid 1943 until 1945 was involved in major action at the front. In military terms his record was excellent: his unit won top ranking for discipline and battle effectiveness, while he himself was twice decorated for personal heroism and promoted to captain. He was brought low by a lack of political caution. For some months he had carried on a correspondence with a fellow officer in another unit, a good friend from Rostov who, like Solzhenitsyn, had developed serious reservations about Stalin and his policies. Assuming that personal mail would be subjected to merely superficial censorship, the two friends had exchanged views on this subject in only slightly veiled fashion.

They were quite mistaken. Solzhenitsyn was arrested at the front in February 1945, brought to Moscow for interrogation, and sentenced to eight years in corrective labor camps for "anti-Soviet agitation" and "malicious slander." The most important phase of his education was about to begin.

Solzhenitsyn served the first part of his sentence in labor camps in the outskirts of Moscow and inside the city itself. In volume 2 of *Arkhipelag GULag* (*The Gulag Archipelago,*

1973–1975), the writer gives an unsparing account of himself during this period, when naiveté and a complete lack of psychological preparation led him to humiliating compromises with his conscience. He was also reaching the point of physical collapse and almost certainly would not have survived had he not attracted the regime's attention with his background in mathematics. It was common practice at the time to put prisoners with specialized training to work in prison research institutes (referred to as *sharashkas*), and in mid 1947 Solzhenitsyn was pulled out of camp and assigned to Marfino, an institute that was charged with designing and producing a telephone scrambler. Apart from a marked improvement of living conditions—there was no exhausting physical labor and the diet was more substantial—the three years he spent there were for Solzhenitsyn a time of great intellectual growth. His Marxist faith had already been shaken to its roots by his earlier labor camp experiences; and at the Marfino *sharashka* he was able to test and realign his evolving views in the process of endless philosophical debates with several friends. In the novel *V kruge pervom* (*The First Circle,* 1968; full version, 1978), Solzhenitsyn's ideological and spiritual odyssey is ascribed to Gleb Nerzhin, a fictional character whose fate has many points in common with Solzhenitsyn's own experience in Marfino.

In 1950, on account of a conflict with the authorities, Solzhenitsyn was expelled from the prison institute and transported to a newly organized camp for political prisoners in Ekibastuz, part of an immense forced-labor empire sprawled over the plains of Soviet Central Asia. The three years at this camp were eventually to provide Solzhenitsyn with rich material for his future work. By turns a common laborer, a bricklayer, and a foundryman, Solzhenitsyn also witnessed a major protest strike by the prisoners and came into contact with numerous individuals who had long histories of incarceration in various Soviet prisons and camps. The implacable routine of the camp

system and its effect on a representative cross-section of the inmate population is depicted in Solzhenitsyn's *Odin den' Ivana Denisovicha* (*One Day in the Life of Ivan Denisovich,* 1962), while many of the accounts he heard from his new acquaintances were later incorporated into *The Gulag Archipelago.*

In 1952 Solzhenitsyn underwent surgery in the camp hospital for the removal of a large cancerous swelling. The procedure was deemed a success at the time, and Solzhenitsyn later related that at a certain point during his convalescence he felt the need to rededicate himself to the Christian faith of his childhood. That same year brought him the depressing news that his wife, who had earlier filed divorce papers for the semblance of dissociating herself from an "enemy of the people," had now finalized the divorce proceeding and was living with another man.

Solzhenitsyn was released from camp in March 1953, shortly after his eight-year sentence had expired. But instead of being granted full freedom, former political prisoners were routinely confined "in perpetuity" to places of internal exile determined by the authorities. In Solzhenitsyn's case this was Kok-Terek, a tiny hamlet on the southern border of Kazakhstan, where the writer eventually received a job as a teacher of mathematics and physics at the local school. All his spare time was now taken up by a feverish haste to record on paper the prodigious amount of verse he had composed in the preceding years. Camp regulations had strictly forbidden inmates from keeping any notes, but Solzhenitsyn had hit upon a method of preserving his thoughts: he cast them in poetic form and committed them to memory, using an elaborate ritual to review the growing text at regular intervals. The major product of this activity was the narrative poem "Dorozhenka" (The way), which allegedly contained over 10,000 lines of verse. Solzhenitsyn later expressed reservations about the poetic quality of this text, and for this reason allowed only small sections to be published, but "Dorozhenka" served him as a repository of his thoughts and feelings during the time of his imprisonment. The title itself is clearly a metaphor for the intellectual and spiritual odyssey of the autobiographical protagonist, set against the kaleidoscopic background of events that he had witnessed. The poem, prefigured in a fundamental manner much of Solzhenitsyn's later work, reflecting both his extraordinary drive to record past experience, and his constant attempt to draw meaning from the raw data of life by subjecting it to the discipline of literary form.

Other works composed and memorized in camp, but recorded in full written form only in Kok-Terek, are *Prusskie nochi* (*Prussian Nights*, 1974), *Pir pobeditelei* (*Victory Celebrations*, 1981) and *Plenniki* (*Prisoners*, 1981). The first two were in fact originally part of "Dorozhenka," but then evolved into independent works. All three are based on the author's experiences in early 1945, at first as an officer in the victoriously advancing Soviet army and then as a prisoner of Soviet counterintelligence.

Some months after settling in Kok-Terek, Solzhenitsyn's ambitious literary plans suddenly appeared to turn moot. He had developed acute abdominal pains that were diagnosed as cancer and probably stemmed from a metastasis of the cancerous growth excised in camp. By late 1953 he was desperately ill and was given only a few weeks to live. Racked by pain and filled with despair that his writings would now be lost, Solzhenitsyn buried them in his garden and undertook an arduous journey to a cancer clinic in Tashkent; his stay there later found reflection in the novel *Rakovyi korpus* (*Cancer Ward*, 1968).

Massive radiation treatment succeeded in shrinking Solzhenitsyn's tumor substantially, and in 1954 he was able to resume his duties as a teacher in Kok-Terek, while continuing to dedicate all his spare time to writing. His next work was another play on the labor-camp theme, ironically entitled *Respublika truda* (Republic of labor, 1981). (The version of this text published under the title *Olen' i shalashovka* [*The Love-Girl and the Innocent*,

1969] was prepared in 1962 in the hope of a Soviet theatrical performance; it represents an abridged and "softened" variant in which Solzhenitsyn also changed the names of many characters.) And in 1955 he began work on what was to become the masterly novel *The First Circle*.

The liberalization that followed Stalin's demise in 1953 had direct consequences for Solzhenitsyn. His sentence of "perpetual exile" was annulled in 1956, and Solzhenitsyn was permitted to return to the European part of Russia. He first took up residence in Miltsevo, a small village about a hundred miles east of Moscow, where he resumed teaching school and using all his spare time to write. The first draft of *The First Circle* was completed here, and Miltsevo became the setting of his famous short story entitled "Matrenin dvor" ("Matryona's Home," 1963).

In the following year the criminal charges that had originally led to Solzhenitsyn's arrest in 1945 were reviewed by one of Nikita Khrushchev's "rehabilitation tribunals" and declared invalid; Solzhenitsyn was issued an official certificate clearing his record. In 1957 he also reinstated his marriage to Natalia Reshetovskaia, moving with her to Ryazan, a provincial town southeast of Moscow, where he soon settled into his by now familiar routine of teaching physics and writing in secret.

The next three years were representative of the astonishing productivity that marked Solzhenitsyn's entire career as a writer. He undertook a fundamental revision of *The First Circle*, laid the groundwork for the project that would eventually grow into *The Gulag Archipelago*, completed a cycle of contemplative prose sketches, composed a screenplay about a camp uprising (*Znaiut istinu tanki* [Tanks Know the Truth], 1981), tried his hand at a play deliberately set outside any specific historical context (*Svecha na vetru* [*A Candle in the Wind*, 1969]), and wrote three prose works of great significance: the narrative that later acquired the title *One Day in the Life of Ivan Denisovich*, and two short stories of more conventional length, "Matryona's Home" and "Pravaia kist'" ("The Right Hand," 1968). All of these works, it must be noted, were written "for the drawer," that is, without the hope of having them appear in print during the author's lifetime.

One Day was the text that was destined to change all that. Following the Twenty-Second Congress of the Soviet Communist Party in October 1961, at which Stalinism had been ringingly denounced, Solzhenitsyn decided to risk submitting his manuscript to *Novyi mir,* the Soviet Union's most respected literary monthly. In *Bodalsia telenok s dubom* (*The Oak and the Calf,* 1975), Solzhenitsyn's account of his uneven struggle with the regime, the writer relates with great verve how clever planning by intermediaries got the text directly into the hands of Aleksandr Tvardovsky, the chief editor, who expressed enthusiasm but had to undertake extraordinary further maneuvers to see the story into print.

The appearance of *One Day* in the November 1962 issue of *Novyi mir* was immediately recognized as an event of great significance. While the West treated it primarily as a political bombshell, the official Soviet interpretation sought to present the story as an excoriation of the abuses of the Stalinist past, now safely and irrevocably gone. For the many millions of ordinary citizens who had come face-to-face with the reality of the camps, however, the impact of the text was of a different order entirely. *One Day* was the first "legitimate" publication to address the camp theme honestly—this after decades of official evasions or outright denials concerning the very existence of the labor camp system. In such a context the story represented a powerful reaffirmation of objective reality, a public acknowledgement that the suffering inflicted—but long denied recognition—had indeed taken place. It was perceived as a restoration of the past and a redemption of lost time, for this reason evoking an emotional response of great intensity. At the same time those who preferred to erase this terrible period of Soviet history from their memory were also profoundly disturbed by *One Day.*

As a result of this publication Solzhenitsyn was inundated with letters. The majority of correspondents expressed fervent approval and gratitude; many described their own camp experiences or offered to do so. A few years earlier Solzhenitsyn had begun sketching out plans for a historical survey of the Soviet penal system, but had abandoned the project as too ambitious. But now fate itself seemed to be summoning him to this task, and in the course of 1963 and 1964 he met privately with many of his correspondents in order to record their accounts in as much detail as possible. Most of this data was eventually incorporated into *The Gulag Archipelago.*

Meanwhile, the wave of liberalization in the Soviet Union that had made the publication of *One Day* possible was already beginning to recede, with immediate consequences for Solzhenitsyn. Increasingly hostile criticism was levelled at his prose works published in *Novyi mir* in the months following the appearance of *One Day* (especially "Matryona's Home"), and his nomination for the Lenin Prize in 1964 was sabotaged at the last moment by floating the shameless allegation that Solzhenitsyn had been a Nazi collaborator during the war. The atmosphere deteriorated further after the late-1964 coup that removed Khrushchev from power. Under the circumstances, Solzhenitsyn's attempts to get a revised and toned-down version of *The First Circle* published in *Novyi mir* were doomed to failure, and the writer decided to have a microfilm of the manuscript spirited abroad in 1964.

Things took another sharp turn for the worse in 1965 when KGB raids on the apartments of two friends resulted in the confiscation of a large volume of Solzhenitsyn's notes, files, and manuscripts of unpublished works. Apart from *The First Circle,* the latter included early plays like *Victory Celebrations,* where the unmistakable expressions of hostility toward the regime could easily serve as grounds for arrest. In fact the authorities soon began making selective use of the confiscated material in an effort to discredit the writer. This development, and

Solzhenitsyn's inability to get his major new work, *Cancer Ward* (written during 1963–1966), into print, seems to have precipitated the writer's resolve to reach his readers in ways defined by himself. In the Soviet Union of the 1960's this meant releasing a copy of the manuscript into the so-called samizdat network, an informal system whereby texts that had not received (or could not receive) official sanction for publication were manually retyped in several copies and distributed chain-letter fashion among like-minded individuals.

In general Solzhenitsyn became increasingly bold in his actions and outspoken in his expression of antipathy for the authorities; the image of him as the tough infighter and master strategist in the struggle with the Soviet regime dates primarily from the post-1965 period. In sharp contrast to his previous tendency to withdraw from the public eye, Solzhenitsyn now made a point of being noticed, firing off eloquent protests, agreeing to give public readings from his works, and even granting interviews to foreign correspondents. His most conspicuous act of defiance at the time was the 1967 open letter to the Soviet Writers' Union in which he bitterly rebuked the organization for its craven acceptance of everything the regime had dished out over the years, from the heavy-handed censorship of literary works to the physical persecution of hundreds of writers. The letter was individually sent to some 250 delegates attending the Fourth Congress of Soviet Writers, but discussion of the topics it raised was blocked by the union's leadership.

Apart from such highly visible activities Solzhenitsyn was moving with even greater resolve behind the scenes. In conditions of utmost secrecy he undertook the gargantuan task of weaving together the data contained in the testimonies he had collected from hundreds of former inmates of Soviet camps and prisons into an 1800-page-long historical overview of the entire system entitled *The Gulag Archipelago.* In 1968 he microfilmed the completed study and had the film smuggled abroad for safekeeping. And a year earlier he had given a signal to proceed with the publication of *The First Circle* in the West. Meanwhile, *Cancer Ward* had crossed the border of its own accord (such was the typical result of samizdat distribution) and in 1968 Solzhenitsyn had the satisfaction of seeing the virtually simultaneous appearance of these two major works in the leading Western countries. The critical reception was overwhelmingly positive, and from now on Solzhenitsyn's formidable international reputation could not but inhibit the Soviet regime from undertaking any extreme actions against him.

But the writer had no intention of resting on the laurels of these victories. With his customary energy he next turned to the vastly ambitious project that he described as the "principal task" of his life. This was the multipart historical epic centered on the Russian Revolution, collectively known as *Krasnoe koleso* (*The Red Wheel*), in which *August 1914* represented the first installment or "knot" (*uzel*). Working with intense concentration in 1969 and 1970, Solzhenitsyn completed the version of this volume that appeared in Paris in 1971. (A substantially expanded edition was published in two volumes in 1983.)

In the meantime there had been new developments in the ongoing duel between the writer and the authorities. In late 1969 Solzhenitsyn was summarily expelled from the Union of Soviet Writers for "antisocial behavior" and views judged to be "radically in conflict with the aims and purposes" of the organization. In the Soviet context this action could be a damaging blow, since it formally closed access to "legitimate" publication and rendered the writer technically unemployed (a punishable offense under Soviet law). In this particular instance, however, Soviet journals were already closed to Solzhenitsyn, and the regime must have been painfully surprised by the outpouring of protest from Western writers and literary associations that followed the expulsion. Moreover, the action of the Writers'

Union apparently played a role in Solzhenitsyn's decision in 1970 to retain a Swiss lawyer in order to look after his interests abroad, which was by Soviet standards an unprecedented arrangement.

In October 1970 the Nobel Prize for literature was awarded to Solzhenitsyn "for the ethical force with which he has pursued the indispensable traditions of Russian literature." In the eight short years since the appearance of *One Day*, Solzhenitsyn had risen to the pinnacle of international fame and had without question become the world's most celebrated living author.

The writer accepted the prize gratefully and expressed the intention of attending the award ceremonies, but a furious campaign launched against him in the Soviet press forced a change of plans, since it seemed likely that he would be barred from returning to his homeland. A further shadow was cast on the event by the refusal of the Swedish government to allow an alternative award ceremony to take place in their embassy building in Moscow, evidently for fear of offending Soviet sensibilities. (No mutually satisfactory procedure could be worked out at the time, and the Nobel insignia were presented to Solzhenitsyn four years later, when the writer was already living in the West.)

At the very time of the Nobel Prize announcement and its aftermath, Solzhenitsyn was in the midst of a painful crisis in his relationship with Natalia Reshetovskaia. He and Reshetovskaia had been steadily drifting apart during the preceding several years, but now matters had come to a head when Solzhenitsyn revealed his relationship with another woman, one that he had no intention of terminating. The distraught Reshetovskaia made an attempt to commit suicide. Her life was saved, but Solzhenitsyn now resolved to press for a divorce, and despite Reshetovskaia's opposition and her appeal to a Soviet court, the break was finalized in early 1973. Shortly thereafter Solzhenitsyn married Natalia Svetlova, a math-

ematician by training, who in due course became his irreplaceable assistant and confidante, the trusted editor of his works, and the mother of his three sons.

Although the press campaign against Solzhenitsyn occasioned by the Nobel Prize soon began to abate, there were signs that the regime was preparing more serious moves. In August 1971 the summer cottage Solzhenitsyn had been using as a retreat was ransacked by a group of KGB operatives during his absence, and a friend who happened to stumble onto the scene was savagely beaten and threatened. Meanwhile, another group of agents was dispatched to Solzhenitsyn's birthplace in the hope of uncovering damaging information about his background. And with the same goal in mind, the Soviet press agency Novosti approached Reshetovskaia, offering to publish her reminiscences of Solzhenitsyn. She agreed, and the Russian version of her heavily doctored text appeared in 1975.

But by far the most ominous development was the mid-1973 arrest of Elizaveta Voronianskaia, a Leningrad woman who had helped Solzhenitsyn in the typing of his manuscripts. After days of relentless interrogation by the KGB, Voronianskaia had revealed the hiding place of a manuscript copy of *The Gulag Archipelago*; soon thereafter she was either murdered or committed suicide. Solzhenitsyn reacted to this tragic news with the only response he considered appropriate: *The Gulag Archipelago* now needed to be published without delay and in its entirety. The corresponding instructions were sent to Solzhenitsyn's Swiss lawyer, and the first volume of the Russian edition appeared in Paris at the very end of 1973, making front-page news around the world.

The impact of *The Gulag Archipelago* in the West can be compared only to the seismic shock produced by *One Day* upon Soviet readers. The facts laid out in Solzhenitsyn's history of Soviet prisons and camps were in themselves not really new, since both specialist studies and numerous memoirs by former inmates had been available in the West for many years. Yet despite this, and despite the de-Stalinization campaign waged by Khrushchev a decade earlier, Western public opinion had to a large degree retained a visceral distrust of information of this sort. It was therefore a measure of Solzhenitsyn's skill as a writer that by the force of his narrative he was able to break this pattern of automatic skepticism, and to convince millions of readers of the stark reality of his portrayal. In this sense *The Gulag Archipelago* will undoubtedly remain the most shattering blow ever delivered to the image of the Soviet Union.

Predictably enough, the Soviet regime reacted to the appearance of *The Gulag Archipelago* with torrents of vituperation. Journalists vied with milkmaids and lathe operators (who had of course not laid eyes on the work in question) in denouncing the author in essays and outraged letters to the editor. Solzhenitsyn was called a psychotic renegade choking with hatred for the country of his birth, a corrupt offspring of embittered class enemies, a despicable Judas dancing to the tune of Western warmongers and Red-baiters, a Nazi sympathizer, a slimy reptile, and so on. There were also threatening phone calls to his Moscow apartment and leering notes in the mail.

Unpleasant as this orchestrated eruption of hatred must have been, Solzhenitsyn was inclined to believe that the storm would blow over, just as the earlier press campaign against him had not led to any further action. This time he was wrong. On 12 February 1974 a large party of KGB agents showed up at his door with an order for his arrest. Solzhenitsyn was taken to Lefortovo prison, subjected to all the humiliating procedures for incoming prisoners, charged with treason, stripped of his Soviet citizenship, and on the next day expelled to West Germany on a plane specially reserved for this purpose. In *The Oak and the Calf* the writer gives an extraordinarily vivid account of these two days and of the inner tumult to which they gave rise.

Solzhenitsyn first set up residence in Zurich (where his wife and family joined him after being allowed to leave the USSR), but soon began to look for a place more suited to his need for privacy, and in mid 1976 he relocated to the United States, settling in Cavendish, a village in a sparsely populated area of southern Vermont.

During his initial years in the West, Solzhenitsyn travelled widely, consenting to a number of appearances and interviews. Some of these became major public events, as for example his television discussion with several short-tempered French intellectuals (April 1975), his blunt remarks in Washington and New York about the illusions of détente (June and July 1975), his speeches to the British on television and radio (February 1976), and his celebrated commencement address at Harvard University (June 1978).

While the interest generated by each of these occasions was considerable—in some cases it was enormous—Solzhenitsyn's public pronouncements did not meet with unanimous approval in the West. Rather, there rose an ever-increasing chorus of dissent, much of it based on genuine disagreement with Solzhenitsyn's message. The writer's belief in the irredeemably evil and hence "unreformable" nature of communism collided with deeply ingrained Marxist sympathies, while his sharp rebuke of the West for what he considered its loss of moral fortitude was deemed shrill and offensive by some. It was charged that the writer's public statements lacked the nuance and complexity that distinguished his literary work. Solzhenitsyn was also assailed by angry critics for his alleged hostility to democracy and to the principle of free speech, for supposedly harboring theocratic and monarchist sympathies, and for willfully ignoring the defects of prerevolutionary Russia while exaggerating those of the contemporary West. Solzhenitsyn's many essays and interviews are a large subject in themselves; suffice it to say here that most of the charges listed above could be substantiated only by wrenching the writer's words out of context. The fact remains, nevertheless, that Solzhenitsyn's hitherto un-assailable public image in the West sustained damage from these attacks and innuendos. And this, in turn, seems to have contributed to his increasing tendency to abstain from com-menting on public issues. Turning his prodi-gious energies inward, Solzhenitsyn began to concentrate on his own work: in 1978 he launched his authorized collected works, and he immersed himself in the historical cycle ini-tiated by *August 1914.*

Solzhenitsyn nevertheless got involved in one other major project. In 1977 he announced the formation of the Russian Memoir Library, an entity visualized both as a repository for unpublished materials bearing on twentieth-century Russia and as a research facility. He appealed to Russian emigrés to submit manuscripts, letters, and photographs in their possession, urged them to write their own rem-iniscences, and promised to publish the most interesting of the materials received. By 1988, eight volumes of the memoir series had ap-peared in print. Solzhenitsyn also sponsored a series of scholarly studies on modern Russian history, and several important titles had been published by the late 1980's. The aim of this undertaking was of course consistent with Solzhenitsyn's entire oeuvre and expressed his overwhelming desire to preserve and rescue from oblivion the true contours of Russian twentieth-century history.

The late 1980's brought promising develop-ments. As the winds of *glasnost* (openness) began sweeping away taboos in Mikhail Gor-bachev's Soviet Union, the long-forbidden name of Solzhenitsyn started to crop up in So-viet publications in various positive contexts. In mid 1988 a Moscow periodical called for an annullment of the 1974 charges against Sol-zhenitsyn and the restoration of his citizen-ship; the response from readers indicated strong support for the proposal. Meanwhile, *Novyi mir,* the journal on the pages of which

Solzhenitsyn had begun his public career as a writer, had succeeded in working out an agree-ment with him whereby selections from *The Gulag Archipelago* were to appear in early 1989, with the novels *The First Circle* and *Can-cer Ward* to follow at a later point. The process of returning Solzhenitsyn to readers in the So-viet Union was due to begin even earlier, with several literary meetings scheduled to coincide with the writer's seventieth birthday on 11 De-cember 1988 and a promised publication of his Nobel Lecture.

But these plans were disrupted at the last moment by the direct intervention of the Polit-buro. Some of the literary gatherings honoring Solzhenitsyn were cancelled outright, those al-lowed to proceed were denied press or media coverage. More important, the publication of *Gulag* in *Novyi mir* was officially pronounced to be out of the question. In what was a star-tling acknowledgement of the power of Sol-zhenitsyn's writings, the party's chief ideolo-gist declared that to publish such works in the USSR would be "to undermine the foundations on which our present [Soviet] life rests" (*The New York Times,* 30 November 1988).

Absolute as this ban seemed to be, it was breached within only a few months. By mid summer of 1989, Solzhenitsyn's essay entitled "Zhit' ne po Izhi" ("Live Not By Lies," written in 1972–1973 and first published by the London *Daily Express* on 18 February 1974 and then in Russian in Paris the next year) had appeared in a number of Soviet periodicals, the classic short story "Matryona's Home" had been repub-lished in the mass-circulation journal *Ogonyok* (June 1989), an Estonian-language monthly had printed a chapter from *The Gulag Archi-pelago, Novyi mir* had published the "Nobel Lecture" (July 1989) and was once again an-nouncing plans to serialize substantial por-tions of *The Gulag Archipelago* on its pages, two large publishing houses were speaking of bringing out editions of selected works, and the leadership of the Writers' Union was said to have voted unanimously for allowing the full text of *Gulag* to be published in the Soviet Union. And thus, despite restrictions and prohibitions the works of Aleksandr Solzhenitsyn began to return to the country for which they were always intended.

WORKS

The study of Solzhenitsyn's works presents certain methodological difficulties. The most fundamental one concerns the textual corpus itself. From 1978 onward Solzhenitsyn oversaw the publication of the authorized *Sobranie sochinenii* (Collected works)[1], but the texts issued in this series often diverge from earlier editions, at times in significant ways. To mention only the most notable examples, *August 1914* grew to almost twice the length of the version published in 1971, *The First Circle* features a completely different plot line in its 1978 edition, and the authorized versions of key works like *One Day* and "Matryona's Home," which were both published in *Novyi mir,* contain passages that could not have appeared on the pages of a Soviet journal in the 1960's.

Some of these changes are simply restorations of texts that had earlier been cut or "toned down" by the author himself as a way of accommodating—or anticipating—the demands of Soviet censorship, others reflect later emendations, still others exhibit a mixture of the two. Any scholarly study should take these variants into account, and there is the further consideration that the extant critical literature is largely based on the earlier editions and could in some cases be textually unsound.

The problem is unfortunately compounded for readers who know no Russian, since beyond the fact that most translators worked with Russian texts that became superseded in the late 1970's and 1980's, the various translated renditions are frequently inadequate, and some contain an inadmissable number of errors.

One other aspect of tangled textual history of Solzhenitsyn's works deserves mention here. The sequence in which Solzhenitsyn's works first appeared in print did not at all correspond to the order in which they were written. The actual chronology became known only later, well after the launching of some spurious notions about the evolution of his thought. Due to the political furor surrounding Solzhenitsyn's name in the 1960's and 1970's, the writer was the subject of much hasty theorizing based on incomplete and erroneous data.

Any approach to Solzhenitsyn must also take into account the literary tradition to which he belongs, since the Russian writer relies on certain assumptions that may not always be familiar to Western readers. Chief among these is the view that literature must not withdraw from the world in quest of aesthetic purity. Together with such predecessors as Tolstoy, Dostoevsky, and Turgenev, Solzhenitsyn believed that the writer must confront issues of great social concern, even if this means coming into conflict with fashionable views or reigning ideologies. In fact it is the writer's moral duty to speak out on such questions, because his special gift of insight gives him the power to discern aspects of reality inaccessible to others. It is unnatural for literature to be artificially separated from the pains and worries of the world.

For the same reason, the Russian literary tradition also rejects any preconceived restriction on what constitutes appropriate form. This point was best articulated by Tolstoy in remarks defending the unusual structure of *War and Peace.* Writing in 1868, Tolstoy claimed that in all of Russian literature "there is not a single artistic prose work, rising at all above mediocrity, which quite fits into the form of a novel, epic, or short story" (*L. N. Tolstoi o literature* [Moscow, 1955], p. 115).

Solzhenitsyn had a similarly unorthodox view of genre conventions, and his prose gravitated toward autobiographical, historical, and

[1] Page references will be to this edition (abbreviated *SS* for *Sobranie sochinenii*) except for items that Solzhenitsyn did not include in the Collected Works series. All translations are by present author.

other nonfictional modes. At the same time those of his works that would seem to be "nonfictional" by design—*The Gulag Archipelago* and *The Oak and the Calf*—were conceived in terms usually associated with aesthetic goals. Such a deliberate confluence of art and reality was a central feature of Solzhenitsyn's writing. Although it had obvious roots in the Russian nineteenth-century tradition, Solzhenitsyn carried it to greater lengths than his predecessors, perplexing critics used to seeing their fiction and nonfiction served in separate, conventionally shaped containers.

Early Works

The earliest work by Solzhenitsyn that has so far appeared in print is *Prussian Nights,* a 1,200-line narrative poem composed in labor camp in 1950. Driving, breathless rhythms usher in a description of the Red Army's tumultuous advance into East Prussia in early 1945, then accompany the portrayal of the looting, arson, rape, and murder that was visited upon the local civilian population with the tacit approval of the Soviet high command.

In *Prussian Nights* the writer traces and effectively dramatizes the painful birth of moral awareness in the first-person narrator who is a witness and participant of these events. At the outset of the poem the narrative voice is not individualized, and we are aware only of the undifferentiated mass of soldiers carried away by their cruelly cheerful savagery ("Let's torch those houses, lads!" [*Prusskie nochi,* p. 7]). Only gradually does a narrator with a separate consciousness emerge, an officer who has deliberately chosen to be an uninvolved observer ("like Pilate" [p. 15]) amid the chaos and destruction that swirl around him. But as the poem progresses, the focus shifts to the growing discord in his mind. He becomes an increasingly willing participant in the injustices committed on all sides, yielding to instincts of greed and sensuality, and drowning out the reproving voice of conscience he makes appeal to

facile slogans like "carpe diem" (p. 55). This is not a solution, however, and the dissonance reaches a crescendo in two episodes that form the heart of the narrative. In the first of these, the narrator is shocked to find himself indirectly responsible for a wanton murder he should have, and easily could have, prevented. Shortly thereafter he sets in motion a squalid plan to trap a timid and quietly attractive German woman into having sex with him. The moral ugliness of this act is manifested with searing force as the narrator dwells on the contrast between his own rapacious yet cowardly scheme and the woman's poignantly meek resignation. His revulsion at himself and the moral awakening to which it leads anticipates the intense focus on ethical values that marks all of Solzhenitsyn's subsequent writings.

After the narrative poem, Solzhenitsyn turned to the genre of the drama, and in the next four years composed a trilogy with the collective title *1945.* It consists of *Victory Celebrations,* a verse play labelled a "comedy" by the author and committed to memory in 1951, *Prisoners,* a play identified as a "tragedy" and containing a mixture of prose and verse (also composed in camp in 1952), and the prose drama *Respublika truda* (completed in exile in 1954).

Technically and stylistically, the plays document the writer's experimentation with literary forms that would best serve as vehicles for expressing his thought, among other things reflecting his distinct movement toward prose. Thematically, the plays exhibit numerous motifs elaborated in the writer's later work. A strong autobiographical basis is evident throughout, with the setting and time in each play related fairly closely to Solzhenitsyn's actual experiences in 1945: a banquet on newly overrun East Prussian territory (*Victory Celebrations*), eye-opening conversations among inmates of a jail operated by Soviet counterintelligence (*Prisoners*), and the abysmally corrupt environment of a labor camp (*Respublika truda*). All three plays also feature an important character who is clearly meant as a version of the real Solzhenitsyn. A conscientious and well-meaning individual, this character is depicted as naively unfamiliar with the new realities he needs to face. But he is also a man determined to learn, and, like later autobiographical heroes of Solzhenitsyn's, a stubborn seeker after truth.

The understandably bitter tone of these early plays is to some extent suggested by their titles. *Victory Celebrations* ostensibly takes its name from a lavish banquet organized to mark a Soviet military victory, yet the battle-hardened veterans who gather there are easily cowed by the insinuating remarks of a rookie officer from SMERSH (the Soviet counterespionage service). Solzhenitsyn is sarcastically pointing out who the true victors are. *Prisoners* is more bitter still, since the incarcerated men in this play have no inhibitions about speaking their minds, and we are treated to a series of devastating critiques of the Soviet regime and of communist ideology. The title also draws attention to the paradox that the majority of the prisoners are actually much freer—intellectually, psychologically, and spiritually—than their ideology-bound captors. The title *Respublika truda* (Republic of Labor), finally, refers ironically to the contrast between the professed goals of the forced-labor camps and their grossly inefficient, graft-ridden, and murderous reality.

While it is probably fair to say that the dramatic trilogy does not measure up to the standards of literary excellence achieved in Solzhenitsyn's later prose, it exhibits considerable flair as well as some very inventive language. But perhaps the trilogy's greatest significance was in serving as a sort of workshop in which Solzhenitsyn could test ideas and images on which he then drew later. One obvious continuity involves characters from the trilogy who resurface under the same or a similar name in a work of prose. Thus Gleb Nerzhin, the author's *porte parole* in the novel *The First Circle,* had made earlier appearances in both *Victory Celebrations* and *Respublika*

truda. And Lev Rubin, the voluble true believer in communism ever at odds with himself and perhaps the most interesting character in *The First Circle,* has a virtually identical predecessor by the same name in *Prisoners.* But the most surprising migratory figure of this kind is Georgi Vorotyntsev, formerly a colonel in the Imperial Russian Army, who is sentenced to death in the soviet jail depicted in *Prisoners.* Since this is clearly the same character who emerges as a central figure in *August 1914* (written almost two decades later) and then reappears in its sequels, we here get an inkling of the complex interrelationships in Solzhenitsyn's vast artistic world.

In 1955 Solzhenitsyn began work on his first novel, *The First Circle,* a text that underwent several revisions, with the definitive ninety-six-chapter version published only in 1978. All the translations into Western languages, however, are based on a substantially different version containing eighty-seven chapters and published in the West in 1968. This odd state of affairs is the result of rapidly changing official attitudes toward Solzhenitsyn in the mid 1960's. In 1962 the novel (in its ninety-six-chapter form) was considered complete by the author, but Solzhenitsyn was then still an obscure physics teacher who could not seriously contemplate publication of his work. Facing an entirely new situation after the appearance of *One Day,* Solzhenitsyn decided that the novel could be made publishable by cutting and altering certain sections that were too politically explosive to appear in a Soviet journal. The result of this pruning and "softening" was an eighty-seven-chapter version of *The First Circle* that was accepted for publication by the editors of *Novyi mir* in 1964, but blocked by the censors. After some further emendations, Solzhenitsyn released this text for publication abroad, where it appeared in 1968. The ninety-six-chapter version, published ten years later in the *Sobranie sochinenii,* basically restores the 1962 text, but also introduces an unknown number of further changes. The complex textual history of the novel thus spans twenty-three years.

The First Circle is based on Solzhenitsyn's experiences during the three years he spent in the prison research institute on the outskirts of Moscow. The title is drawn from Dante's *Inferno,* in which the various circles of hell are enumerated and described. In Dante's scheme the first circle is the region of hell where one finds the souls of virtuous pagans and others who do not deserve the punishment meted out to ordinary sinners. Solzhenitsyn is suggesting an analogy between Dante's idea of a "privileged" section of hell and the special status of the *sharashka* within the Soviet penal system. (Inmates are not forced to engage in physical labor, they are fed reasonably well, and have access to books.)

An enormous cast of characters and a complex narrative structure containing subplots and flashbacks serve two principal goals. The first is to dramatize the quest for moral criteria undertaken by Gleb Nerzhin, an inmate with obvious similarity to Solzhenitsyn himself, as he struggles to find his bearings amid conflicting ideologies and ethical quandaries. The second goal, linked at many levels to the first, is to depict the moral climate of a cross-section of Soviet society during the period of "high Stalinism" (the action is set in late 1949).

The plot connecting these two thematic axes shows substantial differences between the "softened" eighty-seven-chapter version of the novel and the "restored" ninety-six-chapter redaction. In the version familiar from existing translations, a Soviet diplomat named Innokenti Volodin tries to warn a doctor acquaintance against sharing a sample of a Soviet experimental drug with French colleagues at a medical convention: in the paranoid atmosphere of the late 1940's this would be construed as an act of treason. The doctor's telephone is tapped, Volodin's call is recorded, and the hunt for the caller in due course involves the inmates of the *sharashka,* whose work on a voice scrambler gives them some

expertise in voice analysis. In this redaction Volodin's call is motivated by pity, and the psychological background that leads to this act is not elucidated at great length. Since the act is primarily an impulse of simple human decency, perhaps no great build-up is required.

The situation is very different in the ninety-six-chapter version. Volodin here telephones the American Embassy in Moscow to warn of an impending Soviet espionage operation involving nuclear bomb technology. Several chapters in this redaction are accordingly devoted to tracing Volodin's evolution from a privileged and jaded servant of the Soviet regime to an active opponent who is sufficiently moved by hatred of the system to try to foil Stalin's plans of acquiring weapons of mass destruction.

We know from the published memoirs of Lev Kopelev, Solzhenitsyn's fellow inmate in the *sharashka,* that a call to the U.S. Embassy of the type described by Solzhenitsyn did in fact take place, although the personality of the diplomat involved seems to have been quite different. One must assume that the Volodin of the novel gives voice to the author's own disgust at the devastation visited upon the Russian countryside by Soviet policies, and at the string of cynical deceptions that have marked the regime's behavior from the beginning. In this connection one should add that Solzhenitsyn also drew on his own experience in depicting Volodin's initiation into the prison system (shown in both versions of the novel).

Although there are further interesting differences between the two versions of *The First Circle,* the core chapters detailing the complex interrelationships among the prisoners of the *sharashka* are essentially the same in both. Center stage is occupied by Nerzhin and his two fellow inmates, the proud and brilliant elitist Dmitri Sologdin and his ideological antipode, the engaging communist true believer, Lev Rubin. To the extent that Nerzhin is a fictionalized portrayal of Solzhenitsyn himself, Rubin and Sologdin are also based on the real-life prototypes, Lev Kopelev and Dimitri Panin. Both these men wrote memoirs describing their stay in the *sharashka* and their friendship with Solzhenitsyn, thus providing a unique insight into Solzhenitsyn's manner of creating literary worlds from actual experience.

Nerzhin's stance vis-à-vis his two strong-minded friends is one of skeptical independence and committed eclecticism. He learns a great deal from both but refuses to accept their ideological premises. And he is constantly open to insights from other quarters, including such unlikely individuals as the humble, barely literate, but steadfast janitor.

The novel sweeps outward from this central core, pursuing various links between the men inside the *sharashka* and the world outside its walls, and we have the opportunity to glimpse the life of a wide range of Soviet citizens, from impoverished graduate students to members of the elite. We are also given a detailed portrait of Stalin. The aging tyrant is shown as the supreme jailmaster of a system in which he is paradoxically the ultimate prisoner. The ninety-six-chapter version dwells at some length on the suspicion long held by a number of historians that Stalin had been a paid police informer in tsarist Russia.

One interesting aspect of *The First Circle* is the constant attention that is given to the problem of communication in all its forms. Language itself is a theme, and one notes the curious way in which language is shown to resist rational analysis. The inmates of the *sharashka* are hard at work on the design of a voice scrambler (but they have not gotten very far), and they are studying the acoustic features of human speech (but are only beginning to scratch the surface of the subject). Sologdin strains to invent new lexical items so as to avoid using words of foreign origin. (The result is awkward and unintentionally funny.) Rubin struggles to confirm Marxist theory through comparative etymology. (The idea is far-fetched and entirely unpersuasive.) And Stalin labors as hard as his failing mind permits to produce an essay on language. (It is hopelessly muddled.)

But the principal focus is on communications that have been disrupted by force or ideology. Examples are too numerous to list, but the categories include rules forbidding or restricting normal human contact, lies of every description, and ideologically induced false decoding of information. A brilliantly sardonic play on all of these themes is "Buddha's Smile," a chapter presented as a tongue-in-cheek oral account of a mythical visit by Mrs. Roosevelt (referred to as "Mrs. R." in the eighty-seven-chapter version) to a Moscow prison. Everyone in this fable fulfills his role to perfection: the jailers with their preposterously elaborate plan based on the suppression of all truth about the prison and its inmates, the prisoners reduced to naive docility by their utter lack of information about the proceedings, and the visitors in their blind eagerness to believe the Soviet lies. In this instance the lack of communication is of course caricatured, and the theme is more typically presented in bitter and tragic terms.

The First Circle was the first of Solzhenitsyn's works to feature what he called the "polyphonic" principle of construction. (Although the term itself was drawn from the writings of the literary scholar Mikhail Bakhtin, in Solzhenitsyn's usage it refers only to a particular compositional device; certain critics to the contrary, no further link can be demonstrated to the complex theories associated with Bakhtin's name.) As the author defined it, this principle is a means to assure that "each character, as soon as the plot touches him, becomes the main hero" (quoted in Michael Scammell, *Solzhenitsyn*, p. 582). The effect is achieved by shifting the point of view while formally preserving the third-person narrative. In a given section of text (usually a chapter) we become privy to the unuttered thoughts of one particular protagonist, together with his or her subjective vision of the world. In technical terms Solzhenitsyn offers a montage of "authorial" third-person narrative interspersed with interior monologue. It is a remarkably powerful tool for characterization, and in *The First Circle* it is used with great effect to render psychological portraits of Volodin, Rubin, Stalin, and many others. In this connection it is useful to recall that the earliest redaction of the ninety-six-chapter version of the novel was completed in 1957, and that *The First Circle* was thus the first major work undertaken by Solzhenitsyn after the completion of his dramatic trilogy. It therefore seems legitimate to postulate a continuity between the polyphonic method and the dramatic form, with each character in the prose work allowed the equivalent of a chance to deliver a dramatic monologue from center stage.

In the late 1950's and early 1960's Solzhenitsyn turned to short prose, with the most important work from this period being *One Day in the Life of Ivan Denisovich.* Written in 1959, *One Day* demonstrates the method of subjective third-person narrative developed in *The First Circle* but here applied to only one individual, Ivan Denisovich Shukhov. He is a man of peasant origin and no formal education who is currently being held in a Soviet forced-labor camp on the charge of having spied for the Germans. (In reality he has simply escaped from a German POW camp.) The story traces the events of a single day from Shukhov's perspective, beginning with the moment he emerges from sleep at the sound of camp reveille, and ending as he retires to his bunk at night. Nothing particularly dramatic occurs in between these times, and nothing, in fact, is capable of disrupting the relentless camp routine that makes every day alike. But the low-keyed narrative serves only to increase the impact, for the story shocks by understatement, as for example in Shukhov's closing thought that the day just past had been an "almost happy one" (*SS,* vol. 3, p. 120).

A philosophical issue of some import is involved here. Solzhenitsyn's narrator faces the flagrant injustices perpetrated by the camp system without retreating into despair or otherwise giving voice to the alleged meaninglessness of the world that one might expect from a modern work on this theme. Instead of that Shukhov—tough and wily survivor though he is—retains an indestructible sense of moral perspective that informs all his actions. He is, to begin with, stubbornly unreconciled to victimhood, and not for a moment is he deceived about the true essence of the system that has incarcerated him. As a result he never hesitates to cheat the authorities if he can do so without great risk, while at the same time maintaining completely honest dealings with fellow prisoners. He appreciates and respects manifestations of human goodness, as in the case of a pious Baptist prisoner, but he is not ready to accept this creed or anyone else's. Shukhov's guiding principle here and throughout the story is the desire to protect his independence. This also explains why he insists on clinging to certain mannerisms that have no practical importance in a camp, such as making a point of removing his hat during meals.

Other manifestations of this spirit, however, have very explicit significance. Perhaps the most interesting example is the celebrated episode where Shukhov is building a brick wall together with other members of his work brigade. Almost despite themselves, the men begin to put forth their best effort, and Shukhov becomes so caught up in the process that he risks punishment to finish laying a row of bricks after quitting time. Although it is late, he steps back to admire his handiwork: "It was fine. He ran up to take a look over the top of the wall, glancing right and left. Ah, his eye was as true as a level! The wall was perfectly even, his hands had not yet lost their touch!" (*SS,* vol.3, p. 77).

Nikita Khrushchev is said to have admired this scene greatly (thus facilitating the printing of *One Day*), presumably because he believed it to reflect "labor enthusiasm" of the type routinely offered in works of socialist realism. As the above quote makes clear, however, Shukhov is moved not by the desire to contribute to a collective project, but by the need to assert his continuing worth as an individual human being. It is one of the ways in which he resists being reduced to a faceless slave.

Of Solzhenitsyn's other short prose works, the best known by far is "Matryona's Home." Written in 1959, the story is described by Solzhenitsyn as "completely autobiographical and authentic" in that it presents a true account of the writer's stay in the village of Miltsevo in 1956–1957. Since this work is also considered by a number of commentators to be Solzhenitsyn's most perfect literary creation, "Matryona's Home" is a particularly instructive example of the way "art" is not equated to "fiction" by writers of the Russian literary tradition. No necessary link is seen between literary craftsmanship and invention per se; artistry is demonstrated, rather, by the writer's skill in selecting, shaping, and presenting the data of reality within a coherent structure, and by the ability to perceive patterns and analogies.

"Matryona's Home" manifests these principles in many ways, and the opening passage is a good example. We are told in the very first sentence that trains used to slow down at a certain point "for a good six months after it happened" (*SS*, vol. 3, p. 123). What the "it" refers to here is not explained until midway through the story, and the comment lingers in our memory as a troubling and unresolved note. When we eventually do learn that Matryona was killed in an accident at a railroad crossing, the earlier comment takes on the resonance of foreknowledge. The impact of the work is produced by an accumulation of such details of organization.

The story also exhibits a thematic pattern that is repeated frequently in Solzhenitsyn's writings. This is the motif of a quest or mission that ends in failure, but during which something more valuable is acquired by virtue of defeat. In the case of "Matryona's Home," the first-person narrator emerges from his compulsory stay in Central Asia full of yearning for the elusive quality he associates with traditional Russia ("I wanted to efface myself, to lose my-

self in deepest Russia—if it was still anywhere to be found" [p. 123]). But the superficial trappings of this entity do not result in satisfaction: a beautiful village with a melodious name turns out to be unfit for habitation, the landscape of "deepest Russia" is scarred and disfigured by industrial blight, a handsome and dignified village elder is a monster of greed behind his imposing appearance, and the traditional funeral laments performed by the villagers after Matryona's death serve as a convenient front for perpetuating mean-spirited quarrels and jealousies. The ideal Russia the narrator has been seeking so assiduously seems nowhere to be found. Only at the end of the story does he realize, in a flash of illumination, that the qualities he has been looking for have no visible "ethnographic" form: they are moral, spiritual, and transcendent, and they were incarnated in the humble, selfless, and ever-suffering Matryona. She was that "righteous one without whom, as the proverb says, no village can stand" (p. 159).

A similar twist occurs in "Sluchai na stantsii Kochetovka" ("Incident at Krechetovka Station," 1963; the place name was changed from "Krechetovka" to "Kochetovka" in *Sobranie sochinenii*, with the latter form corresponding to a real geographical location). The protagonist in this story, Lieutenant Zotov, is a well-meaning and fundamentally decent man who earnestly desires to understand the precepts of Marxism-Leninism as he tries to subordinate his life to these principles. As a result he uncritically accepts propaganda clichés about the need to be "ever vigilant" against lurking enemy agents and saboteurs, and commits the irreparable blunder of turning over a completely innocent man to the NKVD. (This is a recently drafted actor separated from his unit by the chaos of war.) But even as he lures the alleged infiltrator into the guardroom by a false promise of food—a deceptive little play staged to trap an actor who does not suspect the role he has been assigned—Zotov is stung by the perversity of his own behavior. But the deed cannot be undone, and when Zotov's growing guilt feelings eventually prompt him to inquire about the man he has had arrested, he is more troubled than ever to receive a reply in which the actor's name is badly garbled, followed immediately by the assurance that "we [that is, the NKVD] never make mistakes" (*SS,* vol. 3, p. 255).

This grimly ironic punchline precedes the closing sentence of the story, where we learn of Zotov's inability to drive the painful memory of this incident from his mind "for the rest of his life." The clear implication is that Zotov has failed in his attempt to think and act in terms of orthodox Marxism-Leninism. He has been "corrupted" by having recognized the unbridgeable gap between moral reality and ideological cliché. But this failure is of course a victory in human terms, and the unremitting pain of remorse that Zotov experiences is the assurance of a permanently awakened conscience.

Mention must also be made of Solzhenitsyn's series of seventeen brief sketches written in 1958–1960. The author referred to them collectively as "Krokhotki" (miniature stories) and also characterized them as "poems in prose." The latter designation seems to fit particularly well, since apart from the extreme brevity of these texts (the length ranges from slightly more than a page down to a dozen lines), they exhibit meticulous attention to rhythmic structure, and resemble contemplative poetry in their manner of deriving broad philosophical statements from a single episode or observation. Many of the themes touched upon are familiar from other works of Solzhenitsyn's: a marked distaste for modern secular and mechanical civilization, a love of nature and a particular attachment to the Russian rural landscape, and an acute distress at the desecration of the Russian land by its current masters. At the same time Solzhenitsyn's vision of the past is by no means idyllic. Thus the narrator wanders through a wretched village where the peasant poet Sergei Esenin (1895–1925) had spent his childhood, and reflects on the mystery of the "divine fire" that had come down upon the poet, enabling him to recognize beauty in these depressing surroundings (*SS,* vol. 3, p. 177). And in another piece he broods mournfully about the mute human cost that stands behind the spectacular beauties of St. Petersburg (p. 172).

Other works of short prose include "Pravaia kist'" ("The Right Hand," 1968), another story with a pointed reversal in the ending, "Dlia pol'zy dela" ("For the Good of the Cause," 1963), a longish tale that Solzhenitsyn himself does not consider particularly successful, "Zakhar-Kalita" ("Zakhar-the-Pouch," 1966), about the selfless keeper of a monument on a Russian battlefield, and "Paskhal'nyi krestnyi khod" ("The Easter Procession," 1969), a wrathful denunciation of the barely human mob of gawkers who surround a Russian Orthodox church during the Easter midnight service.

Solzhenitsyn's second major work, *Cancer Ward,* was produced in the years 1963–1966. Although the book is more than 500 pages long, the author insisted on designating it a "tale" (*povest'*) rather than a novel (*roman*), arguing that the latter must treat a larger number of characters in more depth. (*The First Circle* is the only one of Solzhenitsyn's works to which he referred as a novel.) The setting is a cancer clinic in Tashkent in early 1955, and the events described reflect many aspects of Solzhenitsyn's own treatment for an abdominal tumor under similar circumstances. The chief protagonist is Oleg Kostoglotov, a tough, prickly, and assertive former prisoner whose iconoclastic views on politics are matched by his lack of deference for accepted medical procedures.

Beyond the hospital grounds, meanwhile, the attempts of the party leadership to distance itself from the Stalinist legacy are sending shock waves through the system. As this information filters into the ward, Kostoglotov is increasingly drawn into conflict with another patient, a self-important party functionary named Pavel Rusanov. The "Rusanov line" in *Cancer Ward* is quite substantial, with the first chapter describing Rusanov's arrival at the clinic (as seen from his perspective) and several others devoted largely or entirely to him and his relatives. Together with his articulate and aggressive daughter, Rusanov emerges as a sinister representative of the Stalinist past. This explicitly political strand in *Cancer Ward,* taken together with other sections in which political ideology is discussed at some length, led some critics to read the entire work as an allegory about figurative "cancers" on the Russian body politic. While some associations of this type are perfectly appropriate, since every significant work of art is capable of supporting a multitude of symbolic meanings, it would be a gross error to approach *Cancer Ward* on that level alone. The paramount focus of Solzhenitsyn's book is both simpler and more fundamental: it is the drama of human consciousness confronting death. Speaking more broadly, *Cancer Ward* explores the ways in which the proximity or threat of death tests the hierarchy of values that each person brings to the experience. Hence the debates on "ultimate questions" among the patients of the ward, debates in which ideological commitments naturally play a part, but in which most of these commitments offer no answer to the problem of mortality. Physical torment and the fear of death humbles them all alike—earnest Communists, cheerful cynics, grasping careerists, and committed hedonists—and there are moments when we can see even the despicable Rusanov as a suffering fellow human being.

Kostoglotov is the only person in the ward who tries to grapple with the philosophical issues involved. Throughout the text he holds to the belief that "survival at any price" cannot be a goal worthy of a human being. But this position (instinctively held by Ivan Denisovich) does not solve the question of just how high the price can go before it becomes unacceptable, since *some* degree of compromise is inevitable. (Thus Kostoglotov convinces a fearful teenager to go through with an amputation.) Kostoglotov's approach is to keep as well-informed as possible about the treatment he is receiving so as to be able to judge its potential negative effects. To the considerable annoyance of his doctors he tries to monitor their every move and is shocked to discover that the hormone shots that have been prescribed for him will wipe out his virility. Such a sacrifice appears entirely unreasonable to a man starved for feminine companionship after years of enforced bachelorhood—at the front, in prison camp, and in exile. Nor is the problem an academic one, since Kostoglotov is greatly attracted to Zoya, a lively young nurse, while at the same time falling in love with Vera, a high-minded and luminously feminine doctor in the clinic. Fate could not have been more cruel: just as he begins to recover from his primary affliction and as the two women respond positively to his advances, Kostoglotov has to face this new trial. It is a powerful reinforcement of the theme of inescapable physicality that runs through the book. Human beings are in a real sense prisoners of their bodies, and victims of an inscrutable fate.

Yet *Cancer Ward* does not end on this note. With great pain and uncertainty Kostoglotov gropes his way toward a means of overcoming the dark vision of ultimate hopelessness that would otherwise emerge from the text. He chooses the path of renunciation. In what are among the most memorable pages of the book, Kostoglotov decides to return directly to his place of exile upon his release from the hospital, rather than taking advantage of the invitation offered by Vera to stay over at her apartment. (Zoya had made a similar offer.) To depart is the only honest thing to do, he concludes, since he has been warned by the chief doctor that for physical reasons he should not contemplate marriage for some years. Spiritual and ethereal though Vera is, it would be unrealistic, and unfair to her, to place hopes in a purely platonic relationship. Kostoglotov's departure is therefore a conscious act of self-sacrifice, which, however, is not presented in terms of any mystical epiphany. On the contrary, the overwhelming cost of this renunciation is emphasized, but as a free expression of Kostoglotov's moral will it moves him beyond despair toward spiritual liberation.

The years in which this book was being written coincide with the most active phase of Solzhenitsyn's work on *The Gulag Archipelago,* and this proximity has left deep traces in *Cancer Ward.* Oleg Kostoglotov is a former *zek* (labor-camp prisoner), and all his views of life have been irreversibly affected by the harsh experience of life in extremis. This is presented as a mixed blessing at best: while Kostoglotov may have a clearer understanding than others of what really matters in life, the oppressive memories of his past pursue him like a curse, constantly reminding him of a life ruined by unmotivated evil. It is a motif that echoes, and merges with, the equally tragic theme of illness and mortality, reinforcing the somber vision which Kostoglotov struggles to overcome.

The Gulag Archipelago

Gulag: the word is as alien-sounding in Russian as it is in English. Solzhenitsyn combined this acronym, which stands for "Main Administration of Corrective-Labor Camps," with the metaphor of a chain of islands to produce his most famous work, a guided tour of the world of Soviet prisons and camps between 1918 and 1956. While the image of a large body of islands surrounded by sea has an obvious spatial analogy in the network of penal institutions dotting the map of the Soviet Union, the writer is also implying that the contrast between land and water is as great as that between the world of common experience and the special universe of Soviet prisons and camps. The "archipelago" seems to represent an entirely separate dimension of reality, a point that is stressed in the opening of part 1:

How does one get to this mysterious Archipelago? Not an hour goes by without airplanes taking off, ships putting out to sea, and trains rumbling away, all headed in that direction, yet not a single sign on any of them indicates their destination. Ticket agents or the employees of Soviet travel bureaus will be astonished if you ask them for a ticket there. They know nothing either of the Archipelago as a whole nor of any of its innumerable islands; they've never heard of it.

Those who are sent to run the Archipelago enter via the training schools of the Ministry of Internal Affairs.

Those who are sent to guard the Archipelago are inducted through the military conscription centers.

And those who are sent there to die—like you and me, dear reader—enter exclusively and necessarily through the procedure of arrest.

(*SS,* vol. 5, p. 15)

The mythical overtones are unmistakable, for the Archipelago is being compared to the nether world of classical literature: it is a space inaccessible to the ordinary traveller, invisible to common humanity, and, for the average person, attainable only via the ritual of arrest—the death of the former self. (One notes the continuity of this image with the vision of the Soviet penal system as hell that is reflected in the title of Solzhenitsyn's novel *The First Circle.*)

Yet to acknowledge the "otherness" of the Gulag universe, as Solzhenitsyn does here, is not to be reconciled with the deliberate policy of concealment that is associated with it, and the whole thrust of the book is in fact directed toward exposing the ugly secrets of this hidden world. For *The Gulag Archipelago* is above all an act of witness to the reality of the camp system, a monumental effort to reveal an entity the very existence of which had been strenuously denied for decades. To this end Solzhenitsyn marshalled the testimony of over 200 former *zeks,* drawing also on his own experience and on the available literature. Taken as a whole the book stands as an overwhelming "case" brought against the state—and the ideology—that nurtured a monstrous institution behind a facade of enforced silence and mendacious propaganda.

Yet Solzhenitsyn recognized that even a massive collaborative effort of this kind could not do justice to the dimensions of the human tragedy that needed to be brought to light. The subject is too vast even for the combined memories of the hundreds of witnesses that Solzhenitsyn assembled. Indeed, the writer was convinced that no conventional history of Soviet prisons and camps can ever be written, because too much documentary evidence was systematically destroyed, and too many of the victims were silenced forever.

It was in awareness of this problem that Solzhenitsyn turned to the method proclaimed in the subtitle of his work: *Opyt khudozhestvennogo issledovaniia (An Experiment in Literary Investigation*; an alternative translation of the subtitle might be: *Essay in artistic inquiry*). As the adjective in this phrase makes clear, Solzhenitsyn deliberately set out to enlist the devices of literary art in the service of a cognitive goal. To begin with, the narrative exhibits the literary craftsmanship of the author: it has the evocative power that only masterful prose can possess. But Solzhenitsyn's method involves the very specific further step of relying on aesthetic intuition to generalize from what the writer acknowledges to be an incomplete set of facts. Overarching metaphors and clusters of images provide a frame of reference for the events portrayed, thereby infusing seemingly disparate facts with significance. For example, Solzhenitsyn repeatedly likens the Gulag system to a sewer designed to accumulate, channel, and dispose of the "human refuse" that needs to be covertly drained from the surface of "Soviet reality" (part 1, chap. 2). Solzhenitsyn never pretended that this was more than a metaphor, yet it is one that tallies perfectly both with the degrading conditions in which *zeks* were routinely kept (the excremental theme is prominent throughout) and with the squeamish disdain that the authorities displayed toward the prisoners.

The Gulag Archipelago consists of seven parts divided into three volumes and totalling almost 1,800 pages. The text is a complex interweaving of historical exposition with individual case histories (including vividly presented episodes from Solzhenitsyn's own experience), everywhere interspersed with comments, exhortations, questions, and objections that are by turns ironic, bitter, despairing, or melancholy. This running commentary is the most striking stylistic feature of the book, since it assures that the material cannot be read in any "neutral" and detached manner.

Parody is one of the devices Solzhenitsyn uses here with great effect, as when he mimics the phraseology of a communist ideologue who would be expected to voice approval for acts of barbarity described in the text. For example, when a religious community is rounded up for not wishing to join a collective farm, and individual members try to flee from the rafts on which they are being transported to their place of exile, the convoy troops methodically machine-gun them all. The description of this episode ends with a mock exhortation: "Warriors of the Soviet Army! Tirelessly consolidate your combat training!" (*SS,* vol. 7, p. 368).

At other times the subversive edge of the commentary is turned against the author himself, setting up a sort of "interior dialogue" that turns expository prose into drama and demonstrates Solzhenitsyn's continuing affinity for the polyphonic mode. In part IV of *The Gulag Archipelago,* for example, the writer examines the moral and spiritual consequences of incarceration. The first chapter ends with the author making the paradoxical declaration that he is grateful to prison for opening his eyes to moral reality: "Bless you, prison, for having occurred in my life." But this seeming apotheosis is followed immediately by a radical qualification, delivered in sotto voce manner by being enclosed in parentheses: "(But from the burial pits I hear a response: 'It's very well for you to say that—you who've come through alive.')" (*SS,* vol. 6, p. 571).

The Gulag Archipelago is undoubtedly the least "acceptable" of Solzhenitsyn's books from the traditional Soviet point of view, and the reason is not difficult to identify, for Solzhenitsyn was not content to lay the blame for the Gulag system on Stalin alone. While he fully agreed that Stalin had presided over the "flowering" of the murderous system, he cited abundant evidence to show that the roots of the slave-labor empire—both institutionally and in terms of philosophical rationale—went back to the sacrosanct early years of the Revolution when Lenin was at the helm. Fierce intolerance was a central ingredient of Bolshevik ideology from the beginning, and Solzhenitsyn's work documents the inevitable way in which this trait became embodied in the laws and institutions of the new revolutionary regime. For this reason *The Gulag Archipelago* represents nothing less than an attack on the legitimacy of the entire Soviet system. In the words of George Kennan of March 1974, the book is "the greatest and most powerful single indictment of a political regime ever to be leveled in modern times" (quoted in Scammell, *Solzhenitsyn,* p. 878).

The Red Wheel

Solzhenitsyn stated repeatedly that he looked upon his writings on the camp theme as a fulfillment of a solemn moral obligation to the millions who disappeared forever into the abyss of the Gulag world. Immense as this responsibility was, the writer nevertheless regarded it as finite, and in *The Oak and the Calf* he spoke metaphorically of *The Gulag Archipelago* (and the works that preceded it) as a huge boulder that he was able to roll aside in order to get on with the "main task" of his life: a fundamental re-examination of the Russian Revolution.

The original conception for an epic cycle on the theme of the Revolution goes back to 1937, a time when the young Solzhenitsyn was brimming with Marxist enthusiasm. War, arrest, long years of imprisonment, and a near-fatal bout with cancer followed, all contributing to a radical change in Solzhenitsyn's views, but only increasing his desire to delve into the history of this fateful event. Even though he was able to give the subject a great deal of thought over the years (thus Gleb Nerzhin, the author's alter ego in *The First Circle,* compiles voluminous notes on Russian history), other concerns and obligations always seemed to take precedence, and it was only after the spring of 1968—when Solzhenitsyn received word that a microfilm of *The Gulag Archipelago* had been

safely carried across the border to the West—that he felt free to devote his full energy to this project.

The cycle is collectively called *Krasnoe koleso* (*The Red Wheel*) and subtitled *Povestvovanie v otmerennykh srokakh,* a phrase that was translated as "A Narrative in Discrete Periods of Time." As was also the case with the subtitle in *The Gulag Archipelago,* Solzhenitsyn's wording here points very explicitly to the method adopted by the writer in this particular work. The key principle involves rejecting any attempt to encompass the full sequence of historical events. Instead, Solzhenitsyn focused, in extraordinary detail, on relatively brief and sharply demarcated segments of historical time, making no effort to fill in the gaps between these discrete periods. The text allocated to each segment is referred to as a "knot" (*uzel*), a term taken from the mathematical concept of "nodal point," and meant to suggest a moment in history when the central issues of the day had become intertwined in a manner that offered a particularly clear view of the underlying conflicts which were nudging Russia toward the precipice.

The initial plan for the cycle envisaged twenty "knots," each with a separate title corresponding to the time frame covered. "Knot I" is named *August 1914,* and the two immediately following "knots" are *Oktiabr' shestnadtsatogo* (October 1916) and *Mart semnadtsatogo* (March 1917). (It should be noted that Solzhenitsyn's Russian titles refer to dates in the Julian calendar, used in Russia before 1918, which was thirteen days behind the calendar used in the West at this time.) "Knot XX" was to be set in the spring of 1922, and five epilogues were to bring the story up to 1945. This highly ambitious plan had to undergo considerable revision in the course of Solzhenitsyn's work. *August 1914* was first published in 1971, but after the author was expelled to the West in 1974 he came upon new data that begged to be inserted into his cycle, even though most of it predated the time frame of what he had announced to be his first installment. Solzhenitsyn's solution to this problem was to publish a much expanded version of *August 1914* with the title unchanged, but with the added materials prefaced by an internal title page that reads "From Previous Knots." With the starting point of his cycle thus pushed back considerably, and with the burgeoning size of the early "knots" (in *Sobranie sochinenii* edition, Knot I contains just under 1,000 pages, Knot II has almost 1,200, and Knot III has more than 2,800), Solzhenitsyn realized that he would have to cut off his narrative well before the end point he had originally aimed for. Indeed he decided to stop short even of the October Revolution, and according to a statement made in 1987, "Knot IV" (*Aprel' semnadtsatogo* [April 1917]) was to be the final installment in the cycle.

The Red Wheel, like *The Gulag Archipelago* before it, is a troublesome work to define in terms of genre, but the difficulty is here compounded by the substantial change in mode that seems to have occurred after the project had already gotten under way. Thus while the early version of *August 1914* (published in 1971 but reflecting plans conceived many years before) fits the general pattern of the historical novel, the expanded "knot" can no longer be easily accommodated within the novelistic tradition. This is so because the balance between fictional and historical aspects that held in the first edition is sharply altered in the direction of "pure history" by the addition of a 350-page-long insert with no fictional intent whatever. Even more telling is the fact that in the massive four-volume Knot III (published in 1986–1988), the fictional characters introduced in the earlier "knots" become virtually peripheral to the narrative. The general movement away from all fictional constructs and toward dramatized history could not have been more clearly indicated. It should be added that this shift is consistent with the approach stated in Solzhenitsyn's subtitle, for the unbridged gaps in time between the various "knots" are in fundamental conflict with the

literary demands of character development. Since the writer set himself the goal of tracing the ill-starred convolutions that had shaped twentieth-century Russian history, the focus of Solzhenitsyn's narrative is not on individual fates but on the greater tragedy that engulfed the entire nation.

In stylistic terms *The Red Wheel* exhibits the characteristic features developed in Solzhenitsyn's earlier work as well as a number of new literary devices. A prominent example of the former is the "polyphonic" technique (initially elaborated in *The First Circle*), whereby individual characters are given the opportunity to carry the narrative point of view in the section of the text where they are the principal actors. This device is used throughout Solzhenitsyn's historical cycle, with an entire chapter typically being given over to a particular character. In Knot III this creates an unexpected effect due to the extreme brevity of the chapters: the frequent shifts of perspective that result serve to accentuate the sense of disruption and chaos that is central to Solzhenitsyn's description of revolutionary turmoil.

Among the stylistic innovations in *The Red Wheel* the most significant is the manner in which the writer interspersed his prose with diverse materials that are visually set off from the main text: documents in boldface, historical retrospectives in 8-point font, collages of excerpts from the press of the time set in a variety of styles and sizes, "screen sequences" arranged in columns of brief phrases intended to mimic actual cinematic effects, and Russian proverbs printed entirely in capital letters.

The last-named item deserves a special word of explanation. Solzhenitsyn always had the highest regard for Russian proverbial expressions, admiring them as much for their verbal compactness as for their wry wisdom. (In *The Oak and the Calf* the writer relates how he regained composure in times of difficulty by reading collections of Russian folk sayings.) Proverbs appear as independent entries at the conclusion of some chapters in *The Red Wheel,* offering a succinct commentary on the preceding text. For example, at the end of a chapter where Solzhenitsyn describes the public reaction to the news that Prime Minister Stolypin had been seriously wounded in an assassination attempt, the writer gives us a long list of organizations and institutions that rushed to arrange special church services [*molebny*] to be offered for Stolypin's recovery. The bitter irony is that many of these same organizations had earlier been cool or hostile to Stolypin's valiant efforts to restore health and balance to the Russian body politic. The reproach is tersely summed up in the following saying: PRAYERS WERE OFFERED, BUT ALL TO NO PROFIT. (This translation attempts to render the partial rhyme of the Russian original: I MOLEBNY PETY, DA POL'ZY NETU [*SS*, vol. 12, p. 283].)

It is clear that proverbs have a privileged position among the many voices that make up Solzhenitsyn's work: they represent an authoritative "folk judgment," serving a function akin to that of the chorus in Greek tragedy. Together with the cinematic sequences, they provide evidence of the deep mark that the principles of drama have made on the writer's prose.

It should be added that all the proverbs cited by Solzhenitsyn are culled from the glossary of Vladimir Dal, a nineteenth-century lexicographer whose massive compilation of the Russian popular idiom was the writer's principal source and model in his campaign to revitalize the Russian language. It was Solzhenitsyn's belief that the ubiquitous ideological clichés that all too often typified Soviet speech and writing were both a cause and a symptom of the radical impoverishment of the Russian language: the rich linguistic legacy of the past was in danger of being lost forever, together with the nation's historical memory and cultural tradition. The damage could be undone, he believed, by reintroducing the half-forgotten lexical and syntactic structures that had been characteristic of peasant speech. And this was exactly what Solzhenitsyn attempted to do in

The Red Wheel, with results that caused considerable controversy among Russian readers, many of whom find this experimentation unpalatable.

The major thematic concerns of *The Red Wheel* are not difficult to identify. The central one involves the opposition of those individuals in whom a love of Russia prompts efforts to achieve constructive changes, to those who are blinded by ideology-induced hatred or obsessed by self-interest. In Knot I, the principal bearers of the positive impulse are two historical characters, Prime Minister Petr Stolypin and General Aleksandr Samsonov, commander of the Russian forces invading East Prussia in 1914. The assassination of the former by a revolutionary fanatic in 1911 and the betrayal of the latter by highly placed bunglers and cowards at the battle of Tannenberg are the two tragedies that make up the twin core of Knot I, and they become symbolic of the unreconcilable conflicts tearing Russia apart as well as of the ineluctable way in which the best people in the land seem doomed to fail or perish. The further we progress into the cycle, the less resistance there seems to remain to the surging forces of chaos and destruction, forces that Solzhenitsyn chose to associate with the image of a wheel rolling or rotating in an unnatural way. In one of the early screen sequences, a Prussian windmill is engulfed by flame during a battle, and the heat of the fire causes the vanes to begin turning, providing us with the first emblematic vision of a "red wheel":

The radial framework, glowing in red and gold,
   is turning mysteriously,
as though it were a fiery wheel rolling through the
   air.
And then it disintegrates,
crumbling into a shower
of blazing fragments.

                 (*SS*, vol. 11, p. 264)

The image is developed in another screen sequence, where a wheel tears loose from a field ambulance that is careening over a road littered with abandoned equipment:

The wheel rolls on by itself, overtaking the carriage.
It seems to grow bigger all the time,
and bigger still!
It fills the entire screen!
THE WHEEL!—rolls onward, lit by the
   conflagration,
unrestrained,
unstoppable,
crushing everything in its path.

(SS, vol. 11, p. 322)

The Revolution is seen as a similarly furious release of energy, at once spectacular, destructive—and self-destructive. Certainly this is Solzhenitsyn's view of the irresponsible political frenzy that preceded and accompanied the abdication of the tsar. It does not mean, however, that the lack of movement which is a central feature in the depiction of Nicholas is presented as a positive alternative. For Nicholas is shown to reside in what is almost a different plane of reality, a world of static calm barely in touch with the ever-quickening vortex forming around him. Indeed, the tsar seems to relate only to the orderly status quo, and is pathetically incapable of escaping the narrow roles prescribed by court tradition and family obligations. The portrait is at once generous and pitiless, and must be counted among Solzhenitsyn's greatest artistic achievements.

The vision of the tsar imprisoned in patterns of behavior above which he cannot seem to rise brings us to the unresolved—and unspoken— philosophical problem that is present just below the surface of the entire cycle: the issue of inevitability. Since Solzhenitsyn is depicting real events that he obviously deplores, he is at pains to note the many purely accidental occurrences which have contributed to the unfortunate outcome. Yet at the same time his descriptions are so compelling that it is not easy to imagine a result different from the one provided by history. If only the tsar had greater vision and more strength of will to resist psychological pressures, if only military head-

quarters could have been rid of certain bemedaled incompetents, if only. . . . Such sentiments fairly cry out from Solzhenitsyn's text, but the scrupulously historical intent of the narrative keeps the writer from indulging in any tempting fantasies. On the contrary, he uses his fictional apparatus to validate the actual sequence of events instead of exploring lost opportunities. Thus Colonel Vorotyntsev, the principal fictional character of *The Red Wheel* and a man of powerful will and luminous intelligence, in Knot II finds himself immobilized by a marital crisis, thereby echoing the psychological paralysis of the tsar. The tension between what did happen and what might have happened remains painfully clear to every reader, and it is perhaps this quality more than any other that energizes Solzhenitsyn's cycle and provides its tragic coloration.

It is always difficult to sort out the mass of conflicting judgments to which contemporary writers are subjected. Excessive proximity to a subject tends to obscure more than it reveals, and only historical distance allows us to distinguish the true proportions of literary phenomena. Thus few Russians living in the 1820's and 1830's could have guessed that this period in the country's cultural history would eventually come to be known as the Age of Pushkin. And certainly the pompous tsarist ministers who, together with sneering critics and high-society drones, had treated Pushkin with distrust and disdain, could never have imagined that they were destined to shrink in historical memory to their unsavory roles in the great poet's biography.

It is therefore too early to speculate whether the pattern might be repeated, and the decades that have echoed with raucous attacks on Aleksandr Solzhenitsyn's beliefs, credibility, and literary competence might yet be recorded as the Age of Solzhenitsyn.

The perspective of the early 1990's nevertheless permits us to say several things about the writer with a considerable degree of certainty. Aleksandr Solzhenitsyn was without question a major figure in the history of Russian literature. The most powerful talent in the field of Russian prose to emerge in the post–World War II period, Solzhenitsyn must also be regarded as the most formidable single adversary ever to confront the Soviet regime. For that reason he was also an immensely influential figure in the intellectual history of the twentieth century, a writer whose works (especially *The Gulag Archipelago*) modified the political climate in Western countries like France, and whose monumental *The Red Wheel* was clearly destined to affect Russia proper in an equally profound manner. It must also be emphasized that the writer's great impact cannot be dismissed as a fact irrelevant to literature, since the only source of his influence lay precisely in the eloquence of his writing and in the utter persuasiveness of the world he created—or re-created—for his readers. In an age when literature has frequently come to be viewed with cynical disinterest, the works of Aleksandr Solzhenitsyn testify to the explosive power of high art.

Selected Bibliography

EDITIONS

FIRST EDITIONS
PUBLISHED IN THE SOVIET UNION

"Odin den' Ivana Denisovicha." *Novyi mir* 11:9–74 (1962).

"Sluchai na stantsii Krechetovka." *Novyi mir* 1:9–42 (1963).

"Matrenin dvor." *Novyi mir* 1:42–63 (1963).

"Dlia pol'zy dela." *Novyi mir* 7:58–90 (1963).

"Zakhar-Kalita." *Novyi mir* 1:69–76 (1966).

FIRST MAJOR EDITIONS
PUBLISHED IN THE WEST

V kruge pervom. New York, 1968. (The eighty-seven-chapter version.)

Rakovyi korpus. London, 1968.

"Pravaia kist'." *Grani* (Frankfurt) 69: I–X (1968).

Svecha na vetru. Frankfurt, 1969. *Student: Zhurnal avangarda Sovetskoi literatury* (London) 11/12: 1–80 (1968), has marginal textual significance.

Olen' i shalashovka. London, 1969. (An earlier edition [1968] is textually corrupt.)

Avgust chetyrnadtsatogo. Paris, 1971. (The early version of Knot I of *Krasnoe koleso,* superseded by the much-enlarged edition of 1983 in the collected works.)

Arkhipelag GULag. 3 vols. Paris, 1973–1975.

Prusskie nochi. Paris, 1974.

Lenin v Tsiurikhe. Paris, 1975. (A compendium of the chapters dealing with Lenin and drawn from Knots I–IV of *Krasnoe koleso.*)

Bodalsia telenok s dubom. Paris, 1975.

Skvoz' chad. Paris, 1979. (A polemical addendum to *Bodalsia telenok s dubom.*)

COLLECTED WORKS

Sobranie sochinenii. Vermont and Paris, 1978–. (By 1989, eighteen volumes had been published. This edition contains the only complete and authorized texts of the works listed below.)

Vols. 1–2 (1978). *V kruge pervom.* (The ninety-six-chapter version.)

Vol. 3 (1978). *Rasskazy.* (Contains: "Odin den', " "Matrenin dvor," the prose "miniatures," "Pravaia kist'," "Sluchai na stantsii Kochetovka," "Dlia pol'zy dela," "Zakhar-Kalita," "Kak zhal'," "Paskhal'nyi krestnyi khod."

Vol. 4 (1979). *Rakovyi korpus.*

Vols. 5–7 (1980). *Arkhipelag GULag.* (A corrected and augmented version of the work first published in 1973–1975.)

Vol. 8 (1981). *P'esy i kinostsenarii.* (Contains: *Pir pobeditelei, Plenniki, Svecha na vetru, Respublika truda, Znaiut istinu tanki, Tuneiadets.*

Vol. 9 (1981). *Publitsistika: Stat'i i rechi.*

Vol. 10 (1983). *Publitsistika: Obshchestvennye zaiavleniia, interv'iu, presskonferentsii.*

Vols. 11–12 (1983). *Avgust chetyrnadtsatogo.* (This is the expanded version of Knot I of *Krasnoe koleso;* the earlier version was published in 1971.)

Vols. 13–14 (1984). *Oktiabr' shestnadtsatogo.* (Knot II of *Krasnoe koleso*).

Vols. 15–18 (1986–1988). *Mart semnadtsatogo.* (Knot III of *Krasnoe koleso*).

TRANSLATIONS

Translations marked with an asterisk (*) are based on textually dated originals.

———. Knot I of *The Red Wheel.* Translated by

Harry T. Willetts. New York, 1989. [Translation of the enlarged Russian edition of 1983.]

August 1914.* Translated by Michael Glenny. New York, 1972. [Translation of the superseded Russian edition of 1971.]

The Cancer Ward. Translated by Rebecca Frank. New York, 1968.

Cancer Ward. 2 vols. Translated by Nicholas Bethell and David Burg. New York, 1969.

Candle in the Wind. Translated by Keith Armes. Minneapolis, 1973.

East & West. New York, 1980. (Contains the Nobel Lecture, the Harvard commencement address, *Letter to the Soviet Leaders,* and a 1979 BBC interview.)

*The First Circle.** Translated by Thomas Whitney, New York, 1968. (87 chapters).

————.* Translated by Michael Guybon. London, 1968. (87 chapters).

The Gulag Archipelago. Vol. 1* Translated by Thomas Whitney. New York, 1974.

————. Vol. 2* Translated by Thomas Whitney. New York, 1975.

————. Vol. 3* Translated by Harry T. Willetts. New York, 1978.

————.* Edited by Edward E. Ericson, Jr. New York, 1985. (A one-volume authorized abridgment of the above three volumes.)

Lenin in Zurich. Translated by Harry T. Willetts. New York, 1976.

*The Love-Girl and the Innocent.** Translated by Nicholas Bethell and David Burg. New York, 1969.

The Mortal Danger: How Misconceptions About Russia Imperil America. Translated by Michael Nicholson and Alexis Klimoff. New York, 1980; 2nd ed., New York, 1981. (The second edition contains Solzhenitsyn's lengthy reply to his critics.)

The Oak and the Calf. Translated by Harry T. Willetts. New York, 1979.

*One Day in the Life of Ivan Denisovich.** Translated by Max Hayward and Ronald Hingley. New York, 1963.

————.* Translated by Ralph Parker. New York, 1963.

————. Translated by Harry T. Willetts from the authorized text. New York, forthcoming.

Prussian Nights: A Poem. Translated by Robert Conquest. New York, 1977.

*Stories and Prose Poems.** Translated by Michael Glenny. New York, 1971. (Contains "Matryona's House," "For the Good of the Cause," "The Easter Procession," "Zakhar-the-Pouch," "An Incident at Krechetovka Station," and short prose poems.)

Victory Celebrations. Prisoners. The Love-Girl and the Innocent: Three Plays. Translated by Helen Rapp, Nancy Thomas, Nicholas Bethell, and David Burg. London, 1983; New York, 1986. (The translation of the third play is based on an outdated text.)

Warning to the West. New York, 1976. (Contains texts of speeches to the AFL-CIO, to the U.S. Congress, and to British television and radio audiences.)

A World Split Apart. Translated by Irina Alberti. New York, 1978. (The Harvard address.)

BIOGRAPHICAL AND CRITICAL STUDIES

"Avgust chetyrnadtsatogo" chitaiut na rodine. Paris, 1973. (A collection of Soviet samizdat reactions to the early edition of *August 1914.*)

Barker, Francis. *Solzhenitsyn: Politics and Form.* New York, 1977.

Berman, Ronald, ed. *Solzhenitsyn at Harvard: The Address, Twelve Early Responses, and Six Later Reflections.* Washington, 1980.

Carpovich, Vera. *Solzhenitsyn's Peculiar Vocabulary: Russian-English Glossary.* New York, 1976.

Dunlop, John B., et al., eds. *Aleksandr Solzhenitsyn: Critical Essays and Documentary Materials.* Enl. ed. New York, 1975.

Dunlop, John B., et al., eds. *Solzhenitsyn in Exile: Critical Essays and Documentary Materials.* Stanford, 1985.

Feuer, Kathryn, ed. *Solzhenitsyn: A Collection of Critical Essays.* Englewood Cliffs, N.J., 1976.

Gul', Roman Borisovich. *Solzhenitsyn: Stat'i.* New York, 1976.

Hegge, Per Emil. *Mellommann i Moskva.* Oslo, 1971.

Kopelev, Lev. *Ease My Sorrows.* Translated by Antonina W. Bouis. New York, 1983.

Labedz, Leopold, ed. *Solzhenitsyn: A Documentary Record.* 2d ed. Harmondsworth, 1973.

Lakshin, Vladimir. *Solzhenitsyn, Tvardovsky, and "Novy Mir".* Translated by Michael Glenny. Cambridge, Mass., 1980.

Markstein, Elisabeth, and Felix Philipp Ingold, eds. *Über Solschenizyn: Aufsätze, Berichte, Materialen.* Neuwied and Darmstadt, 1973.

Medvedev, Zhores. *Ten Years After Ivan Denisovich.* Translated by Hilary Sternberg. New York, 1974.

Moody, Christopher. *Solzhenitsyn.* Enl. ed. New York, 1976.

Nivat, Georges, and Michel Aucouturier, eds. *Soljénitsyne.* Paris, 1971.

Nivat, Georges, *Soljénitsyne.* Paris, 1980. (This French-language study is the best general introduction to Solzhenitsyn written to date. A Russian translation exists: *Solzhenitsyn.* Translated by Simon Markish. London, 1984.)

Nowikowa, Irene, ed. *Seminarbeiträge zum Werk Aleksandr Solženicyns.* Hamburg, 1972.

Ozerov, N. "Po povodu 'Pis'ma' Solzhenitsyna." *Russkaia mysl'* (Paris), 13 June 1974.

Panin, Dimitri. *The Notebooks of Sologdin.* Translated by John Moore. New York, 1976.

Reshetovskaia, N. *V spore so vremenem.* Moscow, 1975. Translated into English by Elena Ivanoff as *Sanya: My Life with Aleksandr Solzhenitsyn.* Indianapolis, 1975. (This memoir by Solzhenitsyn's first wife, and the equally, but somewhat differently, doctored English version, were co-authored [that is, rewritten] by the Soviet press agency Novosti.)

Scammell, Michael. *Solzhenitsyn: A Biography.* New York, 1984.

Solzhenitsyn: A Pictorial Autobiography. New York, 1974.

Vinokur, T. G. "O iazyke i stile povesti A. I. Solzhenitsyna 'Odin den' Ivana Denisovicha'." *Voprosy kul'tury rechi* (Moscow), 1965, no. 6, pp. 16–32.

BIBLIOGRAPHY

Fiene, Donald M. *Alexander Solzhenitsyn: An International Bibliography of Writings By and About Him.* Ann Arbor, 1973. (For bibliographic guides covering a later period, see the bibliographic sections in the two Dunlop volumes listed above.)

ALEXIS KLIMOFF

STENDHAL
(1783–1842)

LIFE

STENDHAL WAS BORN Henri Beyle. He assumed the most famous of his pseudonyms at the age of thirty-four after signing "Stendhal, cavalry officer" to his witty commentary *Rome, Naples, et Florence* (1817). The Germanic name Stendhal most likely refers to a small town in Brandenberg, where the French general he served as an aide-de-camp, General Michaud, won a minor victory. As a career expatriate and consul in intrigue-ridden Italy, Stendhal had an almost instinctual resistance to seeing his real name appear in cold, hard print. His egotistical legerdemain is astonishing. In his publications, journals, diaries, and correspondence, he coined over two hundred names for himself, some mentioned only once, others again and again; they range from the romantically recurrent Dominique to the lofty comte de Chablis to the bizarre William Crocodile to the downright absurd Polybe Love-Puff.

Near the beginning of his most important autobiographical work, *La vie de Henri Brulard* (*The Life of Henri Brulard*, 1834–1835; surname fabricated), Stendhal asks, "What eye can see itself?"[1] It is only sensible for an artist and autobiographer to try to stand outside himself and look in. When Stendhal did so, he inevitably saw double. His obsessive theme as a novelist and self-memorialist was the delicate relation between the ego and the other where, as often as not, the ego *was* the other. Stendhal's double selves circulate in a double world where actualities betray appearances, where irony turns upon desire, and where ennui levies a rent upon energy. His military career was more logistical than dashing; his amatory career more persistent than consummated; and his diplomatic career more leave time than official service. Stendhal managed to absorb into his multiple beings the elegant pretensions of pre-revolutionary France and the more bourgeois concerns of post-Napoleonic Europe.

Henri Beyle made his way to Paris at sixteen as a student of mathematics, but the plane geometrician soon became a dashing salon dandy. In a career spanning three decades, Stendhal was a would-be writer of comedies, a bureaucrat, an aide-de-camp in Napoleon's Italian army, a failed importer of foodstuffs, an ordnance official, a supply officer during Napoleon's invasion of Moscow, a plagiarist, a critic of music and art, a befuddled lover, a consular diplomat, an autobiographer, a travel writer, a historical commentator, a political journalist, a reviewer of his own and others' books, and a novelist of great scope, subtlety, and wit.

Marie-Henri Beyle was born into the upper bourgeoisie of Grenoble in 1783. His child-

---

[1] Quotations are from the English translations marked with asterisks in the bibliography.

hood was a lifelong bad memory for him; his subsequent career as man and writer reflects his extreme distaste for his local origins and his disdain for the provinces, "the country of barbarians." Henri's father was a well-to-do Grenoble lawyer; his mother, whom he loved to distraction but who died when he was seven, was the daughter of a prominent Grenoble physician, Dr. Henri Gagnon. Dr. Gagnon's own house was but a hundred yards from his son-in-law's, though he never set foot in the latter after his daughter's death. The two households were for the young Beyle rival territories—his father's offering him perpetual strain, his grandfather's perpetual delight.

In his father's home, Henri felt oppressed by the triple threat of his domestic guardians: he and Pauline, a sister to whom he was devoted, fended off a less than angelic father, oddly and inappropriately named Chérubin; another mock angel, Aunt Séraphie; and a devilish Jesuitical tutor, Abbé Raillane. As Stendhal laments in *Henri Brulard,* his hatred of Chérubin, Séraphie, and Abbé Raillane, especially after it became clear to him that his father and his aunt were lovers, "poisoned my childhood." He particularly resented the control exerted over him by those "three devils" in the name of religion, a control that made him detest God in direct relation to the degree that he had worshiped, with a deeply physical sense of deprivation, his dead mother. Idealization of the absent and scorn for the present mark a feature of Henri's youthful imagination that plays itself out fully in the older Stendhal's fiction.

Slightly removed in distance but vastly removed in tone from Chérubin Beyle's household was the rival trio of Dr. Henri Gagnon's family. Grandfather Gagnon, Uncle Romain Gagnon, and Great-aunt Elisabeth match Chérubin, Séraphie, and Abbé Raillane with a liberating vengeance. Dr. Gagnon was an enlightened patron, in contrast to the despotic and parsimonious Chérubin; Uncle Romain a grand libertine lover next to the narrow and hyprocritical Abbé Raillane; and Great-aunt Elisabeth an image of heroic nobility beside the vulgar and jealousy-ridden Séraphie. The transition from his father's house to his grandfather's held symbolic import for Stendhal all his life, providing what Michael Wood calls the option of "another road." Dr. Gagnon's home, in addition to its inhabitants, for whom Stendhal harbored unbounded admiration, contained a magnificent library. Young Henri was allowed to idle in it, read, and do what he preferred above all else—daydream. "My greatest pleasure is dreaming," Stendhal says in *Henri Brulard,* a pleasure he shared with all his admirable literary characters, and a pleasure he no doubt also shared with Jean Jacques Rousseau, whose *Confessions* he first read in his grandfather's library.

Stendhal's early years in Grenoble during the late 1780's and early 1790's coincide with the greater historical drama of the times, the French Revolution and its aftermath. Stendhal later recognized that even as a boy he had made the explicit connection between the injustice of his father's house and the absolutism of the ancien régime. Thus Stendhal's first taste of politics was colored by egocentrism, a tendency that would remain with him for the rest of his life and work itself through the biases of his fictional heroes. Young Henri was a Jacobin primarily because his father was a staunch royalist. The eerie joy with which Stendhal heard his father tearfully report the news of Louis XVI's execution had more domestic resonance than Chérubin might have wished. In *Henri Brulard,* Stendhal mentions how his own loose talk in Grenoble about his father's reactionary politics kept the household in fear that Chérubin would be arrested and perhaps even executed by the town's revolutionary officials. The more paranoid Chérubin and Séraphie grew, the more often young Henri would sneak out to Jacobin meetings, himself convinced that Séraphie had a network of domestic spies after him. In his novels Stendhal was maliciously fond of reimagining a series of father figures who sided violently with the royalist cause (with the exception of the crafty and accomplished Monsieur Leuwen). The thoroughly contemptible Monsieur de Rênal in *Le rouge et le noir* (*The Red and the Black*, 1830) and the absurdly reactionary marchese del Dongo in *La chartreuse de Parme* (*The Charterhouse of Parma*, 1839) have a good deal of Chérubin Beyle in them.

Stendhal's earliest ambitions were for an engineering career. His aptitude for mathematics, he thought, would allow him to escape Grenoble, whose mere mention, according to his own testimony, gave him lifelong indigestion. He found that, unlike his immediate family, mathematics "does not admit of hypocrisy." In 1799 Henri won admission to the École Polytechnique in Paris, but he never attended. Instead, with few prospects and dreary retrospects, he was taken in by his rich and influential cousin Pierre Daru, the minister of war, who gave him a civil service job in his ministry and entrée to the salon world of Paris, a world no longer reserved for blood aristocrats and their minions. Young Henri was driven by "the firm resolve to be a seducer of women, what I should nowadays call a Don Juan."

His resolve, unsuccessfully executed, carried him for barely a year, at which time Daru arranged for his young relative to be sent to Milan as aide-de-camp to General Michaud with a commission as second lieutenant. Stendhal's later attitude toward his new rank is touchingly ironic. When Julien Sorel of *The Red and the Black* enters the garrison town of Besançon to be educated as a cleric, he wants nothing so much as to abandon all such plans in favor of strutting the ramparts as a dandified second lieutenant. But when another of Stendhal's alter egos does precisely that in the garrison town of Nancy at the beginning of *Lucien Leuwen* (1834–1835), he ingloriously falls off his horse and dirties his splendid new uniform.

Stendhal soon became bored with his commission, though he loved Italy from the moment he crossed into it on horseback over the Alps. He was to identify the spirit of that land, in its best manifestations, with the passion, energy, and aesthetic flowering of the Renaissance. Stendhal's admiration for Italy extends even further back, to Etruscan and Roman times and "recalls us most movingly," as Robert M. Adams phrases it, "to the archaic lucidity of the early antique world, to its peculiar, wiry energy and utter lack of sentimentality." When Stendhal crossed the Alps he became what he would remain for the rest of his life, a trans-European, his head in France and his heart in Italy. Though intellectually nurtured by the French Enlightenment, Stendhal felt that his emotional responses were Italianate, "natural and simple." More important, he preferred Italy to France because he felt that his imagination became liberated there just as it had been freed earlier in his grandfather's library. His love of Italy was such that in his *Souvenirs d'égotisme* (*Memoirs of an Egotist*, written 1832) Stendhal imagined his epitaph, the sign of his last remains or the last of his remaining selves, in a manner no Frenchman is apt to do lightly. He gives up his French citizenship to a man with another name: "ERRICO BEYLE / MILANESE / *Visse, scrisse, amò / Quest'anima / Adorava / Cimarosa, Mozart, e Shakespeare / Mori de anni . . . / il . . .* 18—" (He lived, he wrote, he loved / This soul / Worshiped / Cimarosa, Mozart, and Shakespeare). Stendhal fails to mention the one Frenchman he might well have worshiped at least as well as the Italian, the Austrian, and the Englishman—Napoleon.

Stendhal remained in Italy for two years, resigning his commission in 1802 to return to Paris with the intent of launching a new career as a writer of verse comedies. But he could not finish a single play. Indeed, he would labor for days over one line. He complained that the "Castilian spirit" acquired from his great-aunt Elisabeth prevented him "from having the comic genius." Plagued by what Stendhal himself described as monumental laziness, he did little in Paris but attend the theater, taste the other pleasures of the town, and, as he remembers it in *Henri Brulard,* read as much as he could in order to form his mental character. He concentrated on the Enlightenment philosophers to whom his grandfather had exposed him, not only re-reading his beloved Montesquieu and Rousseau but steeping himself in Claude Adrien Helvétius, Étienne Bonnot de Condillac, and Antoine Destutt de Tracy. His allegiance to Destutt's *Ideology,* an argument for the rational-emotional psychology of human activity, became the cornerstone of what Stendhal later called "Beylism," a kind of logic of emotion where the crafty and the elegant pursue happiness with an observant eye and an open heart.

After three years of Parisian life and a surfeit of leisure, Stendhal followed his first mistress, an actress named Mélanie Guilbert (or Louason), to Marseilles, where she had a theatrical engagement. While there in 1805 he tried to turn a profit in the complicated and risky food import business, but ended up counting his losses instead. He separated from Mélanie and returned to Paris in 1806, again to the fold of Cousin Daru's patronage. Stendhal writes that Daru wished above all else to "remove him from vice." Daru set his young cousin up as commissioner of supplies in Brunswick, a position that led to a series of high posts over the next few years, culminating in the office of state auditor in the War Bureau and, in 1810, inspector of the crown buildings.

Stendhal's administrative career took the twists and turns one might expect during the latter days of the Napoleonic regime. In 1812 he traveled with Napoleon's army to Moscow as commissioner of war supplies. In a series of journal entries and many letters to his sister, to Countess Daru, and to friends, he records in brilliant detail the immense complications of supplying an invading army, the spectacle of Moscow's burning, the carousing and drunkenness of Napoleon's conquering troops, and, finally, the panic of the French retreat across the heartland of Russia in the dead of winter. Stendhal suffered the agonies of hunger and frostbite on the retreat, and, of course, the numbing horror experienced by those who witness human death and misery on a large scale. "I am going to be turned into a barbarian," he wrote, "a barbarian lost to the arts." When the retreat was over and Stendhal was recuperating in Germany, he could say: "I saved myself by force of will, for I saw many around me give up hope and perish."

With Napoleon and the remnants of his army back in Europe, Stendhal resumed his duties and eventually participated in the final preparations against the expected Allied invasion of Dauphiné province, one in a series of campaigns that led to the beginning of Napoleon's downfall. During these years of what he considered bureaucratic drudgery and fading military glory, Stendhal practiced what for him was a more notable and flourishing career as amatory campaigner and strategist of love. Behind the somber face and stocky torso of the bureaucrat beat the heart of an obsessed Lothario. With its forays, its tactics, and its intricately timed sieges, love was perhaps the closest parallel to what Stendhal conceived of as military heroism. For Stendhal, love was a timeless venture, a counter to boredom, a contest in the chivalric scheme of things. Though love was subject, like all else in his life and art, to bemused irony, it sustained him in the way it sustains the heroes of his novels.

In his youth Stendhal thought that as a lover he was more in the camp of Rousseau than of Don Juan—he proceeded with too emotional a sense of things to be sure of strategic success. Victor Brombert claims that love for Stendhal "assumes the proportions of a vast allegory of escape." This was still so in his later twenties when he tried to refine and focus his amatory technique in a flirtatious escapade with Countess Daru, his cousin's wife. Had this been anything but a high-flown titillation, it would have been curious repayment to Daru for all his help over the years.

On leave in Milan during 1811 Stendhal

practiced more assiduously the lessons he had learned many years before from his libertine uncle Romain. The first important, that is to say, well-born, woman upon whom Stendhal set or reset his sights was the experienced and beautiful Angela Pietragrua, whom he had met in 1800 during his first stay in Milan. Only eleven years later did he make his conquest, although Angela, a model for the fascinating and proud Sanseverina (Gina Pietranera) of *The Charterhouse of Parma,* said she would have capitulated earlier had the baffled young man merely asked.

After the fall of Napoleon and the restoration of the Bourbon monarchy in 1814, Stendhal added to his retirement pay a small annuity from his mother's family and settled in Milan as Angela Pietragrua's principal lover. Having little to do but avoid the suspicions of the Austrian police in Italy, he initiated his career as music critic, art connoisseur, and social commentator, publishing the largely plagiarized *Vies de Haydn, Mozart, et Métastase* (Lives of Haydn, Mozart, and Metastasio, 1815), an equally plagiarized two-volume *Histoire de la peinture en Italie* (History of Painting in Italy, 1817), and his important *Rome, Naples, et Florence* (1817), the last title admired by no less a luminary than Goethe, who delighted in Stendhal's commentary, even though its author had appropriated material from Goethe's own writings and attributed it to local sources.

In 1819 Stendhal's five-year affair with Angela ended tempestuously. He objected once too often to her string of other lovers. At the same time, he became deeply though hopelessly involved with the one woman in Milan who was to mean more to him than any other in his life, Mathilde Viscontini Dembowski, the estranged wife of a Polish army officer. An extraordinary beauty, she held Stendhal at agonizing distance and made life both miserable and exquisite for him. Mathilde is the implicit, if unmentioned, subject of Stendhal's 1822 treatise *De l'amour (On Love),* an anecdotal fantasia on the psychological features of *l'amour-passion* at the expense of bourgeois or conventional marriage. The document is written under the name of a young man, Visconti, who supposedly died in Volterra, the place where Stendhal's hopes for Madame Dembowski also died in 1821. Stendhal's pseudonym obviously assimilates part of Mathilde's name, Viscontini. Thus Stendhal becomes a version of the woman who obsessed him. Such a notion is made explicit in the marginal note Stendhal scribbled in *On Love* upon hearing of Mathilde's death in 1825: "Death of the author." As Stendhal puts it in *The Red and the Black,* "Every true passion thinks only of itself."

Stendhal's frustrating and frustrated pursuit of Mathilde, or Métilde, as he called her when he called her anything at all, was of such significance that he never tired of representing her in veiled and circumspect forms. She is the never named source for the author's despair in *Memoirs of an Egotist;* the primary model for the beautifully rendered legitimist widow Madame de Chasteller, in *Lucien Leuwen;* and even a sexually aroused parody of herself in a namesake, Mathilde de la Mole, in *The Red and the Black.* Stendhal displays considerable resourcefulness in reimagining the crucial relation of his life; his fictions offer a series of variations on what never actually happened.

In 1821, after seven years in Milan, terribly disappointed in love, and under suspicion by the Austrians for supposed radical activities, Stendhal returned to Paris. His father had died two years before in 1819, and Stendhal hoped to inherit enough money from his estate to sustain an idle life. But he received only a fraction of what he had counted on. Having held Chérubin Beyle responsible for his miserable childhood, Stendhal now held his father posthumously responsible for crippling his finances. It is at this time, as he recalls in *Memoirs of an Egotist,* that he contemplated assassinating the restored Bourbon king, Louis XVIII, and then shooting himself.

Things, however, were to get much better

for the despairing Stendhal. During the early and mid-1820's he became what Joseph Conrad was to dub his hero Martin Decoud of *Nostromo:* a cosmopolitan boulevardier. As correspondent for important English periodicals, including the *Paris Monthly* magazine, *London* magazine, and *Athenaeum,* Stendhal would make extended visits to England to sharpen his wits and enjoy the comforts of liaisons with artfully innocent whores. He frequented the great salons of Paris, especially those of Madame de Lafayette and Madame de Tracy. He took as his mistress Clémentine Curial, the married daughter of the comtesse Reugnot. By the mid-1820's he was thriving. He writes of his life: "I have been a wit since the winter of 1826; before that I was silent out of laziness."

Stendhal's most ambitious venture in this period was a two-part aesthetic treatise, *Racine et Shakespeare* (1823–1825), on the rigidities of classicism and the live currents of romanticism. Having made a case for romanticism and for the necessity of art to follow the dictates of the new, Stendhal turned in 1827 to the novel as the newest and most appropriate form for contemporary artistic expression. He produced a Parisian salon satire, *Armance* (1827), about an ennui-ridden aristocrat, Octave de Malivert, suffering from a hinted-at impotence. Since Octave's complaint seems almost indistinguishable from everyone else's in the narrative, Stendhal explained the specifics of his hero's malady in a letter to his friend Prosper Mérimée, in which he jokingly re-creates a night of love between Octave and his great love, Armance, in Marseilles: Octave is able to provide only what Stendhal calls "ecstasies of the hand." Armance, out of timidity and feminine shame, says nothing. In a marginal note to the novel, Stendhal responds to one of Octave's exclamations on the subject of love by having his hero derisively ask himself exactly how he plans to execute his desires. Later, in his *Memoirs of an Egotist,* Stendhal recalls rumors circulating in Paris about his own impotence after a partic-

ularly unfortunate failure in a Parisian brothel. Octave's complete dysfunction is a version of Stendhal's incidental one, though the real force of impotence in *Armance* is more cultural than clinical. If all this seems a strained idea for a satiric novel, it surely proved so in its realization.

Stendhal's Parisian interlude came to an end in 1830 after the July Revolution and the establishment of the monarchy under the supposedly liberal king Louis-Philippe. Named consul in Trieste, Stendhal was immediately rejected by the Austrians—again, they suspected his liberalism. He was demoted to a lesser post as consul at Cività-Vecchia in the Papal Dominions, a position he was to hold until his death in 1842. In Italy Stendhal renewed his literary and amatory careers with gusto. He proposed marriage to a young woman with whom he had been having an affair, one Countess Cini of Rome (Giulia Rinieri), but her guardian would have none of it; Stendhal's proposal was firmly rejected. An old hand by then at courtship and seduction, Stendhal was apparently less distraught at this turn of events than he might have been earlier.

The failure of the Cini romance was attended by the full flowering of his literary career in all its memorable greatness. "In the career of literature," writes Stendhal, "I still see a crowd of things to be done." The next nine years saw the completion of *The Red and the Black;* work on his autobiographical masterpieces, *Memoirs of an Egotist* and *The Life of Henri Brulard;* brilliant travel commentary in *Mémoires d'un touriste (Memoirs of a Tourist,* 1838) and its incomplete sequel, *Voyage dans le midi de la France (Travel in the South of France);* an unfinished life of Napoleon; a major unfinished novel of near masterpiece status, *Lucien Leuwen;* and a lesser incomplete effort, *Le rose et le vert (The Rose and the Green),* based on his short story "Mina de Vanghel," about an heiress searching in France to escape the boredom of her native Königsberg. In 1839 he finished his collection of stories, *Chroniques italiennes (Italian Chronicles);* published the last of his great novels, *The Charterhouse of Parma;* and, during an illness, worked on *Lamiel* (1840), the foundling heroine of which, after growing up to take and reject a series of aristocratic lovers, was to end up living with brigands in Normandy.

Always a master at parleying leave time into extended sojourns, Stendhal spent a good part of the years from 1836 until his death away from his post and outside Città-Vecchia. He died in Paris in March 1842 from a cerebral stroke, having been in France since the previous year recovering from an earlier stroke. Though he requested that his epitaph name him as Milanese, he died very much a Frenchman and a Parisian.

WORK

To understand Stendhal as a writer requires knowledge of his position in his own century; his admiration, bordering on worship, for Napoleon, whose spirit monopolized the times; his intellectual relation to Enlightenment thought; his stake in the romantic literary movement of the 1820's and 1830's; and his part in shaping the contours of the romantic-realist novel.

For Stendhal, the nineteenth century lacked passion. The radical exile Altamira says to Julien Sorel in *The Red and the Black:* "There's no real true passion left in the nineteenth century. That's why people get so bored in France. The greatest cruelties are committed, yet not from motives of cruelty." The antidote to this "age of boredom" is energy. Energy is a key word; Stendhal uses it again and again to refer to all manner of cultural and personal experience. He writes of energy as a generic necessity in life and art: "I cannot conceive a man without a little *male energy*, constancy, and depth of ideas." And the great women characters in his novels derive their vitality from the same source. As Simone de Beauvoir puts it, "These women are, quite simply, *alive*."

Energy is expressed in individual, national, and institutional vitality. The Renaissance has it in abundance; Enlightenment France has it; Stendhal's Italy has it; parts of some cities (Paris, Milan) have it; none of the provinces has it; Napoleon had it; bourgeois France will never have it; and Stendhal, when not depressed by the people or places that do not have it, has it.

There is a paradox at the heart of Stendhal's attitude toward his own ennui-burdened times, a paradox that turns up in all of his novels. As much as he supported the liberal principles that allowed his age to rebel against the ancien régime in France, he detested the bourgeois ascendancy that came about as a direct result of the Revolution and the Napoleonic system. Politically, the idealist in Stendhal argued for liberalism, but the realist did not absolve for a moment those for whom such principles were framed. He prefers, as he confesses over and again, the court minister to the corner grocer: "I have always, as if by instinct, had a profound contempt for the middle class."

Stendhal's class attitude, part of what he calls his "Beylism," is decidedly aristocratic. He writes in *Henri Brulard* that from the days of his exposure to his grandfather's family, his principles rarely went hand in hand with his preferences: "I must confess that, in spite of my opinions, which were entirely and fundamentally republican, my relations had completely infected me with their aristocratic and reserved tastes." Stendhal half believed what Madame Grandet implies in *Lucien Leuwen* when she asks incredulously, "Are really good manners to be found without noble birth?"

Stendhal's fondness for the aristocracy, however, does not blind him to the real issue of his time, the realignment of class prejudices in which the true aristocrats, men and women of merit, are culturally isolated. He speaks in *Lucien Leuwen* of the "great quarrel that afflicts the nineteenth century: the resentment of rank against merit." This is a central subject in much of his fiction, and in a famous passage of *The Red and the Black* he writes:

> In the nineteenth century when an influential man of good family meets a man of spirit, in the ordinary course of events he either has him put to death, condemned to exile or imprisonment, or humiliates him in such a way that the fellow is foolish enough to die of grief. In this instance, by chance, the man of spirit is not the one to suffer.
>
> (p. 164)

Stendhal is especially exercised when rank is determined by money alone. The minister of the interior in *Lucien Leuwen* explains: "People with money have succeeded to the place and privileges of the great families of the Faubourg Saint-Germain" (2.54). And later in the same novel, Lucien's father points out that the "bourgeoisie has taken the place of the Faubourg Saint-Germain and now the Bank has become the nobility of the bourgeois class." Since the old aristocracy of the ancien régime is out of place, quite literally, in the age of Louis-Philippe, the businessman-king, it responds with a cruelty that verges on sadism. One sees a particularly libidinous version of aristocratic cruelty in *The Red and the Black* when the marquis de la Mole, furious at Julien Sorel for daring to consider marrying his daughter, screams oaths at Julien "partly because he detests him and partly because the novelty of the oaths excites him."

Only one man, Napoleon, seemed capable of truly ennobling the nineteenth century; to this man Stendhal constantly turns his attention in order to gauge his own political vision and political aesthetics. Napoleon inhabited the scene of Europe in various guises and contributed to his time energies that are difficult to articulate let alone measure. Twice Stendhal planned to write at length about him and twice he stopped short. The problem for Stendhal in properly assessing his subject was that one phase of Napoleon's career kept getting in the way of another. As general, Napoleon was

a man whom, as Stendhal writes, "I always worshiped." Stendhal had deep, lasting reservations about what Napoleon wrought as emperor. But he stands in awe of Napoleon insofar as he represents the individual's capacity for expansiveness and energy, but whenever Stendhal brings his powers of political analysis to bear, he recognizes in the legacy of the Napoleonic system the bourgeois monetary and industrial bureaucracy he so despises.

In *Memoirs of an Egotist* Stendhal describes the post-Napoleonic period as a "plunge into the mire," and in *The Red and the Black* he measures what came after Napoleon's "second-hand monarchy" against what Napoleon himself represented:

> Ever since Napoleon's downfall, provincial usage has rigorously banned all manifestations of gallantry. Everyone is afraid of being turned out of his post. Scoundrels seek the support of the Jesuit party, and hypocrisy has made enormous strides even among the educated classes. Boredom is twice as great as ever.
>
> (p. 62)

Stendhal solidified his position in a pamphlet attack on the Saint-Simon utopian industrialists, *D'un nouveau complot contre les industriels* (A New Plot Against the Industrialists, 1825), in which he questions not so much the inevitability of the industrial-bourgeois order initiated under the Napoleonic empire, but its utter gracelessness and vulgarity. The existence of the industrial, bureaucratic class requires no sacrifices of the heart and confers no ennobling of the soul. Nowhere does Stendhal better represent his disgust with this class than in the opening description of the provincial factory owner, Monsieur de Rênal, in *The Red and the Black*. Rênal's nail factory is an expression of the ravages of the industrial order on both the natural landscape and on human sensibility. There is, of course, an implied aesthetic in Stendhal's position. Speaking of the bourgeois regime of Louis-Philippe, Stendhal writes in his third preface to *Lucien Leuwen,* "The nineteenth century . . . introduces the reign of the mediocre, rational, narrow-minded, and *dull* people—that is, from a literary point of view."

Stendhal's antagonism to his age derives in no small part from the realization that he is the child of another, the Enlightenment. As a youth in Grenoble and later in Paris during the first decade of the nineteenth century, his intellectual interests were focused on his Enlightenment forebears, especially those concerned with the way human beings think and feel, that is, with the sensationalist philosphers. Sensationalism in the eighteenth century had nothing to do with the present gaudy aspects of the word, but with the philosophical premises derived from John Locke, David Hume, Montesquieu, Helvétius, Condillac, Rousseau, and Destutt de Tracy—that ideas are essentially sensations and that cognition is directly linked to physical impressions. All is comprehensible to the mind that can chart the course of motives and ideas from their sensate origins. It is for a full understanding of his own behavior, in this respect, that Stendhal kept a journal for over twenty years and forayed so often into autobiography. To be a great poet, young Henri Beyle wrote, "I must know man perfectly."

The essence of Stendhal's psychology in his fiction stems from the notion that impressions, motives, impulses, and ideas are different states of the same phenomenon. A proper understanding of sensation explains the nuances of literary character, the "crystallization" (his coinage) of response that isolates and identifies human actions. As a "sensationalist," Stendhal was able to look with clarity on all manner of impressionable reality and mark, as no other novelist before him and perhaps none after him until Marcel Proust, the progress of the human heart. Honoré de Balzac had greater scope and Jane Austen had a stronger sense of community, but Stendhal had no equal in recording, with incisive yet humane irony, the various agitations of a character's soul.

But when Stendhal names his specific literary allegiance, he suppresses his Enlightenment sympathies and concedes his contemporaneity. He calls himself a romantic, identifying his aesthetics with the arguments he puts forth for romanticism in his *Racine and Shakespeare:*

> *Romanticism* is the art of presenting to different peoples those literary works which, in the existing state of their habits and beliefs, are capable of giving them the greatest possible pleasure.
>
> *Classicism,* on the contrary, presents to them that literature which gave the greatest possible pleasure to their great-grandfathers.
>
> (p. 38)

For Stendhal, romanticism differs from classicism not so much in intent as in potential, and potential is crucial in any theory of generic and formal periodization. Romanticism represents the best resources of what is contemporary for any age. In this way, Stendhal's literary allegiance suits his politics, which also derive from a projection of the truly avante-garde as liberating in contrast to both the ancien régime and the post-Napoleonic order. As the best expression of the imagination in its time, romanticism is a source of literary energy necessary to combat the rigid conventions of the past and the ennui of the present. Stendhal describes his romantic impulse as "this dark spot in my telescope [which] has been a good thing for the characters in my novels; there is a sort of middleclass meanness that they cannot have."

Stendhal's romanticism was Italianate and heroic, even Napoleonic. He defined Napoleon's heroism as that which was "useful" to his time; and his words were virtually identical for literary romanticism: "the expression of qualities that are useful at the time." He does not mean morally useful, resenting as he did the more carefully elaborated and conventional French romanticism of Chateaubriand as a mere rehash of the aesthetics of Christianity or the politics of monarchy. He means that romanticism ought to be generically and aesthetically useful in sustaining the energy of a culture.

The ease with which Stendhal maneuvers from his essentially logical theory of human personality, derived from the Enlightenment philosophers and their *idéologue* followers, to his essentially logical romantic theory of literary usefulness makes him a complex figure of historical accommodation. His career marks the relation between the eighteenth and nineteenth centuries, between cognitive and intuitive reasoning, between the substantial glories of the intellect—clarity, acuity, and grace—and the expansive formation of the romantic soul—growth, grandiosity, and sublimity. Stendhal's Enlightenment allegiance is rooted in a desire for extreme clarity—he writes to Balzac, who had written so glowingly about *The Charterhouse of Parma:* "I see only one rule: to be clear. If I am not clear, *my whole* world is annihilated" (16 October 1840). Yet his romantic ego admits of the fragility and dispersiveness of the self, a self that constantly desires satisfaction and consistently discovers its own insufficiency.

Stendhal alternates between the appeal of the definitive and the appeal of the ineffable: he is at his best when his prose bridges the two, as in his acute analysis of the dangers and attractions that the commonplace romantic phenomenon, nature worship, held for him. He believed that as a child he had a horror of nature because "my father and Séraphie, like the true hypocrites they were, were always extolling natural beauties." Nonetheless, he continues, "without explaining it to myself, I was extremely sensitive to the beauty of the landscape." Here are the two Stendhals in one, the realist and the romantic, the skeptical analyst and the feeling visionary. He is, in this regard, like Rousseau and Rousseau's mimic, Julien Sorel of *The Red and the Black,*

the cynic who also seeks the purification of his soul high in the French Alps, a purification that comes only from nature as the sublime Other.

Stendhal called romanticism a genre, and it is clear he identifies the movement with the subtle and shifting moods of his own efforts in the novel, a form less restrained than others by convention and best able to deal with what is appropriately new. He speaks of his aesthetics in *Henri Brulard:* "I ruminate incessantly on what interests me; by dint of looking at it from different *mental positions,* I end by seeing something new in it, and *I change its aspect."* If Stendhal failed at pure dramatic comedy early in his life, he recognized that the potential of his genius resided with a different genre and a more flexible range of expression. In a discriminating self-assessment, he brackets the double range of his novels, their sympathy and irony: "I can be touched by a tender emotion only after a comic passage." Such a notion explains why he considered his time as a youth spent reading the first important romantic-realist novel of the tradition, *Don Quixote,* so crucial ("the greatest epoch of my life"). He saw in that narrative what he was to create in his own great fiction, not only the comedy of skewed romance, but the sincere and noble expression of the passionate soul.

Stendhal hints at his fictional technique when he cites in *The Red and the Black* a remark he attributes to the abbé de Saint-Réal: "Why, my good sir, a novel is a mirror journeying down the high road. Sometimes it reflects to your view the azure blue of heaven, sometimes the mire in the puddles on the road below." The Azure and the Mire, which sounds like one of Stendhal's titles, might key the two reflexes of his romantic realism. Stendhal's skyward vision is, so to speak, grounded by reality. But its ground is perceptual, not naturalistic, and Stendhal's realism is psychological, not descriptive. As one of the epigraphs in *The Red and the Black* puts it: "For everything I relate, I have seen; and although I may have been deceived in what I saw, I shall certainly not deceive you in the telling of it." What Stendhal wants is authenticity rather than naturalism. Certain novelistic topics, perhaps associated with Balzac, were anathema to him: "I have always had a horror of the gloomy dismal drama based on lack of money, as being bourgeois and too true to life."

When he announces himself as novelistic chronicler, Stendhal is less indebted to the detailed record of a time than to the details of human passions. In subject matter, his fiction deals with the grander gestures of men and women, gestures subject to ironic scrutiny, but never, as in Balzac or later in Gustave Flaubert, ironized beyond human sympathy. Stendhal's sense of event registers from the inside out, as in the brilliant Waterloo chapters of *The Charterhouse of Parma;* there the historical confusion in the narrative mirrors the confusion within the soul and mind of a character whose lot it is to have no historical perspective. To put it another way, when Stendhal says he is the chronicler of a year, in the subtitle of *The Red and the Black,* he does not mean the year in which the action takes place (after all, the key event of that year, the July Revolution, goes unmentioned); he means, rather, that he is a chronicler of the kinds of pressures that impinge upon human beings in time, pressures that both provide the opportunity for displays of imaginative nerve and present obstacles to any kind of action at all.

There is among Stendhal's papers a very late document called "The Privileges of April 10, 1840." It consists of twenty-three articles, all of them intriguing, but one of them (article 21) crucial to understanding his nature as a romantic-realist:

> Twenty times a year, the privileged shall be able to guess the thoughts of all the persons around him at a distance of twenty paces. One hundred twenty times a year, he shall be able to see what whoever he chooses is doing at that time; there is total exception for the woman he loves best.

Realism is insight up to the point where total knowledge of human motive encounters the object of human desire. Love is one mystery that Stendhal's romanticism will not abandon to his enlightened sensibility. Within the controlled honesty of Stendhal's realism is the notion of what it is to have something left to imagine. The very last of his twenty-three articles reveals a faith in art as a kind of transport, a flight of the imagination as visionary. At the age of fifty-seven Stendhal the realist is as much the dreamer as the boy of twelve: "Ten times a year, the privileged shall be transported to the place he chooses, at the rate of a hundred leagues an hour; during the transfer he shall sleep."

THE RED AND THE BLACK

The colors that so appealed to Stendhal as titles—red and black, red and white, rose and green, chartreuse—almost mockingly identify extremes of social coloration that belie the more subtle shades of individual motivation and desire in his characters. Why, then, are some of his works so militantly and garishly titled? These charged colors, of course, signify not so much allegiances as obstacles in Stendhal's fiction. The colors of the title *The Red and the Black,* for example, mark the dangerous boundaries for Julien Sorel between Jacobin and legitimist, salon and church, blood and bile, emotion and austerity.

After the thematic polarities of the title, we are left with the novel's essential symmetry of form, a symmetry that reflects its binary or doubling pattern as a whole. The story of Julien Sorel is based on a famous murder case, that of Antoine Berthet, who returned to his hometown to shoot his ex-mistress in church after his career was frustrated by her family and friends. There is a kind of strange circularity to the melodrama, coming home to roost or passing from one extreme to another. Near the beginning of *The Red and the Black,* before Julien Sorel goes to tutor Monsieur de Rênal's children in Verrières, he wanders into church and sits in the Rênal family pew; there he notices that someone has left a scrap of newspaper or a piece of a pamphlet: *"Details of the execution and last moments of Louis Jenrel, executed at Besançon on . . . "* Everything from the ellipsis of the date of execution to the last syllable of the doomed man's name implies that Julien's alliance with the Rênal household will run a parallel course. Julien ends by returning to the pew to shoot Madame de Rênal after, in a sense, having foreseen his own execution in Jenrel's: "His name ends just like mine."

The question we might ask of such a carefully inscribed structure is the same we might ask of the stark boundary colors that constitute the novel's title: What happens in between? One answer offers itself in the epigraph to the whole of the narrative, a phrase of Georges Jacques Danton, an uncompromising figure of the French Revolution and the Terror: "Truth—Truth in all her rugged harshness." Truth for Stendhal is a quality of narrative voice. But the harshness of Stendhal's truth is eased by a bond of narrative sympathy even for characters not themselves entirely capable of seeing or sensing the full truth about themselves. Stendhal has said of his hero, Julien—who, like the young Henri Beyle in his first serious employment, spells *cela* with two *l*'s—"Julien c'est moi." It was what Flaubert would say of Madame Bovary in a more famous and more androgynous pronouncement. For both novelists, in their characteristically different ways, the "truth" of a main character, that is, the kind of imagination he possesses, is a reflection of the "truth" of the author who imagines him. Stendhal *is* Julien insofar as his authorial sympathies, though never fully complicitous in Julien's

ambition, are never entirely absent from Julien's desire.

The Red and the Black begins with obvious incommensurates: the beautiful mountain setting of provincial Verrières on the border between France and Switzerland and the presence of the inglorious and brutal nail manufacturing plant that constitutes the chief holding of Monsieur de Rênal, the city mayor and provincial industrial aristocrat. His other major holding, of course, is Madame de Rênal, whom he thinks of as a typical woman, hence a "complicated machine." In order to build his plant, Monsieur de Rênal had to turn a stream out of its course and relocate the lumber mill of Julien Sorel's father. The resistance to something as naturally constituted as a stream and the sordid negotiations between a scheming entrepreneur and a double-dealing greedy peasant set the extreme tones or "colors" of a world where force and chicanery are the norms in shaping experience. Such obvious and potent materialism affects sensibility: *"Bringing in money* is the decisive reason for everything in this little town you thought so pretty. A stranger to it, on first arrival there, enchanted by the cool, deep valleys that surround it, imagines its inhabitants are sensitive to beauty."

Stendhal's irony is sweetly savage. Beauty and its moral equivalent, sensitivity, are notably missing from this provincial world in which Julien is nurtured and to which he will return. Just how he will forge his career in the provinces and then in Paris, and, at the same time, fabricate his spirit in both worlds is the driving narrative issue of *The Red and the Black.* I say "fabricate" because that is precisely what Stendhal's important characters have to do. Most often, the forms of behavior and the choices open to them do not coincide with the force of their dreams or the extent of their capacities, as when Julien rejects the very generous offer of his bumpkinish friend, Fouqué, to join him in the timber business:

"This offer put Julien in a bad temper; it interfered with his fantastic dreams."

The course Julien finally settles upon, virtually by default, is a career in the church. The old curé Chélan sees a fire in Julien's nature "which hardly suggests to me the moderate and complete renunciation of all earthly benefits necessary in a priest." For Julien, the fire in his soul is a curious combination of mental energy, hero worship, and willpower that translates in his own mind as a kind of allegorical destiny or fated end: "This secret fire he speaks of is my plan to make my way."

Julien makes his way as one of literature's most extraordinary waifs. After guessing that Monsieur de Rênal pockets a portion of the foundling funds of which he is in charge, Julien none too errantly observes: "I, too, am a sort of foundling, hated as I am by my father, my brothers, and my whole family." At various times in the novel he is made out to be someone's bastard son, as when the marquis de la Mole circulates the story that he is the natural son of an aristocrat brought up in the provinces by a carpenter. In a way, for Julien to accept his true origin is to deny himself the mobility, status, and entrée so necessary to his ambition. Of course, it is the fire of that ambition, masked but sensed, that make so many, including his own family, distrust him. Julien is marginal in almost every way, and that constitutes Stendhal's sustained and sustaining interest in him.

Though Julien has moments of infuriating banality, rarely is he as contemptible as those who block his way or exercise power over him. To put it differently, the only thing he fears in himself is what he sees as contemptible and violent in others. Like so many sensitive heroes in literature, Julien initially knows what he knows only from his reading. But Stendhal places this common motif in ironic perspective when we discover that Julien's books are for him what the Muse is for civilization: total memory. He does not merely read and reflect;

he absorbs. He has the Latin version of the Bible at his complete recall; he can literally repeat the young Rousseau of the *Confessions;* he commits the annals of Napoleon's campaigns to memory; and he memorializes the *Mémorial de Saint-Hélène* by memorizing it. Stendhal's choice of books for Julien is a kind of subtle overview of Julien's career: his literary investiture mixes sacred and secular titles; Rousseau's *Confessions* are of a secular man and Napoleon's place of exile is appropriately sanctified. And it is through the secular byways of a religious career that Julien will negotiate his ambition in Parisian society.

Throughout the novel Julien's memory rather than his intellect proves his most marketable talent, first as tutor in the Rênal household, then as seminarist, then as secretary to the marquis de la Mole, and finally as unwilling co-conspirator in the ultra monarchist cause. This last role, in which Julien is cast because of the usefulness of his memory, touches on a supreme irony in Stendhal's novel: principle and career do not mix. A career for the spirited and energetic does not mean self-realization but self-abandonment, abandonment to a "set" that may or may not possess one's values or any values at all. Stendhal speaks of the fate of men like Julien "endowed with a certain degree of talent."

> . . . these attach themselves with obstinate tenacity to some particular set; and if that set "makes good," all the best things society can give are showered upon them. Woe to the studious man who does not belong to any set; even his minor, doubtful successes will be held against him, and superior virtue will triumph over him by robbing him of these.
>
> (p. 365)

At the same time, there is something in Julien's marginal status that alarms the very sets into which he is absorbed. His brother seminarians hate him for the same reasons his real brothers in Verrières beat him. Julien's nature is so powerfully ambiguous that he is frightened when he looks deeply into his soul. When he says he complies with the dictates of "his master Tartuffe," his hypocrisy buries both the self that performs and the one that frightens. This sort of dual reflex is precisely what occurs in the seminary at Besançon: "Henceforth Julien was on his guard—he had to construct an entirely new character for himself." "Real" character, in the sense of both personal integrity and integrity of self-representation, does not work in the social world of Stendhal's novel; without hypocrisy there is no social character, hence there is no career.

Those who intuit something like hypocrisy in Julien are intimidated by what is real in him. Mathilde de la Mole says: "In this age, in which all energy is dead . . . his energy makes them afraid." And the marquis de la Mole observes: "But deep down in his character, I find something alarming. That is the impression he produces on everyone, so there must be something real in it." Indeed, Julien is alarming because he does not rest easy even in his hypocrisy, or he rests easy only in what can be easily done, like his feats of rote memory.

The question of self-positioning, social and moral, in the course of negotiating one's career is an intriguing one for Stendhal, who senses as no other novelist before him that it is variously treatable but cannot be answered. In one of Julien's moments of anguishing over the course of his life and its direction, he asks himself: "Must one steal? Must one sell oneself? . . . The question pulled him up short. He spent the rest of the night reading the history of the Revolution." Julien's resolve here is less to seek an answer than to avoid being entirely depressed by the question. As Michael Wood trenchantly puts it, "Julien Sorel, like most of us, wants to know who he is, but only on the condition that he is who he wants to be." About Julien's many attempts "in the light of his imagination to interpret life," Stendhal comments: "This is the error of a man of superior quality." Such an error is a ro-

mantic one to its core, and an agonizing one, as we see later when Julien reformulates the question so profoundly troubling for the imagination: "Good God! Why am I what I am?"

There is a paradox at the heart of Stendhal's fiction similar to the paradoxes that mark his own career. To feel oneself truly alive requires an energetic imagination, but the very tendency of that imagination to interpret its surroundings is self-defeating. This paradox explains the sense of liberation Julien feels at the end of the novel when he contemplates the likelihood of execution. Death is the only satisfying prospect for the uncompromising romantic in Stendhal's world. "Wasn't I fine yesterday when I stood up to speak," Julien remarks after his trial. "I was improvising, and for the first time in my life! It's true there's reason to fear it may also be the last." Wittily qualified though his observation is, the paradoxical sense of terminus as true origin is a powerful one in the novel. It is only at the end of a botched career that self-interpretation seems generative: "Julien felt strong and resolute as a man who sees clearly into his own heart." The attempted murder of Madame de Rênal is, among other things, a kind of catharsis of hypocrisy. Julien's character is freed from its performing self by one last performance.

The threat to Julien's energy, however misplaced, and to his liberated spirit, however terminal, is the great plague of the Stendhalian universe: ennui. What makes Stendhal's characters unique is the extent to which they, like the memorable characters of two other masters of romantic comedy, Lord Byron and Alexander Pushkin, can imaginatively identify alternatives, even unsuccessful ones, to the deadening effects of boredom. Thus Julien's first adventure in *The Red and the Black* is precipitated by the extreme ennui of the Rênals' marriage. Of Monsieur de Rênal, Stendhal tells us that Madame de Rênal would scarce "admit she found him boring." In a deft elaboration, she "found Monsieur de Rênal less boring than any other man of her acquaintance." Conditions of life in Verrières are such that Monsieur de Rênal seems less of something that he is unequivocally more of. Madame de Rênal is not herself scintillating, but she has a "somewhat romantic nature" that allows her, once stimulated by her feelings for Julien, to identify what she lacks in her husband. Julien's arrival "had in some way driven boredom from the house." That is to say, Julien drives away Monsieur de Rênal.

In one of Stendhal's bitingly funny passages, he describes an instance of joint surprise in the household. Monsieur de Rênal is surprised at the stone path he finds has been completed during one of his absences, and Madame de Rênal is surprised that he has returned at all: "His arrival was also a surprise to Madame de Rênal, who had forgotten his existence." In a subsequent scene in which Julien and Madame de Rênal are holding hands, Monsieur de Rênal, oblivious to the physical contact between his wife and Julien, occupies himself by throwing stones at a peasant girl who cuts across a corner of his orchard. In his haste to protect his property from trespass, Monsieur de Rênal fails to realize that a more prized possession than his orchard is being trespassed on right in front of his eyes.

As Stendhal argues in *Of Love*, unexciting and nonpassionate relations are, by their nature, conventional. The Rênals' married life in *The Red and the Black* serves primarily as a foil to more vital affairs of the heart: Julien's and Madame de Rênal's or Julien's and Mathilde de la Mole's. Merely because these affairs are exciting, of course, does not free them from other hazards. There is an intricate sequence, for example, in which Madame de Rênal misunderstands why Julien fears the discovery of a small portrait he has hidden in his mattress. Unaware that it is a likeness of Napoleon, she assumes it is one of his mistress, although he has none and never has had. Rather, Julien's desire for love is me-

diated through his worship of Napoleon's career. Later it ironically occurs to Madame de Rênal that perhaps her imagined rival for Julien's affections never slept with him: "Could it be possible my rival never loved him!" Since Napoleon never met Julien, let alone loved him, Madame de Rênal is right for the wrong reasons. But even here the simple fact of Julien's innocence is less interesting than the more complex notion that desire is self-reflexive. As love or hero worship, desire extends out only to reflect back, which is a romantic rather than conjugal form of expression.

Julien's need for Madame de Rênal is predictably different from her need for him. Her need is *need* itself, a desire to possess, even if fleetingly, what she knows is missing from her life. His need is part of his Napoleonic quest for career, something analogous to the pursuit of military fame. Stendhal himself, of course, presents the career of love as equivalent to the desire for military glory—love's intricacies become matters of strategic self-testing and tactical finesse. His journals and diaries repeat the military analogy incessantly, and his fictional characters react to it obsessively. Later in the story, when Julien plans the exciting and amusing conquest of Mathilde de la Mole, love joins glory on the field of victory—Julien feels like "a young Second Lieutenant, who as a result of some astonishing exploit has just been made a Colonel, on the field, by his Commander in Chief."

One of the saving graces of Julien's conception of love as a kind of substitute heroism is rendered by the structural brilliance through which his dangerous love affairs combine the energy of romance with the timing of seduction farce. The several scenes with Mathilde de la Mole are unforgettable in this regard. They transform the usual ennui of the Parisian salon into the thrill of trespass. Mathilde thinks of the affair: "Exposing oneself to danger elevates the soul and preserves it from boredom," and she asks, "What sort of love is that which makes one yawn?" Further, Mathilde says of her love for Julien, mistaking its displacement for reality, "Everything here is on a heroic scale." If Julien is Napoleonic as lover, Mathilde matches him gesture for gesture as Charles IX or Henry III. She is love as historical artifice, her grandest fixation being a fascination with decapitated heads, whether her sixteenth-century ancestor's or Julien's at the end of the novel. Mathilde is a very Salomé to a sequence of John the Baptists.

As for Julien, he can barely comprehend his mistress; perhaps in actuality both lovers are "unconsciously animated with feelings of the keenest hatred towards one another." Julien hates her for the sheer oddity of her nature; she hates him for being low-born and, worse, contemporary. The intense affair has a comic potential to which Stendhal is not blind. For instance, in order to rekindle Mathilde's dying passion at one point, Julien enlists the aid of fifty-three love letters obtained from a Russian friend and prefabricated to court one of Mathilde's rivals, Madame de Fervaques. Julien finds the letters so boring he can barely stay awake transcribing them. Nonetheless, they arouse Mathilde's jealousy, and Julien, confused by this time, reacts with displaced passion: "Dare I tell you that when he got back to his room Julien threw himself on his knees and covered with kisses the love letters given him by Prince Korasoff?" These letters won him a woman he never wanted (de Fervaques) so he could rewin another woman (Mathilde) he ought to have wanted even less. Of course, he has expended all this effort in the first place only because Mathilde seems not to desire him: "I no longer love you, sir; my crazy fancy deceived me." In a gesture that is at best superogatory and at worst absurd, he continues to copy out the rest of the fifty-three letters to Madame de Fervaques after they have served his purpose. His action is a kind of embellishment of ennui masked as energy, a nervous reflex, rather than an appropriate response to circumstance. Thus when Mathilde's love revives, Julien is absolutely un-

sure of it: "Can you promise yourself that you will love me for a week?"

The treachery, lies, and blood-line prejudices let loose by Julien's bizarre encounter with Mathilde de la Mole reveal that, although a marginal character to begin with, Julien has transgressed beyond even his limits. The bourgeois world of his first mistress, Madame de Rênal, reclaims him in the form of a vicious letter concerning his motives, a letter that is both a series of lies (the work of Julien's enemies speaking through her) and a little too close to the truth of his ambitions for Julien's comfort. Julien does not like to consider his motives, which both authenticate and invalidate him. His subsequent attempt to murder Madame de Rênal stems from the severity of his discomfort: she will pay for betraying what is authentic in Julien's heart and what is hypocritical in his soul. At the conclusion of the narrative, Stendhal balances Julien's necessary departure from the bourgeois world of moral exhaustion with his necessary return to it. When that world manages to imprison and sentence him, it does so through a combination of his own misplaced desire and the execution of conventions fatal to his marginality.

LUCIEN LEUWEN

Lucien Leuwen is a title Stendhal suggested to his friend Madame Jules Gaulthier for her novel *The Lieutenant*. He proposed as the subtitle *The Student Expelled from the École Polytechnique*, which reveals, given Stendhal's own earlier career, that in thinking about others he was thinking about himself. Later he saw possibilities for a narrative of his own in the account of a young man expelled from a bourgeois institution for presumed radicalism. Stendhal, who never attended the École Polytechnique he had enrolled in at sixteen, liked to ring changes on imaginary phases of his educational career in the lives of his fictional characters. Octave de Malivert in *Ar-*

mance actually completes his course of study at the school from which Lucien will be expelled.

Stendhal begins *Lucien Leuwen* at the point of his hero's departure from school and, hence, from Paris. He planned a narrative tryptich of sorts. In part one, Lucien, a second lieutenant in the French army, courts Madame de Chasteller, an ultra or legitimist widow in the garrison town of Nancy, where Stendhal conjures up a complete provincial society (army headquarters, bourgeois citizenry, and local aristocracy) not matched in range and tone until Proust's Combrey or Balbec. In the second part of the novel, we follow Lucien to Paris, where Stendhal traces two political careers: Lucien's, as appointments secretary to the minister of the interior, and Lucien's father's, as late-blooming ministerial power. Part two ends with the gloom produced by the elder Monsieur Leuwen's death. Part three, in which Lucien was to serve as embassy official in Rome and, later, to reunite with Madame de Chasteller in Paris, was never written. The general pattern of the whole is simple: Lucien loses a lover in part one, a father in part two, and gains a wife in part three. In essence, the novel would have adhered to the comic form Stendhal never mastered when he tried it years earlier for the theater. He fails to master it here too, though *Lucien Leuwen* has other virtues.

Some critics argue that *Lucien Leuwen* is Stendhal's masterpiece. They do so on the ground that he knew its subjects better than any others he created: the love of a bourgeois gentleman for an aristocratic widow and the politics of the government of Louis-Philippe in the July Monarchy of the 1830's. *The Red and the Black* may be written with greater clarity of design and more controlled pathos; *The Charterhouse of Parma* with more heart and melodramatic abandon; but *Lucien Leuwen* bows to neither in the wit of its dialogue, the equanimity of its tone, and the depth of its political understanding. The novel is rough

and sometimes absurd, however, in its plotting. At the end of part one, for example, Lucien's protracted courtship of Madame de Chasteller is complicated by a scheming town physician, Dr. Du Poirer, who engineers a bizarre end to Lucien's sojourn in Nancy. He convinces Stendhal's gullible hero that he has witnessed his bedridden mistress-to-be give birth to a child supposedly fathered by a previous lover. That the smuggled-in infant is already two months old or that Madame de Chasteller was merely suffering from something like the vapors never occurs to Lucien. He leaves town without ever resolving the matter. By his own admission Stendhal was embarrassed by this plot and abandoned the novel before resolving it.

Given Stendhal's consular position in the government of the July Monarchy, "feeding," as he put it, on the state budget, it would not be surprising if he had felt disinclined to finish or publish *Lucien Leuwen* for other reasons. The narrative is an unrelenting and savage running commentary on scoundrels in scoundrel times. In his published works, Stendhal was of course more forgiving of his government and its policies, but privately the state servant unsheathed his cold, steel pen. He loved to hear his informed friends' damaging assessments of the Parisian and provincial quagmire of Louis-Philippe's regime. He reveled in the corruption, the power brokering, and the stupidity of the monarchy; and he detested it for betraying its liberal trust as much as he detested the Bourbon monarchy of Charles X for disavowing liberalism. Lucien fixes Stendhal's position when he remarks: "It is amusing . . . that the two rivals, Charles X and Louis-Philippe, both on the nation's payroll, while paying the nation's servants with the nation's money, think we are in debt to them personally."

Any dreams of political liberalism Stendhal might have had were stifled in the 1830's. Perhaps the soul requires the dream of political purity to keep itself pure, and perhaps the imagination aspires to political heights to keep the idea of aspiration alive, but the realist intellect soon recognizes the difference between hopes and expectations. When Lucien's mother suggests to her astute husband how splendid it would be to serve as minister so that he might do what is right, Monsieur Leuwen responds: "Something our public would never believe . . . as a people we are too gangrened to understand such things." Liberalism is the problem of the novel, not its solution. With more perspective than Stendhal had in the 1830's, it is possible to see the emergent conflict of the times less as a crisis of liberalism among the monarchists nominally ruling the nation and the bourgeois actually running it, than as a strain between the previously progressive bourgeois orders and the new fermenting proletariat of industrial France. When the minister, Monsieur de Vaize, warns a soon-to-be electioneering Lucien against "those so-called magnanimous sentiments so closely allied to mass insurrection," he is predicting the next phase of political turmoil in Europe. Stendhal's utter distaste for the masses made him reluctant to face, let alone chart, such a turmoil. He would rather, as he does in *Lucien Leuwen*, concentrate his talents on exposing the moribund bourgeoisie than contemplate with glee its replacement.

The series of dirty works that Lucien performs for the minister de Vaize in the second part of the novel go far beyond the failed test of liberal conscience and approach the borders of criminality. Lucien's father wonders: "Now we come to the great difficulty: are you enough of a rogue for such an occupation?" Lucien's reply comes later in a different but apposite context: "Isn't it bad enough to be a rogue in reality, without acting like one?" In his compromised position, Lucien quickly realizes that his adversaries are virtually everyone, not only the minister's public enemies but the minister himself: "When you work in the interest of Ministers, it is not the adversary you have to fear but the men you are working for."

Clearly, Stendhal exercises his powers at the expense of state politics in part two, but the real fictional theme of the narrative is the domination exerted over Lucien by his father, a financial genius known in Paris as the "Talleyrand of the Bourse." The elder Monsieur Leuwen is a witty libertine whose savagery against incumbent politicians is later equaled only by ambitions to replace them with himself and his band of trained acolytes. Lucien and his father are spiritually liberals, although we see them only as time-servers; and Lucien's time is ill served by the attempt, not so much against his will as against his nature, to adjust to the career engineered for him by his father. He recovers from the worst that de Vaize can heap on him, including the incident in which Lucien, while electioneering for the minister in Blois, gets mud thrown in his face and hears an insult that literally turns his soul inside out: "Look how dirty he is! You've put his soul on his face." Lucien, of course, is furious at the insult, which is unfair to his better nature but deeply accurate in regard to his chosen profession. The politician, however, can always take a bath; whether Lucien the man can recover from the blight his father's ambition casts upon him is a more difficult, touchy, and troubling question.

Though Monsieur Leuwen is ironic and witty on the subject of his son, he makes a key admission to Lucien that he loves him with a strange energy, a way of overcompensating for his other inclination to view him as a rival for his wife's affections. Lucien's situation is frustratedly oedipal in that his natural resistance to his father is weakened by his father's cultured fondness for him. Little by little Lucien finds himself absorbed into all his father's wishes, almost as if Monsieur Leuwen can reappropriate his own youth through the life of his son. It is not as if Monsieur Leuwen desires to correct past mistakes; he merely wants to do everything over again. He arranges all: his son's position, his son's advances, his son's future mistress (whose name Lucien keeps forgetting), his son's entire day.

Lucien complains that he has been usurped: "You have taken every minute of my time."

As irritable as Monsieur Leuwen's arrangements make Lucien, partly because of the guilt he feels in not returning what he thinks is the love expended upon him, he fully submits to them. Having lost his only real interest, Madame de Chasteller, there is little in which he can interest himself so as to counter his father's interest in him. As is often the case in Stendhal's fiction, the tensions caused by the situations are also the sources of its comedy. The spectacle of Monsieur Leuwen operating subversively through the son he has a traditional wish to uphold and advance creates some curious reversals. Monsieur Leuwen's main complaint about the conduct of his son's life in Paris is exactly the opposite of what we might expect: "Can a leopard change his spots," the old man asks, "will you ever be wild and frivolous?" When Monsieur Leuwen decides to assume the ministry himself, because he feels that his son has been slighted by Monsieur de Vaize, his decision epitomizes the overall psychological theme of the novel—he replaces Lucien as the main character. Like Oedipus, Lucien can return to center stage only after the death of his father.

In *The Red and the Black,* Stendhal repeats a remark he had published before and would publish again: "Politics in the middle of things that concern the imagination is like a pistol-shot in the middle of a concert. The noise is ear-splitting and yet lacks point." He meant, I suspect, that the details of politics have the same relation to more general notions of politics as the accumulation of details has to the analytical qualities of realism. But if ever it were possible to write a novel with both imagination and political details, *Lucien Leuwen* is it. Politics become fiction, perhaps in the ironic sense of Monsieur Leuwen's famous observation: "Every government, even that of the United States, lies always and about everything; when it can't lie on the main issues, it lies about the details." One would not wish to read *Lucien Leuwen* and ex-

pect to find in it the same sense of formal excitement and economy as in Stendhal's finished novels, but its wealth of social detail, its sinister comedy of corrupt ministries, and its odd version of family rivalries are pleasures not lightly waived by the admirer of Stendhal's work.

THE CHARTERHOUSE OF PARMA

Stendhal's last completed novel, *The Charterhouse of Parma*, was written in an extreme spurt of creative energy. He began it on 4 November 1838 and finished it on 25 December 1838. It was published in April 1839. In broad outline *The Charterhouse of Parma* is the narrative of an intense young man, Fabrizio del Dongo, loved to distraction by his aunt, Gina Pietranera, who in arranging her nephew's life succeeds only in redirecting his love toward someone else, Clelia Conti. The formal elegance and power of the narrative are marred by an abrupt and bizarre conclusion, in which Fabrizio retreats to the charterhouse of the title and dies. Stendhal had written a more reasonably developed ending (now lost), but his publisher wanted to hold down production costs and numbers of volumes. So the novel was halted in its tracks, and the barely mentioned charterhouse remains almost as a vestige of a longer book.

In *The Charterhouse of Parma* Stendhal is interested as always in the formation of character. The task is both a thematic one—what *is* character?—and a narrative one—how does one bring to life a character's fiery soul? Stendhal's important characters circulate in the territory of the novel, especially Parma, without fully accommodating themselves to it, or they assimilate into it on their own terms, which may or may not mean the death of their moral character. The court at Parma is one of the most theatrical settings in world literature for a glorious array of ne'er-do-wells and stooges. Among Parma's petty intriguers and hapless fools are the pasteboard general Fabio

Conti, overseer of the prison at Farnese Tower; the vulgarian minister Rassi, a name that "the common people gave . . . to mad dogs"; the scheming libertarian Marchesa Raversi; the extraordinary prince Ernesto IV, who becomes furious at "the sight of happiness"; the princess Clara Paolina of Parma, "who, because her husband had a mistress . . . imagined herself to be the most unhappy woman in the universe, an idea which had made her the most boring one"; and the prince's mistress, Marchesa Balbi, whose face was hopelessly wrinkled by the "continual habit of smiling, while inwardly she was yawning."

The Stendhalian theme of ennui appears early in the novel, this time in its Italian dimension: "These people had been living in a state of boredom for the last hundred years." For the Italian, according to Stendhal, ennui is counterbalanced by natural passion; for the Frenchman, the antidote to ennui is a kind of turning inward and a destructive vanity. The Italian has the sincerity of his desire to extend or participate in an order made habitable by the morality of passion: "The Italian wishes to be happy through moral love, or failing that, physical love. The Frenchman through self-love." There is no truth in the Frenchman's nature. When Fabrizio imputes cowardice to the French troops in the opening military scene of *The Charterhouse of Parma*, he also charges them with hypocritical emptiness: "With these Frenchmen you're never allowed to speak the truth if it offends their vanity." Italians suffer less from vanity than from overactive imaginations: "Italian hearts are much more tormented than ours by the suspicions and wild ideas which a burning imagination presents to them, but on the other hand, their joys are far more intense and more lasting."

If truth is rearranged by vanity in France, it is rearranged by intrigue and subterfuge in the principalities of Italy, especially those fearful of Austrian hegemony: "In despotic courts, the first skillful intriguer manages to arrange the *truth,* just as fashion manages to do so in

Paris." Stendhal plays between the notions of appearance and actuality; fabricated truth (whether in fashion or by design) serves as the basis for power. In Italy of the nineteenth century, the intrigue-obsessed imagination is more destructive than liberating: "Fear makes people cruel."

Something terribly manipulative, even fearful, is bound to happen to Fabrizio del Dongo in Parma, because he is one of those Stendhalian naifs whose hearts are filled with a liberality of spirit without comprehending the realities of power. Fabrizio, like Julien Sorel, is a libertarian with no real politics, a republican without a republican cause. Though he loves the liberal newspapers of France, he does not for a moment believe in the democratic ideas that they propound: "The desire for liberty, the vogue and the cult of the *greatest good of the greatest number,* over which the nineteenth century has lost its head, were nothing in his eyes but a heresy that would pass like all the others."

Fabrizio is a Francophile largely because of his boyhood dream of serving with the armies of Napoleon. As was the case for Julien Sorel, Napoleon serves Fabrizio as much as Fabrizio desires to serve Napoleon. Napoleon offers the prospect of escape from the dullness of home. At home, of course, Stendhal locates the archetypal reactionary father, the marchese del Dongo, "who was so great a lord, and with whose fat, pasty face, false smile, and boundless hatred for the new ideas you are already acquainted." Since the novel hints that Fabrizio is, in fact, the natural son of a French officer, a passing fancy of his mother's, he is returning to his true origins in seeking his destiny abroad. He wishes to fight with Napoleon against the Allies, perhaps at Waterloo. However, Fabrizio can never be sure that he has been there even after taking part in the battle. He wonders: "Have I really taken part in a battle? It seemed to him that he had, and he would have been supremely happy if he could have been certain of this." Was it Waterloo? What part did Fabrizio play? Was he playing a part in the almost metaphysical sense of misidentity? Is his destiny self-authenticated or just some horrible burlesque joke? Fabrizio, through a series of plot complications, wears the uniform of a hussar who died in prison. This seems an omen: "I have, so to speak, inherited his identity . . . and that without wishing it or expecting it in any way! Beware of prisons! The omen is clear, I shall have much to suffer from prison." The omen works its way through the novel's plot. Ironically, Fabrizio will feel the liberation he had sought on the Napoleonic battlefield only when he is later imprisoned. The enclosed space with a view turns out to be much more sublime than the territory of the dead and dying in Belgium.

Fabrizio marches onto the Napoleonic field like a Renaissance Italian hero: "He saw springing up between himself and them that noble friendhsip of the heroes of Tasso and Ariosto." But instead he faces the vulgar reality of the French soldiers who hound him, humiliate him, and desert him in battle. Later, in prison, he contemplates the heroic again, this time as a state of mind, exulting that his spirit is nobler than his condition: "Can I be one of those men of valor of whom antiquity has furnished the world with certain examples? Am I a hero without suspecting it?"

The prospect of authentic heroism is still troubling Fabrizio at the conclusion of the novel, when his quest for a chivalric destiny is muddled by an almost uncontrollable lust. Clelia Conti, virtually harangued by Fabrizio into a sordid affair, meets him only in the dark of night; and Fabrizio, freed by his supposed magnanimity of soul, becomes the possessive and slightly crazed lover whose miscalculated impetuosity contributes to the death of his mistress and their child. It is at this point in the narrative that Fabrizio takes leave of Parma and retires to the charterhouse on the Po. The institution of the title is mentioned only once in the novel, on its last page, as a kind of retreat from what passion has wrought. Thus the novel ends with escape

rather than accommodation, a recourse that places the sensibility of Stendhal's characters (and perhaps of his readers) in another realm.

The authenticity that is so important to Stendhal's *Charterhouse* is evoked ironically by the motif of passports that appear and reappear in the novel: "Especially in the neighborhood of the Po, everyone's conversation turns on passports." Such a motif allows Stendhal his full range of dramatic wit and stylistic irony. Passports are something of a priority to diplomats, and, as documents in the Austrian-Italian police state, they substitute for vitality itself. The document breathes more life than the individual because without it the individual may not breathe at all. Or, in a bureaucratic sense, without a passport the individual is not himself, and, in all probability, is someone else. Of course with fake passports—and the novel is filled with them—authenticity takes on an entirely new dimension. Who one is becomes as much a political as a metaphysical question, whether asked of Fabrizio the hero, or of Fabrizio traveling under the passport of a man who sells barometers in France, or of Fabrizio under the passport of a citizen of Modena.

The best, or most proficient, characters in Stendhal's novels negotiate their own identities and control the authenticity of others'. In *The Charterhouse of Parma*, Fabrizio is controlled and maneuvered by his overadmiring and overzealous aunt, the duchess Sanseverina, and her lover, the brilliant count Mosca della Rovere Sorezano. The duchess and the count are Stendhal's most spectacular courtiers, she understanding fully the nature of court life, where there is "nothing real, or capable of surviving disgrace, save money," and he a man of two driving desires, love and ambition. Count Mosca is an exemplary Stendhalian character, a "Beyliste" who pursues happiness through total awareness. Mosca will do everything, even more than his conscience ought to allow him, to secure what he desires. But it is characteristic of the power of Stendhal's fiction (at the expense of Stendhal's program for living) that in Mosca's moment of greatest potential, when it is within his power to draw up a document that will bring the prince of Parma to his knees and ensure the happiness of the woman in the world he most desires, he wavers.

The scene is an appropriate one with which to conclude this essay. The duchess Sanseverina is desperate to attain a pardon for her nephew Fabrizio, and she threatens to leave Parma if she does not succeed. (Fabrizio had in self-defense killed a scoundrel during a brawl over a woman.) Prince Ernesto IV is desperate to keep the duchess in his principality—because he has plans for making her his mistress, because he fears the boredom of his court without her, and because he anticipates the scandal she would spread abroad about his rule. Count Mosca is summoned to the scene, having no idea what the precise nature of the requests and threats are. After some tense negotiation, Ernesto agrees to sign an unconditional pardon for Fabrizio under Parmesan law. But in drawing up the document for the duchess, Mosca's "courtier's soul was scandalized," and he strikes the document's key phrase, *"These unjust proceedings shall have no consequence in the future."* Of course, the proceedings have deep consequences in the future, both for Mosca's affair with the duchess and for Fabrizio's course with Parmesan justice. The striking of the phrase provides a tyrant with a power he will later exercise.

In this scene Mosca, the lover, sacrifices a great part of himself, his lover's heart, to his political brain. Mosca is done in by an impulse that makes his soul express itself cautiously before it releases itself amorously. The import of his action can be grasped only when the full theme of the novel is grasped, a twofold theme merging at all levels: love and power. Mosca is deeply and genuinely in love with the duchess, and when he utters the language of love his idiom is hyperbolic and self-sacrificial. At a moment's notice he seems willing to give up ambition and power to escape Parma with Sanseverina. But in the scene with Ernesto, when the duchess speaks *her* language of power, a language motivated by intense love for her nephew, Mosca can compete only with a kind of understatement, the opposite of hyperbole, in which he enacts his idiom by deleting a phrase in an agreement. He witnesses the duchess' display of passionate negotiation for her nephew, so he modulates his whole being from lover's accessory to ruler's protector. Mosca's gesture is extraordinary. It is not so much his sense of loyalty to a particular tyrant as his diplomatic sensibility (and his fragile love) that the *"unjust proceedings"* scandalize. Mosca proves himself instinctually *homo politicus,* a man whose ambition is routinized, whose calculation is habitual. His public reflexes are more potent than his private love.

Once an individual's habits have gone public, so to speak, the private self is forever compromised. It is difficult to determine in Stendhal's fiction (or even in his larger vision) just how fatal Mosca's error is, just what alternatives are open to a thinking and feeling man, just how far Stendhal's own romantic integrity goes, just how far he would allow any man the quest for purpose that goes under the drab name of career. And it is difficult to determine in Stendhal's best work whether one is more ridiculous in striving for a balance of public and private selves or more hapless in having attained that balance.

Selected Bibliography

EDITIONS

INDIVIDUAL WORKS
Vies de Haydn, Mozart, et Métastase. Paris, 1815.
Histoire de la peinture en Italie. Paris, 1817.
Rome, Naples, et Florence. Paris, 1817.
De l'amour. Paris, 1822.
Racine et Shakespeare, I. Paris, 1823.
Racine et Shakespeare, II. Paris, 1825.
Armance. Paris, 1827.
Promenades dans Rome. Paris, 1829.

Le rouge et le noir. Paris, 1830.

Chroniques italiennes. Paris, 1837–1839.

Mémoires d'un touriste. Paris, 1838.

La chartreuse de Parme. Paris, 1839.

Le journal. Paris, 1888.

La vie de Henri Brulard. Paris, 1890. Written 1835–1836.

Souvenirs d'égotisme. Paris, 1892. Written 1832.

Lucien Leuwen. Paris, 1901. Unfinished; written 1834–1835.

COLLECTED WORKS

Correspondance. Edited by Henri Martineau and V. Del Litto. 3 vols. Paris, 1962–1968. Pléiade edition.

Oeuvres complètes. Edited by Henri Martineau. 72 vols. Paris, 1927–1937.

Oeuvres intimes. Edited by Henri Martineau. Paris, 1966. Pléiade edition.

Romans et nouvelles. Edited by Henri Martineau. 2 vols. Paris, 1966–1968. Pléiade edition.

TRANSLATIONS

Armance. Translated by C. K. Scott Moncrieff. London, 1928.

* *The Charterhouse of Parma.* Translated by Margaret R. S. Shaw. London, 1958.

———. Translated by C. K. Scott Moncrieff. New York, 1962.

Lamiel. Translated by T. W. Earp. New York, 1952.

* *The Life of Henri Brulard.* Translated by Catherine Alison Phillips. New York, 1925.

* *Lucien Leuwen.* Translated by Louise Varèse. 2 vols. New York, 1950.

* *Memoirs of an Egotist.* Translated by T. W. Earp. New York, 1958.

On Love. Translated by H. B. V. (under the direction of C. K. Scott Moncrieff). New York, 1947.

The Private Diaries of Stendhal. Translated by Robert Sage. Garden City, N.Y., 1954.

* *Racine and Shakespeare.* Translated by Guy Daniels. New York, 1962.

* *The Red and the Black.* Translated by Margaret R. B. Shaw. New York, 1959.

———. Translated by Lloyd C. Parks. New York, 1970.

———. Translated by Robert M. Adams. New York, 1969. Useful for critical apparatus and appended essays.

———. Translated by C. K. Scott Moncrieff. New York, 1926.

BIOGRAPHICAL AND CRITICAL STUDIES

Adams, Robert M. *Stendhal: Notes on a Novelist.* New York, 1959.

Alter, Robert. *A Lion for Love: A Critical Biography of Stendhal.* New York, 1979.

Arbelet, Paul. *La jeunesse de Stendhal.* 2 vols. Paris, 1919.

Blin, Georges. *Stendhal et les problèmes du roman.* Paris, 1954.

———. *Stendhal et les problèmes de la personalité.* Paris, 1958.

Blum, Léon. *Stendhal et le beylisme.* Paris, 1930, 1947.

Brombert, Victor. *Stendhal et la voie oblique.* New Haven, Conn., 1954.

———. *Stendhal: Fiction and the Themes of Freedom.* New York, 1968.

———, ed. *Stendhal: A Collection of Criticial Essays.* Englewood Cliffs, N.J., 1962.

Del Litto, Vittorio. *La vie intellectuelle de Stendhal: Genèse et évolution de ses idées (1802–1821).* Paris, 1962.

Green, F. C. *Stendhal.* Cambridge, 1939.

Gutwirth, Marcel. *Stendhal.* New York, 1971.

Hazard, Paul. *Stendhal.* Translated by Eleanor Hard. New York, 1929.

Hemmings, F. W. J. *Stendhal: A Study of His Novels.* Oxford, 1964.

Josephson, Matthew. *Stendhal.* Garden City, N. Y., 1946.

Levin, Harry. *Toward Stendhal.* Murray, Utah, 1945.

Martineau, Henri. *Le coeur de Stendhal.* 2 vols. Paris, 1952–1953. The standard biography.

———. *L'Oeuvre de Stendhal.* Paris, 1951. Revised ed. 1966.

May, Gita. *Stendhal and the Age of Napoleon.* New York, 1977.

Prévost, Jean. *La création chez Stendhal.* Marseille, 1942; Paris, 1951.

Richardson, Joanna. *Stendhal.* New York, 1974.

Stendhal-Club, 1958– . Periodical containing a variety of material on Stendhal, his works, his times.

Strickland, Geoffrey. *Stendhal: The Education of a Novelist.* Cambridge, 1974.

Taine, Hippolyte. ''Stendhal.'' In *Nouveaux essais*

de critique et d'histoire. Paris, 1909. Reprint of the original 1804 essay.

Tillett, Margaret. *Stendhal: The Background to the Novels.* London, 1971.

Wood, Michael. *Stendhal.* Ithaca, N.Y., 1971.

BIBLIOGRAPHIES

Del Litto, Vittorio. *Bibliographie stendhalienne, 1947–52.* Grenoble, 1952.

————. *Bibliographie stendhalienne, 1953–70.* 4 vols. Grenoble, 1958–1974.

Martineau, Henri. *Petit dictionnaire stendhalien.* Paris, 1948.

Royer, Louis. *Bibliographie stendhalienne, 1928–1933.* Editions du *Stendhal-Club* nos. 30, 33, 34. Grenoble, 1930–1934.

MICHAEL SEIDEL

ALEXIS DE TOCQUEVILLE
(1805–1859)

I

ALEXIS DE TOCQUEVILLE was one of the greatest, perhaps the greatest, of the political thinkers and historical writers of the nineteenth century. The principal support of such a claim is the lasting power of his writing. Often during the twentieth century, in different places and on different occasions, the few books that Tocqueville wrote have been rediscovered by people who thereafter became his respectful admirers. His reputation survives not only because of the excellence of his work but because the history of the last hundred and fifty years confirms the impression, again and again, that when we read him we are in the presence of a great mind whose judgment is virtually unerring, whose insight is often profound, and whose vision is startlingly applicable to our own times. That his vision has been much more accurate than that of Karl Marx or other nineteenth-century radicals has been recognized on occasion; such comparisons have been increasingly easy to prove. It is less often recognized that Tocqueville gains in comparison not only with utopians and radicals but with the great conservatives such as Edmund Burke, Joseph de Maistre, and Juan Donoso Cortés, as well as with the great liberals such as John Stuart Mill, Thomas Macaulay, and Lord Acton.

Tocqueville is the premier thinker of the democratic age. One of his admirers in the nineteenth century, the German philosopher Wilhelm Dilthey, ranked him among the three greatest political thinkers of all time, with Aristotle and Machiavelli. Yet Tocqueville is not very widely known.[1] In France historians and political thinkers devoted relatively little attention to him for almost a century after his death. The reason for this neglect was the customary prevalence of certain climates of opinion and intellectual fashions; but there is another condition that, even at this time of writing, has been an obstacle to the universal recognition of Tocqueville's importance. This condition is the unclassifiable nature of Tocqueville's ideology and achievement. Was Tocqueville a historian or a sociologist? Was he a conservative or a liberal? Was he an aristocratic skeptic or a believing Catholic? These are secondary questions about which there exists no intellectual or academic consensus to this day.

Tocqueville was an aristocrat who came to believe that democracy was inevitable; but the purpose of this belief was neither opportunism nor an accommodation to what seemed to him obvious. He saw his own aristocratic past and the unfolding democratic present with detachment, denying neither the former nor the latter. He was not the kind of aristocrat who

---

[1] His very name, especially in the English-speaking world, is often erroneously written: when not preceded by his first name it should be Tocqueville, not ''De Tocqueville.''

1673

chooses to become a democrat; and he saw in the coming of democracy more than a social or economic development: he thought he detected in it the hand of God. "I cannot believe," he once wrote,

> that God has for several centuries been pushing two or three hundred men toward equality just to make them wind up under a Tiberian despotism. Verily, that wouldn't be worth the trouble. Why He is drawing us toward democracy, I do not know; but embarked on a vessel that I did not build, I am at least trying to use it to gain the nearest port.

This passage contains the essence of his historical vision. Tocqueville believed that the movement toward democracy—which, in his view, had begun earlier than historians and people in general were accustomed to think—was the great overriding theme of the historical evolution of the West, perhaps even of the entire world. The structure of Tocqueville's thought and his view of human nature differed entirely from those of the materialists and of Marx. Yet Tocqueville did not share the prevalent liberal view of history either, the one espoused and expressed by the historian Lord Acton, to the effect that the history of mankind is the essential unfolding of the history of liberty. Tocqueville's view of democratic evolution was clear, but he was fully aware of its complex nature, the main element of its complexity being the relation between its often contradictory elements of equality and liberty. His concentration on this subject would alone justify the recognition of Tocqueville as a latter-day Aristotle; yet Tocqueville, even more than his famous predecessor Montesquieu, knew that modern mass democracy is not comparable to the democracy of the Athenian city-state, that it is a new historical phenomenon. Tocqueville's political thinking was realistic and existential, not abstract and theoretical.

II

Tocqueville was born in 1805 of an ancient noble family of Normandy, whose title and land dated from the eleventh century. His parents had barely escaped the guillotine; his maternal great-grandfather, the famous political and legal thinker Malesherbes, had not. Perhaps in consequence of these harrowing experiences (the hair of Tocqueville's father had turned white at the age of twenty-two) the family life of the Tocquevilles had none of the airy worldliness of the French aristocracy of the eighteenth century; it was closely knit, religious, and affectionate, as well as protective of an only child who maintained his love and respect for his parents throughout his life. This respect was not only filial but also intellectual. His understanding and appreciation of the royalist and traditionalist convictions of his father went hand in hand with his understanding and defense of the democratic evolution of the world.

When the July Revolution of 1830 put an end to the rule of the last Bourbon king of France, Tocqueville was twenty-five years old; indeed, his twenty-fifth birthday came on the day when Charles X left Versailles forever. At dawn on the next day Tocqueville saw a melancholy historical scene that moved him to tears: the cortege carrying the king and his family into exile.

His father had been an important official in the last Bourbon regime. Most of his friends were convinced legitimists; Tocqueville was not. He had no illusions about the bourgeois regime of Louis-Philippe, but he had no illusions about the possibility of a Bourbon restoration either. After some soul-searching he took the oath of allegiance to the new government. But his restless mind was already looking ahead. Less than a month after the upheaval in July, and less than two months before he took the oath, he wrote to a friend: "I have long had the greatest desire to visit North America: I shall go there to see what a great republic is like; my only fear is lest, during that time, they establish one in France." He and his close friend Gustave de Beaumont managed, not without difficulty, an assignment from the government to study the American prison system; but the scope of their interest was rather more spacious than that.

They left in early April 1831, landed in the United States by mid-May, and returned to France nine months later. The product of their extensive (and at times dangerous) travels was three separate works: a study of the American penitentiary system; a romantic novel by Beaumont about slavery in America; and Tocqueville's own *Democracy in America*, of which the first volume was published in 1835 and the second in 1840.

Democracy in America is the great outstanding book about the United States in particular and about democracy in general. Its immediate success was due both to its inherent qualities and, perhaps even more, to the contemporary state of affairs: in the 1830's the United States was the only well-established democratic republic in the world. This kind of uniqueness was alone sufficient to stimulate interest in its description and analysis. The unequaled merit of *Democracy in America* appears when we consider that Tocqueville's work remains interesting, valuable, enduring, and thought-provoking long after the United States has ceased to be the solitary example of a democracy. *Democracy in America* has stood the test of time, which is astonishing when we bear in mind the changes in the institutions and population of the United States from what they were some hundred and fifty years ago.

In this encyclopedic and philosophical work, which covers nearly all of the institutions and characteristics of the American government and the American people, some of Tocqueville's observations and conclusions should have inevitably become outdated. Yet such instances are remarkably few. Perhaps the only one worth noting is Tocqueville's description of the power of the presidency and,

indirectly, of the federal government. These at that time seemed weaker than the powers of Congress and the states. What is remarkable is that this youthful foreign aristocrat should have had such an acute and profound comprehension of the American character. True, he had prepared himself well for his American journey by extensive reading; he knew English, and had had for some time a particular interest in the laws and institutions of England; yet it remains a rare occurrence that the best and most enduring book about a nation should be written by a foreigner.

The reason for this exceptional feat lies in Tocqueville's singular genius. This singularity can be seen in the method, style, and philosophy of *Democracy in America*; but the unity of this method, style, and philosophy does not derive solely from the subject of this first work. It reappears in Tocqueville's other books, written fifteen or twenty years later and dealing with different subjects.

The first volume of *Democracy in America* consists of two parts: the first and shorter one is a description of American self-government and political institutions; the second is a description and analysis of democratic government and majority rule in the United States. The first part is composed of eight chapters, the second of ten: but most of these chapters, especially the most important ones, are divided into numerous subchapters, and it is within these subchapters that Tocqueville's method—or, more precisely, the structure of his thought—is apparent. These subchapters are short, often hardly more than a page each. They consist of paragraphs that seldom run to more than a few lines. This kind of composition reflects the author's personality: Tocqueville's mind was quick, restless, and impatient. Yet the working of these qualities enhances, rather than diminishes, the value of what he has to say, for the compressed wisdom of his generalizations and the quiet profundity of his insights make them memorable. Here are a few examples:

[On the freedom of the press] I admit that I do not feel toward freedom of the press that complete and instantaneous love which one accords to things by their nature supremely good. I love it more from considering the evils it prevents than on account of the good it does.

(1.11)

[On democracy and envy] One must not blind oneself to the fact that democratic institutions most successfully develop sentiments of envy in the human heart. This is not because they provide the means for everybody to rise to the level of everybody else but because these means are constantly proving inadequate in the hands of those using them. Democratic institutions awaken and flatter the passion for equality without ever being able to satisfy it entirely.

(1.13)

[On universal suffrage] Those who consider universal suffrage a guarantee of the excellence of the resulting choice suffer under a complete delusion. Universal suffrage has other advantages, but not that one.

(1.13)

[On the budget and the costs of democratic government] There is in democratic societies a stirring without precise aim; some sort of prevailing feverish excitement finds expression in innovations of all sorts, and innovations are almost always expensive.

(1.13)

[On the enduring benefits of democracy] The vices and weaknesses of democratic government are easy to see; they can be proved by obvious facts, whereas its salutary influence is exercised in an imperceptible and almost secret way. Its defects strike one at first glance, but its good qualities are revealed only in the long run.

(1.16)

[On the danger of majority rule] My greatest complaint against democratic government as organized in the United States is not, as many Europeans think, its weakness, but rather its irresistible strength. . . . I am not asserting that at the present time in America there are frequent acts of tyranny. I do say that one can find no guarantee against it there and that the reasons for the government's moderation must be sought in circumstances and in mores rather than in the laws.

(1.16)

[On the races in the United States] When they have abolished slavery, the moderns still have to eradicate three much more intangible and tenacious prejudices: the prejudice of the master, the prejudice of the race, and the prejudice of the white.

(1.18)

The most famous and most often quoted passage in *Democracy in America* is at the conclusion of the first volume:

There are at the present time two great nations in the world, which started from different points, but seem to tend towards the same end. . . .

All other nations seem to have nearly reached their natural limits, and they have only to maintain their power; but these are still in the act of growth. All the others have stopped, or continue to advance with extreme difficulty; these alone are proceeding with ease and celerity along a path to which no limit can be perceived. The American struggles against the obstacles that nature opposes to him; the adversaries of the Russian are men. The former combats the wilderness and savage life; the latter, civilization with all its arms. The conquests of the American are therefore gained by the plowshare; those of the Russian by the sword. The Anglo-American relies upon personal interest to accomplish his ends and gives free scope to the unguided strength and common sense of the people; the Russian centers all the authority of society in a single arm. The principal instrument of the former is freedom; of the latter, servitude. Their starting-point is different and their courses are not the same; yet each of them seems marked out by the will of Heaven to sway the destinies of half the globe.

(Reeve-Bowen trans., 1.18)

What is the principal theme of *Democracy in America*? It is that American society is a living illustration of the possibility of a more or less orderly democracy, and that consequently both the conservative and the radical European views of democracy ought to be revised. Tocqueville's conservative contemporaries were wrong in believing that democracy inevitably leads to anarchy and chaos; the opposite is rather true: the universal acceptance of majority rule leads to slowness in the movements of thought, to conformity, and to the danger not of anarchy but of tyranny exercised by the majority. On the other side, the radicals were wrong in believing that the establishment of majority rule would suffice to ensure the freedom and happiness of people; these depend far more on the workings of certain laws, habits, and beliefs, including religion: in short, the character of a people influences its political institutions rather than the reverse. In the first volume of *Democracy in America* Tocqueville gradually rises to this theme, as the book advances from a description of American institutions to an analysis of American democratic society and its problems.

The first volume was published in 1835 in Paris. Despite the skepticism of its publisher, it was an instant success. Tocqueville became famous overnight: his work and his wisdom were praised in many quarters, primarily among the conservative liberals who formed what was perhaps the last great generation of French political thinkers in the 1820's and 1830's. Because of their judicious acclaim Tocqueville was then, and has been often since, classed among this group, known by the somewhat misleading adjective *doctrinaires*. Let me repeat, however, that he transcended such categories for many reasons, one of them being his awareness that the world was facing a new development of such scope and extent that the existing political categories were no longer sufficient; as he himself wrote, "a new science of politics was necessary for a new world."

The composition of the second volume of *Democracy in America* took twice as long as the first. Published in 1840, it was less of a success. Unlike the first, it received a number of severely critical reviews. Today we can see that the second volume is even more important than the first, more timely in its details and richer in its contents.

We note, first of all, that the title of the entire work is as accurate as it is honest. *De la démocratie en Amérique* (About Democracy in America) is not, as most people assume, a book principally about America; it is a book principally about democracy. And in this respect there is a subtle but significant difference in emphasis between the two volumes. Whereas it may be said that the main direction of Tocqueville's interest in the first volume is America even more than it is democracy, in the second volume it is democracy even more than it is America. The connection between the two volumes is nonetheless organic. Already, toward the end of the first volume, Tocqueville had written:

> Those who, having read this book, should imagine that in writing it I am urging all nations with a democratic social state to imitate the laws and mores of the Anglo-Americans would be making a great mistake; they must have paid more attention to the form than to the substance of my thought. My aim has been to show, by the American example, that laws, and more especially mores, can allow a democratic people to remain free. But I am very far from thinking that we should follow the example of American democracy and imitate the means that it has used to attain this end, for I am well aware of the influence of the nature of a country and of antecedent events on political institutions, and I should regard it as a great misfortune for mankind if liberty were bound always and in all places to have the same features.

> (1.17)

The second volume of *Democracy in America* has no subchapters. The volume has four parts, each consisting of twenty or more short chapters, except for part 4, a kind of conclusion, which has only eight. Throughout, however, all the terse, lucid, and aphoristic characteristics of the first volume appear again. The titles alone of some of these chapters suggest the form of Tocqueville's thought: "Why the Americans Show More Aptitude and Taste for General Ideas than Their English Forefathers"; "How Religion in the United States Makes Use of Democratic Instincts"; "How American Democracy Has Modified the English Language"; "Some Characteristics of Historians in Democratic Times"; "Why Some Americans Display Enthusiastic Forms of Spirituality"; "How an Aristocracy May Be Created by Industry"; "Why Great Revolutions Will Become Rare"; "Why the Ideas of Democratic Peoples About Government Naturally Favor the Concentration of Political Power"; "What Sort of Despotism Democratic Nations Have to Fear."

The succinctness in the second volume of *Democracy in America* is even more pronounced than in the first. The chapter "Some Characteristics of Historians in Democratic Times," for example, consists of forty-eight sentences in fifteen paragraphs; yet many of these paragraphs contain a particular argument so condensed and profound that it would be sufficient for an entire book, indeed, for the kind of book that could establish the reputation of a thinker. "I am very well convinced," Tocqueville writes,

> that even among democratic nations the genius, the vices, or the virtues of certain individuals retard or accelerate the natural current of a people's history; but causes of this secondary and fortuitous nature are infinitely more various, more concealed, more complex, less powerful, and consequently less easy to trace, in periods of equality than in ages of aristocracy, when the task of the historian is simply to detach from the mass of general events the particular influence of one man or of a few men. . . .
>
> M. de Lafayette says somewhere in his *Memoirs* that the exaggerated system of general causes affords surprising consolations to second-

rate statesmen. I will add that its effects are not less consolatory to second-rate historians; it can always furnish a few mighty reasons to extricate them from the most difficult part of their work, and it indulges the indolence or incapacity of their minds while it confers upon them the honors of deep thinking. . . .

> Those who write in democratic ages have another more dangerous tendency. . . . To their minds it is not enough to show what events have occurred: they wish to show that events could not have occurred otherwise. They take a nation arrived at a certain stage of its history and affirm that it could not but follow the track that brought it thither. It is easier to make such an assertion than to show how the nation might have adopted a better course. . . .

> If this doctrine of necessity, which is so attractive to those who write history in democratic ages, passes from authors to their readers till it infects the whole mass of the community and gets possession of the public mind, it will soon paralyze the activity of modern society and reduce Christians to the level of the Turks.

> Moreover, I would observe that such doctrines are peculiarly dangerous at the period at which we have arrived. Our contemporaries are only too prone to doubt of human free-will.
>
> (Reeve-Bowen trans., 2.1.20)

Probably the most important part of the second volume of *Democracy in America* is its concluding chapters. Tocqueville's argument here rises to its highest level; and these chapters also reveal a subtle and important change in his mind. In "What Sort of Despotism Democratic Nations Have to Fear" Tocqueville begins by saying that during his travels in the United States he became aware of the relatively novel danger of democratic despotism; "a more accurate examination of the subject, and five years of further meditation, have not diminished my fears, but have changed their object." He no longer dwells on the relative weakness of the central power in a democracy; rather the contrary. "If despotism were to be established among the democratic nations of our days," it would be wholly different from despotism in the past:

"It would be more extensive and more mild; it would degrade men without tormenting them. . . . [The] same principle of equality which facilitates despotism tempers its rigor.

I think, then, that the species of oppression by which democratic nations are menaced is unlike anything else that ever before existed in the world; our contemporaries will find no prototype of it in their memories. . . . The old words *despotism* and *tyranny* are inappropriate. . . . The first thing that strikes the observer is an endeavoring to procure the petty and paltry pleasures with which they glut their lives. . . .

Above this race of men stands an immense and tutelary power, which takes upon itself alone to secure their gratifications and to watch over their fate. That power is absolute, minute, regular, provident, and mild. It would be like the authority of a parent if, like that authority, its object was to prepare men for manhood; but it seeks, on the contrary, to keep them in perpetual childhood: it is well content that the people should rejoice, provided they think of nothing but rejoicing. For their happiness such a government willingly labors, but it chooses to be the sole agent and the only arbiter of that happiness; it provides for their security, foresees and supplies their necessities, facilitates their pleasures, manages their principal concerns, directs their industry, regulates the descent of property, and subdivides their inheritances: what remains, but to spare them all the care of thinking and all the trouble of living? . . .

I have always thought that servitude of the regular, quiet, and gentle kind which I have just described might be combined more easily than is commonly believed with some of the outward forms of freedom, and that it might even establish itself under the wing of the sovereignty of the people.

(Reeve-Bowen trans., 2.4.6)

It appears from the above that Tocqueville foresaw the tendency that many social and political thinkers a century later were still unwilling to recognize: the possibility that the age of aristocratic society and government would be succeeded by bureaucratic society and government rather than by a true democracy, even though Tocqueville did not use the term "bureaucracy." In any event, the last sentence of the magisterial work sums up his historical and political vision: "The nations of our time cannot prevent the conditions of men from becoming equal, but it depends upon themselves whether the principle of equality is to lead to servitude or freedom, to knowledge or barbarism, to prosperity or misery."

III

We have seen that the publication of the first volume of *Democracy in America* suddenly made the young Tocqueville a public figure. What followed were thirteen superficially uneventful years, the middle period of Tocqueville's life. I write "superficially," because beneath the external signs of an honorably progressing career there were evidences of frequent disillusionments, depressions, and torment.

Between 1835 and 1848, the thirtieth and the forty-third years of his life, Tocqueville was elected to the Chamber of Deputies and to the French Academy. He traveled in England, Ireland, Algeria, Switzerland, and Germany. He published the second volume of *Democracy in America* and a number of minor writings; the *Democracy* was being published in many translations across Europe and in the Americas. He married a middle-class Englishwoman from a respectable family who had served as a governess in France for years; Marie Mottley was several years older and several inches taller than her husband, an earnest and intelligent woman with a difficult temperament who bore him no children.

Tocqueville suffered from a weak chest; the progressive disease of his lungs grew worse through the years. He was now a respected public personage, but not a very successful political figure. He took part in the political life of France out of a sense of duty rather than out of ambition. He wanted to help channel the democratic tide in the direction of decency and order. Many people disliked the serious and Olympian tone of his utterances; he seemed like Aristides the Just in the heedless democracy of Athens. On the evidence of his contemporaries we may add that his speeches in the Chamber were unduly learned, sometimes lengthy, and delivered without much oratorical talent. Yet at least one of Tocqueville's speeches became famous. On 29 January 1848 he spoke in the Chamber, accurately predicting that a revolution was brewing. "Gentlemen," he said,

> my profound conviction is that we are lulling ourselves to sleep over an active volcano. . . . When I consider what has been, at different times and epochs of history among different peoples, the effective reason why ruling classes have been ruined, I note the various events and men and accidental or superficial causes, but believe me, the real cause, the effective one, that makes men lose power is that they have become unworthy to exercise it. Consider the old monarchy, gentlemen. It was stronger than you, stronger because of its origin; it was better supported than you are by ancient customs, old mores, and old beliefs; it was stronger than you, and yet it has fallen into dust. Why did it fall? Do you think it was because of some particular accident? Do you think it was due to one particular man, the deficit, the Oath of the Tennis Court, La Fayette, or Mirabeau? No, gentlemen, there is another cause: the class that was ruling then had, through its indifference, selfishness, and vice, become incapable and unworthy of ruling.
>
> (*Recollections,* Lawrence trans., pp. 14–15)

He implored his colleagues in the Chamber to change the spirit of the government, because another great revolution was around the corner. His prophetic speech was received with apathy and ridicule. What Tocqueville had foretold came about less than a month later.

The memory of this speech, together with the reputation of Tocqueville's intelligent advocacy of an orderly democracy, led naturally to his leadership of the committee that was to write the constitution of the Second French Republic. During the deliberations a short but bloody second insurrection, in June 1848, turned the tide of sentiment and opinion more conservative. In December 1848 Louis-Napoleon was elected president of France. For the next two years he governed with the support of the Assembly, and in 1849 he appointed Tocqueville foreign minister. Tocqueville performed his duties with much energy and intelligence during a difficult and eventful period of French and European history. The fires of the 1848 revolutions had not yet died out: there was a war of independence in Hungary, a war in northern Italy; French troops were sent to Rome to crush the republican rebellion there and to restore the pope to his see. In October 1849 Louis-Napoleon dismissed the conservative-liberal cabinet of which Tocqueville was a prominent member. Tocqueville did not return to political life.

There was worse to come. Tocqueville accurately foresaw the political future: Louis-Napoleon would be supported as dictator by the majority of the people; his regime would be a new kind of democratic Caesarism. Tocqueville had only contempt for the Left radicals who in June 1848 had attempted the first socialist revolution in France; but he immediately realized that the fear-ridden reaction against the Left, equally contemptible, was a new phenomenon consonant with the development of democracy. It meant the appearance of a new radical Right, supported by masses of people out of fear of revolution and out of their sentiments of nationalism and respectability. "The insane fear of socialism," Tocqueville, this opponent of socialism, wrote in a letter, "throws the bourgeois headlong into the arms of despotism. . . . The democrats have served the cause of the absolutists. But now that the weakness of the Red party has been proved, people will regret the price at which their enemy has been put down."

It would be wrong to think that during the political phase of Tocqueville's career he wrote little. His literary dedication was exceptionally strong. But the largest part of his writings was unpublished on his death, and a good part remains unpublished even today. His friend Beaumont later said that "for one volume he published he wrote ten; and the notes he cast aside as intended only for himself would have served many writers as copy for the printer." Apart from his shorter writings and speeches in the 1840's, he kept up a very large correspondence. To put down his thoughts on paper, whether in letters to friends or only for himself, remained a necessity for Tocqueville throughout his life. Between 1849 and 1852, while the devolution of the French parliamentary democracy to the imperial regime of Napoleon III was progressing, Tocqueville's mind and body were racked with suffering. The cold and damp winters in the Tocqueville château in Normandy were bad for his lungs; and he complained that his state of mind was painfully agitated and depressed. In 1850 his doctors advised him to spend a winter further south; they also said that he ought to occupy his mind with other than political concerns. In Italy, at Sorrento, he began to write his recollections of the turbulence of the revolutionary years 1848–1849. He did so for his eye alone, one of the reasons for this discretion being his reluctance to make public the often caustic portraits of some of his friends and political associates. His manuscript, entitled *Souvenirs*, was eventually published by his great-nephew . in 1893, thirty-four years after Tocqueville's death.

The *Souvenirs* (later translated as *The Recollections of Alexis de Tocqueville*) are perhaps the best of all possible introductions to Tocqueville's mind. They are obviously the most personal of his published books. Again we are in the presence of an extraordinary work, because of the character and the genius of its author. Again its contents demonstrate the unique and uncategorizable character of Tocqueville's achievement. The *Souvenirs* transcend the limits of what is called a memoir or a history. They are a kind of autohistory, a history written in the first-person singular, but not because of their author's dominant preoccupation with himself. The book is a participant's history, springing from the realization that history is participant knowledge par excellence. In this book, as also in some of his other writings, Tocqueville demonstrates—without, however, arguing the philosophical point—the inadequacy of the Cartesian and scientific separation of the universe into object and subject, the separation of the observer from the matter observed.

Tocqueville's purpose was to describe some of the things and some of the people he saw in 1848 and 1849—or, rather, some of the things he saw that he saw. He begins the book with an avowal:

> Now that I am out of the stream of public life and the uncertain state of my health does not even allow me to follow any consecutive study, I have for some time in my retreat turned my thoughts to myself, or rather to those events of the recent past in which I played a part or stood as witness. The best use for my leisure seems to be to go back over those events, to describe the men I saw taking part in them, and, if I can, to catch in this way and engrave on my memory those confused features that make up the uncertain physiognomy of my time.
>
> Along with this decision of mine goes another to which I shall be equally faithful: these recollections are to be a mental relaxation for myself and not a work of literature. They are written for myself alone. These pages are to be a mirror, in which I can enjoy seeing my contemporaries and myself, not a painting for the public to view. My best friends are not to know about them, for I wish to keep my freedom to describe myself and them without flattery. I want to uncover the secret motives that made us act, them and myself as well as other men; and when I have understood these, to state them. In a word, I want to express myself honestly in these memoirs, and it is therefore necessary that they be completely secret.

(*Recollections*, p. 3)

He returns to this theme later in the work: "I do not want to write a history of the 1848 Revolution. I am merely trying to retrace my own actions, thoughts, and impressions during that time." And again, after meditating on the difficulty of describing human motives and purposes: "Nevertheless I want to try to discover myself in the midst of this labyrinth. For it is only right that I should take the same liberties with myself as I have taken, and will often take again, with so many others."

These "liberties" are essentials in his gallery of portraits. Here are a few examples:

[His friend Dufaure, who did not come to the Chamber of Deputies on 24 February 1848, the first day of the revolution] Weakness was certainly not the reason, for I have subsequently seen him very calm and unmoved in much more dangerous circumstances. I think that in his concern for his family he must have wanted to put them in safety outside Paris first. His private and his public virtues, for he had both in great measure, did not march in step, for the former always came first; we saw things go that way more than once. In any case, I cannot count that as a great crime. Virtues of any sort are rare enough, and we can ill afford to quibble about their type and relative importance.

(pp. 38–39)

[Jean Pierre Sauzet, the president of the Chamber] He got easily excited over the smallest matter, so you can imagine what state he was in then. I found this excellent man—for such he was in spite of well-meaning bits of trickery, pious fibs, and all the other petty sins that a timid heart and vacillating mind could suggest to an honest soul—I found him, I say, walking about in his room, a prey to strong emotions. M. Sauzet had handsome but undistinguished features, the dignity of a cathedral verger and a large fat body with very short arms. When he was restless or upset, as he nearly always was, he would waggle his little arms convulsively in all directions like a drowning man. His manner, while we talked, was strange; he walked about, stopped and then sat down with one foot tucked under his fat buttocks, as he usually did in mo-

ments of great agitation; then he got up and sat down again without coming to any conclusion. It was a great misfortune for the House of Orleans to have a respectable man of that sort in charge of the Chamber on such a day; a bold rogue would have been more use.

(pp. 45–46)

[In the midst of the upheaval the two sons of Louis-Philippe appeared in the Chamber.] The count of Paris had a boy's thoughtlessness combined with a prince's precocious impassivity. Beside them stood the duke of Nemours, buttoned up in his uniform, erect, stiff, cold and silent: a post painted to look like a lieutenant-general. In my view he was the only man in real danger that day. All the time that I watched him exposed to this peril, his courage remained the same: taciturn, sterile, and uninspired. Courage of that nature was more likely to discourage and dishearten his friends than to impress the enemy; its only use would be to enable him to die honorably, if die he must.

(p. 48)

[Ledru-Rollin, the leader of the radical party] At that time, the nation saw Ledru-Rollin as the bloody image of the Terror. They regarded him as the evil and Lamartine as the good genius, mistakenly in both cases. Ledru was nothing but a great sensual sanguine boy, with no principles and hardly any ideas; he had no true courage of mind or heart, but he was also free of malice, for by nature he wished all the world well and was incapable of cutting an enemy's throat, except perhaps as an historical reminiscence or to please his friends.

(p. 110)

[On 24 June 1848 a committee of the Assembly appointed Tocqueville as a commissioner, one of a group including the deputies Cormenin, Crémieux, and Goudchaux; their job was to move from barricade to barricade, to encourage the National Guards fighting the battle of Paris. Tocqueville's portraits of his colleagues, too long to cite here, are full of acute but good-natured insights. Here is his summary.] I have always found it interesting to follow the involuntary effects of fear in the minds of men of

ALEXIS DE TOCQUEVILLE

intelligence. Fools show their fear grossly in all its nakedness, but the others know how to cover it with a veil of such fine and delicately woven, small, convincing deceits that there is a pleasure in contemplating this ingenious labor of the intelligence.

(p. 150)

[Toward the end of the uprising Thiers meets General Lamoricière, who won the battle of Paris.] M. Thiers came up and threw his arms round Lamoricière's neck, telling him he was a hero. I could not help smiling at that sight, for they did not love each other at all, but danger is like wine in making all men sentimental.

(p. 161)

[About the Assembly near the end of the uprising] The President called the Assembly together only at long intervals for short periods; and he was right to do so, for Assemblies are like children in that idleness never fails to make them do or say a lot of silly things. Each time the sitting was resumed, he himself told us all that had been learned for certain, during the adjournment. This President, as we know, was Sénard, a well-known lawyer from Rouen, and a courageous man; however, the daily comedy of the bar had from his youth led him to contract such an inveterate habit of acting that he had lost the faculty of truthfully expressing his real impressions, if by chance he had any. Inevitably he would add some turgid phrases of his own to the acts of courage he was narrating, and when he expressed the emotion which he, I think, really felt, in sepulchral tones, with a trembling voice and a sort of tragedian's hiccup, he even then seemed to be acting. Never were the ridiculous and the sublime so close, for the deeds were sublime and the narrator ridiculous.

(pp. 153–154)

Space does not permit my adding Tocqueville's two or three portraits of Louis-Philippe, masterpieces of historical and psychological description though they are. Like those just quoted, they show their author's talent for depicting human beings and their characters. This ability rarely comes out in *Democracy in America,* where Tocqueville deals principally with institutions and society as a whole, rather than with individuals. A second feature worth observing is that each of Tocqueville's portraits ends with, indeed is summed up by, an epigram about human nature itself. This is not only the result of intelligent artistry or the French style. The *Souvenirs* embody Tocqueville's deep understanding of human nature— the main requirement of a great historian. Thus it is not only the subject matter of the *Souvenirs* but the very substance of their author's thought that is historical.

Here is how Tocqueville saw the first days of the Revolution of 1848:

As I left my bedroom . . . the 24th of February, I met the cook who had been out; the good woman was quite beside herself and poured out a sorrowful rigmarole from which I could understand nothing but that the government was having the poor people massacred. I went down at once, and as soon as I had set foot in the street I could for the first time scent revolution in the air; the middle of the street was empty; the shops were not open; there were no carriages, or people walking; one heard none of the usual street vendors' cries; little frightened groups of neighbors talked by the doors in lowered voices; anxiety or anger disfigured every face. I met one of the National Guard hurrying, rifle in hand, with an air of tragedy. I spoke to him but could learn nothing save that the government was massacring the people (to which he added that the National Guard would know how to put that right). It was always the same refrain, which, of course, explained nothing to me. I knew the vices of the July government all too well, and cruelty was not among them. I consider it to have been one of the most corrupt, but least bloodthirsty, that has ever existed, and I repeat the rumor only to show how such rumors help revolutions along.

(p. 36)

The *Souvenirs* are more than a historical account. They contain the principles of Tocqueville's historical philosophy. We have seen that Tocqueville had predicted the coming of

1683

the Revolution of 1848. He had made an even more trenchant prediction in October 1847, which he decided to quote in the beginning of his *Souvenirs*. "The time is coming," he states,

> when the country will again be divided between two great parties. The French Revolution, which abolished all privileges and destroyed all exclusive rights, did leave one, that of property. Property holders must not delude themselves about the strength of their position, or suppose that, because it has so far nowhere been surmounted, the right to property is an insurmountable barrier; for our age is not like any other. . . . Soon the political struggle will be between the Haves and the Have-nots; property will be the great battlefield; and the main political questions will turn on the more or less profound modifications of the rights of property owners that are to be made.
>
> (p. 12)

In this respect, as in so many others, Tocqueville was ahead of Marx and of the socialist thinkers after him. Unlike them, however, Tocqueville did not for a moment believe that the struggle between the haves and have-nots would be the culmination of the history of mankind. He did not believe in economic man. Tocqueville did not think that the coming revolution would be anything but another act in the intermittent drama of violent shocks whereby the cause of equality was advanced in France by different people at different times. Already in the second volume of *Democracy in America* Tocqueville made the startling proposition that great revolutions were bound to become rare. In 1848, in the midst of the fighting, he remarked how there was something flashy and make-believe in this revolution:

> . . . there was absolutely no grandeur in this one, for there was no touch of the truth about it. We French, Parisians especially, gladly mingle literary and theatrical reminiscences with our most serious demonstrations. This often creates the impression that our feelings are false,

whereas in fact they are only clumsily tricked out. In this case the quality of imitation was obvious. . . . It was a time when everybody's imagination had been colored by the crude pigments with which Lamartine daubed his *Girondins*. The men of the first revolution were still alive in everybody's mind, their deeds and their words fresh in the memory. And everything I saw . . . was plainly stamped with the imprint of such memories; the whole time I had the feeling that we had staged a play about the French Revolution, rather than that we were continuing it.

> (pp. 52–53)

Before that riotous day he wrote: "Nowhere did I see the seething unrest I had witnessed in 1830, when the whole city reminded me of one vast boiling cauldron. This time it was not a matter of overthrowing the government, but simply letting it fall." Throughout the *Souvenirs* Tocqueville insists on the marked differences among the revolutions of 1789, 1830, and 1848; and at the same time, on the frequently misleading and falsifying influence of the memories of these revolutions on the minds of all kinds of people, including Louis-Philippe and himself. More remarkable still, on occasion Tocqueville is able to distinguish—and he is driven by his honesty to describe—the difference between his impression of certain events when he first experienced them and the sometimes dissimilar impressions that came to his mind later and the conclusions he drew from them. One of the most engaging passages in the *Souvenirs* is Tocqueville's recollection of his argument with his friend J.-J. Ampère during the early days of the revolution:

> All the indignation, grief and anger that had been piling up in my heart since the morning suddenly erupted against Ampère; and I addressed him with a violence of language which makes me a little ashamed whenever I think of it and which only such a true friend as he would have excused. [He then reconstructs his own diatribe, and ends:] After a lot of shouting, we both

agreed to leave the verdict to the future, that enlightened and just judge who, unfortunately, always arrives too late.

(p. 68)

In sum, the *Souvenirs* are not only an incomparable account of the revolutionary year 1848–1849 in France and a set of clues to Tocqueville's character; they are not only excellent illustrations of his historical talent; but they also give us his view of history:

> For my part, I hate all those absolute systems that make the events of history depend on great first causes linked together by the chain of fate and thus succeed, so to speak, in banishing men from the history of the human race. Their boasted breadth seems to me narrow, and their mathematical exactness false. I believe, *pace* the writers who find these sublime theories to feed their vanity and lighten their labors, that many important historical facts can be explained only by accidental circumstances, while many others are inexplicable; and lastly, that chance, or rather the concatenation of secondary causes, which we call by that name because we can't sort them all out, is a very important element in all that we see taking place on the world's stage. But I am firmly convinced that chance can do nothing unless the ground has been prepared in advance. Antecedent facts, the nature of institutions, turns of mind and the state of mores are the materials from which chance composes those unexpected events that surprise and terrify us.

(p. 62)

IV

While he was writing his *Souvenirs*, during the winter of 1850–1851 in Sorrento, the idea of a book on Napoleon arose in Tocqueville's restless mind. He began to compose his first notes even though he was ill and weighted down by the gloomiest thoughts about the future of France. By December 1852 his mind had seized upon a different plan. He would write a book describing the main features of the French Revolution and include Napoleon. Because of his illness he was again advised to move away from Normandy, at least for a time. He and Madame de Tocqueville found a country house near Tours. A fortunate circumstance attended him there: he was able to search through the provincial archives in Tours, where he was assisted by the excellent archivist Charles de Grandmaison. Tocqueville now extended further the scope of his projected work. He would deal not only with the French Revolution and Napoleon but with the origins of the Revolution. He immersed himself more and more in that subject, which became the first volume of a projected two-volume work. Again the title was precise: *L'Ancien régime et la révolution (The Old Régime and the French Revolution)*. Published in June 1856, it received a critical acclaim not dissimilar from that of the first volume of *Democracy in America* twenty-one years before.

The Old Régime and the French Revolution is the most conspicuous example of Tocqueville's powers as a historian. The writing is of the same high quality as that of his earlier works, and his philosophy is of course unchanged. Yet two new features are worth noting. One is the evidence of Tocqueville's talent for archival research—that is, his knack for finding what is significant, illustrative, vivid, and telling in all kinds of materials. The other is his individual style of historiography. In *The Old Régime and the French Revolution* Tocqueville's method is more topical than chronological. He is interested in why as well as in how things happened; and the why is often wrapped up in the how. As we found apt illustrations in his chapter titles before, so we may learn about the cast of his thought from these:

> How the chief and ultimate aim of the Revolution was not, as used to be thought, to overthrow religious and to weaken political authority in France.

(Gilbert trans., 1.2)

Why feudalism had come to be more detested in France than in any other country.

(2.1)

How administrative centralization was an institution of the old régime and not, as is often thought, a creation of the Revolution or of the Napoleonic period.

(2.2)

How the desire for reforms took precedence of the desire for freedom.

(3.3)

How certain practices of the central power completed the revolutionary education of the masses.

(3.6)

And so on. The main theme of the book is that many of the practices of the old regime, foremost among them administrative centralization, were responsible for the actual ills as well as the restlessness that plagued France and the French people before 1789. The emphasis on these origins of the French Revolution was something very new at the time. Yet *The Old Régime* is not a thesis-history; Tocqueville knew very well that great events are seldom the results of a single string of causes.

One of the main achievements of Tocqueville the historian is his revision of many standard notions about the origins of the Revolution. It is not true that the Revolution brought about a radically new kind of government: the vice of modern democratic rule, excessive centralization, had begun under the old regime. It is not true that royal abuses provoked the outbreak of the revolt: violence broke out where royal power proved the mildest, and counterrevolution was to rise in the west of France, where the feudal rules had lingered on longest. It could not be denied that in 1788–1789 there was a noble, generous, virile spirit in the air; on the other hand there was much pretense, vanity, and opportunism. "Une règle rigide, une pratique molle": rigid

rules and weak enforcement marked the character of the old regime. The clergy was neither ther weak nor corrupt: "I began to study the old society with many prejudices against the clergy; I finished full of respect." The revolutionary government adopted the worst administrative habits of the old regime, without recognizing that in this matter, as well as in many others, continuity proved to be even stronger than change.

"It is not my purpose," Tocqueville wrote in his foreword, "to write a history of the French Revolution; that has been done already, and so ably that it would be folly on my part to think of covering the ground again. In this book I shall study, rather, the background and nature of the Revolution."

We saw earlier that Tocqueville transcends ideological and academic categories; as is the wont of genius, his spirit also transcended his times. Tocqueville, who is all too often described as an admirable nineteenth-century thinker, a conservative liberal of a time and place now hopelessly remote, possessed a mind that had both eighteenth- and twentieth-century characteristics. His writings—if only by the fine clarity of his prose—bear many of the marks of the eighteenth century, when history was part and parcel of literature, in the broad and honorific sense. The lucidity, the economy, the aphoristic quality, and the symmetrical structure of many of his chapters put Tocqueville in the company of Montesquieu, Voltaire, and Gibbon. In these respects he has more in common with them than with the professional historians of the nineteenth century. Nor does his view of the nature of history accord with that of the nineteenth century. To him history is not a science possessing an ascertainable method. His view of history, based on his understanding of human nature, is akin, rather, to that of the few independent thinkers of the twentieth century who regard the application of scientific method to human affairs as unworkable and unduly restrictive of meaning.

A generation after Tocqueville's death the

French critic Émile Faguet wrote that the task Tocqueville "set for himself was to penetrate beneath accidental history to solid history, or beneath history to the physiology of peoples." From this correct analysis Faguet, however, came to the wrong conclusion: that Tocqueville was a sociologist rather than a historian. Yet Faguet missed the key to Tocqueville's historiographical talents. When Faguet wrote, more than eighty years ago, the texture of history had not yet changed. At that time it seemed still reasonable to concentrate on the history of the politically conscious classes; history was past politics and politics present history. Since then, it has become obvious that given the social and democratic character of our age the requirements of history writing must change; it is no longer reasonable to concentrate exclusively on the actions of the leading protagonists of the politically active classes and separate what Faguet called "surface" history from what lies "beneath" it. This Tocqueville already knew. The importance of *The Old Régime and the French Revolution* is not only that it is an extraordinarily enlightening and instructive interpretation of the French Revolution; it is also an extraordinarily instructive new type of history.

Tocqueville implicitly and, at times, explicitly refutes many of the dogmas of modern professional history writing. He is not only among the earliest to note that political history is no longer enough; he sees that the politically active classes may become powerless, and that their abdication of leadership is a development often more decisive than the alleged demands and decisions of the people. Revolutions are seldom made by the conscious dynamism of the people; yet Tocqueville rejects both the fatalistic notion that accidents govern history and the deterministic notion that people are moved by predetermined material motives. History is made by men, to whom God has given free will. He saw the historian's task as being moral as well as artistic. In his notes he often wrote: "What I am going to paint," "what I am trying to portray." He

wished to paint rather than to chronicle, and he sought to detect the latent tendencies of the human heart and mind rather than to ascertain and explain regularities. His purpose was description rather than definition, comprehension rather than narration.

While Tocqueville was writing the first volume of *The Old Régime and the French Revolution* he was thinking more in terms of a European revolution. He considered that what had happened in France in 1789 was but the first phase of an epoch of European revolutions that, sixty years after the storming of the Bastille, was still going on. The European revolution, in turn, was but part and parcel of a greater movement toward social democracy, at the core of which stood the fundamental problem of the relation of liberty to equality, as well as that of democracy to Christianity. By the time the first volume was published he was well on his way through the second. Of the second volume we have his outline: it was to consist of five books, of which two (books 1 and 3) were almost completed; the rest consists of half-completed passages and notes to himself.

That Tocqueville died before he could finish this work was, and remains, a tragedy. As in the case of *Democracy in America*, the second volume might have been even more impressive than the first. The portions we have suggest this judgment. Book 1 deals with France immediately before the Revolution, book 3 with the coming of Bonaparte. In book 1 Tocqueville draws attention to the history of the *parlements*, those aristocratic assemblies that in 1788 initiated the attack on the old regime. The title of the fourth chapter reads: "How, Just When They Thought Themselves Masters of the Nation, the *Parlements* Suddenly Discovered That They Amounted to Nothing."

Perhaps the most brilliant completed portion of the volume (quoted in *The European Revolution and Correspondence with Gobineau*) is book 3, which treats France before the Consulate:

Between fear of the royalists and of the Jacobins, the majority of the nation sought an escape. The Revolution was dear, but the Republic was feared lest it should result in the return of one or the other. One might even say that each of these passions nourished the other; it was because the French found precious certain benefits ensured them by the Revolution that they feared all the more keenly a government which might interfere with these benefits. Of all the privileges that they had won or obtained during the previous ten years, the only one that they were disposed to surrender was liberty. They were ready to give up the liberty which the Revolution had merely promised, in order to finally enjoy the benefits that it had brought.

("How the Republic Was Ready to Accept a Master")

The parties themselves, decimated, apathetic, and weary, longed to rest for a time during a dictatorship of any kind, provided only that it was exercised by an outsider and that it weighed upon their rivals as much as on themselves. This feature completes the picture. When great political parties begin to cool in their attachments without softening their hatreds, and at last reach the point of wishing less to succeed than to prevent the success of their opponents, one should prepare for servitude—the master is near.

It was easy to see that this master could rise only from the army.

("How the Nation, Though Ceasing to Be Republican, Remained Revolutionary")

What a portrait of Napoleon Tocqueville could have given us. We have some of its features in the notes he left behind; they startle us with his many insights.

The last of Tocqueville's notes sums up his view of the Revolution:

Generally speaking, people are not very ardent or indomitable or energetic in their affairs when their personal passions are not engaged. Yet their personal passions, however vivid they may be, do not propel them either very far or very high unless these passions keep growing before their own eyes, unless they seem to justify themselves by being related to some greater cause for the service of mankind.

It is because of our human sense of honor that we are in need of this stimulant. Add to passions born of self-interest the aim to change the face of the world and to regenerate the human race: only then will you see what men are really capable of.

That is the history of the French Revolution.

Its narrowminded and selfish nature led to violence and darkness; its generous and selfless elements made its impulse powerful and great.

Tocqueville's books about the French Revolution are the clearest evidence that he was a modern historian. And yet, because of the deplorable habit of thinking in intellectual compartments, it is seldom that he is recognized as such. An interesting list could be compiled from the names of those who have asserted that Tocqueville was a conservative, a liberal, a historian, a sociologist, an aristocrat, a democrat, a Christian, an agnostic. In quite a few instances the commentators contradict themselves; at times Tocqueville is assigned to contradictory categories within the same monograph, essay, or review. Yet his books about the Revolution are crystal clear. They show, for instance, that while he did not believe that the voice of the people is the voice of God, neither did he believe that it was the voice of the devil. He was not one of those who thought that a nation has the right to go beyond its natural interests to impose ideas on others and arrogate to itself the role of teaching the world; yet he did not believe in a narrow concept of national interests either. He was not a French nationalist or a European imperialist; yet he did not assume that the achievements and the ideals of every nation and every civilization are of the same worth. He condemned the old regime as well as the Revolution and found virtues in both.

The Revolution, therefore, is hortatory history. I have suggested that it is hardly possible to comprehend Tocqueville's writings without considering the moral purposes of their author. In turn, it is only with these moral purposes in mind that one can avoid some of the mistaken conceptions of Tocqueville and his work. If the main concern of *Democracy in America* was the future of democracy, that book also reveals Tocqueville as more than a conservative democrat or a liberal aristocrat. If the main concern of the *The Revolution* included the future of France and of Europe, it also reveals Tocqueville as more than an old-fashioned historian or a forerunner of sociology. His preoccupation with the evolving relationship of Christianity and democracy, revealed in his letters and later writings, shows that he was neither a "progressive" Catholic nor an aristocratic skeptic, but a great Christian thinker and a magnanimous spirit.

V

During the summer of 1858 Tocqueville's physical condition worsened. He had to give up work on his book. In June he suffered a hemorrhage in one lung. His wife was also ill. In October his doctor in Paris recommended that they go south again. The next month they arrived in Cannes, completely exhausted. By February his health had improved a little. As always, he devoted considerable time and effort to correspondence with his friends. His last letters were dictated a week before he died, on 16 April 1859.

Next to his health, the most important development during Tocqueville's last months concerned his religion. Soon after they had arrived in Cannes the Tocquevilles began to look for a nursing sister. Since his illness prevented him from going to church, he asked one of the sisters to read him the prayers of the mass. The bishop of Orléans came to visit; he and another priest said mass in Tocqueville's rooms. He made his confession, took communion, and died at peace with himself and with his church.

These events were contested during the century that passed after Tocqueville's death. Certain people, especially certain intellectuals, claimed that Tocqueville's last religious acts were questionable, since they had been undertaken out of respect for the wishes of his wife. The support of their claim rests on a statement by Beaumont, as well as on an earlier phrase written by Tocqueville himself: "Je crois mais je ne puis pratiquer"—"I believe but I cannot practice"—a phrase that attests to Tocqueville's intellectual and moral scrupulosity, rather than to disbelief. He had been brought up by an admirable tutor, the abbé Lesueur; around the age of sixteen, Tocqueville said, he had recognized that his Christian beliefs were no longer unconditional.

The evidence for his private religious practices during the middle phase of his life remains fragmentary; the evidence for his religious practices during the last phase of his life is not. It is not only that the statement by Beaumont is contradicted by many other accounts and letters by Tocqueville's friends and members of his family. In 1962 this writer found three separate accounts by the nursing sisters in the archives of their congregation; published in the July 1964 issue of the *Catholic Historical Review*, they confirm the facts and attest to the sincerity of Tocqueville's religious acts.

Why lay stress on these private matters? For two reasons. First, they may help to answer the third among the series of questions previously posed: Was Tocqueville a historian or a sociologist? a liberal or a conservative? a skeptic or a believing Catholic? Second, his concern with religion appears with increasing frequency in Tocqueville's correspondence during the last decade of his life when, together with self-questioning about his own faith, the problem of the compatibility of religion with democracy became one of his deepest preoccupations. There are evidences of this already in his *Democracy in America* in the 1830's.

Tocqueville's correspondence was voluminous. Of the twenty-one volumes planned for the still uncompleted edition of his collected works, eleven or twelve will consist of letters. They are still being discovered in French family archives and in the stocks of manuscript dealers. The scope of his correspondence is amazing. It deals with innumerable topics of lasting interest. The letters about England, Germany, and Russia deserve minute attention. The quality of the writing is as high as that of his finished books. Tocqueville had often thought that he was solitary, but he put great value on his friendships. He was driven by a need to express his thoughts to his friends. His letters served him as a diary would another thinker. In them we find the germ of ideas Tocqueville would later develop in a book. For example, Tocqueville to Pierre Freslon, 10 August 1853:

> In reading the correspondence of the ministers of Louis XV with their subordinates, you see a crowd of little embryo professors of imperial administrative law. So true is this that the better one is acquainted with the old regime the more one finds that the Revolution was far from doing either all the good or all the harm that is supposed; it may be said rather to have disturbed than to have altered society. This truth springs up in all directions as soon as one ploughs the ancient soil.

Among the most important of these letters are those that Tocqueville wrote to Arthur de Gobineau. Gobineau met Tocqueville in the early 1840's. In 1849 he served as Tocqueville's secretary. During the 1850's they saw each other relatively seldom; but Gobineau tried out some of his theories in his letters to Tocqueville, whose reactions to Gobineau's ideas—and later to Gobineau's book *The Inequality of the Human Races*—are trenchant and extremely important. They are summary statements of the beliefs of the Catholic Tocqueville; and they are principal arguments for the incompatibility of Christianity with a philosophy of history dependent on conceptions of race. They also illustrate the idealism

of Tocqueville, who wrote his friend Louis de Kergorlay in 1835, twenty years before the development of his dialogue with Gobineau:

> Do what you will, you can't change the fact that men have bodies as well as souls—that the angel is enclosed in the beast. . . . Any philosophy, any religion which tries to leave entirely out of account one of these two things may produce a few extraordinary exemplars, but it will never influence humanity as a whole. This is what I believe, and it troubles me, for you know that, no more detached from the beast than anyone else, I adore the angel and want at all costs to see him predominate.

This passage, by no means an isolated one, shows the Pascalian element in Tocqueville's thought. Like his temperament and his faith, his views of human nature and of human knowledge were not Cartesian.

Tocqueville had little appetite for methodical philosophy, though on occasion he did not hesitate to criticize certain passages in Aristotle or Plato. Yet the processes of Tocqueville's thought were exquisitely philosophical. He saw, for example, that in human beings the relations of cause and effect are far more complex than in other organisms, let alone in the physical world. This perception is manifested in Tocqueville's discovery that revolutions often break out not when the pressure on people is the greatest, but when that pressure has recognizably begun to lessen. In short, the mechanical laws of the physical universe do not automatically apply to the human universe. As Tocqueville wrote in one of his last letters to Gobineau, in 1858: "A hypothesis which permits the prediction of certain effects that always recur under the same conditions does, in a way, amount to a demonstrable truth. [But] even the Newtonian system has no more than such a foundation." In this respect, too, Tocqueville's mind ran ahead of the nineteenth century. His ideas accord with those of some of the greatest twentieth-century thinkers, such as the Spanish philosopher José Ortega y Gasset, the French radical Christian humanist Georges Bernanos, and the German physicist-philosopher Werner Heisenberg.

We have seen that the recognition of Tocqueville has been far from universal and often inadequate, even though his literary legacy is unusually rich in scope and extent. We know much about his ideas, about the inclinations of his mind, and even about his religious and other beliefs. We know less about his private life. Many of his contemporaries resented Tocqueville's detached intelligence; they imputed to him an air of self-conscious superiority. Yet Tocqueville was a warmhearted human being, often to the point of excitability. His physical appearance was unprepossessing: he was small, thin, and nervous. The true nature of his nobility resided in his soul. In one of his notes he wrote: ''Life is neither a pleasure nor a pain, but a serious spiritual business which it is our duty to carry through and to terminate with honor.''

Selected Bibliography

EDITIONS

INDIVIDUAL WORKS

De la démocratie en Amérique. Vol. 1. Paris, 1840.
————. Vol. 2. Paris, 1860.
L'Ancien régime et la révolution. Paris, 1856.
Souvenirs. Paris, 1893.

COLLECTED WORKS

Oeuvres complètes. Edited by Gustave de Beaumont. 9 vols. Paris, 1860–1866.
Oeuvres complètes. Edited by J. P. Mayer et al. Paris, 1951– . Of the projected twenty-one volumes, sixteen had been published as of 1985, including two double volumes of *De la démocratie en Amérique.*

TRANSLATIONS

Alexis de Tocqueville: Recollections. Translated by George Lawrence and edited by J. P. Mayer and A. P. Kerr. Garden City, N.Y., 1970.

Democracy in America. Translated by Henry Reeve. New York, 1862. Revised by F. Bowen and Phillips Bradley. New York, 1945, 1961. Includes bibliography.
The European Revolution and Correspondence with Gobineau. Translated with introduction by John Lukacs. New York, 1959. Contains unfinished portions of Tocqueville's projected second volume of *The Old Régime . . .* as well as the Gobineau correspondence.
Journeys to England and Ireland. Translated by George Lawrence and J. P. Mayer. New Haven, Conn., 1958. Paperback edition, Garden City, N.Y., 1968.
Memoir, Letters, and Remains of Alexis de Tocqueville. Translated by Henry Reeve and edited by Gustave de Beaumont. New York, 1862.
The Old Régime and the Revolution. Translated by Stuart Gilbert. New York, 1955.
The Recollections of Alexis de Tocqueville. Translated by Alexander Taxeira de Mattos. New York, 1896.

BIOGRAPHICAL AND CRITICAL STUDIES

Alexis de Tocqueville: Livre du centenaire 1859–1959. Paris, 1960.
Corral, Luis Diez del. *La mentalidad política de Tocqueville con especial referencia a Pascal.* Madrid, 1965.
Drescher, Seymour. *Tocqueville and England.* Cambridge, Mass., 1964.
Lamberti, Jean Claude. *La notion d'individualisme chez Tocqueville.* Paris, 1970.
Marcel, R. P. *Essai politique sur Alexis de Tocqueville avec un grand nombre de documents inédits.* Paris, 1910.
Mayer, J. P. *Alexis de Tocqueville: A Biographical Essay in Political Science.* New York, 1940. Revised ed. with additional essay, New York, 1960.
Pierson, G. W., ed. *Tocqueville and Beaumont in America.* New York, 1938.
Redier, Antoine. *Comme diasit M. de Tocqueville.* Paris, 1925.
Zetterbaum, Marvin. *Tocqueville and the Problem of Democracy.* Stanford, Calif., 1967.

JOHN LUKACS

LEO TOLSTOY
(1828–1910)

IN NOVEMBER 1855 Count Leo (in Russian: Lev) Tolstoy arrived in Saint Petersburg directly from the Crimea, where he had participated in the war with the European powers and had observed the siege of Sevastopol. The disastrous war was being brought to a close. Nicholas I, after ruling despotically for thirty years, had died in February, and the heir, Alexander II, was expected to undertake long-delayed reforms, including the abolition of serfdom. Everyone felt that an era of Russian history was ending. The time was ripe for the advent of a new generation of writers. At this propitious moment Tolstoy entered the circle of literati grouped around the influential journal *Sovremennik (The Contemporary)*.

Tolstoy was already well known by reputation to the Saint Petersburg writers who welcomed him. His first work, *Childhood*, had appeared in *The Contemporary* in 1852 and had been greeted by almost unanimous praise from all the factions that made up the contentious Russian literary scene. Ivan Turgenev, whose *Sportsman's Sketches* had established him as the leading writer of the day, wrote to the editor of *The Contemporary:* "This is a sure gift. Write him and encourage him to continue. Tell him, in case he may be interested, that I welcome, hail, and applaud him." *Childhood* had been followed by *Boyhood* (1854) and several short stories, but when Tolstoy came to Saint Petersburg he was hailed as the author of *Sevastopol Sketches,* the first two of which had appeared in *The Contemporary* earlier in 1855.

Sevastopol Sketches had electrified the public with their accounts of the Russian soldiers' suffering and heroism under continual bombardment in the besieged city. "The hero of my tale is truth," Tolstoy had written, and the precision of his account, combined with an elevated and sonorous lyricism, had impressed upon his readers the tragedy of war. The second sketch, "Sevastopol in May," began: "Already six months have passed since the first shot whistled from the bastions of Sevastopol and plowed the earth at the enemy's fortifications, and since that time thousands of bombs, cannonballs, and bullets have not ceased to fly from the bastions to the trenches and from the trenches to the bastions, and the angel of death has not ceased to soar above us." In his role as war correspondent Tolstoy had gone far beyond "dispatches from the front" to evolve a style combining factuality with prophetic vision. He was greeted on his arrival in Saint Petersburg both as the hero of Sevastopol (his role in the fighting had in fact been slight) and as the hope for the future of Russian literature.

The Saint Petersburg writers expected Tolstoy to take up the career considered appropriate for a Russian literary man in the mid-nineteenth century. He would ally himself with one of the factions, announce his ideological position on the literary and social questions debated by the intelligentsia, and settle down as a regular contributor to one of the journals, probably *The Contemporary*, where all his work to date had been published. They reckoned without Tolstoy's independent character. He lost no time in establishing himself as wholly different in his habits and attitudes from members of the Russian intelligentsia. He quarreled with Turgenev, rejected the ideological positions of all the factions, and played the role of officer and aristocrat to the hilt by visiting in society, carousing at night with gypsies, and sleeping until two in the afternoon. The intellectuals reached their verdict, ''a wild man,'' and yet still they courted him, eager to acquire so much talent and energy for the service of their cause.

In subsequent decades, as in the 1850's, Russian literary men continued to regard Tolstoy as a valuable national property to be exploited for the glory of Russian literature. His life and work continued to be bound inextricably with the vicissitudes of national life and yet to express the concerns of each decade in ways peculiarly his own. The pressures of these forces, national and individual, shaped that mythical ''Tolstoy'' possessed by the modern reader. Virginia Woolf thought him the very type of the alien element in the Russian character that prevents Russian literature from ever being wholly accessible to Europeans. Yet Tolstoy seems far more the world's than Russia's, too large to be confined within a single national tradition or even a single historical period.

With Tolstoy's debut the constellation of writers whose work would make the Russian novel a powerful voice in world literature was complete. The tide of novels began by the end of the 1850's and continued with undiminished force up to 1880. In this period Tolstoy wrote two works, *War and Peace* (written 1863–1869) and *Anna Karenina* (written 1873–1876), that have become accepted into the world's common fund of literature. He is the author of other original and ingratiating works that continue to hold the reader's affection, among them *Childhood* (1852), *Family Happiness* (1859), *The Cossacks* (1863), *The Death of Ivan Ilich* (1886), *Master and Man* (1895), *Father Sergius* (1911), and *Hadji-Murad* (1912). These and a few more items compose his purely literary legacy, but he also wrote strange, powerful, polemical works— *The Kreutzer Sonata* (1891), *A Confession* (1884), *What Is Art?* (1897–1898), *Resurrection* (1899)—that are an inseparable part of our modern conception of Tolstoy.

Beyond that, Tolstoy's own life has become a part of our literary tradition. Boris Eikhenbaum observes that in another epoch Tolstoy would not have been a writer. Tolstoy entered literature because in the Russian conditions of the time, literature was the arena open to independent action. There was scarcely another possibility for setting one's own course. One could retreat and become the manager of one's estate—Tolstoy's grandfather and father had taken this path, and Tolstoy would try it in his turn—but then one lost the possibility of influencing public life. In spite of his hatred of the ideological polemics that drained Russian life of all force of action, Tolstoy entered the public arena repeatedly. His energies spread out beyond literature into pedagogy, social thought, and moral philosophy. Again and again he sought to turn the gold coin of his fame as a writer into public influence.

In the last decades of his life Tolstoy publicly repudiated his earlier literary career to devote himself to the moral betterment of humankind. He succeeded in becoming the spokesman for a great ethical position and achieved world influence and renown. His creed was based on the realization in daily life of the ethical principles of Christ—a freely chosen life of simplicity and poverty, resistance to evil through the force of one's example, and nonviolence in every sphere of life from the personal to the national. He had thirsted from youth to play the role of a great prophet. That desire was justified by his consciousness of his genuinely great powers, but the wish was sometimes so transparent that it dismayed Maxim Gorky, who wrote in his memoirs:

> I was always put off by that stubborn, despotic aspiration to turn the life of Count Leo Nikolaevich Tolstoy into "The Life of the Saintly Father Our Blessed Boyar Leo." . . . He had been planning to "suffer" for a long time; he expressed his sorrow that he hadn't succeeded; but he wanted to suffer not simply, not from a natural wish to test the stubbornness of his will, but from a clear and, I repeat, despotic intention to strengthen the yoke of his religious ideas, the burden of his teaching, to make his prophecy irrefutable, to consecrate it in people's eyes by his suffering and to force them to accept it, you understand—force them!
>
> (*Sobranie sochinenii*, Moscow, 1963, vol. 18, p. 75)

Tolstoy's life and work are tied to a place more surely than any other Russian writer's. Yasnaya Polyana, the estate where he spent his early childhood, where he later brought his wife, where they raised a large family, and where he wrote his books and became a prophet of moral awakening, was in a profound sense his home. He once answered "Where were you born?" on a playful family questionnaire with "At Yasnaya Polyana on the leather couch." Yasnaya Polyana means "serene fields," and it is located in the central Russian heartland near Tula, some few hours' drive south of Moscow.

We can speak of a Yasnaya Polyana idyll that dominates Tolstoy's life and work to the end of the 1870's. Yasnaya Polyana was bound up in Tolstoy's thinking with the continuity of his family and its traditions, with the dream of finding a place where he could lead a life of moral integrity and productive work, and with the desire to secure a retreat from the corrupting influence of society at large. How he dreamed upon the theme of Yasnaya Polyana is revealed in a remarkable letter he wrote from the Caucasus in 1852 to his Aunt Toinette:

> Here is how I imagine the happiness that awaits me in the future. The years pass and I find myself, already no longer young, but not yet old, at Yasnaya. My affairs are in order, I have no worries or problems. You are still living at Yasnaya. You have grown a little older, but you are still active and in good health. Life goes on as before: I work in the morning, but we are together almost all day. After dinner in the evening I read something aloud to you that you won't be bored listening to. Then conversation begins. I tell you about my life in the Caucasus, you recount your recollections of the past, of my father and mother. You tell me the horror tales that we used to listen to with frightened eyes and open mouths. We recall those who were dear to us and are no longer living. You cry and I do, too, but with reconciled tears. We talk of my brothers who come to visit us and of dear Mashenka [Tolstoy's sister], who will visit her beloved Yasnaya with the children for several months every year. We will have no acquaintances. No one will come to bother us and spread gossip. A beautiful dream, but I allow myself to dream of even more. I am married. My wife is gentle, kind, and loving and she loves you as I do. Our children call you "grandmother." You live upstairs in the big house, in that room where grandmother used to live. Everything in the house is the way it was when papa was alive, and we continue to live that life, only changing roles: you will take on the role of grandmother, I the role of papa, though I don't hope ever to deserve it, my wife, that of mama, our children, our role. Mashenka will be in the role of both the aunts, but not unhappy as they were. Even Gasha [Toinette's servant] will be in the place of Praskovya Isaevna [the former housekeeper]. The only thing missing is a person who could replace you in relationship to the whole family. We won't find such a wonderful loving soul. No, you will not have a replacement. . . . If you made me the Russian emperor, if you offered me Peru, in a word if a fairy godmother appeared with a magic wand and asked me what I want, I can say

in all honesty with hand on heart: Just one thing, to realize my dream.

(*Sobranie sochinenii*, vol. 17, p. 56)

Three generations of life at Yasnaya Polyana provided Tolstoy with material that would become the backbone of his novels. Yasnaya Polyana had been the estate of his formidable grandfather Prince Nicholas Volkonsky, who had retired there when he incurred the czar's disfavor and himself became disillusioned with public life. Prince Volkonsky had risen to prominence during the reign of Catherine the Great, attaining the rank of *général en chef* and serving as ambassador extraordinary to the king of Prussia. Tolstoy's mother, Princess Marya Volkonsky, had spent her girlhood at Yasnaya Polyana, educated there by her widowed father in the spirit of the philosophes, who were his chief reading and the major influences on his own mind and sensibilities. The figure of his grandfather loomed large in Tolstoy's imagination, as did in a very different way the figure of his mother. Yasnaya Polyana had been in his grandfather's generation a symbol of the independence of the nobility from the court and administration, a place where reason and order and the pursuits of the mind were dominant, and the place where his mother had quietly nurtured in herself the moral sentiments and spiritual aspirations that later set the tone for her family.

Princess Marya's married life at Yasnaya Polyana formed the second generation of the idyll, the one Tolstoy harks back to in his letter as the model for his own future life. Prince Volkonsky had kept his daughter with him beyond the age when she should have married, and it was only after his death that her relatives, finding her possessed of a surprising and dangerous independence, grew alarmed and sought a husband for her. They found one in the handsome, socially brilliant Count Nicholas Tolstoy, who had been forced to seek a wealthy bride because his father had squandered the family fortune.

Nicholas Tolstoy brought with him to live at Yasnaya Polyana his widowed mother, a spoiled, aristocratic grande dame with a strong sense of her rank. From time to time his sisters Alexandra and Polina, and Tatyana Ergolskaya ("Toinette"), a relative, stayed with the family. Toinette had grown up with the Tolstoy children and was in love with Nicholas, whom she hoped to marry, but in a self-sacrificing spirit native to her character she stepped aside to permit the family fortunes to be saved. Tolstoy recognized the ready-made novel in his parents' marriage and Aunt Toinette's role and incorporated it into *War and Peace*.

Marya Tolstoy won over her new relatives by her lively and gentle temperament and settled down to bear Nicholas five children, the fourth being Leo, born 28 August 1828. The family idyll was cut short by the untimely death of Marya Tolstoy soon after the birth of her last child, a daughter, when Leo was not yet two years old. Aunt Toinette took over the task of mothering the children and became, as Tolstoy was to say, the most important influence on his life.

The high spiritual ideal that came to Tolstoy from the tradition of his mother's life is central to the Yasnaya Polyana idyll. He had in his possession his mother's papers—her diaries, notebooks, and letters. They reveal that Princess Volkonsky was a highly educated, even intellectual, woman. Her reading encompassed history, travel notes, philosophy, and moral instruction. Among authors whom she read and in many cases translated were Laurence Sterne, Blaise Pascal, Voltaire, Alphonse de Lamartine, Jean Jacques Rousseau, and Georges de Buffon, as well as many now-forgotten authors of sentimental admonitions and instructive tales. Princess Marya took seriously the discipline of self-improvement that was enjoined upon her by her reading. Pious and sentimental by temper, she kept watch on her own spiritual development and was concerned as a mother that her children should develop their moral potentialities. After her marriage she read Rousseau's *Émile* together with her sister-in-law and engaged her in discussion of pedagogical theory. She kept a notebook on the methods she employed to mold the spirit of her oldest son, Nicholas.

Princess Marya also had literary aspirations. In her girlhood she had kept the other girls spellbound at balls by narrating stories to them. Her papers include her poems; accounts of trips she made; a moral fairytale, "The Forest Twins," about the transformation of simple shepherdesses into princesses; and a story, "The Russian Pamela," about the love of a prince's son for a poor girl. Her writings express the simple noble sentiments: that the meaning of life is found only in virtue, that only truth is worthy of human suffering and striving, that happiness lies in the aspiration to well-being of those around us, and that it is easier to bear poverty than to avoid becoming attached to wealth.

Along with her sincere dedication to the search for the moral life, Princess Marya also gives an impression of gaiety, thirst for experience, and appreciation of the larger life. According to one story, her mortal illness was caused by her fall from a swing when she had swung up with too much abandon. She was bitterly disappointed when Czar Alexander I passed along the road near Yasnaya Polyana in 1823 and she saw only his carriage from afar without getting a glimpse of his person. She admired the czar and took an interest in monarchs as actors in the great affairs of state. She felt herself to be a woman of the highest class, the daughter of a man who had been a participant in history. She felt at home among great aspirations. They were in some sense her own, in spite of her personal modesty.

The atmosphere of moral striving, self-examination, and the search for the good lingered on at Yasnaya Polyana after her death. It was reflected in her sister-in-law Alexandra's meek Christianity; in Aunt Toinette's preservation of the tradition of Marya's goodness and spirituality; in Toinette's self-abnegating

service to the family; and in the influence of the oldest son, Nicholas, on the younger children. Tolstoy was less than two when his mother died, but the high-minded tone of Yasnaya Polyana continued to shape his development up to twelve years of age, when, after the death of his father, he went to live with his Aunt Polina in Kazan. Indeed, the rules inculcated by the Yasnaya Polyana tradition were those Tolstoy used to measure his conduct to the end of his life. There came to be a recognizable Tolstoy family tone, which made the poet Afanasy Fet say about the three of the four brothers he knew:

I am convinced that the underlying type of all three Tolstoy brothers is identical, as identical as the type of maple leaves, in spite of all the variations of their features. And if I tried to develop that thought, I would show to what degree was characteristic of all three brothers that passionate enthusiasm, without which one of them could not have become the writer, L. Tolstoy. The difference in their relationship to life consists in the way in which each of them withdrew from an unsuccessful dream. Nicholas quenched his transports with skeptical irony, Leo left his unrealizable dream with silent remorse, and Sergey with painful misanthropy.
(*Vospominanie*, Moscow, 1890, vol. 1, p. 296)

Tolstoy's life is one of the best-recorded of any writer's. He kept diaries for most of his adult life, and he inspired those around him to keep diaries, so that for many periods of his life we have multiple accounts of his daily actions and states of mind. Self-analysis was not only his habit but his pleasure. In his youth he read many of the same authors who had formed his mother's sensibility, in particular Rousseau and Sterne, from both of whom he learned to examine the immediate flow of experience. Tolstoy kept his diaries from 1846, when he was eighteen years old, to his death in 1910. He interrupted them for only one significant break, from 1865 to 1878, when he had established his own domestic idyll at Yasnaya Polyana and was occupied in composing *War and Peace* and *Anna Karenina*.

Tolstoy's diaries are his indispensable aid to following and shaping his inner life. They are both retrospective and projective. Particularly in youth he spent much time laying out programs of action for himself:

> What will be the aim of my life in the country during the next two years? (1) To study the entire course of legal sciences needed for the final examination at the university. (2) To study practical medicine and some medical theory. (3) To study languages: French, Russian, German, English, Italian, and Latin. (4) To study agriculture, both theoretical and practical. (5) To study history, geography, and statistics. (6) To study mathematics—the gymnasium course. (7) To write my dissertation. (8) To attain an average level of accomplishment in music and painting. (9) To write rules. (10) To acquire a certain understanding of the natural sciences. (11) To write compositions in all the subjects that I will be studying.
>
> (*Sobranie sochinenii*, vol. 19, p. 40)

Boris Eikhenbaum remarks that in fact the writing of rules was the main point of Tolstoy's activity. His programs of moral improvement and steps to social success were as ambitious as his programs of self-instruction. The grandiose plans were never realized. Indeed, their primary purpose seems to have been to allow Tolstoy to record in his diary all the ways in which he fell short of them, a task he undertook with gusto. Nevertheless, the programs were indispensable to Tolstoy's development as a writer. In his fiction, as in his life, a motive force was the program of moral action. His compensatory imagination caused him to remake reality, to project onto the past or the future the forms that suited his inner sense of how things should be. His work is distinguished by its documentarity: it is full of the details and events of his own observed and lived reality. Yet whatever story he took, whether from his own life or from the lives of others, he reshaped it to suit his rules, his pro-

grams. Eikhenbaum calls Tolstoy's diaries of youth the laboratory in which he worked out his craft. They were also the workshop in which he constructed the programs of values he hoped to advance through his life work.

We see Tolstoy casting about in the diaries for a role to play in the world. He is full of great ambitions: he thinks now of writing a history of Europe in the nineteenth century, now of founding a religion, now of writing a code of laws, now of becoming a famous writer. In this period from 1847 to 1852 his brothers regarded him as a failure. He dropped out of his law course at the University of Kazan; he tried to manage his estate but grew tired of the task and abandoned it; he went to Saint Petersburg planning to enlist as a cadet, but decided against it. He spent his time drinking, womanizing, gambling his inheritance away. He dreamed of bettering his lot by marrying an heiress. Finally, his brother Nicholas, in a desperate attempt to save him, took him off to the Caucasus, where by serving as a volunteer Leo won an officer's commission.

In the undemanding and isolated conditions of a Cossack border station Tolstoy began writing in earnest and produced the work that established him as a writer, *Childhood*. Yet he was not satisfied that he had found an occupation answering to his need, and the search in the diaries continued, through his stay among the Saint Petersburg intelligentsia, through his retreat once more to Yasnaya Polyana, through two trips abroad, and through a passionate involvement in pedagogy. In 1862 he married eighteen-year-old Sofya Andreevna Behrs, brought her straight to Yasnaya Polyana, and began at last to establish the domestic idyll he had elaborated with such pleasure to his Aunt Toinette. In the next decade he wrote his great novels and ceased to write his diary.

In 1878, when he once again became engaged in a search for a great and significant task that would give meaning to his life and change the world, Tolstoy returned to his diary. His spiritual crisis resulted in the repudiation of his earlier life and work and the rejection of the wealth he had accumulated through his literary efforts and the good management of his estate. His wife could not accept this new program, which contradicted the whole of their lives together and threatened to impoverish their children. The children divided into parties, some taking the side of their mother, some of their father. Thus the diaries of his last decades, begun as an aid to his inner search, became inadvertently the history of a family drama, which culminated in 1910 when Tolstoy, old and in ill health, left his home to escape his wife's importunities and to find the ideal life of spirituality and poverty that his beliefs bound him to. He died at the railway station at Astapovo on 7 November 1910.

The diaries were not only the record of but a weapon in the struggle between Tolstoy and his wife, which still seizes the popular imagination as powerfully as any of his fictions. In these last years of his life a veritable war of diaries was waged in the Tolstoy family. Not only did Sofya Andreevna keep her own diary, expressly to counter the pernicious story she suspected her husband of constructing for posterity; not only did one or another of the children keep diaries; but Tolstoy himself kept two diaries, a "public" diary, accessible to his wife and others, and a secret one for himself alone. In the battle among the members of the family for the right to tell the story, the physical possession of the diaries became a matter of concern. Tolstoy's disciple Vladimir Chertkov, the self-appointed guardian of the moral awakening that Tolstoy's name was attached to, persuaded Tolstoy to surrender the diaries to him. Sofya Andreevna took this as a profound betrayal of her role as wife, companion, and literary secretary to her husband. She suspected that Tolstoy had made a secret will depriving her and the children of the rights to his works after his death. Chertkov in fact had persuaded him to do so. The loss of the diaries instigated her desperate opposition and led to Tolstoy's final departure.

Thus Tolstoy, who had coveted the power that the written word could have if it was wholly given over to truth, found his own diaries invested with a power that he could never have anticipated. Throughout his life Tolstoy was disturbed by writing that was not ultimately serious, by writing that emphasized the aspect of pleasure and play (this was his objection to William Shakespeare, whom he found too pliant to be moral). Seeking to find a form in which truth itself would be the hero, he constantly changed his literary direction. His diaries, the searching record of his own aspirations and experiences, were in many ways the very foundation of the Tolstoyan aesthetic.

When Tolstoy sent the manuscript of his first work, *Childhood*, to N. A. Nekrasov in 1852 for publication in *The Contemporary*, he wrote to him by way of introducing the work: "This manuscript comprises the first part of a novel, *Four Epochs of Growth*." *Childhood*, and as much of the tetralogy as Tolstoy completed, is shaped by the notion of a self unfolding in time, in responsive sympathy with its surroundings and experiences. The emphasis on growth and formation, and the consequent fluid image of the self, was to become a keystone of Tolstoy's vision as artist. Though Tolstoy did not invent this view of the self, he devoted a lifetime of creative work and thought to its examination. Indeed, we might say that this vision of the self, which has lately come to be called "expressivist," was at the heart of those far-flung endeavors and generous expenses of energy, mind, and emotion that characterized this man's prodigious life.[1]

Rousseau had written of the "expanding plenitude" that "extends our being." Johann Gottfried von Herder took his cue from Rousseau and worked out a unified scheme for the relationship of self to external reality. Herder sought to find again a single center from

---

[1] The term "expressivist theory" was coined by Isaiah Berlin: see his *Vico and Herder*, New York, 1976.

which everything the individual does flows inevitably. In the thought of Herder and those who followed him, a program of life that would be conducive to the natural unfolding of the self's potentialities had been elaborated. In *Childhood* Tolstoy shows himself well aware of the program. Indeed the structure of the work is directly derived from it, and Tolstoy assiduously moves through the series of formative experiences that had become touchstones of the life of feeling: maternal love, sympathetic concern for those less fortunate than oneself, religious exaltation, responsiveness to natural beauty, desire for artistic self-expression, friendship, romantic love, death.

In his tracing of the child's awakening sense of moral responsibility, Tolstoy focuses in particular on Nikolenka's developing sense of his own fortunate position in society and the unfortunate position occupied by those of lower rank, a sense that the psychologist Robert Coles dubbed "entitlement." Turgenev's *Sportsman's Sketches*, written in the tradition of George Sand's country romances and the village stories of the German moralists, had set a new standard for depicting members of the lower classes. The unfortunate—who included tutors and governesses as well as servants and peasants—must be shown fully to be persons in the light of the new standard of selfhood. They must be shown to have aesthetic and moral sensibility, to enjoy the full play of consciousness in which the significance of life was now felt to reside. In his sketches of the tutor Karl Ivanych, the old housekeeper Natalya Savishna, the holy fool and pilgrim Grisha, Tolstoy creates portraits of members of the lower classes who have rich inner lives. The child Nikolenka develops sentiments of pity and justice in response to the full feelings he observes in them.

As the boy's capacity for self-expression flowers, Tolstoy reveals a damaging paradox in expectations of self-expression. In the programmatic chapter "Childhood" he emphasizes what is unique to early childhood, the child's pure sensations and the unfettered responses to the misfortunes of others. Later, life spoils the child's pure feeling. As the child's moral awareness is developed, his exposure to society develops a corresponding insincerity. For the first time we see the struggle between purity and the knowing consciousness that shapes so much of Tolstoy's work.

Even before the time of Rousseau the myth of the noble savage had provided one image of an untrammeled freedom in which the self could develop apart from the corrupting influence of society. Whereas European writers looked to America as the locus of their fantasies, the Russians found a promised land within their own borders, and the Russian romantic writers hastened to glorify the Caucasus, with its exotic peoples and wild, majestic scenery. Tolstoy began his novel of life in the Caucasus, *The Cossacks*, in the early 1850's during his service there, but he published it only in 1863. The Greben Cossacks, whom Tolstoy lived among and observed in his border station, were Russians belonging to the sect of Old Believer schismatics. They had retreated into the wild border area in earlier centuries to escape persecution and in modern times had taken on the duty of defending the border in return for the right to preserve their own customs and self-government. They were not exactly "noble savages," but they were simple people living in close touch with nature and with considerable freedom by Russian standards, since most peasants in Russia were bound to the land and hence to the owners of the land.

The Cossacks is filled with much closely observed ethnographic detail, but its main interest lies in Tolstoy's depiction of the psychology of his hero, Olenin, a young man from the landowning class who has come from Moscow to escape the empty life he has been leading in society and to find new purpose in the romantic Caucasus. He has formed an image of life there from books. The novel traces the gradual displacement of Olenin's romantic image with one more true to life, still noble but infused with the actual complexity of reality itself. Olenin has dreamed that he will meet and marry a beautiful Cossack girl. Soon after his arrival he settles upon the lovely and aloof daughter of his landlord, Maryanka, but discovers that she is to be betrothed to a young Cossack, Lukashka. Lukashka is for Olenin the perfect image of what he himself longs to be, a "brave," courageous and a superb horseman. He kills a hostile Chechen tribesman and feels no remorse, only triumph in his skill and bravery. For Lukashka everything is straightforward: he does his duty at the cordon, he drinks and enjoys himself on leave at the border station, and he plans to marry Maryanka and settle down to the life of his forefathers. Olenin is civilized. Self-consciousness complicates and, in the end, spoils everything. Trying to befriend Lukashka, he merely bumbles and draws Lukashka's suspicion and hostility. The proud Maryanka is curious about the lodger, but she comes to feel contempt for him and spurns him for Lukashka. Nothing is left for Olenin but to leave the station and return to his own society, unburdened of his illusion that he, a pampered, civilized man, can become a Cossack.

Much of the Cossacks' nobility derives from their immersion in simple, useful work that fills their time and gives their lives meaning. Maryanka is usually shown at her chores— milking, driving the goats to pasture, harvesting the grapes. Though the Cossacks' activities render them in some measure prosaic, they still remain beyond Olenin's reach, images of the ideal Other with whom the self cannot merge. Tolstoy has created a remarkable figure in the old Cossack Eroshka, a hunter and himself something of an outcast in the village, who lives in the old way. He is the village's storyteller, the repository of the legends of a golden age in which the Cossacks, untouched by civilization, lived like the Chechen tribesmen, truly noble savages. Eroshka also has something about him of the legendary trickster who survives through cunning. His acquisitiveness, his willingness to

manipulate Olenin for his own ends, his lack of fidelity either to Olenin or to his favorite, Lukashka, are passed over as the godlike attributes of a simple nature that has not been spoiled by the complex ethical codes of civilized society. In the ways that count, reverence for life and knowledge of nature, Eroshka is pure.

After the publication of *Childhood* and the *Sevastopol Sketches* the critic Nikolay Chernyshevsky wrote that Tolstoy was chiefly interested in "the psychological process, its forms, its laws, the dialectic of the soul." Methods of depiction of the inner life were further developed in *The Cossacks* and culminated in the great interior monologues of *War and Peace*. Chernyshevsky went on to say:

> Count Tolstoy's attention is turned most of all on how some feelings and thoughts develop out of others; he is interested in observing how a feeling, arising spontaneously from a given situation or impression and submitted to the influence of memories and the force of combinations projected by the imagination, turns into other feelings, then again returns to the starting point and again and again wanders away, being transformed along the whole chain of recollections; how a thought, born of the first sensation, leads to other thoughts, is drawn farther and farther, merges daydreams with real sensations, dreams of the future with the reflection of the present.
>
> (*Polnoe sobranie sochinenii*, Moscow, 1947, vol. 3, p. 422)

In *The Cossacks* Olenin's experience of the Caucasus and the consequent change in his own apprehension of reality constitute the story. Though the work is by no means structured according to the Jamesian "point of view," Olenin's consciousness defines the form of the novel. For long chapters we are apart from Olenin while Tolstoy tells us about the life of the station from the ethnographer's point of view, and yet the very objectivity of these passages is tied to Olenin. That the station has its independent life, of which he is not a part, is the lesson he must learn. Events find their meanings in his consciousness, as he discovers the essential truth that an objective world exists apart from himself. Thus the novel is both objective and subjective: objective in insisting on the presence of the larger world, subjective in focusing on the process of Olenin's development. It was Tolstoy's habit to diffuse his energies into many projects; some came to fruition decades after they were begun, others remained forever incomplete. His major novels crown whole decades of work, uniting in monumental, collage-like summations the themes and devices of lesser works. *War and Peace* comprehends the exploration of self worked out in the *Childhood* trilogy, the modes of consciousness and self-testing of *The Cossacks*, the domestic theme of *Family Happiness*, and the battle detail of the *Sevastopol Sketches*. At the same time it stretches the possibilities of all these thematic spheres. The nature of Tolstoy's imagination was such that combination led to new possibilities.

War and Peace belongs to the small group of literary works that seem placed beyond ordinary standards of literary judgment. It meant much personally to Tolstoy, for it demonstrated that he could realize the large ambitions that had haunted his imagination from childhood. He had the good fortune to understand the grandeur of the project as he embarked upon it. He wrote to his relative Alexandra Tolstoy:

> I have never before felt my powers of mind and even of moral force so free and so ready for work, and I do have work. That work is a novel of the period 1810–1820, which has occupied me entirely since the autumn. I am a writer now with the full force of my soul and I write and think as I have never written and thought before.
> (*Polnoe sobranie sochinenii*, Moscow, 1953, vol. 61, p. 23)

The work occupied seven years of Tolstoy's life—1863 to 1869. The monumentality of the task can be assessed through the novel's archive, which amounts to thousands of manuscript pages (and far from all of the drafted materials survive). Many episodes were redrafted numerous times. Other episodes were created and then found no place. Tolstoy often redrafted an episode once again when he had the page proofs in hand.

I have spoken of a Yasnaya Polyana idyll that provided a center for Tolstoy's imaginative projections of how life should be lived. *War and Peace* is saturated by the themes of the idyll. At its heart is the imagined world of Yasnaya Polyana's past during the time of Prince Volkonsky and after Marya's marriage to Nicholas. Though Tolstoy incorporates much factual material from the family tradition, he works it into his notion of how things might ideally have been had everything cohered to give his parents' lives their deepest significance. The documentary and visionary sides of Tolstoy's work come together here. We see how profoundly Yasnaya Polyana (called Bald Hills in the novel) was for him a space of the imagination in which the peculiarly Tolstoyan world could be invented. In keeping with the family history so firmly associated in Tolstoy's mind with Yasnaya Polyana, the novel is organized as the history of two families, the Rostovs and Bolkonskys. Indeed, we may speak of these families as collectively composing two of the major characters.

In the story of the Bolkonsky family Tolstoy transparently re-creates the epoch of his mother's girlhood, which was spent with her father at the country estate. The Bolkonsky family manifests collective characteristics: high-minded seeking for the good, devotion to duty, and self-denial. In Tolstoy's rich fictional world the making of discriminations among things that are like is paramount; each member of the family must be distinguished by his individual style of adherence to the general pattern of the family character. In old Prince Bolkonsky, duty and the renunciation of society are the product of cold reason and fierce pride. Princess Marya's devotion to duty is mediated by her pietism into personal humility and self-sacrifice for others. The Bolkonskys' spiritual elevation is extended to a wholly fictional character, Prince Andrey, who is attached to the family. In Prince Andrey, the Bolkonsky qualities of character are manifested on a new, ideal plane as greatness of soul and capacity to turn the intellect to the fundamental questions of the meaning of life and death.

The Rostovs are associated with Tolstoy's father's family in much the same way that the Bolkonskys are associated with his mother's family. Old Ilya Rostov, whose profligate ways land his family in penury, harks back to the spendthrift Ilya Tolstoy. Madame Rostov is a portrait of Leo's doting and proud Tolstoy grandmother. Nicholas Rostov is drawn from Tolstoy's father but incorporates much of the youthful experience of Leo himself. The marriage of Nicholas to Marya is taken from the story of his own parents' marriage, rethought and idealized. Sonya plays the role in the family of Tatyana Ergolskaya. The Rostov family character is defined by spontaneity, which gives them the ability to live in harmony with their physical natures and to escape the suffering and distortion of self caused by the analytical and self-examining mind so characteristic of the Bolkonskys. Nicholas represents the Rostov character in its mundane expression, but again Tolstoy has added a character who raises the family principles to their ideal embodiment. In Natasha Rostova, Tolstoy shows the principle of spontaneity achieving a purity of expression that elevates it to the quality of a life force. Natasha, too, has her prototypes: Tolstoy's sister-in-law, Tatyana Behrs, and his wife, Sofya. But she is tied less to the detail of a specific life than Princess Marya, and this endows her with the freedom of action Tolstoy gives to his purely fictional heroes, Andrey and Pierre.

One central character, Pierre Bezukhov, stands apart from the families. He embodies the free search for the self's most just expression. If Tolstoy projected into Andrey his own longing to be perfectly comme il faut, to be a man of aristocratic hauteur and noblesse oblige, in Pierre he embodies his own capacity for falling into error while seeking the good. In Pierre we see how the man of good character whose moral sense is intact is nevertheless turned aside from the right path by the complexities of reality, by his own baser desires, and by his failure to stand up to those of less rectitude. Significantly, the great moments in Pierre's life are rare moments of assertion of will when circumstance, desire, and action come into conjuction. Yet in the end his very passivity makes him open to a larger vision of the world than any other character can encompass.

Just as there are family heroes in *War and Peace*, so there are family villains, the Karagins and the Kuragins. They embody self-seeking worldliness and tone-deafness to the inner moral voice. Tolstoy has achieved in the Kuragin family—old Prince Vassily, Anatole, and the beautiful Hélène—a brilliant portrayal of lack of moral intuition. The very flatness in the depiction of these characters is made to seem not a result of Tolstoy's artistic decision, but the fault of their own truncated natures. The Kuragins are the chief agents of evil in the lives of the protagonists: Hélène by marrying Pierre turns him temporarily away from his pursuit of virtue; Anatole comes near to seducing Natasha, the greatest moral crisis in her life. The Kuragin viciousness is underscored by the presence of a demonic figure of evil, the sinister officer Dolokhov, friend of Anatole and agent of vice and death.

In this comprehensive design Tolstoy finds room to accommodate all the seemingly disparate values that the program of self-formation had specified as necessary to the fully expressed self: intellect and nature, spirit and body. The true expression of spontaneous feeling is discriminated from false self-indulgence, the harmonious relationship with the physical self from corrupting vice. The principle of growth itself, rather than the destiny of any character, is Tolstoy's subject, and so the destinies of this large array of characters cross and recross, not so much to form a plot as to show the vicissitudes of the self's development through time.

It is his interest in time as the medium of growth that leads Tolstoy to his interest in history. Each individual has a private life lived in the interior of the consciousness, full of meaning for him but closed to others. Social organization is introduced at the level of family life, where the potentialities of self are shaped by the pressures of family principles and interaction among members of the group. At its most abstract, time becomes history, in which the individual is situated in the flux of the human mass that bears so inexorably upon him that his acts take on new meanings, extraneous to his own understanding or his own intentions.

The historical event is produced by the confluence of innumerable wills. Kings, being subject to the same forces as others, are deceived in their illusions of power: "The king is history's slave." Those whom conventional histories have glorified as the movers of human destiny share the common human condition of being subject to the flux of events that they are part of and that they cannot see from their position within the flow. Yet Tolstoy does not assert the dominance of chance. The individual wills and acts of men cohere in ways unseen by them to form a grand design. Napoleon is petty and laughable because he believes that his smallest action has great consequences. The actual forces that bring the French across Europe in 1812, that lead to a Russian victory, and that then bear the Russian and allied armies to Paris seem to Tolstoy to reflect the will of providence, but those forces are not discoverable because their multiplicity is incommensurate with our ability to know.

War and Peace brings to perfection the special Tolstoyan verisimilitude by which he is able to suggest a world infinitely expansive and therefore coterminous with our own experience of reality. It is Tolstoy's gift to see that the eternal qualities of people, objects, situations can be found in entities that appear different at first glance. He needs both documentarity—precision of factual detail, especially as observed by the eye—and abstraction—the fixed and immovable truth of things. Between these two poles the forms of cohesion, the ways in which truth indwells in the detail, are myriad, and that abundance gives Tolstoy the large freedom of discrimination and invention from which the rich fictional world of the novel is elaborated.

The final volume of War and Peace was published in December 1869. By January 1870 Tolstoy was casting about for a new topic. He made a number of false starts, though as early as February 1870 he thought of writing the story of the fall of a married woman of high society. It took several years for the mass of possibilities to crystallize into the structure of Anna Karenina. Still, the conjunction is telling: readers are still discussing the epilogue of War and Peace, still debating whether it is plausible that the delightful Natasha Rostova should turn into a domestic frump, and it comes into Tolstoy's head to write a novel about a fallen woman. Anna Karenina is related to the epilogue of War and Peace in a curious way. The characters of the latter meet in the epilogue as survivors in a genuine sense. Russia has undergone a grave crisis in the War of 1812. The two families at the center of the novel have undergone crises parallel to the national one. Each has lost a son. The characters who remain have regrouped their forces in strategic marriages, Pierre to Natasha, Nicholas to Marya. They have undergone much, have risked much, and have come through. The mood of the epilogue well justifies Tolstoy's original title, "All's Well That Ends Well." There is behind War and Peace a strong compensatory force. Even death is shown to exalt the dying and to educate the living into spiritual mysteries. Everything that bears down upon humanity can be reconsidered, reformed. The novel can be a compensation for what life itself withholds from us.

Turning to *Anna Karenina*, we find the opening sentence: ''Happy families are all alike; every unhappy family is unhappy in its own way.'' We begin with the Oblonsky household, where everything is in disorder because the wife has discovered her husband's affair with the governess. On the opening page we encounter a number of generic terms for family members: ''the wife,'' ''the husband,'' ''the children,'' ''the English governess,'' ''the French governess,'' ''the cook,'' ''the kitchenmaid,'' ''the coachman''; but where in *War and Peace* the epilogue shows us an array of characters all beautifully fitted into their roles as ''the wife,'' ''the husband,'' ''the children,'' ''the maid,'' here everything is awry. From the first paragraph we see the beginnings of a movement that will go directly counter to the movement of *War and Peace*: not reconciliation, flowering, compensation, but dissolution, chaos, death.

The shift in emphasis is striking in the character of Stiva Oblonsky, Anna's brother. Stiva is most full of that vital force that Tolstoy has honored in *War and Peace*. He is plump with life's juices. We have a keen sense of his fleshly presence: we constantly know where the parts of his body are and what they are feeling. In a difficult moment, Nicholas Rostov comes to the realization that ''one could kill and rob and yet be happy.'' Stiva is such a person who can be happy out of his sheer excess of physical vitality even though he is in a painful and morally untenable situation. Pondering the difficult situation with his wife, he asks, What am I to do?

He could find no answer, except life's usual answer to the most complex and insoluble questions. That answer is: live in the needs of the day, that is, find forgetfulness. He could no longer find forgetfulness in sleep, at any rate not before night . . . consequently he must seek forgetfulness in the dream of life.

(*Sobranie sochinenii*, vol. 8, p. 10)

We have come a long way from the world of *War and Peace;* its rich affirmation of present experience has now become ''the dream of life,'' even for so spontaneous and earthly a presence as Stiva Oblonsky. Only forgetfulness can assure happiness.

As the novel progresses, the recognition of the equivocal nature of human happiness is ever more harshly impressed on us. It is the very stuff of Anna's story, but we come to the same recognition in the situation of the chief male character, Constantine Levin, who, after achieving the marriage he wants and starting a family, suddenly finds himself hiding a piece of rope so that he won't be tempted to hang himself with it. The novel reaches its climax in a scene that powerfully evokes hatred of life. Anna has left her husband and gone to live openly with her lover, the socially brilliant officer of the guards Aleksey Vronsky. But giving in to desire brings them both unhappiness. Anna's husband refuses to allow her custody of their son. A debauched but hypocritical society refuses to accept Anna after she has openly flouted its rules of decorum. Vronsky is prevented from achieving the brilliant career that his position and capabilities should have ensured him. Anna fears the loss of his love and turns her anger and dissatisfaction against him. The relationship grows colder and colder, more full of anger and blame, until a break seems imminent.

A desperate Anna sets out to confront Vronsky, whom she suspects of going to the country for the day to court a young woman of good society. Here Tolstoy goes entirely into Anna's consciousness and shows us the world through her inner chaos, which is driving her to destruction. Through Anna's vision we see a kaleidoscope of broken images. We are situated wholly within her ugly vision of the world. Everything that she sees fills her with loathing, seems grotesque and hateful. The word "vision" is critical here. The eye is a powerful instrument for Tolstoy. He relies greatly on *seeing* in itself as the foundation of truth. Sight is the major organizing principle of Tolstoy's texts. It reveals to us what words conceal in the telltale gesture or the inadvertent expression of the face. As Anna approaches her death she attains the summit of the capacity to see—her sight is called a "searchlight." Though Tolstoy fixes us firmly within her point of view by repeating that her horrific vision is "what she thought she saw," it would be wrong to dismiss what is seen as a crazy woman's distorted vision. Her insight has its own powerful truth:

> Where did I leave off? At the point that I cannot imagine a situation in which life would not be a torment; that we all have been created in order to suffer, and that we all know this and try to invent means of deceiving ourselves. But when you see the truth, what are you to do?
> (*Sobranie sochinenii*, vol. 9, p. 386)

Where Stiva can find forgetfulness in "the dream of life," Anna *sees* and cannot *not see.* Anna comes to a conclusion that is fully motivated in the circumstances: "Why not put out the candle?" Where *War and Peace* affirms the power of life to make something even of pain and grief, *Anna Karenina* shows us that life has infinite capacity to harm and that we are helpless before it.

In the epilogue to *Anna Karenina* the survivors are once again gathered together, but "survivor" in this novel means a very different thing. In *War and Peace* we see a group of people who by undergoing disaster have grown fully to be themselves and have found a deserved happiness. In *Anna Karenina* the survivors are people maimed by life, diminished rather than augmented by the experience of living. Even Levin, who has saved

himself for the time being by a tenuous faith, seems vulnerable.

Anna Karenina is not all dejection. As in *War and Peace,* much of its charm comes from fresh and vivid scenes of the joy of life: Levin skating or, later, taking part with the peasants in mowing; the happy consummation of healthy and productive love in Levin and Kitty; even Anna's deep gladness and vitality before it is irreparably damaged. Nowhere else in Tolstoy do we have so full a feeling of his protean energies and vivid responsiveness combined with so intense an insight into how that very life-energy can bring on loathing of life. At bottom *Anna Karenina* does not hold out a great deal of hope, and it is understandable that Tolstoy, soon after writing it, in the tide of his great crisis, rejected it and all his past works—works that had led him to this evil intensity of vision.

In the epilogue to *Anna Karenina* Tolstoy says of his autobiographical (or, in Lidia Ginzburg's phrase, "autopsychological") hero Levin, "Thus he lived, not knowing and not foreseeing the possibility of knowing what he was and why he lived on earth, and tormented by his ignorance to such a degree that he feared suicide, and yet with all this, firmly laying down his own special defined road in life." The years of writing *Anna Karenina* had been for Tolstoy a time of what William James, using Tolstoy as an exemplary case of the kind of religious conversion that is precipitated by the loss of all sense of meaning in life, called "anhedonia."

In 1869, while on a trip to Penza province to buy land, Tolstoy had experienced during a night spent in the little town of Arzamas an inexplicable terror, which he described in a letter to his wife:

> For two days I have been tormented by anxiety. Three nights ago I spent the night at Arzamas, and something unusual happened to me. It was two o'clock in the morning, I was terribly tired, wanted to sleep and wasn't sick. But suddenly, there came over me such a depression, fear, hor-

ror as I have never experienced before, and that God grant no one to experience.

(*Sobranie sochinenii*, vol. 17, p. 322)

In 1880 he described the occasion in an unfinished, posthumously published story titled *Notes of a Madman*. In his nighttime fear the narrator asks, "What is bothering me, what am I afraid of?" and hears the answer:

"Me," inaudibly answered the voice of death. "I am here." A chill ran over me. Yes, death. It comes, it is here, and it shouldn't be. If I were really facing death, I could not be experiencing what I was experiencing. I would be afraid. But now I was not afraid, but saw, felt, that death was coming, and at the same time felt that it shouldn't be there. My whole being felt the necessity, the right, to life and at the same time that death was occurring. And that internal division was terrible.

As Tolstoy was coming out of his crisis he began to draft versions of his new creed, which resulted in *A Confession* (finished in 1882).

The answer that Tolstoy found and that made it possible for him to go on to the full, new career that stretched from 1880 to 1910 was, in James's words,

that his trouble had not been with life in general, not with the common life of common men, but with the life of the upper, intellectual, artistic classes, the life which he had personally always led, the cerebral life, the life of conventionality, artificiality and personal ambition. He had been living wrongly and must change. To work for animal needs, to abjure lies and vanities, to relieve common wants, to be simple, to believe in God, therein lay happiness.

(*Varieties of Religious Experience*, p. 180)

As James remarks, Tolstoy had drunk too deeply of the cup of bitterness ever to forget its taste, but his discovery had given him something to live by.

Tolstoy's *A Confession* inaugurates a new style in his writing, one that dominates the work of the final thirty years. This austere, aphoristic, often biblical style is both closer to conversational forms of the language and more solemn than the narrative style of his earlier literary work. Tolstoy had always preferred the omniscient, authorial narrative to the use of the point-of-view because it gave him the opportunity to unify in a Godlike perspective the many vantages of his characters and even to speak from time to time as God or as a prophet who has access to fundamental truths. In the period after *A Confession* the style of his writings, both fiction and nonfiction, is that of an author who seems at one with the deity. The time of the narrative is often retrospective: Tolstoy summarizes whole epochs of his characters' lives in a discourse that moves inexorably toward the truths he wants to unfold. At its best, in such works as *The Death of Ivan Ilich* and *Father Sergius*, the style achieves scriptural solemnity; at other times it is coercive.

Tolstoy's lifelong preoccupation with death reached its greatest intensity in the crisis that resulted in *A Confession*. Death had been a persistent theme in his work from the beginning. In *Childhood* Nikolenka's premonition of his mother's death is borne out in actuality at the end of the volume. The narrator of "Notes of a Billiard Marker" describes the elevation he expects death's nearness to bring. In the third of the *Sevastopol Sketches* Tolstoy tries his hand for the first time at the tour de force that he became master of—the description of a man's thoughts as he is dying, up to the extinction of consciousness. One of his best works in the years before *War and Peace* is "Three Deaths" (1859), in which he likens the peasant's meek acceptance of death to the natural and unconscious passing of a tree, contrasting these "proper" deaths unfavorably with the death of a landowner.

The two great novels are shaped by the deaths of pivotal characters. Tolstoy said of Prince Andrey that he had intended to have him die at Austerlitz but then "took pity on him and spared him." Prince Andrey is attached to the Bolkonsky family, that is, to the avatars of Tolstoy's mother's family, the Volkonskys, and hence is connected in the fabric of Tolstoy's imagination to his own dead mother. Old Prince Bolkonsky's death is described in detail in the novel; it is the means both for Marya's own recognition of the boundary between life and death and for the renewal of her capacity to live. In the epilogue we are given clues that Princess Marya herself will die young, leaving a bereft husband and young children. In spite of his initial sparing of Prince Andrey, Tolstoy discovered nevertheless that he must let him die to complete the thematic economy of his novel. So, after much of the novel was set in type, Tolstoy changed the ending he had planned; he wrote into the galley proofs the remarkable passages describing Prince Andrey's delirium at Mytishchi (the famous "hovering fly" scene) and then created the episode in which Prince Andrey on his deathbed discovers that death is an awakening.

The expressive philosophy that so influenced Tolstoy always had a catch in it. With its emphasis on process it tends to suggest that the person cannot be whole until the life is complete. It thus opens the way to a glorification of death. Rousseau had already given the hint in his celebrated conclusion to *La nouvelle Héloïse,* with the transfigured Julie on her deathbed. That life is process and therefore inimical to perfect love is one of the truths Prince Andrey expresses in his deathbed inner monologue. Anna Karenina's death achieves no such great philosophy; it is only a release from the torments that the conflict between physical vitality and moral purpose have imposed upon her. But for Tolstoy the question of what kind of meaning might be inherent in the experience of dying remained critical.

Soon after his crisis, as soon as he could bring himself to think again about writing fiction, Tolstoy began a story that is very likely the greatest ever written on the theme of death, *The Death of Ivan Ilich.* Tolstoy's brother Sergei teased him by saying of the story: "They praise you because you discovered that people die. As if no one would have known it without you." In spare and solemn language Tolstoy recounts the story of one Ivan Ilich, a successful judge who, having fallen and struck his side while hanging drapes in his new quarters, becomes ill and begins the slow decline toward death. The first part of the story describes the reactions of his colleagues and his family after his death. We see mundane society life continuing its frivolous concerns, untouched by the mystery of extinction. The second part of the story opens with a straightforward statement of its moral: "The story of Ivan Ilich's life was most simple and ordinary and most terrible." Thus from the start we know that Ivan Ilich will die and what the significance of his life has been. Tolstoy turns our attention to the process: Ivan Ilich by living an ordinary life killed his finest impulses; suffering and death redeem him.

Tolstoy was fond of the proverb "Il faudra mourir seul" (One dies alone), and the story brilliantly evokes the increasing isolation of the dying from the process of the living. Whereas in *War and Peace* Tolstoy had shown that it is natural for the survivors to retreat from the knowledge of death possessed by the dying, in order that they may go on living, in *The Death of Ivan Ilich* he is merciless toward those of the world who stand apart from Ivan Ilich's death. It is as though Tolstoy, seeing that he is growing old, increasingly consumed by his fear of death, resents those around him whose lives will inevitably go on once his own stops.

Like many of Tolstoy's works, the story was suggested by an incident that came to his attention: he heard about the death of Ivan Ilich Mechnikov, a judge of the Tula court who died of cancer in 1881 and was said to have expressed remorse on his deathbed for his unproductive life. Mechnikov's brother, a well-known scholar and revolutionary, commented that although his brother was a careerist,

> and I don't like careerists, how much richer his psychological register was than what Tolstoy has done with his hero! That's what enlightenment means, I thought, if even such an artist as Tolstoy found it necessary to turn the soul of his vulgarized hero into a square of poorly cleaned parquet.
>
> (*Vospominanie*, Moscow, 1967, vol. 2, p. 157)

That Tolstoy did reshape Mechnikov's story is clear from one detail known to us: it was to his wife that the real Ivan Ilich confided his sense of his misspent life, while in Tolstoy's story the wife is much too limited and unresponsive to be the recipient of such confidences. Nevertheless, Tolstoy has gained an artistic advantage by the simplification of his character. The painter Kramskoi remarked on the story's biblical quality. By subtracting all the things that make a man's life and character rich, by reducing Ivan Ilich to banality, Tolstoy makes him into the perfect test case of death's power to transform. In Prince Andrey we see a great nature realizing its capacities in death, but *Ivan Ilich* affirms the capacity of even the most ordinary and unheroic life to find significance in death. In spite of its solemnity *Ivan Ilich* is an optimistic story, as the Gospels are optimistic stories.

Tolstoy had taken seriously Rousseau's assertion that it is society—"high society" in particular—that corrupts. After his spiritual crisis he took on the task of making himself over as best he could into a simple man. If he could not escape the torturing consciousness of the educated man, he could, he believed, at least refrain from living the artificial and corrupting life of one. That his new view came directly out of the principles of the expressive philosophy that had formed him in his youth is clear from his late statement of his aesthetic principles, *What Is Art?* In the expressive

view of Herder and others, all activities of life are expressions of self, but in particular those that have their foundations in feeling or the creative impulse. The century separating *What Is Art?* from Herder and other thinkers in the expressive vein had shown up the paradoxes in a view that bases its primary value on self and yet struggles to attain exalted ideals of service and brotherhood. Yet Tolstoy strives mightily once again to reconcile the axiom that art comes out of the artist's need for self-expression with the moral imperative that art must serve social welfare. Clearly the contradiction can be eliminated if we look to the artist's own moral health: if his soul is pure, then his self-expression will inevitably serve truth. This formulation satisfied Tolstoy, if few others.

Following his own precepts, Tolstoy determined to write only works that would be morally beneficial. To some extent this meant writing tracts, putting together daybooks of uplifting quotations, engaging in polemics with those who were embarked on an evil path (including the church and the czar), and writing educational materials for the peasantry. But Tolstoy by no means ceased to write fiction, and some of his most powerful works—works in a style different from that of his early ones—belong to the last thirty years of his life. Tolstoy was preoccupied with the temptations society puts in the way of its educated members. He was striving to find the way back to the simplicity and faith he saw in the lower classes. These preoccupations shape all his later work. They manifest themselves in two ways: the harsh exposé of society as it is and the uplifting depiction of exemplary figures who show the way to virtue.

In this last period Tolstoy seemed obsessed by the harmful consequences of relations between the sexes. In the 1850's he had examined the institution of marriage in *Family Happiness*, where he had followed the line of Jules Michelet and Pierre-Joseph Proudhon, conservatives on the "woman question." Like them he asserted that woman's destiny is to marry and have children, that romantic love is a threat to the sanctity of the family, and that tender feelings should be put aside in marriage, to be replaced by devotion to children and to the husband as the father of the children. At the time he wrote *Family Happiness* Tolstoy had not yet had any experience of marriage, and after concluding the work he became embarrassed by the "nonsense" he had indulged in. He hoped for much from his own marriage, and in many ways got much. (Victor Shklovsky is right when he says, "He chose the fate that he needed and the woman that he needed was Sofya Andreevna.") *War and Peace* reflects his domestic happiness in its good marriages, although Pierre's mistaken marriage to the debauched Hélène is a warning about the power of a bad woman. In *Anna Karenina* marriages go awry, but we still have before us the successful example of Levin and Kitty.

Beginning in the 1880's Tolstoy was at constant war with his wife over his desire to dispose of his property and lead the life of a simple man. From then on his treatment of marriage among the upper classes was merciless: marriage, he believed, concentrates the vices of society. *The Kreutzer Sonata* calls for absolute chastity within marriage. Its protagonist, Poznyshev, has murdered his wife out of jealousy over her lover, but he comes to the conclusion that he was to blame for her infidelity by introducing his wife to sensuality: "If I had known what I know now, all would have been different. On no account would I have married her. . . . I would not have married at all." Beethoven's sonata has been the spur to the wife's illicit passion, and thus corrupt art is implicated as another avenue through which base society appeals to man's evil impulses. Tolstoy's passionate indictment of marriage in *The Kreutzer Sonata* was no doubt influenced by his continuing sexual need for his wife, which, together with his sense of duty to family, prevented him from realizing the virtuous life he sought.

At the end of the 1880's and throughout the 1890's Tolstoy worked on another of his summations, the novel *Resurrection.* The family idyll disappears entirely as the organizing principle of the long work. Now attention is focused on a society in dissolution from top to bottom. The scenes of Tolstoy's new panoramic vision take place in the ruined villages, the unjust courts, the prisons, and on the road to Siberian exile. The protagonist, Nekhlyudov, while serving as a member of the court, comes across a woman of the lower classes, Katyusha Maslova, whom he had seduced and abandoned in his youth. He resolves to marry her to save her from a life of degradation. He strives to get her freed from prison, but society opposes his righteous desire at every turn. In the end Katyusha marries the virtuous revolutionary Simonson instead, but Nekhlyudov has been transformed by his exposure to Russia's poverty and injustice; as the novel ends he sits down to read the Gospels.

Resurrection has never achieved the popularity of Tolstoy's other long novels, perhaps because it lacks the underlying structure of romance that shapes the others, for all their realism. Here Tolstoy's compensatory imagination is focused on showing how society can be overcome and the path of virtue found, rather than on the attainment of personal happiness.

The good peasant had always seemed to Tolstoy to be the answer to society's corruption. He often introduces a variant of the figure at the end of a work, where, as an icon of the exemplary life, it brings the fluidity of Tolstoyan character and time to stasis. In *Childhood* the narrative is rounded off with the story of the old housekeeper, Natalya Savishna, who has sacrificed her own happiness for the mistress and children, but who remains unembittered, her declining years illuminated by her childlike faith. Riding away from the Cossack station, Olenin sees the simple life of Eroshka and Maryanka, continuing as if he did not exist. Pierre's grave doubts about the meaning of life are resolved by his acquaintance in French captivity with the peasant Platon Karataev, whose unresisting accommodation to all life shows Pierre how to overcome evil. Levin, when in such spiritual pain that he contemplates suicide, is saved by the words of faith uttered by an old peasant.

The need to show the true virtue of the peasants becomes increasingly pressing as Tolstoy repudiates the upper classes more forcefully. Thus, in *Ivan Ilich* the peasant Gerasim's calm certainty of right behavior and unselfconscious attentiveness to his master's needs show up society's false attitude toward death. Yet Tolstoy can make Gerasim an exemplary figure precisely because he holds his imagination aloof from any inquiry into Gerasim's desires, psychological processes, or circumstances of life. Falsity enters because of what is left unsaid.

Elsewhere Tolstoy had tried to fill that lack by applying his searching realistic method to the life of the peasants. As early as the 1850's he had started the novella *Polikushka* (1863), which gives an unremittingly bleak picture of village life while fixing the blame on the structure of society. In the 1880's he turned his attention to the plight of town peasants whose moral foundations had been destroyed by their uprooting from the patriarchal way of life. In his play *The Power of Darkness* (1887) he seized on an incident that came before the Tula court: a peasant had married a well-off widow, then forced the widow's daughter to have sexual relations with him. When the daughter bore a child, the peasant smothered the baby to hide the evidence of his illicit relationship. Subsequently, a marriage was arranged for the daughter, but at the betrothal the peasant was seized by guilt and confessed his crime to the assembled crowd. Tolstoy turned this sensational event into a brooding parable of fall and salvation. Keeping close to the details of the original story for the most part, he added two almost allegorical figures: Akim, a saintly peasant, and Matryona, a force of primitive evil. The parents of the weak and criminal Nikita, they struggle for possession of his soul. Nikita's confession affirms that the power of faith is still alive in the peasants in spite of their degradation by city life.

Throughout his inquiry into peasant life, Tolstoy held to the irreducible fact on which their virtue was founded: they worked. In his short novel *Master and Man* (1895) Tolstoy lays out this opposition with stark simplicity. The "master" is now only a merchant and not even a member of the spoiled aristocratic class, but even his little bit of privilege has taken him away from the plain truths accessible to the poor. Moved by greed, he sets out in a snowstorm to acquire a piece of land. He and his driver, Nikita, are overpowered on the road by the storm's fury, and the merchant achieves enlightenment before his death, coming to realize that the true goal of human life lies in mutual concern.

Summaries of Tolstoy's work in the late period make it sound hollowly moralistic, but the great works like *Master and Man* transcend their didacticism through perfection of style. Tolstoy's late work retains the documentary precision of detail of his early work. At his best, he wrote beautiful parables that combine keen realistic observation with the inevitability of prophetic truth.

The plight of the educated man trying to find his way back to elemental virtue was close to Tolstoy, and many of his most powerful works of the last period address it. The protagonist of *Father Sergius* is an aristocratic officer, reminiscent of Prince Andrey, who retires from the world to enter a monastery. The occasion for his leaving society is his discovery that the woman of good family to whom he is betrothed has been the mistress of Czar Nicholas I. Out of pride he determines to become a monk, to set himself above the czar who has had the power to ruin his life with impunity. He excels in his career in the church as he excelled in the military, eventually becoming a famous holy man who is sought out by crowds of people for advice and cures.

Though Father Sergius achieves genuine elevation of spirit, he is still prey to pride and sexual desires. At length he leaves the monastery and makes his way to a woman whom he knew in youth. The widow Pashenka embodies Tolstoy's new sense of Christian duty. Though she does not attend church or remember to observe the rituals, she devotes herself cheerfully and wholeheartedly to the service of those around her. Sergius comes to the conclusion, "I lived for people under the pretense of living for God; she lives for God, imagining that she lives for people." Under the influence of her example, Sergius becomes a poor pilgrim and devotes his life to doing good to those he meets.

Throughout his career Tolstoy had shown a genius for projecting the lives and thoughts of the rulers of men, beginning in *War and Peace* with his depictions of Napoleon and Alexander I. In his late period he returned frequently to the czars and boldly treats them with the freedom of invention he employs with fictional characters. In his late unfinished work "The Deathbed Notes of the Elder Fyodor Kuzmich" Tolstoy deals with a persistent rumor concerning Alexander I. The story current among the people asserted that another man was buried in the czar's place and that Alexander had taken up a new life as a monk. Tolstoy had been haunted by the vision of a soldier running the military gauntlet (such episodes figure in "After the Ball" and in *Hadji-Murad*), and he makes the sight of a soldier being beaten the incident that triggers the czar's final resolve to quit his exalted life. Some parts of the story, in which Tolstoy has the czar recount his childhood memories of his brother Constantine and of life at the court of Catherine the Great, hark back to *Childhood* in their precise evocation of the child's experiences. Tolstoy's intention is to show that in the child who will be czar we find the same impulses of goodness, the same alertness to insincerity, that are in other children. The czar's story is a variant, at the uppermost reaches of society, of the common story, the corruption of the child as he is fitted for his role in society.

The lives of rulers figure largely in Tolstoy's last great work, the short novel *Hadji-Murad,* in which Tolstoy harks back to a figure who had fascinated him in his youth. During Tolstoy's stay in the Caucasus, the lieutenant of the Muslim leader Shamil's forces, Hadji-Murad, a famous warrior, had come over to the Russians. At the time it had seemed to Tolstoy that this was an act of cowardice, but in his subsequent study of the period he came to the conclusion that Hadji-Murad was a victim of the circumstances of his life. Once again Tolstoy created a panoramic view of society, incorporating his major themes into a major summary work. The difference is that he was now able to achieve that breadth in a work a fraction of the size of *War and Peace.*

From the line soldiers in the little border station who are waiting in ambush when the news comes that Hadji-Murad is about to come over, Tolstoy moves up through the ranks of society, to the governor, Vorontsov, at Tiflis and finally to Nicholas I himself. Parallel to this movement he shows the Chechens' society from bottom to top, concluding with the ruler, Shamil. In his dispassionate tone he treats every character equally, whether soldier or czar, with the exception that he has more sympathy for the forces that mold the soldiers' lives. At every level Tolstoy emphasizes that each person is mainly caught up in his private concerns, his family, his own desires. What is vital to one man is unimportant or of unequal significance to another. But the ruler's state of mind is different, for his momentary whims have far-reaching consequences that affect the lives of many men. Hadji-Murad is caught between the "policies" of Nicholas and Shamil and is in the end destroyed by them.

In his final years Tolstoy came to be called the "second czar," because the government was afraid to touch him. He was the only man in Russia besides the czar who could speak his mind forthrightly with impunity. He had earned that freedom through the power of his work and his example. When he took up his pen to speak of czars as though they were men like himself, he proved that writing can be, as he had dreamed, a real power in the world.

Selected Bibliography

FIRST EDITIONS

INDIVIDUAL WORKS

Childhood (Detstvo). Short novel. *Sovremennik (The Contemporary)* 9 (1852).

"The Raid" ("Nabeg"). Story. *Sovremennik* 3 (1853).

Boyhood (Otrochestvo). Short novel. *Sovremennik* 9 (1854).

"Sevastopol in December" ("Sevastopol v dekabre mesyatse"). Sketch. *Sovremennik* 6 (1855).

"Sevastopol in May" ("Sevastopol v mae"). Sketch. *Sovremennik* 9 (1855).

"The Woodfelling" ("Rubka lesa"). *Sovremennik* 9 (1855).

"Sevastopol in August, 1855" ("Sevastopol v avguste 1855 goda"). Sketch. *Sovremennik* 1 (1856).

"Two Hussars" ("Dva gusara"). Story. *Sovremennik* 5 (1856).

Youth (Yunost). Short novel. *Sovremennik* 1 (1857).

"Three Deaths" ("Tri smerti"). Story. *Biblioteka dlya chteniya* (Library for Reading) 1 (1859).

Family Happiness (Semeinoe schastie). Short novel. *Russkii vestnik* (Russian Messenger) 7 and 8 (1859).

"Who Teaches Whom to Write, We the Peasant Children, or They Us?" ("Komu u kogo uchitsya pisat, krestyanskim rebyatim u nas ili nam u krestyanskikh rebyat?"). Pedagogy. Yasnaya Polyana, 1862.

The Cossacks (Kazaki). Short novel. *Russkii vestnik* 1 (1863).

Polikushka. Short novel. *Russkii vestnik* 2 (1863).

War and Peace (Voina i mir). Parts 1 and 2 in *Russkii vestnik* (1865–1866). Separate publication, Moscow, 1867–1869.

Alphabet (Azbuka). Stories for children. Moscow, 1872. Revised as *New Alphabet (Novaya azbuka)* and *Russian Books for Reading (Russkie knigi dlya chteniya)*. Moscow, 1874.

Anna Karenina. Novel. *Russkii vestnik* (1875–1877). Separate publication, Moscow, 1878.

A Confession (Izpoved). Written 1879–1882. First published Geneva, 1884, due to censor's forbidding publication in Russia. First Russian publication, Moscow, 1906.

"What People Live By" ("Chem lyudi zhivy"). Story. *Detskii otdykh* (Children's Recreation) 12 (1881).

"Where Love Is, God Is" ("Gde lyubov, tam i bog"). Story. Moscow, 1885.

The Death of Ivan Ilich (Smert Ivana Ilicha). Short novel. Moscow, 1886.

"How Much Land Does a Man Need?" ("Mnogo li cheloveku zemli nuzhno?"). Story. *Russkoe bogatstvo* (Russian Wealth) 4 (1886).

"Three Hermits" ("Tri startsa"). Story. *Niva* (Field) 13 (1886).

"Yardstick" ("Kholstomer"). Short novel. In *Sochineniya grafa L. N. Tolstogo*. Moscow, 1886.

"What Then Must We Do?" ("Tak chto zhe nam delat?"). Essay. Geneva, 1886. First Russian publication, Moscow, 1906.

The Power of Darkness (Vlast tmy). Play. Moscow, 1887.

The Kreutzer Sonata (Kreitserova sonata). Short novel. Moscow, 1891.

The Fruits of Enlightenment (Plody prosveshcheniya). Play. Moscow, 1891.

Master and Man (Khoziain i rabotnik). Short novel. *Severnyi vestnik* (Northern Messenger) 3 (1895).

What Is Art? (Chto takoe iskusstvo?). Essay. *Voprosy filosofii i psikhologii* (Problems of Philosophy and Psychology) (1897–1898).

Resurrection (Voskresenie). Novel. Moscow, 1899.

Father Sergius (Otets Sergei). Short novel. Written 1889–1900. Published posthumously in Moscow, 1911.

"The Living Corpse" ("Zhivoi trup"). Play. Written 1897–1900. Published posthumously in *Russkoe slovo* (Russian Word) (23 September 1911).

"After the Ball" ("Posle bala"). Story. Written 1903. Published posthumously, Moscow, 1911.

Notes of a Madman (Zapiski sumashedshego). Short novel. Written 1884–1903. Published posthumously, Moscow, 1912.

Hadji-Murad (Khadzhi-Murat). Short novel. Written 1896–1904. Published posthumously, Moscow, 1912.

"I Cannot Remain Silent" ("Ne mogu molchat"). Essay. Published simultaneously in newspapers in England, France, Germany, Italy, and Russia. 1908.

COLLECTED WORKS

Polnoe sobranie sochinenii. 90 vols. Moscow, 1928–1955. Fullest edition, but editing of some artistic texts leaves much to be desired.

Sobranie sochinenii v dvadtsati tomakh. Moscow, 1960–1965. Revised 1978–. Current standard edition for artistic texts.

TRANSLATIONS

Tolstoy Museum. *L. N. Tolstoi v perevodakh na inostrannye yazyki.* Moscow, 1961. Lists all known translations of Tolstoy's works 1862–1960; individual entries printed in language of the translation, so non-Russian readers can use this volume to find English translations.

The Works of L. Tolstoy. Translated by Louise and Aylmer Maude. New York and London, 1928–1937. Includes Aylmer Maude's biography of Tolstoy, all the major works and many of the minor ones, and a selection of the major articles.

BIOGRAPHICAL AND CRITICAL STUDIES

Bayley, John. *Tolstoy and the Novel.* London, 1966.

Canadian-American Slavic Studies (Winter 1978).

Christian, R. F. *Tolstoy: A Critical Introduction.* London, 1969.

———, ed. *Tolstoy's Letters.* 2 vols. New York, 1978.

———. *Tolstoy's "War and Peace": A Study.* Oxford, 1962.

Davie, Donald, ed. *Russian Literature and Modern English Fiction: A Collection of Critical Essays.* Chicago, 1965.

Eikhenbaum, Boris. *Tolstoi in the Seventies.* Ann Arbor, Mich., 1980.

———. *Tolstoi in the Sixties.* Ann Arbor, Mich., 1980.

———. *The Young Tolstoi.* Ann Arbor, Mich., 1972.

Gibian, George, ed. *Anna Karenina.* New York, 1970. The Maude translation; backgrounds and sources; essays in criticism. Norton Critical Edition series.

———. *War and Peace.* New York, 1966. The Maude translation; backgrounds and sources; essays in criticism. Norton Critical Edition series.

Gifford, Henry, ed. *Leo Tolstoy: A Critical Anthology.* Harmondsworth, 1971.

Goldenweizer, A. B. *Talks with Tolstoy.* Translated by S. S. Koteliansky and Virginia Woolf. New York, 1969.

Gorky, Maxim. *Literary Portraits.* Translated by Ivy Litvinov. Moscow, 1961.

Institut d'études slaves. *Tolstoi aujourd'hui. Colloque international Tolstoi.* Paris, 1980.

Jones, Malcolm, ed. *New Essays on Tolstoy.* Cambridge, 1978.

James, William. *Varieties of Religious Experience.* New York, 1902. Reprinted 1936.

Kuzminskaya, Tatyana A. *Tolstoy As I Knew Him.* New York, 1948. Translation of *My Life at Home and at Yasnaya Polyana* by Tolstoy's sister-in-law.

Lukács, Georg. "Tolstoy and the Development of Realism" and "Leo Tolstoy and Western European Literature." In *Studies in European Realism.* New York, 1974. Pp. 103–132, 133–158.

Mann, Thomas. "Goethe and Tolstoy" and "Anna Karenina." In *Essays of Three Decades.* New York, 1947. Pp. 93–175.

Matlaw, Ralph, ed. *Tolstoy: A Collection of Critical Essays.* Englewood Cliffs, N.J., 1967.

Reminiscences of Lev Tolstoi by His Contemporaries. Moscow, 1961.

Shestov, Lev. *Dostoevsky, Tolstoy and Nietzsche.* Athens, Ohio, 1969.

Shklovsky, Victor. *Lev Tolstoy.* Moscow, 1978.

Steiner, George. *Tolstoy or Dostoevsky: An Essay in the Old Criticism.* New York, 1959.

Tolstoy on Education. Translated by Leo Wiener, with an introduction by Reginald Archambault. Chicago, 1967.

Tolstoi, Lev Nikolaevich. *Last Diaries.* Translated by Lydia Weston-Kesich, edited and with an introduction by Leon Stillman. New York, 1960.

Tolstoy, Sophia. *The Final Struggle: Countess Tolstoy's Diary for 1910. With Extracts from Leo Tolstoy's Diary of the Same Period.* New York, 1980.

Troyat, Henri. *Tolstoy.* Translated by Nancy Amphoux. Garden City, N.Y., 1967.

Wasiolek, Edward. *Tolstoy's Major Fiction.* Chicago, 1978.

BIBLIOGRAPHIES

Bibliografiya literatury o L. N. Tolstoi, 1917–1973. 4 vols. Moscow, 1960–1978.

Leo Tolstoy: An Annotated Bibliography of English-Language Sources to 1978. Metuchen, N.J., and London, 1979. Lists criticism and commentaries.

PATRICIA CARDEN

IVAN TURGENEV
(1818–1883)

MANY CRITICS NOW consider Ivan Turgenev the most dated of the great masters of the novel in nineteenth-century Russia. His exquisitely planned, finely wrought books are "faded," they say; the political issues that concerned him have long since lost their immediacy; his approach is sentimental, even mawkish; he supplies nourishment only to "those who find meat and drink in clouds and nymphs," in the words of an unkind contemporary scholar. So runs the standard list of complaints about the most civilized and cosmopolitan of Russian writers. And indeed there is some truth in them. Turgenev cannot boast the verbal exuberance and astounding inventiveness of a Nikolay Gogol; the profound energy and conviction of a Feodor Dostoevsky, wrestling with problems of a sort our age thinks very relevant; the epic sweep of description and inquiry to be found in Leo Tolstoy; the painstaking attention to detail and psychological analysis of an Ivan Goncharov. Yet despite all this, Turgenev displays strengths that led the American author and editor Albert Jay Nock to call him "incomparably the greatest of artists in fiction"—or Virginia Woolf to describe his books as "curiously of our own time, undecayed, and complete in themselves"—and which ensure that he will continue to be read both in his native country and in the West for as long as we can foresee. The intellectual fashions may be against him at the moment and may remain so for some time, but Turgenev has never been totally eclipsed, and such a fate is scarcely likely to befall him in the near future.

Turgenev wrote primarily brief novels and short stories. He was a master of literary form and a superb stylist, with a command of the Russian language that was the envy of his contemporaries. His skill at painting with words, especially in his nature descriptions, has never been surpassed. Turgenev was a genuine literary professional. As he was independently wealthy, he had time to polish his efforts, for he did not depend on literature for his living (an economic reason for the inordinate length of many Russian novels is that Russian writers of the nineteenth century were paid according to the number of pages they produced). He watched the contemporary political scene closely, and any reader who wishes to obtain a detailed understanding of Russian intellectual and political life of the mid-nineteenth century is well advised to read Turgenev. He was a subtle student of human psychology, especially as it manifests itself in the relationships between men and women. He was concerned with the great questions of life and death, too, and although his responses to them were shallower than those of Dostoevsky or Tolstoy, much more akin to those of Mikhail Lermontov before him or Anton Chekhov after, it remains true that to study Turgenev carefully is to gain a fuller appreciation of life. Such strong points as these guarantee that, for all his weaknesses, Turgenev will continue to occupy a secure niche in the pantheon of his country's greatest authors.

Ivan Sergeevich Turgenev was born on 28 October 1818 in the town of Orel, located in the heartland of Russia. Orel was not far from the Turgenev family estate at Spasskoe, which later became the writer's principal Russian retreat. His mother, who evidently loved to dominate those under her authority, repelled the young Ivan by her cruelty to her serfs. His handsome father, who died in 1834, was content to let his wife manage the estate while he pursued local females more attractive to him than his spouse. After 1827, for the greater part of the year the family resided in Moscow, returning to Spasskoe only in the summer. Thus from childhood Turgenev was intimately acquainted with the life of a Russian country estate, that small fiefdom which could be culturally and economically almost independent, and which he made the setting for much of his later fiction.

Turgenev was first educated at Moscow boarding schools, then tutored at home, in the best tradition of the Russian gentry, for several years before he entered Moscow University in the fall of 1833. Moscow University was, intellectually speaking, the place to be at that juncture. An entire generation of talented men, including the poet Lermontov, the novelist Goncharov, the journalist and revolutionary Alexander Herzen, the radical poet Nikolay Ogarev, and the critic Vissarion Belinsky, found spiritual sustenance there—sometimes within the lecture halls, more often outside them, in student circles of their own. Moscow University nurtured the great intellectual generation of the 1840's in Russia, many of whose members had had their careers terminated or interrupted by 1850, though not before they had stamped their impress on Russian intellectual life. Despite this, Turgenev soon elected to desert Moscow for Saint Petersburg University, arriving just in time to attend lectures in world history given there by

Gogol and graduating in 1837, at the age of eighteen.

Never again would Turgenev spend as many as eighteen years uninterruptedly in his homeland. In the spring of 1838, feeling that his undergraduate days had given him no more than the bare rudiments of an education, he set out for the source of European enlightenment, the University of Berlin. Thus began his lifelong odyssey through Europe. From September 1838 to September 1839, Turgenev spent most of his time in Berlin, following the latest developments in German philosophy and gaining entrance to the world of Teutonic culture. But it was also in Berlin that he met the semi-legendary embodiment of Russian culture of the time, Nikolay Stankevich. Stankevich, who has come down to us as the prototype of the pure, idealistic Russian intellectual of the 1830's, died an untimely death at twenty-seven in 1840, only a short while after he and Turgenev had met again, this time in Rome, and become close friends. Turgenev has left us a highly spiritualized portrait of him in the character of Pokorsky in the novel *Rudin* (1856). It was also in 1840, and again in Berlin, that Turgenev made the acquaintance of the famous anarchist Mikhail Bakunin. Their mutual interest in German philosophy created a tight though short-lived bond between them, and one that spawned embarrassing consequences when Turgenev visited Bakunin's multitudinous brothers and sisters for a few weeks at the end of 1841: a sister of Bakunin's fell extravagantly in love with him, and he extricated himself from the situation only with some difficulty. His reluctance to become involved with Bakunin's sister did not spring from any antipathy toward women: he had evidently been introduced to sex early on by a peasant woman, and just at the end of 1841 another peasant woman at Spasskoe was carrying his daughter, Pauline, born in the spring of 1842. Turgenev saw to her upbringing, and in the 1860's succeeded in marrying her off to a French businessman despite her illegitimate origins.

IVAN TURGENEV

Affairs of the heart did not overwhelm the life of the mind, however. Turgenev spent the academic year 1840–1841 at the University of Berlin, and in the spring of 1842 took his examinations for the degree of master of philosophy at Saint Petersburg University. From 1842 through 1847 he lived chiefly in Saint Petersburg, though he took several trips to Moscow, Spasskoe, and western Europe.

The year 1843 saw the initiation of two relationships that were perhaps the most fateful of Turgenev's life, with the critic Belinsky and the singer Pauline Viardot. Although he had known Belinsky's articles for some time, Turgenev first met the foremost Russian critic of the nineteenth century, that man "exceptionally dedicated to truth," as he put it in his reminiscences written twenty-five years later, in the summer of 1843. The two subsequently spent long hours in philosophical discussions of great intensity: Turgenev later recalled that when he once interrupted a conversation of theirs to wonder about dinner, Belinsky remonstrated with him quite seriously, "We haven't yet decided the question of God's existence, and you want to eat!" Just as he had done with Stankevich, Turgenev spent time with the mortally ill Belinsky, in Salzbrunn in 1847, less than a year before Belinsky died of tuberculosis in Saint Petersburg at the age of thirty-seven.

Turgenev's connection with Pauline Viardot, one of the most famous singers of her day, was of a different sort. In 1840 she had married Louis Viardot, an art historian and critic some twenty years her elder. She met Turgenev while on tour in Moscow in 1843, at which point there began one of the most extraordinary ménage à trois arrangements in the history of literature. From then until 1883, a span of forty years, Turgenev's thoughts were rarely far from her, and for long periods of time he lived near the Viardots. The three were almost inseparable, and Turgenev and Louis Viardot died within months of each other. Turgenev's attachment to Pauline Viardot (it may possibly have been platonic) pre-vented him from ever thinking seriously of marrying. In a way he possessed a complete family, but his "wife" was bound to another man and his daughter was the offspring of a woman he cared nothing for. The situation hardly seems to have been satisfactory.

In the Saint Petersburg period of his life, between 1842 and 1847, Turgenev did not keep at any very definite formal employment for long. Most of his energies were devoted to literature. His first, immature effort, the dramatic poem "Steno" (1834), had been composed in verse, the dominant genre of the 1830's. But his initial serious effort, the narrative poem "Parasha," dated from 1843 and was subtitled "A Short Story in Verse," in an obvious reference to the subtitle of Alexander Pushkin's *Eugene Onegin* (1824–1831), "A Novel in Verse." Belinsky dedicated a lengthy article to "Parasha," commending it warmly for being composed in "splendid poetic verse" and "imbued with a profound idea and completeness of inner content." For some time Turgenev continued to work the same vein, producing such narrative poems as "A Conversation" (1843) and "The Landowner" (1845), in addition to a quantity of lyric poems. Simultaneously, however, he tried his hand in other areas; for example, plays and some short stories in prose, especially "Andrey Kolosov" (1844), in which the narrator generously resolves to take up a young woman jilted by one of his best friends, only to discover that when she responds to his overtures he loses interest and shamefacedly drops her too. It is clear that in his earliest stories and poems Turgenev has already treated the chief themes of his career, most especially that of love gone awry. This fact has been obscured to some extent, however, by the fact that toward the end of the 1840's he made a slight but significant detour in his literary development. The first hint of this was the appearance in 1847 of the initial sketch of a group that eventually constituted *A Hunter's Notes* (1852).

This piece, "Khor and Kalinych," was subtitled "From a Hunter's Notes" by an editor and tucked away in the miscellaneous section of *The Contemporary*, the leading literary journal of the day. In it the author, with great richness of detail and psychological skill, delineates the distinct and contrasting personalities of two serfs. Each is shown as a full and interesting human being, and each is shown—so subtly as to make it seem almost incidentally—as weighted down by his servile status and unconvinced that his lot has genuinely improved of late. This story, along with a few others published by the end of 1847, caused Belinsky to conclude that Turgenev's future lay precisely along the lines of the hunting sketches, rather than those of his early poetry. If the critic was not wholly right in this estimate, he was entirely correct in remarking that a "chief characteristic" of Turgenev's talent was his inability "accurately to create a character whose like he had not encountered in reality"—that reality must always serve as Turgenev's touchstone.

Though the sketches in *A Hunter's Notes* have remained among Turgenev's highest achievements, they are not the most typical of his works, for later on he reverted to the type of story illustrated by "Andrey Kolosov." For the time being, however, he accepted Belinsky's prescription, publishing further peasant sketches individually and then collecting them under the general title *A Hunter's Notes* (a final three were added as late as 1874). In his last years Turgenev used to congratulate himself on the contribution his book had made to the emancipation of the serfs in 1861. And indeed his claim was probably substantial. The book made a solid political point while not ceasing to be art.

The chief thrust of *A Hunter's Notes* as a whole continued to be the characterization of peasants as human beings, but human beings diminished by an officially sanctioned system of enslavement. The peasant boys in "Bezhin Meadow" who sit about a fire of an evening telling one another frightening tales, Kasyan with his pungent personality in "Kasyan of Krasivaya Mecha," Khor and Kalinych—all

are unforgettable portraits. The reader also remembers the almost unconscious cruelty of the landowners who are accustomed to giving their serfs short shrift: "The way I see it, if you're a master then be a master; if you're a peasant then be a peasant," one of them says in "Two Landowners." However, it would be an error to think of the entire collection as structured around a contrast between admirable peasants and bestial landowners. Some landowners, though perhaps feckless, are depicted as genuinely interested in their peasants' welfare; and the serfs are often drawn as not particularly honest (Turgenev noted as one of their main characteristics a tendency to lie purely for the sake of lying) and occasionally downright repulsive, as in the scene of the drunken, swinish peasants at the conclusion of "The Singers." Moreover, the author is interested in a number of things with no direct bearing on social relationships: he transmits the folk beliefs of the common people, or investigates the manner in which individuals face the immediate prospect of death ("A Country Doctor" is a poignant story of a lonely, incompetent doctor who falls deeply in love with a dying young woman he cannot save). Turgenev is also concerned with aesthetic matters: he gives an extraordinarily detailed description of the singing competition in "The Singers," and what most readers remember from the welter of detail—the quantity of detail that makes it difficult to recall the outline of any particular story is perhaps the book's main weakness—is his magnificent nature descriptions. The final sketch, "Forest and Steppe," consists entirely of unsurpassed lyrical word-painting.

Turgenev's best-known single story dedicated to the unfortunate condition of the serfs is "Mumu" (1852), not included in *A Hunter's Notes*. Much anthologized in the Soviet Union today because of its relatively overt social criticism, the tale describes the hard lot of a deaf and dumb serf who for lack of any other object forms an attachment to a dog, but has even this small solace taken from him through the unheeding cruelty of his captious, elderly female owner. The hero, Gerasim, is drawn as a very positive character despite the physical affliction that makes him a trifle peculiar and for which no one can be held responsible; but few of those around him, including his fellow serfs, make any effort to ease his situation. His position would have been trying enough had he been a free man, but the far-reaching powers over him granted to his owner by the institution of serfdom certainly intensify his misfortunes. "Mumu" stands as Turgenev's most forthright indictment of the system of serfdom.

Over the years when the stories in *A Hunter's Notes* were appearing, Turgenev wrote other works as well. In 1849, while living abroad, he wrote a work of cardinal importance for all Russian literature, "Diary of a Superfluous Man," published in 1850. The phrase "superfluous man" has since become the mightiest cliché in the criticism of nineteenth-century Russian literature, utilized as it now is to link Pushkin's Onegin, Lermontov's Pechorin, Goncharov's Oblomov, and several other literary creations as essentially positive characters unjustly treated by contemporary society. But it was Turgenev who, through his story, gave the phrase its first wide currency, even though his hero, Chulkaturin, is more psychologically than socially or politically superfluous. The work is cast in the form of a diary kept by Chulkaturin in the last days before his death, which occurs on April Fools' Day, appropriately enough. Though the consciousness of his impending demise weighs on both Chulkaturin and the reader, Turgenev underlines the complete indifference of nature toward the fortunes of her creatures, of whom man is only one: there is a constant and jarring discord between the budding life of the incipient spring in which the narrative is set and Chulkaturin's morbid sickliness.

Chulkaturin is a sensitive though excessively self-conscious individual, capable of analyzing himself as well as others with impressive penetration. This is especially the case now, when he is summing up his life; but at the same time he realizes that in the actual situations he looks back on, he either acted totally inappropriately or misinterpreted the deeds and attitudes of others. The most central of Chulkaturin's characteristics is his "superfluity," his quality of always being a "supernumerary." "Evidently nature had not counted on my putting in an appearance," he says, "and therefore treated me like an uninvited and unexpected guest. . . . All during the course of my life I constantly found my place already occupied, perhaps because I looked for that place where I should not have." The narrative illustrates this apparently almost fated trait of his life: he has hopes of winning the love of a young lady but is frustrated by the appearance of a dashing nobleman who wins her heart instead; when he attempts to defend her honor he merely earns her hatred; at the end he "magnanimously" resolves to cover for her sins, only to discover that yet another rival has preceded him. Nothing remains for him but to acquiesce first in his own humiliation, then in his own dissolution. Chulkaturin is an outstanding literary creation: he is both sufficiently individualized and sufficiently generalized to endure in the treasury of world literature.

Given Turgenev's general literary approach, one might expect him to be interested in writing for the stage, and indeed for a time it seemed he might leave a large body of dramatic writing. Beginning with a brief piece in a Spanish setting dating from 1843, Turgenev produced some ten plays of varying length before abandoning the genre permanently after 1852, largely for extraliterary reasons: the theatrical censorship at the time was unusually strict, so that he despaired of even getting his plays published, much less staged. And later on, when the situation improved, he somehow failed to try his hand at the drama again.

Turgenev's finest play—one that remains a staple of the Russian repertory to this day and is often presented on Western stages as well—is *A Month in the Country*, written in 1850. A play of Chekhovian mood created before Chekhov was born, it is based on a situation reminiscent of Turgenev's own relationship with the Viardot family. The hero, Rakitin, is a freeloader and a devotee of the lady of the house, whose husband is too preoccupied with managing the estate to pay her much heed. However, Rakitin is also an educated man with a morbid sensitivity to the beauties of nature. The world of the estate—outwardly idyllic but inwardly full of discontent and potential unhappiness—is disturbed by the arrival of a young tutor, whose unaffected naturalness and energy awaken the love of both the jaded mistress of the estate, Natalya Petrovna, and her seventeen-year-old ward, Vera. Rakitin follows the situation almost as an external observer and, though at first incredulous, soon realizes that the only solution is for both him and the tutor, Belyaev, to take their leave. Rakitin then departs for the future of a lonely bachelor; Belyaev leaves for the more important things he presumably has the capacity to achieve; Vera escapes what has become an intolerable situation at home by accepting the proposal of a kind but dull man thirty years her elder; and Natalya Petrovna subsides into the rut of existence on her husband's well-managed estate. Thus the tutor's brief stay on the estate precipitates a whole series of crises: the situation of the characters at the end is very different from what it was at the beginning, and the majority of them are worse off than before. The entire piece is imbued with an autumnal atmosphere: everyone's situation is somehow out of joint, and there are no real prospects for improvement. *A Month in the Country* encountered difficulties with censorship: it could be published only in modified form, with Natalya Petrovna a widow rather than a wife, in 1855, and not in its original version until 1869.

The period during which Turgenev established his literary reputation was not a propitious one for Russian literature: the years 1848 to 1855, from the European revolutions to the death of Czar Nicholas I, are now called the "epoch of censorship terror." Herzen, sensing what was below the horizon, left his homeland in 1847 never to return; Belinsky died an early death in 1848; Dostoevsky was exiled to Siberia for subversive activities in 1849. During this period Belinsky's name could not be mentioned in print, and any hint of disloyal intent was blue-penciled by the censors. At first Turgenev was not especially affected by these conditions. Between 1847 and 1850 he traveled extensively in western Europe, particularly France and Germany, and though he may have been regarded by some in the government as a carrier of the revolutionary virus, nothing untoward happened to him until 1852. Then, ironically enough, he suffered for writing an obituary extolling Gogol, politically the most conservative of the great Russian writers, whom Belinsky had attacked scathingly not long before his own death. But evidently the government did not care to see any writers praised, and Turgenev was jailed in Saint Petersburg for a month, though not under very arduous conditions, for his friends could visit him freely and his meals were brought to him from outside. Thereafter, from May 1852 to November 1853, he was exiled to Spasskoe, which he had inherited after his mother's death in 1850, returning to the capital only at the very end of 1853.

The year 1855 saw the opening of a new era in the history of nineteenth-century Russia. When the country was far along toward losing the Crimean War, Nicholas I, remembered as the greatest tyrant among the czars, was succeeded by Alexander II, the "czar-liberator," who decreed the emancipation of the serfs in 1861. The beginning of Alexander's reign was a period of high hopes: it saw the lightening of the censorship and a resultant quickening of intellectual life. In addition, the 1850's witnessed a transition from the philosophical idealism of the 1840's to the politically radical activism of the 1860's. If the first half of the decade was a period of stagnation, the second was a time of ideological reorientation. It was then that the consistent old-line liberal Turgenev noted the first hints of trouble from those to his political left. This occurred when *The Contemporary*, under the editorship of his old friend Nikolay Nekrasov, began a process of radicalization under the guidance of the radical critics Nikolay Chernyshevsky and Nikolay Dobrolyubov. Chernyshevsky and Dobrolyubov were impatient with Turgenev's absorption with what they considered trivial affairs of the heart at a time when all honorable people were expected to be worrying about political and social problems. Turgenev never denied the importance of social problems, but at the same time he defended the artist's independence and his right to deal with other subjects he felt were also significant. Chernyshevsky and Dobrolyubov gradually took Nekrasov along with them, and after they had insulted Turgenev irreparably, the latter broke with both *The Contemporary* and Nekrasov.

By the end of the 1850's Turgenev was famous as the "great poet of the doomed love affair," to use Alfred Kazin's phrase of a later date. "Faust" (1856), a "Short Story in Nine Letters," displays several major themes in Turgenev's writing: the potentially malign influence of artistic literature on the minds of people unprepared to cope with it; an awareness of the supernatural intervening in human life; the violent, sudden snatching of the fruits of love from between outstretched hands: "What there was between us flashed by instantaneously, like lightning, and like lightning bore death and destruction." Some years after their first acquaintance the hero of "Faust" meets the heroine, now married to a pedestrian husband. Though the heroine's late mother had strictly forbidden her ever to read fiction, the hero, who could never comprehend the reason for this prohibition, begins to visit her estate and recite Goethe's *Faust* to her. The poem wreaks such a change in her character that the relationship between hero and heroine develops to the stage where each avows love for the other. On her way to the assignation that would have led to the consummation of their passion, however, the heroine is stopped by her mother's apparition. She returns home with a mysterious ailment to which she succumbs in two weeks, leaving the hero to the standard lonely future.

Just as in "Faust," artistic literature, represented in this instance by Pushkin's foreboding lyric "The Upas-Tree" (1828), plays a crucial role in the story "A Quiet Spot" (1854). A brief work that took Turgenev six months to compose, it is not particularly successful, partly because of the excessive number of plot lines but primarily because the heroine's character is delineated so sketchily that her final decisive act of committing suicide seems insufficiently motivated. The reader may surmise, however, that she is designed as a deeply passionate though disciplined soul compelled to live among potential or actual philistines, and that the impression made on her mind, so unaccustomed to artistic literature, by her reading of Pushkin's poem triggers her fatal decision.

In his love stories of the 1850's Turgenev rings the changes on the basic theme of the abrupt denial of love's fruits. "Asya," for example, written in Rome at the end of 1857 after the author had weathered a spiritual crisis, and published in 1858, may be viewed as one of the most characteristic of Turgenev's love stories. The tale is set in Germany rather than on a Russian estate, but the foreign environment serves primarily to bring the Russian characters—the narrator, N.; Gagin; and the latter's illegitimate half-sister, Asya—closer together than they might have been in a native setting. A consuming love sweeps over the heroine, reducing her to a state of physical illness. But when she offers her love to N. during the climactic scene, and he must accept or reject her on the spot, he declines to do either but instead temporizes wordily. To be sure, he quickly realizes his error and within twelve hours is prepared to grasp the opportunity presented him, but he is too late:

the Gagins depart, and he is unable to trace them. At the time he consoles himself with the thought that other opportunities may present themselves, but he is wrong: "Condemned to the loneliness of an old bachelor, I live out my dull years, but I preserve as something sacred her little notes and a faded geranium, the same blossom she threw me from the window once upon a time."

"First Love," a long short story of 1860, is among the most autobiographical of Turgenev's writings, being based in large measure on the situation in his own family, with his philandering father married to an unattractive and older woman. As is the case with "Asya," the story is recalled through the prism of intervening years by a hero for whom the events described were crucial; the impressions are those of a youth of sixteen not fully cognizant of what is happening about him, as recalled and interpreted by an older man. The narrator describes his first passion for a beautiful but impoverished noblewoman, Zinaida, a capricious and independent young woman who completely dominates her suite of admirers but submits to the narrator's father, a man who values independence and freedom above all. The reader must take some pains to piece together the history of the love affair between Zinaida and the father, for the narrator himself perceived it only fragmentarily, being most concerned with his own emotions upon first falling in love. And certainly the story is a masterpiece of psychological analysis in its description of the reactions of a boy in this state who realizes that he faces a successful rival in his own father, whom he greatly admires. But even successful love engenders disaster: the father dies of a stroke soon after the affair is terminated, leaving as a legacy the words, "My son, fear woman's love; fear that happiness, that poison"; Zinaida, after bearing an illegitimate child, makes the best marriage she can but dies a mere four years later. In "First Love," as in many of Turgenev's other works, love is like a disease that can re-

sult only in damage: it ruins one's life if unrequited, it ruins one's life if requited. The temporary joys it brings must be paid for in excessive measure.

Turgenev is now remembered as a novelist, though, even more than as a short-story writer. Although he did not get around to separating his novels from his short stories until 1880, Turgenev wrote six of them: *Rudin A Nest of Gentlefolk* (1859), *On the Eve* (1860), *Fathers and Sons* (1862), *Smoke* (1867), and *Virgin Soil* (1877). His novels differ from his short stories in that the latter deal primarily with personal emotions and love conflicts, whereas the former also treat broader social questions. However, even in the novels Turgenev's interest remains focused on his heroes' distinct personalities. He once remarked that he always began from a personality rather than an abstract idea, and thus it is not surprising to find him supplying his heroes with detailed prehistories either in his notes for a novel or in the novel itself, and setting them very carefully in historical context. Another hallmark of Turgenev as literary artist was the externalizing of his characters' psychology. He rejected Tolstoy's method of analyzing his heroes' psychological motives directly and at length. The artist, he held, should be a "secret psychologist": Turgenev knows quite as well as Tolstoy how his heroes think and feel, but he causes them to express their internal experience through words and external actions, so that the reader must deduce their inner feelings from outward signs, just as in real life. To be sure, Turgenev's characters occasionally deliver themselves of monologues that are more closely allied to Tolstoy's approach, but on the whole the reader is presented with a substantial task of interpretation in dealing with Turgenev's writing.

A famous article of Turgenev's, published in 1859 under the title "Hamlet and Don Quixote," is worth considering briefly as a key to his view of life and literature. In this piece Turgenev postulates the Hamlet type and the

Quixote type as polar opposites in human character. To Turgenev's mind, Don Quixote represents primarily "faith," "faith in truth located beyond the individual." Don Quixote dedicates his life to a cause outside himself. This makes him appear mad to some, and it indisputably bestows a considerable monotony upon his mind: "He knows little, but he does not have to know much." At the same time, he is "the most moral creature in the world," this insane knight. Hamlet is quite the opposite: he represents "analysis first of all, and egotism, and therefore lack of faith." Though an egotist, Hamlet is simultaneously too skeptical to believe in himself. Though intelligent, he finds his own internal resources insufficient. His weapon is irony, where Don Quixote's is enthusiasm. Don Quixote would not fear to seem foolish in the eyes of the world, whereas Hamlet thinks there is nothing worse than this. Hamlet despises this life and wishes he could end it, but he is still too much attached to it to make any serious attempt to do so. Turgenev does remind us, though, that Hamlet suffers much more intensely than Don Quixote: the latter undergoes only physical discomfort inflicted by others, whereas Hamlet tortures himself spiritually.

The first of Turgenev's novels, *Rudin*, contains a central hero constructed largely on the pattern of Hamlet. Composed in six or seven weeks during the summer of 1855 at Spasskoe, it was published early the following year in *The Contemporary* and in a separate edition a few months later. The setting for the story is yet another isolated Russian estate, where Rudin appears abruptly and unexpectedly. When he leaves a short time later, everything remains outwardly much as it was before, but inward tensions have been created that will markedly alter the fortunes of the individuals in the group Rudin finds there. This group includes Darya Mikhailovna, the imperious and vain mistress of the estate; her daughter, Natalya, the book's heroine; a neighboring land-owner, Volyntsev, who at first refrains from making an open avowal of his love for Natalya but who eventually wins her as his wife; the sycophant and secret sensualist Pandalevsky; the embittered misogynist and poseur Pigasov; and the earnest tutor Basistov. All of these are affected in one way or another by Rudin, especially by his flair for rhetoric, the "music of his eloquence." Words are Rudin's stock in trade. "Some of his hearers very likely did not understand precisely what he was talking about," the author comments, "but his breast heaved, some sort of curtains were withdrawn before his eyes, and something radiant flared up before him." After listening to him for a time Darya Mikhailovna calls him a "poet," and Turgenev emphasizes the fact the Rudin is often carried away by the music of his own eloquence in what is indeed a rather poetic fashion.

Rudin almost desperately uses words as a cover for his lack of inner emotion. Toward the end of the novel one character remarks that "Rudin has the nature of a genius," only to be corrected by another: "There is a touch of genius in him, . . . but nature—that's the whole thing, he really has no nature." There lies within Rudin an emotional void he strives to fill with words and intellectual convictions, but cannot. He is a man lacking in passion who feels that he should be passionate. But his predilection for intellectual analysis and verbalization destroys any possibility of true emotional commitment. In his student days he wrecked a love affair in which one of his friends was involved by insisting on analyzing it and informing other people about it. In the novel he does the same thing to his own love affair: when Natalya offers herself to him without reservations, he knows he should respond but can feel nothing. He therefore attempts to counterfeit the appropriate emotions, but fails, and afterward loses Natalya because he cannot take positive action at the time required. He tries to justify his failure in a lengthy analytic letter written to her when he leaves, but words simply cannot compensate for his lack of substance. At the end of the novel as originally published, Rudin is depicted dejectedly and aimlessly wandering through Russia.

Apparently, though, Turgenev was uncomfortable about leaving his hero in such an existential limbo, for in 1860 he took the unusual step of adding to the novel an epilogue presenting him in a slightly more favorable light. Rudin himself tells of several projects that he had undertaken but that had all come to naught because of his inability to accomplish anything practical. At the same time, he is reconciled with an old university classmate, who had been very much against him during the body of the novel; and the author grants that the uttering of the right words at the right time may be a form of action. At the end, in a scene whose appropriateness is open to some question, Turgenev brings Rudin to the Parisian barricades of June 1848 and there has him perish, shot through the heart, after the Revolution has already been put down. Thus in the final accounting he does prove capable of action, though fate decrees that even this shall be abortive.

Turgenev had been planning his second novel, *A Nest of Gentlefolk,* as early as 1856, but circumstances prevented serious work on it before a sojourn at Spasskoe in 1858. The book was written in the latter half of that year and published in early 1859 (publication early in the year is a nearly constant pattern with Turgenev's novels). Though *A Nest of Gentlefolk* was received by his contemporaries with approbation, its popularity has not stood the test of time, and it is now among the least read of his novels.

In the years immediately following 1855 Turgenev was for some reason at his most Slavophile or Russophile. Toward the conclusion of *Rudin* he had caused a character for whom he obviously felt some sympathy to make a strong statement against cosmopolitanism and to define the source of Rudin's unhappiness as his ignorance of Russia. "Russia can get along without us," he says, "but none of us can get along without her. Woe to him who thinks he can, and double woe to him who actually does!" In *A Nest of Gentlefolk* Turgenev continued to work along lines such as these. This should not be taken to mean that he abandoned his Western predilections, but he did at that time look most sympathetically on the Russian traits of his heroes and most unfavorably on certain aspects of Western culture. This is exemplified by the history of the father of the book's hero, Lavretsky. The father was a scatterbrained Anglophile who tried to bring Lavretsky up as a rootless European. However, not only does Lavretsky rediscover the positive values of his native land, but his father is transformed into a Russian in the bad sense when he suddenly goes blind, wanders across Russia seeking a cure, and dies a crotchety Russian landowner of the classical type. Aside from this, in *A Nest of Gentlefolk* Turgenev also devotes a great deal of attention to the problem of the family as the foundation-stone of any society. He provides Lavretsky with the most extensive family history of any of his major characters, tracing his ancestors back several centuries and dwelling in much more detail than is usual even for him on Lavretsky's immediate family. In like manner, the "nest" of the title is a family nest depicted in loving detail at the end of the book. Lavretsky has nothing to do with its existence, but he appreciates the principle of human continuity that it embodies.

Lavretsky himself is a likable man with scholarly inclinations who is trapped between two women representing the poles of womankind in Turgenev's fiction. His wife, Varvara Pavlovna, is unredeemable: she exploits her husband, is blithely unfaithful to him with insignificant men, makes demands on him when she has nowhere else to turn, and generally blights his life. She is one of several women in Turgenev who feed their egos by exercising power over men. For a time, misled by a false report of her death in Paris, where he has left her in order to return to Russia, Lavretsky is deceived into thinking he can find true happiness with the book's heroine, Liza, the most ethereal, most moral, and strongest-willed of Turgenev's women. Intensely religious, Liza is disturbed by the notion of loving a man promised to another woman, even if the latter be dead. In a brief scene of suppressed passion, the two seem on the verge of happiness until all is suddenly destroyed by the reappearance of Varvara Pavlovna. Liza interprets the return of Lavretsky's wife as divine punishment for her spiritual insolence and resolves to take up life as a nun in a distant convent. Lavretsky is soon abandoned by his wife once again. The novel ends with a vignette describing Lavretsky's visit years later to Liza's convent. As he watches her pass by a few feet from him, "only the lashes of the eye turned toward him trembled slightly, she merely bent her emaciated face lower—and the fingers of her clasped hands, intertwined with prayer beads, clenched more tightly." In these external signs may be read the extent of Liza's inner strength.

One of the most dynamic male characters Turgenev ever created was Insarov, the Bulgarian hero of his third novel, *On the Eve*. The author began the book in the summer of 1859 while taking the waters at Vichy, although he had been nurturing the idea for it since 1855, when a friend had given him a manuscript describing an unfortunate love between a Bulgarian man and a young Russian woman. Completed in the autumn at Spasskoe, it appeared in the January 1860 issue of the *Russian Herald*, the journal in which Turgenev would publish for some years following his break with *The Contemporary*, despite its conservative politics and his general dislike for its editor, Mikhail Katkov.

On the Eve sharply contrasts the Russian male—in the persons of Shubin, an artist of ability and intelligence but lacking in constancy, and Bersenev, a good man and a scholar who ends by producing articles on such trivial topics as "On Certain Peculiarities of Ancient German Law in the Matter of Judi-cial Punishments"—and the dedicated Russian female in the character of Elena Stakhova. The single-minded Insarov is the only one who can satisfy her aspirations and meet her standards. Having grown up an independent soul, Elena has reached just the right age for love when she first meets Insarov, at that time a student in Moscow, in the period preceding the outbreak of the Crimean War in 1853. Insarov is totally devoted to the goal of freeing his country from its Turkish occupiers, and it is this complete dedication that makes him one of the most Don Quixote–like characters in Turgenev's fiction. The analytical Shubin presents the major traits of Insarov's character admirably in two sculptures he does of him. The first is a realistic bust in which his features are "honorable, noble, and bold," but the second depicts him as a rearing ram in whose countenance are expressed "dull pomposity, fervor, stubbornness, clumsiness, and narrowness." But the first Insarov is the one who remains predominantly in the reader's mind and the one who inspired Dobrolyubov to write his famous article "When Will the Real Day Come?" in which he lauds Insarov while at the same time looking to the appearance of his Russian counterpart in the near future.

Once Insarov and Elena meet, the plot develops rapidly. Elena takes the initiative in pressing her love on him. Though he knows a revolutionary should have no family ties, he accepts her when she agrees to support his cause wholly and make no demands of her own on him. She thereupon abandons her family and Russia to go with her husband to Bulgaria to fight for liberation. Evidently, however, the pair have upset the balance of fate by their actions. Insarov contracts an illness while attempting to make arrangements for his wife to accompany him. He recovers, but falls ill again in Vienna and finally in Venice, where he dies before regaining his native soil. It is Insarov himself who raises the question of whether his illness is not punishment, and perhaps it is—a sign that personal happiness cannot be combined with dedication to a political cause. Then, too, Insarov is a prime example of his creator's belief that if a man of action appears on the scene before history is ripe for him (after all, the Crimean War ended in Russia's defeat and the continued enslavement of Bulgaria), some indefinable force will cut him down. The final pages of *On the Eve* contain lengthy though inconclusive ruminations on the meaning of a death that cuts short such a significant life, ruminations grounded in the tension between Turgenev's innate philosophical nihilism and the optimism of a man with a goal, like Insarov. Turgenev could not himself believe with such conviction; however, he admired those who could, even though he was persuaded they were doomed to failure.

Nihilism as a political rather than a philosophical phenomenon was central to Turgenev's next and finest novel, *Fathers and Sons* (more precisely, *Fathers and Children*). He later wrote that he had first conceived of the book upon meeting an unnamed provincial doctor who impressed him as representative of a particular social type, which he then embodied in the novel's hero, Bazarov. Commencing work on the manuscript in October of 1860, he completed the first version about a year later, then spent the last months of 1861 revising the text and agonizing over whether he ought to publish it at all in view of the widespread political unrest among the peasantry and students following the emancipation of the serfs in the spring. But the editor Katkov knew a good novel when he saw one—he published Tolstoy and Dostoevsky as well as Turgenev—and substantially decided the matter for him, bringing it out in the February 1862 issue of the *Russian Herald*. In the summer of that year it appeared in a separate edition, with the addition of a dedication to Belinsky.

Fathers and Sons was composed with at least two major ends in view: to contrast representatives of the best in the older and younger generations and to demonstrate that the idealistic theories of the young, however admirable in the abstract, could not withstand confrontation with the realities of life.

The ideological standard-bearer of the older generation is Pavel Petrovich Kirsanov. An Anglophile and a man of cultivation, he is also a bachelor embittered by a long-term enslavement of passion to a captious and mysterious noblewoman. In his mouth Turgenev placed the major tenets of his own generation: a belief in principles as a guide to action; admiration of civilization and its accomplishments coupled with a denial that anything essential can be accomplished by brute force; a conviction that an enlightened aristocracy is essential for the well-being of the nation; respect for the proprieties and customs of social intercourse. His opponent, Bazarov, the primary representative of the younger generation, resembles him in many facets of his emotional and psychological makeup but differs from him sharply in his philosophical approach to life. Bazarov is the great "negator," the quintessential "nihilist" (though Turgenev did not invent the word, he gave it popularity as a tag for the political radicals of the 1860's). He denies any validity to existing customs and social structures, insisting that they be swept away and space cleared for something better to be built; he refuses to recognize received authorities and even scoffs at medicine, though he is studying to be a doctor; he denies that human beings possess any individuality: for him they are simply "copies," constituent parts of a social collective; he tends to equate evil with illness, which can be eliminated by altering the social order; he lacks any appreciation of art and aesthetics generally. Philosophically he is a thorough materialist. The intellectual clashes between Pavel Petrovich and Bazarov, intensified by their instinctive personal dislike for each other, constitute an important part of the book. Essentially these are debates rather than discussions. Since neither is genuinely willing to listen to the other, no meeting of minds occurs, but Bazarov usually bests his opponent because he is quite willing to push his arguments to their logical extreme on provocation, whereupon Pavel Petrovich can only gape. Later on the enmity between them results in a duel, which Bazarov wins, physically and then also spiritually, by magnanimously binding his opponent's wounds.

But if Bazarov gains the philosophical battle with Pavel Petrovich, and through him with the older generation as a whole, he loses the struggle with life. The very duel with Pavel Petrovich supplies an example of this: though Bazarov in theory rejects the notion of honor and dueling as a social institution, when he is actually challenged his pride causes him to accept the duel. The clearest instance of the failure of his doctrines to bear up under the testing of real life is his love for Odintsova, the book's beautiful but cold heroine, who does not mind flirting with him so long as the involvement does not become serious and disrupt her placid routine. Bazarov thinks love solely a matter of physiology: if one cannot "achieve one's aim" with one woman, drop her and find another. And in fact it is Odintsova's physical beauty that first attracts him: a physical lust akin to malice drives him to make his confession of love to her. But when Odintsova refuses him, Bazarov to his own amazement discovers that he cannot put her out of his mind. He keeps coming back to her in the hope that she may relent, and at the end summons her to his deathbed to bid her farewell. In this and other ways Bazarov partially falls prey to the "romanticism" of which he is so contemptuous. His theory of sexual attraction turns out to be invalid.

After love, death is the final irrational factor Bazarov had not reckoned with. Like Insarov, he is felled before he actually accomplishes anything: while dissecting a corpse he cuts himself and falls ill because no disinfecting substance is immediately available. Before the conclusion he grasps more clearly the mysteries of existence. "Yes," says the great negator on his deathbed, "just try to negate death. It negates you instead, and that's all there is to it."

After *Fathers and Sons* appeared, the question of the author's intent in writing it was paramount in the minds of the radical literary critics who discussed it. Dmitry Pisarev and his journal *Russian Word* argued that Turgenev had simply tried to be objective in picturing the younger generation, and that a young person should be quite pleased with Bazarov's portrayal. To be sure, Turgenev had included the figures of Sitnikov and Kukshina, two intellectual and moral travesties of Bazarov, but it had to be admitted that such people as these actually existed in reality and did no credit to the radical movement. Pisarev thus felt that there was nothing intentionally "antinihilist," or deliberately directed against the young radicals, in the book. But the other and more influential segment of the radical intelligentsia, led by Chernyshevsky and Dobrolyubov's heir, Maksim Antonovich, assailed Turgenev vigorously for having slandered the younger generation, declaring that, since he stood revealed as a reactionary, all of his previous novels should be consigned to oblivion. When Turgenev visited Saint Petersburg in the spring of 1862, he found to his dismay that those he considered his enemies welcomed him, while those he would have liked to think were his allies scorned him. Some, he later recalled sadly, had informed him then that they had burned photographs of him "with a hawhaw of contempt." In April 1862 Turgenev wrote a lengthy letter to a group of Russian students at Heidelberg University, defending his creation of Bazarov, proclaiming in the standard political idiom that his entire work was directed "against the gentry as the dominant class," and throwing up his hands at the students' claim that the idiotic Kukshina was his most successful character. But such was the intellectual atmosphere in Russia at the time that all his protestations availed him little.

The decade of the 1860's was a sharp-edged but seminal one in Russian intellectual history. The hopes aroused by Alexander II's accession to power were crowned by the emancipation of the serfs in 1861 and lesser but still important reforms, as of the courts, in subsequent years. But Chernyshevsky, Dobrolyubov, Pisarev, and their allies, the descendants of the philosophical radicals of the 1840's, were not content with even these substantial changes: they went on to demand much more. The agitation for drastic change reached a crescendo in 1862, after the radicals had denounced the emancipation as a hoax, but it was quelled in that year through such actions as the suspension of *The Contemporary* and *Russian Word*, the imprisonment of Chernyshevsky and Pisarev, and most especially the outbreak of a rebellion in Poland in early 1863, which rallied public opinion to the government's side. Thereafter, deciding that the arson and university closing of 1861–1862 had served little purpose, those hard-core radicals who were prepared to give their lives for the cause embarked on a course of individual terrorism against high government officials. A deflected shot fired in April 1866 at Alexander II in the heart of Saint Petersburg inaugurated the era dominated by assassins and bomb throwers, an era that culminated in the successful assassination of Alexander fifteen years later but that continued sporadically into the twentieth century. It is these terrorists, most of whom paid with their lives for their deeds, who were called "nihilists" by western Europeans in the 1870's and 1880's.

The relations between the old-style liberals like Turgenev and the younger generation of the 1860's were delicate at best. Turgenev felt nearer to the radical than the conservative camp; he took pains to cultivate the young radicals, explain his attitudes to them, and reach some sort of understanding with them. But in the 1860's they for the most part would not have him, and he was compelled willy-nilly to ally himself with the more conservative elements of the Russian literary world, publishing in their chief organ, *Russian Herald,* during most of the decade. He could not condone the violence and terrorism perpetrated by the radicals, but at the same time he remained convinced that they were essentially correct in their outlook. Thus it was that many years later, in a brief prose poem, Turgenev wrote sadly of his attempts to tell the truth, only to be met with disdain from "honorable souls." All he could do, he felt, was continue on his path and hope that eventually he would be understood. "Pummel me, but be healthy and well-fed" was the slightly masochistic way he put it.

The unexpectedly violent reaction to *Fathers and Sons* gave Turgenev pause. Indeed, for about a year after its publication he wrote virtually nothing of consequence. Then he reappeared bearing an odd concoction, begun some years before, entitled "Phantoms." When he printed it at the beginning of 1864 in a new journal edited by Dostoevsky, he went to great lengths to emphasize its apolitical character, subtitling it "A Fantasy" and equipping it with a brief introduction in which he asked the reader to take it at face value and not read anything into it. "Phantoms" is a series of disjointed sketches with an anonymous narrator whisked about nocturnally by a supernatural being called Ellis. Ellis is able to transport him at will not only through space but also through time: for example, she shows him Julius Caesar's legions marching in the days of imperial Rome's glory. During one of these nightly episodes, however, Ellis is attacked by a mysterious creature the narrator recognizes as death. He recovers consciousness lying on the ground near a beautiful woman, who embraces him passionately and promptly vanishes.

One of the few minor items Turgenev wrote in the years following "Phantoms" was another series, this time of brief ruminations, entitled "Enough" (1865) and subtitled "Passages from a Dead Artist's Notes." "Enough" is Turgenev at his sentimental and self-pitying worst, consisting as it does of meditations on melancholy themes of lost happiness, the indifference of nature, the inevitability of destruction and the void, all done in a mood redolent of Arthur Schopenhauer. The work ends with a Shakespearean quotation in English: "The rest is silence."

Though this retreat from literature was only temporary (among his friends his repeated declarations of intent to abandon literature forever became something of a joke, and Dostoevsky used them to embarrassing effect in his nasty caricature of Turgenev as Karmazinov in *The Possessed* [1871–1872]), his experiences of 1862 did alter the "mix" of his writing significantly. To be sure, he wrote two more novels, but they now appeared at less frequent intervals—whereas he published four between 1855 and 1862, he put out only two from 1862 to 1877—and the relative importance of the "mysterious" or the "supernatural" in his fiction increased. Turgenev did not believe in God, and superficially it might seem he would be little interested in supernatural phenomena. Yet he was haunted by a suspicion that there was something more to life than meets the eye. In 1864 he composed a small story entitled "The Dog," in which he described something that may have been an apparition—but then may have had a natural explanation too. He ventured no answer to the question with which he begins and concludes the story: "But if we allow the possibility of the supernatural, the possibility of its intrusion into real life, . . . then what role is left for common sense?"

"Knock . . . Knock . . . Knock" (1870), set in the romantic 1830's, is written in a similar vein. Its hero, Lieutenant Teglev, appears to others to be a "fatal" type who bears the seal of a man of destiny (in speaking of him, the narrator makes the interesting comment that a belief in fate is equivalent to a belief in the "significance of life"). Each of the individual occurrences in the chain leading to Teglev's decision to take his own life has a completely natural explanation, but the way in which they combine is at the very least mysterious: the overall pattern seems "fated," although at one point Teglev must do some forcing to fit a major event into the pattern. Here, as in "The Dog," Turgenev left himself a way out so that he would not have to commit himself irrevocably to the proposition that the supernatural does play a role in human life.

As the 1860's wore on, Turgenev renewed his interest in the political novel—his last two novels were even more political than the first four. He began writing *Smoke* around the end of 1865, dropped it for a time, then published it in early 1867 in the *Russian Herald*, despite some disagreements over it with Katkov. Curiously enough, this work is built around a love affair of a typically Turgenevian stripe, but one in which the man, Litvinov, is determinedly and avowedly apolitical. The author masterfully develops the love conflict around the question of whether Litvinov will succeed in wrenching his beloved, Irina, from the stifling world of Russian high society in which she is embedded in the German resort town of Baden-Baden, or whether she will enslave him with chains of passion and make of him a "kept man" to whom she can repair for surcease from the banality of the social circles in which she moves. In the end she proves too weak, too permeated by the poisons that have circulated about her for so many years, to leave her husband and his social milieu and follow Litvinov; and since Litvinov is exceptionally strong among Turgenev's heroes and demands all or nothing from her, the two part. At the novel's conclusion it is for once the woman who has missed her opportunity and become embittered, while Litvinov is able to renew his relationship with his former fiancée.

The political aspects of *Smoke* are treated in conjunction with Litvinov and his love affair, though he is more an observer of political discussion than a participant in it. Turgenev delineates with acid pen the generals, high bureaucrats, and stultified nobility who constitute Irina's circle and who are incapable of a single original or even intelligent thought. In many cases he denies them the dignity of full names, designating them by initials. Even the tolerant Litvinov can find no redeeming features in them. The opposite end of the political spectrum is represented by the members of the Gubarev circle, which Litvinov visits on occasion. Though they waste their time in pointless wrangling, and though many of them eventually return to Russia and become petty despots, Turgenev feels that they are not really bad people at heart, but simply misguided ones. The rightist and leftist groups resemble each other in a number of ways, but their creator is noticeably inclined toward the latter.

Turgenev advanced many of his own favorite notions through an admirable but weak character in *Smoke*, Potugin. Potugin is what Litvinov is in danger of becoming: a man so helplessly in love with Irina that he trails about after her to do her bidding. In lengthy conversations (or monologues, to put it more precisely) with Litvinov, Potugin sets forth his political and philosophical views, as, for instance, that Russia has contributed nothing to the progress of humankind and that Western civilization holds the only promise for Russia's future development. Potugin believes firmly in the West, but without rejecting his homeland even though he sees it in a jaundiced light.

In view of Turgenev's "plague on both your houses" political approach in *Smoke*, it is not astonishing that he was reviled from all sides for it. Members of the establishment resented being pictured as empty-headed reactionaries, and the radicals took offense at the depiction of the Gubarev circle, which was in fact one of Turgenev's most "antinihilist" creations. Pisarev, the chief radical critic still on the scene at the time, continued to display understanding for Turgenev, but even he criticized him for abandoning the line he had followed in creating Bazarov and turning instead to such a socially insignificant hero as Litvinov.

During the bulk of the 1860's, from 1864 to 1870, Turgenev resided near the Viardots in Baden-Baden. He made an average of one trip a year to Russia to keep abreast of developments, but fundamentally he was now living abroad and merely visiting his homeland. Toward the end of the decade the political situation in Russia eased noticeably, so at that time he published his reminiscences of Belinsky as well as a series of comments "On the Subject of *Fathers and Sons*," in which he fell victim to the compulsion felt by many of the "antinihilist" novelists to justify their books, so badly "misunderstood" by their readers. Ordinarily these efforts did their authors little good, and Turgenev's was no exception to the rule.

If Turgenev was at his most Slavophilic in the later 1850's, while writing *A Nest of Gentlefolk*, he was at his most Slavophobic at the conclusion of the 1860's. He was a European, he used to say then, and not particularly a Russian: "So bin Ich . . . ganz und gar Deutsch" (I am totally and completely German), he wrote to a correspondent in 1870. It is thus the more ironic that the conflict of that same year between France and Germany, two great bearers of Western civilization, drove him from his European nest: after the outbreak of hostilities the Viardots, being French citizens, had to leave Germany, and Turgenev followed them, first to London, then to France. And it was in France that the Russian-German lived from then on.

During the 1870's, while residing in France and continuing to pay occasional visits to Russia, Turgenev maintained relationships with certain of the greatest French writers of that day on a footing of at least equality, and sometimes superiority. He wrote and spoke French and German with native fluency and could handle English with some competence, a rare accomplishment for a nineteenth-century Russian. His vast correspondence, which has only recently been brought together in something resembling its entirety, was conducted in any one of four languages, and contains an immense mass of interesting commentary on contemporary literary and political events. Henry James, who first met Turgenev in 1875, declared him "the richest, the most delightful, of talkers," and found him and his work fascinating, although he was grieved that evidently Turgenev had no such high opinion of his, James's, writing. At the same time, as James emphasized in his memoirs of Turgenev, he was not at all gallicized: "No sojourner in Paris was less French than he," James recalled. And indeed the brothers Goncourt record in their journal not only samples of Turgenev's stimulating table talk, but also the fact that he discoursed mostly about Russia and things Russian. All of this speaks of the ambivalence of his character: in Russia he was a European, in Europe a Russian.

Turgenev's closest literary associates in Paris included Alphonse Daudet, Gustave Flaubert, and Émile Zola. Daudet recollected first meeting Turgenev at Flaubert's. Daudet being unusual among Frenchmen in that he was familiar with Turgenev's work, and Turgenev being unusual among authors in that he loved music, the two had much in common. Turgenev and Zola also got along well—Turgenev evidently had a hand in arranging for him to write a series of articles for the leading Russian liberal monthly, *Herald of Europe*, between 1875 and 1880—but there must have been some powerful temperamental differences between them. Thus the Goncourts record that once the two quarreled about love: Zola maintained that the only thing special about this emotional state was the prospect of copulation, while Turgenev argued that it was an extraordinary phenomenon distinct from its material and physiological aspects. Temperamentally Turgenev was probably closest to Flaubert in these years. He spent many evenings in conversation at his home, and their friends felt the two almost made a couple, with Turgenev playing the feminine role. Daudet commented that sometimes in nature "feminine souls are embodied in titanic forms" (Turgenev was a man of large build), and James remarked that Turgenev and Flaubert each "had a tender regard for the other," mixed with some compassion for Flaubert on Turgenev's part.

At the very time that Turgenev was living abroad and consorting so extensively with foreigners, however, in his writing he manifested a deep interest in peculiarly Russian themes. In "A Strange Story" (1869) he describes a mad wandering Holy Fool attended by a girl of good family who has found in him a leader before whom she can humiliate herself. Though he does not sympathize with the form it has taken, Turgenev cannot help admiring the strength of her devotion. "A King Lear of the Steppes," a long short story published in 1870 and since unduly neglected by students of Russian literature, is extraordinarily Russian in its execution despite the fact that it takes its title and plot idea from English literature. The hero of the story is a landowner named Kharlov, a man of immense build and of undisputed authority over his two daughters, their husbands, and his peasants. But when he sees in a dream a black foal, which he interprets as a symbol of impending death, he resolves to distribute his earthly goods to his heirs before his demise, confident that they will continue to revere him as before even without any material motive for doing so. Unhappily, he is mistaken, for once they obtain title to his property his heirs gradually deprive him of what little he has retained until finally they drive him from the estate altogether. Up to this point Kharlov's pride has kept him from complaining, but an almost chance remark kindles his rage: what he has created he can also destroy, he thinks to himself. In the concluding scene he mounts the roof of his former house and sets to wrecking it with his bare hands until he falls to the ground and injures himself so severely that he shortly dies. "A King Lear of the Steppes" is remarkable not only for the drama of its plot but also for its language, based on the colloquial style of the narrator and on peasant speech, and for its treatment of certain facets of the Russian character, not all of them positive.

Turgenev's interest in things Russian did not submerge his internationalist approach. "Torrents of Spring" (1872), his lengthiest work aside from his novels, presents a Russian hero involved with an Italian heroine in a German setting (Frankfurt and Wiesbaden) of thirty years before. Its plot is reminiscent of that of *Smoke,* although the hero, Sanin, is much weaker than Litvinov. It begins as something unusual for Turgenev, an account of love apparently fulfilled, with Sanin meeting a crucial test of resolution that enables him eventually to win a promise of marriage from the beautiful Gemma against substantial obstacles. But precisely when the reader has been lulled into the belief that Turgenev is after all capable of picturing successful love, the author abruptly drops his hero into the abyss of abject enslavement to the most predatory heroine he ever created, Polozova. Polozova, a wealthy woman of peasant origin, finds meaning in her life solely by enslaving men through the power of lust: at the moment of her triumph over Sanin, "her eyes, wide and so light they seemed white, expressed nothing but pitiless insensitivity and the satiety of victory." As a result of Polozova's intervention, Sanin loses his self-respect as well as his fiancée, and ends as one of the most embittered of Turgenev's numerous stand of lonely, middle-aged bachelors. Life, he muses to himself in the introduction, is not so much a stormy sea as a calm one with transparent waters. But beneath this superficially benign surface are many mysteries and many evils: on the "dark, slimy bottom" there are "hideous monsters," "all life's infirmities, sicknesses, griefs, insanity, poverty, blindness," any one of which may at any moment rise to the surface and capsize the boat in which the observer floats. The catastrophic shift in Sanin's fortunes illustrates this danger, and there is much in "Torrents of Spring" to justify Turgenev's referring to it as an "abortion" and remarking to a correspondent that he had conceived of it as full of blue sky and the song of larks, but it had turned out a poisonous toadstool: "I have never been so immoral," he added. The novelette, as it were, took on an evil life of its own under the author's pen.

Turgenev's sixth and last novel, *Virgin Soil,* appeared in early 1877 in the *Herald of Europe.* He worked over it for many years, composing thumbnail biographies of chief characters for his own use, but this did not guarantee the success of the final product, artistically the weakest of his novels. Evidently his prolonged residence in western Europe and his lack of contact with Russian reality sapped the vitality of an art that sought to deal with contemporary times. The critics condemned *Virgin Soil* roundly on its publication, and the verdict of later generations has not been appreciably more generous.

Virgin Soil is the most political of Turgenev's novels, being an attempt to trace the early history of the "movement to the people" that began about 1868. The "movement to the people" was based on the notion that radical students and intellectuals should conduct propaganda and agitation among the peasantry in order to make them a revolutionary force. But the ideas the young people preached were too foreign to the outlook of the peasantry, and the entire movement proved a fiasco. Turgenev wrote *Virgin Soil* largely to demonstrate how and why the radicals failed despite their good intentions.

The book's principal hero is Aleksey Nezhdanov, who comes from an established family: his father was a high-ranking officer, and he has been given a first-rate education by a strict Swiss schoolmaster. His very inner being is aristocratic, moreover: his fine facial features are an external reflection of his love of the beautiful and his sensitive intellect. One of his major weaknesses as a revolutionary is a tendency to write poetry, an inclination he carefully conceals after joining the radical movement. The novel's climax occurs when he sallies forth in peasant clothing to enlighten the common people, only to discover that he cannot "simplify" himself to the degree required, and that furthermore he cannot overcome his instinctive aversion to some nasty peasant traits. The conflict between his inborn instincts and his intellectual convictions leads to self-destruction, in one of the few instances where a Hamlet-like Turgenevian personage goes so far as to take his own life. In Nezhdanov's personality the ideal enters into an irreconcilable contradiction with the real.

There are those in *Virgin Soil* who remain faithful to the cause, however: the plain-looking Mashurina, who loves Nezhdanov with an unrequited love, and the energetic Markelov, who also discovers it is no simple matter to conduct agitation among the peasantry. A species of ideological barometer in the novel is Marianna Sinetskaya, who deserts her guardian's home to run away with Nezhdanov but refuses to marry him until he commits himself totally to her. This Nezhdanov cannot bring himself to do, but by means of a letter written before his suicide he joins her with the character offered as the book's positive hero, Solomin. Solomin, a practical man who operates along English lines, manages a factory on his estate. He springs from the common people and is not a great talker, but he displays "common sense" in his judgments. Turgenev clearly hoped the future would belong to him.

The radical critics violently disputed Turgenev's assessment of the class to which the future might belong, and he, as usual, attempted to mollify them by agreeing with them as far as he could. But they would not be placated, despite the novel's satirical thrusts against the aristocratic establishment. These were embodied especially in the person of Kollomeytsev, a pseudo-Westernizer who, though outwardly charming and graceful, is in fact a cruel exploiter of his peasants and a deep-dyed reactionary. Another despicable personage is Valentina Mikhailovna Sipyagina, reminiscent of such predatory Turgenevian females as Natalya Petrovna (*A Month in the Country*) in her rivalry with her ward, and of Polozova ("Torrents of Spring") in her desire to bind the naive Nezhdanov to herself by the bonds of love in order to inflate her own ego. Still, the erotic element, though important, is relatively less central in *Virgin Soil* than in any of the other novels.

Turgenev received honors as well as abuse in the latter half of the 1870's. In 1875 he settled for what remained of his life at Bougival near Paris, not far from the Viardots. He continued his excursions to Russia, as in the late summer of 1878, when he was reconciled with Tolstoy and visited the latter's estate at Yasnaya Polyana. But he made his most triumphal return to his homeland during a visit to Saint Petersburg and Moscow during the first months of 1879. At this time he was extensively feted by his fellow liberals in Russian society, and responded with pleasure to the evidences of his popularity among the reading public. Shortly thereafter, in June 1879, he journeyed to England to receive the honorary degree of doctor of civil law from Oxford University, a token of esteem from a nation he esteemed, and that he therefore cherished.

Almost exactly one year later, in June 1880, Turgenev participated in ceremonies connected with the unveiling of a monument to the great Russian poet Alexander Pushkin in Moscow. The festivities remain one of the outstanding public occasions in the history of Russian literature. Many leading writers were in attendance, and Dostoevsky in particular delivered the most famous speech of his career then. Turgenev chose to be cautious in defining Pushkin's place in Russian letters. He was ready to dub him the first "poet-artist" in Russian literature, he was willing to acknowledge him as the synthesizer of Russian literary language, but he would not crown him the "national poet" in the same sense in which Shakespeare and Goethe were considered the national poets of their respective homelands. Such ambiguity, however honest it may have been intellectually, did not suit the tenor of the occasion.

After the publication of *Virgin Soil* Turgenev's relatively sparse production was limited to short pieces. "A Desperate Character" (1881) presents an absorbing analysis of a certain type of personality that cannot stand the proprieties of staid bourgeois society and seems desperately bent on its own destruction. "The Song of Triumphant Love," also dating from 1881, is unusual in that it is set in sixteenth-century Ferrara instead of contemporary Russia or Russia of the recent past, and in that it deals with plainly supernatural occurrences, though in the form of a legend, connected with an unsuccessful love. A unique treatment of the theme of love and death is offered in "After Death" (later known as "Klara Milich"), written in 1882, the last full year of the author's life. The hero, a sensitive, lonely young man named Aratov, inspires love in a singer and actress, Klara Milich, though they have not met at the time. A strong-willed character who has promised to "take" the man she loves if she ever encounters him, she commits suicide onstage after an abortive attempt to bring Aratov to her feet during an interview in Moscow. Having failed to conquer him in this world, she returns to capture him in the next: Aratov falls in love with her after her death, sees her in dreams and visions, and ends by passing blissfully through the gate of death to join her. "Klara Milich" is one of Turgenev's most powerful statements on the exceptional nature of love, which can overcome the grave.

At the twilight of his writing career Turgenev effected something of a return to the poetic attempts of his first years in the *Poems in Prose,* brief lyrical vignettes on various subjects of usually not more than a page, and sometimes only a few lines. Written at different times between 1878 and 1882, each of them is carefully dated. Though frequently oversentimental, they treat many themes that had long been constants in Turgenev's work, and at the very least they are instructive as indices to his thinking in those years. Certain of them embody distillations of a philosophy of life derived from many years of observation of humankind's weaknesses and related to the capsule one-sentence aphorisms on human behavior with which he studded his novels and stories from the beginning, and some of which could be quite cynical. Philosophically speaking, however, the center of gravity of the

Poems in Prose lies not in such vignettes as these but in pieces on more serious, usually very pessimistic, subjects. One theme is the indifference of nature to human aspirations, which early received notable expression in the introduction to his "Excursion to the Woodlands" (1857): in the presence of the great forest, Turgenev wrote then, man "feels that the last of his brothers might vanish from the face of the earth, and not a single needle on these pine branches would twitch." Similarly, in "Conversation" the Jungfrau and the Finsteraarhorn look down distantly on the world below at intervals of thousands of years and express their satisfaction when the frenzied activities of antlike human beings in the lowlands cease and all is frozen and quiet. When the narrator inquires of personified nature in "Nature" what she is turning her attention to at that moment, she replies that she is strengthening the muscles of the flea so that he may more easily escape his enemies. To the narrator's protestations about human values, she remarks that she cherishes human beings no more and no less than any other of her creatures. One of the few prose poems with a religious coloration is "Christ," in which Jesus is perceived as a man with a face "like all other human faces" who by implication incorporates everything human within himself.

Two of the most famous sketches from the *Poems in Prose* deal with Russia and its domestic political situation. "The Threshold" points up both the dedication of the Russian revolutionaries and Turgenev's ambiguous attitude toward them. Questioned before being permitted to pass through a door, a girl says she is ready to die herself or commit a crime; she even realizes that she may one day lose faith in the cause to which she now dedicates herself. As she enters then, two voices accompany her, the first crying "Fool!" as the second responds "Saint!" In "The Russian Language," dated June 1882, Turgenev found moral sustenance in the tongue of which he was such a master: "In days of doubt, in days of gloomy meditation upon the fate of my homeland—you alone are my strength and support, oh great, mighty, honest, and free Russian language! Were it not for you how could we help despairing over everything done at home? But one must believe that such a language can have been given only to a great people!"

The most persistent theme in the prose poems, however, is that of death. It is central to the reminiscence of Turgenev's last meeting with Nekrasov. Its inevitability and unexpectedness are underlined in "The Old Woman" and "Tomorrow." It is treated allegorically in "The Insect," a tableau of a crowded hall into which flies a large and menacing insect. Everyone sees it and retreats from it in horror except its victim, who expires when it stings him on the forehead. The stolid resignation or deep despair of the common people when faced with the death of loved ones is the subject of two sketches. But in two others, both of them for some reason associated with sparrows, Turgenev sounds a note of hope or defiance: in "We Will Still Put Up a Fight" he draws inspiration from the cocky cheerfulness displayed by a family of sparrows while far above them circles the hawk who can destroy them any time he chooses; and in "The Sparrow" the mother bird's readiness to defend her young against an immense dog causes Turgenev to meditate: "Love, I thought, is stronger than death and the fear of death. Life maintains itself and develops only through that, through love."

Turgenev had long been preoccupied with death, of course. It had concerned him in some of his earliest works, and once in 1872, while discoursing at Flaubert's, he commented that he had always somehow been surrounded by "an odor of death, of nonbeing, of dissolution," a death that he defined as the inability to love. The predominance given the subject in the *Poems in Prose* became immediately relevant to his life when he fell ill with cancer in April 1883. From that time on the die was cast, though he experienced periods of temporary improvement. He continued his literary work when he could, publishing some new pieces and laboring over an edition of his collected writings, but death, however imagined—a black foal in "A King Lear of the Steppes," the more conventional skulls in one of the *Poems in Prose,* or a monkeylike creature huddled in a boat and holding a flask of dark liquid in a striking dream of Aratov's in "Klara Milich"—would not forever be denied. On 3 September 1883, Turgenev died at Bougival after an extremely painful illness. "His end," Henry James wrote, "was not serene and propitious, but dark and almost violent." This remark points to depths within Turgenev that he himself could not plumb, though he was aware of their existence.

At the end the expatriate was returned to Russia. In Paris, prominent Frenchmen paid tribute to his memory at the station from which he began his last journey, and in Saint Petersburg crowds gathered to escort his coffin to a niche in the Volkovo cemetery. There Turgenev lies in a section set aside for literary men, among those, like Dobrolyubov, who were his enemies in life, and those, like Belinsky, who were his friends. Death, as he had said of Nekrasov, reconciles all.

Selected Bibliography

EDITIONS

INDIVIDUAL WORKS
"Diary of a Superfluous Man." Moscow, 1850.
A Hunter's Notes. Moscow, 1852.
A Month in the Country. Moscow, 1855.
Rudin. Moscow, 1856.
A Nest of Gentlefolk. Moscow, 1859.
On the Eve. Moscow, 1860.
Fathers and Sons. Moscow, 1862.
Smoke. Moscow, 1867.
Torrents of Spring. Moscow, 1872.
Virgin Soil. Moscow, 1877.

COLLECTED WORKS
Turgenev's individual works were ordinarily published in contemporary journals, then shortly

thereafter (in the case of novels particularly) in separate editions. His collected works were issued in multivolume editions several times during his lifetime (in 1860–1861, 1865, 1869–1871, and 1880, for example) and his complete works in 1883 and many times thereafter. During the Soviet period there have been several multivolume selected or complete editions of his works (in 1949, for example, and from 1953 to 1958). The edition upon which all scholarly work must now be based, however, is the *Polnoe sobranie sochinenii i pisem v dvadtsati vosmi tomakh* (Complete Works and Letters in 28 Volumes, Moscow and Leningrad, 1960–1968), which allots 15 volumes to his works and 13 to his extensive correspondence. This edition may be supplemented, but it is unlikely to be superseded for many years.

TRANSLATIONS

Constance Garnett long ago rendered the bulk of Turgenev's writing into English in *The Novels of Ivan Turgenev*, including his short stories (15 vols., London, 1894–1899). Translations of individual works in this century are almost too numerous to mention. A convenient selected edition, though poorly translated and not very extensive, is *The Vintage Turgenev* (2 vols., New York, 1960). The hundredth anniversary of Turgenev's death saw the publication of two excellent annotated editions of his letters: A. V. Knowles, editor and translator, *Turgenev's Letters* (New York, 1983); and David Lowe, editor and translator, *Turgenev: Letters* (2 vols., Ann Arbor, Mich., 1983).

BIOGRAPHICAL AND CRITICAL STUDIES

Brodianski, Nina. "Turgenev's Short Stories: A Revaluation." *Slavonic and East European Review* 32:70–91 (December 1953).

Carr, E. H. "Turgenev and Dostoevsky." *Slavonic Review* 8:156–163 (June 1929).

Chamberlin, William Henry. "Turgenev: The Eternal Romantic." *Russian Review* 5:10–23 (Spring 1946).

Folejewski, Zbigniew. "The Recent Storm Around Turgenev as a Point in Soviet Aesthetics." *Slavic and East European Journal* 6:21–27 (Spring 1962).

Freeborn, Richard. *Turgenev: The Novelist's Novelist.* New York, 1960.

Garnett, Edward. *Turgenev: A Study.* London, 1917.

Gettman, Royal. *Turgenev in England and America.* Urbana, Ill., 1941.

Howe, Irving. "Turgenev: The Politics of Hesitation." In *Politics and the Novel.* New York, 1957. Pp. 114–138.

Kagan-Kans, Eva. "Fate and Fantasy: A Study of Turgenev's Fantastic Stories." *Slavic Review* 18:543–560 (December 1969).

————. *Hamlet and Don Quixote: Turgenev's Ambivalent Vision.* The Hague and Paris, 1975.

Ledkovsky, Marina. *The Other Turgenev: From Romanticism to Symbolism.* Würzburg, 1973.

Lerner, Daniel. "The Influence of Turgenev on Henry James." *Slavonic and East European Review* 20:28–54 (December 1941).

Lloyd, John A. T. *Ivan Turgenev.* London, 1942.

Lowe, David, *Turgenev's "Fathers and Sons."* Ann Arbor, Mich., 1983.

Magarshack, David. *Turgenev: A Life.* London, 1954.

————, ed. and trans. *Ivan Turgenev: Literary Reminiscences and Autobiographical Fragments.* New York, 1958.

Mandel, Oscar. "Molière and Turgenev: The Literature of No-Judgment." *Comparative Literature* 11:233–249 (Summer 1959).

Matlaw, Ralph. "Turgenev's Art in *Spring Torrents.*" *Slavonic and East European Review* 35:157–171 (December 1956).

————. "Turgenev's Novels: Civic Responsibility and Literary Predilection." *Harvard Slavic Studies* 4:249–262 (1957).

Moser, Charles. "Turgenev: The Cosmopolitan Nationalist." *Review of National Literatures* 3(1):56–88 (Spring 1972).

Peterson, Dale. *The Clement Vision: Poetic Realism in Turgenev and James.* Port Washington, N.Y., 1975.

Pritchett, V. S. *The Gentle Barbarian: The Life and Work of Turgenev.* New York, 1977.

Ripp, Victor. *Turgenev's Russia: From "Notes of a Hunter" to "Fathers and Sons."* Ithaca, N.Y., and London, 1980.

Sayler, O. "Turgenieff as a Playwright." *North American Review* 214:393–400 (September 1921).

Schapiro, Leonard. *Turgenev: His Life and Times.* New York, 1978.

Sergievsky, Nicholas. "The Tragedy of a Great Love: Turgenev and Pauline Viardot." *American Slavic* and East European Review 5:55–71 (November 1946).

Waddington, Patrick. *Turgenev and England.* New York, 1981.

Wilson, Edmund. "Turgenev and the Life-Giving Drop." In *Ivan Turgenev: Literary Reminiscences and Autobiographical Fragments,* by David Magarshack, editor and translator. New York, 1958. Pp. 3–64.

Woodcock, George. "The Elusive Ideal: Notes on Turgenev." *Sewanee Review* 69:34–47 (January–March 1961).

Woolf, Virginia. "The Novels of Turgenev." *Yale Review* 23:276–283 (Winter 1934).

Yarmolinsky, Avrahm. *Turgenev: The Man, His Art and His Age.* New York, 1959.

BIBLIOGRAPHIES

Yachnin, Rissa, and David Stam. *Turgenev in English: A Checklist of Works By and About Him.* New York, 1962.

CHARLES A. MOSER

VOLTAIRE
(1694–1778)

IT IS IMPOSSIBLE to say whether Voltaire, Jean Jacques Rousseau, or Denis Diderot made the greatest contribution to the French Enlightenment. However, there is no doubt in my mind that Voltaire was the most representative writer of his age: first because his life spanned most of the century and second because he was involved in almost every important event of his time.

His contemporaries were impressed not only with the number of his works but also with their quality and diversity. Voltaire experimented in every genre, and in almost all succeeded in being the best in his day. This assured him a large following in the most varied fields, even those that normally had only a few readers, such as the area of religious controversy. This large audience, which has seldom been stressed, is extremely important in explaining why his propaganda was so effective, why it took the form of witty and entertaining stories or articles, and why it provoked such angry reactions from those who could not tolerate the deliberately irreverent treatment of serious matters.

Voltaire's life, his character, and his books were conditioned by the battle he waged for sixty years against the strongest conservative force of the time, the Catholic church, and, more generally, all revealed religions.

At first glance the odds seem disproportionate; and Voltaire would have been crushed had he directly attacked such a formidable adversary. However, the idea for this unthinkable war did not come to him all at once. It began with disrespectful jokes and a refusal to accept the sacred, which often provoked clumsy reprisals. Progressively, as Voltaire's audacity grew, he became aware of his mission and of the weaknesses of his apparently indestructible enemy.

Against force and tyranny—the church had almost unconditional backing from the state—Voltaire could not consider a frontal attack, which would have annihilated him immediately. He had to invent a strategy of false submission and apparent innocence that made his reader an accomplice and that gave him the opportunity to use all the weapons of irony, satire, and wit. Such political necessity ensured his literary triumph. The writings that directly express his thoughts or his sensitivity—his plays and poetry, which were so admired by his contemporaries—have now lost their appeal, but the same ideas expressed in an ambiguous form, from a dual point of view, retain their freshness and their relevance.

Voltaire waged a guerrilla warfare that was courageous and disinterested in its principle but unscrupulous in the means he deployed in order to win. He was the champion of liberty, but he did not fight so much *for* it as *against* intolerance and fanaticism. For Voltaire, intolerance and fanaticism found their main ally in the religion of his time.

VOLTAIRE

He was not against God (in fact, he was a deist), but against his earthly representatives who meddled in world affairs. Long before the eighteenth century, priests and monks had been the subject of suspicion and mockery, but it is Voltaire, in my opinion, who inaugurated modern anticlericalism of the brand still widespread in France today.

Naturally, Voltaire was hated and scorned by devout Roman Catholics and by conservatives. Even his death in 1778 did not bring an end to the campaigns against him. Eleven years later, the Revolution of 1789 would take place, with all of its social and political upheavals, followed by Napoleon, the Restoration, the July Monarchy, the Revolution of 1848, the Second Empire, and the Third Republic. Each time the church attempted to regain lost ground, new editions of the works of Voltaire would appear as antidotes. Liberals and anticlericals would make him their champion, while the right wing would endlessly defame him as a kind of monster. The posthumous battle lasted about one hundred and fifty years and did not cease until conservatives had to accept the division of church and state. Anticlericalism, no longer historically justified, became unfashionable.

The strategy invented by Voltaire's enemies was quite simple. In the events of his life (which he did not try to conceal), in his jokes about himself, and, most of all, in his letters (where he expressed himself freely), his foes would look for anything to belittle him or to show his baseness of character. They even praised his talent in order to underscore the bad use to which he put it. They would then extract passages from his works, which they quoted out of context, and would point to his incessant contradictions, purporting to show his frivolity, his incapacity to think seriously: he made mockery of that which he could not understand. At the beginning of the twentieth century, one critic summarized this conception of Voltaire in a formula that gained wide popularity and is still often quoted today: "Voltaire is a morass of clear ideas." It was not Voltaire's fault if the critic was not intelligent or honest enough to understand him. In fact, no judgment could have been more incorrect; a modern scholar, Ira Wade, has justly insisted on the organic unity of Voltaire's work.

Voltaire's message was clear—critics have always emphasized his clarity—since obscure propaganda would be, by definition, bad propaganda. When the reader has finished *Candide* (1759) or the *Dictionnaire philosophique* (*Philosophical Dictionary*, 1765) he has not the slightest doubt about the intentions of the author. However, the presentation of ideas is complicated by the literary achievements of the text, by the comic invention, and by the impossibility of the scholar's resolving its deliberate ambiguity into unity. There is no great writer without mystery.

LIFE

A detailed biography of Voltaire would require eight to ten volumes, not only because his life was extremely active and linked to almost all the important events of the century but also because for sixty years he continually attracted the attention of his contemporaries.

Prior to Voltaire authors played secondary roles in the society of their own times, and so they depended upon the generosity of a patron. We know very little about François Rabelais, Jean de La Fontaine, Molière, or Jean de La Bruyère. Those whose lives are well known to us owe it to the fact that they were noblemen, like François de La Rochefoucauld, or almost saints, like Blaise Pascal, whose biography, written by his sister, is in fact a hagiography.

With Voltaire everything changed. First, he lived in the company of the best society; second, his huge fortune afforded him respectability; and finally, a mixture of flattery, wit, and idealistic conviction enabled him to be accepted and to establish the rights of talent next to those of birth and money. Settled in Ferney, he became "King Voltaire" and treated with irony and respectful familiarity the princes, lords, and ladies who came to visit him or with whom he corresponded. With Voltaire, the man of letters became a personality, and after the democratization wrought by the French Revolution this new status would allow men such as François René de Chateaubriand, Alphonse de Lamartine, and Victor Hugo, when they had achieved literary fame, to launch successful political careers.

Although the adult life of Voltaire as a writer is well known to us, we have very little information about his childhood and adolescence—basically anecdotes told by Voltaire himself as jokes, which sometimes makes them unreliable. In spite of frequent references to himself in his letters, he did not feel the need to reveal himself—a trend not yet in vogue. When he began his *Mémoires* in 1759, he started the story of his life with his meeting with Madame du Châtelet; he was then forty years old. One must wait for Rousseau in his *Confessions* and *Émile* for the child to appear in literature.

François-Marie Arouet, who would later take the name Voltaire, was born in February or November 1694 in Paris or in a Parisian suburb. The place and time deserve attention. We may say that over half of the numerous French comic writers (Molière, Boileau, Voltaire, Beaumarchais, Musset, Courteline, and others) were born or brought up in Paris. The percentage is too large to be mere coincidence. The date of birth is still more important. When Louis XIV died in 1715 (a date that marks the end of the century more clearly than the conventional date of 1700), Voltaire was twenty-one and his education was completed; he had already accepted or rejected the ideas and clichés of the age. At this date, Rousseau and Diderot were three and two years old, respectively. They belonged to the generation of Louis XI. Since Voltaire lived to be very old and wrote until his death, we have a tendency to forget this difference in ages when we compare him to the two other famous writers of the Enlightenment.

Voltaire's father was a *notaire*, an important appointed position among French men of law that does not have an equivalent in the Anglo-Saxon judicial system. Without being truly affluent, he was well off, and Voltaire would never have to earn a living from writing; this security contributed to his freedom and independence.

His mother, Marie Daumart, belonged to the upper middle class (and, some biographers even say, the lower nobility). Clearly, this was a time of upward social mobility for the family. Madame Arouet died when François-Marie was seven. It is, therefore, not surprising that he mentioned her very little.

The couple had five children, two of whom died shortly after birth. The eldest, Armand, who was nine years older than Voltaire, completed his studies at the pro-Jansenist school of Saint-Magloire; he became a fanatical religious Jansenist and was a member of the sect of the *convulsionnaires*. Needless to say, the brothers never got along. On the other hand, Voltaire loved his sister very much, and when she died during his exile in England, he was deeply grieved. Later, his sister's three children would have an important role in his life.

From 1704 to 1711 Voltaire studied with the Jesuits at the collège Louis-le-Grand. To be sure, his father had no desire to repeat with his youngest son the experience of the oldest. At Louis-le-Grand, Voltaire was a brilliant student, winning in the same year the prize for Latin discourse and for Latin verse. He received an excellent classical education. He developed his taste for literature and made many friends who were to be of great service to him in his future struggles. During these college years, Voltaire does not seem to have rebelled against the religious instruction, which probably had little effect upon him but gave him an intimate knowledge of the enemy.

Later on, his opinions of his education were contradictory. He publicly praised his teachers and for a long time put himself under their protection, either to gain their support with the authorities or to pass off his audacious writings as attacks that singled out Jansenists. If he failed in his efforts to divide his enemies, he succeeded in neutralizing the Jesuits up until the 1750's. After that time, the violence of his polemic no longer permitted compromise. The Jesuits condemned him forcefully; he rebutted their arguments in very amusing pamphlets that helped expel the Jesuits from France. However, Voltaire regretted having thus played into the hands of the Jansenists.

Whenever Voltaire spoke about education, his opinion was almost always unfavorable. In school he learned "some Latin and nonsense." His studies did not appear to him to be adapted to the needs of society. He taught himself the scientific knowledge that he deemed indispensable for an enlightened *philosophe,* as well as learning English and Italian.

We are very poorly informed about his life once his studies were completed. He came into conflict with his father when he refused to embark upon a law career, choosing instead to become a poet. His father sent him to Holland in the company of the French ambassador. Having just arrived, he fell in love with a young French girl, Olympe du Noyer, nicknamed Pimpette. Her mother, however, who made a living publishing a newspaper, wanted her daughter to marry a rich man. She made a scandal, and Voltaire was sent back to France. (A few years later, when Voltaire had become famous, the mother published his love letters to Pimpette in her newspaper, omitting only the passages where she was unfavorably depicted. Pimpette was therefore inscribed in the margins of literary history.) There was now an open conflict between father and son. To avoid prison, Voltaire had to enter a law practice. There he met a clerk, Thieriot, who also loved poetry, with whom he was to form a faithful friendship, although Thieriot was not always trustworthy.

Voltaire did not, however, allow himself to be dissuaded from literature; his vocation was imperious. His blossoming poetic talent opened the doors of the Society of the Temple, composed of blasé aristocrats and skeptical poets who sang the praises of love and wine. The libertine, of whom the most extreme example was Molière's Don Juan in the play of that title, was often a *débauché,* and at the same time an unbeliever. He deplored the unnatural morality of the church as much as its dogma. In this dual form, the libertine trend ran through the whole eighteenth century, and very often Voltaire found himself similarly criticized for his risqué jokes and his sarcasms against the Bible and revealed religions.

He also frequented the château of the duchesse du Maine, where, at this time, he probably wrote his first prose narratives. It was as a poet, however, that he expected to become famous, and he began acquiring his reputation with satirical poetry. The château of the duchesse du Maine was a center of opposition to the regent, Philippe d'Orléans, whom Voltaire violently attacked in several anonymous poems. The reaction was not slow in coming: Voltaire was exiled and found a haven at the château of the duc de Sully. But the lesson did not serve him well. In 1717 he was arrested and taken to the Bastille, where he remained imprisoned for eleven months. Most critics have a tendency to speak lightly of this detention without trial. This is due largely to Voltaire's own attitude: he never sought to complain; he joked about and even profited from his stay in prison by writing. He would later be on good terms with the regent and depict him in his historical works as a good prince. This lack of resentment is noteworthy, for it contrasts sharply with the violence of his protests when he felt that an injustice had been committed, whether it affected him personally or concerned others.

At this time Voltaire was working on two major projects, a tragedy and an epic poem, both the most highly respected genres in the literary hierarchy of the period. A success could confer fame upon their author overnight. Soon after leaving prison, he had *Oe-*

dipe (1718) staged; it was a triumph that would last the century. Voltaire did not hesitate to take on a subject that had already been treated by Sophocles and Pierre Corneille; it was indicative of the breadth of his ambition. Actually, the imitation of Corneille and of Jean Baptiste Racine is still considerable in this work, but already one may find typical Voltairean themes: the injustice of the gods and the greed of priests:

> Priests are not what frivolous people suppose,
> Our gullibility constitutes all of their art.

At this time he worked on an epic poem, *La henriade* (originally published in 1723 under the title *La ligue*), and would contribute significantly to making Henri IV a popular figure. Here, too, there was imitation, this time of Vergil's *Aeneid,* but with a plea against religious fanaticism built on the sound historical foundation of the wars of religion of the sixteenth century. "I do not decide between Geneva and Rome" was an often quoted line. Despite a strong Catholic attack against this parallel between "Geneva and Rome," the poem was a great success throughout the eighteenth century. People knew whole cantos by heart, and it seemed that France finally had an epic to rival those of the Greeks, the Romans, the Italians, and the English. Today the *Henriade* is unreadable because the blending of daring ideas—for the time—and classical prose has lost its charm. We see only the weak versification and the commonplace imitation of antiquity.

Voltaire's reputation as a poet, his wit, and his improvisational talents opened all doors to him. He continued to frequent aristocratic circles, which had helped launch him, but only because he enjoyed such company. Ambition was not a sufficient motivation for him. He never went to the influential literary "salons," which he despised for reasons we do not know; he possessed all the requisite qualities to shine there. He loved the life of the châteaus, all the while complaining that his pleasures prevented him from working as he would have liked. For beneath his epicureanism and his continual mockery of self and others, Voltaire was at heart very serious. During this period he wrote two tragedies, which enjoyed limited success. He had amorous adventures with actresses and noblewomen, went to court, and began to build his fortune. His career as a worldly poet was becoming well established when an incident occurred involving the chevalier de Rohan, who was a scion of one of the most illustrious families of France.

Voltaire and the chevalier had argued, probably in the presence of the famous actress Adrienne Lecouvreur. Naturally insolent and disrespectful, quick to answer, Voltaire had forgotten the distance that separated a successful poet from a nobleman. The chevalier decided to remind him of it. Voltaire was a dinner guest of the duc de Sully; he was called to the door; he went down quite unsuspectingly and was caned by Rohan's lackeys, the chevalier all the while cheering them on. When he returned to the dinner table determined to seek justice for this attack, he realized that no one supported him: the prejudices of caste played fully against him. The reaction of the public was the same. They blamed the chevalier but felt that Voltaire was in the wrong for having been involved in such a quarrel. His stature as the greatest playwright and the only epic poet of France was not of sufficient importance. Voltaire then decided to avenge his honor with arms. Concerned at the prospect of a duel, Rohan's family had the authorities arrest Voltaire, who was, for a second time, incarcerated in the Bastille. Fifteen days later he succeeded in having his imprisonment commuted to exile, and in 1726 Voltaire left for England.

The three-year stay in Britain was crucial in the life of Voltaire: his character was strengthened by the injustice he suffered, and he found in England openly expressed confirmation of all the ideas that were already his.

His first task was to master the language in order to study at close hand a people whose mores and institutions were so different from those of the French. After a few months—his facility was astounding—he knew the language well enough to write directly in English a book marked by the imprint of his personal style; all that his English friends had to do was to eliminate his mistakes.

Little is known about Voltaire's existence during these three years, for he stopped almost all correspondence with his country. Lord Bolingbroke, who had known him well in France, introduced him to his Tory friends, and through him Voltaire became acquainted with Alexander Pope and Jonathan Swift. Horace Walpole, the English ambassador to Paris, wrote a letter of recommendation to his brother Robert, the Whig prime minister, and Voltaire, as a canny businessman, was able to find financial backing in England for the publication of *La henriade,* which he had not been allowed to publish in France. The undertaking was a resounding success.

In England, Voltaire was not to resume the glamorous and dissipated life of the aristocracy. He had come to study and to learn. He had discovered William Shakespeare, Isaac Newton, and John Locke. No one has ever been, I believe, a greater promoter of reputation than Voltaire. He made England fashionable and made Shakespeare known on the Continent, despite all the reservations he had about the latter's genius. He contributed to the dissemination of the ideas of Newton and of Locke. He also discovered freedom of conscience in matters of religion, as well as the importance attached to commerce by the English, and he returned to France determined to have his compatriots profit from his experience.

Upon his return to France, Voltaire's activity was remarkable and could be explained only by the accumulation of materials gathered in England. He wrote the tragedy *Brutus* (1730), which was not wholly successful; *Zaïre* (1732), which was an unmitigated

triumph and remained for a very long time in the repertory of the Comédie Française; his first historical work, *Histoire de Charles XII, roi de Suède* (History of Charles XII, 1731); *Le temple du goût* (Temple of Taste, 1733), bantering literary criticism; and finally *Lettres philosophiques* (*Philosophical Letters,* 1734).

Voltaire's return did not imply that he was on good terms with the authorities. In fact, they considered him a troublemaker, and their opinion was confirmed by the stir that marked the appearance of each new work. France was then ruled by an ambitious old man, Cardinal de Fleury (the de facto prime minister), who, like all men in charge, wished only to govern in peace the way he wanted. Deeply religious, he had contempt for freethinkers but did not consider them dangerous; he was afraid only of Jansenists. His hostility was due to the fact that Voltaire became involved in topics that were not in his field and did not show proper respect. If his ironic comments had been made with less verve and talent, they would have passed unnoticed. But since Fleury did not intend to destroy Voltaire, the persecution was clumsy and ineffective.

The first incident was caused by Voltaire's poem on the death of Adrienne Lecouvreur, his favorite actress and close friend. Because she had not renounced her acting career on her deathbed, she was refused a Christian burial. Voltaire protested against this barbaric tradition and contrasted her fate with that of the English actress Anne Oldfield, whose ashes had been deposited in Westminster Abbey. Then the *Histoire de Charles XII* had to be published clandestinely, because the praise of Stanislas, the ex-king of Poland and father-in-law of Louis XV of France, could have offended the present king of Poland. The *Temple du goût* generated a scandal that we cannot understand today. It is so obviously a playful piece of literary criticism that we wonder how the public could have been offended by disrespectful remarks about famous authors of the past. But people were so incensed that they were still resentful when the *Lettres philoso-phiques* appeared.

How could Voltaire, usually such a realist, have hoped that the prudent Cardinal de Fleury would support such a daring and ironic book? Perhaps he expected that by adding to its twenty-four letters on the English a twenty-fifth on Pascal, the great Jansenist of the previous century, he would get the tacit protection of a government whose main concern was Jansenism. Certainly, he was encouraged at first. But when the book was published, the reactions were so violent that no one dared take the risk of defending it. The parlement ordered the *Lettres* to be burned publicly, and Voltaire escaped prison only by taking flight. He could not deny his authorship, and for years the sentence of the parlement would be used as a threat whenever he published an objectionable book. This was a regrettable consequence of the persecution, because in the *Lettres philosophiques* Voltaire had found the way of expressing his true talent. And it took twenty years before he was in a position to write again in this dangerous vein.

Meanwhile, he was making his fortune by using his literary connections to invest his money with the most successful financiers of the kingdom. His wealth was unheard of for a man of letters; not only did it assure his independence, but it also gave him status and power and allowed him to live his last twenty years as a great philanthropic lord.

It was during that period that he started a love affair with Gabrielle Émilie Le Tonnelier de Breteuil, marquise du Châtelet, a woman of the highest rank who was married and the mother of two children. Such a liaison was not uncommon in the eighteenth century. Madame du Châtelet was a brilliant woman, coquettish and sensual, and was an intellectual with a serious interest in the sciences. She published a book on Leibniz, translated Newton, and wrote on biblical subjects. In an era when the education of women was totally neglected, Madame du Châtelet was a phenomenon, and her scientific achievements were re-ceived either with admiration or with incredulity and mockery, depending upon what people thought of her and Voltaire. In any case, the couple never passed unnoticed.

The influence of Madame du Châtelet on Voltaire was considerable. Was that influence good or bad? It is a debatable point and of little interest. When he had to run away after the publication of the *Lettres philosophiques,* he sought refuge at Cirey, the marquise's castle, close to the Lorraine border. Cirey became their literary and scientific shelter. Working in the footsteps of his friend, Voltaire became interested in physics and chemistry and studied with his usual fervor. He felt that in the age of experimental sciences no one could expect to be a true *philosophe* without a solid scientific background. Despite the seriousness and the quality of his research, I do not think that Voltaire ever intended to become a major scientist. His literary vocation was too compelling and his reputation as a poet, playwright, and historian too well established to imagine that he was planning a new career.

In fact, his experiments in physics and chemistry did not prevent him from devoting a large part of his time to poetry. It was during the Cirey period that he wrote some of his most successful tragedies, *Alzire* (1736), *Mahomet* (1742), and *Mérope* (1743); without a doubt, in the eyes of his contemporaries, he was the equal of Corneille and Racine. He also wrote a *Discours en vers sur l'homme* (Discourse in Verse on Man, 1738), which was put on a level with Pope's *Essay on Man.* And, in his leisure time, he composed an erotic, sacrilegious mock epic, *La pucelle* (The Maid), which was not intended for publication and was read to friends at Cirey for their amusement. Published many years later (1755), the poem was an enormous success. People learned whole cantos by heart, and during the French Revolution many aristocrats went to the guillotine reciting the little impious lines of *La pucelle,* to show their courage and their detachment.

It was during the years at Cirey that Voltaire and an admirer, the crown prince of Prussia, began to exchange letters. And very soon this correspondence, despite the mandatory praises and compliments from both parties, became remarkably interesting and lively. Their friendship remained the same when the crown prince became Frederick II, king of Prussia. Nothing astonished contemporaries more than this relationship between a poet and a powerful monarch. The correspondence benefited the two: it made Frederick a champion of the new philosophical trends, while it assured Voltaire of a powerful protector and gave him great prestige among the French aristocracy. Of course, they were both too clever not to realize that this friendship made them two of the most original people of the century.

Frederick had no greater desire than to entice Voltaire to Berlin. Madame du Châtelet was condemned by her situation to remain in France; she felt the danger of such an invitation and opposed her lover's move to the court of Prussia, even on a temporary basis. Three times between 1740 and 1743 Voltaire met with the king, the first two times privately, the third time entrusted by two French ministers with a secret diplomatic mission.

In 1740 the philosopher-king, having just written *Anti Machiavel* (corrected by Voltaire, who also attended to its publication), abandoned his principles, attacked Austria, and annexed Silesia. France joined him in an unjust war to take advantage of Austria's weakness. The road to Vienna seemed open. However, quarrels between French generals and the indecisiveness of Cardinal de Fleury (he was almost ninety) made them miss the opportunity. Under the inspiration of Empress Maria-Theresa, a vigorous counterattack was launched, and the French troops, who had ventured as far as Prague, had to beat a hasty retreat during the winter. Frederick profited from these events to conclude a separate peace with Austria that assured him the possession of Silesia and left France alone in the fight against Austria and England.

In January 1743 Cardinal de Fleury died and was not replaced. The French ministers, left to themselves, hoped for peace because they were incapable of waging war. The only way to bring Austria to a settlement was to persuade Frederick II to take up arms again. But the important faction in favor of war at Versailles, with the duchesse de Châteauroux, the king's mistress, at its head, sought the same goal, although to achieve not peace but victory. Two of the ministers, Amelot (minister of foreign affairs) and the comte de Maurepas (minister of the navy), asked Voltaire, though they did not entirely trust him, to approach the king of Prussia and find out what his intentions were, without informing the rival faction in Versailles of his mission. The secret was not intended to fool Frederick; otherwise Voltaire would have been a spy and lost the king's friendship. This point explains why Voltaire took so few precautions in hiding the motives of his visit.

He was admirably received, stayed longer than the duties of his role as goodwill diplomat required, much to the chagrin of Madame du Châtelet, and returned having succeeded in his mission. Unfortunately for Voltaire, the friends of the duchesse de Châteauroux were watching, and they showed Frederick that it was in his interest to make a treaty through the strong war party that would not abandon him, in turn, if he again took up the struggle. The shrewd king of Prussia made the dismissal of Amelot a condition for his alliance. The minister's disgrace deprived Voltaire of any reward. But he was again well received at court. Madame de Châteauroux died that very year and was quickly replaced. The king's new favorite, Jeanne Antoinette Poisson, Madame d'Étioles, who became the marquise de Pompadour, had great admiration for Voltaire. Thanks to her support, he was made king's historiographer and gentleman of the bedchamber (1745); the following year he entered the French Academy.

Voltaire was too intelligent and too impatient to be a good courtier. He did not aspire to a political career; he wanted only to secure his freedom as a writer by being on friendly terms with those in power. It took him years of unpleasant experiences to realize that his only protection was to be far away, out of reach, and financially independent. But it was not long before Voltaire and Madame du Châtelet made imprudent remarks and were forced to leave Versailles. They went to the castle of the duchesse du Maine, in Sceaux, where he wrote his first major philosophical tale, *Zadig* (1747). Then they moved to Lorraine, to the court of Stanislas, the ex-king of Poland.

After fifteen years the relationship between Voltaire and Madame du Châtelet had changed. She fell in love with Jean François de Saint-Lambert, a young officer who was also a poet; became pregnant; and died a few days after giving birth, in 1749.

Voltaire's grief was great but brief. He returned to Paris and went back to writing. His enemies rallied around an old playwright, Prosper Jolyot de Crébillon, whom they pretended to consider a genius in order to belittle Voltaire. Irritated by the unjust comparison, the author of *Zaïre* decided to remake his rival's tragedies so that the public could decide who was better. The project was ill conceived: Crébillon was a very old man, and he had Madame de Pompadour's backing. Obviously Voltaire's tragedies were far superior to Crébillon's; this did not mean that they were good, and the public's support was not strong enough to deter the cabal.

The king of Prussia had renewed his invitations and made enormously tempting offers to induce Voltaire to come to Berlin. Madame du Châtelet was dead. Why should he stay among his ungrateful compatriots? In 1750 Voltaire left for Prussia—despite the warnings of his friends, who feared the friendship of a king for a commoner.

The first months of Voltaire's stay with Frederick were enchanting. Each of them tried to conquer the other, and both succeeded. This was the philosophical freedom Voltaire had always dreamed of. Soon, however, the inequality of their respective positions, the difficulty of sharing stardom, the biting irony of their remarks provoked a cooling off. Voltaire made illegal investments, and the king reacted too quickly. Frederick was surrounded by French scientists and writers, and they were not happy with the arrival of such a famous poet, whose friendship with the monarch seemed a threat to their position. They repeated some of the comments that Frederick and Voltaire had made privately. The jokes were witty; they appeared nasty. Prussia was definitely not a haven of peace.

Voltaire's reaction was the usual one: he worked. During his stay in Prussia he published *Micromégas* (1752), one of his best-known philosophical tales, and he wrote *Le siècle de Louis XIV* (The Age of Louis XIV, 1751). The "Sun King" was not popular in the middle of the eighteenth century, and such a rehabilitation was an act of courage. Voltaire was no longer the historiographer of the king of France, but he wanted to show that he was continuing his functions. If he had left for Prussia, it was to have the freedom that the impartial writing of history required. The reaction of the authorities proved he was right. The book, which later was considered a patriotic undertaking, could not be printed in France, because the government saw in the apology for Louis XIV an ironical criticism of its own shortcomings. This, of course, did not prevent the book from being very successful.

Soon a scientific quarrel—stupid, like most quarrels—brought the Swiss scientist Samuel Koenig up against the Frenchman Pierre Louis Moreau de Maupertuis, president of the Berlin Academy. Maupertuis succeeded in having Koenig expelled from the Berlin Academy. Frederick supported Maupertuis because he was its president; Voltaire backed Koenig because he was shocked by the arbitrary decision made by the Academy. Voltaire had an intolerance for injustice; his reaction was violent, because emotional, and it is this emotional reaction, dissimulated under a cover of irony, that readers encounter whenever Voltaire feels that somebody's rights have been severely violated.

Frederick had clearly taken sides in favor of Maupertuis, which made a reply extremely difficult. And this was the reason for the king's intervention. But it was always dangerous to provoke Voltaire. He took advantage of a general authorization to publish given to him by Frederick—though he knew full well it did not apply to the case—and he wrote a very funny but devastating satire, *La diatribe du docteur Akakia* (1752). Maupertuis was not a mediocre scientist, but the *Diatribe* ruined his reputation. The king countered by having the pamphlet burned by the hand of the executioner. In Paris people were startled by the news.

The two men realized that they had gone too far; they renewed their friendship, but the charm had vanished. Under the pretext of poor health, Voltaire solicited and obtained permission to return to France. He started out very slowly, stopping at all the princely and ducal courts of Germany, where he was treated with honor and distinction. During his trip, he continued to ridicule Maupertuis and outclassed him in this battle of wits. When Voltaire was deeply incensed, it was extremely difficult to make him give up the fight.

During their honeymoon period, Frederick had given to Voltaire a book of his poetry, of which there were only a few copies printed on account of their impieties. Was he afraid that Voltaire would publish it or let copies circulate? Did he want to remind his old friend that it was risky to challenge a king? Or did he simply try to teach him a lesson that the zeal of his agents exaggerated? It is difficult to say; the king never attempted to justify his decision. Voltaire was on his way back to France when he was arrested at Frankfurt (1753) and detained until he surrendered the volume of poetry. Unfortunately, the book was in the traveler's baggage, and it was a long time before it arrived. This search and seizure was a deliberate infraction of international law, for Frankfurt was an imperial city, and Frederick

had no jurisdiction over the city. When Madame Denis, Voltaire's niece, joined her uncle, she was also guarded by Prussian deputies. Both of them protested loudly, trying to attract the attention of the world to this denial of justice. Finally they were released and took up their route to France, but by now the scandal had done Voltaire great harm; he was coming back as a fugitive. It also hurt Frederick, but to a lesser degree.

In Alsace, where he had stopped, Voltaire learned that his presence was not wanted in Paris, and even less at Versailles. Louis XV did not like him and Madame de Pompadour dared not speak in his favor. Besides, at the moment, she resented his departure for Prussia. Voltaire's morale was very low. He was sick—for eighty-four years, the duration of his life, he would be sick—with the feeling of impending death. He wanted to find a place where he could rest, study, and write; and such a place was denied him.

Madame Denis had become his mistress. From Paris, where she was trying to mitigate the obstacles to her uncle's return, she wrote him that she was pregnant, but she had a miscarriage and Voltaire was hurt by the news. He liked children and doubted after this accident that he could have any, considering his age and the condition of his health. Everything was amiss. Suddenly a manuscript of his world history that had been stolen from Frederick during the Austrian war was published in a distorted and truncated form. The name of the author was withheld, but the style was unmistakable. With its malicious distortions, it could not have appeared at a worse time, and Voltaire had the feeling that it was the last of Frederick's tricks to prevent him from finding a refuge. First he had to write a correct history of the world, which became the *Essai sur les moeurs et l'esprit des nations* (An Essay on the Manners and Spirit of Nations, 1756); then he tried to settle somewhere in the provinces, as Paris was out of the question.

In Lyons he was welcomed by the population, acclaimed at the Lyons academy; but the

VOLTAIRE

cold reception of Cardinal de Tencin, archbishop of the city, was a serious warning. Finally he bought the estate of Saint-Jean, near Geneva, through an intermediary, because the laws of Geneva forbade Catholics to acquire property on the territory of the Helvetian Republic. I would not be surprised if the irony of being refused on account of his Catholicism was a determining factor in his move to Geneva. The name "Saint-Jean" was changed, of course, and the place became famous as "Les Délices." For the winter, he rented another house in Lausanne. Immediately, his health improved; his morale was as good as ever, and he found himself ready to become involved and to intervene. Soon he was in trouble with the local pastors, whom he had judged *philosophes* because they were liberal. The subject of the dispute was the theater. It was prohibited by laws dating back to John Calvin. But Voltaire, who loved tragedy and considered it an instrument of propaganda far superior to church sermons, had a theater built at Les Délices (he had had one in Cirey, another in Paris—amateur theater was in fashion during the whole century). The actors were members of the Geneva aristocracy, and so were the spectators. The pastors did not appreciate such an infraction of the law, coming from a man who had promised not to create problems. Jean Jacques Rousseau, of whom Voltaire would be the archenemy, did not like the presence of such a man in his country and interfered in the quarrel with his celebrated *Lettre à M. d'Alembert sur les spectacles* (Letter to M. d'Alembert on Theater); Voltaire realized once more that he had not yet found the place where he wanted to finish his days.

Important events were happening in succession. On 1 November 1755, All Saints' Day, while everyone was praying in churches, a terrible earthquake occurred in Lisbon. At first it was reported that one hundred thousand people had died. This high toll—which was later found to have been exaggerated—and the circumstances surrounding the event deeply affected Voltaire, who succeeded in communicating his emotion to all of Europe. But the catastrophe did not affect him personally. His reaction was emotional but on a secondary level; it could take a philosophical aspect. How was it possible to reconcile this earthquake with the doctrine of Optimism? How could one still believe in a benevolent providence? Almost immediately Voltaire wrote his *Poème sur le désastre de Lisbonne* (Poem on the Lisbon Earthquake), which was widely read but met with strong objections from the theologians, notably the Protestant pastors. Voltaire would remember this opposition when, three years later, he took up the subject again in an ironic and negative way, in *Candide.*

In 1756 war broke out again. Voltaire hated war and in all his works denounced its cruelty and absurdity. This time the alliances were reversed: France and Austria fought against Prussia and England in what was to be the Seven Years War. Frederick was now the enemy: Voltaire had not forgotten the Frankfurt episode, and from his border he applauded the Prussian setbacks and encouraged the French troops to avenge him. However, he was clever enough to realize that a crushing defeat of Prussia would result only in a rupture of the European equilibrium. He resumed his correspondence with Frederick and tried to act as a mediator to put a halt to this useless butchery. No government took these negotiations too seriously. Meanwhile, the French were destroyed by the Prussians at Rosbach, and Frederick was no longer interested in peace overtures. The war ended disastrously for France in 1763. The indifference of providence (as shown at Lisbon) was matched by the stupidity of mankind (as shown by war), and suddenly Voltaire could not tolerate the situation.

But, to understand his reaction, we have to keep in mind that in the midst of this turmoil Voltaire himself was enjoying a rather pleasant existence. His difficulties with the Protestant pastors had convinced him that his establishment in Switzerland made him too

1751

dependent on Geneva's authorities. So he bought two estates in France near the Swiss border and settled in Ferney, which he made famous. Now, with two residences in each country, he felt secure against persecution from either side as long as he observed certain rules of prudence in his fight. Understanding the opposition between his comfortable position and the troubles of the world, he wrote his friend Thieriot in 1759: "I am so happy that I feel ashamed." His most famous story, *Candide*, begun in 1758 and published in 1759, was born of this dichotomy.

Candide was, with the *Nouvelle Héloïse* of Rousseau, the best seller of the eighteenth century. This does not mean that contemporaries saw all the impact we find in it today. Voltaire felt the need to confront once more the problem of evil. But this time he was truly angry and determined not to accept any solution that was a compromise. The doctrine of Optimism, to be valid, implied that humanity sees the universe from God's point of view. And this is what Voltaire had done in *Zadig*, where an angel explains the universal arrangement of things. Already Zadig had objections to raise, but how could one argue with an angel? In *Candide*, Voltaire had decided to see the world through men's eyes, the only real vision, and what he discovered was abominable. He ferociously accumulated catastrophes to make the optimist's stand untenable. But life's lack of meaning did not prevent it from being worth living. With or without an optimistic explanation, man had hope. And from so many disasters and cruelties came a lesson of courage and indulgence, given by the terrestrial "moths," as Micromégas called them.

A witty story like *Candide* contained jokes about dogmas and against priests, but, on the whole, God was spared because the structure of the book implied his elimination from his creation. The radicalism of the concept prevented *Candide* from being directly antireligious.

The point is worth mentioning, for immediately afterward Voltaire started the great antireligious campaign that would use most of his time and energy for his last twenty years. "Écrasez l'infame" (Crush the infamous), he wrote to his friends as a motto at the end of his letters, and by "infamous" he meant all the evils stemming from revealed religions and probably those religions themselves. Of course, because he lived in France and was addressing his Catholic compatriots and the enlightened elite of Europe, it was upon Christianity that his blows fell the hardest.

Why did Voltaire start these systematic and dangerous attacks at an age when people are generally searching for peace and quiet? First of all, he belonged to the rare category of persons who become bolder and almost irrepressible with success and the passing of years. Instead of being afraid to lose what they have gained, they realize that age and fame have brought them security, and they derive advantage from this. Voltaire was rich, independent, and relatively secure at his Swiss border, though he knew he was taking risks. But he could count on the protection of powerful friends at Versailles, such as the duc de Choiseul, head of the government, and the marquise de Pompadour. Also, nearly half a century of propaganda had had its effect: enlightened ideas were widely circulated, and Voltaire had a large number of supporters who were eager to read his work. Furthermore, he had discovered and carried to the point of perfection the weapon—the short and witty article, pamphlet, poem, or story—with which he hoped to win the battle. Finally, he was compelled to intervene to defend the Encyclopedists, who were under the fire of the conservative forces, suddenly aware of the progress of impiety and of the danger it represented for the church.

Around 1760 the battle was raging and the very existence of the *Encyclopédie* was threatened. Everybody in the philosophic camp was looking in the direction of Ferney for help. It came immediately.

Voltaire's method was very simple. He would write a short, sarcastic text, then have

1752

it printed in Geneva and smuggled into France, where it would be widely read. The work would appear anonymously—or under a false name, generally amusing—and this would be enough to stop any action of the police, because no one, in fact, was really anxious to discover the perpetrator. Naturally, the style was so unmistakably Voltairean that few people were fooled.

Voltaire's first targets were those laymen or ecclesiastics who had attacked him or the philosophers, and single-handedly he destroyed some of the writers of the conservative party by covering them with ridicule. The government did nothing to prevent him; he was so amusing, and besides, he had never been the aggressor. Simply, some people, among those who pretended to be neutral, thought he was hitting too hard and too long. By a curious paradox, his devastating attacks against those mediocre writers assured them a small place in posterity by linking their names to his.

Having wiped out his opponents, Voltaire was free to carry on his fight against the church. The war was waged on enemy territory, which meant that Voltaire chose the subjects he wanted to deal with in his attacks and treated them the way it pleased him. The irony of his short publications made refuting them difficult. A serious reply was out of the question, but a witty one required wit, and who could compete with him in his specialty? The simple fact that he treated sacred matters with total irreverence—or with an obviously simulated respect—made the exegete's position impossible, because a scholarly or religious controversy cannot develop without a certain atmosphere of dignity and seriousness. He had proceeded the same way in *Candide* and ridiculed Optimism by refusing to discuss a metaphysical theory in its usual and proper philosophical context.

What struck Voltaire's contemporaries the most during this period were his efforts to redress the judicial errors of his time and to obtain the acquittal or rehabilitation of the victims of these errors. Since three of these cases,

and the most celebrated ones—the Calas, Sirven, and chevalier de La Barre affairs—were related to religion, there has been a tendency to consider these interventions as episodes in Voltaire's struggle against the church. To be sure, Voltaire was not a man to pass up such an opportunity to strike the enemy, but one must not forget that he saved or tried to save innocent people in cases where religion was not involved. Humble people were not mistaken: it was the champion of justice, not the denunciator of church abuses, whom they later acclaimed.

The Calas affair has always been singled out because it was the first one and probably the most dramatic. It can be summarized as follows: A Protestant merchant from Toulouse, Jean Calas, had been accused of murdering his son to prevent him from converting to Catholicism. After some hesitation, he declared (and his family backed his testimony) that his son had committed suicide. The Parlement of Toulouse, by a small majority, sentenced him to death after first submitting him to the wheel. During the entire ordeal and until his death, Calas swore he was innocent. Impressed by such fortitude, the parlement did not dare extend the condemnation to the rest of the family, though they had to have been accomplices if Calas were guilty. This situation would later be fully exploited by Voltaire as a proof of their innocence. However, his first reaction had been negative. Living near Geneva, a Protestant city, he had heard of the case, but the possible fanaticism of the father horrified him as much as the parlement's cruelty. Nevertheless, he met with the youngest of Calas's sons, who convinced him that his father was innocent. Voltaire wrote to friends who were in a position to know the truth, or at least to give him information. Everyone advised him not to antagonize the church and the powerful Parlement of Toulouse.

Almost seventy, Voltaire undertook the impossible task of having the sentence reversed when there existed no higher court than the

Parlement of Toulouse. To arrive at this result, he decided to appeal to public opinion, which would judge the judges. Because the burden of proof rested on the accusers, he did not try to ascertain whether young Calas had committed suicide, but set out to prove that he could not have been murdered by his family. He spent his time, his money, and his energy to exonerate Jean Calas. He wrote his celebrated *Traité sur la tolérance* (Treatise on Tolerance, 1763), and enlisted the help of his friends, his correspondents, and the *philosophes.* He tried to convince Empress Catherine II of Russia, the king of Prussia, the German princes, the nobles of Louis XV's court, the Parisian salons, even members of the clergy. He supplied the lawyers with arguments, rewrote their conclusions. He restrained the zeal of the Protestants in Geneva in order not to alienate the moderate Catholics. Finally, the king's council, yielding to the pressure of public opinion, decided to review the case and rehabilitated Jean Calas's name. The Parlement of Toulouse never agreed to register the new verdict.

Voltaire had become "King Voltaire," as one critic called him. It was fashionable for enlightened people to make a pilgrimage to Ferney. Between visits the old man continued to write assiduously. He dictated twenty letters a day, wrote tragedies that he staged in his theater, short stories (among them "L'Ingénu," 1767), pamphlets, and antireligious works of all kinds. The most famous of those is the *Dictionnaire philosophique* (1765).

Voltaire took his role as lord of Ferney very seriously. Endowed with remarkable common sense, he tried by all possible means to improve the well-being of his peasants. Using his charm and his literary prestige, he succeeded in having laws modified to favor his province. For political reasons Geneva was persecuting some of her watchmakers. Voltaire attracted them to his estate, assured them religious freedom, built them houses, created watch and silk stocking factories, and almost ruined himself in this enterprise. But he was a shrewd philanthropist. He used his contacts with kings and princes to acquire new outlets for his commercial ventures. In short, he was the benefactor of his little town, and it is only just that today the town is called Ferney-Voltaire.

In February 1778, at the age of eighty-four, Voltaire decided to return to Paris. He had written a tragedy, *Irène,* and wanted to direct the rehearsals, make the necessary corrections, and attend its performance. His arrival gave rise to widespread enthusiasm. A delegation from the French Academy came to greet him, as did a group of actors representing the Comédie Française. Anyone with a name in the nobility, literature, or the arts came to pay him a visit. Only the clergy and the government abstained. For five months he was the main topic of conversation. He managed to receive each visitor, to say a polite or witty word of thanks. Then he would rush to his study and correct his tragedy, or work on a new one he was writing. *Irène* was a triumph. People realized that it could not be compared to *Zaïre* or to *Mérope,* but it was still a tour de force coming from the pen of an octogenarian.

Exhausted by such intensive work and so many honors, Voltaire could not attend the first performance, but when he went to the sixth he was given an ovation such as no author had ever received before. After the performance his bust was brought to the stage and crowned with laurels, while Madame Vestris (Lucia Elizabeth Mathews), who had played Irène, read a poem improvised by a spectator in Voltaire's honor. When he left the theater, admirers unhitched his horses from his carriage and escorted him back to his house.

Soon afterward he fell gravely ill, and newspapers were full of reports of his declining health. Priests tried to persuade him to meet his death in an edifying manner. Voltaire wished to have a decent burial, without scandal, but he did not want to sign the retractions that the church sought from him. He died on 30 May 1778 without having altered his stance. Later some zealous bigots pretended that he had expired in horrible agony and supplied repulsive details, but no witness ever substantiated these rumors.

To avoid any confrontation with the church, the government permitted the abbé Mignot, Voltaire's nephew, to take away his uncle's body, which was placed in a coach as if he had gone to Ferney and died during the trip. The only possibility then left to Mignot was to have the body buried in the Abbey of Scellières, which belonged to him. The church accepted the fait accompli without too much protestation.

In 1791, during the Revolution, the National Assembly organized imposing ceremonies for the transfer of Voltaire's ashes to the Panthéon. For a century and a half he remained the symbol of opposition to the church.

WORKS

Voltaire's output was enormous and remarkably varied. This diversity, which so impressed his contemporaries, was detrimental to his future reputation. Whenever a writer tried to succeed in a given genre, Voltaire was in his way. He was fully aware of the risk he was taking. More than once he said: "One does not pass to posterity with such baggage." Nonetheless, he cultivated a versatility that allowed him to reach a very large audience. All the works of propaganda were aimed at an immediate success, but at the same time Voltaire took every opportunity to revise his books in order to secure them long-lasting fame.

Unfortunately, the books that he revised are not the ones that we read today. A revolution in taste occurred. On one hand, all the volumes that seemed major contributions during his lifetime are now forgotten. On the other hand, his stories, his pamphlets, his light poetry—all these witty texts that he wrote so easily and that were accepted with playful indulgence by the connoisseurs as the relaxation of a great mind—seem brand-new today.

For his contemporaries—and for a third of the nineteenth century—Voltaire was first and foremost the poet of his age, the only deserving French epic poet, the playwright who had written the most moving and dramatic tragedies as well as a remarkable didactic poem. But this part of his work is dead, and this is why Voltaire as poet can quickly be dispensed with.

The Tragedies

For the eighteenth-century critic, if Voltaire had a chance to survive it was as a dramatic poet. Today his tragedies cannot endure comparison with those of Corneille and Racine. Modern scholars condemn them on several grounds:

1. They are imitations of seventeenth-century plays, despite the author's attempts to renew the genre.

2. They offer no psychological insight. Voltaire was more interested in dramatic situations than in character delineation.

3. Voltaire was a resourceful playwright who knew how to create good roles. If his plays were often performed for over a hundred years, it was at the request of famous actors who found in these tragedies an opportunity to display their talents. When read, the plays lose much of their interest.

4. Too often the characters express the ideas of the author rather than their own feelings. Human interest is destroyed by propaganda.

All these considerations are true by our standards, but it was for these very reasons that Voltaire's tragedies, alloys of novelty and imitation, appeared so original at the time. The most celebrated plays were *Zaïre* (1732) and *Mérope* (1743).

The Comédie Française was a repertory

theater, regularly attended by the same people, much like those theaters frequented by opera or ballet buffs today. Its public was extremely conservative and ill-disposed to innovation. Many times Voltaire tried to break away from tradition; he was praised for his boldness when the idea was well received, but quite often plays failed, despite the author's reputation, because the novelty had not been appreciated. Borrowing from Shakespeare, he tried to give more intensity to the drama; he departed from the Greeks and the Romans and used subjects taken from French history, from China, or from the New World. By introducing religious conflicts and the ideas of tolerance and fanaticism on the stage, Voltaire renewed tragedy enough to please his public. The propaganda contained in the plays was less bold than that expressed in the anonymous books, but it was accepted with less resistance. And since spectators were more numerous than readers at the time, the stage was a perfect vehicle for Voltaire. Today his ideas have been so totally accepted that they seem commonplace. Despite some felicitous lines, the plays appear to us to be utterly conventional.

This judgment applies even more to Voltaire's epic, and didactic, poetry. His light verses are still charming, but few people read light poetry today.

The Histories

Voltaire was the first modern historian. His three major works—*Histoire de Charles XII, roi de Suède* (1731), *Le siècle de Louis XIV* (1751), and *Essai sur les moeurs et l'esprit des nations* (1756)—are still read for pleasure and profit.

The *Histoire de Charles XII* is the biography of a chivalric hero at the beginning of the eighteenth century. Voltaire had little affinity with him and did not attempt a solid psychological portrait of this strange prince. The book's principal merit rests on the quick pace of the narration, on the suspense created by the unfolding of this incredible life, which the reader has to accept without justification because it is true. Commentators at the time called the work a "novel," which, to some extent, was a compliment to the writer's talent, but such a label also seemed to cast doubt on the value of his documentation. This indirect reproach was unfounded. Voltaire, although he had not spent years in libraries as a modern scholar would have done, was nevertheless very well informed, notably by those who had been closely connected with the king in his adventures. His story is quite reliable. Obviously, Voltaire was attracted to the subject by its literary potential. His research was adequate; it would otherwise have ruined the book. At the time, history came closer to art than to science. We must keep in mind that Voltaire always addressed a large public and not a group of scholars. For such readers good and entertaining writing was as important as accuracy, a point that specialists find difficult to accept.

Commentators have found little fault with the *Histoire de Charles XII*. However, they generally agree that the book does not have the substance and impact of the later works, the *Siècle de Louis XIV* and the *Essai sur les moeurs*, which they more actively criticize. These latter works are indeed more ambitious in scope, and polemical intentions play a much greater role.

The *Siècle de Louis XIV*, as the title clearly indicates, is not the biography of a monarch, but the tableau of an era particularly remarkable for its literary and artistic achievements. Louis XIV was at the same time the promoter of and the one responsible for this glorious period, which to Voltaire made the seventeenth century in France the equal of the age of Pericles in Greece, of Augustus in Rome, and of the Medicis in Florence, the four ages in which human civilization has reached its apogee. For Voltaire, the world was evolving in cycles; it tended toward progress, but once a limit had been reached it would be followed by a period of decadence. Very often he admitted that the writers of his time did not approach the masters of the seventeenth century; however, in his century people were better thinkers.

In the *Siècle,* Voltaire succeeds in defining and imposing on posterity the concept of French classicism, which has remained almost unchanged up to the present day. It is for that reason that Voltaire's most determined detractors—for the most part, conservatives and church supporters—have always appreciated the "patriotic" qualities of a book that placed on such a pedestal a literature that owed so much to Catholicism and monarchy, these two symbols of order.

However, if Voltaire's taste caused him to admire the accomplishments of the seventeenth century, he was equally sensitive to the harmful philosophy of the time, to the century's excessive religious zeal, which led to persecutions. Nothing could excuse Louis XIV for the revocation of the Edict of Nantes in 1689, which provoked a massive emigration of Protestants.

In the 1750's Louis XIV's memory was not popular, especially in the countries where French Protestants had settled. Many critics of the time loathed the *Siècle* as a panegyric of the late king. They did not notice that the work ends on an ironic note, with two chapters devoted to Catholic ceremonies in China. Nor was the irony perceived by nineteenth-century scholars, who simply regretted the faulty composition of a good book. This did not surprise them, as they always found shortcomings in Voltaire's literary structure.

The book contains a number of flaws. By grouping the facts into categories instead of following a chronological order, Voltaire introduces clarity but destroys the suspense and the interrelationship of events; this also leads to repetitiousness. Voltaire's explanations are generally correct, but he shows little interest in finding the deep causes of events.

Voltaire's study was new in many aspects:

the emphasis is placed neither on a period nor on a privileged person; history replaces biography. Civilization was the key factor in his choice of time span. Military events, generally so prominent, are given less importance; literary, artistic, and scientific achievements are emphasized instead. The grand style of the Roman historians is abandoned. The *Siècle de Louis XIV* is written with lucidity, elegance, and simplicity. No attempt is made to re-create the atmosphere of the time; rather, this is a model of analytical study.

The *Essai sur les moeurs* is a world history that starts where Jacques Bénigne Bossuet's celebrated *Discours sur l'histoire universelle (Discourse on Universal History)* left off. This choice was justified, not by the fear of confronting too strong a rival, as has been said—the two works are totally different in every respect—but by a desire to limit the study of history to more modern times, about which documentation was available and known facts were not distorted by legendary or fantastic accounts, pagan or Christian. In Voltaire's work no nation or group receives preferential treatment, as do the Jews in Bossuet's *Discours.* He also rejects the idea of a providence conducting people's destiny. Events are related to one another, the smallest ones having sometimes unforseeable consequences. This process, as detailed by Voltaire, could be termed hazard or determinism, but his lack of direction does not give the reader a feeling of fatalism. An explanation of this type was not new. It was summed up in a famous sentence of the very Catholic Pascal: "If Cleopatra's nose had been longer, the face of the world would have been changed."

Of course, the *Essai* has many weaknesses. It was too ambitious an undertaking for the science of the period. Voltaire makes many erroneous judgments that are simply what the specialists believed at the time. More than once, he is carried away by his antireligious biases and purposefully alters facts. One has simply to open the book to realize that Vol-

VOLTAIRE

taire does not try to hide his polemical intentions. Irony permeates this serious book and gives it a particular flavor. Despite its lapses and prejudices, I would recommend its reading to anyone desirous of gleaning a first knowledge of general history. Modern encyclopedias are safer, but none are as entertaining or give a clearer overall picture; it is a matter of style.

The late-eighteenth-century historians paid tribute to Voltaire as their precursor, but the great nineteenth-century historians did not share those sentiments. Their judgment of Voltaire was generally severe, because their preoccupations were so different. In my opinion, Voltaire was not really a historian; he was, rather, a moralist.

This affirmation may seem paradoxical when one considers the number of his historical works, the solidity of the information, and the success they enjoyed. But his goal was never to re-create bygone eras, nor to unearth lost systems of thought, nor to rearrange facts in their chronological order. Local atmosphere and strange folkways never attracted him; he was searching for permanent behaviors in time and space. If men's motivations were constant, then lessons could be drawn from the study of the past. History had a moral value; it was a source of examples to imitate or avoid.

It may be said that the entire philosophical movement of the French Enlightenment rested on the primacy accorded to the experimental sciences. For Voltaire the moralist, history was a recollection of past experimentation. If he condemned Christianity, it was because experimentally, or historically if one prefers, it had failed: this religion of love and peace had only provoked wars and persecutions. Every time Voltaire attacked a theory or an institution, it was never because he opposed its principles, but because it was historically or experimentally unsound. He did not proceed differently in *Candide* when he submitted a metaphysical concept to the test of daily reality, as will be discussed below.

The Lettres philosophiques

Voltaire was forty when he published the *Lettres philosophiques;* he had a long literary career behind him. The *Lettres* followed *Oedipe*, the *Henriade, Brutus*, the *Histoire de Charles XII, Zaïre*, and the *Temple du goût* and did not appear very different, though perhaps a bit more daring and scandalous, than the previous works. No one, not even those who prosecuted the *Lettres*, perceived that the work was the first major attack against the ancien régime (the name by which the government was known before the Revolution of 1789). The volume is composed of twenty-four letters about England, plus a twenty-fifth on Pascal. It is not a matter of describing a country little known to the French; the work is not a travelogue. A charming letter on suicide, full of picturesque details, was omitted from the book because it did not match the others. Critics who have reproached Voltaire's silence on the weaknesses of the English system have not understood the polemical intentions of the author. By forcing his reader to become conscious of ways of thinking different from his own, Voltaire meant to make him recognize that certain ideas heretofore accepted without discussion, out of habit, were often illogical, contrary to common sense, and contrary to the individual's own interests and those of humanity.

To hide what was actually propaganda in his presentation of England, Voltaire adopted a superior and detached tone, profoundly mocking, and he treats serious and difficult topics in a playful manner, which makes them entertaining to digest. There is no rhetoric in these letters; the author does not want to be convincing. From the very first lines, he is right, his opponent wrong. No explanation is furnished; it is contained within the letter.

The first seven letters are devoted to religion, proving how important the subject already was for Voltaire. Four letters deal with the Quakers, while the Episcopalians, Presbyterians, and Socinians are allotted one apiece.

VOLTAIRE

This proliferation of sects in England contrasted with the situation at the time in France, where Catholicism was the state religion. Voltaire's thesis is that persecution assures the survival of minority churches; the dominant church, therefore, has every interest in practicing tolerance. If there is only one religion in a country, it will be oppressive; if there are two, civil war will be certain; but if there are thirty, they will coexist peacefully. These seven letters are a plea for tolerance.

The Quakers were a small sect with little influence. Why, then, did the author grant them such a choice place? The favorable treatment in the first letter made many critics believe Voltaire to be sympathetic to the Quakers. Arguments in their favor were not lacking—they were tolerant; they hated war; their small number made their enterprises less than fearsome—but nonetheless, they were religious fanatics. The way in which Voltaire ridiculed them in the third letter, while giving an account of their history, should have clearly shown his satirical intentions. If he placed them in the limelight, despite their negligible influence, it is because their singular behavior, their dress, their way of speaking were comical and allowed Voltaire to create an ironical climate for the whole book. The demolishing of institutions is taken up in an atmosphere of gaiety and lightheartedness that is the trademark of Voltairean satire—serious in its content, funny in its form. Instead of directly attacking Catholic sacraments, which would immediately warn the reader of the polemical nature of the letter, he has them criticized by a heretic. Shocked by these extravagant impieties, the good Catholic—that is, Voltaire—tries to reply. Unfortunately, his answers are weak, and soon he does not bother contradicting arguments that are so obviously wrong. This twisted way of presenting the subject introduces comedy and laughter into religious controversy. The satirical aspect of Voltaire's talent implies that equal importance should be given to ideas and to the way in which they are expressed. Thoughts are simple, almost obvious, as if there were little point in discussing them; their ambiguity lies in the manner of their exposition, and it is because the difficulties are located at the level of the narration that Voltaire's style has been so rarely studied to date.

The letters deal with politics, commerce, English science (Newton, Locke), and English literature (particularly Shakespeare). Though Voltaire is speaking only of England, a comparison with France is always implicit. Praise is limited to areas where improvements could be made. The letters on literature show exactly Voltaire's intention: Shakespeare, in his opinion, was not the equal of Corneille or Racine, but by judiciously borrowing some of the action and movement of the English theater, French tragedies could be renewed and perfected.

The twenty-fifth letter is a refutation of some of Pascal's *Pensées* and has very little to do with England. The only connection with the first seven letters is religion. However, the continuity of style and tone is strong enough to maintain the book's unity.

Voltaire's sense of polemics recognized in Pascal the archenemy at a time when Pascal was not yet the champion of Catholic apologetics. In letter 25 he examines some of the *Pensées* and writes down the critical reflections that they inspired in him. These are reading notes, not a systematic refutation. Voltaire feigns deep respect for Pascal. When he underlines a fault in reasoning, or an obscurity, he immediately explains that the great man would have made appropriate corrections if he could have reviewed his manuscript. However, beneath this banter, the argumentation is serious and focuses on three main points:

1. The anthropocentrism of Pascal, which attributed to man an exceptional place in Creation since he alone had a nostalgia for the lost Paradise. For Voltaire, this was too great a conceit. Man was no more a mystery than all the other beings; he was only a part of nature (this stand was developed in *Micromégas*).

2. The hatred of Pascal for diversion that impeded man's concentrating his thought on the only important thing, his salvation. By seeking pleasure, glory, and more generally all worldly values, he allowed himself to be distracted from a condition too painful to tolerate. Countering Pascal, Voltaire made himself the apologist of luxury (*Le mondain*, 1736), then of work and useful accomplishment (*Candide*). Man, he said, was born to act, not to contemplate. To the selfish values of sainthood he opposed the social concern of the enlightened philosopher.

3. The pessimism of Pascal, whom Voltaire called "the sublime misanthrope." Life was better than Pascal presented it in order to justify the sacrifice of this existence in the expectation of eternal bliss.

In 1734, countering Pascal's pessimism, Voltaire refused the consolation of religion because he considered that life could be pleasant if one knew how to make good use of it. In 1759, fighting Leibniz's optimism, he offered a terrible picture of human misery, yet maintained that life was worthy of being lived without the help of a metaphysical system. Facing the extremes, he was satisfied with a commonsense solution. Besides, he did not have to prove that he was right—simply that his adversaries were wrong.

The Contes philosophiques

Today the *Contes philosophiques* (Philosophical Tales) are considered Voltaire's masterpieces and rightly so. He did not invent the genre, but adapted it to his talents and to the exigencies of his struggle. He carried it to such a point of perfection that he had relatively few imitators.

What was a philosophical tale? As the name indicates, it was a short story designed to demonstrate a philosophical idea. Why this recourse to fabulation? Because the theory under consideration, generally supported by great scholars and widely accepted, could not be proven right or wrong dialectically. The subject often touched on metaphysics and ethics: freedom and determinism, God, the problem of evil, man's fate. These were questions lacking a sure answer. If someone won an argument on one of these matters, it simply meant that he was a better debater. Consequently, Voltaire refused a theoretical discussion that led nowhere and decided to submit the ideas to experimentation. He imagined a story—an imitation of life—that would be used as a test for a philosophical concept. Under such circumstances it would seem that the narration was just a pretext for the confrontation of ideas, but the contrary was true. The story was ironical and conceived in order to make the reader laugh at the expense of the partisans of the exposed system.

In fact, from the very beginning the test was rigged. The theory was never given a chance to win, and the reader, having a good time, became an accomplice of the author. The metaphysical discussion, which would have killed interest in the story, was almost totally eliminated and reduced to the use of a jargon as unconvincing as that of the doctors in Molière's comedies.

Voltaire's procedure can be explained by concentrating on *Candide*, the best-written and the most famous of the philosophical tales. At issue in *Candide* was the theory of Optimism, which justified the presence of evil in a universe created by an almighty and good God. Because he was good, God necessarily created the best possible world. If we do not agree with this assertion, it is because we have a limited vision and cannot conceive of the whole universe. If—and this is obviously pure supposition—we were in God's position, we would recognize his wisdom and benevolence. Voltaire was not convinced. After the earthquake of Lisbon and the Seven Years War, he decided he could no longer be content with suppositions that did not console and could be socially harmful.

It is possible that a war, seen from remote headquarters, may be perceived as a brilliantly executed maneuver, but for the soldier who is on the front line it is more likely a succession of absurd moves, of privations, of sufferings, of perils of all kinds. In *Candide* there is no remote vantage point; we are with a small group of survivors, frightfully exposed for no reason, whose main preoccupation is to escape one menace after another. There is no sign whatever of the presence of God in the entire story.

The attack on Optimism is twofold. First, it ridicules Optimism as such and the assertion that all is well. The author carefully avoids ever contradicting this assertion. On the contrary, each character (with one exception, the pessimist) approves it. But as soon as someone makes an optimistic comment, a catastrophe immediately occurs. The system is contradicted by facts; obviously, no metaphysical theory can resist such an arrangement of events. The reader accepts this manipulation because he has to laugh at the characters' conceited predictions and their automatic contradiction by the facts.

Second, Optimism presupposed an absolute determinism: there was not a single effect without a cause. Voltaire was basically of this opinion, although he sometimes vacillated on the point. However, this opinion, logically sound, had dangerous moral implications. If the world were determined, man would not be free; if he were not free, he would cease to be responsible for his actions, and consequently ethics would no longer exist. To solve the problem in *Candide*, Voltaire made Pangloss, the champion of Optimism, ludicrous. Pangloss makes extravagant speeches, full of nonsense, which are enough to render his determinist stand ridiculous. Having declared with great satisfaction that there is no effect without a cause, he seeks to illustrate the point, and here is the example he gives: "Note that noses were made to wear spectacles, so we wear spectacles." Even if the reader agreed that there is a final explanation for everything, he would probably think that noses were made for breathing rather than wearing spectacles.

The reader laughs at these incredible errors in a seemingly philosophical story because he is not looking for an accurate answer. Voltaire was not trying to give his own opinion; he wanted only to show how far one could be carried by strict adherence to a metaphysical system. When Voltaire was on the defensive (for example, when he tried to justify his deist God to the atheists in the *Histoire de Jenni*, 1775) he had no better arguments to put forth than had the supporters of Optimism. But in *Candide* Voltaire was on the attack and waged the war in the best way to support his demonstration. Not once did he attempt to understand his opponent's position. There is very little room for good faith in a polemical and sarcastic work.

Metaphysics, which many considered to be the subject of the story, was reduced to a jargon without much sense and always used at an inopportune time; this sufficed to render it ridiculous. The vocabulary of Leibniz was from the outset made laughable by its use in a heavily erotic context. The vulgarity of the scene was attenuated by this unexpected euphemistic language, which nobody could take seriously after such treatment.

One may wonder how it is that *Candide*, having killed the theory of Optimism (but not ordinary optimism, which is as widespread today as it was in the eighteenth century), could have survived its victory. It is because, behind the metaphysical system, the story deals with the problem of evil.

Nobody had ever given a good explanation of the presence of evil, and Voltaire had no answer to offer; in his opinion, there was no need for such an answer. Man had an instinct for self-preservation that allowed him always to believe—sometimes against all logic—that his situation would improve. To tell him that all was well when all went wrong was an insult to his intelligence and to his sensitivity. Furthermore, to think that all was for the best in the best of all possible worlds introduced a fatalism and a dangerous laissez-faire attitude that impeded necessary reforms. It was precisely because the eighteenth century had seen that things needed to be redone that it was so optimistic and eager for change. The lesson of *Candide* is easy to discern in a single reading, without searching for any hidden meaning in one or several revealing chapters: man is so weak, so irrational, so easily cruel, that he should treat his fellow men with indulgence and pity; he should never add to their current misery in the name of principles that are beyond his reason; he should help his fellows to undo their prejudices and errors. Such a result would be an extraordinary accomplishment, which we may not hope to attain but toward which we cannot contribute too much. Voltaire's optimism was born of his realistic view of the world. In areas where great progress has been made—in the social order, for example—Voltaire's modest claims were surpassed, and he now appears to be a reactionary. Where there has been no change—in ethics, for example—Voltaire has remained the champion of liberty.

The plot of *Candide* may be summarized as follows. Candide's love for Cunégonde warrants his being ejected from the "castle" by the young girl's parents. After innumerable ups and downs that lead the protagonists into many countries of Europe and to America, they are finally all reunited in Constantinople. Candide marries the now-ugly Cunégonde, buys a farm, and with his friends cultivates his garden.

The book is comical, making one laugh from the first line to the last. It is a nonpsychological biography, an adventure story without suspense, a love story that is neither sentimental nor erotic, a historical novel whose chronology is pure fantasy, a travelogue without local color. Yet all these negatives do not prevent this short novel from being a masterpiece. How does this come about? Through its style, to be sure, but more precisely through the rapidity of motion and coldness of tone that are in continual contradiction with the succession of dramatic scenes.

Candide is recounted at an accelerated pace. If you skip a page, you have no idea what country you are in or what is happening. The catastrophes multiply beneath the characters' feet without anyone taking the trouble to be astonished at the fury of fate, as if the exceptional lot of these little creatures was that of all humanity. This exaggeration—which the reader easily accepts, for it is comical and an endless source of laughter—serves to destroy the theory of Optimism by ridding history of all its dramatic connotations. Usually death, an unjust condemnation, a kidnapping, are pathetic events. When they are multiplied, as in *Candide*, they lose their intensity. When two or three calamities occur on a single page, tragedy turns to comedy. The reader has no time to pity the fate of the protagonists or to share their suffering. He looks on with detachment, from afar, all the more so because the characters themselves never think of complaining. Once one catastrophe has been bridged and before a new one irrupts, they again take up their lives as though nothing had befallen them. They limit themselves to recalling the list of their misfortunes in ludicrous shorthand, which becomes a series of comic litanies. Evil is ubiquitous, no matter what the champions of Optimism say. We may regret it, but we cannot change man's fate.

The impression of speed is further accentuated by Voltaire's style. He proceeds in short sentences, linking them as little as possible. It is the extreme logic of thought in the midst of this incoherent narrative that maintains the thread of the narration. As for the comic effects, they work through accumulation without any single one attracting attention and stopping the reader in passing. A moment after a comic device is introduced it is modified, regrouped, and reused in such a way that one would need ten lines to comment on one line of *Candide*. The renewing of invention is all the more incredible because the narrative seems linear, without complexities, and because the rapidity of the action hides the richness of the orchestration. Of course, a subjective element is added: since the reader is having fun, he has the impression that time is quickly passing and that the story, which consists of an accumulation of digressions, acquires an organic unity; but this unity is essentially a consequence of the way *Candide* is written.

The falsely dramatic story is told in a disinterested tone, which permits the author to push the scenes toward utter outrage. He is certain that the reader will not be duped by these exaggerated situations at which he can only laugh, for nothing is more amusing than a melodramatic effect that fails. Voltaire has his characters in the tales speak in almost the same language he gives to the heroes of his tragedies, but these speeches occur at the most inopportune times for passionate or sorrowful expressions—which is all that is needed to render them ridiculous.

Candide unfolds under the sign of the superlative: "All is for the best in the best of all possible worlds." If we accept such a constant exaggeration so easily, it is because the tone is never in unison with the narrative. This deviation puts a distance between the reader and the elements of the narrative—plot, characters—and such distance is common to all great comic novels.

The characters speak of their misadventures as if they had befallen someone else or as if their woes were not basically different from the sufferings of other human beings. In the end they attest to the omnipresence of evil. The story that each one tells is different, but the result is identical. The likeness in style of the adventures is underlined by the use of the same language, whatever the rank or education of a particular character. They naturally have all the qualities of unimpeachable witnesses: memory, good judgment, detachment, sincerity (even when they lie, nobody notices).

In this respect they are Voltaire's marionettes, and he manipulates them as he pleases. This aspect is further accentuated by the comic nature of the book: for example, the repetition of certain scenes, which makes them easily predictable. We know, for instance, that as soon as Cunégonde meets a man she will seduce him and in turn be forced to submit to his desires. The element of surprise lies in the manner in which the scene is presented and in the angle of focus.

This unidimensionality, open to criticism in a psychological novel, offers advantages in a comic story. No preparation is needed to justify the scenes; the author is free to accelerate, slow down, or interrupt the narrative as he likes. It is an animated cartoon, not a movie with real actors.

Nevertheless, since ambiguity is the rule in Voltaire's ironic world, the marionettes, simple witnesses to evil, possess characteristics of their own that are not requisites of propaganda. Thus Pangloss, the true absentminded professor, is at the same time endowed with a remarkable sexual appetite, and his misfortunes result as much from his escapades with females as from his unfortunate Leibnizian philosophy. Candide is naive, but although his naiveté is often mentioned, the hero learns his lesson from experience and is not far, by the end of the book, from symbolizing man's small wisdom. Beneath its apparent simplicity and its extreme clarity, *Candide* is an ambiguous and complex masterpiece.

In another philosophical tale, *Micromégas* (1752), two extraterrestrial beings—Micromégas, who comes from the planet Sirius, and a dwarf, who comes from Saturn (and is a dwarf only in contrast to his companion, for he is "one thousand fathoms high")—discover our globe (or "globule") in travel. Just as *Candide* is a false adventure story, so *Micromégas* is a false science-fiction story. Voltaire made every effort to render this fantastic tale as natural as possible, not to persuade us of its credibility but to show that on their scale the two giants are identical to man, because the relationship between capacity and achievement, pleasure and suffering remains constant.

To some extent, the story is a satire of man's unjustified conceit. The pretense that the universe has been created for his own sake becomes a joke when told to the inhabitants of other worlds, whose only reply is laughter. Of course, no eighteenth-century reader believed in the existence of either Micromégas or the Saturnian. All the same, anthropocentrism, that manifestation of human pride, remained tainted with ridicule.

When he wrote *L'Ingénu* (1767), Voltaire was seventy-three years old. Nevertheless, gaiety and a quick pace triumph in the entire first half of the story. At the same time, Voltaire was in the thick of his battle against the Catholic church; religion is thus at the root of almost all the mishaps that befall the story's protagonists. The *Ingénu* preached Voltaire's familiar themes of tolerance and hatred for fanaticism and prejudice. But it posed problems for commentators: the story read more like a novel; the historical background was more carefully delineated than in *Candide*; there was no attack on a preconceived notion or on a metaphysical system; toward the end of the story the tone changed abruptly and, while still being ironic, was permeated by drama. Suddenly Voltaire stopped laughing and decided that the demonstration would be more convincing if the events became moving.

Here again, as in so many of his propaganda works, the world is seen through the eyes of a young and naive outsider whose common sense is used to denounce the incoherences and abuses of humanity's ways of being and thinking. The character evolves during the story and learns how to draw a lesson from his experience—a short lesson, for Voltaire did not wish to substitute new errors for those he was combating. For the first time in any story, a collection of self-satisfied imbeciles appears, announcing the future characters of Gustave Flaubert.

The Mémoires

The *Mémoires* were written in the same year as *Candide* (1759), at a time when Voltaire's irony and literary talent were at their peak. They are excellent and yet are among the least known of his works. For the most part, this is due to the circumstances of their publication. The book dealt ironically with Voltaire's political associations with the most prominent personalities of his time. To justify such treatment he depicted the world as an insane arena in which events never materialized in the expected way. Such a satirical work could not appear during the author's life. It was only after Voltaire's death that a few clandestine copies circulated. The *Mémoires* were really published with the collection of the complete works of Voltaire and appeared at the end, where they passed unnoticed.

The reader of today will be somewhat hindered by the many allusions to forgotten events; a joke that needs footnotes is never very funny. But still the *Mémoires* are very pleasant reading. Historically speaking, they are remarkably accurate, despite the distortions produced by the continual derision poured on the protagonists. A few years before the Revolution of 1789, some people were shocked by the lack of respect shown for a king—in this case, the king of Prussia. Only Frederick was not disturbed. Under the mockery, he recognized that his malicious friend had paid homage to his tremendous originality.

The Antireligious Campaign of Voltaire

Some of Voltaire's best works belong to this campaign, and yet, on the whole, they enjoy a bad reputation. Paradoxically, this bad reputation is due to the campaign's success. Voltaire's militant anticlericalism seems cumbersome now that the church plays a more modest role in Western society. In the eighteenth century, most exegetists did not accept a figurative interpretation of Scripture. Voltaire thus repeatedly denounced everything in the Bible that was either scientifically or historically impossible, or even that he considered poetically feeble or morally shocking

VOLTAIRE

even to an enlightened reader. Voltaire found endless pleasure in these attacks. Nowadays, his relentlessness seems excessive and narrow-minded.

Voltaire constantly repeats himself, but this is propaganda, and all advertisement is based on repetition. In any case, it must be admitted that Voltaire seems to have been obsessed with certain themes. We must keep in mind that the ironic, the sarcastic Voltaire was a man of passion—angry, emotional. As an example, on 24 August 1572 there had been a vicious massacre of Protestants in Paris. On each anniversary of that day, two centuries later, Voltaire took to his bed with a fever.

Voltaire's Correspondence

There is no critic today who does not admire these letters, though it is unlikely that many people have read the hundred volumes they represent. Their historical and literary interest is considerable, but it is difficult to discuss them as a whole. An author writes letters, not a correspondence; a correspondence is the task of an editor. Voltaire wrote thousands of letters to all kinds of people on all kinds of subjects. He also had instructions to give on the staging of his plays and on the appropriate measures for carrying on the fight for the Enlightenment. Above all, he quickly realized what a good instrument of propaganda his letters could be. They were so witty, so graceful, that those to whom they were addressed read them aloud to their friends. They were copied, read elsewhere, printed in journals. They became a mechanism of pressure for Voltaire in obtaining satisfaction for his innumerable requests.

On the whole, the letters are of an exceptional quality. The style is more familiar than that of the stories; metaphors and puns are more frequent. Many of them mix verse and prose, written with equal facility. Nowhere can we find a clearer example of Voltaire's mastery, especially when we remember that

almost all these letters were dictated and posted without corrections.

CONCLUSION

No one contributed more than Voltaire to the political, religious, social, and judicial evolution of his time. All the reforms that he fought for have been adopted. He denounced prejudice and injustice. He was a great popularizer. He made England fashionable; he recognized the genius of Shakespeare, Newton, and Locke and built them a European reputation. Through his books Henri IV and Louis XIV became popular—but he was also held responsible for the overthrowing of the French monarchy.

Voltaire has been considered both a revolutionary and a conservative; yet there is remarkable unity to his life and to his writings. His influence was enormous, since he reached very large audiences and explained to them the most serious problems in a language that they could easily grasp. Never did a century so much influence an author, and never did an author so much influence his century.

From a literary point of view, almost alone in his time he maintained the cult of poetry (tragic, epic, didactic, light); he introduced the concept of modern history; he was among the best letter writers; and finally, he created a genre, the philosophical tale—and his *Candide* is one of the masterpieces of world literature.

These are some of the reasons why Voltaire is so much alive today.

Selected Bibliography

EDITIONS

INDIVIDUAL WORKS
Romans et contes. Paris, 1959.
Lettres philosophiques. Paris, 1961.
Dictionnaire philosophique. Paris, 1967.

VOLTAIRE

COLLECTED WORKS

Oeuvres complètes. Edited by Louis Moland. 52 vols. Paris, 1877–1885.

Oeuvres complètes de Voltaire. Edited by Theodore Besterman et al. Geneva and London, 1968– . Still in progress. Includes the complete correspondence.

TRANSLATIONS

"Candide," "Zadig," and Selected Stories. Translated by Donald Frame. Bloomington, Ind., 1961.

Philosophical Letters. Translated by Ernest Dilworth. Indianapolis, 1961.

Philosophical Dictionary. Translated by Peter Gay. New York, 1962.

BIOGRAPHICAL AND CRITICAL STUDIES

A worthy and detailed biography of Voltaire has so far not been published. The available works about him are out of date, unscholarly, too favorable, or too prejudiced. The following list includes works that are either relatively recent or useful about some specialized aspect of his life.

Barber, William H. *Candide.* London, 1960.

Besterman, Theodore. *Voltaire.* New York, 1969.

Brumfitt, J. H. *Voltaire, Historian.* London, 1958.

————, and Gerard Davis. *"L'Ingénu" and "Histoire de Jenni."* Oxford, 1960.

Lanson, Gustave. *Les lettres philosophiques.* Paris, 1909.

————. *Voltaire.* Translated by Robert Wagoner. New York, 1966.

Mason, Haydn. *Voltaire.* Baltimore, 1981.

Mitford, Nancy. *Voltaire in Love.* New York, 1957.

Pomeau, René. *Candide.* Oxford, 1980. Critical edition in French.

————. *La religion de Voltaire.* Paris, 1956.

Ridgway, Ronald. *La propagande philosophique dans les tragédies de Voltaire.* Geneva, 1961.

Rousseau, André-Michel. *L'Angleterre et Voltaire.* 3 vols. London, 1976.

Sareil, Jean. *Essai sur "Candide."* Geneva, 1967.

————. *Voltaire et les grands.* Geneva, 1979.

Wade, Ira. *The Intellectual Development of Voltaire.* Princeton, N. J., 1969.

JEAN SAREIL

RICHARD WAGNER
(1813–1883)

FRIEDRICH NIETZSCHE WROTE in *Toward a Genealogy of Morals* that the artist is, "after all, only the presupposition of his work, the womb, the soil, at times the dung and manure on which and out of which it grows—and accordingly, in most cases, something one must forget if the work itself is to be enjoyed." Richard Wagner engrossed Nietzsche's thoughts as he wrote this passage.

To an extraordinary extent Wagner's operas—so abundant in tonal beauties—are sublimations of ignoble ideas and instincts, sublimations of that ruthlessness and fanaticism many of his admirers put out of mind when under the spell of his compelling, captivating, powerful music. Finding his ideology troubling, indeed, embarrassing, they either ignore or deny it. To shut one's eyes to his ideology is, perhaps, consoling to those without intellectual curiosity and thus without interest in the cultural meaning of his whole achievement; but denial is utterly in vain: the monumental record of Wagnerian thought survives in his own hand—the prose works, so fascinatingly rich in mental perversities.

I

During the great decades of Wagnerism (1880–1920), Wagner's essays were considered prodigious in style and profound in substance, their significance attested by both the few devotees who had read them and the many who had not. The composer's followers celebrated him as a philosopher of commanding literary power in the tradition of Friedrich Hegel, Ludwig Feuerbach, and Arthur Schopenhauer—indeed, as a master who had put such predecessors quite in the shade. It was the supposed universality of his genius that captured the imagination and made him appear matchless, his adherents hailing his impostrous role of commentator, critic, aesthetician, and social, political, and racial theorist no less fulsomely than his musical genius. For the most part, in matters Wagnerian his disciples stripped themselves of reason, discrimination, and judgment.

Political and racial elements buttressed German Wagnerism. However, for the French symbolists and those in the related English aesthetic movement, Wagner's clamorous nationalism, vulgar anti-Semitism, and ritual vegetarianism had less attraction. Rather, his theories of art stirred in them intimations of the ineffable, of secret and marvelous things. For a variety of reasons, in which the magic of his music played the most consistent part, men of talent the world over entangled themselves to varying degrees in Wagnerism, among them the junior Rossettis, Algernon Charles Swinburne, John Galsworthy, Aubrey Beardsley, George Bernard Shaw, Alphonse

Daudet, D. H. Lawrence, Paul Verlaine, Stéphane Mallarmé, Charles Baudelaire, Paul Valéry, Camille Saint-Saëns, César Franck, Henri Duparc, Ernest Chausson, Vincent d'Indy, Gabriele D'Annunzio, and Walt Whitman.

Societies of Wagnerism, enlisting the talented, the amateur, and the philistine, proliferated. One of the century's most complicated and fascinating movements, it proved especially attractive to the young, many of whom became cultists obediently manifesting an understandable idolatry of Wagner's music, a no less ardent (if less comprehensible) admiration of his poetry and prose, an inflexible antagonism toward the Jews, and a scornful contempt for any contemporary composer save their master.

Among the few consolations of Hugo Wolf's tragic life were his pilgrimages to Bayreuth, the very heart of the cult, the site of Wagner's theater (the *Festspielhaus*), and of his press. Wolf embraced Wagner's vegetarianism and particular loathing of Johannes Brahms and attempted—happily, rather unsuccessfully—a stern anti-Semitism. For his part, young Gustav Mahler was less doctrinaire: born of Jews, he made no effort to repudiate them; nor could he summon up anything but respect for Brahms; but he did follow the teaching of his revered Wagner by renouncing animal flesh, an act he believed would speed the arrival of the cleansed and regenerated Wagnerian world promised by Bayreuth.

Of course, for such sensitive and gifted young men, Wagner's music counted above all else. It stirred them to the depths and cast the spell that entangled them in the rest of his work. After a performance of *Parsifal* at Bayreuth, Wolf threw his head into his hands and sobbed. Franck's pupil, the young Guillaume Lekeu, fainted and had to be carried from the *Festspielhaus* as the prelude to *Tristan* unfolded; Emanuel Chabrier, no longer a youth—he was close to fifty—reportedly shed tears during the same performance. Two generations of Wagnerites surrendered themselves to the monumental pathos, to the overwhelming presence of the Wagnerian drama. At twenty-five, Richard Strauss still trembled merely thinking about the sound of Wagner's orchestra.

The eventual downfall of Wagnerism was hastened by the plethora of nonsense published by its leading journals: in Germany Wagner's own *Bayreuther Blätter;* in France the *Revue wagnérienne;* in England *The Meister.* The less sense Wagnerians made the more they understood one another: both the fallaciousness of Wagnerian theory, so carefully wrapped in pseudoprofundities, and the foolishness of Wagner's prose stood forth—unwittingly laid bare by his own devotees.

From the time Wagner's comprehensive essays began to circulate, many had questioned the quality of Wagnerian thought. In the 1890's the Viennese critic Eduard Hanslick, one of the most distinguished and persistent opponents of Wagnerism, predicted that within a short time "the writings of the Wagnerites will be looked upon in amazement as the relics of an intellectual plague." During the preceding decade, Nietzsche, once a Wagnerite, wondered how he had been capable of taking Wagnerism seriously; he too had come to recognize it as a malady: "Is Wagner a man at all?" he asked. "Is he not rather a disease?" Some twenty years Hanslick's junior, Nietzsche realized how enduring the infection would prove; he sensed the terrible future. The new generation of Wagnerites would include Houston Stewart Chamberlain, Alfred Rosenberg, and Adolf Hitler, all of whom found refreshment and inspiration not only in the master's scores but in his prose. Many of its motifs were to reappear in the design of the disasters Nazism visited upon the world. Bizarrely compelling in their earnestness and with a weird, sinister logic of their own, Wagner's writings set in motion vibrations dangerous to culture itself; and no simplification, however consoling, can mask the fact that the ethical problems they pose implicate Wagner's music dramas as well.

II

Wagner (born on 22 May 1813) looked upon his operas as projections into art of all he wished to accomplish as a social and political reformer, his aesthetic theories and stage works being, in his eyes, but implements of this higher purpose. The lion's share of his prose writings elaborate this social/political/aesthetic composite that, over the years, he untiringly reiterated and amplified. He would certainly knit his brows at attempts to separate his art from the ideas from which it grew. He was proud of his didactic program meant to restructure the Germanic world, and he ceaselessly lamented the failure of most of his contemporaries—especially those in power—to pay attention to his teachings. (One suspects that in his subconscious Wagner appreciated his true purpose and concern—the creation of great music—which, in his prose, he so often confused with his message.) He laboriously raised a strange house few desired to enter apart from a small group of faithful commentators whose murky writings then worked on the nervous systems of a later and troubled generation; his theoretical ramblings—especially his racial theories—became a legacy to be exploited and carried to its logical and appalling conclusions in the century following his own. Wagner left the "solution" to those more reckless than he.

His earliest serious interests were literary. While a student at Dresden's Kreuz School he enjoyed a reputation as a poet and began a giant, demoniacal tragedy, *Leubald*, awkwardly pieced together from elements taken from Shakespeare, Goethe, and Heinrich von Kleist—from the beginning his way with words was ungracious. A performance of Goethe's *Egmont* with Beethoven's incidental music brought him revelation: *Leubald*, too,

required music to achieve its full effect; he immediately sought instruction in composition. He had moved from word to tone but would soon reverse the procedure. His next adolescent attempt for the stage was a pastoral play modeled on Goethe's *Laune des Verliebten* (The Lover's Whim) and with music suggested by Beethoven's Sixth Symphony. Wagner later recalled: "While I wrote the score on one page, I had as yet not even considered a text for the following."

His verse became an extension of his musical inspiration. Indeed, he came to speak of setting his librettos to music as a process of recollection, an exercise in remembering—or sometimes tortuously struggling to remember—that first musical impulse. Too often composing became for him, in his own words, a question of: "'How did it go?' instead of 'How is it?'; not 'How is it to be?' but 'How was it?' and then having to search about until one finds it again." "It is not my way," he explained (in a letter to Karl Gaillard on 30 January 1844) quite early in his career,

to select any pleasing material, put it into verse, and then ponder how to add suitable music to it. Were I to proceed in this way, I would expose myself to the inconvenience of having to inspire myself twice, which is impossible. My way of creating is quite different: to begin with, only that material can appeal to me which displays to me not only poetical but also, and at the same time, musical significance. Before starting to write a verse or even to sketch a scene, I am already intoxicated by the musical aroma [*Duft*] of my creation; I have all the tones, all the characteristic motives in my head so that when the verses are finished and the scenes put in order, the opera proper is also finished for me, the detailed musical treatment being rather a calm and considered afterwork that the moment of real creation has preceded.

(*Richard Wagner Briefe*, p. 154)

The poetic idea of the unfolding dramatic situation incited a tonal correlative, which in turn called forth the almost simultaneously fitted text in a seemingly fated fusion of tone and word.[1]

His prose, alas, had no such intoxicating origins. Yet the effort to traverse it should be made. One suffers the infelicitous poetry of his librettos for the rewards of their musical investiture; his tangled prose also offers recompense: an understanding of Wagner's purpose in constructing the giant machine of his so-called *Gesamtkunstwerk* (the all-embracing work of art) and a recognition of the forces that forged this purpose. The essays lay open the thinking that engendered the initial "intoxication" and with it Wagner's first apprehension of the music; they convey whatever may be known of the origins themselves.

III

Except for his autobiography, Wagner's prose is rarely read. Stretching in time from an aspiring young composer laboring in Paris at his first consistent literary attempts to the disordered scribblings of a celebrated master dying in Venice, it includes journalistic articles and reviews, polemic essays, and ambitious speculative treatises. Of the influences that helped form this almost half-century of writing, among the first was Heinrich Heine. A fellow student in Leipzig, one Schröter, introduced Wagner to works—probably the *Reisebilder* (1826–1831)—of the Rhenish poet, whose light and elegant manner of expression

the young Wagner would all too briefly attempt to imitate during his first stay in Paris. Another source was E. T. A. Hoffmann, especially his *Fantasiestücke in Callots Manier* (1814–1815). In *My Life* Wagner recalls this youthful enthusiasm: "I really lived and moved amid Hoffmann's artistic, ghostly apparitions." More lasting impressions derived from two of his mentors: the convoluted syntax of both his uncle, Adolf Wagner, a scholar, literary critic, and translator resident in Leipzig, and a young teacher at the university, Christian Hermann Weisse—already a respected Hegelian—the obscurity of whose lectures on aesthetics set the young man aflame. For a while Wagner's diction became so complicated that he could not be understood, and his elder brother Albert grew concerned at his mental state. Abstruseness was to remain an essential of the Wagnerian literary manner.

As a prose writer Wagner's earliest attempts are uncharacteristic of his more mature work. Having written his first opera, *Die Feen* (The Fairies), during 1833, in the German romantic idiom of Felix Mendelssohn, Carl Maria von Weber, and Heinrich Marschner—a complicated, haunted northern world of chivalry and supernatural forces—he suddenly and unexpectedly trumpeted forth a newfound admiration of the simplicity and warmth of the Mediterranean temperament. Prompted by the novelist Heinrich Laube, a leader of progressive German youth, the young composer took Vincenzo Bellini as his new idol and Italian sensualism as his new ideal, tendencies characterizing his second opera, *Das Liebesverbot* (The Ban on Love), and discussed in two of (his earliest) articles of 1834. The first, "Die deutsche Oper" ("On German Opera"), appeared in Laube's *Zeitung für die elegante Welt*; the other, "Pasticcio," in the *Neue Zeitschrift für Musik*, Robert Schumann's new periodical. For the moment Wagner saw the Latin spirit as a symbol of freedom, the Teutonic temper as the essence of puritanical narrowness. His articles con-

---

[1]Wagner's purely literary works are for the most part of a disagreeableness painful to comtemplate—his play, *Eine Kapitulation: Lustspiel in antiker Manier* (*A Capitulation*, 1870), for example. The mass of his music composed without connection with words—marches, salon pieces—has a similar distinction. Exceptions are his splendid libretto for *Die Sarazenen* (*The Saracen Woman*, 1841–1842) and his sketch of a drama called *Die Sieger* (*The Victors*, 1856). But since both came into being without initial musical stimulus, he could not find suitable ways of providing them with scores. At best they served to contribute literary elements to later works, the first to *Tannhäuser* and *Die Walküre* (*The Valkyrie*), the second to *Parsifal*.

demned the Germans as too intellectual, too learned to create warm, human figures on the stage. Mozart, he admitted, had succeeded, but only with the aid of Italian song—erudition being the source of every German ill. Through Bellini he sought simple, noble beauty in song and with it the operatic image of true life.

A third article concentrated its fire on German operatic music. Its delight in the orchestral, Wagner insisted, created a tawdry scene of boundless disorder, a patched and doctored jumble in which countless pedantic commentaries from the orchestra fought for attention and distracted the mind; in contrast, the Italians, especially Bellini, could apprehend a dramatic situation vocally with clear and firm melodic strokes. This paean to the enrapturing qualities of Bellinian song appeared anonymously in the Riga *Zuschauer* in December 1837. Wagner had been gaining experience as a conductor in the grubby theaters of one provincial German town after the other: Würzburg, Magdeburg, Königsberg, and then Riga. By the time he quit the Livonian capital, he had again changed his artistic course by his new predilection for grand opera, the pompous genre recently fabricated by Gasparo Spontini and Giacomo Meyerbeer; with them as his models, he began the composition of his mammoth *Rienzi.*

Wagner's way of quitting a job usually took the form of flight from his creditors. His exit from Riga was particularly undignified, for he also had to evade the police. By way of Prussia and then England he eventually made his way to Paris in 1839. There he had no success and sustained himself by fresh borrowing, by working as a musical hack, and by turning out a series of stories and articles for the *Gazette musicale*, a magazine owned by the German publisher Moritz Schlesinger. Writing in German—which the *Gazette* put into French—Wagner adopted a light, readable style, a watered mixture combining the weirdness of E. T. A. Hoffmann and the sparkle of Heine. Some of the tales are not without fine effect,

especially two interrelated narratives: "An End in Paris," whose autobiographical burden is the unhappy lot of an impecunious German musician in the glittering capital, and the moving "Pilgrimage to Beethoven," a fictional account of the same artist's visit to the master. Here Wagner provided a startling adumbration of his future mode of expression relative to his music dramas. He has Beethoven declare that were he to write an opera after *Fidelio*, he would abandon the "number" opera—"no arias, duets, trios, none of the stuff with which they patch together operas today"—and instead create true musical drama by opposing "the wild, unfettered elemental feelings, represented by the instruments, to the clear, definite emotion of the human heart as represented by the human voice." The "Pilgrimage" was a first step toward the essays of Wagner's Swiss period, that climacteric in his development as a theorist.

In Paris he also became correspondent for a Dresden newspaper, the *Abendzeitung*, dispatching to it the German originals of some of his *Gazette* articles and additional observations on the local musical life. To August Lewald's journal, *Europa* (Stuttgart), he sent a pair of witty pieces (1841): "Parisian Amusements" and "Parisian Fatalities for the Germans," the latter ending with a prayer for the redemption of the thirty thousand Germans living in the French capital. He was striving to keep his name alive in his homeland and to demonstrate his attachment to it.

"On German Music" (1840), his first contribution to the *Gazette*, had revealed the depth of his enthusiasm for grand opera as offered at the great Paris Opéra, an especially magniloquent and calculated kind of historical pageant accompanied by music, an ingenious genre brought to its ultimate point by a German, Giacomo Meyerbeer, in *The Huguenots.* Wagner had fully done with his Italian flirtation and his concomitant contempt for the operatic ability of his countrymen. The article hailed the particular and historic gift of the Germans to "denationalize" themselves in the realm of opera:

> The universal tendency of which the German spirit is capable made it easy for the German artist to naturalize himself on foreign terrain. German genius appears to be almost destined to seek out among its neighbors what is not native to its motherland, to lift this above its narrow boundaries and thereby create something universal for the entire world.

"On German Music" was not only a tribute to Meyerbeer's methods but also an avant-courrier for *Rienzi*, that Brobdingnagian grand opera, which, Wagner hoped, might outdo Meyerbeer and topple him from his throne.

The longer he lingered in Paris the more Wagner prized things German. As German history, medieval German literature, and Teutonic myth increasingly commanded his interest, his Meyerbeer fever subsided: *The Huguenots* now seemed to him too contrived, its composer an artful charlatan. Wagner's failure to make an impression on Paris made him resent Meyerbeer's extraordinary success all the more; resentment turned to anger, anger to hatred. Moreover, Meyerbeer was a German and a Jew, two words Wagner had come to regard as mutually exclusive: he no longer looked upon Meyerbeer as a representative of the German spirit. Henceforth, an almost pathological anti-Semitism would play its baleful part in the development of Wagnerian theory, which—ironically—availed itself boldly and unashamedly of constituents of Meyerbeer's art while characterizing them as newly born and of immaculate Aryan strain.

With the completion of *Rienzi*, set under the brilliant sun of Rome, Wagner began work on a new opera, *Der Fliegende Holländer (The Flying Dutchman)*, which unfolds amid the mists and wild cliffs of the Scandinavian fjords. Both works received their premieres soon after Wagner's return to Dresden (1842), where he had quickly been named *Kapellmeis-*

ter of the Royal Theater. The triumphs that had eluded him in Paris he finally met on his native soil.

By the end of his seven-year tenure of the Dresden podium, Wagner had added *Tannhäuser* and *Lohengrin* to his creations and become a famous if increasingly difficult man, with a tendency to inflate his domestic, personal, and professional problems into transcendant political, moral, and artistic issues. Moreover, he had grown to see himself and his art as *the* quintessential expressions of the German spirit. Most of his major essays—tracts might be a more accurate word—would take the form of attempts to substantiate this extraordinary claim, a bizarre manifestation of an ego that astounded even Bismarck.

Despite outward success, Wagner realized that audiences remained indifferent to the national elements coloring his work since the *Dutchman*. They looked upon *Tannhäuser* as they did upon *Rienzi* or *Huguenots*—that is, as splendid grand opera—and showed little interest in his crescent, ponderous Germanism. In *Lohengrin*—it would not be staged until after his departure from Dresden—he had made the affairs of the Reich the very fulcrum of the action: the hero, just before his embarkation, is favored with a vision of an invincible Germany. Wagner faced the fact that he commanded a vogue based on a misconception of his aims, an acknowledgment that determined his new course: to bestir himself to help bring about those immediate political changes that would pull the mask of complacency from the eyes of the German public and thus begin its transformation into a knowledgeable assembly dedicated to his true meaning. The route to the permanent revitalizing of German politics and culture lay—he was certain—in a complete reform of Germany's operatic tradition. With the ambitious intention of creating a new kind of Teutonic music drama, he devoured the *Volsunga Saga*, the *Nibelungenlied*, the Eddic poems, the writings of the brothers Grimm, and other works on the

Nordic tales. He put on paper "Der Nibelungen-Mythus als Entwurf zu einem Drama" ("The Nibelungen Myth as Scheme for a Drama")—it contains the essence of the later *Ring*—and from it derived a dramatic poem, *Siegfrieds Tod* (*Siegfried's Death;* later titled *Götterdämmerung,* or *The Twilight of the Gods*). When provided with its musical score, it was to stand forth—so he imagined—as the first of his major instruments of German rebirth. But they could come into being only when he had cleared his way of two stumbling blocks: German officialdom (had not Saxon courtiers ignored his "Draft for the Organization of a German National Theater . . . "?) and the Jews. He extolled revolution and anti-Semitism: "The real artwork cannot be created now but only prepared for, yes, by revolutionary means, by destroying and beating down all that deserves to be destroyed and beaten down."

During several days of civil war in Dresden, Wagner was in the center of revolutionary activity. The rising failed, and by a providential escape he eluded indictment for treason and a possible death sentence. He sought refuge in Switzerland, awaiting there the pan-European conflagration he felt certain to be in preparation and devoting his time to writing: "I myself must come, and those who are interested in my artistic being must come with me, to a clear understanding." He determined to make his position and purpose unmistakable in a series of treatises: "It is most essential that I accomplish this work and send it into the world before going on with my immediate artistic production."

Wagner had anticipated something of the ambitious polemic of his Swiss period in *The Wibelungs,* written shortly before his Nibelung scenario. In that essay he attempted to sort out and codify his reading and thinking on the Rhenish myths of Siegfried and the Nibelung Hoard and their relation to German history. By the time he arrived in Switzerland, he was ready to offer the world a master plan

and the rationale of his future activities. He intended it to bestow critical legitimacy on his coming Nibelung music drama whose purpose, in turn, was to lead the Germans back to the essential greatness and profundity of their national spirit, to redeem a nation degraded and led astray by the seductions of Parisian and Jewish pseudoart.

Four tracts completed in Switzerland represent the very heart of Wagnerian thought: *Die Kunst und die Revolution* (*Art and Revolution,* 1849), *Die Kunstwerk der Zukunft* (*Artwork of the Future,* 1849), *Das Judentum in der Musik* (*Jewry in Music,* 1850), and *Oper und Drama* (*Opera and Drama,* 1851). They set forth a bizarre and complicated dialectic of dramatic and musical art.

The first discussed Athenian drama, which had brought together the arts of poetry, music, dance, and design in a profound civic and religious expression; only revolution, Wagner maintained, could free the Germans from a materialism hindering the emergence of a similar and equally great communal utterance in their midst. If the Greek artwork, as he recognized, could not be reborn, its spirit could be born anew in Germany.

The second essay described both Wagner's conception of the Folk (the epitome of all who feel a *gemeinschaftliche Noth,* a common and collective want) and his special perception of the fate of the Greek dramatic synthesis: after its decline and disintegration, he asserted, the individual arts had gone their egoistic, separate ways; having in the present time reached the limits of these divided routes, they now longed to reunite, languishing for absorption, dissolution, and redemption in a new Germanic universal artwork. Its creator could be only that unique poet through whom the unconscious, unfettered genius of the Folk might rise to consciousness.

Jewry in Music arraigned the Jew as the materialist hindering the pure instincts of the German Folk from realizing the artwork of the future through its own Teutonic Aeschylus.

The Jew, Wagner reasoned, must therefore be eliminated from German life.

The final link in this speculative tetralogy, having sweepingly surveyed operatic and dramatic history, proceeded to describe—or, as will be seen, purported to describe—the philosophy and technique of Wagner's coming composite artwork, with its close relation between word and music and its expanded orchestral eloquence that would utter the unspeakable. *Opera and Drama* postulated a compound of verse and its parallel vocal melody. The poet's part, presenting the conceptual elements, would beget the musician's vocal line. The latter was to interpret the text through artfully calculated juxtapositions of rhythm, accent, pitch, and key relationships. The resulting congruity of verse and musical phrase was to be further confirmed both by an orchestra providing harmonic modulations and instrumental color appropriate to the stage situation and by dramatically compatible contributions on the part of singing actors. The orchestra with its many tongues would take over the operatic tasks traditionally assigned to the chorus. The artwork was to be unified by a system of motifs, reiterating and stressing the conditioning forces of the drama. Toward this end, certain musical phrases were to be extracted from their positions under their correlative verses and repeated by voice or orchestra in later dramatic situations whenever ideas associated with the original words had particular pertinence. As well as recalling the emotional content of past thoughts, the motif could also awaken foreboding. Accordingly, through a subtle integration of word and tone, the conceptual was to be conveyed in terms of the musical.

To summarize this quartet of treatises: revolution was to provide the political atmosphere in which the *Gesamtkunstwerk* might flourish; the German Folk, itself, would bring it into being by inspiring the national poet; those not truly of the Folk and thus inimical to its need for the *Gesamtkunstwerk* were to be weeded out; the poetic/literary elements in the *Gesamtkunstwerk* would form the fecundating element and affect as offspring the music and other participating arts.

Tortuous in style, speciously reasoned, and often historically inaccurate, the Swiss essays became the peculiar rock upon which Wagner built his church; and this despite the fact that in *Opera and Drama* he described a creative process the very opposite of his own. Eager to present the German-speaking world with music dramas that would establish him as the new national poet, yet at the same time acutely aware of the limited intellectual respectability enjoyed by most musicians, he thought it politic to claim to be first of all a poet. In *Opera and Drama* he pretended that his music flowed from his verse; that, notwithstanding the powerful floods of music engulfing his so-called poetry, the word had the superior power and functioned as the dominating, regulating element of his music dramas. From this false assertion there grew with the years a maze of amorphous explanations, desperate defenses, and perplexing contradictions, a labyrinth through which many of his succeeding articles would wind. He never contrived publicly to extricate himself from this dilemma of his own creation, though to his second wife, Cosima, he later confided the depth of his embarrassment concerning *Opera and Drama:* "I know what Nietzsche didn't like in it—it is the same thing . . . that set Schopenhauer against me: what I said about words. At the same time I didn't dare say that it was music that produced drama, although inside myself I knew it."

Uneasiness about the paramount role assigned to the word in *Opera and Drama* had inspired Wagner to cite the finale of Beethoven's Ninth Symphony as rendering the *Gesamtkunstwerk* historically legitimate. In the *Artwork of the Future* he maintained that in this movement Beethoven had become a musical Columbus: exploring the seemingly shoreless sea of absolute music, he had caught sight of the undreamed-of coast of the Wagnerian music drama, this great climax of the

Ninth, in which a symphonic web discoursed upon sung poetry, anticipating the Wagnerian synthesis. (In the famous recitative for low strings Wagner claimed to sense the point of decision on Beethoven's part: his instruments, pressing toward articulateness, could of necessity but call to their aid the human voice and thus prepare for the Wagnerian music drama.) *Opera and Drama* in turn espoused Germanic myth as the worthiest subject for such discourse but held that it must proceed one voice at a time, ensembles (duets, trios, and so forth) being censured, along with formal arias, as Italianate and hence un-German.

In *Opera and Drama,* Wagner also pondered the language of his projected national drama. Writing librettos had always set him on thorns.[2] Despite his youthful belletristic pretensions, both the verse and plan of *Die Feen* had been foolish and shamelessly slipshod. The remarkable improvement evident in the literary quality of *Das Liebesverbot* must be credited to Shakespeare, whose *Measure for Measure* here provided both model and inspiration; lacking these, the verse of *Rienzi* returned to the deplorable level of *Die Feen*'s. Though by the time of Wagner's Paris–Dresden period he had taken Eugène Scribe as exemplar, the books of the *Dutchman, Tannhäuser,* and *Lohengrin,* their fine poetic moments notwithstanding, revealed a hand incapable of mastering the mechanism of the well-made play. Yet by this time the shortcoming was made good by music, much of it so magical and imposing that it transformed the faulty librettos, rendering them convincing and covering their frequent solecisms and awkwardness. Only the increasingly long narratives, designed to explain what more skillful dramatists would have woven into the body of the plot, defied the metamorphosing powers of

Wagner's music; it is a problem he never overcame.

Opera and Drama also outlined a course by which Wagner hoped to find a permanent solution for his difficulties with texts, at least in respect to diction: his Nibelung tragedy would put to use the old alliterative verse called *Stabreim.* Forsaking formal metrical patterns and terminal rhyme, he would instead rely on pithy accented first syllables and explosive consonants, vigorous devices in which he believed to have glimpsed the deepest roots of the German language. Moreover, the dense and concise configurations into which *Stabreim* could be hammered offered Wagner a compensatory opportunity for musical expansiveness.

Wagner's Nibelung drama grew to gigantic proportions as, adding to the material already in his Nibelung scenario, he developed it into theatrical form and penned three expository dramas elucidating the series of mythic, cosmic events leading to the catastrophe, the death of Siegfried. Wagner ended (1852) with a cycle of poetic dramas called *Der Ring des Nibelungen (The Nibelung's Ring),* a trilogy preceded by a prologue—and thus often termed a tetralogy—consisting of *The Rhinegold, The Valkyrie, The Young Siegfried* (later simply *Siegfried*), and *The Twilight of the Gods.* The titles of the *Ring* operas as we know them today were fixed by the summer of 1856.

Thus the *Ring* grew from the piling up of antecedent dramas designed to elucidate those that followed. At the same time, Wagner retained tracts of repetitive narrative in all of the units in order to permit them independent lives on the stage. From these circumstances—in addition to his frequent need, even in the ordinary course of events, to turn to narrative when his dramatic craft failed— were born the celebrated longueurs of the *Ring.* Thus Wagner brought into being a bizarre genre, not without elements of precedent in the dramas of Germany's greatest poet, Goethe: a series of expanded narrative and reflective monologues masquerading as drama,

---

[2]Today only the most believing Wagnerian disciples maintain the claim that Wagner's librettos are self-sufficient works of art or that he was as great a poet and playwright as a musician. It is the marvelous music that carries the *Gesamtkunstwerk.*

a masquerade made convincing by great music. In general, the *Ring* dramas are inert and passive, Wagner's characters either chronicling past events or expressing their reactions to the woeful situations in which they, for the most part, find themselves. They narrate, argue, meditate, or lament, but rarely act. Though in the *Ring* (and in *Tristan* and *Parsifal*), a bit of stage action often has the force of an event, Wagner's supreme artistic moments remain these subjective deliberations, for they provide opportunities for a kind of music that turns seemingly unhistrionic cogitations into powerful drama.

IV

Even before completing the four dramatic *Ring* poems—which he himself hailed as the greatest ever written—he had turned to the German-speaking world and, in a largely autobiographical pamphlet, *Eine Mitteilung an meine Freunde* (*A Communication to My Friends*, 1851), appealed for financial help to bring about the poetic and musical realization of the *Ring* and its mounting at a specially appointed festival. (The *Communication* remained the richest source of biographical facts concerning Wagner until the appearance of *My Life.*)

Banned from returning to German lands after his revolutionary escapade, he sought to guide from a distance the increasing number of Wagnerian productions in his homeland. He wrote *Über die Aufführung des Tannhäuser* (*On Performing Tannhäuser*) in August 1852 and at the end of the year issued a similar pamphlet on the mounting of *Dutchman;* these instructions were forwarded to theaters evincing an interest in these operas. By this time he had renounced the unrealistic idea of making tiny Zurich the center of Wagnerian activities, evidently his hope while putting together his article "Ein Theater in Zurich" ("A Theater in Zurich," 1851).

His prolonged involvement with prose works did not really steal for literature energies better devoted to music: as a composer he had found himself in a virtually complete musical paralysis since the completion of the prelude to *Lohengrin* in August 1847. Though the music of the *Ring* was shaping itself in his inner ear, he remained unable to gather his musical strength, impotent to dredge the notes from the depths and put them on paper. It is doubtful that any other major composer ever suffered so long a musical drought.

Not until September 1853 did the hour come and the music of the *Ring*'s opening scene begin to rise to the surface of his consciousness. He proceeded to compose the score of *Rhinegold*, that of *Valkryie,* and the first two acts of *Siegfried* over a period of almost four years, completing the orchestral sketch of the latter on 30 July 1857. But at the point when Siegfried was approaching the fire-enclosed Valkyrie rock to awaken Brynhild from her magic slumber, Wagner suddenly put aside all work on the *Ring;* he had thrown himself into the affairs of a quite different kind of hero. By 20 August he had begun to sketch the libretto of *Tristan.*

Since his Dresden days he had known the story of Tristan, but only after the poet Georg Herwegh (also a German exile in Switzerland) introduced him to the philosophy of Arthur Schopenhauer did Wagner awaken to the musical and dramatic possibilities of the tale. He now interpreted Tristan's character in terms of Schopenhauerean disaffirmation and negation. Wagner had borrowed many ideas from Goethe: not only the disaffected hero and the mother goddess or "Eternal Feminine" as his savioress, but also the concept of a transfiguring renunciation. But studying Schopenhauer made Wagner apprehend this motif—in Goethe one of quiet withdrawal—in terms of violent annulment; he came to see in the figure of Tristan the very essence of this annihilative spirit. Wagner now identified himself not with the mythological, heroic Siegfried exalting action and victory but with a medieval knight preaching self-extinction and oblivion. In short, Wagner was no longer attuned to the *Ring:* as the Tristan theme increasingly took possession of him, it drove from his mind the robust and at times boisterous music of *Siegfried* and replaced it with intimations of those chromatic harmonies of passion and sorrow now inseparable from the very idea of Tristan and his beloved Isolde. Wagner's creative energies first reawakened in *Rhinegold,* fully flowing in *Valkyrie,* and then blocked in *Siegfried,* had found a new channel. He finished the score of *Tristan* in Lucerne on 6 August 1859.

His journey from the joyous Siegfried to the melancholy Tristan had been prepared by two disappointments: the collapse of his marriage (long foundering) and the failure of the revolutionary movement. In the great capitals of Europe uprisings had come and gone, leaving matters much as before. In particular, Louis Napoleon's coup—the preparation for the second French empire—had made Wagner despair of Europe's artistic and political future. Ironically, it was this new emperor who indirectly helped restore him to his homeland. Napoleon III had commanded a production of *Tannhäuser* at the Paris Opéra, for which occasion Wagner rewrote and expanded whole sections of the work. Armed with whistles and flageolets, a group of socialites, eager to embarrass Napoleon and to show disapproval of Wagner in particular and of Germans in general, turned the performances (March 1861) to shambles. News of the shameful demonstrations made Germans close ranks behind a composer whom foreigners had come to regard as a symbol of the nation. At home complete amnesty was but a matter of time. By March 1862 the last barrier had fallen: his native land of Saxony lay open to him.

With the completion of *Tristan,* Wagner was still unready to resume work on the *Ring.* Instead, he returned to a plan conceived as early as 1845: to write a light comedy about Hans Sachs and the Meistersinger as a kind of satyr play following the tragedy of Tannhäuser, a comic, Aristophanic complement to the heavier work. (The rewriting of *Tannhäuser* in Paris had evidently rekindled the project.) Moreover, comedy was the genre most likely to open the doors of German theaters. Wagner had not had a premiere since that of *Lohengrin* in 1850. The unfinished *Ring* was locked in his desk, and the enormous difficulties in the orchestral and vocal parts of *Tristan* for the moment precluded its performance. Somehow he had to start a flow of new royalties: Hans Sachs was needed to open the sluice.

The language of *Tristan und Isolde,* with its extravagant, often grotesque, alliterations, repetitions, and forced rhyme, is so overwrought and at times so private that phrases frequently yield more mood and effect than sense. Indeed, without the help of the poem's prose draft many turns of the plot would remain incomprehensible. In its own way no less heavily mannered—though it often descends to doggerel—the poem of *Die Meistersinger von Nürnberg* is at the same time buoyed up by the charming and quaint folk vocabulary coloring many of its pages, terminology Wagner borrowed from Johann Christoph Wagenseil's famous study of the Meistersinger and their customs. In its attempt to succeed as a well-made play, *Meistersinger* does not carry the day as felicitously as the earlier *Liebesverbot,* the device of the exchanged clothes and identities in the second act, for example, completely missing the mark. With such details Wagner was utterly helpless. In any case, *Meistersinger* emerged as a traditional historic grand opera and announced Wagner's return to this Parisian genre, to the line of *Rienzi* and the middle acts of *Tannhäuser* and *Lohengrin.* Fittingly, he wrote and completed the poem in the French capital (December 1861–January 1862). Retreating from the scenic complexities, the transformations and magic, of the *Ring*—even if finished, it appeared doomed to remain a silent score—he had come back to a more practical, yet no less impressive, kind of theater. Moreover, his mood had changed: he no longer identified himself with Tristan's longing for self-dissolution; though relinquishing his beloved Eva, Hans Sachs remains very much of the world. In its earliest stages of creation, *Meistersinger* seemed to pour from the composer, who found himself writing down the music as he simultaneously framed the libretto. Such had not been the case since the pastoral drama of his youth. He was to finish this masterly score years later and under extraordinary patronage.

V

In 1864 the young king of Bavaria, Ludwig II, summoned Wagner to Munich, there to live under royal protection and, free from material care, to devote himself to completing the *Ring.* Ludwig determined to give his capital a monumental theater in which model performances of Wagner's works might be given, and the composer began to organize his thoughts about a complementary conservatory in which to train singers, instrumentalists, and conductors in his style. The result was his "Bericht an Seine Majestät der König Ludwig II von Bayern über eine in München zu errichtende deutsche Musikschule" ("Report to His Majesty Ludwig II, King of Bavaria, Concerning a German Music School To Be Erected in Munich," March 1865), the kind of work in which Wagner showed himself at his best: his discussion of the state of music education in Germany reveals the astute professional who had built his career on the podiums of the nation's provincial theaters; for whole stretches his writing is incisive, businesslike, and without the more usual flow of nonsense on racial, social, and political matters. In much the same spirit he had, a year and a half before, written *Das Wiener Hof-Operntheater* (*The Vienna Opera House*), a pamphlet urging that the great theater rising on the newly created *Ringstrasse* adopt the organizational procedures of the Paris Opéra, whose methods he so admired. For a while he had imagined that Vienna would be his final home, the scene of his crowning endeavors.

In Munich Wagner's major error was to assume that his operatic projects would become one with Bavaria's governmental policies and that the concept of artistic and political rejuvenation through his music dramas would spread from this new center to all of greater Germany. He was perhaps surprised by the long memory of the Bavarian court, which looked on him with deep suspicion because of his involvement in the Dresden insurrection. To allay this animosity, Ludwig asked him soon after his arrival to define his political thinking of the moment. From this request had grown the essay "Über Staat und Religion" ("On State and Religion") of July 1864. It maintained that he had "never descended to the province of politics proper." Limited creatures like police officials—those who judge only from outward appearances—had accused him of being a revolutionary; a sensitive statesman like Ludwig, Wagner declared, could never make such a mistake. This defense was completely mendacious: he had been over his head in political intrigue. But in truth Wagner was no longer the firebrand of Dresden. The revolutionary, having experienced a period of resignation and apathy nourished by Schopenhauer, had returned to honor the authoritarianism and monarchism so dear to him since youth. "On State and Religion" celebrated the king as a kind of superman. The *Ring*, born of the revolutionary spirit, now tortured its creator with seemingly insoluble problems of adjustment and revision: during his Munich days he had no clear idea of how to end it, much less how to explain it.

During the autumn of 1865, for the king's instruction, Wagner had begun a political journal. (It appeared later in revised form under the title "Was ist deutsche?" ["What is German?"].) Here he scorned the revolutionary disturbances of the late 1840's as "un-German," the very concept of democracy, in fact, being un-German, "a completely translated thing," a French concept foisted on the nation by its Jewish press. He condemned not only the Jews—"the completely alien element" corrupting the German Spirit—but also the Prussians: "The German . . . sees himself . . . squeezed between Junker and Jew." Redemption for Germany, that is, salvation from contaminating Franco/Judaic/Hohenzollern influences, could come only from that prince who had made the Wagnerian music drama the very center of his thought and endeavor. Such observations lay bare how few ideas really make up Wagnerian "thought": his so-called metaphysics and politics, hailed as revelation by his disciples, boil down to a few preposterous ideas, repeated, expanded, and only slightly varied through the decades.

The brilliant premiere of *Tristan und Isolde* (*Tristan and Isolde;* Munich, 10 June 1865) demonstrated that Wagner's presumed unsingable and unplayable operas were, indeed, singable and playable. He now appeared unassailably entrenched in Bavaria. But it was not long before his arrogance, as formidable as his musical genius, led him to a fatal blunder: he sent to a local newspaper an article—under the shield of anonymity, so he thought—that painted the monarch as more faithful to Wagnerian interests than to those advocated by his cabinet. Wagner had done the unthinkable in terms of etiquette by exploiting his friendship with the king in print. Court and public were coming to look on him as a danger to the state. A royal request bade him leave the kingdom, and on 10 December 1865 he once again departed for exile in Switzerland.

VI

Whatever his disappointment in respect to Wagner's character and judgment, Ludwig persisted in his idealism concerning Wagnerian opera. He continued his lavish support of the composer, who settled on a splendid estate near Lucerne and returned to the score of *Meistersinger.* Coincident with work on its final act, he began (September 1867) a long essay, "Deutsche Kunst und deutsche Politik" ("German Art and German Politics"). He had resumed his self-imposed role of mentor to the nation.

The passing months, the preoccupation of the press with the conflict between Austria and Prussia (in which, to its cost, Bavaria took the Hapsburgs' part), and Wagner's residence in Switzerland had helped cool Munich's hostility toward him. Ludwig could now anticipate visits from his friend, whom he expected personally to supervise the premiere of *Meistersinger* at the Royal Theater. Tensions had relaxed to such a point that Wagner found himself encouraged to dispatch to Munich on a regular basis contributions to the *Süddeutsche Presse,* a new government newspaper sustained by both treasury funds and the king's personal benefactions. Wagner was expected to concern himself only with material appropriate to the section on the arts. The very title of his first contribution, "German Art and German Politics," should have put the editor, the famous Julius Fröbel, on guard; he must have known that Wagner saw the two as one.

"German Art and German Politics" (which was to appear in fifteen installments) is essentially an expansion of Hans Sachs's final address to the German Folk in the third act of *Meistersinger,* a famous tirade disparaging French, and extolling German, art. The series, which, alas, lacks the antidote of the tirade's magnificent music, appeared anonymously; but as usual the idiosyncratic style betrayed the author from the first. Unashamedly, he served up his usual terrine of clichés, hardly bothering even to freshen them. Once again he expected the public to digest such stale nuggets as the degeneracy of the French, the shallowness of their art, the contrasting vigor of the German Folk destined through the instrumentality of the *Gesamtkunstwerk* to civilize the globe, and so forth. Most shocking to contemporary readers was Wagner's panegyric (in the ninth installment) on the young assasin who in 1819 had struck down the celebrated Weimar-born playwright, August von Kotzebue, distinguished for having brought a particularly Parisian flair and facility to his dramas. Germans sympathetic to things French were, according to Wagner, seducers of German youth, betrayers of the German Folk; the only truly German response to those like Kotzebue—Wagner implied—was the dagger.

The astounding inappropriateness of such material to an official Bavarian publication makes one wonder why the government permitted the articles to continue beyond the first few. Perhaps Ludwig held back from one issue to the next in the hope that Wagner's arguments might take a happier turn. But by the thirteenth installment both palace and cabinet realized that matters had reached an intolerable pitch, Wagner's anti-French and anti-Prussian bias threatening to disturb Bavarian foreign policy. A sudden royal order required whatever remained of the type to be broken up: "German Art and German Politics" vanished from the pages of the *Süddeutsche Presse.* A period of estrangement between Wagner and Ludwig ensued. It ended when the triumphant premiere of *Meistersinger* (Munich, 21 June 1868) rekindled their dedication to what originally had been the main and mutual goal of their friendship: the completion of the *Ring.*

Since those parts of the cycle already in score still remained unperformed, few realized that, though *Rhinegold* and the first two acts of *Valkyrie* to a limited extent followed the spirit of the Swiss essays, its concluding act revealed a thickening orchestral fabric betokening a dramatic change in Wagner's apprehension of the relation between the word and its accompanying music. Yet, if the Nibelung scores remained a sealed book to Wagnerites, many of those who had heard *Tristan and Isolde* must have recognized it as violating almost every prescription of *Opera and Drama:* the composer, it appeared, had drawn the pen through the Wagnerian commandments. How could he maintain his pretense that the word remained the regulating and dominating element in his works? *Tristan* showed itself not an opera or music drama (the term Wagner preferred) but a symphonic poem with auxiliary vocal parts. In measure after measure sweeping musical tides washed the libretto, drenching the knotty text in orchestral sound, reducing it to an overall incomprehensibility from which there fitfully emerged those repeated words and phrases Italian librettists call *parole sceniche.* Moreover, the lovers, ignoring the injunction of *Opera and Drama* to sing alternately, joined their voices at the climax of their great duet.

In *Meistersinger* Wagner departed even further from his own orthodoxy; in fact, he now threw all of it to the winds: putting aside his declaration that myth alone provided themes worthy of the German stage, he here offered a historical grand opera in the manner of Meyerbeer. The closed Italian forms he had once denounced in Switzerland reappeared: arias, marches, ensembles (including a quintet), elaborate massed choruses, a ballet, and a rousing crescendo finale. Only initiates knew that in the opening act of *Siegfried* Wagner had provided the hero with two swaggering arias. Yet even at this point Wagner, ever wishing to present himself as primarily the poet, refused publicly to deny the validity of his Swiss pronouncements; almost to the end of his life he attempted, through reinterpretation, to harness them anew, to bring them into harmony with a view utterly denying their very basis: as early as 1857 in his open letter to Princess Marie Wittgenstein (published as "Über Franz Liszts symphonische Dichtungen" ["On Franz Liszt's Symphonic Poems"]), he had accepted Schopenhauer's estimate of music as the highest art.

During the years following the completion of *Tristan and Isolde,* Wagner had begun the attempt to resolve this aesthetic predicament. A sheaf of essays bears witness to his continuing struggle to force his mind along paths essentially alien to his temperament—he rarely found himself at home in the realm of abstract thought—and to persuade his followers (and himself) that his principles and his practice could yet be reconciled, that his open endorsement of music's superiority over the other arts did not contradict his Swiss pronouncements concerning reciprocal relationships within the *Gesamtkunstwerk,* that the author of *Opera and Drama* could lie at Schopenhauer's side in peace.

He found himself turning back to attitudes enunciated in his pre-Swiss writings. Two of his articles for the *Gazette musicale* ("Über deutsches Musikwesen" ["On German Music"], 1840; and "'La Reine de Chypre' von Halévy" ["Halévy and the Queen of Cyprus"], 1842) had extolled music as the superior component in opera. His "Zukunftsmusik" ("Music of the Future"), written in September 1860, acknowledged music as the more powerful agent in its union with poetic drama, the latter now being described as playing a mediating role between Schopenhauer's metaphysical, ideal world of music and the conceptual, material world of the listener: the libretto was the "plastic expression" meant to clarify music's abstract language of feeling, while poetry had as its ultimate goal the longing "to ascend" to music. Nevertheless, poetry, for its part, did provide an essential lack in music: the capacity to reply to the question, "Why?" Only when poetic drama joined music and related it to phenomena could this disturbing but indispensable question be answered. Yet, ironically, these arts, when united, had the power to transport auditors into an ecstatic state in which no inquiries were made and all answers given—a superb evocation of the intoxicating effect of the *Tristan* score. The poet was to be measured by what he left unsaid; the musician, echoing the poet's silence, was to speak the unutterable.

Ingenious as this mystification was, it did not disguise the fact that things had indeed changed: no longer, as in *Opera and Drama,* did Wagner describe music as a parallel and derivative expression of the words. Though he persuaded himself that "Music of the Future" pictured a *Gesamtkunst* structure in which the planes of music and dramatic poetry mutually penetrated and supported one another, the essay really described a fabric held aloft mainly by the musician.

With his return to grand opera and the creation of *Meistersinger,* Wagner made even more determined efforts to deck out his works with an elaborate theoretical apparatus, to bestow Germanic philosophic status on a genre that was, in reality, a somewhat sybaritic product of the Parisian boulevards. The imposing final act of *Meistersinger* is permeated with the concept of life and art as mutually reflecting dream mirrors. "On State and Religion" of 1864 had touched upon the concept of the theater as a series of ideal dream images *(Wahngebilde).* The idea owed much to Schopenhauer's *Parerga and Paralipomena.* Using it as his point of departure, Wagner began mythologizing his music dramas as emanations of the Metaphysical Will, which, he indicated, informed his genius through the allegory of dreams and visions (or apparitions), music paralleling the former, drama the later. By the time of his essay *Beethoven* (1870), he was postulating the additional concept of telepathic aural expressions paralleling the ocular, all of these experiences occurring simultaneously in the case of his brain, which thus received nothing less than composite communications from the Metaphysical Will. He had traveled light-years from the phenomenal correlatives of the Swiss essays by means of this highly idiosyncratic adaptation of Schopenhauerean theory.

The improved literary style, ingenious dialectic, and poetic insights of Wagner's *Beethoven* owe not a small debt to his discussions with a new young friend, Friedrich Nietzsche, who was at this very time writing his first large-scale work, *The Birth of Tragedy from the Spirit of Music.* Though still a devoted

Wagnerite and no doubt flattered to catch echoes of his own voice in Wagner's essay, Nietzsche was not slow to recognize that, despite great adroitness, it represented a hopeless attempt to reconcile the irreconcilable: Wagner continued to build a theory of opera on Schopenhauerean principles—principles that really denied the genre.

In *Beethoven*, however, Wagner discarded nearly all pretense concerning *Opera and Drama. Beethoven* hailed music as the towering component in the *Gesamtkunstwerk—*drama (with its stage action) being music's visible but subordinate complement, verse the element of least significance. At most, Wagner now maintained, poetry evoked the mood that evoked the music—the last really a plaintive plea that the reader recognize at least some thread of continuity in Wagnerian theory.

Über die Bestimmung der Oper (The Destiny of Opera), an address Wagner delivered to the Berlin Academy in 1871, continued the course set in *Beethoven*, the *Gesamtkunstwerk* here emerging as essentially a synthesis of music—the principal element—and mimetic action. Since the margin of improvisation open to actors of the spoken word shrank on the operatic stage because of the musical score's restricting demands, Wagner saw the composer's role as that of a ventriloquist speaking through the singers and the orchestra and thereby bestowing on the whole the necessary spirit of the extempore. Though in his article "Über die Benennung 'Musikdrama'" ("The Name 'Music Drama'") of 1872, he continued to exalt the transfiguring role of music in the *Gesamtkunstwerk—*here he spoke of music's "ancient dignity as the very womb of drama"—Wagner could never free himself of the ambivalence that had prompted him in the preface to *The Destiny of Opera* to declare it to be in complete agreement with *Opera and Drama,* which he had in fact reissued in a new edition in 1868. He continued to insist that though everything was different, nothing had changed.

VII

When the scandal attendant on his love affair with Cosima von Bülow—a daughter of Franz Liszt and the wife of Wagner's disciple Hans von Bülow—reawakened the old antagonisms in Munich, Wagner recognized that the premiere of the completed *Ring* could never be realized there. Abandoning his ties to Bavaria and King Ludwig, he turned for patronage to Prussia and the house of Hohenzollern, a move to the side of power: Prussia's minister-president Bismarck, having prevailed in greater Germany by both arms and diplomacy, had herded the German states he permitted to survive (excepting defeated Austria) into a reborn German empire with Berlin as its capital and with its king as emperor; with the defeat of the army of Napolean III at Sedan (1870), the Prussians had become suzerains of the Second Reich. During this period Wagner began to yearn for a theater of his own in some small German city—he eventually chose the Franconian town of Bayreuth—where he might bring the entire *Ring* to performance. The court at Berlin, so he believed, would help him achieve this end. The Prussians whom, for Ludwig's sake, he had formerly denounced as enemies on a par with the French and the Jews, now received his fulsome praise. By the end of the Franco-Prussian War he had determined to complete the *Ring* as a tribute to Prussia's new and ascendant position in Europe.

Wagner did not grow mellow. Quite early he had admitted to Liszt that hatred of the Jews had become as necessary to his nature "as gall is to the blood," and with the passing years this motif possessed him more and more, tenaciously invading his conversations, letters, and articles. On this subject he was to end not far from mad. In addition, the Franco-Prussian War drew the worst from him, his undying hatred of the French producing the jingoistic poem "An das deutsche Heer vor Paris" ("To the German Army Before Paris," dispatched via Lothar Bucher to Bismarck himself) and the tasteless farce *Eine Kapitulation (A Capitulation)*, which ridiculed the sufferings of the population during the siege of Paris.

Bismarck and the Prussian royal family remained aloof: they looked on Wagner as the adornment of King Ludwig's cultural preserve and did not want to appear to be poaching on Bavarian terrain. Though Wagner had yoked his *Ring* to the Prussian chariot by turning the Bayreuth project into a pan-German venture centered in Berlin—he first called the Bayreuth Theater the "National Theater"—his hopes of luring substantial sums from the Hohenzollern proved illusory. Moreover, the public sale of certificates in the Bayreuth enterprise continued to be embarrassingly light, despite his tours through the Reich during which he conducted concerts and attended endless banquets, fund-raising efforts that drained his strength. He had yet to complete *The Twilight of the Gods;* he struggled to find the time and energy.

His travels did permit him to take stock of singers and personnel in Germany's opera houses in his search for the artists to bring the *Ring* to life on the Bayreuth stage. He recorded his impressions in an article, "Ein Einblick in das heutige deutsche Opernwesen" ("A Glance at the Condition of Contemporary German Opera," 1873). A happy return to the finest period of his prose, Wagner here recapturing the roguish spirit of many of his pieces for the *Gazette musicale* as he discoursed on what he knew best: professional music-making. His witty, biting descriptions spared neither fools nor incompetents, especially in his hilarious accounts of productions of his *Dutchman, Tannhäuser,* and *Lohengrin.* Articles of this type—workaday, light, instructive but eschewing the philosophic—found Wagner at his most readable; one thinks, for example, of his brisk and entertaining "Erinnerungen an Auber" ("Reminiscences of Auber") of 1871. Not only Berlin's reticence in respect to Bayreuth but the Reichstag's bestowal of equality of citizenship on the Jews made him veer from Prussia in outrage and disgust. He turned back to King Ludwig and wooed him again. In the end the king provided the capital needed to turn Bayreuth into a Wagnerian principality: he built and equipped the theater (or *Festspielhaus*) and constructed and furnished a palatial residence for the composer—*Haus Wahnfried.* Wagner took possession of it on 28 April 1874 to begin a reign that ended with his death (13 February 1883), a period during which Wagnerism—in which his prose works played no small part—took institutional shape.

VIII

The first Bayreuth Festival, consisting of the three premiere performances of the complete *Ring,* unfolded during August 1876. By the following autumn Wagner had begun to express the hope that the existence of the *Festspielhaus* would make Bayreuth *the* educational center of German national art: in this unique theater a new generation might be trained to take part in model performances of the masterpieces of the German lyric stage with the focus of attention on his own works from *Dutchman* to *Parsifal.* The latter was already taking form on paper; suffering from a serious heart complaint, Wagner recognized in *Parsifal* his final opera.

The plan for this Bayreuth academy collapsed, but out of his didactic mood came the founding of the official journal of Wagnerism, the *Bayreuther Blätter (Bayreuth Leaves),* originally intended as the Wagnerian academy's literary organ. Its main purpose was to give the aging and increasingly weary master a forum from which to address Wagnerites the world over—Wagner Societies had come into being not only on the Continent but in England and America too—though its pages were open to other writers as well. Initially, Wagner had looked forward to appointing

Nietzsche its editor, but the philosopher's turning into the leading apostate from Wagnerism made him choose instead the wealthy young Prussian and fanatical Wagnerite Hans von Wolzogen. Under his aegis—more correctly, under that of Cosima Wagner, whose instrument he became—the journal's maiden issue appeared early in 1878.

The completion of *Parsifal* became a race with death; Wagner tired easily, and there were periods during which memory refused his summons, a frightening state of affairs for a master accustomed to describe composing in terms of recollection. Amid these frustrations—and thus parallel with his intermittent exertions on the score of *Parsifal*—he ground out a group of articles of a bizarre cast of thought for the *Bayreuther Blätter:* "Religion und Kunst" ("Religion and Art," 1880) and its three supplements entitled "Was nützt diese Erkenntniss?" ("What Avails This Knowledge?" 1880), "Erkenne dich Selbst" ("Know Thyself," 1881), and "Heldentum und Christentum" ("Heroism and Christianity," 1881), the last greatly influenced by Arthur de Gobineau's *Essay on the Inequality of Races.* Since Wagner regarded the journal essentially as a means to apprise subscribers of "the obstacles to a noble development of the German artistic capacity . . . and the efforts necessary to conquer them," it is not surprising that these contributions were liberally laced with anti-Semitism. But it was but one of many—and often related—themes in this series of preposterous rambles that too often revealed the accelerating corruption of his faculties. One encounters such leitmotifs as the ethnologic superiority and innate nobility of the Teutonic Aryans, their godly descent and their destiny as world rulers, the inferiority of all other races, the crossing of races and the decline of racial pride, Germany's racial crisis, the possibility of the nation's racial regeneration—and with it the necessity that the Jews vanish—the Aryan as innate Schopenhauerean, the reestablishment of society and salvation through an Aryan Jesus. Most insis-

tent in their return are irrational denunciations of vivisection and an equally irrational advocacy of vegetarianism, both positions resting on a grotesque perversion of Darwin's *Descent of Man:* it had made Wagner conclude that, since man descended from the beast, man and beast must share the same substance, the salvation of the Cross thus extending to beast as well as to man and to vegetation too—a blessed state of affairs Gurnemanz celebrates in his Good Friday discourse in *Parsifal.* Wagner presented these ideas most completely in "Offenes Schreiben an Herrn Ernst von Weber, Verfasser der Schrift: 'Die Folterkammern der Wissenschaft'" ("An Open Letter to Herr Ernst von Weber, Author of the Book: *The Torture-chambers of Science,*" 1879). In Weber, a former African explorer and diamond miner, Wagner found a fellow crusader against vivisection.

Wagner had in fact built the book of *Parsifal* from these shabby materials. Yet, despite much in it that is morally monstrous, the libretto proved to be Wagner's most ingeniously wrought; though the text suffers from passages of astounding turgidity (the "blood" arias of Amfortas, for example), there are nevertheless many moments of surpassing lyric expressiveness. For its part, the subtle music of *Parsifal* with its superb tone painting betrays nothing of the struggle that accompanied its realization. Nietzsche, who recognized *Parsifal* as "a work of malice, of vindictiveness, of poison secretly brewed to envenom the prerequisites of life, a *bad* work . . . an outrage on morality," also acknowledged the skillfulness of its literary construction and the overwhelming beauty of its music. In many ways Wagner's final opera was his most accomplished. Moreover, it epitomized the ambiguities of the *Gesamtkunstwerk;* to quote Nietzsche's magnificent summing-up: "As musician, Wagner belongs among the painters; as poet, among the musicians; as artist, really among the actors."

Sixteen performances of *Parsifal*—the premiere (26 July 1882) and fifteen repetitions—

made up the second Bayreuth Festival. Some two and a half years earlier, during a search for the health and calm needed to complete the opera, Wagner had vacationed in Naples and there devoted himself to the completion of what would become his most widely read literary work—his autobiography, *My Life,* which he had begun to dictate to Cosima in 1865. It was to appear in a private edition meant exclusively for the eyes of King Ludwig and a few intimates; only in some indefinite future, Wagner calculated, would it be used as the basis of an ''official'' biography.

In *My Life* Wagner concealed and misrepresented incidents in his past. The protégé of the Bavarian king, for example, found it politic to forget his active role in the Dresden revolution, just as the lover of Cosima thought it equally wise to describe the often affectionate years with his first wife, Minna, as utterly hateful, and his turbulent and celebrated affair with Mathilde Wesendonk as of little account. In general, his many post-factum manipulations and suppressions approached the scandalous as he attempted to edit a new Wagner into existence.

From the very start of his labors on the autobiography, Wagner had planned to stop when he reached May 1864, the month the royal summons had brought him to Munich. Immediately beyond this point lay the complications of his relationship with Cosima. The Wagner who first sat down to dictate *My Life* had but recently thrown himself into the unpredictable adventure of having a passionate affair with the person to whom he was dictating—the wife of his closest friend. With good reason the composer desired to defer to the remote future any official description of this period about which he was, at the moment, concocting various and often conflicting informal explanations: for the forseeable future, he realized, a persuasive authorized account lay beyond even his powers of invention. He therefore imposed on Cosima—almost a quarter of a century his junior—the duty of one day completing the story of his life

from the spring of 1864 to the day of his death. Toward this end she began a diary on 1 January 1869, soon after she had once and for all abandoned her husband to join Wagner. Yet she could never face up to the embarrassing gap between the end of *My Life* and the first page of her diary, a period during which she had passed back and forth between the two men. Eventually she left the literary solution to Carl Friedrich Glasenapp whom, after Wagner's death, she chose as his official biographer.

Thus, despite its imposing length, *My Life* is but a torso: it breaks off before the truly great triumphs of Wagner's career. The first three volumes of the private printing appeared between 1870 and 1875, the fourth and final part in 1880, the public edition of the whole reaching the press in 1911. The book varies in style. That Wagner often dictated it after concluding the main business of his day is too frequently reflected in sluggish paragraphs. Still they sometimes give way to sudden spurts of energy as he returns to the animated manner of his days at the *Gazette musicale.* He holds the reader most firmly when exercising that causticity renowned in his conversation. His descriptions, for example, of the premieres of *Liebesverbot,* of the Paris *Tannhäuser,* of Spontini and Karl Ritter as conductors, of the peculiarities of Liszt's personality, are extraordinarily incisive and witty too. Not surprisingly, part 4 finds Wagner at low ebb: it details his least interesting years (1861–1865), and there was little humor left in him by 1880.

Though the letters of Richard Wagner remain outside the compass of this essay, it should at least touch on them. This vast trove—approximately five thousand specimens survive—offers not only a broader and more complete picture of him and his artistic development than does *My Life,* but also a more accurate and spontaneous view. The letters show him marvelously varied: comradely and warm toward his boyhood chum Theodor Apel; moving and often full of love for his wife Minna; political and violent in mood and diction in his outbursts to his Dresden friend Theodor Uhlig; pretentious and schoolmasterish toward Mathilde Wesendonk; highly mannered—a nineteenth-century late baroque style unto itself—in dispatches to Ludwig of Bavaria; down-to-earth, a kind of prose he easily recaptured when writing to members of his family; Jovian, in communications to those concerned with the business of the Bayreuth Festival. An element in common binds these diverse approaches: through most of his letters run, like threads of scarlet, passages of romantic exaltation and lamentation, arias of love, woe, and hate in which he quits the world of the cogitative to wander in the realm of the impulsive and compulsive. Here is the intrinsic Wagner.

He arrayed instinct against reason[3]: to be a successful Wagnerite one had to deny the intellect—an injunction Nietzsche, for one, found unendurable. Wagner's magnification of instinct led him to the doctrine of the unerring impulses of the German Folk and into the dark waters of the collective right and freedom, in which individualism and dissimilitude are subdued in a mass destiny—only a short distance from the perilous concept of an infallible leader as symbolic extension of the Folk's wisdom. In some marvelous and poetic way Wagner saw himself—in his words, "the most German of Germans"—filling this role. Nevertheless, he shied from detailing the means by which his countrymen might achieve what he called the "great solution," a course of conduct in which, having "overcome

all false shame," they would then "not shrink from ultimate knowledge" ("Know Thyself"). In an elaborate afterthought to *Jewry in Music,* published in 1869, he remarked: "Whether the deterioration of our culture can be arrested by a violent ejection of the malefic foreign element I have no capacity to judge, since that would require forces with whose existence I am unacquainted."

As a political and social thinker, Wagner was a major precursor of Adolf Hitler. The Führer revered Wagner's prose works, emulated their turgid style, enthroned him as artistic god of the Third Reich, and acted on many of the ideas in the essays, especially the late ones. Indirectly, Wagner played a devastating role in Europe's political history. From the pages of the *Bayreuther Blätter* grew a cult of militant Wagnerism. Encouraged by Cosima and given a sharper focus by Wagner's son-in-law, Houston Stewart Chamberlain, in his *Foundation of the Nineteenth Century,* this accumulating tradition provided Hitlerism—via Alfred Rosenberg—with many of its most virulent features. The mythology of Wagnerism became the mythology of Nazism; there are few of Wagner's prejudices that did not become part of Nazi culture.

With Hitler's arrival in power, it did appear that Wagner's art might be swallowed by its own hypotheses; many—especially those who read and pondered his prose works—turned from him in horror. Yet his art soars beyond concepts reconcilable with the figure and acts of this wicked and arrogant little man. For his music he could tap deep wells of spirit from which rose streams of compassion, the gigantic framework of his creations enclosing blooms as delicate, intimate, and moving as a Schumann song. Even his most bitter detractors have never been able to dismiss Wagner as he dismissed others. Both Nietzsche and Hanslick extolled his vital musical enchantment, that most precious of his gifts; it works the charm that renders his artistic synthesis—however bogus its theory—valid on its own extravagant terms.

---

[3]In his many essays the great composer rarely discussed technique. An anomaly, "Über die Anwendung der Musik auf das Drama" ("The Application of Music to Drama," 1879), touches on the methods he called into play to unify his operas, Wagner emphasizing the difference between the structural demands of opera and those of the symphony, especially in regard to tonality and motivic manipulation. A more typical Wagnerian quality dominates "Über das Dirigiren" ("On Conducting," 1869–1870)—essentially, a recommendation that in matters of tempo, phrasing, and tone color the opera house become the model for the concert hall, the ultimate end being the stirring impression. In any case, Wagner maintained, only the pure-bred German musician with his inherent spontaneity, certainly not the Jew with his pseudoculture, possessed the gift of finding the proper rendering.

Selected Bibliography

EDITIONS

The first two collections are the "classical" editions of Wagner's prose and poetry and are the ones most often found in European and American libraries.

Sämtliche Schriften und Dichtungen. 12 vols. 5th ed. Leipzig, 1911.

Gesammelte Schriften und Dichtungen in zehn Bänden (Goldene Klassiker-Bibliothek). 10 vols. Berlin, Leipzig, Vienna, and Stuttgart, n.d.

Richard Wagner Briefe. Edited by John N. Burk. Frankfurt, 1953.

TRANSLATIONS

Richard Wagner's Prose Works. Translated by William Ashton Ellis. 8 vols. New York, 1966. This is a photographic reprint of the K. Paul 1892–1899 London edition. Ellis succeeds in making Wagner's prose even more difficult to read in English than in German; moreover, the translation is often treacherously wrong. Still, it is the only rendering of the *Gesammelte Schriften* prose in English.

BIOGRAPHICAL AND CRITICAL STUDIES

Barzun, Jacques. *Darwin, Marx, Wagner.* 2nd rev. ed. Chicago, 1981.

Boucher, Maurice. *The Political Concepts of Richard Wagner.* Translated by Marcel Honoré. New York, 1950.

Donington, Robert. *Wagner's "Ring" and Its Symbols.* New York, 1963.

Gutman, Robert W. *Richard Wagner: The Man, His Mind, and His Music.* New York, 1968. This is the standard one-volume life of Wagner, which forms the basis of much of the material in this essay.

Hanslick, Eduard. *Vienna's Golden Years of Music, 1850–1900.* Translated and edited by Henry Pleasants III. New York, 1950.

Newman, Ernest. *The Life of Richard Wagner.* 4 vols. New York, 1933–1946. The grandest, most monumental life of Wagner in any language. The reader, however, must bear in mind that it was written before the opening in 1950 of the Burrell Collection with its hundreds of items of Wagneriana.

————. *The Wagner Operas.* New York, 1949.

Shaw, George Bernard. *The Perfect Wagnerite.* Chicago and New York, 1904.

Stein, Jack M. *Richard Wagner and the Synthesis of the Arts.* Detroit, 1960.

Stein, Leon. *The Racial Thinking of Richard Wagner.* New York, 1950.

Viereck, Peter. *Metapolitics: The Roots of the Nazi Mind.* New York, 1961.

Zuckerman, Elliott. *The First Hundred Years of Wagner's "Tristan."* New York and London, 1964.

ROBERT W. GUTMAN

ÉMILE ZOLA
(1840–1902)

ÉMILE ZOLA WAS born on 2 April 1840. His birth harks back to the days of Louis-Philippe, king of the French. So what are Zola's titles to the exceptional treatment he is receiving, in and out of France, as a living figure? Obviously, I daresay overwhelmingly, the part he played in the Dreyfus affair is a prime factor. Nowadays, to a surprising number of moderately cultured people, those exotic syllables, Zola, spell courage and decency. The paunchy, myopic man with the beribboned pince-nez, never a shining knight in his physical appearance, has achieved the recognition Anatole France promised him as "a moment of the conscience of mankind." This, be it noted, is a posthumous, indeed comparatively recent, development. No one should suppose, for instance, that the transfer of Zola's remains to the Panthéon (1908), which followed shortly upon the rehabilitation of Captain Alfred Dreyfus, united friends and foes in at least a display of esteem for the dead man's character. Far from it! Contrived as a political gesture by the then premier (none other than Zola's old comrade-in-arms, Georges Clemenceau), the ceremony was marred by vociferous protests from the rightist faction and by an attempt on the life of Dreyfus himself. It is no exaggeration to say that only the trials of World War II rid Zola's name of its former, divisive virulence.

In the United States, too, Zola was a beneficiary of World War II or of events that led to it. For a long time his American fortunes had pursued a wholly predictable course. When Honoré de Balzac ceased to be anathema to self-respecting families, Zola replaced him as the main proponent of Gallic materialism and godlessness—and as purveyor of smut extraordinary. To be sure, he, unlike Balzac, had earned a similar reputation at home: Jules Barbey d'Aurevilly dubbed him "the Michelangelo of the gutter"; François Mauriac vividly recalled how his parents referred to chamber pots as "the zolas." The French, however, proved to be lusty customers of whatever the devil had to offer, whereas the American public, such as it was, labored under a sense of guilt. As late as 1927, Ernest A. Boyd depicted Zola in the garb of the anti-Christ. Then, on the eve of the war, linked, it would seem, to a feeling of revulsion against Adolf Hitler's malevolence, especially against his persecution of Jews, a dramatic change occurred: Hollywood, mirabile dictu, was responsible for it. Woefully inaccurate in its detail, but saved by the grace of Paul Muni's performance, a screen version of Zola's life lifted him bodily from the realm of the damned into that of the heroes of thought. The Dreyfus affair supplied the necessary pathos, and, incidentally, enough "punch lines" were delivered to bruise the sensitivities of the French government, whose censors banned the film for twenty years and then insisted on substantial cuts.

ÉMILE ZOLA

Zola was not born a fighter: he molded himself into one. As a youth he had displayed escapist traits that were indicative of a thoroughly romantic makeup. Later he took his espousal of naturalism to represent a repudiation of those early tendencies. Still later, however, he himself entertained few illusions that, on escaping escapism, he had uprooted his romanticism as well.

The poet in him came from the South, unmistakably. There remained throughout, to Zola's literary stance, a wordy, almost rhetorical touch that bespoke its Mediterranean origins. Until he went to Paris—to stay and to struggle—the accident of his birth in the capital weighed but lightly against the fifteen formative years (1843–1858) that he spent, for the most part, at Aix-en-Provence. Nor do his near-Parisian roots on the maternal side alter the picture significantly. When, at the age of twenty, Émilie Aubert married forty-four-year-old François Zola, a native Dalmatian, half-Italian and half-Greek, she, to all practical purposes, entered the typically southern world of her husband.

A civil engineer of some merit, but prone to embark upon highly speculative ventures, the elder Zola died in 1847, leaving his family in dire financial straits. He was still a citizen of Venice. So was young Émile, according to French law, until he became of age and could apply for naturalization papers. Some day his political enemies would brand him a *métèque* (a foreigner, an interloper)—about the worst insult in their vocabulary.

The next ten years tell a tale of endless court battles fought by François Zola's widow to stem the tide of oncoming ruin and ensure a proper education for her son. When the boy finally entered secondary school, he was late in his studies and inordinately shy. Luck had it, however, that he came under the protective wing of two older schoolmates, the sons of well-established local families, one of whom, Paul Cézanne, was also destined for fame as an artist. For several years, on Sundays and holidays, the three companions roamed the countryside, drinking in the poetry of nature along with that of their favorite poets. Victor Hugo was their first god, soon joined, then eclipsed, by Alfred de Musset. Musset, the nonchalant roué par excellence, was already on his way to the strange destiny that made him a healer of adolescent pangs, adept at dissolving them into wisps of idealized love. Chalk him up, paradoxical though it may seem, as Zola's original master and prompter. Musset it was who "taught me how to weep"—delicious tears, of course, while waiting for bitter ones. Musset it was who peopled the sun-drenched, lavender-scented solitudes of Provence with a number of "love-fairies," all to become one, in due time, as the imaginary dedicatee of the *Contes à Ninon* (Tales for Ninon, 1864).

There is today, with increasing frequency, another, a tragic side to Provençal inspiration. The murderous sun and wind, and the primitive passions they foster, supply the underlying theme of many a novel by Jean Giono, Thyde Monnier, or Henri Bosco. Zola may have shown the way in some passages of *Les Rougon-Macquart* (1871–1893); but, as a general rule, I cannot see that he forged a specific link between the greed of his Provençal creatures and the ruggedness of their habitat. His one novel of the soil has the plenteous Beauce for its locale. The Rougons are small-town products. They, and the Macquarts, too, fall prey to the mistral, Provence's ruling wind, only in the sense that modern conditions make it, spiritually speaking, a germ carrier, laden with the miasmas of political intrigue and urban civilization. All in all, Zola's vision of Provence remained that of an earthly paradise, perhaps lost forever, which he drew from limbo on at least one occasion when he wanted to conjure up a tableau of luxuriant love amidst the complicities of nature. I refer, of course, to that fantastic creation of his—the sheltered, impossibly huge park in *La faute de l'abbé Mouret* (*The Sin of Father Mouret*,

1875), where the hero and his child-mistress play Adam and Eve, and the name of which, aptly enough, happens to be "le Paradou."

In 1858 Madame Zola moved to Paris in search of work and assistance. Émile, for his part, entered the Lycée Saint-Louis; he was a badly confused youth whose scholastic averages fell precipitously. At nineteen, in his kind of situation, there was no recourse except to quit school and look for employment. He found none, or none that mattered, until February 1862, when he became a shipping clerk in the publishing firm of Hachette & Co. A biographical sketch, written at a later date for the benefit of Alphonse Daudet, reads in part: "The years 1860 and 1861, abominable. Not a penny to my name, literally. Whole days without food. . . . Sort of happy, nevertheless. Interminable walks across Paris, especially along the quays, which I adored." Note this last: the siren had sung her song; the poor devil was hopelessly smitten.

It is not easy to measure the impact of Paris on Zola's imagination. Paris, to him personally, became the crucible of every manly experience, intellectual as well as emotional. This accounted for still another romantic relationship, though far less elemental, hence far less elementary, than had been his with Provence. Where dream meets reality, the clash is bound to have complex reverberations. It took Zola a lifetime to sort his feelings in the matter. The late novel that bears Paris' name will restore it to its pristine splendor as the City of Light. Midway through the novelist's career it will stand again and again in the image of the modern metropolis, whose brazen law crushes or degrades human values. Yet on other occasions, the perspective appears to reverse itself: Paris emerges as a victim, perhaps the most pitiable of them all, its soul and body violated by the ruffians of the Second Empire. Just now, to the famished newcomer in his garret, it appears to him as a kind of siren whose cruel whims fill him with alternate moods of despair and anger.

When chance contacts in the house of Hachette finally enabled Zola to break into print, his sparse readers were treated to a battle royal between the "Provençal," or Musset-in-pink, and the "Parisian," or Musset-in-black, brands of emotionalism. The *Contes à Ninon*, his maiden effort, fairly dripped with maudlin sentimentality; and surprisingly, this vein did not dry out for ten more years; *Nouveaux* [New] *contes à Ninon* appeared in 1874. Dark, drab, desolate romanticism, on the other hand, informed *La confession de Claude* (*Claude's Confession*, 1865), Zola's earliest full-length novel. This story of bohemian life, told in the first person, with strong autobiographical overtones, recounts a young man's pathetic attempts at redeeming both the prostitute who had initiated him and himself in the process. But stark though they are, and reminiscent of Musset's *Confession d'un enfant du siècle* (*Confession of a Child of the Century*, 1836), Claude's juvenile effusions end on the hopeful note—possibly an echo from Hugo's *Les misérables* (1862)—that whoever "tears the fabric of the night" may "hasten the slow and majestic rise of the day." Even his imperial majesty's prosecutor general, who frowned at the vividness of some of the scenes, had to concede that the book on the whole did not offend public morality.

Late in 1865, Zola—never a philanderer, by the way—entered into a serious affair with Gabrielle-Alexandrine Meley, whom he was to marry in 1870. Shortly afterward (January 1866) he resigned from his job in order to embark upon a journalistic career. This was a calculated risk. Potentially, at any rate, it meant money—the sinew of independence. It also meant a tribune, an audience, an intoxicating sense of power.

Zola left us an enormous legacy of newspaper and magazine articles. Those he collected (nine volumes in all) represent only a fraction of his output. Any but the briefest comments thereon would cause the present essay to burst at the seams. Let it be clear, however, that if poetry expressed Zola's first nature, journalism became his second. The one tended to abstract him from the world; the other brought him back with a vengeance. Literary chronicler, art critic, political columnist, social reporter, he achieved identification with his times through this journalistic ubiquity. He also discovered the advantages of prepublishing his novels in serialized form and, initially at least, was not above serving up a couple of potboilers (*Le voeu d'une morte* [A Dead Woman's Vow], 1866; *Les mystères de Marseille* [*The Mysteries of Marseilles*], 1867). All in all, nevertheless, he took his responsibilities most seriously. Unlike Gustave Flaubert or the Goncourt brothers, he did not mind "dirtying his hands" in the give-and-take of public controversy: so much so that even his fictional work may be said—not the least bit disparagingly—to be journalistic in essence. By divesting the word of its ephemeral connotations, only to retain what journalism meant to him *as a vehicle,* one arrives at a fair understanding of Zola's mental processes. Half his writings, novels included, ring in some *vérité en marche*—as did, specifically, his last campaign in Clemenceau's newspaper *L'Aurore.* And surely, *J'Accuse* would make a handsome caption for the other half.

It is fitting to remark at this point that Zola, fervent crusader though he was, never evinced an interest in active politics, never carried a "party card," never courted elective office, never spoke on the issues in anyone's name save his own. Even *J'Accuse* (*I Accuse,* 1898), with its stress on the first person, was to be the public utterance of a private citizen. Its author, in other terms, was basically the same man whose *Confession de Claude* had romantically asserted the individual's prerogative to cry out his feelings (*vivre tout haut*); the same man who, at the age of twenty-six (1866), published his first collection of critical essays as *Mes haines*—my hatreds—and another (on the annual art exhibition) under the title *Mon salon*—my salon. As his outlook steadily widened, running the gamut from emotional to aesthetic to social experience, so did his need for self-expression.

There is every reason to suppose that Zola's political sympathies, at the outset of his career, were already oriented to the left. Yet his concept of the creative artist as supreme among individuals threatened to make a shambles of whatever democratic principles he may have had. Next to the conservative pundits, whose fiats and taboos stifled the progress of art, hoi polloi—obtuse, sheeplike, fainthearted—were the target of his contempt: for it was they who recoiled at the boldness of the Goncourt brothers' *Germinie Lacerteux* (1864) or burst out laughing before a Manet canvas. But where do you draw the line between the people as common people and what is called "the public"? Zola—the young Zola—did not quite know and did not care: "Frankly," he averred, "I would sacrifice humanity to the artist." By much the same token, he rebuked the critic Hippolyte Taine himself, who submerged the artist under the mechanical forces that govern the world. As if an invention counted for anything outside the inventor; as if a work of art were not "a corner of nature reflected through the author's temperament!" This oft-quoted formula recurs three times in *Mes haines* and *Mon salon,* then rather startlingly, after a nine-year interval, in a study on Alexandre Dumas *fils.* By that time (1875) Zola was an avowed disciple of Taine and fast becoming a social-minded writer. Paradox, or contradiction? Neither, I venture to say. He was henceforth reasonably satisfied that he could reconcile a fiercely personal stance with the exigencies of humanitarian concern. He likewise saw himself as temperamentally suited to become a surveyor of temperaments.

The word "temperament" plainly belongs to the vocabulary of psychophysiology. It has always been reminiscent of Galen's old theory of humors. In the late eighteenth and early nineteenth centuries the Ideologues used it, or reasonable equivalents, to counteract and dispel the animistic implications of the word "character." When Zola happened on the scene, their influence had been running through two separate channels. The straighter current had carried far enough to produce Taine's massive, monistic-mechanistic philosophy and, of late, to receive Charles Darwin's powerful contribution. On the other hand, the more circuitous romantic route had allowed for a great deal of compromise. Romantic writers were not hardcore materialists and conceived of a spiritual world over, above, and in conjunction with that of physical necessity. The latter was not ignored, however, and claimed an ever-growing share of their attention. Jules Michelet, whose impact on the young Zola looms uncommonly large, made almost a fetish of physiological causes in his *Tableau de la France* and his disquisitions on *La femme* (*Woman*, 1860) and *L'Amour* (*Love*, 1858). Nor could it be denied that, from Balzac's *Comédie humaine* (*Human Comedy*, 1842 ff.) to the Goncourts' *Germinie Lacerteux*, by way of Flaubert's *Madame Bovary* (1857), the novel crystallized along increasingly "clinical" lines. By 1866 the gap was about to close between harder and softer determinists—and Zola seemed predestined to close it. How and how much he hovered on the threshold of decision may be gathered from the following pronouncement—wherein, incidentally, he stumbled on a future title of his: "What we do nowadays is take a *bête humaine* [human animal] and study him *within the margin of freedom* left him by his environment" (italics mine).

The protagonists of Zola's next two novels—*Thérèse Raquin* (1867) and *Madeleine Férat* (1868)—are indeed human brutes, swayed by the "fatalities" of their nerves, blood, and flesh. It matters little that Thérèse and Laurent end as criminals, whereas Madeleine and Guillaume certainly do not. Both stories are "autopsies" in Zola's words, "case studies" in our own—one verging on the exceptional and the other falling squarely into it.

Case number one arises from a trite enough "triangle" situation. Thérèse's pitifully inadequate husband seals his doom when he brings his friend, Laurent, into the family circle. In the course of a boat ride wife and lover drown him and camouflage the deed as an accident. A kind of visceral revulsion (about the only "remorse" soulless creatures can feel) grips them when the body is recovered from the Seine and they are called upon to identify it. The corpse keeps intruding, in a quasi-physical way, upon the murderers' days and nights—until, finally, they commit suicide under the very eyes of the victim's paralyzed mother, who has known their secret for some time and gloats mutely over their demise.

Case number two purported to illustrate the "law" enunciated in Michelet's *L'Amour*, to the effect that he who impregnates or even merely possesses a virgin remains her "spouse" for all time. Nothing whatever may erase the original imprint: so much so that children by a second husband are likely to resemble the first. Faithful to the script, Zola drags Madeleine through the whole harrowing experience, and makes doubly sure of the result by having her conceive in the room she once shared with her lover. The macabre denouement, as improbable as the episodes that led to it, brings death to the child, suicide to Madeleine, and insanity to the father.

There is some unfairness in pooling together the awkwardly contrived machine that is *Madeleine Férat* and a near-masterpiece such as *Thérèse Raquin*. Ideologically, however, they belong to the same transitional period and conceal a residue of caution beneath their outward boldness. True enough, the "margin of freedom" enjoyed by Zola's characters had shrunk to practically nil. True again, he now (for the first time) called himself a "naturalist writer" and flaunted, as an epigraph to the second printing of *Thérèse Raquin*, Taine's famous dictum "Vice and virtue are products, like vitriol and sugar." Yet it is symptomatic that even then he paid little heed to the *race*, or heredity, ingredient that surely, to a simon-pure physiologist, must be paramount in controlling the chemistry of temperaments. Neither story enlightens us very much as to the antecedents of the dramatis personae. Where they are concerned the word "product" does not point to a definite hereditary legacy. Slaves they are, but to the primordial instincts that rule the animal kingdom at large, and then to *moment* and *milieu* in the narrowest sense—namely, to the circumstances of time and place that throw them together.

Not until the winter months of 1868–1869 was the last piece of the puzzle allowed to fall into position. The hard-driving novelist spent part of that time poring over medical books, among them *Traité philosophique et physiologique de l'hérédité naturelle* (Philosophical and Physiological Treatise on Natural Heredity, 1847–1850) by Dr. Prosper Lucas. Its author assumed an air of authority—mostly unwarranted—that may or may not have deceived Zola into endorsing his thoroughly deterministic conclusions. That he appropriated those is, of course, a matter of record; but he permitted himself an aside or two that leave some doubt as to the depth of his conviction. One needs a hypothesis, Zola reflected, "whether or not it is accepted as indisputably true." Or again: "Let me take a philosophical prop, for the sake . . . of connecting my books with one another. Materialism may be the best bet, for it believes in forces that will require no explaining." Quite refreshing, this dash of humor (one hopes it *is* humor), as Zola braces himself for the grim, twenty-five-year exertion that will produce *Les Rougon-Macquart.*

Unlike Balzac, who began with hardly any preconceptions at all, then codified his system some twelve years and one hundred works later, Zola, the engineer's son, drew the most elaborate blueprints, only to depart from them, consciously or not, on many occasions. At least the substance of his voluminous preliminary notes may readily be found in modern editions and monographs; but whoever is unable to wade through them will find a substitute of sorts in *Le docteur Pascal* (*Doctor Pascal*, 1893), the last novel in the series, part of which comprises a recapitulation and interpretation of what has gone on before. The author achieved this perilously didactic purpose by creating one member of the Rougon tribe with whom he could identify. At his death in 1873 Dr. Pascal Rougon is supposed to have left behind him an impressive "natural and social history of his family under the Second Empire"—in other terms, right down to its subtitle, a dummy replica of *Les Rougon-Macquart.* Poetic license is involved here, whereby the good doctor, revived in print twenty years after his official demise, surveys his creator's progress over the intervening decades and, more significantly still, endorses the conscientious qualms and modified viewpoints that such a long travail necessarily entailed.

For the benefit of his niece and pupil, Clotilde, Pascal displays his pride and joy—the family tree that Zola had drawn at a very early stage, no later than 1869 or 1870, then made public, in quasi-final form, as an appendix to *Une page d'amour* (*A Love Affair*, 1878). Rooted in Plassans (that is, Aix-en-Provence), the "stump" is represented by Adélaïde Rougon née Fouque, still alive in 1872 at the age of one hundred and four, but neurotic from birth and definitely insane since 1851. She had borne three children: one, Pierre, by her husband, a hard-working gardener; two, Ursule and Antoine, by her lover, a disreputable smuggler named Macquart. The three branches had proliferated, even becoming knotted through the marriage of François Mouret, Ursule's son, to Marthe Rougon, Pierre's daughter. By 1872 Adélaïde's descendants number about thirty. All exemplify in varying degrees "the laws of nerve and blood irregularities that as the result of a primal organic lesion break out among members of a family."

An obedient disciple of Prosper Lucas, Pascal has adopted his nomenclature of hereditary components and done "as scientific a job as possible" of apportioning them in each and every case. Yet he expresses reservations that were Zola's in 1893 but may not have been his at the outset. Who can ever hope not to miss an important collateral contribution? Most of all, how much credit should be given an infant discipline that, temporarily at least, straddles the frontier between poetry and science proper?

> Poets walk as pioneers, in the vanguard; oftentimes they discover virgin territory and point to forthcoming answers. *There* lies a margin all their own—that which separates the truth already conquered, already definitive, from the unknown whence will be extracted the truth of tomorrow. . . . What an immense fresco stands to be painted, what a colossal human comedy or tragedy awaits its writer, in the form of heredity—the very genesis, you might say, of families, societies, and the entire world!

Granted, by now, that heredity provides the theme for all human manifestations, natural and instinctive, the products of which we call virtues and vices. But understood, too, that milieu and moment play the variations. Milieu and moment rise henceforth to their full stature as a spatial and temporal climate—a living stage of Darwinian proportions, made to order for the strong, treacherous to the weak: all the more so, in modern times, as it keeps shifting at an accelerated pace. The Rougon-Macquart story, Pascal muses,

> epitomizes that of the Second Empire from Louis-Napoleon's coup d'etat to the Sedan defeat. . . . Our folk issued from the people; they spread all over contemporary society; they invaded all fields, carried, as it were, on the tidal wave of present-day cravings.

Ambivalent feelings—again the later Zola's feelings—pervade this verdict. Still very much to the fore, in 1893, is his detestation of an era when materialistic principles (not bad in themselves: how could they be, to a materialist?) became perverted at the hands of schemers, speculators, and social climbers. Yet he has the doctor contending that civilization is better than the sum of its parts—that the life current, even as it crosses a wasteland of dregs and scoria, retains its inherent majesty and will purge itself in due time.

Such buoyant hopes may have had their germ in Zola's attitude toward the Franco-Prussian War. Exempt from conscription as a widow's son, he spent most of the wartime months in unoccupied southern France. Thus he was spared the permanent scars that closer experience inflicted upon some of his future disciples (Guy de Maupassant, Joris-Karl Huysmans, and others), causing them to wallow in stark pessimism and think of themselves as a "lost generation." What is more, the swift collapse of the regime presented him with a providential finis to his contemplated saga. Until then, the fortunes of the Rougon-Macquarts stood open-ended, so to speak, and no Tarpeian rock could clearly be seen near the Capitol. As Fate took a hand, Zola shed a tear for the innocent but welcomed the punishment visited upon the guilty. Shocking or not, his concept of war—of that particular war—was in the biblical tradition of Joseph de Maistre. At the outbreak of hostilities, a violent article of his had exhorted "fifty thousand French soldiers on the bank of the Rhine" to refuse to fight for the imperial government. With the Sedan capitulation and the subsequent overthrow of that government, he viewed the catastrophe as a purifying process, still unspeakably cruel in its immediate repercussions, yet therapeutic in the long run.

Seven novels span a first period, 1871–1877, through which the author tried his formula upon a long-reluctant public. Both in form and in substance, this subcycle exhibits characteristics that faded toward the end.

Initially at least, the Rougons dominated the scene. They enjoyed, over the Macquarts, the advantage of legitimacy; and with it, a driving spirit, a native shrewdness, that their underprivileged cousins did not possess in equal proportion. *La fortune des Rougon (The*

Fortune of the Rougons, 1871), volume 1 of the series, written before the war, *La conquête de Plassans* (*A Priest in the House,* vol. 4, 1874), and *Son Excellence Eugène Rougon* (*His Excellency,* vol. 6, 1876) show Pierre Rougon's eldest son, Eugène, masterminding his family into a position of commanding local power and himself into the highest of state functions. In this particular group the first novel is easily the best; but no small interest attaches to Zola's recital of the excellency's career, modeled in large part after that of Eugène Rouher, Napoleon III's minister of state for seven years. Its merit lies in the small nuggets of universal truth that Zola managed to extract from his consideration of modern "machine politics" and "government by cronies."

Aristide, Pierre Rougon's second son, takes over in the second volume, *La curée* (*The Kill,* 1872). To him the lower forms of gratification: money, women, luxury. A matter of days after the coup d'etat, he "swoops down" on Paris like a vulture. Under the assumed name Saccard (it would not do to embarrass brother Eugène), he makes, loses, and recoups millions through the wild real-estate speculations that attended Baron Haussmann's program for the beautification of the capital. His second marriage to a woman much younger than himself is a purely financial transaction that leads him to tolerate an affair between her and his grown son, Maxime. The most scabrous episodes of this liaison take place in the hothouse of Saccard's mansion and introduce the reader to an early device of Zola's, symbolistic in essence, that emphasizes the mimetic influence of environment. Maxime and his stepmother literally grow into "flowers of evil," almost indistinguishable from the huge poisonous plants that witness and condone their vicious disport.

Volume 3 in the cycle (1873) interrupted the Rougon parade long enough to bring forward a major Macquart figure. *Savage Paris* is as far as English translators ever went in rendering its title, *Le ventre de Paris.* An early one

passed it off as *The Flower and Market Girls of Paris.* Flower and market girls indeed! Lying and jutting out before us is the city's belly— namely, the central market (*les Halles*), a shining new structure (1854) at the time of the action. Smelly, oily, greasy, meaty, cheesy as you please, its opulence comes off, mimetically once again, on the shopkeepers who thrive in its shadow. This is the kingdom of the Fat, and Lisa Quenu, Antoine Macquart's elder daughter, stands very nearly enthroned as its queen. No Rougon would aspire to her kind of royalty, founded as it is on ungrateful chores and the practice of petit-bourgeois virtues. The Rougons own the law, sometimes make it, and gamble under its cover. Not so the Macquarts. Outsiders they are and misfits they remain for the most part; but the few among them who do not topple from various heights or drift aimlessly may be expected to learn the hard way about the exact price of security and respectability. Take honest Lisa, encamped in her delicatessen store, for a rare illustration of how a "reformed" Macquart is apt to turn into a pillar of society. When brother-in-law Florent, a political subversive, becomes a liability, she betrays him to the police and has him sent back to the penal colony whence he came.

Implicit in Zola's very premises, the theme of the fall followed closely upon that of the rise and began asserting itself with *La faute de l'abbé Mouret* (vol. 5). Mention has been made earlier of the walled Paradou, or Zola's version of a Provençal Garden of Eden, where young abbé Serge Mouret convalesces after an attack of brain fever and is nursed by sixteen-year-old Albine, the park attendant's niece. A love story unfolds, wringing from the author's pen a torrential but final outflow of the same metaphoric "correspondences" that ran through *La curée* and *Le ventre de Paris.* Albine, herself, is a flower of that paradise; from the flowers and from the trees, to whose song of songs her inner ear is attuned, she asks and receives "thunderous" encouragement as she leads Serge along the path of temptation; and when she realizes that she is a woman after all, with a balance of unfulfilled desires that no vegetable, or even unthinking animal, can possibly experience, she still wants to die as a flower among flowers, on a bed of hyacinths and tuberoses whose sweet "symphony" slowly asphyxiates her. But what of Serge's so-called transgression? It is definitely not related to the breaking of his chastity vows: for Zola views priestly celibacy as a monstrous imposition, virginity as an abnormal state, and sexual intercourse—provided it does not elude the procreative ends of nature—as the life-giving sacrament. For a clue to his meaning, one must turn once more to omniscient Dr. Pascal. The following is a portrait of Serge's uncle as he revisits the Paradou's site—long after the garden has been torn down:

> He, Pascal, was a scholar, a clear-sighted man. He did not believe in an idyllic humanity living in a land of milk and honey. He saw, instead, the evils and the taints; he had spread them out, probed, cataloged them for thirty years; and all he needed was his passion for life, his reverence for the energies of life, to throw him into a perpetual joy: whence flowed his love of others, a fraternal emotion, an empathy detectable even under his rough exterior of an anatomist and the factitious impersonality of his studies.

This is Zola describing Zola as he saw himself eighteen years after the publication of *La faute de l'abbé Mouret*. Which strands had led from it to *Germinal* (1885) and *La terre* (*Earth*, 1887), which would lead further to *Les trois villes* (*Three Cities*, 3 vols., 1894–1898) and *Fécondité* (*Fruitfulness*, 1899), were by then becoming apparent. And so was the true "error" of abbé Mouret. The Paradou had vanished like a dream. The Paradou *was* a dream. Serge, henceforth a poor parish priest slowly dying from consumption, had been doomed to fall into the realities of the world-in-exile symbolized by the communities nearby—a world in which grim, obdurate peasants, ploughing the earth and their women alike,

toiled in utter blindness for the harvests of the future.

Thus far established critics had paid scant attention to Zola's novels. *La faute de l'abbé Mouret*, for the first time, drew some lively comment—severe as a rule and most of it denouncing this "outrage" to "the noble spiritualism of Christianity" (Barbey d'Aurevilly). But it remained for *L'Assommoir* (*Drunkard*, vol. 7, 1877) to unleash a literary storm second only to the controversies that *La terre* was to arouse ten years later.

L'Assommoir carries the reader hundreds of physical and spiritual miles from the fairylike Paradou—to a Parisian faubourg ominously called "de la Goutte d'Or" (of the Golden Drop) from what, in olden days, must have been a tavern sign. In due course the scene narrows down to one of the saloons with which the neighborhood is liberally sprinkled. Old man Colombe's establishment stays nameless: we merely know that it is an *assommoir*—a "knock-out bar"—similar to others and the epitome of them all. The feeling of epic simplification becomes reinforced through further pinpointing—this time to the evil heart of the house, the "rot-gut dispenser":

> The attraction of the place was, toward the back, on the other side of an oak railing, in a glass-encased courtyard, the distilling machine working in full view of the patrons—a mess of long-necked alembics, of retorts reaching underground, a hellish kind of brewery in front of which boozing workers stood a-dreaming.

Such procedure evolved from Zola's previous uses of symbolism, but it was not the same procedure. Gone was the former sense of identification and quasi-parity between actors and surroundings. As Zola developed the pattern of failure, the logic of the system compelled him to stress the ascendancy of things. He could not become more of a materialist, but he could—and did—write "of mice and men," sometimes locked in uneven combat against the forces of nature, sometimes ensnared in traps of their own making.

The pernicious powers that issue from l'assommoir radiate and fester like a cancer. They shatter the comparative happiness of the Coupeau household. In the wake of a bad accident, the husband, a roofer by trade, loses his zest for work and takes to drink. The wife, Gervaise, struggles for a while and keeps her laundry shop going, but moral decay is contagious. When Coupeau brings in Lantier, a former lover of hers, by whom she had had three children before marriage; when, under the eyes of Anna (Nana), her legitimate daughter, sordid episodes follow, her will, never too strong, breaks down completely: she in turn becomes an alcoholic and dies at forty-one, "slowly, horribly, exhausted by pain and misery." A most moving creation, this sister of Lisa Macquart's—and as pathetic, as lovable, in her defenselessness as the matron of les Halles was sturdy and coldly aseptic.

A practical lesson (de la morale en action) according to its author, L'Assommoir hovered on the brink of didacticism. That it stayed clear of this pitfall redounds to Zola's eternal credit. However, while its predecessors (La faute de l'abbé Mouret excepted) were framed in the political context of the Second Empire, L'Assommoir broached the much larger social question and testified to the awakening of a man's social conscience. There was abundant justification for Zola's claim that he presented French readers with the first piece of fiction ever devoted to the lower classes, the first that "smelled of the common people," the first that "did not lie." One may well wonder how in heaven some leftist critics found cause to reproach him for slandering the workingman. They missed the clear implication that society at large was responsible, not only for the prosperity of public malefactors such as père Colombe, but for the systematic degradation and subjection of the have-nots.

The proletarian "smell" came forth by means of an unheard-of stylistic device. Not content to record conversations in the vernacular, Zola also reported the thoughts of his characters. Thus, through a very extraordinary blend of direct and indirect discourse, L'Assommoir achieved a consistent atmospheric flavor. It did so at considerable risk, if only because slang forms are notoriously ephemeral. Beginning with the title word itself, which no longer applies in that particular sense, examples of obsolescence have been garnered in an effort to discredit Zola's "philological experiment." The least this writer can say is that, on preparing, in 1937, a French-English glossary of one chapter of L'Assommoir, he found nine-tenths of its vocabulary to be miraculously fresh. Louis-Ferdinand Céline's Voyage au bout de la nuit (Journey to the End of Night, 1932) was five years old at the time and already showing symptoms of linguistic arteriosclerosis.

Purists grumbled, mixing their criticism with ideological objections; but the public recovered from initial shock quickly enough to send the book through thirty-five printings in a few months. Unofficially assisted by Zola himself, William Busnach converted Gervaise's story into a melodrama that ran for three hundred consecutive performances. Dance halls echoed to the rhythms of L'Assommoir-Polka. Decorative plates representing scenes from the novel were sold at popular prices. First-year royalties enabled the author to purchase, in the suburban village of Médan, on the banks of the Seine, the "rabbit hutch" that was to grow into a somewhat pretentious country house, a famous literary rendezvous, and, posthumously, the Émile Zola Foundation for sick children of poor families. Fame, wealth, status symbols—all those bourgeois increments abruptly and paradoxically heralded the golden age of naturalism.

The golden age of naturalism extended from L'Assommoir to La terre, a period of exactly ten years (1877–1887). This means—well, almost—that it was that of Zola, of "Zola tout seul" (Zola alone), as an opponent remarked somewhat later. Whatever following he built never boasted a concerted strategy, let alone a unified doctrine: more about this in a moment. In the last analysis, Zola's continued success stemmed from his own ways with the public (if one excepts some unimpressive forays into the theater) and his consummate skill in throwing the opposition off balance. By far the major part of his strength lay in a bold assessment of what he could accomplish, as a man of letters and would-be indoctrinator, within the frame of bourgeois reference that he felt no need and no urge to subvert. Somewhat different from the Zola of *Mes haines*, the mature Zola chose to trust to the intelligence of the average individual; and alone, it would seem, on the literary scene of his day, he wrote for wide consumption without heaping either flattery or scorn on the heads of his readers. He appointed himself physician extraordinary to a sick society, not its coddler or high executioner. This presupposed, between doctor and client, a bond of confidence and even complicity. The patient must be saved, not only from himself, but from those whose personal or political advantage it was to pronounce him in the best of health; in today's parlance, he must be dissociated from the "establishment." There was no other meaning to Zola's dictum: "The republic will be *naturaliste*—or it will not be."

The novelist's popularity reached a new peak in 1880. This, by all odds, should have been his brightest year so far. It was not. As we shall see, private woes descended upon Zola and left him a profoundly disturbed man. Yet most of the intended harvest was in before the lightning struck—quite enough to make him the master of that particular hour.

In 1880 he published *Nana*. As a follow-up to *L'Assommoir* Zola had elected to produce a novel of the "psychological" variety, classically restrained under a romantic title (*Une page d'amour*, vol. 8 of *Les Rougon-Macquart*). This, of course, put into effect the grand design he had evolved to keep the critics guessing. Could it be, after all, that Zola was no unredeemable blackguard? *Nana* rang out the

answer. *Nana* was another "leaf" taken from the book of love—but the starkest imaginable, one that divested sexual desire or intercourse of the last shreds of idealization. *Nana* raised (or lowered) Woman to the status of a mythical force, at work to corrupt and disrupt society "between her snow-white thighs." A blind force, by the way, a mere instrument, wholly unconscious of its evil destination. But the instrument of whom—or what? On the one hand, Nana's story provided the true sequel to *L'Assommoir*: not only in the literal sense that the heroine was Gervaise's and Coupeau's daughter, but insofar as she, like her parents, had been preordained from birth to become chattel for the privileged few. Yet on the other hand, any illustration of that old theme—the devil and the flesh—tends to establish man's lust, even the rich man's lust, as a law of nature; willy-nilly, it restricts to hypocrisy, to stuffy righteousness, the guilt of the upper classes. In short, the deterministic system to which Zola was beholden detracted somewhat from the value of *Nana* as a moral and social document. Such as it was, however, the book evoked from the conservative press all the boos its author confidently expected. Reviewers called him an ignoramus (which he *was*, to a large extent, in the ways of profligacy); they branded him an impotent maniac, haunted by unfulfillable erotic dreams. But the public, also as expected, took to *Nana* like fish to water. Only hours after the volume went on sale, its publisher ordered ten thousand copies added to the first printing. Throughout the years few other works from Zola's pen ever outsold *Nana* in France—and none abroad.

In 1880 *Les soirées de Médan* (Evenings at Médan) was also published. How many remember today that this collection of six short stories about the Franco-Prussian War, written by Zola and the five young habitués who gathered around his table every Thursday evening, provided the initial vehicle for Maupassant's incomparable *Boule-de-suif*? The host, for his part, offered "L'Attaque du moulin"

("The Attack on the Mill")—a contrived narrative, with romantic overtones, that barely overstepped the threshold of honest mediocrity. Nevertheless, the undertaking afforded concrete evidence that, for the time being at least, Zola had mustered the loyalties of quite a few promising neophytes. They responded, if truth must be told, to the robustness of his character far more than to his personal brand of aesthetics. Almost to a man, they eschewed complete identification with his "scientific" tenets; but long after they had gone their separate ways, one of them (Huysmans) was heard to exclaim: "Ah! quels reins [what loins he has], ce Zola!"

And 1880 was the year of *Le roman expérimental* (*The Experimental Novel*). It was yet another "Médanien," Henry Céard, who, in 1879, drew his host's attention to Dr. Claude Bernard's fourteen-year-old *Introduction à l'étude de la médecine expérimentale* (*Introduction to the Study of Experimental Medicine*, 1865). Céard came to rue his initiative, so avidly did Zola take up this little classic and begin appropriating its contents. *Le roman expérimental* stops short of being a plagiarism only because it professes to be one. The author avowed his intention to "entrench himself" behind Claude Bernard and proceeded to liken the play and interplay of his fictional characters to that of chemical compounds in a test tube. Critic after critic has underscored ever since the childishness of such mechanistic postulates as applied to the workings of literary creation. What should be said in defense of an otherwise indefensible theory is that it was good propaganda. Zola, who flattered himself that he knew how to "drive wedges" into people's minds, had deliberately calculated the impact of this heavy blow. It stamped him in the public eye as the "practical sociologist" he wanted to be.

But 1880 was also a year of mourning. Two losses in succession—that of Flaubert, whom he revered, and that of Zola's mother—threw the novelist into a state of depression. It took immense effort on his part to carry on amid signs that he was prone to morbid fears and mental disturbances. A preoccupation with death—with his own death, final, irremediable, since he no longer expected to have children—crept diffusely into his current work, never to ebb, at least in significant degree, until his liaison with Jeanne Rozerot, from 1888 on, rekindled his zest for living and gratified his paternal yearnings. Those intimate adumbrations were to lend unusual color and poignancy to several of his forthcoming novels—not inconsiderably to that entitled *La joie de vivre* (*Zest for Life*, 1884).

Conceived in the waning months of 1880, but gestated over a period of years, *La joie de vivre* did not appear till 1884. It was to have been called "La douleur" (Sadness), and the dramatic reversal of titles was neither stoically nor sardonically intended. Zola's protagonist, Pauline Quenu, does exemplify the joy of living in the very special sense that she is the lay counterpart of a sister of mercy. The daughter of Lisa, the queen of *les Halles*, she has miraculously escaped the curse of heredity or, at any rate, transferred to good deeds, to the renunciation of personal gain, the purposefulness that her mother brought to acquisitive ends. Yet Pauline, by the very nature of her mission, inhabits a vale of sorrows, just as surely as Alfred de Vigny's Eloa, the angel of compassion, inhabited a world of evil. Thus, *La joie de vivre*, unique as such in Zola's production, projects the image of a divided man and author, whose humanitarian resolves identify him with his heroine and whose broodings with the recipients of her charity.

Let no one believe that Zola, unsettled though he was, could remain silent for long. While waiting for *La joie de vivre* to mature, he added installments ten and eleven to the *Rougon-Macquart* series. Octave Mouret, abbé Serge's brother, served as a connecting link between *Pot-bouille* (Steaming Cauldron, 1882) and *Au bonheur des dames* (*Ladies' De-*

light, 1883). Throughout the former this ambivalent character assumes a fair share of the petty intrigues and sordid amorous encounters that take place within the walls of an apartment house; in the latter, he presides regally over the management of a department store and, on making his first million, proposes marriage to the most devoted (and least corruptible) of his saleswomen. Both works are substandard—for a Zola, that is—but show him still playing cat-and-mouse with the pundits. Whereas *Pot-bouille* resembled *Nana* in its savage depiction of bourgeois (this time lower-middle-class) appetites, its successor sounded like a hymn to free capitalistic enterprise. What kind of person was this Monsieur Zola anyway? Hardly had the "troglodytes" given their accolade to the "safe" doctrines embodied in *Au bonheur des dames,* than the irrepressible trouble-monger let go of his towering masterpiece in the form of a quasi-socialistic novel.

Germinal, Zola's epic of the coal mines, is essentially the story of a strike and of its repression at the hands of the army. The action is set in 1864—the year the First International was born; the year, too, when the government of Napoleon III granted French labor the right to strike while denying it the right to organize. This crude formula, an invitation to bloody conflict, endless litigation, or both, prevailed until March 1884, at which time the Third Republic extended de jure recognition to most labor unions.

March 1884—note the date. When Zola drew the first sketches of *Germinal,* shortly after the new year, he may have had it in mind to assert the prerogatives of an "experimental" novelist and press for quick adoption of the new law. As it happened, events robbed him of that privilege. Parliament acted under the sting of a long and bitter strike that broke out on 21 February at the mines of Anzin in northern France. The disturbance, on the other hand, provided Zola with a "live" background, far better suited to his broader pur-

poses than the documentation he had culled on the subject of labor unrest from specialized books. He rushed to Anzin, mingled with the miners, interviewed managers of the struck companies, even insisted on descending into a pit. As a result, the novel throbs with barely suppressed excitement and indignation.

Yet it is not a "socialist" novel, at least not in the modern sense of the word. The title itself, borrowed from the revolutionary calendar of 1792, strongly suggests that its ideological roots plunge all the way back into the eighteenth century. Moreover, no little symbolic significance attaches to the fact that 1885, the year of *Germinal*'s unveiling, also was that of Victor Hugo's death and apotheosis. Had Zola planned to don the old seer's mantle, his timing could not have been better; for *Germinal* was in effect an updated version of *Les misérables*—a reminder that both physically and spiritually people were born and created to breathe the open air, not the foul vapors of subterranean depths. But nowhere does the writer commit himself to the violent therapeutics of either Pierre Proudhon or Karl Marx; nowhere does he uphold the principle of class struggle and advocate a proletarian takeover. There is indeed some evidence that the Paris Commune of 1871 had left a sour taste in his mouth; that his sporadic contacts, through Ivan Turgenev, with Russian political refugees (Peter Kropotkin, Mikhail Bakunin, and Peter Lavrov, after whom he fashioned Souvarine in *Germinal*) increased his abhorrence of radical means; and that his subsequent interview (1886) with Jules Guesde, the French Marxist leader, all but confirmed him in the belief that the "pie-in-the-sky" promises of socialism were pure demagoguery.

As a warning, however, or as a prophecy, *Germinal* purported to be, and was, and remained ever after, Zola's most solemn utterance in the realm of "practical sociology." It presented the ruling classes with, according to him, an inescapable dilemma: either they would atone for their shameless exploitation of the downtrodden, of those they confined to the level of beasts, or they would sign their own death warrants. Piecemeal legislation of the "too little and too late" variety could not possibly prevent the "germination" of a "black and vengeful army" whose explosive potential was more than enough to "blow the earth to bits."

Germinal surpasses *L'Assommoir* in that it is built on a heroic scale. The spotlight no longer falls on a handful of workingmen, but on the toiling, suffering masses presented as an entity; no longer on their ill-spent idle hours, but on a lifetime bereft of idle hours—unless you count as such the moments they devote to procreating, in mechanical abandon, the galley slaves (or avengers?) of the future. The devouring monster who faces them is no longer a mere alembic, a provider of oblivion, ensconced in a neighborhood tavern; it is the consortium known as the *Régie* (governing board), whose decrees, issued in Paris and carried out by local subordinates, resemble those of a remote and implacable deity. By no means does this aggrandizement result in a lack of individual characterization; yet such is Zola's absolute mastery that personal lives appear to be—indeed are meant to be—submerged within the pulsating, swirling, random life of the whole. The mob scenes for which *Germinal* is justly famous serve to emphasize its emblematic quality. So does the invisibility of the *Régie*. So does the gnawing feeling, implanted on page after page, that both camps, however unevenly, are but the tools of a third force, call it fate if you will, tortuously engaged in leading humankind, through blood, sweat, and tears, to an unknown destination.

Germinal has all the features and—so the author hopes—the cleansing power of a Greek tragedy. When the strikers, driven into submission by hunger and rifle fire, show a disposition to resume work, Souvarine, the dreamy nihilist who until then had cloaked himself in contemptuous aloofness, blows up the mine and floods it. An ambivalent gesture—not in his eyes, to be sure, but from the lofty dialectical standpoint that Zola maintained throughout his career: a trauma is a purge; every night brings promise of the dawn.

Insofar as the wretched miners of *Germinal* have a leader, the part falls to Étienne Lantier, youngest of Gervaise Macquart's illegitimate children. He is cast in the not-too-savory role of a self-taught, youthful militant whose immature notions cannot provide inspired guidance and gradually estrange him from his followers. As he departs for Paris in a fit of enraged frustration, we are given broad hints that he will sink to the level of raw politics—perhaps become the prototype of the corrupt labor chieftain. This, in our day, might supply the kernel of a resounding, cynical success story. Not so with Zola. In true Darwinian (and puritanical) style, he dooms his inadequate hero to ultimate failure and oblivion. From the family tree one learns that Étienne will participate in the Paris Commune of 1871, be tried, and languish thereafter as a deportee in faraway New Caledonia.

This, in turn, supplies a clue to the meaning of *L'Oeuvre* (*The Masterpiece* 1886), next to appear in the series. Granted, the externals of *L'Oeuvre* thoroughly differ from those of *Germinal*. It was to be the novel of the art world—a world with which Zola was long since conversant; and it was to lay bare the dilemmas of creativity, many times removed from the so-called social question. Yet in broad philosophical terms the new book again raised the social question par excellence: where should the weary pilgrims of the century go? The change of milieu was not so abrupt as appeared at first sight: art, too, had its "establishment," its oppressive *Régie*, its angry young men, its crusaders and fumbling pioneers, its traitors and agents provocateurs. The moment remained exactly the same: a murky period precariously suspended between past and future, a time for anguish and soul-searching. Moreover, the "race" factor, in *L'Oeuvre*, looms as ominously as ever. Claude Lantier, the main character, is

Étienne's flesh-and-blood brother; and far more disinterested, far more appealing though he is, his career, mutatis mutandis, follows the same downward path.

A painter by vocation, Claude is largely self-made and plagued with a lack of intellectual discipline that causes him to squander his natural gifts. He, too, has a diseased mind: his pursuit of originality turns to frenzy and impotence and warps his sense of values, both human and artistic. He, too, will end in abject failure: not a *raté* (failure) in the mediocre sense—rather a near-genius, who either overshot or undershot the mark and, at the time of his self-inflicted death, leaves "nothing of note, absolutely nothing" behind him.

Was Claude's figure drawn in the pseudo-likeness of Édouard Manet, or Cézanne, or both? Was he set up as a straw man, the better to burn them in effigy? Speculation has been rife on the subject. Quite undeniably, Zola was no longer an ardent admirer and defender of the new school of painting. He still clamored for revolutionary ways of "seeing" and "rendering," still upheld the "regenerators" as regenerators, but questioned, unwisely it now appears, the permanent value of their achievements. In due time he dubbed both Cézanne and Manet "unfulfilled geniuses," with more than a suggestion that Cézanne sinned through exuberance, and Manet through some sort of anemic deficiency. Only to that extent, however, did they (and others, no doubt) pose as models for Claude Lantier. Zola fully exercised the novelist's privilege to extract one composite character from multiple reality. He did not tax his erstwhile friends with pathological tendencies other than those of a century at large—from which he, Zola, considered himself a sufferer just as well. Actually, the more one analyzes Claude's final, abortive "masterpiece"—a nude allegory of Womanhood who rises against a bustling Parisian background, whose haunches and navel are painted a bright vermilion, whose gilded thighs resemble the pillars of an altar, whose genitals flower into a "mystical rose"—the more one is reminded, not of anything that ever came from a contemporary brush, but of the aberrations of decadent symbolism as shown—a little later—in the literary works of fin-de-siècle illuminati.

L'Oeuvre, in fact, is above all else an autobiographical novel—the most intimate Zola ever wrote and as such quite possibly the most moving. Not only does it overflow with memories of his childhood in Provence and struggling years in Paris, but it documents the spiritual crisis that had opened in 1880 and shaken his aplomb almost to the breaking point. As late as 1886 *L'Oeuvre* instituted a manner of Don Quixote–Sancho Panza, or Eusebius–Florestan, dialogue within himself. Ever since *La confession de Claude*, that very name, Claude, sometimes used by Zola as a nom de plume, had held strange associations with the romantic and, in his eyes, erratic side of his nature. By way, it would seem, of exorcising his demons, he sent Claude Lantier to a calamitous death and camped alongside him the far steadier figure of Pierre Sandoz, a professional writer and the lifelike image of Zola the plodder, of Zola the would-be believer in the "no-nonsense" of science and the virtues of patient endeavor. Yet the book closes on a very ambiguous note. Standing over Claude's grave, Sandoz chides himself for "cheating with life" as his friend never did: in other terms, for issuing under false pretenses works that he knows in his heart of hearts are no more authentic and viable than Lantier's own compositions. Were this to be accepted literally, Sandoz's abrupt resolve (*allons travailler!* [let's get to work]) would sound very hollow indeed, and *L'Oeuvre* might be called a bleak admission of failure on the part of Zola the poet and Zola the scientist.

As it happened, the fortunes of both took an unexpected turn. The romantic demons had not been exorcised after all. They returned in full fury and, more surprisingly still, they, not Sandoz's sedate gods, pointed the way to ultimate liberation. Ostensibly *La terre* was to forge another link—the fifteenth—in a long chain of "experiments." Today, however, with the benefit of hindsight, we realize that this controversial work, in fact and in effect, broke the pseudo-scientific spell under which the novelist had been laboring for years.

The sociological intent of *La terre* is indeed obscure. Although one episodic character can be heard advocating agrarian socialism, by no means does he propound the author's views. Farmers, even the more substantial among them, are shown to suffer from a variety of economic ills; but Zola appears to be reasonably satisfied that they themselves bear a measure of responsibility for their plight. Briefly, the peasants, unlike industrial workers, were one of the oldest social classes in existence; they stood within reach of the ancestral dream—ownership of the land; yet having thrown off the shackles of serfdom, they remained slaves to the flinty qualities that had won the struggle for them—their rapaciousness, their guile, their insatiable animal hunger.

One would hesitate to say that Zola felt out of sympathy with the peasantry, but it must be admitted that his saga of the countryside breathed none of the warmth and little of the urgency that not so long before pervaded the pages of *Germinal.* Despite the fact that the novelist went through his usual paces, revisiting his mother's native Beauce for on-the-spot documentation, the suspicion arises that the end product, qua novel, was primarily a rhetorical exercise based upon literary reminiscences. It was meant to relegate to their proper place the bucolic fantasies of George Sand—and in this it succeeded admirably. It also invited comparison with Balzac, whose unfinished fresco, *Les paysans* (The Peasants, 1844), bid fair to count among his greatest: perhaps a good enough reason this direct challenge to an awesome predecessor lacked the imaginative power Zola had brought or would bring to several others. As an observer of the rural scene he contributes little that is intrinsically new and seems content to accentuate

Balzacian traits. From Fourchon to Fouan, from Courtecuisse to Bécu or Lequeu, from Mouche to Mouche (pure coincidence?), family names retain their punlike, sometimes half-obscene quality. Greed and murderous hatred, not to mention uninhibited lust, supply the main motivations, as they had done in *Les paysans*—only more so. Cunning remains the peasant's favorite weapon, but violence, already present in Balzac, is markedly on the increase. Comic relief turns to positive ribaldry. Where Balzac had made a wry jumble of human and animal life on the farm, Zola pointedly juxtaposes the insemination of cows and that of women, or again the birth of a calf and that of a child.

Harsh though it may sound, this estimate of *La terre* does not purport to exonerate its original detractors. The work should have been recognized for what it was, for what the author intuitively felt it to be: "the living poem of the soil"; or, more accurately perhaps, the poem of man's incestuous attachment to the earth; the poem of Cybele as mother and mistress: equally demanding in both roles, yet strangely sparing at times, or at least capricious, in the dispensation of her bounties. It is a poem as removed from the paradisiacal climate of the Paradou garden as reality can be from a midsummer night's dream. The poem of fecundity, yes, but of fecundity through human fecundation. The earth's womb must be penetrated, the seed sown, the fruit reaped; people must sweat and people must die, so that "the bread of life may spring from the land." In this respect at any rate, *La terre* far outdistanced Balzac's conceptions. Out of its manure-scented chapters there issues, willynilly, a paean to civilization: for no matter how close to the brute man is depicted to be, he is also credited with a dim sense of direction and purposefulness. But for him the planet will forever remain a desert or a jungle.

La terre proved to be another popular success—probably for the wrong reasons. It did portend, however, profound changes in Zola's status within the literary world. The first blow, a painful one no doubt, came from the ranks. Editorialized by *Figaro* on 18 August 1887, the famous "Manifeste des Cinq" (Manifesto of the Five) violently upbraided Zola's "betrayal," his "descent into unadulterated filth," and the "Hugoesque inflation" that robbed his characters of any credibility. The five young signatories were not the Médan habitués, of course, but they had been fellow travelers up to that point. They were, to be exact, followers of Daudet and Edmond de Goncourt, who, out of sheer jealousy, either inspired their diatribe or secretly chuckled over it; and it may well be that as a result of their action, the Médaniens themselves felt badly shaken. *La terre* caused to explode not only an accumulation of petty rancors, but also the intellectual differences that separated Zola from even his most loyal retinue. Always tenuous at best, naturalist unity fell to pieces within the space of a few years. Meanwhile conservative critics, ever on the lookout for a chink in Zola's armor, had pounced on their long-awaited opportunity. Less than two weeks after the publication of the "Manifeste des Cinq," Ferdinand Brunetière, official spokesman for the *Revue des deux mondes*, was blazoning the fact that "the master had finally alienated his disciples" and proclaiming *urbi et orbi* "the bankruptcy of naturalism."

It is entirely conceivable that the threatened dispersal of naturalism did not displease Zola altogether. Let his opponents cry havoc as long as the general public stayed solidly and unquestioningly behind him. (It did. Not even the utter chastity of his next book, *Le rêve* [*The Dream*, 1888], almost perverse in its contrast to *La terre*, could disconcert and discourage his readers.) Furthermore, let naturalism disintegrate if it must and if the net result should be a sense of emancipation he, Zola, had come to crave as much as anyone else. The day was approaching when he would assume a sanguine mood and offer himself as a valedictorian for the whole movement. The future, he prophesied to Jules Huret in 1891,

> belongs to the man or men who will plumb the soul of modern society; who, having rid themselves of excessively rigid doctrines, will prove amenable to a more plausible, softer-hearted acceptance of life. I am looking forward to a broader, more complex representation of the truth, to greater openness in our understanding of mankind, to, shall we say, a classical coming of age of naturalism.

Whereupon, the same reporter tells us, his buoyant interlocutor had blurted out: "And mind you, if I live long enough, I'll do them myself—the things *they* want!"

Whence this truculent exercise in benignity? Whence this new upsurge of self-confidence? By the time of the Huret interview, few were those among Zola's acquaintances who did not know or suspect the answer. Madame Zola herself was about to learn that ever since the last months of 1888 her husband had been carrying on an affair with her former seamstress, Jeanne Rozerot, an attractive and reasonably literate woman in her early twenties. Originally, at least, the aging novelist had fallen prey to what he himself described as a "recrudescence of life"—to what his contemporary, Paul Bourget, aptly called "the demon of twelve-noon"; but, as we know, there was nothing in him of the profligate, nor was Jeanne a sordid adventuress. Their attachment became unbreakable when she bore him a daughter and a son. Over and above his pangs of remorse Zola's paternal pride led him to profess a renewed ability to "move mountains." He weathered his wife's anger, which relented only at length and then solely for the sake of the children. Not the least of a number of ironic twists was that being a father—even out of wedlock— gave him an added sense of bourgeois respectability. He now had a stake in the future. Yesterday the ribbon of the Legion of Honor; tomorrow—why not—a seat in the French Academy: and would Monsieur Brunetière be red in the face! Membership in the academy never materialized, but what matters to posterity is that the dialogue between life and death that ran steadily through Zola's novels no longer was allowed to end on a note of despair.

As might be expected, this shift in inspirational values did not occur overnight. It was in fact, to follow a jagged course through the remaining volumes of *Les Rougon-Macquart. Le rêve*, a romantic idyll and perhaps something more: perhaps a spiritual purge in the aftermath of *La terre*, antedates Zola's liaison; yet it coincides with his first "dreams" of amorous rejuvenation and must have assumed, in retrospect, a premonitory character: for, of its several drafts, one took up the ancient theme of the senescent guardian falling helplessly in love with his ward. *La bête humaine (The Human Beast*, 1890), on the other hand, and to a lesser extent *L'Argent* (Money, 1891) testify to the stubbornness of old habits. Only in *La débâcle* (1892) and *Le docteur Pascal* (1893) did Zola's new (or renewed) gospel sound loud and clear.

With the world of railroads as its background, *La bête humaine* bid fair, and indeed purported, to be still another probe into the scope and meaning of material progress. As a devotee of science, Zola could ill afford not to celebrate the wonders of the railroad track and its contribution to "the exchange of ideas, the transformation of nations, the mingling of races, the ultimate unification of the planet." Yet he chose (Was it a choice? Was it not, rather, a kind of compulsion?) to underline the mechanical or mechanizing aspects of technological advance. There is a futuristic coloring to his vision of Jacques Lantier, the engineer, grafted, so to speak, onto his engine, *la Lison*, as one with it in a vertiginous sexual embrace. It is, however, an unequal and darkly symbolic embrace. The life of the machine suffuses that of the man, empties his mind of whatever rational processes may have

been his, restores him to his feral origins. Thus the story evolves into a recital of wanton crime and bloody murder. It goes even further than did *La terre* in stressing the animality of human beings. Whereas the epic of the fields found a layer of civilization deeply embedded within the human beast, that of the railroads exposes the human beast under a thin crust of civilization.

Through the expedient of returning Saccard, the protagonist of *La curée*, to center stage, Zola presumed to open to his readers the sanctum sanctorum of modern capitalism—namely, the stock market. A rash venture on his part, since he knew nothing of its operations, never owned a share in his life, never even possessed a bank account. The true wonder, then, is not that *L'Argent* should fall far short of being a masterpiece, but that it should be as competent a novel as it actually is. Zola's informants did their homework, with the result that, structural weaknesses notwithstanding, *L'Argent* today remains unrivaled as a portrayal of the stock exchange and would need few transpositions to evoke for us not the distant saga of speculation under the Second Empire, but that, closer to our times, of the Staviskys in France or the Insulls in America. Saccard's financial schemes, as well may be imagined, come to a crash in a kind of götterdämmerung atmosphere, with hosts of hapless victims left wailing across the night. Yet surprisingly enough, Zola does not issue a blanket indictment of his hero. Saccard's recklessness is taken to be but a malformation or misuse of the creative urge that makes the world go round. Not a little sophistry attaches to this judgment, whose devious purpose it is to bring out an analogy with love. Money has no odor; money is what money manipulators make it. Likewise—and this is a note not heard in Zola's novels since *La faute de l'abbé Mouret*—none of the filth that is being stirred in the name of love can defile love itself.

Should war, both foreign and civil, be defended, or excused, on roughly the same dialectical grounds? Should we look upon it as an illustration of Darwin's "haughty and heart-rending" law of necessity—then make a text and pretext of that very premise to assert: "War is life itself. . . . None but the warlike nations ever prospered. A nation perishes the minute it disarms"? This was the tenor of a Zola article published in *Figaro* on the twenty-first anniversary of the Sedan capitulation and generally considered to be a blurb for his forthcoming novel, *La débâcle.* A while ago, this article and the novel itself came under heavy criticism from an otherwise very sympathetic commentator, Henri Guillemin, who sees in them a damaging concession to the "establishment" (remember: Zola coveted a seat in the French Academy!) and a white-washing of the retrograde policies followed after Sedan—up to and including the savage repression of the Commune uprising. We shall, in these pages, adopt a kindlier view of Zola's motivations. We made it clear that he had a flair for publicity and was not above making opportunistic moves. We also took note of the fact that while his heart beat to the left, his head tended to lean to the right in vague fear of the "red peril" that somehow the writing of *Germinal* had conjured up before his eyes. It is no less true, however, that he had been toiling for twenty-five years on the fundamental assumption that his appointed task was to cleanse the Augean stables of the Second Empire. For twenty of those twenty-five years he had regarded Sedan as a deed of immanent justice that closed one era and opened another. What he wrote in 1891 he could have written in 1871 just as well—that Sedan was relevant, "not merely in terms of war," but also and chiefly as "the collapse of a dynasty and the tumbling down of an age."

How, then, could Zola, without tearing up the fabric of his work, without repudiating its conclusions, acknowledge publicly—whether or not he acknowledged privately—that nothing was changed and that not even the trauma of Sedan had been able to raise France from the trough of corruption? Short of becoming an out-and-out revolutionary, the author of *Les Rougon-Macquart* was bound to express temporary faith in the Third Republic and long-term confidence in the due process of evolution. Thus *La débâcle* re-intones the litanies so often encountered in earlier novels—only magnified by the euphoria of new-found love and parenthood. Over the Sedan holocaust, over Paris still ablaze in the wake of fratricidal war, an immaculate sky keeps singing "of eternal nature, of eternal humanity," of "the renewal promised to all who hope and who labor."

By no means an impeccably constructed novel, *La débâcle* stands nevertheless as one of Zola's most impressive achievements. It is a work of great scope and power, not unworthy of comparison with Leo Tolstoy's *War and Peace* (1862–1869). Sweepingly majestic in its description of the battlefields, crystal clear in its reconstruction of strategic or tactical maneuvers, masterly in its handling of enormous masses of people, it shows Zola at his narrative and epic best. Yet the emphasis appears to be on individuals, combatants and noncombatants alike. There is merit in the author's later boast that he discarded, once and for all, the trappings, the flourishes, the heroics of the conventional war tale, substituting for them the naked truth: that of the smoke, the noise, the bloodshed, the stench, the pent-up brutality, the visceral fears, the cries of the wounded, the involvement of innocent bystanders—civilians, women, children. This may be the reason, at a time when the Franco-Prussian War (and the Commune) remained very much a topical subject, when veterans were just about reaching the reminiscent age, the success of *La débâcle*—Zola's biggest best-seller—exceeded all expectations. This may also be the reason the army took a dim view of it. One prominent general averred that he was "shocked"; another chided the author for presenting reality "under noxious aspects." No better proof is needed that if perchance Zola tried appeasing the establishment, part at least of the establishment refused the bait—thus setting the stage for the open break that was to be precipitated by the Dreyfus affair.

To all practical or hopefully practical purposes, then, the debacle of the imperial regime signaled that of the Rougon-Macquart tribe, so that the nineteenth book of the series brought it to its logical end. Since, however, in keeping with Zola's philosophy, every end calls for a beginning, the twentieth and last volume would provide that beginning. We have already given proper consideration to the recapitulative aspects of *Le docteur Pascal* and should be content at this time to lay stress on the strong emotional impulse that made it a thinly veiled transposition of Zola's personal love story. Pascal Rougon "weds" his niece Clotilde (without benefit of clergy), and has a child by her. That, unlike Zola, he had been a lifelong bachelor removes from him the "stigma" of adultery; that he is at least ten years older than his creator when he becomes a father accentuates further, not indeed the incongruity of his "marriage," but on the contrary its Ruth-and-Boaz quality, the symbolic beauty, the invincible promise, the sanctity of it. To J. van Salten Kolff, on 22 February 1893, he wrote:

> It was courageous, on concluding this history of the terrible Rougon-Macquart family, to have it give birth to a last child: the unknown child, perhaps the messiah of tomorrow. A mother nursing her child, isn't that continuing the world—and redeeming it?

As it happened, Zola did not wait for the messiah of tomorrow. Almost two full years before finishing *Les Rougon-Macquart*, shortly after the Huret interview of 1891, he set out to "rid himself of excessively rigid doctrines" and achieve "greater openness in [his] understanding of mankind." This was tantamount to instituting himself the messiah of today.

In a sense he had never been anything else.

To show his true colors as a kindred spirit to the Hugos and the Michelets, all he had to do was throw away the paraphernalia of the "experimental novel" and pick up the pilgrim's staff that had lain within reach in a corner of his laboratory. What is more, *Le docteur Pascal* made it clear that this could be done without renouncing one's scientific tenets: it was just a matter of endowing modern technology and modern economics with a spirituality of their own. The conflict between science and religion, between progressive and traditional values, would be resolved through a return to fundamentals. Universal love—not only human brotherhood, but a Saint Francis–like extension of it to every living thing—would eventually lead to universal peace and harmony. In a world whose inexhaustible bounties could be rationally developed and distributed, even the Darwinian concepts upheld in *La débâcle* would lose their dire pertinence.

Zola saw no contradiction between his tolerance of war as a means of surgical purification—when the tree is diseased and the rotten branch must be cut off—and his advocacy of nonviolence in a society pure and mature enough to turn its technical knowledge into an instrument of social justice. He, not unlike Tolstoy, acquired the conviction that by divesting the New Testament of its supernatural envelope, by breaking the Church's monopoly over it, one could extract from its teachings the charter of the future. And, again not unlike Tolstoy, he saw the artist as the apostle of the new faith. As if in anticipation of André Gide's famous axiom that good feelings make for bad literature, he, in the last decade of his life, endeavored to prove exactly the opposite.

Alas, he did not succeed. There are, to be sure, passages of great force and brilliance in Zola's triptych *Les trois villes: Lourdes*, 1894, *Rome*, 1896, *Paris*, 1898; and in the unfinished *Quatre évangiles* (Four Gospels: *Fécondité*, 1899; *Travail*, 1901; *Vérité*, posthumous, 1903; and the fourth "Justice", never written). This enormous production, however, while it bears witness to the author's unflagging stamina, is decidedly anticlimactic from a literary standpoint. It takes uncommon courage to follow abbé Pierre Froment's spiritual journey from Lourdes, the shrine of "naive faith and illusion"—through Rome, the hardheaded metropolis of political Catholicism—to Paris, where he finally resolves to abandon his cassock and become a lay worker in the service of justice and human love. Of the three novels involved, the least unrewarding is probably *Paris*, if only because a certain grandeur attaches to the implicit contrast between the Paris of the Rougon-Macquart era and the new Paris of the coming century, hopefully reinstated to its former role as the capital of Thought.

But then nothing less than heroism is required to withstand the heavy rhetoric, the utopian arbitrariness, the utter unreality of Zola's *Évangiles*. Even their symbolism descends at times to sheer puerility: the "gospels" were to unfold the life story of Pierre Froment's four sons, pointedly christened Mathieu, Luc, Marc, and Jean after the four evangelists; the patronymic itself, Froment (*wheat* in French), becomes an obvious emblem of fertility; Mathieu's wife, Marianne, borrows her given name from the woman in the Phrygian cap who traditionally personifies the French republic; and that happy couple gives birth to twelve children who in turn present them, on their diamond wedding anniversary, with 134 grandchildren and great-grandchildren. Were it not for lack of space, we might be tempted to probe more deeply into the whys and wherefores of Zola's messianic intemperance; we might even reach some instructive and not altogether damning conclusions; yet, one of them would have to be that if *La débâcle* came reasonably close to emulating Tolstoy's *War and Peace*, none of Zola's subsequent works even remotely offers itself as a counterpart to Tolstoy's *Resurrection* (1899).

If we are to believe Daudet—but *is* Daudet believable?—Zola's irruption into the Dreyfus case was primarily due to his fondness for the limelight. This would be presupposing that he himself was aware of a decline in his creative powers and anxious to divert his energies into other than literary channels. The inference would also be that, for the first time in years, he grievously misjudged public reaction. As a result of his gesture, his popularity faded overnight, never to return in full panoply until long after his death.

Reasons for this are not far to seek. For many months after Captain Dreyfus was found guilty of treasonable acts (22 December 1894) and deported to Devil's Island, few if any outside his family challenged the verdict. Still stung by its defeats, the nation at large was riding a wave of jingoism that made the army—or its decisions—virtually untouchable. Then, Dreyfus was a Jew. The image of the Jews as an alien element, bent on capturing all control and subverting all traditional values—was being kept successfully in the forefront of public consciousness by the likes of Édouard Drument, the venomous author of *La France juive* (Jewish France, 1886), whose newspaper, *La libre parole* (The Free Word), had been founded for the express purpose of spreading the anti-Semitic creed. So it is that when Zola, long before becoming interested in the Dreyfus case per se, rose in defense of the Jews (*Pour les Juifs* [For the Jews], *Figaro*, 16 May 1896), he was already contradicting the prevalent mood and aligning himself with the fractious, "intellectual," minority.

Only the salient facts about Zola's intervention and subsequent trial—this affair within an affair—may be recalled here. Late in 1897, when the finger of evidence began pointing away from Dreyfus and to a fellow officer, Major Ferdinand Esterhazy; when the latter was forced to request a hearing, ostensibly to "clear his name," Zola, through a series of articles and brochures, joined in the demand for a review of the Dreyfus sentence. Esterhazy's swift acquittal by a court-martial (11 January 1898) effectively quashed this move and prompted Zola to write his impassioned *Lettre à M. Félix Faure, Président de la République.* Published 13 January in Georges Clemenceau's *L'Aurore,* known to posterity under the title *J'accuse,* which Clemenceau gave it, this "letter" inculpated the entire military hierarchy—here and there somewhat randomly for lack of adequate proof, but with unerring accuracy in its overall assumption that the army was concealing its mistakes and saving face at the expense of common justice. A libel suit instituted by the government inevitably followed, and Zola was condemned to the maximum penalty of one year in prison and a 3,000-franc fine (23 February). Having lost on appeal (18 July), he was prevailed upon by Clemenceau and others to evade the sentence—on the grounds, it would seem, that this was the only way to keep the Dreyfus case open. A reluctant Zola stole away to England and remained there until June of the following year, when he was still technically liable to arrest but the march of events made it fairly safe for him to return. In his absence the tangled truth had begun unraveling: a high officer had committed suicide; Esterhazy had fled and issued from abroad a confession of sorts; orders were going out to bring Dreyfus back for a retrial. As Dreyfus stepped on French soil, Zola called his homecoming "a rebirth" and the results of his campaign "a harvest of uprightness, equity, and infinite hope."

It did not take him long to realize how mistaken he was. Unable to exonerate Dreyfus without incriminating senior officers, the military court chose to recondemn him . . . with extenuating circumstances! He who should have been acquitted was awarded instead a magnanimous presidential "pardon." The "Dreyfus crusade" fizzled out—partly because Dreyfus himself, an army man whose mental processes did not differ basically from those of his accusers, chose to discourage it and wait six more years for his total rehabilitation (15 July 1906). Meanwhile an amnesty bill designed to liquidate the affair as expediently as possible was rammed through parliament and defended by the premier, René Waldeck-Rousseau, in the crudest terms imaginable: "Amnesty," he said, "does not judge, does not ac-

cuse, does not acquit: it ignores." Last-minute "Dreyfusists" prepared to make hay out of the labors of early "Dreyfusards." Young Charles Péguy complained mournfully that "every mystique degenerates into politics."

Zola, for his part, went on fighting. *La vérité en marche* (Truth on the March, 1901), a collection of his writings throughout the Dreyfus affair, contains—apropos of the "pardon" and on the subject of amnesty—vigorous protests against the guileful policies followed by the government. There can be no question, however, that Zola's former assertive tones ("Dreyfus is innocent. I swear it. I pledge my life. I pledge my honor. . . . I may be smitten here, [but] I shall conquer") were giving way to those of disbelief and frustration: "I stand in dread . . . in sacred terror. . . . The impossible [has] come to pass. . . . Future generations will shudder in shame," and so on. A veteran of many journalistic brawls, but a novice in the field of action, Zola was visibly shaken. Indomitable, yet shaken. Mudslinging and derision had taken their toll:

> Zola's a big pig,
> The older he gets, the stupider he is;
> Zola's a big pig,
> Let's catch and roast the silly pig.

He had earned the suffrage of part at least of the intelligentsia; a book of homage had been presented to him (1898) under the patronage of a Franco-Belgian committee that included, besides Clemenceau, Maurice Maeterlinck and Émile Verhaeren; but the first words of dedication read—all too ominously: "The people learn their lesson even as they stone those who love them."

The posturing, the prophesying, the anathematizing—and the resultant stoning—were part and parcel of the romantic heritage that Zola, wisely or not, had chosen to assume in later years. After half a century or so he was reechoing Hugo's hyperbolic claim that he would scale the heavens in order to steal the truth; that, if thunders should bark, *he* would roar. Whatever megalomania is involved here may be a character trait—it certainly was in Hugo's case; but its deeper significance must be assessed in the context of romantic vaticination. Sooner or later, with Hugo and Zola, there comes a time when the man subsumes himself into the poet; when his commitment to self-expression reaches the visionary level; when the word becomes the Word in so spontaneous a manner that even self-conceit acquires the colors of self-abnegation.

It is, I believe, extremely revealing that Zola should have sworn to Dreyfus' innocence "by my forty years of toil, by the authority that such labor may have given me." This is at once romantic nonsense and the reason Zola's championship of Dreyfus is still remembered, whereas other participants in the drama are readily forgotten. Let us face it: we went, we are still going, through experiences that dwarf the Dreyfus case; Zola's involvement in the specific issues thereof has, really, no greater relevance to our times than Voltaire's effort on behalf of Calas; but what matters in modern terms is that he entered the fray, not as a high-minded politician (assuming the breed exists), not as a man of action, not even as a writer systematically *engagé* in the Sartrean sense of the word, but as a *clerc* (Julien Benda's expression), *as a man of thought*, whose devotion to principles, and to principles only, prepared, nay, designated him for this extraordinary assumption of risk and responsibility.

Zola died a strange accidental death, on 29 September 1902, when carbon monoxide fumes from a defective chimney asphyxiated him in his sleep. Talk of foul play arose immediately and is still being intermittently revived. There is little evidence to support it—the most likely explanation is that Zola fell a victim to ingrained, unhealthy habits of another age that some of us are old enough to remember: lighting coal fires in the bedroom—closing windows hermetically—bolting inside doors for added privacy. The sensational aspects of that death lay much less in its manner than in its timing at the hands of fate. In one of the most eloquent and substantial tributes that the event elicited (there were many hollow ones), Gabriel Trarieux had this to say:

> He died at the top of his strength, his faculties still unimpaired. Among all ways of dying this is one to be envied. There are those who deplore that he was denied well-earned returns, a happy old age, the inevitable apotheosis, the vast emotional outpouring that took place, on a starry spring night, around the peaceful coffin of Victor Hugo. Of small importance, however, in the face of the gestures of survivors. I, for one, am of the opinion that the style of his funeral—which was his last battle—suited best that incorrigible warrior, far too bitterly dedicated ever to become a patriarch. Clashing hurrahs and outrages are an apotheosis, too, and the proof that one still lives. This kind of an apotheosis Hugo also would have known if he had died on the morrow of his *Châtiments*.

Selected Bibliography

EDITIONS

INDIVIDUAL WORKS

Contes à Ninon. Paris, 1864.

La confession de Claude. Paris, 1865.

Mes haines. Paris, 1866.

Le voeu d'une morte. Paris, 1866.

Les mystères de Marseille. Marseilles, 1867.

Thérèse Raquin. Paris, 1867.

Madeleine Férat. Paris, 1868.

La fortune des Rougon. Paris, 1871. Vol. 1 of *Les Rougon-Macquart, histoire naturelle et sociale d'une famille sous le Second Empire* (hereafter *RM*).

La curée. Paris, 1872. Vol. 2 of *RM*.

Le ventre de Paris. Paris, 1873. Vol. 3 of *RM*.

La conquête de Plassans. Paris, 1874. Vol. 4 of *RM*.

Nouveaux contes à Ninon. Paris, 1874.

La faute de l'abbé Mouret. Paris, 1875. Vol. 5 of *RM*.

Son Excellence Eugène Rougon. Paris, 1876. Vol. 6 of *RM*.

L'Assommoir. Paris, 1877. Vol. 7 of *RM*.

Une page d'amour. Paris, 1878. Vol. 8 of *RM*.

Le roman expérimental. Paris, 1880.

Nana. Paris, 1880. Vol. 9 of *RM*.

Pot-bouille. Paris, 1882. Vol. 10 of *RM.*
Au bonheur des dames. Paris, 1883. Vol. 11 of *RM.*
La joie de vivre. Paris, 1884. Vol. 12 of *RM.*
Germinal. Paris, 1885. Vol. 13 of *RM.*
L'Oeuvre. Paris, 1886. Vol. 14 of *RM.*
La terre. Paris, 1887. Vol. 15 of *RM.*
Le réve. Paris, 1888. Vol. 16 of *RM.*
La bête humaine. Paris, 1890. Vol. 17 of *RM.*
L'Argent. Paris, 1891. Vol. 18 of *RM.*
La débâcle. Paris, 1892. Vol. 19 of *RM.*
Le docteur Pascal. Paris, 1893. Vol. 20 of *RM.*
Les trois villes: Lourdes. Paris, 1894.
Les trois villes: Rome. Paris, 1896.
Les trois villes: Paris. Paris, 1898.
Les quatre évangiles: Fécondité. Paris, 1899.
Les quatre évangiles: Travail. Paris, 1901.
La vérité en marche. Paris, 1901.
Les quatre évangiles: Vérité. Paris, 1903.

COLLECTED WORKS
Oeuvres complètes. 48 vols. Paris, 1906.
————. Notes and commentaries by Maurice Le Blond (Zola's son-in-law). 50 vols. Paris, 1927–1929.
————. Edited by Henri Mitterand. 15 vols. Paris, 1966–1970. A far richer and more truly critical edition than Le Blond, above.
Les Rougon-Macquart, histoire naturelle et sociale d'une famille sous le Second Empire. Edited by Henri Mitterand. 5 vols. Paris, 1964–1967.

TRANSLATIONS

The Debacle. Translated by L. W. Tancock. Baltimore, 1972.
Doctor Pascal. Translated by Vladimir Kean. London, 1957.
The Dream. New York, 1888.
Earth. Translated by Ann Lindsay. New York, 1955.
The Experimental Novel. Translated by Belle M. Sherman. New York, 1964.
Germinal. Translated by Havelock Ellis. New York, 1937.
————. Translated by L. W. Tancock. Baltimore, 1961.
The Heirs of Rabourdin. Translated by Teixeira de Mattos. London, 1894.
His Excellency. Translated by Alec Brown. London, 1958.
The Human Beast. Translated by Louis Colman. New York, 1948.

The Kill. Translated by Teixeira de Mattos. London, 1958.
Ladies' Delight. Translated by April Fitzlyon. London, 1958.
A Love Affair. Translated by Jean Stewart. New York, 1957.
Madeleine Férat. Translated by Alec Brown. New York, 1957.
The Masterpiece. Translated by Thomas Walton. London, 1957.
Modern Marriage. Translated by Benjamin R. Rucker. New York, 1893.
The Mysteries of Marseilles. Translated by Edward Vizetelly. New York, 1976.
Nana. Translated by George Holden. Baltimore, 1972.
Paris. Translated by Edward Vizetelly. New York, 1898.
A Priest in the House. Translated by Brian Rhys. New York, 1957.
Restless House. Translated by Percy Pinkerton. New York, 1953.
Rome. Translated by Edward Vizetelly. New York, 1896.
Savage Paris. Translated by David Hughes and Marie-Jacqueline Mason. New York, 1955.
Shell Fish. New York, 1911.
The Sin of Father Mouret. Translated by Sandy Petry. Englewood Cliffs, N.J., 1969.
Theresa. New York, 1952.
The Three Cities. Translated by Edward Vizetelly. New York, 1894.
Three Faces of Love. Translated by Roland Gant. New York, 1968.
Truth. Translated by Edward Vizetelly. London, 1912.
Zest for Life. Translated by Jean Stewart. Bloomington, Ind., 1956.

CORRESPONDENCE

Correspondance. Edited by B. H. Bakker. Paris, 1978.
Émile Zola's Letters to J. van Salten Kolff. Edited by Robert Judson Niess. Saint Louis, 1940.
Paul Cézanne's Letters. Edited by John Rewald and translated by Marguerite Key. New York, 1976.

CRITICAL STUDIES

Barbusse, Henri. *Zola.* Translated by Mary Balairdie Green and Frederick C. Green. New York, 1932.

ÉMILE ZOLA

Bédé, Jean Albert, *Emile Zola.* New York, 1974.

Brown, Calvin Smith. *Repetition in Zola's Novels.* Athens, Ga., 1952.

Carter, Lawson A. *Zola and the Theatre.* New Haven, Conn., 1963.

Grant, Elliott Mansfield. *Émile Zola.* New York, 1966.

Hemmings, Frederick William John. *Émile Zola.* Oxford, 1966.

————. *The Life and Times of Émile Zola.* London, 1977.

Hewitt, Winston R. *Through Those Living Pillars: Man and Nature in the Work of Émile Zola.* The Hague, 1974.

Josephson, Matthew. *Zola and His Time.* New York, 1969.

Kranowski, Nathan. *Paris in the Works of Émile Zola.* New York, 1966.

Patterson, J. G. *A Zola Dictionary.* London, 1912.

Richardson, Joanna. *Zola.* London, 1978.

Schor, Naomi. *Zola's Crowds.* Baltimore, 1975.

Vizetelly, Edward. *Émile Zola, Novelist and Reformer.* New York, 1904.

JEAN-ALBERT BÉDÉ

CHRONOLOGICAL LIST OF SUBJECTS

The Middle Ages and the Renaissance

The Age of Reason and the Enlightenment

The Romantic Century

CHRONOLOGICAL LIST OF SUBJECTS
The Twentieth Century

SUBJECTS BY LANGUAGE

ANGLO-SAXON
See ENGLISH

DANISH
Andersen, Hans Christian
Dinesen, Isak
Kierkegaard, Søren

ENGLISH
Beowulf
Dinesen, Isak

FRENCH
Anouilh, Jean
Balzac, Honoré de
Beauvoir, Simone de
Camus, Albert
Colette
Descartes, René
Dumas PÈRE, Alexandre
Flaubert, Gustave
Gide, André
Hugo, Victor
Ionesco, Eugène
La Fontaine, Jean de
Malraux, André
Maupassant, Guy de
Molière
Montaigne, Michel de
Proust, Marcel
Rabelais, François
Romance of the Rose
Rousseau, Jean Jacques
Saint-Exupéry, Antoine de
Sand, George
Sartre, Jean-Paul
Stendhal
Tocqueville, Alexis de
Voltaire
Zola, Émile

GERMAN
Brecht, Bertolt
Freud, Sigmund
Goethe, Johann Wolfgang von
Grass, Günter
Hesse, Hermann
Kafka, Franz
Luther, Martin
Mann, Thomas
Nietzsche, Friedrich
Rilke, Rainer Maria
Wagner, Richard

ITALIAN
Boccaccio, Giovanni
Dante Alighieri
Machiavelli, Niccolò
Petrarch
Pirandello, Luigi

LATIN
Aquinas, Thomas, Saint
Augustine, Saint
Boccaccio, Giovanni
Dante Alighieri
Descartes, René
Erasmus
Luther, Martin
Petrarch

NORWEGIAN
Ibsen, Henrik

OLD NORSE
Norse Sagas

SUBJECTS BY LANGUAGE

RUSSIAN
Babel, Isaac
Chekhov, Anton
Dostoevsky, Feodor
Gorky, Maxim
Pasternak, Boris
Pushkin, Alexander

Solzhenitsyn, Alexander
Tolstoy, Leo
Turgenev, Ivan

SPANISH
Cervantes, Miguel de
García Lorca, Federico

LIST OF CONTRIBUTORS

CHARLES AFFRON
New York University
HONORÉ DE BALZAC

MARGUERITE ARCHER†
Lehman College,
City University of New York
JEAN ANOUILH

TEODOLINDA BAROLINI
University of California,
Berkeley
GIOVANNI BOCCACCIO

JEAN BÉDÉ
ÉMILE ZOLA

JULIA CONWAY BONDANELLA
Indiana University
PETRARCH

PETER BONDANELLA
Indiana University
NICCOLÓ MACHIAVELLI

GERMAINE BRÉE
Vilas Professor Emerita,
University of Wisconsin
ALBERT CAMUS

JUDITH BUTLER
Johns Hopkins University
JEAN-PAUL SARTRE

PATRICIA CARDEN
Cornell University
LEO TOLSTOY

STEPHEN CRITES
Wesleyan University
SØREN KIERKEGAARD

GORDON CUNLIFFE
University of Wisconsin
GÜNTER GRASS

JOSEPH P. DANE
University of Southern
California
MEDIEVAL DRAMA

RICHARD DANNER
Ohio University
JEAN DE LA FONTAINE

LENNARD J. DAVIS
Brandeis University
GUSTAVE FLAUBERT

DORIS L. EDER
ANDRÉ MALRAUX

MARTIN ESSLIN
Stanford University
BERTOLT BRECHT

INGA-STINA EWBANK
University of Leeds
ISAK DINESEN

DONALD M. FRAME†
National Humanities Center
MICHEL DE MONTAIGNE

GREGORY FREIDIN
Stanford University
ISAAC BABEL

W. M. FROHOCK†
Hunter College
ANDRÉ MALRAUX

PAUL H. FRY
Yale University
JEAN JACQUES ROUSSEAU

JOHN GEAREY
Graduate School of the
City University of New York
JOHANN WOLFGANG VON GOETHE

RICHARD B. GRANT
University of Texas
VICTOR HUGO

RONALD GRAY
Emmanuel College,
Cambridge
HENRIK IBSEN

V. H. H. GREEN
Lincoln College, Oxford
SAINT THOMAS AQUINAS AND
SCHOLASTICISM
MARTIN LUTHER

ROBERT W. GUTMAN
RICHARD WAGNER

ROBERT W. HANNING
Columbia University
BEOWULF AND ANGLO-SAXON
POETRY

F. W. J. HEMMINGS
University of Leicester
ALEXANDRE DUMAS PÉRE
MARCEL PROUST

MICHAEL HOOKER
Bennington College
RENÉ DESCARTES

LAURA KENDRICK
Dalhousie University
MEDIEVAL SATIRE

ALEX KLIMOFF
Vassar College
ALEXANDER SOLZHENITSYN

JOHN LUKACS
Chestnut Hill College
ALEXIS DE TOCQUEVILLE

LIST OF CONTRIBUTORS

ANNE McCLINTOCK
Columbia University
SIMONE DE BEAUVOIR

PATRICK J. MAHONY
Université de Montréal
SIGMUND FREUD

GUY DE MALLAC
*University of California,
Irvine*
BORIS PASTERNAK

GITA MAY
Columbia University
GEORGE SAND

JAMES V. MIROLLO
Columbia University
RENAISSANCE PASTORAL POETRY
RENAISSANCE SHORT FICTION

CHARLES A. MOSER
George Washington University
IVAN TURGENEV

MARK MUSA
Indiana University
DANTE ALIGHIERI
PETRARCH

MARTIN J. NEWHOUSE
FRIEDRICH NIETZSCHE

JOHN OLIN
Fordham University
ERASMUS

D. D. R. OWEN
University of St. Andrew
ARTHURIAN LEGEND

SHARLENE POLINER
Princeton University
FRANÇOIS RABELAIS

OLGA RAGUSA
Columbia University
LUIGI PIRANDELLO

JOHN RICHETTI
Rutgers University
GUY DE MAUPASSANT

JAMES ROLLESTON
Duke University
RAINER MARIA RILKE

VINIO ROSSI
Oberlin College
ANDRÉ GIDE

JEAN SAREIL
Columbia University
VOLTAIRE

PAUL SCHACH
University of Nebraska
NORSE SAGAS

HAROLD B. SEGEL
Columbia University
MAXIM GORKY

MICHAEL SEIDEL
Columbia University
MOLIÈRE
STENDHAL

J. THOMAS SHAW
*University of Wisconsin—
Madison*
ALEXANDER PUSHKIN

ERNEST J. SIMMONS†
FEODOR DOSTOEVSKY

WALTER H. SOKEL
University of Virginia
FRANZ KAFKA

J. P. STERN
University College, London
THOMAS MANN

JOAN HINDE STEWART
*North Carolina State
University*
COLETTE

RALPH TARICA
University of Maryland
ANTOINE DE SAINT-EXUPÉRY

EUGENE VANCE
University of Montreal
SAINT AUGUSTINE

BRUCE WARDROPPER
Duke University
MIGUEL DE CERVANTES

ARNOLD WEINSTEIN
Columbia University
FEDERICO GARCIA LORCA

WINTHROP WETHERBEE
University of Chicago
THE ROMANCE OF THE ROSE AND
MEDIEVAL ALLEGORY

MATTHEW H. WIKANDER
Columbia University
EUGÈNE IONESCO

THOMAS G. WINNER
Boston University
ANTON CHEKHOV

THEODORE ZIOLKOWSKI
Princeton University
HERMANN HESSE

JACK ZIPES
*University of Wisconsin—
Milwaukee*
HANS CHRISTIAN ANDERSEN

COMPLETE LIST
OF SUBJECTS IN THE
PARENT SET

European Writers comprises 261 essays on continental authors and their works, arranged chronologically from Prudentius to Milan Kundera. Of these, 252 directly concern individual authors or anonymous works. In a few cases related writers are addressed in the same essay: for example, the Goncourts, the Poetic Realists (Storm, Keller, and Meyer), or the French novelists of the eighteenth century (Prévost, Laclos, and Constant). An additional 9 essays focus on genres or themes.

SUBJECTS IN THE PARENT SET

CHANSON DE ROLAND AND THE *CHANSONS DE GESTE*

CHAUTEAUBRIAND, FRANÇOIS RENÉ DE

CHEKHOV, ANTON

CHÉNIER, ANDRÉ

CHRÉTIEN DE TROYES

CLAUDEL, PAUL

COCTEAU, JEAN

COLETTE

CONSTANT, BENJAMIN

CORNEILLE, PIERRE

CROCE, BENEDETTO

D'ANNUNZIO, GABRIELE

DANTE ALIGHIERI

DELACROIX, EUGÈNE

DESCARTES, RENÉ

DIDEROT, DENIS

DINESEN, ISAK

DOSTOEVSKY, FEODOR

DUMAS PÈRE ALEXANDRE

DÜRRENMATT, FRIEDRICH

EÇA DE QUEIROZ, JOSÉ MARIA

EKELÖF, GUNNAR

ELYTIS, ODYSSEUS

ERASMUS

FÉNELON, FRANÇOIS DE SALIGNAC DE LA MOTHE

FERREIRA DE CASTRO, JOSÉ MARIA

FLAUBERT, GUSTAVE

FONTANE, THEODOR

FOSCOLO, UGO

FOUCAULT, MICHEL

FREUD, SIGMUND

FRISCH, MAX

GARCÍA LORCA, FEDERICO

GAUTIER, THÉOPHILE

GENET, JEAN

GEORGE, STEFAN

GHELDERODE, MICHEL DE

GIDE, ANDRÉ

GINZBURG, NATALIA

GIRAUDOUX, JEAN

GOETHE, JOHANN WOLFGANG VON

GOGOL, NIKOLAY VASILIEVICH

GOLDONI, CARLO

GOMBROWICZ, WITOLD

GONCHAROV, IVAN

GONCOURT, EDMOND LOUIS ANTOINE DE, AND JULES ALFRED HUOT DE

GORKY, MAXIM

GOTTFRIED VON STRASSBURG

GRASS, GÜNTER

GRILLPARZER, FRANZ

GUNNARSSON, GUNNAR

HAMSUN, KNUT

HARDENBERG, GEORG FRIEDRICH PHILIP

HAŠEK, JAROSLAV

HAUPTMANN, GERHART

HEBBEL, FRIEDRICH

HEINE, HEINRICH

HERDER, JOHANN GOTTFRIED VON

HESSE, HERMANN

HOFFMANN, E. T. A.

HOFMANNSTHAL, HUGO VON

HÖLDERLIN, FRIEDRICH

HUGO, VICTOR

HUYSMANS, JORIS KARL

IBSEN, HENRIK

IONESCO, EUGÈNE

JARRY, ALFRED

JIMÉNEZ, JUAN RAMÓN

JOHNSON, EYVIND

KAFKA, FRANZ

KAZANTZAKIS, NIKOS

KELLER, GOTTFRIED

KHLEBNIKOV, VELIMIR

KIERKEGAARD, SØREN

KLEIST, HEINRICH VON

KLOPSTOCK, FRIEDRICH GOTTLIEB

KOSZTOLÁNHYI, DEZSÖ

KRLEŽA, MIROSLAV

KUNDERA, MILAN

LA ROCHEFOUCAULD, FRANÇOIS VI, DUC DE

LA BRUYÈRE, JEAN DE

LACLOS, PIERRE-AMBROISE-FRANÇOIS CHODERLOS DE

SUBJECTS IN THE PARENT SET

LA FONTAINE, JEAN DE

LAFORGUE, JULES

LAGERKVIST, PÄR

LAMPEDUSA, GIUSEPPE TOMASI DI

LAXNESS, HALLDÓR

LECONTE DE LISLE, CHARLES MARIE

LEOPARDI, GIACOMO

LERMONTOV, MIKHAIL YURIEVICH

LESAGE, ALAIN-RENÉ

LESSING, GOTTHOLD EPHRAIM

LUKÁCS, GYÖRGY

LUTHER, MARTIN

MACHADO, ANTONIO

MACHIAVELLI, NICCOLÒ

MAETERLINCK, MAURICE

MALLARMÉ, STÉPHANE

MALRAUX, ANDRÉ

MANDELSHTAM, OSIP

MANN, HEINRICH

MANN, THOMAS

MANZONI, ALESSANDRO

MARINETTI, FILIPPO TOMMASO

MAUPASSANT, GUY DE

MAURIAC, FRANÇOIS

MAYAKOVSKY, VLADIMIR

MÉRIMÉE, PROSPER

MEYER, CONRAD FERDINAND

MICHELET, JULES

MICKIEWICZ, ADAM

MILOSZ, CZESLAW

MOBERG, VILHELM

MOLIÈRE

MONTAIGNE, MICHEL DE

MONTALE, EUGENIO

MONTESQUIEU

MONTHERLANT, HENRY DE

MORAVIA, ALBERTO

MUSIL, ROBERT

MUSSET, ALFRED DE

NERVAL, GÉRARD DE

NIBELUNGENLIED, THE

NIETZSCHE, FRIEDRICH

NOVALIS

OLESHA, YURI

ORTEGA Y GASSET, JOSÉ

PASCAL, BLAISE

PASCOLI, GIOVANNI

PASTERNAK, BORIS

PAVESE, CESARE

PÉREZ GALDÓS, BENITO

PERSE, SAINT JOHN

PESSOA, FERNANDO

PETRARCH

PIRANDELLO, LUIGI

PRÉVOST, ANTOINE-FRANÇOIS

PROUST, MARCEL

PRUDENTIUS

PUSHKIN, ALEXANDER

QUASIMODO, SALVATORE

QUENEAU, RAYMOND

RABELAIS, FRANÇOIS

RACINE, JEAN

RICHTER, JEAN PAUL

RILKE, RAINER MARIA

RIMBAUD, ARTHUR

RITSOS, YANNIS

ROBBE-GRILLET, ALAIN

ROMANCE OF THE ROSE, THE, AND MEDIEVAL ALLEGORY

RONSARD, PIERRE DE, AND THE PLÉIADE

ROUSSEAU, JEAN JACQUES

SADE, DONATIEN ALPHONSE FRANÇOIS, MARQUIS DE

SAINT-EXUPÉRY, ANTOINE DE

SAINTE-BEUVE, CHARLES-AUGUSTIN

SAND, GEORGE

SARRAUTE, NATHALIE

SARTRE, JEAN-PAUL

SCHILLER, FRIEDRICH VON

SCHLEGEL, FRIEDRICH VON

SCHNITZLER, ARTHUR

SCHOPENHAUER, ARTHUR

SEFERIS, GEORGE

SILONE, IGNAZIO

SIMENON, GEORGES

SIMON, CLAUDE

SUBJECTS IN THE PARENT SET

SÖDERGRAN, EDITH
SOLZHENITSYN, ALEXANDER
STAËL, MADAME DE
STENDHAL
STORM, THEODOR
STRINDBERG, AUGUST
SVEVO, ITALO
TAINE, HIPPOLYTE
TASSO, TORQUATO
TIECK, LUDWIG
TOCQUEVILLE, ALEXIS DE
TOLSTOY, LEO
TRAKL, GEORG
TSVETAEVA, MARINA
TURGENEV, IVAN
TYCHYNA, PAVEL

UNAMUNO, MIGUEL DE
UNDSET, SIGRID
UNGARETTI, GIUSEPPE

VALÉRY, PAUL
VALLE-INCLÁN, RAMÓN DEL
VEGA, LOPE DE
VERGA, GIOVANNI
VERLAINE, PAUL
VESAAŚ, TARJEI
VICO, GIOVANNI BATTISTA

VIGNY, ALFRED VICTOR DE
VILLON, FRANÇOIS
VITTORINI, ELIO
VOLTAIRE

WAGNER, RICHARD
WALTHER VON DER VOGELWEIDE
WEDEKIND, FRANK
WEIL, SIMONE
WIELAND, CHRISTOPH MARTIN
WITKIEWICZ, STANISŁAW IGNACY
WOLFRAM VON ESCHENBACH

YOURCENAR, MARGUERITE

ZAMYATIN, YEVGENY IVANOVICH
ZOLA, ÉMILE

Themes and Genres

THE ARTHURIAN LEGEND
THE CID IN EPIC AND BALLAD
MEDIEVAL DRAMA
MEDIEVAL SATIRE
NORSE SAGAS
RENAISSANCE PASTORAL POETRY
RENAISSANCE SHORT FICTION
TROUBADOURS AND TROUVÈRES
THE WELL-MADE PLAY

ACKNOWLEDGMENTS

The following pamphlets in the Columbia University Press Series *Columbia Essays on Modern Writers* have been revised by their authors for *European Writers* and have been reprinted here by special arrangement with Columbia University Press, the publisher.

Archer, Marguerite: *Jean Anouilh*
Copyright © 1971 Columbia University Press

Esslin, Martin: *Bertolt Brecht*
Copyright © 1969 Columbia University Press

Brée, Germaine: *Albert Camus*
Copyright © 1964 Columbia University Press

Simmons, Ernest J.: *Feodor Dostoevsky*
Copyright © 1969 Columbia University Press

Rossi, Vinio: *André Gide*
Copyright © 1968 Columbia University Press

Ziolkowski, Theodore: *Hermann Hesse*
Copyright © 1966 Columbia University Press

Sokel, Walter H.: *Frank Kafka*
Copyright © 1966 Columbia University Press

Frohock, W. M.: *André Malraux*
Copyright © 1974 Columbia University Press

Stern, J. P.: *Thomas Mann*
Copyright © 1967 Columbia University Press

Ragusa, Olga: *Luigi Pirandello*
Copyright © 1968 Columbia University Press

Moser, Charles: *Ivan Turgenev*
Copyright © 1972 Columbia University Press

Bédé, Jean-Albert: *Émile Zola*
Copyright © 1974 Columbia University Press

ACKNOWLEDGMENTS

The publishers additionally wish to thank
the following for permission to quote from
published editions and translations.

"Michel de Montaigne": Quotations reprinted from *The Complete Essays of Montaigne,* translated by Donald M. Frame, with the permission of the publishers, Stanford University Press. © 1958 by the Board of Trustees of the Leland Stanford Junior University.

"Alexander Pushkin": Quotations from *The Letters of Alexander Pushkin* © 1963 by J. Thomas Shaw. Originally published by Indiana University Press and University of Pennsylvania Press. Reprinted in paperback, copyright © 1967 by the Regents of the University of Wisconsin. The author gratefully acknowledges the permission granted by the University of Wisconsin Press.

"Rainer Maria Rilke": Excerpts of poetry from *Samtliche Werke.* Reprinted by permission of Insel Verlag, Frankfurt. Excerpt from "Burnt Norton" in *Collected Poems 1909–1962,* copyright 1936 by Harcourt Brace Jovanovich, Inc., copyright © 1964, 1963 by T. S. Eliot, reprinted by permission of Harcourt Brace Jovanovich, Inc., and Faber and Faber Ltd.

"Aleksandr Solzhenitsyn": Excerpt from "The Wheel" from *Sobranie Sochineii,* vol. 11, Editions YMCA Press, Paris.

INDEX

A

"À Albert Dürer." *See* Hugo, Victor

"À la fenêtre, pendant la nuit." *See* Hugo, Victor

"À la Feuille de Rose, Maison Turque" ("At the Rose Leaf, Turkish Brothel"). *See* Maupassant, Guy de

À la recherche du temps perdu. See Proust, Marcel, *Remembrance of Things Past*

À l'ombre des jeunes filles en fleurs. See Proust, Marcel, *Remembrance of Things Past* (*À la recherche du temps perdu*), *Within a Budding Grove*

"À propos de Beckett." *See* Ionesco, Eugène, *Antidotes*

"A qualunque animale alberga in terra." *See* Petrarch, *Canzoniere*

Abba, Marta, Pirandello and, 1294b, 1295a

"Abbot and the Learned Lady, The." *See* Erasmus

Abélard, Peter, 54a

Sic et non (*Yes and No*), 54b–55a

Abindarraez y Jarifa, Montemayor's *Diana* and, 1427a

"About Holy Church." *See* Rutebeuf, "De Sainte Église"

"About Love." *See* Chekhov, Anton, "O lyubvi"

Above the Barriers. See Pasternak, Boris

Abraham, Karl, Freud and, 578a

Abraham (O.T. patriarch)

in Kierkegaard's *Fear and Trembling,* 891b–892a

in Mann's *Joseph and His Brothers*, 1013b

Abraxas (Gnostic deity), in *Demian*, 742b, 745b, 746b

"Absage." *See* Hesse, Hermann

Abstemius, La Fontaine and, 920b–921a

Absurd, theater of the, Ionesco and, 842b–843a, 843b

Absurdism

Camus and, 314a–323a

Grass and, 712a–713a

Sartre and, 1596b

Académie Française

Hugo's election to, 772b

La Fontaine and, 905b

"Academy of Pataphysics," 830a

Acción Popular, Lorca's death and, 628b

Account of a Journey from Paris to Limousin. *See* La Fontaine, Jean de, *Relation d'un voyage de Paris en Limousin*

Acta Augustana. See Luther, Martin

Acting, profession of, in France and England, 1746b

Acts of the Apostles, The. See Gréban, Simon

Actuelles: Chroniques. See Camus, Albert

Ad Nepotianum. See Jerome, St.

"Ad se ipsum." *See* Petrarch

Adages. See Erasmus

Adagiorum chiliades. See Erasmus, *Adages*

Adagiorum collectanea. See Erasmus, *Adages*

Aðalhending, in *dróttkvæt* stanzas, 1200b

Adam of Bremen, *History,* 1203b

Adam de la Halle, 1058b–1061a

Jeu de la feuillée, 1057a, 1059b–1060a, 1060b

Jeu de Robin et Marion (Play of Robin and Marion), 1057a, 1059a, 1060b–1061a

Adamov, Arthur, Anouilh and, 32b

"Adebar." *See* Grass, Günter, *Gleisdreieck*

Adelard of Bath, 56a

Adieu. See Balzac, Honoré de

Adler, A. P., Kierkegaard and, 879b

Adler, Alfred, Freud and, 578a, 587a

Admonitions for Peace on the Twelve Articles. See Luther, Martin

Adolescence, sexuality and, in Colette's *The Ripening Seed*, 403a–405a

Adolphe. See Constant, Benjamin

Adonis. See La Fontaine, Jean de

Adultery

in Chrétien's poems, 88b

in Maupassant's works, 1035b–1036a, 1038a, 1043a

See also Flaubert, Gustave, *Madame Bovary;* Tolstoy, Leo, *Anna Karenina*

Advantages of Windfowl, The. *See* Grass, Günter, *Die Vorzüge der Windhühner*

"Aerial Ways." *See* Pasternak, Boris, *Rasskazy* (*Stories*)

Aeschylus, *Oresteia, Iphigenia in Tauris* and, 666a, 666b

Aesop, La Fontaine's *Fables* and, 904b, 908b

Aesthetic autonomy, of Rilke, 1462b, 1463a

Aesthetics

Brecht's left-wing, 282a

Kierkegaard and, 888b–891a, 895a–b

Marxist, 296b, 297a

Sartre and, 1603a–1605b

INDEX

INDEX

All Men Are Mortal. See Beauvoir, Simone de

All My Sons. See Miller, Arthur

All Said and Done. See Beauvoir, Simone de

Allegory

    in Augustine's *Confessions,* 112a

    Camus and, 330a

    in Chekhov's "The Steppe," 367b

    in Christian interpretation of classical
        literature, 1065a

    in Hugo's works, 771a

    medieval, **1491a–1517b**

    in Rabelais's works, 1396a, 1396b

"Allegory of poets" (Dante), 420a

"Allegory of theologians" (Dante), 420a

Allemann, Beda, on Rilke and Mallarmé,
    1473b, 1476b

Alliteration

    in Anglo-Saxon poetry, 232b

    in *Fljótsdæla saga,* 1220b–1221a

All'uscita. See Pirandello, Luigi

Allusion, in Malraux's works, 992a–b

Almogaver, Juan Boscán, Petrarchan influence,
    1284b

"Alone and filled with care." *See* Petrarch,
    Canzoniere "Solo et pensoso i più deserti
    campi"

Alonso, Ruiz, Lorca's death and, 628b–629a

Alouette, L'. See Anouilh, Jean, *The Lark*

Alsfelder *Passion,* 1066b

Also sprach Zarathustra. See Nietzsche,
    Friedrich, *Thus Spoke Zarathustra*

Alte und der neue Glaube, Der. See Strauss,
    David

Altercazione. See Medici, Lorenzo de'

Altersstil, of Hesse, 757a

Alzire. See Voltaire

Amadas and Ydoine, 1506a

"Amante liberal, El" ("The Generous Lover"),
    348a–b

Amaranta. See Casalio

Amatory Disillusions. *See* Zayas y Sotomayor,
    Maria de, *Desengaños amorosos*

Amatory and Exemplary Tales. *See* Zayas y
    Sotomayor, Maria de, *Novelas amorosas
    y exemplares*

Amatory Happenings and Wonders in Eight
    Exemplary Novellas. *See* Montalbán,
    Juan Pérez de, *Sucesos y prodigios de
    amor en ocho novelas ejemplares*

Amatory Improvisations. *See* Medici, Lorenzo
    de', *Selve d'amore*

Ambiguity, Camus and, 332a

Ambra. See Medici, Lorenzo de'

Ambrose, St.

    Augustine and, 108a, 108b, 110a

    Hexameron, Boccaccio's use of, 265a

Amédée. See Ionesco, Eugène

Amelius, 449b

American literature, twentieth century, Kafka
    and, 852b

Amerika. See Kafka, Franz

Amica delle mogli, L'. See Pirandello, Luigi

Aminta. See Tasso, Torquato

Amis et Amile, 1064a

"Among the Intelligentsia." *See* Gorky, Maxim,
    My Universities

"Amor che ne la mente mi ragiona." *See* Dante
    Alighieri, *Convivio*

*Amor de Don Perlimplín con Belisa en su
    jardín, El. See* García Lorca, Federico

Amor fati, Nietzsche's view of, 1173b, 1187a

"Amor pastorius." *See* Petrarch

Amori senza amore. See Pirandello, Luigi

"Amorous Shepherd, The." *See* Petrarch, "Amor
    pastorius"

Amours de Psyché et de Cupidon, Les. See La
    Fontaine, Jean de

Amphion. See Proust, Marcel

Amphitryon. See Kleist, Heinrich von; Molière;
    Plautus

Amy, Pierre, 1377b

"An die Musik." *See* Rilke, Rainer Maria

Anabaptists, Luther and, 942a–b

Anacreon, influence on Renaissance pastoral
    poetry, 1414b

Analogy

    argument from Aquinas on, 69b

    in Augustine's *On the Trinity,* 120a

"Analyse der Phobie eines fünfjährigen
    Knaben." *See* Freud, Sigmund

"Analysis of a Phobia of a Five-Year-Old Boy."
    See Freud, Sigmund, "Analyse der
    Phobie eines fünfjährigen Knaben"

Analytical Studies. *See* Balzac, Honoré de,
    Études analytiques

Anatomy of the Novella. See Clements, Robert;
    Gibaldi, Joseph

Ancien régime, Voltaire's opposition to,
    1758b–1760a

INDEX

INDEX

INDEX

Anthony, St., Flaubert and, 554a

Anthropocentrism, Voltaire on, 1759b,
    1763b–1764a

Anti Machiavel. See Frederick II of Prussia,
    king

Antibarbari (The Antibarbarians). *See*
    Erasmus

Antichrist, Der. See Nietzsche, Friedrich, *The
    Anti-Christ*

Anti-Christ, The. See Nietzsche, Friedrich

Anticlericalism, Voltaire and, 1741a–1742a,
    1752a–1753b, 1757b–1758a,
    1764b–1765a

Antidotes. See Ionesco, Eugène

Antigone. See Alfieri, Vittorio; Anouilh, Jean;
    Cocteau, Jean; Sophocles

Antigone, Beauvoir and, 200a

Antigone des Sophokles, Die (*The Antigone of
    Sophocles*).

Antimémoires. See Malraux, André,
    Anti-Memoirs

Anti-Memoirs. See Malraux, André

Anti-Semite and Jew. See Sartre, Jean-Paul

Anti-Semitism
    and the Dreyfus affair, 1789a–b, 1809a–1811a
    Freud and, 579a
    Nietzsche and, 1181a, 1195a
    in twentieth century Russia, 137a
    of Wagner, 1167a, 1181a
        admission of, 1782b
        German nationalism and, 1773a, 1779a
        in journals, 1784a
        Meyerbeer and, 1772a
        Wagnerism and, 1767b

Antithesis, in *Hrafnkels saga,* 1216b

Antokol'skii, Pavel, on Pasternak's *Early
    Trains,* 1244b–1245a

Antonio of Brescia, 62a

Antonovich, Maksim, on Turgenev, 1729b

Antony. See Dumas père, Alexandre

Anxiety
    Freud's concept of, 578b
    Kierkegaard and, 893a–894a
    Sartre and, 1601b–1602b

"Apellesova cherta" ("The Apelles Mark"). *See*
    Pasternak, Boris, *Rasskazy* (*Stories*)

"Apocalypsis Goliae Episcopi" ("Revelation of
    Golias the Bishop"), 1092a

Apollinaire, Guillaume, 1318b

Apollo

Daphne and, in Petrarch's *Canzoniere,*
    1273a, 1276a, 1276b

in Rilke's "Archaic Torso of Apollo," 1479b

Apologue, La Fontaine and, 905a, 908b–909a,
    923a

"Apology for Raymond Sebond." *See*
    Montaigne, Michel de, *Essays*

Apprendre à marcher. See Ionesco, Eugène

*Apprenticeship and Travels of Wilhelm
    Meister, The. See* Goethe, Johann
    Wolfgang von

Aprel' semnadtsatogo. See Solzhenitsyn,
    Aleksandr, *The Red Wheel*

"Après une lecture de Dante." *See* Hugo, Victor

April 1917. *See* Solzhenitsyn, Aleksandr, *The
    Red Wheel*

Apuleius, Lucius
    Golden Ass
        Flaubert and, 560a
        influence on Renaissance short fiction,
        1435a

"Aquesta gens, cant son en lur gaieza." *See*
    Peire Cardenal

Aquinas, Thomas, St., **53a–77b**
    on Aristotle's *De fallaciis,* 58b–59a
    Augustine and, 103a
    Catena aurea (*The Golden Chain*), 63a,
        63b–64a, 64b
    Compedium theologiae (*Compendium of
        Theology*), 67a
    Contra doctrinam retrahentium a religione
        (*Against the Doctrine of Defection
        from the Religious Life*), 65b
    Contra errores Graecorum (*Against the
        Errors of the Greeks*), 63a
    *Contra impugnantes Dei cultum et
        religionem* (*Against the Assailants of
        God*), 62a
    Dante and, 413b
    De aeternitate contra murmurantes (*On
        Eternity Against the Critics*), 70a
    De angelis (*On Angels*), 67a
    De anima (*On the Soul*), 66a
    De divinis nominibus (*On the Divine
        Names*), 64a
    De ente et essentia ad fratres et socios meos
        (*On Being and Essence*), 60b
    De hebdomadibus (*On Axioms*), 62b
    De ingressu puerorum in religione (*On Entry
        of Boys into Religious Life*), 65b

INDEX

INDEX

INDEX

B

INDEX

INDEX

INDEX

INDEX

INDEX

INDEX

INDEX

INDEX

INDEX

INDEX

INDEX

D

INDEX

INDEX

Deeds That Have Now Become Words. *See* Pirandello, Luigi, "Fatti che or son parole"

Deep Song. See García Lorca, Federico

Défense et illustration de la langue française (Defense and Illustration of the French Language). *See* Du Bellay, Joachim

Defensiones theologiae divi Thomae Aquinatis. See Capreolus, John

Defoe, Daniel, *Journal of the Plague Year,* 836a, 837b

Deguileville, Guillaume, *Romance of the Rose* and, 1514b

De-historicization, in works of Ionesco, 837b–838a

Del modo di trattare i popoli della Valdichiana ribellati. See Machiavelli, Niccolò

Delacroix, Eugène, Flaubert on, 569b

Deleitar aprovechando. See Tirso de Molina

Délices, Les, Voltaire's activities at, 1751a

Délire à deux. See Ionesco, Eugène

Delo Artamonovykh. See Gorky, Maxim, *The Artamonov Business*

Deloney, Thomas, translation of Des Périers nouvelles by, 1453a

"Deluge at Norderney, The." *See* Dinesen, Isak

Demagoguery, Mann's *Mario and the Magician* as metaphor of, 1008a–1009a

Dembowski, Mathilde Viscontini, Stendhal and, 1653a–b

Demian. See Hesse, Hermann

Demi-monde, Le. See Dumas fils, Alexandre

Democracy
  despotism and, Tocqueville on, 1678b–1679b
  Tocqueville on historical evolution toward, 1674a

Democracy in America. See Tocqueville, Alexis de

Demons
  in Alsfelder *Passion,* 1066b
  in Descartes's *Meditations on First Philosophy,* 440b–441a, 442a, 444a
  in Greban's *Passion,* 1070a

Demos. See Camus, Albert

Demoustier, Charles-Albert
  Dumas père and, 512a
  Lettres a Émile sur la mythologie, 512a

Deor (Anglo-Saxon poem), 232a

Dépit amoureux, Le. See Molière

Depression, Kierkegaard and, 879a, 880b–882b

Derenkov, Andrei, 705b

Dernier amour, Le. See Sand, George

Dernier jour d'un condamné, Le. See Hugo, Victor

Dernière Aldini, La. See Sand, George

Derzhavin, Gavriil, Pushkin and, 1342b–1343a

Des Amts-Vogts Josuah Freudel Klaglibell gegen seinen verfluchten Dämon. See Richter, Jean Paul

"Des Jacobins." *See* Rutebeuf

Des Périers, Bonaventure
  Marguerite of Navarre as patron of, 1452b
  Nouvelles récréations et joyeux devis (Novel Pastimes and Merry Tales), 1452b–1453a

Des vers. See Maupassant, Guy de

Descartes, René, **431a–452b**
  Beauvoir and, 195a, 200a
  Compendium musicae, 433a
  Discours de la méthode (Discourse on Method)
    Meditations and, 439b
    organization of, 437a–b
    publication of, 436b
    three dreams in, 434a–b
    on unity of knowledge, 433b–434a
  Le monde, 436b
  Meditations on First Philosophy, 437b–438a, 439b–441a, 441b, 441a–442b, 443a–444a, 444a–445b, 445b–447a, 450b, 451a, 452a
  Montaigne and, 1155b, 1156a
  Passions de l'âme (The Passions of the Soul), 451b
  Principia philosophiae (The Principles of Philosophy), 443a, 450b–451b

"Descent into Reverie." *See* Hugo, Victor, "La pente de la rêverie"

Descent of Man. See Darwin, Charles

Deschamps, Eustache
  on Bohemians, 1082b–1083b, 1088a
  on financial experts, 1091a–1092a
  on Hundred Years' War, 1100b–1102a
  strophic poetry and, 1110b
  wordplay of, 1109b

Description of the Method Used by Duke Valentino in Killing Vitellozzo Vitelli, Oliverotto da Fermo, and Others. See Machiavelli, Niccolò, *Descrizione del modo tenuto del duca Valentino . . .*

INDEX

"Description of a Struggle." *See* Kafka, Franz, "Beschreibung eines Kampfes"

Descrizione del modo tenuto del duca Valentino nello ammazzare Vitellozzo Vitelli, Oliverotto da Fermo, il Signor Pagolo e il duca di Gravina Orsini. See Machiavelli, Niccolò

Desengaños amorosos. See Zayas y Sotomayor, Maria de

"Deserter, The." *See* Babel, Isaac, "Dezertir"

"Desire spurs me." *See* Petrarch, *Canzoniere,* "Voglia mi sprona"

"Despedida." *See* García Lorca, Federico

"Desperate Character, A." *See* Turgenev, Ivan

Desportes, Philippe
  Bergeries, 1416a
  Petrarchan influence, 1284a

Despotism, democratic, Tocqueville on, 1678b–1679b

Detective fiction
  Ionesco and, 818a
    Victims of Duty, 822b, 823a, 843b

Determinism
  in Balzac's works, 165b–166a
  Voltaire on, 1761a–b

Deti solntsa. See Gorky, Maxim

Detstvo. See Babel, Isaac; Gorky, Maxim, *Childhood*

"Detstvo Liuvers." *See* Pasternak, Boris, *Rasskazy* (*Stories*)

Deutsche Messe, Die. See Luther, Martin

"Deux amis." *See* Maupassant, Guy de

"Deux archers, Les." *See* Hugo, Victor

Deux poètes, Les. See Balzac, Honoré de

Deuxième sexe, Le. See Beauvoir, Simone de, *The Second Sex*

Deviat'sot piatyi god. See Pasternak, Boris

Devil
  in Goethe's works
    Faust, 675a–b
    Urfaust, 673b
  Luciferin Dante's *Divine Comedy,* 427a
  in "Pange lingua, necem Petri qui turbavit Angliam," 1108a
  in Redentin Easter play, 1068a

Devil and the Good Lord, The. See Sartre, Jean-Paul

Devil's Pool, The. See Sand, George

Devin du village, Le. See Rousseau, Jean Jacques

Devotional literature, Kierkegaard and, 897a

"Dezertir." *See* Babel, Isaac

"Di Grasso." *See* Babel, Isaac

"Di pensier in pensier, di monte in monte." *See* Petrarch

"Di sera, un geranio." *See* Pirandello, Luigi

Diable et le bon Dieu, Le. See Sartre, Jean-Paul, *The Devil and the Good Lord*

Dialectic
  Abelard's *Sic et Non* on, 55a
  in Augustinianism, 57b
  Brecht and, 288b, 300b
  Ibsen and, 811a
  in scholasticism, 53a–54b
  in universities, 57a

Dialoge aus dem Messingkauf. See Brecht, Bertolt

Dialogue
  internal, allegory and, 1505b–1506a
  in medieval secular drama, 1071a–b

Dialogue Concerning the Two Chief World Systems. See Galilei, Galileo

"Dialogue of the Dogs, The." *See* Cervantes, Miguel de, *Exemplary Tales* (*Novelas ejemplares*), "El coloquio de los perros"

Dialogue on Dramatic Poetry. See Eliot, T. S.

Dialogue on Language, A. See Machiavelli, Niccolò, *Discorso o dialogo intorno alla nostra lingua*

Dialogues: Rousseau juge de Jean-Jacques. See Rousseau, Jean Jacques

Dialogues with the Characters. *See* Pirandello, Luigi, "Colloquii coi personaggi"

Dialogues de bêtes. See Colette

"Dialogues familiers sur la poésie des prolétaires." *See* Sand, George

Diamant des Geisterkönigs, Der. See Raimund, Ferdinand

Diamant, Dora, 851b

Diamond of the King of Spirits, The. *See* Raimund, Ferdinand, *Der Diamant des Geisterkönigs*

Diana. See Gil Polo, Gaspar, *Diana enamorada;* Montemayor, Jorge de, *Los siete libros de la Diana;* Pérez, Alonso, *Segunda parte de la Diana*

Diana e la Tuda (*Diana and Tuda*). *See* Pirandello, Luigi

Diana enamorada (Diana in Love). *See* Gil Polo, Gaspar

INDEX

INDEX

Discourse on the Origin of Inequality. See Rousseau, Jean Jacques, *Discours sur l'origine de l'inégalité parmi les hommes*

Discourse on Remodeling the Government of Florence, A. See Machiavelli, Niccolò, *Discursus florentinarum rerum post mortem iunioris Laurentii Medices*

Discourse on the Sciences and the Arts. See Rousseau, Jean Jacques, *Discours sur les sciences et les arts*

Discourse in Verse on Man. See Voltaire, *Discours en vers sur l'homme*

Discourse on Voluntary Servitude. See La Boétie, Étienne de, *Discours de la servitude volontaire*

Discourses on Dante. See Boccaccio, Giovanni, *Esposizioni sopra il Dante*

Discourses, The. See Machiavelli, Niccolò

Discoveries. *See* Ionesco, Eugène, *Découvertes*

Discursus florentinarum rerum post mortem iunioris Laurentii Medices. See Machiavelli, Niccolò

Discussions. See Firenzuola, Angelo, *Ragionamenti*

Disguise, Kierkegaard and, 882b–883a

Disputed Questions of Truth. See Aquinas, Thomas, St., *Quaestiones disputate de veritate*

Dissertation on Modern Music. See Rousseau, Jean Jacques

"District Behind the Lines, A." *See* Pasternak, Boris, "Uezd v tylu"

Diu Krône. See Heinrich von dem Türlin

Diván del Tamarit (Divan). See García Lorca, Federico

Divers jeux rustiques (Diverse Rustic Diversions). See Du Bellay, Joachim

Diversions, The. See Parabosco, Girolamo, *I diporti*

Diversity, theme of, in Montaigne's *Essays*, 1147a–b

"Dives eram et dilectus." *See* Hugh Primas

Divine, in Dinesen, 453a

Divine Comedy. See Dante Alighieri

Divine intervention, in Rousseau, 1535b–1536a

Divorce Judge, The. See Cervantes, Miguel de, *El juez de los divorcios*

"Divortium." *See* Petrarch

"Djinns, Les." *See* Hugo, Victor

"Dlia pol'zy dela." *See* Solzhenitsyn, Aleksandr

"Dnevnik." *See* Babel, Isaac

Döblin, Alfred, Grass and, 733a

Dobrolyubov, Nikolay
  Dostoevsky and, 487a
  Turgenev and, 1723a, 1727b

Docteur amoureux, Le. See Molière

"Docteur Héraclius Gloss, Le" ("Doctor Heraclius Gloss"). *See* Maupassant, Guy de

Docteur Pascal, Le (Dr. Pascal). See Zola, Émile

Doctor Faustus. See Mann, Thomas

Doctor Zhivago. See Pasternak, Boris

Doctor's Duty, The. See Pirandello, Luigi, *Il dovere del medico*

"Doctor's Visit, A." *See* Chekhov, Anton, "Sluchay iz praktiki"

Doctrinaires (French political thinkers), Tocqueville and, 1677a

Documentary novels, Zola's Rougon-Macquarts series, 1794a–b, 1795b–1808a

"Dog, The." *See* Turgenev, Ivan

Dog Years. See Grass, Günter

Dogmatism, theme of, in Ionesco's *Hunger and Thirst*, 835b, 836a

Doktor Faustus. See Mann, Thomas, *Doctor Faustus*

"Dolci rime d'amor ch'i'solìa, Le." *See* Dante Alighieri, *Convivio*

Doll's House, A. See Ibsen, Henrik

"Dom s mezoninom." *See* Chekhov, Anton

Domenichi, Ludovico, *Facetie, motti et burle (Jokes, Witticisms, and Pranks)*, anecdotes in, 1442b

Dominicans
  Aquinas and, 58b, 59a, 62b, 65b, 66b, 74b
  Luther and, 934b–935a
  in Rutebeuf's "Des Jacobins," 1084a–1085a
  University of Paris and, 61b–62a

Don Giovanni. See Mozart, Wolfgang Amadeus

Don Juan. See Brecht, Bertolt; Byron, George Gordon, Lord; Molière

Don Juan, in Pushkin's *Stone Guest*, 1363b–1364a

Don Quixote. See Cervantes, Miguel de

Doña Rosita la soltera (Dona Rosita, the Spinster). See García Lorca, Federico

Donati, Forese, 412a

Donation of Constantine, 423a–b

Donaueschingen *Passions*, 1066a–b

Doni, Antonfrancesco

INDEX

I marmi (*The Marbles*), novellas as sources
for, 1444a
Panchatantra translated by, 1444b
"Donne ch'avete intelletto d'amore." *See* Dante
Alighieri, *Vita nuova*
Donne, John
influence on pastoral lyric, 1419b
"The Bait," pastoral argument in, 1419a–b
"Twickenham Garden," Arcadia in,
1403b–1404a
"Don't fret, don't cry, don't pine . . . ." *See*
Pasternak, Boris, *Second Birth* (*Vtoroe
rozhdenie*), "Ne volnuisia, ne plach', ne
trudi . . ."
Doppelgänger
Andersen and, 24a
in Pirandello's *The Late Mattia Pascal,* 1298a
Doppelroman, Hesse's *Narcissus and
Goldmund* as, 751b
"Dorozhenka." *See* Solzhenitsyn, Aleksandr
Dorp, Martin, Erasmus and, 540b
Dort, Bernard, 825a
Dorval, Marie, Sand and, 1578b
Dostigaev i drugie (Dostigaev and Others). *See*
Gorky, Maxim
Dostoevsky, Feodor, **479a–501b**
"A Faint Heart," 483a
"A Gentle Creature," 492b, 496a
A Raw Youth, 496b–497b
Belinsky and, 481a–483b
"Bobok," 496a
Camus and, 311b, 331a
Chekhov and, 375a
Crime and Punishment (*Prestuplenie i
nakazanie*), 490a–491b
The Three of Them and, 696a
"Diary of a Writer," 496a–b
Doctor Faustus and, 1015a
Epoch magazine, 488b–489a
Hesse on, 745b–746a
interpretation of Pushkin's *The Gypsies,*
1349b
Kafka and, 852a
literary celebrity, 139b
"Mr. Prokharchin," 483a
Netochka Nezvanova, 483a–b
Notes from Underground (*Zapiski iz
podpol'ia*), 489a–490a
Rilke and, 1475a
Poor Folk, 481a–482a

Pushkin's *Covetous Knight* and, 1362a
Solzhenitsyn and, 1630b
The Brothers Karamazov (*Brat'ia
Karamozovy*), 497b–499b
Doctor Faustus and, 1015b
The Double, 482a–b
"The Dream of a Ridiculous Man," 496a
The Eternal Husband, 493b–494a
The Friend of the Family, 486a–b
The Gambler, 491b
"The Heavenly Christmas Tree," 496a
"The Honest Thief," 483a
The House of the Dead, 487a–b
The Idiot (*Idiot*), 492a–493b
The Insulted and the Injured, 487b–488b
"The Landlady," 483a
"The Life of a Great Sinner," 494a–495a
"The Peasant Marei," 496a
The Possessed (*Besy*), 147a, 484a–b,
494b–496a
Thomas Mann on, 1019b
Time (magazine), 486b–487a, 488b
Turgenev and, 1731a
"Uncle's Dream," 485b–486a
"Vlas," 496a
Western values and, 1182a
"Winter Notes on Summer Impressions," 488b
Double, The. See Dostoevsky, Feodor
Doubt
hyperbolic, in Descartes's *Meditations on
First Philosophy,* 440a–b, 441b–442a,
448b
in Rabelais, 1392a–b
Dovere del medico, Il. See Pirandello, Luigi
Dowry legend, 1062a–b
Drama
Aristotelian conception of, 297a
Brecht's theory of, 281b, 285b, 291a–291b
didactic, Brecht's *Schulopern,* 283a
French, antitheater, 32b
gestus in, 291a–292b
Goethe and, 297a
Greek, Wagner on, 1773b
Hugo's work in, 763a–b, 772b
Ibsen's use of verse in, 792b
Ionesco on, 818a–b
Marxist, 290b, 295b–296a, 296b
Maupassant's work in, 1029a–b
medieval, **1051a–1074b**
English, 1052a, 1068b–1069a

E

INDEX

INDEX

F

INDEX

Fables
  Aesopian, influence on Renaissance short
    fiction, 1434a
  La Fontaine on, 908a, 908b
Fables choisies. See La Fontaine, Jean de
Fabliaux
  influence on Renaissance short fiction,
    1437a–b, 1449b
  Rabelais and, 1381a
Fábula de Polifemo y Galatea. See Góngora,
  Luis de
Facetia (joke), in Renaissance short fiction,
  1441b–1443a
Facetie, motti et burle. See Domenichi,
  Ludovico
Fâcheux, Les. See Molière
Facial imagery, in Rilke, 1469a–b, 1470a
Fact and Fiction. See Goethe, Johann Wolfgang
  von, *Dichtung und Wahrheit*
Fact and fiction, in Dinesen's tales, 454b–455b
Facta et dicta memorabilia. See Valerius
  Maximus
Faerie Queene, The. See Spenser, Edmund
Fáfnismál, 1220a
Fail, Noël. *See* Du Fail, Noël
"Faint Heart, A." *See* Dostoevsky, Feodor
Fair Unknown
  Chrétien de Troyes and, 91b
  earliest version of, 91a–b
Fairies, The. *See* Wagner, Richard, *Die Feen*
Fairy tale
  in America, 18a
  of Hoffmann, Hesse's *Steppenwolf* and, 749b
  See also Andersen, Hans Christian; Pushkin,
    Alexander
Fairy Tale of My Life, The. See Andersen, Hans
  Christian
Fairy Tales Told for Children. See Andersen,
  Hans Christian
Faith, religious
  in Hesse's "Ein Stückchen Theologie," 751a
  in Ionesco's plays, 835a, 835b, 843a
  Kierkegaard and, 887b, 891b–892a, 896b–898a
  reason and, Aquinas on, 72b
Faithful Shepherd. See Guarini, Giambattista,
  Pastor fido
Faithful Shepherdess, The. See Fletcher, John
Fall, The. See Camus, Albert
Fall Wagner, Der (*The Fall of Wagner*). *See*
  Nietzsche, Friedrich

"Fallen Laurel, The." *See* Petrarch, "Laurea
  Occidens"
Fal'shivaia moneta. See Gorky, Maxim
"Fama tuba dante sonum." *See* Archpoet
"Fame with its trumpet blowing." *See* Archpoet,
  "Fama tuba dante sonum"
"Familiar Dialogues on the Poetry of the
  Proletarians." *See* Sand, George,
  "Dialogues familiers sur la poésie des
  prolétaires"
Familiaries. See Petrarch, *Rerum familiarium
  libri*
Family
  Augustinian trinitarianism and, 118b–119a
  disintegration of
    in Gorky's fiction, 693a–b, 694b–695a,
      704b
    in Mann's *Buddenbrooks*, 998a–999b
"Family Affair, A." *See* Maupassant, Guy de, "En
  famille"
Family Happiness. See Tolstoy, Leo
Family Idiot, The. See Sartre, Jean-Paul
Family romance, Freud's concept of, 576b
Family saga, Zola's Rougon-Macquarts series,
  1794a–b, 1795b–1808a
Famine, in Chekhov's "The Wife," 370b
Fanal bleu, Le. See Colette
Fantasies and Sketches. See Andersen, Hans
  Christian
"Fantôme de Staline, Le." *See* Sartre, Jean-Paul,
  The Ghost of Stalin
Farce
  German, of Wagner, 1783a
  Hávarðar saga Ísfirðings as, 1218b
  historical evolution of, 1116b–1117a
  medieval, 1071a, 1072a
  typical characters and plots, 1117a
Færeyinga saga, 1203a
Fascism
  German, 1194b
  Mann's *Mario and the Magician* and, 1009a
  Pirandello and, 1294b
  Rhinocéros and, 827a
  in *The Lesson*, 820a
Fastnachtspiele, 1071a
Fastoul, Baude, 1060a
Fatal Skin, The. See Balzac, Honoré de, *La peau
  de chagrin*
Fate
  Anouilh's view on origin of, 37a

INDEX

Ibsen plays filmed, 810a
Ibsen's *Doll's House,* 810a
Pirandello
    As You Desire Me, 1295a
    La canzone dell'amore, 1295a
Filocolo. See Boccaccio, Giovanni
Filostrato. See Boccaccio, Giovanni
Fils naturel, Le. See Diderot, Denis
"Fils, Un." *See* Maupassant, Guy de
Fin de Chéri, La. See Colette
Fin de Satan, La. See Hugo, Victor
Financiers, in Deschamps' satire, 1091a–1092a
Finnboga saga ramma, 1219b, 1220a
Fiore, Il (*The Flower*), Dante and, 424b
Fiorenza. See Mann, Thomas
Fire imagery
    in Hesse's prose, 736a, 746b
    in Ionesco's *The Bald Soprano,* 818b–819a
Firenzuola, Angelo
    novellas of, 1444b–1445a
    Ragionamenti (*Discussions*), 1445a
Firm of Nucingen, The. See Balzac, Honoré de,
    La maison Nucingen
First Circle, The. See Solzhenitsyn, Aleksandr
First Decade. See Machiavelli, Niccolò,
    Decennale primo
First Grammatical Treatise, The, 1202a
"First and Last Declaration, A." *See*
    Kierkegaard, Søren
"First Long Railroad Ride, The." *See* Kafka,
    Franz, "Die erste lange Eisenbahnfahrt"
"First Love." *See* Babel, Isaac, "Pervaia liubov";
    Gorky, Maxim, "O pervoi liubvi";
    Turgenev, Ivan
First Man, The. *See* Camus, Albert, *Le premier*
    homme
Fischer, S. (German publisher), Hesse and,
    738a
Fischer-Dieskau, Dietrich, on Nietzsche and
    Wagner, 1169a
Fitch, Clyde, Ibsen's influence on, 809b
Fitzgerald, F. Scott, Babel and, 134b
"Five Songs." *See* Rilke, Rainer Maria, "Fünf
    Gesänge"
Flaminio, Marcantonio, *lusis pastorales* of,
    1413a–b
Flashback technique, Anouilh's use of, 49a
Flaubert, Gustave, **553a–574b**
    "A Simple Heart," 572a
    Bouvard and Pécuchet, 570b–572a

Cocagne, 146b
"Hérodias," 565a, 572b
Kafka and, 848b, 852a
L'Éducation sentimentale (*Sentimental
    Education*), 553a, 554a, 555b–557b,
    567a–570b, 1029a
    Paris in, 176b
Madame Bovary, 554a, 561b–565a, 1029b,
    1034b
    Proust's *Remembrance of Things Past* and,
    1322b
    Maupassant and, 1025b, 1026a–1028b,
    1029a–b, 1030a–1031a, 1032a, 1034b,
    1048b
Memoirs of a Madman, 554a
on Montaigne, 1157a
November, 554a–555b
Proust and, 1317b, 1326a
"Saint Julian the Hospitaller," 565a, 572b
Salammbô, 146b, 565a–567a
Sand and, 1590b–1591a
Sartre and, 1612b–1617a
The Temptation of Saint Anthony,
    557b–558b, 565a
Turgenev and, 1733a
Fletcher, John, *The Faithful Shepherdess,*
    Guarini's influence on, 1424a
Fletcher, John, and Beaumont, Francis, *The
    Triumph of Death,* Bandello as source
    for, 1447b
Fleury, Cardinal de, Voltaire and,
    1746b–1747a
Fleury Play Book, 1062a, 1062b
Fliegende Holländer, Der. See Wagner,
    Richard, *The Flying Dutchman*
Flies, The. See Sartre, Jean-Paul
Fliess, Wilhelm, Freud and, 577b, 583a,
    584a–b, 589a
Flight of the Lindberghs, The. See Brecht,
    Bertolt, *Der Flug der Lindberghs*
Flight, The. See Ionesco, Eugène, *La soif et la
    faim* (*Hunger and Thirst*), *La fuite*
Flight theme, in Ionesco's *A Stroll in the Air,*
    831a, 831b
Flight to Arras. See Saint-Exupéry, Antoine de,
    Pilote de guerre
Fljótsdæla saga, 1220b–1221a
Flokkr, 1200b
Flood. See Grass, Günter

1877

INDEX

INDEX

INDEX

G

INDEX

Gil Polo, Gaspar, *Diana enamorada* (Diana in Love), influence on pastoral romance, 1426a, 1426b–1427b

Giono, Jean, Camus and, 311b

"Giornata, Una." *See* Pirandello, Luigi

Giotto, Dante and, 412a

"Giovane donna sotto un verde lauro." *See* Petrarch, *Canzoniere*

Giovanni del Virgilio, Dante's epistolary eclogues to, 1407b–1408a

Giraldi, Giambattista
Egle as tragicomedy, 1421a
Gli ecatommiti (*The Hundred Stories*), 1447b–1448b
Orbecche, Senecan tragedy and, 1448b
tragicomedy and, 1421a

Giraudoux, Jean
modernization of myth, 36b
Siegfried, Anouilh and, 33b

Girl with the Golden Eyes, The. See Balzac, Honoré de, *La fille aux yeux d'or*

"Girl's Confession, A." *See* Proust, Marcel, *Les plaisirs et les jours*

Gísla saga Súrssonar, 1218a–b, 1219a

"Gitanilla, La." *See* Cervantes, Miguel de

Giuoco delle parti, Il. See Pirandello, Luigi

Gizur (Icelandic bishop), 1201b

Gladkov, Aleksandr, Pasternak's conversation with, 1244b

"Glance at a Contemporary Effort in Danish Literature, A." *See* Kierkegaard, Søren

Glasperlenspiel, Das (*The Glass Bead Game*). *See* Hesse, Hermann

Gleisdreieck. See Grass, Günter

Gleoman, in Germanic society, 231a

Gluttony, in Rabelais's *Fourth Book*, 1394a–b

Gobineau, Arthur de
Essay on the Inequalities of Races, 1784a
Tocqueville and, 1690a–b

God. See Hugo, Victor, *Dieu*

God
"death of", in Nietzsche, 1182b, 1186a
as deceiver, in Descartes's *Meditations on First Philosophy*, 440b, 444a–b, 445a
Dumas's view of, 518a, 523a
existence of
Aquinas on, 68a–69a
Augustine on, 124b
in Descartes's *Meditations on First Philosophy*, 443a–444a, 446a–447a

Hugo's view of, 777b–780b, 783b–784a
knowability of, in Augustine's *Confessions*, 112a
as last end of man, Aquinas on, 73a
in Mann's *Joseph and His Brothers*, 1013b, 1014a
Maupassant's view of, 1041a
nature of
Aquinas on, 68a, 69a–b
Scriptum super Sententias on, 60a–b

Godly Feast. *See* Erasmus, "Convivium religiosum"

Gods, pagan, Augustine's *City of God* on, 115a–b

Goethe és kora (*Goethe and His Age*). *See* Lukács, György

Goethe, Johann Wolfgang von, **655a–680b**
allegory and, 1502a–b
Altersstil of, 757a
Andersen and, 15a–b
Brecht and, 285b–287b, 293a, 297a
Clavigo, 658a–b
Dichtung und Wahrheit (*Poetry and Truth*), 656b, 660a
Die Leiden des jungen Werthers (*The Sorrows of Young Werther*), 659a–662a, 665b, 667a, 669a, 674b
Die natürliche Tochter (*The Natural Daughter*), 668b
Die Wahlverwandtschaften (*Elective Affinities*), 669b, 670b–671a
Dinesen and, 466b
Dostoevsky and, 480b
Egmont, 663a–664b
Faust, 287a, 656a–b, 659a, 668b, 671a, 671b–678a
Egmont and, 663b, 664b
Ibsen and, 789a
Iphigenia in Tauris and, 666b
Mann's *Doctor Faustus* and, 1015b, 1016a
Pasternak's *Doctor Zhivago* and, 1246b
personal experience and, 657a
Gide and, 632a
Götz von Berlichingen, 658a–659a, 663b, 664b
"Helena," 668b
Hesse and, 737b
in Hesse's *Steppenwolf*, 750a, 750b
Iphigenia in Tauris (*Iphigenie auf Tauris*), 664b–665a, 666a–b, 668a, 668b

INDEX

INDEX

INDEX

H

H. C. Andersens Levnedsbog 1805–1831. See Andersen, Hans Christian

Hadji-Murad. See Tolstoy, Leo

Hahn, Reynaldo, Proust and, 1318b

Hákon the Old of Iceland, king, 1221a–b

Hákonar saga gamla. See Sturla Thórdarson

Half-line, in Anglo-Saxon poetry, 232b–233a

Halldórs þáttr Snorrasonar, 1206a

Halle, Adam de la. *See* Adam de la Halle

Hallfreðar saga, 1206a–b

Hamann, Johann Georg, on poetry, 657b

Hamburger, Käte, on Rilke, 1478a

Hamburgische Dramaturgie, The (The Hamburg Dramaturgy). See Lessing, Gotthold Ephraim

Hamlet. See Shakespeare, William

"Hamlet and Don Quixote." *See* Turgenev, Ivan

Hampton, Christopher, *Tales from Hollywood,* 1010a

Handbook of the Christian soldier. *See* Erasmus, *Enchiridion militis Christiani*

Hænsa-þóris saga, 1217b

Hańska, Madame, Balzac and, 161b–162a

Hanslick, Eduard, Wagnerism and, 1768b

Happiness, in Camus, 317a, 320b–321a

Happy Death, A. See Camus, Albert

Happy Warriors, The. See Laxness, Halldór, *Gerpla*

Harald Fairhair
  in sagas of Snorri Sturluson, 1210a
  skaldic poetry and, 1200b
  in *Vatnsdœla saga,* 1212a

Harðar saga, 1219a

Hardy, Alexandre, Guarini's influence on, 1423b

Hardy, Thomas, Proust and, 1321b

Harlem, in Lorca's poetry, 611b–613b

"Harry the Steppenwolf." *See* Hesse, Hermann, "Vom Steppenwolf"

Hartmann von Aue, Chrétien's *Erec et Enide* and, 94b

Hašek, Jaroslav, Mann's *Confessions of Felix Krull* and, 1019a

Hasidism, Kafka and, 849a

"Háttatal." *See* Snorri Sturluson, *Edda*

Hattingberg, Magda von, 1465b

Haufniensis, Vigilius. *See* Kierkegaard, Søren

"Haunted House, The." *See* Pirandello, Luigi, "La casa del Granella"

Hauptmann, Gerhart, Ibsen's influence on, 809b

Hauspostille. See Brecht, Bertolt, *Manual of Piety*

Hauvette, Henri, *Boccace,* 256a

Hávarðar saga Ísfirðings (Saga of Howard the Halt), 1218b–1219a

Hayman, Ronald, on Nietzsche, 1195b

He Who Says Yes/He Who Says No. See Brecht, Bertolt

"He?." *See* Maupassant, Guy de, "Lui?"

Headbirths; or, The Germans Are Dying Out. See Grass, Günter

Heaven, Augustine on, 113a

"Heavenly breeze that breathes in that green laurel, The." *See* Petrarch, *Canzoniere* "L'Aura celeste che 'n quel verde lauro"

"Heavenly Christmas Tree, The." *See* Dostoevsky, Feodor

Hebbel, Friedrich
  Herod and Mariamne (Herodes und Mariamne), 794a
  on Ibsen, 791a–b
  Maria Magdalena, 794a

Hebel, Johann Peter, *Unverhofftes Wiedersehen (The Unanticipated Reencounter),* 25b

Hedda Gabler. See Ibsen, Henrik

Hedonism, in Gide's *Fruits of the Earth,* 648b–649a

Hegel, Georg Wilhelm Friedrich
  dialectic, 811a
  education of, 737a
  Ibsen and, 791a, 792a, 811a
  Kierkegaard and, 895b–896a
  Mann's *Magic Mountain* and, 1005a
  master-servant notion, Andersen and, 24a
  on philosophy's development, 1176b

Hegius, Alexander, Erasmus and, 530a

Heiberg, Johan Ludvig
  Andersen and, 10b–11a
  Kierkegaard and, 882b

Heiðarvíga saga (The Story of the Moor-killings), 1207b

Heidegger, Martin
  Grass and, 721a–722a
  Kierkegaard and, 894a

INDEX

INDEX

INDEX

INDEX

INDEX

INDEX

1899

INDEX

INDEX

K

INDEX

INDEX

INDEX

INDEX

INDEX

M

INDEX

INDEX

INDEX

Marcuse, Herbert, Thomas Mann and, 1004b, 1005a

Mare au diable, La. See Sand, George, *The Devil's Pool*

Marguerite de Valois. See Dumas père, Alexandre, *La reine Margot*

Marguerite of Navarre
Heptaméron, 1451b–1452b
Boccaccio's influence on, 1449b, 1451a–b
pastoral poetry of, 1415a
patronage of, 1452b

Maria Magdalena. See Hebbel, Friedrich

Mariage de Figaro, Le. See Beaumarchais, Pierre-Augustin Caron de, *The Marriage of Figaro*

Marie Antoinette of France, queen, in Dumas's works, 510b, 513a, 517a–518a

Marie de France, Brother Róbert and, 1221b

Marie Tudor. See Hugo, Victor

Marigo, Aristide, 421b

Mariia. See Babel, Isaac

Marini, Giambattista, Petrarchan influence, 1284a–b

Mario und der Zauberer (*Mario and the Magician*). *See* Mann, Thomas

Marionette, che passione!. See San Secondo, Rosso di

Marionettes, Dinesen and, 469a

Marionettes, What Passions They Feel!. *See* San Secondo, Rosso di, *Marionette, che passione!*

Marivaux, Pierre, Anouilh and, 43b, 44a

Markish, Simon, on Isaac Babel, 137a–b

Marlowe, Christopher
Machiavelli and, 973b
Mann's *Doctor Faustus* and, 1017a
"The Passionate Shepherd to His Love," 1419a

Marmi, I. See Doni, Antonfrancesco

Marot, Clément
La Fontaine and, 907a
pastoral poetry of, 1415a
Petrarch and, 1284a

Marriage
Ibsen's *A Doll's House*, 795b–796a
Kierkegaard and, 894b–895a
Molière on, 1117b–1118b
in Tolstoy's works
Anna Karenina, 795b–796a
Family Happiness, 1709b–1710a

Marriage of Figaro, The. See Beaumarchais, Pierre-Augustin Caron de

Marshlands. See Gide, André

Mart semnadtsatogo. See Solzhenitsyn, Aleksandr, *The Red Wheel*

"Martirio de Santa Olalla." *See* García Lorca, Federico

Martoglio, Nino, Pirandello and, 1293a

Marvell, Andrew
pastoral poetry of, 1419b
"The Garden"
Arcadia in, 1403b–1404a
complexity of, 1419b

Marx, Karl
on exile, 1009b
Gorky and, 683b

Marxism
aesthetics and, 296b, 297a
Beauvoir and, 209a, 213a
Brecht and, 281b, 282b, 284a, 285b, 286a, 290b, 293a, 295b–296a, 296b
Camus and, 323b
drama and, 290b
existentialism and, 202a
Sartre and, 1609b–1612a
Zola and, 1801b

März (journal), Hesse and, 739a

Masaryk, Thomas G., *Spirit of Russia*, Dostoevsky and, 480a

Maschera e il volto, La. See Chiarelli, Luigi

Maschere, Le. See Machiavelli, Niccolò

Masculine principle, in Hugo's works, 771a–b

Mask and the Face, The. *See* Chiarelli, Luigi, *La maschera e il volto*

Masks, in Hugo's works, 779a

Masks, The. See Machiavelli, Niccolò, *Le maschere*

Masochism, Rousseau and, 1520a

Mason, Eudo, on Rilke, 1464b

Masquerades, Camus and, 313a–b, 319a

Masson, Paul, and Colette, 392b

Master Bellringers, The. See Sand, George, *Les maîtres sonneurs*

Master Builder, The. See Ibsen, Henrik

"Master Glass." *See* Cervantes, Miguel de

Master and Man. See Tolstoy, Leo

Masterpiece, The. See Zola, Émile, *L'Oeuvre*

Masuccio Salernitano, *Novellino*, 1443a–1444a

Mat'. See Gorky, Maxim, *Mother*

INDEX

INDEX

Moral Letters to Sophie. See Rousseau, Jean
Jacques
Morality
art and, in Mann, 1006a
Camus and, 327b
Nietzsche on
Christianity and, 1188b–1189b
creation of, 1192b
eternal recurrence and, 1193b–1687a
"master morality," 1187b–1188a
Overman and, 1189b–1192a
self-discipline and, 1193b
value systems of, opposing, 1187b–1188b
will to power and, 1192b–1193b
in *Romance of the Rose,* 1495b
spirituality and, in Mann's *Joseph and His
Brothers,* 1011b
Tolstoy on literature and, 1709a–b
Morality plays, 1071a, 1071b–1072a
Moralized Ovid, 1065a
More, Thomas, Erasmus and, 532a, 541b
Moreno, Marguerite, and Colette, 392b
Morgenlandfahrt, Die. See Hesse, Hermann
Morgenröte. See Nietzsche, Friedrich
Moriae encomium. See Erasmus, *The Praise of
Folly*
Morkinskinna, 1215a
Morlini, Girolamo, *Novellae,* 1444b
Mornay, Philippe de, Montaigne and, 1149a
Morny, Mathilde de ("Missy"), 393b
Morozov, Savva, Gorky and, 684a
Morris, William, *Völsunga saga* and, 1222b
Morsa, La. See Pirandello, Luigi
Mort heureuse, La. See Camus, Albert, *A Happy
Death*
Mort très douce, Une. See Beauvoir, Simone de,
A Very Easy Death
Mortality
in Ionesco's plays
Exit the King, 832b
Jacques, 820a–b
Morte Darthur. See Malory, Sir Thomas
Moschus
Lament for Bion, Renaissance pastoral elegy
and, 1404b–1405a
Renaissance pastoral poetry and,
1404b–1405a
Moscow Art Theater
Chekhov and, 361a, 363a, 363b, 383a

Gorky and, 683b, 699a
Moses Saved. See Saint-Amant, Girard, *Moyse
sauvé*
Mother. See Gorky, Maxim
Mother
in Flaubert's writings, 555b
Freud's concept of, 583b
in *Narcissus and Goldmund,* 752b
relationship with son, in Camus, 315a–318a
Mother Courage and Her Children. See Brecht,
Bertolt
"Mother Savage." *See* Maupassant, Guy de, "La
mère Sauvage"
Mother, The. See Brecht, Bertolt
Motion
Aquinas' *Summa theologica* on, 68b
physics of, Descartes vs. Gassendi, 449a–b
"Motiv der Kästchenwahl, Das." *See* Freud,
Sigmund
Motor Show, The. See Ionesco, Eugène, *Le salon
d'automobile*
Mots, Les. See Sartre, Jean-Paul, *The Words*
Mouches, Les. See Sartre, Jean-Paul, *The Flies*
Mountain Giants, The. See Pirandello, Luigi
"Mountain That Gives Birth, The." *See* La
Fontaine, Jean de, *Fables,* "La montagne
qui accouche"
Mourgues, Odette de, *La Fontaine: "Fables,"*
919b
Mousquetaire, Le. See Dumas père, Alexandre
"Moya zhizn." *See* Chekhov, Anton
Moyse sauvé. See Saint-Amant, Girard
Mozart and Salieri. See Pushkin, Alexander
Mozart, Wolfgang Amadeus
Don Giovanni, 1131a
in Hesse's *Steppenwolf,* 750a, 750b, 751a
"Mr. Prokharchin." *See* Dostoevsky, Feodor
Mrs. Morli, One and Two. See Pirandello, Luigi,
La signora Morli, una e due
"Mstitel." *See* Chekhov, Anton
Muette de Portici, La. See Auber, Daniel
François Esprit
Mulatto, The. See Andersen, Hans Christian
Mule sans frein, La
Chrétien de Troyes and, 91b, 99a
Gawain in, 99a
"Mum and the Sothsegger," 1092b–1093a
"Mumu." *See* Turgenev, Ivan
Munich, Wagner in, 1778a–1779a

INDEX

Murder, Camus and, 326a–327a

Muri Easter play, 1057a, 1067b–1068a

Murner, Thomas, Luther and, 944a

Musco, Angelo, Pirandello and, 1293a–b

Muse du département, La (*The Muse of the District*). *See* Balzac, Honoré de

Muse française, La. See Hugo, Victor

"Muse of the Twentieth Century, The." *See* Andersen, Hans Christian

Musée imaginaire de la sculpture, Le. See Malraux, André

Muses galantes, Les. See Rousseau, Jean Jacques

Music

    Augustine on, 126b–127b

    in Chekhov's works, 376a–b, 383a

    Luther and, 945a

    in Rilke's works, 1474a, 1475a, 1482a

    Rousseau and, 1520a–1521b

    Wagner and

        admiration for Italian, 1770b–1771a

        libretto, 1769b–1140a, 1774a–1775b

"Music for Brass." *See* Grass, Günter, *Die Vorzüge der Windhühner* (The Advantages of Windfowl), "Blechmusik"

"Music of the Future." *See* Wagner, Richard, "Zukunftsmusik"

Music-Hall Sidelights. See Colette, *L'Envers du music-hall*

Musil, Robert

    Hesse's *Beneath the Wheel* and, 738b

    Pirandello and, 1313b

    on Rilke, 1461a, 1461b, 1462b, 1467a

Musset, Alfred de

    Confessions of a Child of the Century (*La confession d'un enfant du siècle*), 179a, 1791b

    Sand's affair with, 1578b–1581a

    Zola and, 1790b–1791b

Mussolini, Benito

    Machiavelli and, 974a

    Rilke and, 1464b

Must We Burn Sade?. See Beauvoir, Simone de

Mutter Courage und ihre Kinder. See Brecht, Bertolt, *Mother Courage and Her Children*

Mutter, Die. See Brecht, Bertolt, *The Mother*

"Muzhiki." *See* Chekhov, Anton

My Apprenticeship. See Gorky, Maxim

My Apprenticeships. See Colette, *Mes apprentissages*

"My Belief." *See* Hesse, Hermann, "Mein Glaube"

"My First Goose." *See* Babel, Isaac, "Moi pervyi gus"

"My good fortune is late and slow in coming." *See* Petrarch, *Canzoniere,* "Mie venture al venir son tarde et pigre"

My Interviews. *See* Gorky, Maxim, "Moi interv'iu"

"My Italy." *See* Petrarch, *Canzoniere,* "Italia mia"

"My Life." *See* Chekhov, Anton, "Moya zhizn"; Nietzsche, Friedrich, "Mein Leben"

My Life. See Wagner, Richard

My Memoirs. See Dumas père, Alexandre, *Mes mémoires*

My Mother's House. See Colette, *La maison de Claudine*

"My Notes: Odessa." *See* Babel, Isaac, "Moi listki: Odessa"

My Sister, Life. See Pasternak, Boris

"My Travelling Companion." *See* Gorky, Maxim, "Moi sputnik"

My Universities. See Gorky, Maxim

Mystery plays, 1065b–1070b

    German, 1066a–1068b

    miracle plays and, 1061b

Mysticism

    Christian

        in Augustine's *On the Trinity,* 118b

        Luther and, 933a–b

Myth, Wagner and, 1167a–b

Myth of Sisyphus, The (*Le mythe de Sisyphe*). *See* Camus, Albert

Mythology

    Christian

        in German Easter plays, 1067b

        Jeu de Saint Nicolas and, 1063b

        in miracle plays, 1065a

    classical, Anouilh's modernization of, 36b–37a, 38b

    comparative, miracle plays and, 1061b

    Hebrew, Mann's *Joseph and His Brothers* and, 1010a–1014a

    in Middle Ages, 79a

    Norse, *See* Norse sagas

1923

INDEX

O

INDEX

INDEX

P

INDEX

INDEX

Peasants, The. See Balzac, Honoré de, *Les paysans*

"Peasants, The." *See* Chekhov, Anton, "Muzhiki"

Peau de chagrin, La. See Balzac, Honoré de

Pecham, John, vs. Aquinas, 66a, 66b, 71b, 74b

Pechat' i revolutsiia (Russian journal), Babel's articles in, 135b

Pecorone, Il. See Ser Giovanni Fiorentino

Pedro de Urdemalas. See Cervantes, Miguel de

Peer Gynt. See Grieg, Edvard; Ibsen, Henrik

Péguy, Charles, Proust and, 1319a

Peire Cardenal, "Aquesta gens, cant son en lur gaieza" ("These people, when they are in good spirits"), 1109b–1110a

"Penal Colony, The." *See* Kafka, Franz

Penitential Psalms. *See* Petrarch, *Psalmi poenitentiales*

Pensaci, Giacomino!. See Pirandello, Luigi

Pentamerone, Il. See Basile, Giambattista, *Lo cunto de li cunti*

"Pente de la rêverie, La." *See* Hugo, Victor

Perception
  Augustine on, 120a
  Sartre and, 1595b–1596a

Père Goriot, Le. See Balzac, Honoré de

"Père, Le." *See* Maupassant, Guy de

"Père Milon, Le." *See* Maupassant, Guy de

Peredur, 85b

"Perekhod cherez Zbruch." *See* Babel, Isaac

Pérez, Alonso, *Segunda parte de la Diana* (The Second Part of the Diana), influence on pastoral romance, 1426a, 1426b–1427b

Perjury, Augustine on, 129a

Perlesvaus, Gawain in, 100a

Persiles y Sigismunda. See Cervantes, Miguel de, *The Trials of Persiles and Sigismunda*

Persius
  on Horace, 1089a
  Marcabru and, 1107a

Personification
  allegory and, 1504a–1506a
  in classical literature, 1104b–1105a
  in Dante's *Vita nuova*, 421a
  in medieval satire, 1107b

"Pervaia liubov." *See* Babel, Isaac

Peshkov, Aleksey Maksimovich. *See* Gorky, Maxim

Pessimism

in Maupassant's works, 1040b
  Voltaire on, 1760a

Peste, Le. See Camus, Albert, *The Plague*

Peter I the Great, czar of Russia, in Pushkin's works, 1351a–1352b, 1357b

Peter Camenzind. See Hesse, Hermann

Peter of Gaveston, 1108a

Peter of Hibernia, 58b

Peter Lombard
  Dante and, 413b
  Sententiae in IV libris distinctae (*The Four Books of the Sentences*), 55a–b, 60a–b

"Peter and Rosa." *See* Dinesen, Isak

Petit de Julleville, L., 1064b

"Petit poisson et le pêcheur, Le." *See* La Fontaine, Jean de, *Fables*

Petit prince, Le. See Saint-Exupéry, Antoine de

Petite Fadette, La. See Sand, George, *Little Fadette*

Petite Molière, La. See Anouilh, Jean, and Barrault, Jean-Louis

"Petite Roque, La." *See* Maupassant, Guy de

Petrarch, **1255a–1287b**
  "Ad se ipsum" ("To Himself"), 1258b
  Africa, 1259b, 1260a, 1260b–1262b, 1276a
  "Amor pastorius" ("The Amorous Shepherd"), 1264b
  "Argus," 1264b
  on Aristotle, 1268a
  Boccaccio and, 255b–256a, 273b–274b, 275a–b
    on the Griselda story, 272b, 274a
  Bucolicum carmen (Bucolic Song), 1264a–1265b
  Canzoniere, 1255a–b, 1259b, 1263b, 1272b–1282b
    "A qualunque animale alberga in terra" ("For whatever animals dwell on earth"), 1276a
    "Anima che diverse cose tante" ("Soul, who see so many different things"), 1277a
    ballads, sonnets, and madrigals, 1280b
    "Benedetto sia 'l giorno" ("Blessed be the day"), 1282a–b
    canzoni and sestinas, 1280b–1281a
    "Chi vuol veder quantunque po Natura" ("Whoever wishes to see"), 1276b

1936

INDEX

INDEX

INDEX

INDEX

rustic, etymology of term, 1406a

vernacular, Augustine's *On Christian Doctrine* and, 123b

Poetry of Banditry, The. See Veshnev, V., "Poeziia banditizma"

Poetry and Truth. See Goethe, Johann Wolfgang von, *Dichtung und Wahrheit*

Poet's Bazaar, A. See Andersen, Hans Christian

"Poeziia banditizma." *See* Veshnev, V.

Poezye. See Mickiewicz, Adam

Poggio Bracciolini, Gian Francesco, *Liber facetiarum* (Book of Jokes), 1441b–1442a

Poggioli, Renato
  on Chekhov's "The Darling," 379b–380a
  The Oaten Flute, on pastoral poetics, 1420a

Pogrom, in Babel's writing, 140b, 143a, 143b, 145b

Point Counter Point. See Huxley, Aldous

Point of View for My Work as an Author, The. See Kierkegaard, Søren

"Pois l'iverns d'ogan es anatz." *See* Marcabru

Poissenot, Bénigne, *L'Esté,* 1453b

Poissons rouges ou mon père ce héros, Les. See Anouilh, Jean

Polak, Ernst, Kafka and, 851a

Polemical satire. *See* Satire

Polemicism
  in *Beowulf,* 223b
  in oral cultures, 222b

Polikushka. See Tolstoy, Leo

Polish Flag. *See* Grass, Günter, *Die Vorzüge der Windhühner* (The Advantages of Windfowl), "Polnische Fahne"

Political theory, of Tocqueville, 1673b–1674a, 1675a–1679b, 1690b

Politics
  Anouilh's literary response to, 46b–47a
  of Aquinas, 73b–74a
  Augustine's *City of God* and, 117a
  Camus and, 323b
  Flaubert on, 553a–b, 570a
  French
    Hugo's career in, 772b–773b
    Sand and, 1589b
    Tocqueville and, 1677a
  German
    Grass and, 722a–726a
    Luther and, 929a–949b
    Wagner and, 1773a, 1778a–1780a
  of Hesse, 754a

Ibsen on, 789b

Machiavelli's view of, 953a–975a
  factions, 968b–969a

repression in, in Gorky's fiction, 691a

Sartre and, 1596b, 1603b, 1606a–1610a

Zola on, 1792a–b

Poliziano, Angelo
  anecdotes by, 1442b
  Orfeo, Renaissance pastoral drama and, 1420b
  pastoral scholarship of, 1414b
  Sylvae, contribution to Renaissance pastoral poetry, 1410b

"Polnische Fahne." *See* Grass, Günter, *Die Vorzüge der Windhühner*

Polonskii, V., on Babel's *Red Cavalry*, 154b

Poltava. See Pushkin, Alexander

Pontano, Giovanni
  De sermone (*On Discourse*), anecdotes in, 1442b
  Lepidina, Renaissance pastoral poetry and, 1411a, 1412b
  Melisseus innovation of, 1410b–1411a

Poor Bitos. See Anouilh, Jean

Poor Folk. See Dostoevsky, Feodor

"Poor Folks." *See* Hugo, Victor, "Les pauvres gens"

Poor laborer persona, in medieval satire, 1100a

"Poprygunya." *See* Chekhov, Anton

Populists, Russian, in Gorky's *Children of the Sun,* 700b

Poquelin, Jean-Baptiste. *See* Molière

Porphyry, *Isagoge,* 53a

Porretane, Le. See Sabadino, Giovanni

Porte étroite, La. See Gide, André

Porto Empedocle, Sicily, Pirandello and, 1290b

Porto, Luigi da
  Romeo and Juliet
    Masuccio's influence on, 1444a
    structure of, 1432b

Poshlost, 367b

Poslednye. See Gorky, Maxim

Possédés, Les. See Camus, Albert, *The Possessed*

Possessed, The. See Dostoevsky, Feodor

Posteritati. See Petrarch

Posthumous Writings and Poems of Hermann Lauscher, The. *See* Hesse, Hermann, *Hinterlassene Schriften und Gedichte von Hermann Lauscher*

INDEX

INDEX

Processions
    in English cycle plays, 1069a
    in medieval drama, 1065b–1066a
Proclus, *Elements of Theology*, 55b
Progress, idea of, Machiavelli's view of,
    964b–965a
"Project for the Constitution of Corsica." *See*
    Rousseau, Jean Jacques
Project of a Universal Science. *See* Descartes,
    René, *Discours de la méthode*
"Promenade" ("A Walk"). *See* Maupassant,
    Guy de
Promenades et souvenirs. *See* Nerval, Gérard de
"Promeneur dans Paris insurgé, Un." *See* Sartre,
    Jean-Paul
*Promessi sposi, storia milanese del secolo XVII
    scoperta e rifatta da Alessandro Manzoni*.
    See Manzoni, Alessandro, *The Betrothed:
    A Milanese Story of the Seventeenth
    Century Discovered and Retold by
    Alessandro Manzoni*
Prométhée mal enchaîné, Le. *See* Gide, André,
    Prometheus Misbound
Prometheus Misbound. *See* Gide, André
Promontorium somnii. *See* Hugo, Victor
Propaganda
    Nazi, German intellectuals and, 1018a
    of Voltaire, 1741a–1742b, 1764a–1765a
Propertius, Petrarch's *Canzoniere* influenced by,
    1273b
Property, in Rousseau, 1540a
Prophet persona, in medieval satire,
    1097b–1098a
Prophets, procession of, in medieval drama,
    1058b
Propos rustiques. *See* Du Fail, Noël
Propp, Vladimir, on plot in the traditional story,
    224b
"Propter Sion non tacebo." *See* Walter of
    Châtillon
Prose Edda. *See* Snorri Sturluson, *Edda*
Prostitution, in Maupassant's works,
    1031a–1032b, 1033a–b
Protestant Reformation
    criteria of truth and, 438a–b
    Erasmus and, 543a–546b
    Luther and, 929a–949b
Protestantism
    medieval drama and, 1073a
    Montaigne on, 1153a, 1155a

"Protsessy." *See* Vaksberg, Arkady
Proudhon, Pierre-Joseph, treatment of women,
    1709b
Proust, Adrien, 1317a–b
Proust, Marcel, **1317a–1340b**
    Colette and, 408b
    Hesse and, 757a
    Jean Santeuil, 1319a–b, 1320b, 1334a
    Les plaisirs et les jours (*Pleasures and Days*),
        1319a
        "A Girl's Confession," 1334a
    Pirandello and, 1313b
    Remembrance of Things Past (*À la recherche
        du temps perdu*)
        Cities of the Plain (*Sodome et Gomorrhe*),
            1319b, 1321b–1322a, 1322a, 1324b,
            1326a, 1326b
        cyclical structure, 1323a
        genre of, 171b, 179b
        Jean Santeuil and, 1319b
        narration, 1320b–1321a
        Pléiade edition, 1320a
        plot, 1321a–1323a
        style, 1338b–1339a
        Swann's Way (*Du côté de chez Swann*),
            1319b, 1320b, 1321b, 1322a, 1326a,
            1328b–1330a, 1332a–b, 1333b, 1334a
        The Captive (*La prisonnière*), 1319b, 1322a
        The Fugitive (*La fugitive*), 1319b, 1322a
        The Guermantes Way (*Le côté de
            Guermantes*), 1319b, 1321b, 1324b
        Time Regained (*Le temps retrouvé*), 1319b,
            1322a, 1323b, 1327a, 1338a–b
        Within a Budding Grove (*À l'ombre des
            jeunes filles en fleurs*), 1319b,
            1321b, 1327b, 1328a, 1333b, 1335a
    Sand and, 1571a
    Sartre on, 191a
    Weil and, 190a
Proust, Robert, 1318a–b
"Provando la commedia." *See* Pirandello, Luigi
Proverbs, Solzhenitsyn's use of, 1642b–1643a
Providence, in Dumas's works, 517b–523a
Provincial Celebrity in Paris, A. *See* Balzac,
    Honoré de, *Un grand homme de province
    à Paris*
Prozess, Der. *See* Kafka, Franz, *The Trial*
Prozess der Jeanne d'Arc zu Rouen, Der. *See*
    Brecht, Bertolt, *The Trial of Joan of Arc at
    Rouen*

1944

INDEX

Prudentius
  Psychomachia (*The Battle for Man's Soul*), 1504a–1505a
    "Bataille des vices contre les vertus" and, 1103a
"Prudoterie," 925a
Prussian Nights (*Prusskie nichi*). *See* Solzhenitsyn, Aleksandr
Psalmi poenitentiales. See Petrarch
Psalms
  Augustine on, 128a
  Erasmus and, 549a–b
  Luther and, 932a
Pseudo-Dionysius, Aquinas and, 63b–64a
Pseudonyms
  Camus and, 313a
  Dinesen and, 453b
  Kierkegaard and, 877a–878a
  Stendhal and, 1649a
Psyche (Greek mythology), Chekhov's "The Darling" and, 379b–380a
Psyche, human, in Balzac's works, 169b
Psychoanalysis
  Freud and, 579a–582b, 590a–592b
  of Hesse, 740b–741a, 741b, 748b
  Nietzsche and, 1194a
  Sartre and, 1601a–b
  See also Freud, Sigmund
Psychologia Balnearia. See Hesse, Hermann, *Kurgast*
Psychologie de l'art, La. See Malraux, André, *The Psychology of Art*
Psychology
  allegory and, 1505a–1506a
  Kierkegaard and, 893a–894a
Psychology of Art, The. See Malraux, André
Psychology of the Imagination, The. See Sartre, Jean-Paul
Psychology of the Unconscious. See Jung, Carl, *Wandlungen und Symbole des Libido*
Psychomachia. See Prudentius
Psychopathology of Everyday Life, The. See Freud, Sigmund, *Zur Psychopathologie des Alltagslebens*
Public life, Montaigne on, 1151a
Público, El. See García Lorca, Federico
Pucelle, La. See Voltaire
Puddles. *See* García Lorca, Federico, "Remansos"

Pugachev, Emilian, revolt of, Pushkin and, 1345a, 1370a–1371a
Puissances du désert, Les. Malraux, André
Punin, Nikolai, Pasternak's intercession for, 1231b
Punishments. See Hugo, Victor, *Châtiments*
Punitive fantasies, of Kafka, 857b–858a, 859a–b, 863b–864a, 865b, 869a–b
Puns, in medieval satire, 1109a–b
Puntila and Matti, His Hired Man. See Brecht, Bertolt
Puppet, man as (Pirandello), 1300b
"Puppeteer, The." *See* Andersen, Hans Christian
Pur et l'impur, Le. See Colette
Pure and the Impure, The. See Colette, *Le pur et l'impur*
Purgatorio. See Dante Alighieri
Purgatory, in Dante's *Divine Comedy*, 427a–b
Purge, The. *See* Anouilh, Jean, *Épuration*
Purity of Heart Is to Will One Thing. See Kierkegaard, Søren
"Pus s'enfulleysson li verjan." *See* Marcabru
Pushkin, Alexander, **1341a–1373b**
  A Journey to Erzurum, 1345b
  Angelo, 1345a
  Boris Godunov, 1344a, 1360a–1361b
    permission to publish, 1344b
  Count Nulin, 1350a–b
  Dostoevsky and, 480b
  Eugene Onegin, 1343b, 1344a, 1344b, 1345a, 1352b–1355b
  Feast in Time of the Plague, 1345a, 1364a–b
  "I Have Raised to Myself a Monument," 1358a–b
  "I Remember a Wondrous Moment," 1356b–1357a, 1359a
  "In the Country," 1357b
  lyrics, 1355b–1360a
  "Mistress into Maid," 1369a
  Mozart and Salieri, 1345a, 1362b–1363b
  "Nereida," 1356b
  "No, I Do Not Value," 1357a
  Poltava, 1351a–1352a
  Ruslan and Lyudmila, 1343a, 1346b–1347a
  The Blackamoor of Peter the Great, 1344b
  The Bronze Horseman (*Mednyi vsadnik*), 1345a, 1351b, 1352a–b
  The Captain's Daughter (*Kapitanskaya dochka*), 1345b, 1370a–1371a

Q

INDEX

INDEX

INDEX

INDEX

INDEX

INDEX

INDEX

INDEX

T

INDEX

"Theater of the grotesque," Pirandello and, 1293b

Theater-in-the-theater (*teatro nel teatro*), Pirandello and, 1295b, 1305b, 1308a, 1312a

Théâtre de l'Equipe, Le, 309a

Théâtre Libre-Antoine (Paris), naturalist plays, 809b

"Theme of Three Caskets, The." *See* Freud, Sigmund, "Das Motiv der Kästchenwahl"

Themes and Variations. See Pasternak, Boris

Theocritus
    Idylls, 1404a
    Lament for Daphnis, Renaissance pastoral elegy and, 1404b–1405a
    Renaissance pastoral poetry and, 1404a, 1405a–1406a

Theodoricus (Norwegian cleric), *Historia de antiquitate regum Norwagiensium* (*History of Norwegian Kings from Ancient Times*), 1202b

Theologia naturalis. See Sebond, Raymond

Theologica Germanica. See Luther, Martin

Theology
    Aristotelianism and, 56a
    of Augustine's *On the Trinity,* 117b
    of Augustinians, 57b
    in Greban's *Passion,* 1069b–1070a
    Kierkegaard and, 882a–b
    Luther and, 929a–949a
    systematic
        in Aquinas' *Summa theologica,* 64b–65a
        in Peter Lombard's *Sententiae,* 55a

Theory of Color. See Goethe, Johann Wolfgang von

Theosophy, Pirandello and, 1296b

"There Is a Difference." *See* Andersen, Hans Christian

There Was a Prisoner. See Anouilh, Jean, *Y'avait un prisonnier*

Thérèse Raquin. See Zola, Émile

"These people, when they are in good spirits." *See* Peire Cardenal, "Aquesta gens, cant son en lur gaieza"

These Pleasures. See Colette, *Le pur et l'impur*

Theseid of the Nuptials of Emilia. *See* Boccaccio, Giovanni, "Teseida delle nozze d'Emilia"

Theseus. See Gide, André

Thibaudet, Albert, Montaigne and, 1157b

Þiðreks saga, 1223b

"Thieves." *See* Chekhov, Anton, "Vory"

Thieves' Carnival. See Anouilh, Jean

Think It Over, Giacomino!. See Pirandello, Luigi, *Pensaci, Giacomino!*

Third Book. See Rabelais, François

Thjódólf of Hvin, "Ynglingatal" ("Enumeration of the Ynglings"), 1210a

Thomas Aquinas, St. *See* Aquinas, Thomas, St.

Thomas, Augustus, Ibsen's influence on, 809b

Thomas of Brittany
    Tristan, Tristrams saga and, 1221b
    Tristan story and, 90b, 95a

Thomas à Kempis, *The Imitation of Christ* (*Imitatio Christi*), French Evangelicals and, 1376b

Þórðar saga hreðu (*The Story of Thórd Tumult*), 1219a–b

Þorgils saga ok Haflioða, 1221a, 1222a

Thorlák Runólfsson, 1203b

Thorlák Thórhallsson, 1203b, 1205b

Þorláks saga helga, 1205b

Thormód, *Þorgeirs drápa,* 1207a

Þormóðar þáttr, 1206a, 1207a

Þorsteins þáttr stangarhöggs (*The Story of Thorstein Staff-struck*), 1217a–b

Thought
    Augustine on, 120b
    existence and, in Descartes's *Meditations on First Philosophy,* 441b, 442a–b, 447b
    source of, in Descartes's *Meditations on First Philosophy,* 443a–b, 444a

Thought-Forms. See Leadbeater, C. W.

"Thoughts on Dostoevsky's *Idiot." See* Hesse, Hermann, *Blick ins Chaos* (*In Sight of Chaos*), "Gedanken zu Dostojewsky's *Idiot*"

Thousand and One Nights, influence on Renaissance short fiction, 1436a

Three clerics legend, 1062b

Three Essays on the Theory of Sexuality. See Freud, Sigmund, *Drei Abhandlungen zur Sexualtheorie*

Three Musketeers, The. See Dumas père, Alexandre, *Les trois mousquetaires*

Three Sisters, The. See Chekhov, Anton

Three of Them, The. See Gorky, Maxim, *Troe*

Three Truths. See Charron, Pierre, *Trois Veritez*

"Three Years." *See* Chekhov, Anton, "Tri goda"

INDEX

death theme, 1707b

diaries, 1697b–1699b

Family Happiness, 1694b, 1702a, 1709b–1710a

Father Sergius, 1694b, 1707b, 1711b–1712a

Four Epochs of Growth, 1699b

Gorky and, 682a, 682b, 683b, 686a, 706a

in the Crimea, 706b, 707a–b

The Lower Depths, 699b

Hadji-Murad, 1694b, 1712a, 1712b

"How Much Land Does a Man Need?,

"Chekhov's "Gooseberries" and, 377b

Kafka and, 850b

letter to Alexandra Tolstoy, 1702a

letter to Aunt Toinette, 1695b–1696a

literary celebrity, 139b

Master and Man, 1694b, 1711b

Notes of a Madman, 1707a

Pasternak and, 1229a, 1249b–1250a

peasantry in works of, 1710b–1711a

Polikushka, 1711a

Resurrection, 1694b, 1710b

Rilke and, 1463b

Sevastopol Sketches, 1693a–b, 1701b, 1702a

death theme, 1707b

Solzhenitsyn and, 1621a, 1630b

The Cossacks, 1694b, 1700b–1702a

narrator's voice, 152b–153a

The Death of Ivan Ilich, 1694b, 1707b, 1708b–1709a, 1711a

"The Deathbed Notes of the Elder Fyodor Kuzmich," 1712a

The Kreutzer Sonata, 1694b, 1710a

The Power of Darkness, 1711a–b

"Three Years" and, 375b

War and Peace (Voina i mir), 1694a, 1696b, 1701b, 1702a–1705a, 1710b–1711a

death theme, 1707b–1708a, 1708b

epilogue, 1704b–1705a, 1708a

form, 1630b

Proust's *Remembrance of Things Past* and, 1322b

treatment of marriage, 1710a

What Is Art?, 1694b, 1709a–b

Chekhov on, 368b–369a

Zola compared with, 1808b–1809a

Tolstoyanism

Chekhov and, 362b, 367b–369a, 370a, 370b, 375b

in "Gusev," 371b

in "My Life," 374b

Tomashevskii, Boris, on Mayakovsky, 140a

"Tombe, La" ("The Tomb"). *See* Maupassant, Guy de

Tonight We Improvise. See Pirandello, Luigi, *Questa sera si recita a soggetto*

Tonio Kröger. See Mann, Thomas

Torquato Tasso. See Goethe, Johann Wolfgang von

"Torrents of Spring." *See* Turgenev, Ivan

Totalitarianism

Ionesco's *Rhinocéros* and, 827b

Kafka and, 863a

Totem and Taboo (Totem und Tabu). See Freud, Sigmund

Totemism, Freud's concept of, 586a–587a

Tour de Nesle, La. See Dumas père, Alexandre

Tourneur, Cyril, on Ibsen, 811b

Tous les hommes sont mortels. See Beauvoir, Simone de, *All Men Are Mortal*

Toute compte fait. See Beauvoir, Simone de, *All Said and Done*

Toutounier, Le. See Colette

Towneley cycle plays, 1069a

Trabajos de Persiles y Sigismunda, Los. See Cervantes, Miguel de, *The Trials of Persiles and Sigismunda*

Traditional story

Beowulf as, 224a–226a, 237, 238b

characteristics of, 224a–b

Grettis saga as, 225a–b

Traditionalism

in *Beowulf,* 223b–224a

in oral cultures, 222b–223a

Traffic jams, in plays of Ionesco, 824b, 841b

"Tragedia di un personaggio, La." *See* Pirandello, Luigi

Tragedy

Apollinian versus Dionysian, 1172b–1173b

in French literature

Camus and, 320a–b

Ionesco's *Exit the King* and, 832a–b

"Tragedy of a Character, The." *See* Pirandello, Luigi, "La tragedia di un personaggio"

Tragic, the, Sartre and, 1595b

Tragicomedy

Guarini's defense of, 1421a–b, 1423a

origins of, 1421a–b

"Trahison de la comtesse de Rhune, La." *See* Maupassant, Guy de

INDEX

U

INDEX

INDEX

INDEX

INDEX

INDEX

Y

INDEX